The English M

D0628653

The English Mystery Plays

Rosemary Woolf

Somerville College, Oxford

UNIVERSITY OF CALIFORNIA PRESS

Berkeley and Los Angeles

University of California Press
Berkeley and Los Angeles, California

First Paperback Printing 1980
ISBN 0-520-04081-3
Library of Congress Catalog Card Number 72-82226

Printed in the United States of America

1 2 3 4 5 6 7 8 9

Contents

Conclusion

Appendices

Preface

The subject of this book is the four cycles of mystery plays, York, Chester, Towneley (Wakefield) and the *Ludus Coventriae*. Unfortunately there are no modern editions of the cycles although all four need re-editing (new editions of them are in hand). This lack has presented difficulties both in regard to general bibliographic and linguistic problems (especially in the discussion of the revision of the cycles undertaken in Chapter XIII of the present work) and also to the precise problem of quotation. I have taken quotations from the old editions still in use, except that I have occasionally emended the text (emendations being indicated and explained in the footnotes) and I have punctuated quotations from the *Ludus Coventriae*. In all quotations, whether English or Latin, I have normalised the spellings *u*, *v*, and *w*, and where manuscript abbreviations have been retained in the printed texts I have expanded them.

My debt to earlier writers on the mystery plays will be obvious throughout and I gratefully acknowledge it. In addition I would like to thank the friends and colleagues who have helped me in various ways, and in particular Miss Barbara Harvey, Miss Lotte Labowsky and Mrs Olive Sayce. I am especially grateful to Mrs Catherine Byron who checked most of the footnote references and quotations in the text and to Mrs Clare Matthews who helped me correct the proofs: remaining inaccuracies are my own.

The Background

Latin Liturgical Drama

The influence of Latin liturgical drama upon the mystery plays is paradoxically both important and negligible: important in that vernacular religious drama would have been inconceivable as a form had not the liturgical offices of Easter and Christmas come to include passages of drama; negligible in that it is only in trivial instances that the mystery plays draw upon liturgical drama as a direct source. The relationship between the two is therefore much finer and more elusive than was supposed by early scholars, who held the theory that the mystery plays were in origin liturgical drama, which, having outgrown the confines of the physical structure of the church and the religious framework of the liturgy, was transferred to the marketplace and performed in English. This interpretation of the evidence is untrue for at least two substantial reasons. Firstly, liturgical drama never left the church but co-existed with the mystery plays almost throughout their lifetime. It has been estimated that of the five or six hundred plays enumerated by Young about half belong to the fifteenth century or later, in other words to the period when vernacular plays flourished throughout western Europe. There are records of liturgical plays in England until the fifteenth century and there is no reason to doubt that they continued until suppressed in the sixteenth century with the rest of the Latin liturgy. In Roman Catholic countries, such as Spain, some churches retained liturgical drama until the eighteenth century.

Secondly, there was no steady evolutionary growth in liturgical drama towards an ever higher degree of representationalism, this growth reaching its fullness in the fourteenth century when the mystery plays were first composed.[1] In a graph designed to chart this kind of development, liturgical drama would not climb in a steady line, but would be shown to zig-zag across the centuries, the highest peak occurring in the twelfth. It is to this century that nearly all the longest and most elaborate examples of Latin liturgical drama belong. Thereafter there was little new invention (the Barking Harrowing of Hell or the Avignon Presentation of the Virgin in the Temple are rare exceptions), and throughout the remaining centuries of the Middle Ages churches adopted the dramatic ceremonies of Easter and Christmas according to their preference and according to what customs they respected. In general they preferred the briefer forms as the very many fourteenth- and fifteenth-century manuscripts of these bear witness; it is even likely that in some churches there was in the later period a deliberate reversion to simpler forms, though the loss of manuscripts usually makes the detection of this kind of variability impossible. It is, however, noticeable that Young's arrangement of texts in order of degree of amplitude occasionally leads to the chronological reversal of texts from the same cathedral or monastery.[2]

Whilst the term development cannot be applied to the course of liturgical drama after the twelfth century – thereafter we can only study the history of its use – it may be applied, though with caution, to the period spanned at the one end by the few lines dramatising the Visit of the Three Marys to the Sepulchre (commonly called the *Visitatio*) and at the other by the complete, though miniature, plays of the Resurrection. The caution lies in not seeing this development as a manifestation of a blind tendency towards full representationalism and in not measuring the success of each text by its advance towards this end. The reasons for the development were historically precise and various: the learned religious who composed the more extended texts of the *Visitatio* probably did so initially through a desire for liturgical embellishment or a propagandist concern to instruct the laity, whilst later they probably recognised the nature of the dramatic office and amplified upon tradition with conscious literary awareness.[3] As one would expect in such circumstances, the texts, if arranged chronologically, show no even progress towards a fully dramatic play, but in these terms sometimes regress and sometimes advance by leaps and bounds. There is, however, no exact correlation between the dramatic effectiveness of the texts and their progress towards dramatic form: one of the arts of the liturgical authors was to exploit the emotive possibilities of the liturgical context, and, as we shall see, some of the most striking of the texts are technically hybrid in form.

The question of how the dramatic ceremony of the *Visitatio* itself came to be composed is one that can only be discussed in a tentative and exploratory way: the surviving evidence for liturgical customs in the ninth and tenth centuries is far too slight for any certainty to be reached. But the kind of explanation that must be sought is one which accounts for the *Visitatio* in terms of some variation in liturgical order, which could reasonably have been made without the reviser recognising that by his innovation he had made a step of crucial significance across the dividing line between dramatic liturgy and drama.

4

For reasons that have nothing to do with literature, the Church had in its structure and liturgy conditions from which drama might accidentally develop. It possessed, for instance, the outward phenomena of a theatrical performance, a building, an audience, and men speaking or singing words to be listened to and performing action to be watched. Within this framework there were more precise resemblances which might be heightened in a variety of ways. Choirs sang the psalms and other pieces antiphonally and therefore when two adjoining verses consisted of question and answer they might momentarily seem to be engaged in dialogue. The singing of the Passion narratives in Holy Week, though different speakers did not take part (as was once thought), were made dramatic by musical indications to different speakers,[4] and dramatic speech elsewhere, particularly if it was that of Christ, could be given corresponding musical expression. Action as well as words could have a dramatic character. From the ninth century onwards the action of the mass and other offices had been interpreted allegorically.[5] Whilst often the discrepancy between liturgical action and New Testament signification would have been far too great for there to be any dramatic effect, sometimes there were notable coincidences which, to the instructed at least, would have seemed more like mime than allegory: an interesting example is the parallelism between the priests carrying thuribles in procession in order to cense some sacred object, such as the altar, and the Marys bearing spices to the tomb in order to anoint the body of Christ.

Whilst mimetic action in the liturgy is fairly rare, verbal impersonation is extremely common: to take the simplest examples, when a choir sings the *Magnificat* they impersonate the Virgin, when the *Nunc dimittis* Symeon. Such liturgical impersonation, however, is a far cry from dramatic impersonation. What was essential to the emergence of drama was that the two types of liturgical impersonation should be brought together, so that the dramatic words normally sung by clergy and choir solemnly stationary became united to the mimetic action which had not hitherto been accompanied by words implying impersonation. The earliest surviving text of the *Visitatio*, in which this combination can be seen, is that of the *Regularis concordia*: this was the code of monastic customs, based upon French models, which Dunstan and Æthelwold compiled for the English Benedictine monasteries towards the end of the tenth century.[6]

The kernel of dramatic dialogue in the *Visitatio* is earlier found as a trope in manuscripts of the first half of the tenth century from Limoges and St Gall.[7] Tropes were liturgical pieces composed for singing and bore approximately the same kind of relationship to the regular liturgy as does the hymn. The text of the *Concordia*, which is slightly longer than that of the earlier trope, is as follows:[8]

> Quem quaeritis in sepulchro, Christicolae?
> Ihesum Nazarenum crucifixum, o caelicola.
> Non est hic. Surrexit sicut praedixerat; ite
> nuntiate quia surrexit a mortuis.
> Alleluia. Resurrexit Dominus, hodie [resurrexit] leo
> fortis, Christus, filius Dei. Deo gratias, dicite eia!
> Venite et videte locum ubi positus erat Dominus, alle-
> luia, alleluia.
> Surrexit Dominus de sepulchro, qui pro nobis pependit
> in ligno, alleluia.
> Te Deum laudamus

This dialogue between the three Marys and the choir is accompanied by two important pieces of action. At the beginning, before the angel's initial question, the Marys, carrying thuribles, make their way to the sepulchre, reaching it as though at the end of a journey; and later, when the angel has summoned them to look into the sepulchre, the Marys do so, laying down their thuribles and picking up the linen-cloth, which they then display as they sing 'Surrexit Dominus de sepulchro'. There are various other dramatic touches in terms of costume and mimic gesture, to which we shall return, but it is reasonable to postulate an original combination of these words with these actions as the germinal starting-point for all later developments.

In the *Concordia* the *Visitatio* provides the narrative conclusion of three other striking, though more symbolically mimetic, ceremonies, the *Adoratio, Depositio* and *Elevatio*:[9] all four are linked by continuity of theme and by the use throughout them of one dramatic property, namely the cloth which represents the grave-clothes of Christ. The oldest of these ceremonies is the *Adoratio*, a custom of eastern origin, which was adopted in Rome in the seventh century and thereafter became widespread in the west.[10] By the tenth century this rite had become highly infused with devotional and dramatic feeling. Two deacons held a veiled cross or crucifix before the congregation[11] and sang the *Improperia* or Reproaches, in which Christ rebukes His people for unkindness, 'Popule meus, quid feci tibi'.[12] During the singing of the Reproaches the Cross was gradually uncovered,[13] and at the end it was laid fully unveiled upon the altar and a series of Christocentric prayers followed: finally the Cross was venerated by each member of the congregation in turn kissing the wood. Although this ceremony is not dramatic in a technical sense, anyone who has seen it nowadays will know that in the heightened emotional feeling of the day it conveys very powerfully the feeling of dramatic action and in particular a sense that the figure of Christ addresses the congregation: the very fact that it is not coherent drama paradoxically enhances its imaginative intensity.

The ceremonies that follow, the *Depositio* in which the Cross used for the *Adoratio* was 'buried' in a linen cloth and the *Elevatio* in which the Cross was restored to the altar before the congregation was admitted for the mass of Easter morning, seem to have been of distinct origins. In later custom the *Depositio* and *Elevatio* could be of the Cross or of the Host or of both.[14] There is, however, some evidence that in their original form the Host only was used and that the ceremonies initially served only a practical purpose.

Among the many variations in eucharistic custom in the early Middle Ages one was important in contributing to the development of the ceremonies. It was an ancient habit in the church to mark the solemnity and mourning of Good Friday by singling it out as the one day in the liturgical year on which mass might not be celebrated. But by the ninth century this spiritual abstinence had been modified by the introduction of the Mass of the Presanctified in which, though mass was not said, communion was given from the sacrament reserved from the mass of Maundy Thursday. The sacrament was thus brought to the altar on Good Friday for communion and (wherever it was the custom to reserve the sacrament) the remnant would then be returned to the place of reservation and brought out again for mass on Easter Sunday. The place of reservation used to contain the sacrament for the Mass of the Presanctified was traditionally some place apart, its actual container a tower-shaped vessel which was understood to symbolise Christ's tomb.[15] With the intensity of feeling that from the ninth century onwards became focused upon the Good Friday liturgy it seems that the purely practical return of the sacrament to the place of reservation on Good Friday acquired a devotional and commemorative significance. The earliest evidence for this is the life of Bishop Ulrich of Augsburg written in the tenth century by a contemporary:[16] it gives a description of the many liturgical customs which Ulrich performed with great devotion, including the burial of the Host on Good Friday and probably the raising of it on Easter Sunday, though the second action is not described as clearly as the first.[17]

There is no way of locating the precise place in which the Cross was first buried instead of the Host, though it is likely to have been in

Southern Germany or Lorraine;[18] nor is it possible to reconstruct with certainty the process of thought which led to this substitution. The life of Ulrich provides the earliest instance of the one, the *Concordia*, some decades later, of the other. It seems reasonable, however, to suppose that when the symbolic significance of the return of the Host to the place of reservation came to overshadow its practical necessity, the object of the symbolic ceremony became the cross or crucifix, which in the ceremony of the *Adoratio* had come so closely to represent Christ on the Cross. The Cross thus became the chief symbolic object which connected these ceremonies when they were performed in succession, as in the *Concordia*. But there was also the symbolic accessory of the cloth, and it is this which provides the tangible link between the *Elevatio* and the *Visitatio*.

It is clear from various sources that when the Host was buried, it was covered in a cloth corresponding to the corporal and pall, already used in eucharistic ceremonies as a sign of reverence: analogously, when the Cross was buried, it was wrapped in the cloth which had previously veiled it and which now expressly symbolised the grave-clothes:[19] this cloth was necessarily left behind on Easter morning when the Cross was raised and returned to the altar. Obviously one of the clergy could have removed this object, no longer needed, discreetly and expeditiously but, by the tenth century, iconographic influences suggested a further symbolic usage for the discarded cloth. In this period the moment in the Resurrection story which in art was taken to symbolise the whole was the visit of the three Marys to the sepulchre, and in this scene the empty grave-clothes were always visually stressed; in iconography it was they, and not the risen Christ Himself, that demonstrated the truth of the Resurrection. There is evidence of a further mimetic ceremony centring upon the cloth, which was at first liturgically mimetic, not dramatic.

An adaptation of the *De officiis* of Amalarius contains a ceremony of this kind: though it is preserved in a manuscript of the eleventh century, the ordinal itself, according to the late Dom Wilmart, is earlier, conceivably even of the ninth century.[20] This ordinal prescribes that, after the *Elevatio*, the *sudarium* shall remain in the sepulchre until the *Te Deum* at the end of matins and that the sepulchre shall be 'visited' after the third respond (that is immediately before the *Te Deum*). Nothing is said of an acted *Quem quaeritis* and it is reasonable to infer that the Visit to the Sepulchre was processional rather than dramatic.[21]

The account of the *Visitatio* in the Ordinal from Toul (which is related to the *Visitatio*) may cast some light upon the nature of a non-dramatic Visit to the Sepulchre.[22] This ceremony begins with a procession of clergy to the sepulchre, some of them bearing candles and thuribles, and ends with the abbot ceremonially censing the sepulchre. The responsory, *Angelus domini*, accompanies the latter action, whilst at the beginning the third respond for matins (which describes how the women bought spices and went to the tomb)[23] is repeated a second time in order to serve as a processional. Embedded in this processional ceremony is an acted *Quem quaeritis*, which makes a very apt sequel to the third respond, continuing its narrative in dialogue form: so appropriate is it that it may even have been composed precisely for this position, in which technically it may be described as a trope of the *Te Deum*.[24] In Toul the *Quem quaeritis* was acted in the sense that the number of performers was dramatically correct, one cleric singing the part of the angel and three that of the Marys, in contrast to the presumably earlier form in which, though two singers took the part of the angels, the procession of clerics gave the responses of the Marys.[25] But, though there is acting in this sense, the processional frame prevents an effect of full impersonation.

The supposition that the *Visitatio* prescribed by the ordinal based on the *De officiis* was similar to the processional part of the ceremony at Toul is of course hypothetical. But the implications of the Toul ordinal are less uncertain: for here the acted *Quem quaeritis* is quite clearly part of a procession, which had as its purpose a visit to the sepulchre which had been used for the *Depositio* and in which the *sudarium*, in which the Cross had been wrapped, still remained. That a liturgical procession would be deliberately devised to enclose an acted *Quem quaeritis* seems an improbable development; but that the processional *Visitatio* came first, that the unique conjunction of dramatic words and matching action encouraged the singing of the words of the Marys by the dramatically correct number of clerics, and that the procession thus became redundant and was abandoned – this seems a plausible sequence of events, though not one that can be fully documented.[26]

A comparison of the Toul *Visitatio* with that of the *Concordia* shows how readily the limited dramatic enactment of the former could change into genuine impersonation. The comparison is the easier to make because the text of the *Quem quaeritis* is identical in both. In the *Concordia* the third respond again opens the ceremony, but it is not sung by a procession but by the choir, while the three clerics, taking the part of the Marys, make their way to the sepulchre; furthermore these clerics do not proceed in formal liturgical order, but go slowly and wanderingly, as though searching for something (a touch of surprisingly realistic mime). A bit of mime was also devised to make a convincing transition between the Mary's Alleluia and the angel's summons to them to look in the tomb, an undramatic sequence made naturalistic by the Marys apparently turning away from the sepulchre too soon. Finally whereas at Toul, the choir joined in the antiphon, 'Surrexit Dominus de sepulchro', in the *Concordia* the Marys retain this as their own dramatic proclamation.

In the Toul ceremony the liturgical present and the historical past, dramatically re-created, repeatedly intermingled in the one ceremony: the 'sepulchre', for instance, was at one moment the historical tomb in which Christ was buried and which the Marys sought, at the next a constructed Easter sepulchre in church, appropriately censed by the abbot. In the ceremony of the *Concordia* this mingling of dramatic and liturgical is effectively reserved to the conclusion, when the prior replying to the Marys' announcement of the Resurrection joyfully gives out the *Te Deum*.[27] The retention of the *Te Deum* as part of the dramatic representation was not only moving but also crucial from the point of view of dramatic developments, for it meant that the dramatic passage was not constricted by the limits of what the framework of the office could enclose: instead of seeming an intrusion in the office of matins, it became rather an interlude between the end of matins and the beginning of lauds.

The form of the *Visitatio* seems to have remained fairly constant for about a hundred years: the only variation consists in the co-existence with it of a shorter version without the last two antiphons accompanying the display of the grave-clothes (it may be conjectured that this text would be devised or preferred by churches that adopted the *Visitatio* but not the *Depositio* and *Elevatio*).[28] When later the *Visitatio* was elaborated, the process consisted of bringing more and more of the appointed gospel for the Easter mass, Mark xvi. 1-7, into the dramatic performance. Thus the visit of the Marys to the spice-merchant (*unguentarius*) might be added at the beginning and the race of Peter and John to the tomb and the Appearance to Mary Magdalene at the end. Whereas the earliest version was moving only as the culmination of the Easter story, which up to this point had been only liturgically enacted, the rare texts to include all these elements acquired the pattern and completeness of a play: an opening scene which stresses the Marys' sad belief that Christ is dead, the reversal of feeling in the angel's announcement of the Resurrection, a scene in lower key in which the apostles themselves visit the tomb, and the final emotionally powerful dénouement in which the risen Christ appears.[29]

Full plays of this kind survive only from the latter part of the twelfth century, but sources for the individual episodes survive from the close of the eleventh or the beginning of the twelfth. The scene of the *Unguentarius* is first extant in the pages of the Ripoll Troper,[30] which has been dated at the end of the eleventh or the beginning of the twelfth century:[31] it may either be a Catalan invention or have been borrowed by the Benedictines from one of the many French houses with which they had connections, these including Fleury and Limoges.[32] That it was common in the liturgical drama of southern France has been plausibly argued by Mâle on the evidence of its representation in sculpture.[33] The earliest record of the race between Peter and John is also of the turn of the century, but of German origin. Since this incident turns upon the display of the grave-clothes, either by the Marys to Peter and John or by the disciples themselves, it is not surprising that the Augsburg Ordinal to contain it includes the series, *Depositio*, *Elevatio* and *Visitatio*.[34] The first known occurrence of the *Hortulanus* episode is in a Norman-Sicilian *Peregrini*, which survives in a manuscript dated 1132–7,[35] but its position there is so strangely unchronological, namely after the Appearance to the disciples at Emmaus, that it seems likely to have been borrowed from its proper place in a *Visitatio*, which itself would be of French-Norman origin. As we shall see later, this episode was acted in England well before the end of the twelfth century.

Though these manuscripts in terms of dating provide only a *terminus a quo*, the coincidence in time between them strongly suggests that the *Visitatio* underwent no development until about the end of the eleventh century. It seems possible that it was its association with the liturgical ceremonies of Good Friday that for so long exercised a restraining influence upon festive and dramatic elaborations. At any rate, when in the second half of the tenth century an analogous Christmas scene (which had no solemn liturgical antecedents) was invented, it was followed by a full play, not almost two centuries later, but within about thirty years.

Between the years 1050 and 1100 various types of Christmas play are found. The starting-point was a trope modelled upon the *Quem quaeritis* and sung on Christmas Day. In it the interlocutors, later identified as the midwives of apocryphal tradition, ask the shepherds whom they seek, 'Quem quaeritis in presepe, pastores, dicite?', and the shepherds reply, 'Salvatorem Christum Dominum…'; the Christ-Child is then pointed out to them, 'Adest hic parvulus cum Maria matre sua' and the piece ends with a celebratory *Alleluia*. This dialogue is not only linked to the Easter *Quem quaeritis* by verbal echoes and analogous structure, but is also exactly parallel to it in religious meaning: the one demonstrates that Christ is risen, the other that Christ is born. Eleventh-century texts of this trope survive from many churches of France and northern Italy,[36] but since the manuscripts to contain them are all *troparia* (which would record the words only and not the manner of delivery), we cannot tell whether the dialogue was sung in such a way as to imply any dramatic impersonation. But, since in all these eleventh-century manuscripts the Christmas *Quem quaeritis* serves as a trope of the Introit of the third mass of Christmas Day, it is unlikely that the degree of impersonation ever exceeded that recorded at Novalesa, in which there is dramatic propriety in regard to the number of singers and the altar symbolises the crib.[37]

Genuine dramatisations of the Visit of the Shepherds, which incorporate this trope, occur normally at the end of matins and before the first mass of Christmas Day. This Christmas play (commonly called the *Officium pastorum*), however, remained extremely uncommon and fairly unelaborated throughout the Middle Ages (the fullest version, which comes from Rouen, will be discussed below). Its comparative rarity has sometimes been explained by the theory that the preferred form of Christmas drama was the *Ordo prophetarum*, the prophets' play in which a succession of Old Testament prophets foretold the coming of Christ. The *Ordo prophetarum*, however, seems also to have been an uncommon play: only three full texts of it survive, those of Limoges, Laon and Rouen,[38] and in Rouen at least it co-existed with an *Officium pastorum*. The division therefore seems to be rather between the few churches which favoured dramatic offices on Christmas Day and the many that did not. A possible explanation for the general reluctance to devise or adopt a play on Christmas Day is that of shortage of time: the ancient customs of celebrating three masses on Christmas morning must have considerably disrupted the liturgical time-scheme, leaving no time for additional embellishments to the liturgy.

A way, however, was found of representing the Visit of the Shepherds on a festive day other than Christmas: this consisted of combining it with an Epiphany play of the Visit of the Three Kings (the *Officium stellae*), the link being made by an unbiblical encounter between the approaching Kings and the three shepherds departing from the manger. This incident is one of the many expansions to the Visit of the Three Kings, expansions that cannot be related in historical order, since the earliest texts containing them all cluster round the end of the eleventh century. Of this early group the most ample is that from the Cathedral of Freising. It is a remarkable play for so early a date. Though it does not show the freedom of invention that characterises the later drama from the Fleury Play-book and Benediktbeuern, the Freising play is entirely comparable in the range of episode included.³⁹ It begins with the angels' announcement to the shepherds and ends with the Massacre of the Innocents, the latter being fairly elaborately prepared for by a scene at the court of Herod with speaking parts for messengers, soldiers and scribes, whilst at the end Herod's anger at his deception by the Magi is expressed in a quotation from Sallust's account of the Catiline conspiracy, 'Incendium meum ruina extinguam'.⁴⁰ The only incident not included in the Freising play is the lament of the mothers of the Holy Innocents under the biblical figure of Rachel weeping for her children. Freising, however, is one of the few places to have a separate *Ordo Rachelis* (the other texts being from the Fleury Play-book and Limoges).

It is clear from this brief account of the growth of liturgical drama that, whilst the beginnings lay in a verbal dramatic fragment which made narrative sense only in the context of the liturgy, the later tendency was to make the narrative complete in itself by dramatising the whole of the appointed gospel for the day along the same lines; furthermore, that the Epiphany play gathered into itself a dramatisation of the appointed gospels for both Christmas Day and the feast of the Holy Innocents as well as that for the Epiphany itself. This kind of unliturgical accretion, however, did not usually occur in the treatment of the Resurrection. The chronologically appropriate extension to this was Christ's encounter with the disciples on the Road to Emmaus: this is the subject of the gospel for Easter Monday and dramatisations of it are usually confined to that day. It is only the long and rather eccentric thirteenth-century play from Tours, which, after the Appearance to Mary Magdalene, proceeds to the Appearance to Thomas,⁴¹ the latter normally being the concluding scene of the more extensive plays of the *Peregrini*.

So short an account of Latin liturgical drama can best be concluded by a consideration of the drama of one particular place: for a summary that ranges over the whole of western Europe, covering countries which are now France, Belgium, Germany, Spain, Italy, Austria and Czechoslovakia, can necessarily give little impression of what was happening in any particular area. The most useful ecclesiastical province at which to look is that of Rouen. Texts of all the main types of liturgical drama from Rouen survive in manuscripts of the twelfth to the fifteenth century: it is therefore possible to examine a whole set of plays from one area and also to observe in part their development from one century to another. More importantly it was Rouen that supplied the exemplars of most of the Anglo-Latin liturgical drama of the Middle Ages, and since, as we shall see, there exist various references to this, but, with one exception, no texts, a knowledge of Rouen drama in the twelfth century serves as a helpful background to an otherwise tantalisingly uninformative list.

The earliest mention of liturgical drama in Rouen itself occurs in the *De officiis* of Jean d'Avranches, a work representing the customs of Rouen and completed in 1167:[42] among the customs described by Jean are an *Officium sepulchri* and an *Officium stellae*. No texts are provided but in a later twelfth-century manuscript of the *De officiis* an *Officium pastorum* and *Officium stellae* have been inserted.[43] Though no earlier texts from Rouen itself survive, fairly reliable indications of the manner and contents of its plays at a much earlier point in time can be gained from three Norman-Sicilian liturgical manuscripts, the earliest of which has been dated 1132–7 (it is of course the Rouen rite which the Norman princes, accompanied by high ecclesiastics, carried to Sicily after their final conquest of the island). Between them the Sicilian manuscripts furnish two texts of the *Visitatio*, two of the *Peregrini* and one of the *Ordo stellae*. All these dramatic offices recur in Rouen manuscripts of the thirteenth, fourteenth and fifteenth centuries. The only play not recorded for Rouen by the end of the twelfth century is the *Ordo prophetarum*, but this should not be taken as evidence that Rouen only adopted a prophets' play at a late date, since the type of liturgical manuscript to contain it, namely an *ordinarium* or a *troparium*, is lacking from Rouen until the fourteenth century.[44]

The two twelfth-century Sicilian texts of the *Visitatio* contain none of the episodes added to the Visit to the Tomb.[45] In one of them, however, the two lines of lament given at the beginning to each of the Marys lend a rounded movement lacking to the briefest texts. The three later Rouen versions, however, agree in having a sparse version of the Visit itself but in adding to this the Appearance to Mary Magdalene.[46] It is a curiosity of the Rouen tradition that the Appearance to Mary Magdalene can also be annexed to the *Peregrini*. This arrangement is found in the earliest and also fullest version of the *Peregrini*, that in the Sicilian gradual, dated 1132–7.[47] The first part of this play is of standard type, consisting of a dialogue excerpted from Luke xxiv. 13–35, with narrative links sung by the choir, while the conclusion, as often, is the

Appearance of Christ to Thomas. Interposed between these, however, is the Appearance to Mary Magdalene, which is then linked to the Emmaus scene by the apportionment of the dramatic centre of the sequence, *Victimae paschali*, between Mary and the Emmaus disciples who ask the question, 'Dic nobis, Maria, quid vidisti in via?', which in other versions of the *Visitatio* is asked either by the choir or by Peter and John.[48] Though the later Sicilian text consists solely of the Emmaus scene, with its biblically-based dialogue, the thirteenth-century Rouen text extends to the dialogue between Mary and the Emmaus disciples; the *Hortulanus* scene itself, however, is omitted.[49] The reasonable inference from this evidence is that the *Hortulanus* is of early origin in Rouen, beginning in its natural place as part of the *Visitatio*, and then by an eccentric variation becoming transferred to the *Peregrini*, from which it was again gradually eliminated.

The *Officium pastorum* is also particularly connected with Rouen: indeed on extant evidence it is true to say that amplifications upon the Christmas *Quem quaeritis* belong solely to this province.[50] The earliest version of the *Officium pastorum* to survive from Rouen (that in the late twelfth-century manuscript of the *De officiis*) has already added to the earlier trope by prefacing it with the Annunciation to the Shepherds. The dialogue of this scene, however, is restricted to that of Luke ii. 10–15, stripped of narrative: an angel *in excelso* (presumably in the gallery of the church) sings the angelic message, 'Nolite timere . . .', and more angels then appear upon either side of him to sing the 'Gloria in excelsis Deo'. The shepherds then reply, 'Transeamus usque Bethleem', and the Adoration follows with the dialogue of the *Quem quaeritis*. The later versions of the *Officium pastorum*, one recorded in the thirteenth, the other in the fourteenth century, show two minor developments. One consists of the insertion of two hymns to be sung by the shepherds, 'Pax in terris nunciatur', which replaces their briefer 'Transeamus . . .', and 'Salve, virgo singularis', a hymn to the Virgin which takes the place of the *Alleluia* declaring the birth of Christ. The other feature is that the shepherds 'rule the choir' during the subsequent mass and lauds, singing some of the responses; the dramatic impersonation comes fully to life again when at the beginning of the lauds the choir asks them the question adapted from the *Victimae paschali*, 'Quem vidistis, pastores, dicite?' and the shepherds reply, 'Natum vidimus et choros angelorum'. This inextricable mingling of liturgical and dramatic seems to be characteristic of developments in liturgical drama devised later than the twelfth century: we shall see the same feeling for liturgical-dramatic effects, operating freely without concern for consistent dramatic impersonation, in the Barking *Visitatio* to be discussed later.

The most ample versions of the *Officium stellae* are those, respectively, from Sicily and the *De officiis*.[51] The Sicilian version is fullest at the beginning, covering the meeting of the Magi together, the messenger bringing them to the court on Herod's instructions, a scene at Herod's court, and the encounter with the shepherds; but the play ends fairly abruptly after the Adoration with the angel's warning followed by a hymn. The other twelfth-century version follows a similar pattern but at the end returns to Herod's court, where Herod's son proposes violent action against the Child, whilst the soldiers urge Herod to 'vindicate his wrath' by the massacre, and the play ends with Herod brandishing the naked sword which the soldiers have offered him. Very different are the versions found in Rouen manuscripts from the thirteenth to the fifteenth centuries in which the subject is reduced to the assembling of the Magi and their Adoration of the Child:[52] there are no shepherds, no messenger, and, most important of all, no Herod (at most some texts permit the meeting with Herod to be described in narrative form in a response sung by the choir). This massive curtailment of the play, with the expunging of Herod from the text, certainly represents a preference for simpler forms, and perhaps originally some nervousness occasioned by the attacks on liturgical drama made by ecclesiastics such as Gerhoh of Reichersberg, who amongst specific objects of complaint had mentioned the raging of Herod.[53]

The last Rouen play to be mentioned is the *Ordo prophetarum*, which resembles those from Limoges and Laon; there are some distinctive stanzas common to all three. In all three the pseudo-Augustinian sermon, setting out the Jewish and gentile prophecies of Christ, is dramatised by the simple method of impersonation:[54] while members of the choir ask each figure for his prophecy, the reply comes from individual figures appropriately dressed, who speak the prophecies, not in the prose of the sermon, but in agreeable stanza form. At Rouen, as at Laon, the few prophecies that had been uttered in striking historical circumstances are more elaborated, Balaam and his ass and the Children in the fiery furnace.[55] In general, however, as both source and subject-matter requires, this play remains impressive in a formal and ceremonial way, and indeed in its lack of plot can scarcely be appropriately called drama.

It was in the twelfth century, before the loss of Normandy in 1204, that England had the opportunity to adopt liturgical plays from Rouen. As will be clear from the above account the range of plays available was large and they were at their period of maximum elaborateness. It is quite likely that there was an *Ordo prophetarum* and certainly there was a *Peregrini* which may well have extended to the Appearance to Thomas. The *Visitatio* included the Appearance to Mary Magdalene but none of the other possible developments. There was an *Officium pastorum*, possibly beginning with the angelic announcement to the shepherds; whilst the most dramatically ambitious *Officium stellae* was available which gave to Herod a substantial role. Though Anglo-Latin drama could have been influenced by other models, Rouen would initially have furnished its major sources.

The actual history of Latin liturgical drama in England after the Norman conquest has largely to be pieced together from scraps of evidence of various kinds. With the notable exception of the fourteenth-century Barking play, no texts survive. The late Anglo-Saxon *Visitatio*, described in the *Regularis concordia*, must have fallen into disuse with the Norman abbots' tacit decision to ignore this work. Its successor, the *Constitutions* of Lanfranc, based upon the customs of Bec and Cluny, does not mention this ceremony, a silence that possibly implies rejection.[56] The *Constitutions*, though primarily composed for the Benedictine house of Christchurch, Canterbury, was adopted by other monasteries, though its observance was not imposed upon them.[57] The lack of reference to liturgical drama in the *Constitutions* was not perhaps tantamount to a prohibition of it. The great monastery of St Albans, for instance, which received a copy of the *Constitutions*, when Lanfranc sent one to his nephew, Paul, then Abbot of St Albans, may nevertheless have practised liturgical drama in the twelfth century.

There are many indications which suggest an informed interest in drama at St Albans in this period. That an *Officium stellae* and a *Peregrini* play formed part of their Christmas and Easter ceremonies has been very convincingly argued by Professor Pächt on the basis of the iconography of the illuminations in the *St Albans Psalter*.[58] Amongst the many telling resemblances that he describes are, the presence of a soldier in the Herod scene, apparently suggesting the massacre, and the emphasis upon the Emmaus story, with the dialogue invariably excerpted from Luke written in the top left-hand corner of one of the illustrations,[59] and another showing the unhistorical linking of the Appearance to Thomas with the Emmaus story, which was characteristic of the fuller *Peregrini* plays. If St Albans had liturgical drama, it would undoubtedly have been borrowed from Rouen, since it was from that province that a succession of its abbots came, and in particular, Geoffrey of Le Mans, abbot from 1119–46. It is a particularly strong link in the chain of evidence that the distinctive features of the St Albans miniatures are all to be found either in the Sicilian texts or in the twelfth-century manuscript of the *De officiis*.

There is evidence that by the end of the twelfth century one other Benedictine monastery, that at Eynsham, had a substantial Easter play, which included the conversation of Peter and John (and therefore perhaps the race) and the Appearance of Christ to Mary Magdalene. The evidence for this is found in the *Vision of the Monk of Eynsham*:[60] this account of a vision of hell was written by Adam, the author of the *Magna Vita* of St Hugh of Lincoln, and the vision, dated 1196, was that of his brother, who was then a novice in the monastery of Eynsham; the narrative was undoubtedly written within a few years after the date given. In the preface to the vision, which describes the strange sickness of the novice in Holy Week, there is a circumstantial account of some of the Easter customs, which includes a brief summary of the episodes of the Easter play.

Whilst it is not surprising that St Albans, which was pre-eminent amongst English Benedictine monasteries in the twelfth century, should have adorned its liturgy with drama, the existence of drama in the small monastery at Eynsham may at first sight seem strange. That it was put on to honour some great visitor cannot be the explanation, since, according to the *Vision*, its performance was *annua consuetudine*. The explanation probably lies in the connection between Eynsham and Lincoln, for to the Bishop of Lincoln belonged the right of patronage,[61] and the *Magna Vita* describes the visit of Hugh to Eynsham in 1196, when the election of a new abbot was made.[62] Adam, then sub-prior, shortly afterwards became Hugh's chaplain and then his biographer. It seems likely therefore that Eynsham adopted an Easter play through the influence of Lincoln. As we shall see later, entries for expenses in account books show that liturgical drama flourished there in the fourteenth and fifteenth centuries. These records, however, begin only in 1304, and the Eynsham play may therefore be taken as an interesting indication of Lincoln customs in the preceding century. It is generally agreed that the Lincoln use, drawn up towards the end of the eleventh century under Remigius, was influenced by that of Rouen, and that the influence of Rouen continued in the twelfth century. It is therefore very tempting to see a direct connection between our earlier inference that the Rouen *Visitatio* before 1130 included a *Hortulanus* scene, and the presence of this episode in the Eynsham play, which by 1196 could be called an annual custom.

It has usually been thought that whilst on the one hand Lanfranc's

Constitutions inhibited or prevented the performance of liturgical drama in English Benedictine monasteries, so also did the Sarum Use exclude liturgical drama from secular churches. The Sarum Use, which was widely adopted, contains the ceremonies of the *Depositio* and *Elevatio* (and hence most churches had Easter sepulchres), but not the *Visitatio*, and in this it is paralleled by the uses of York and Lincoln. However, just as monasteries might sometimes perform liturgical plays, despite the discouraging silence of the *Constitutions*, so also the great cathedral churches often went their own way on this issue. In the south only Salisbury itself seems to have had a liturgical play: a cathedral inventory dated 1214–22 includes the item, 'Coronae duae de latone ad representationes faciendas', presumably crowns for the Magi in an *Officium stellae*.[63] In the north at least four cathedral churches had plays, York, Lincoln, Lichfield and Norwich. The Statutes of Lichfield Cathedral (namely those of Hugh de Nonant, revised in the thirteenth and fourteenth centuries) show that there was performed there an *Officium pastorum*, a *Visitatio sepulchri* and a *Peregrini*.[64] The York Statutes, probably dated about 1255, provide for an *Officium pastorum* and an *Officium stellae*.[65] A Norwich ordinal, dated 1265–78, refers to a *Visitatio*.[66] Lincoln, as we have seen, probably had a *Visitatio* in the twelfth century, and the entries in the account books show that in the first quarter of the fourteenth century it had an *Officium stellae* and *Peregrini*, and by the end of the century an *Ordo prophetarum*.[67] The dates are of course those of the earliest surviving references and in no way indicate the period in which liturgical drama was first adopted in these cathedral towns.

Unfortunately these entries in statutes, ordinals and account books can give no indication of the length of the plays nor of any freedom of invention that might have been displayed in them. The sole testimony to English practice is an ordinal from the convent of Benedictine nuns at Barking, which includes a text of Easter dramatic ceremonies. Though the manuscript is of the late fourteenth or fifteenth century, the ceremonies can be dated more precisely, since a rubric records that they were instituted by Katherine of Sutton (abbess 1363–76).[68] Related to the Barking text is the Easter drama preserved in a fourteenth-century processional from the church of St John the Evangelist in Dublin,[69] though the historical nature of this relationship is not known and cannot be inferred from the texts themselves. They are alike in containing a fairly similar version of the play of the *Visitatio* and a very rare symbolic enactment of the Harrowing of Hell.[70]

In outline and in much of the dialogue the *Visitatio* clearly belongs to the Rouen tradition. The laments of the Marys as they approach the tomb consist largely of the lines found in the Sicilian *Visitatio*,[71] whilst their exchanges with the angel and the dialogue of the *Hortulanus* episode correspond closely to the three Rouen texts of the *Visitatio*.[72] Only the ending of the play seems to represent a departure from Rouen customs, in that it consists of an encounter between Mary Magdalene and the disciples of Christ, anonymous here, but in the Dublin version identified as Peter and John. Whilst the inclusion of this scene might suggest either independent English custom (it occurred at Eynsham) or confirm other hints of indirect German affiliations, it is interesting to note that this apportionment of the *Victimae paschali* between the Emmaus disciples and Mary Magdalene is also found in the Sicilian *Peregrini*.[73] Though this play is a little more eclectic in its use of sources than this summary indicates (some of the dialogue is found elsewhere only outside the Rouen tradition and a few of the antiphons, according to Young, are on present knowledge peculiar to it), it can in general be characterised as formal and highly derivative. The only small point of dramatic interest arises from the special circumstances of its performance, namely the naturalistic feature that the Marys are played by women: this is a rare decorum in regard to sex, confined throughout the Middle Ages to the churches of nunneries.[74]

Whilst this fourteenth-century *Visitatio* is substantially the Rouen play of two hundred years before, the dramatic ceremony which precedes the *Elevatio* may well be a new invention. This representation of the Harrowing of Hell is an interesting example of vivid liturgical symbolism that lacks the naturalism and consistency of genuine dramatic form. In preparation for the ceremony the abbess with the whole convent of nuns and some priests go into a side-chapel and close the door, and therein they signify (*figurantes*) the souls of the holy patriarchs in Limbo awaiting Christ's descent into hell. Another priest approaches the door, accompanied by two deacons, one of them carrying a Resurrection Cross, by two boys carrying lighted candles, and by other priests and clerks. At the threshold the priest sings the antiphon, *Tollite portas*, the verse from Psalm xxiv, long understood as Christ's summons to hell to open its gates. This antiphon is sung three times, the *clerici* repeating it, and each time the priest beats upon the door with the Resurrection Cross: the door then opens. The traditional question put in reply to Christ's command, 'Quis est rex gloriae?', is not used, no doubt because it would have implied impersonation of the devil,[75] but instead those within the chapel sing the antiphon *A porta inferi*, expressing the patriarchs' plea for their release.[76] The whole convent then streams out, carrying palms and lighted candles, and go in procession to the sepulchre, the priest leading them and himself entering the sepulchre. From the sepulchre is then raised, not the wound-marked carving of Christ, which had been detached from the Cross and 'buried' there after the *Elevatio*,[77] but the Host, which is then carried in a monstrance and shown to the congregation during the singing of the antiphon, 'Christus resurgens'. The procession in making its way to the high altar is said to figure 'per hoc quomodo Christus procedit post Resurrexionem in Galileam, sequentibus discipulis'.[78]

This is manifestly not a play, largely because there is an obviously deliberate unwillingness to have Christ impersonated fully and consistently. Though the priest is said to represent the person of Christ, to the beholder it must rather have seemed that the high priest and his attendant clergy corporately represented Him, both words and properties (i.e. Cross and candles) being distributed amongst them. Furthermore after the *Elevatio*, it is the Host, carried by the priest, and not the priest himself, who is the risen Christ. The procession, led by the priest, also changes in dramatic meaning, signifying at first the redeemed led by Christ from Limbo, but later how Christ preceded the disciples into Galilee. The latter signification of course may be no more than a learned allegorical comment upon the action (it does not occur in the Dublin analogue), but in that case one has simply an example of dramatic impersonation dissolving into non-dramatic liturgical action. These discrepancies in no way impair the powerfully dramatic effect of the ceremony: indeed this may well have been a more moving ceremony than the fairly naturalistic *Visitatio* which was to follow. At any rate it is interesting to see that Barking in the later fourteenth century was happy to invent (or, if not, adopt) a mimetic ceremony, splendid in itself but, purely in terms of dramatic form, very retrogressive.

It may seem from this necessarily brief account of Latin liturgical drama in England that in the Middle Ages plays were far rarer here than in France and the Empire: this indeed is the common view of scholars. It must be borne in mind, however, that there is never sufficient manuscript evidence surviving for any great church for us to be able to say with certainty that it possessed no liturgical drama. The problem is that plays might be copied in any of the many different types of service book used in the Middle Ages, ordinals, breviaries, tropers, antiphonars, and occasionally graduals and processionals.[79] Therefore one could only know that a particular cathedral or monastery at any given period did not have any liturgical drama if a full set of service books from it survived: the devastation of liturgical manuscripts at the Reformation, however, has led to our never having anything like this complete evidence. Since, for instance, York and Lincoln had plays, one wonders whether the other great northern cathedral church of Durham also did so. But from Durham there survives only one gradual and breviary dated from the thirteenth to fourteenth centuries.[80] From this nothing at all can be safely inferred.

The final question is that of the influence of Latin liturgical drama upon the English mystery plays. It is clear in general that the liturgical drama, rather than literary sources, provided an abiding authoritative model for the mystery cycles. It is perhaps notable that of the four cathedral cities known to have had Latin drama, York, Lincoln, Lichfield and Norwich, three also had mystery cycles: Lichfield, which alone did not, was too small a town to support so large and expensive an enterprise. The argument of course must not be reversed: Chester was not a cathedral town in the Middle Ages and it would be rash to infer from the Chester cycle that the Benedictine Abbey of St Werburgh performed liturgical drama, and Wakefield seems to have adopted the custom of an annual mystery cycle on the model of the archdiocese of York.

But though vernacular plays owed the fact of their existence to liturgical drama, any other debt was minuscule. The most important part of the cycles, namely the Passion sequence, could not derive from liturgical models, as churches continued to represent the Passion on Good Friday by the more decorous and reticent means of symbolism (the Passion plays of the twelfth century are not properly liturgical drama).[81] There were also no liturgical plays on the subject of events momentous in divine history, but uncommemorated in the festivals of the calendar, the Fall of the Angels, the Creation of the World and the Fall of Man. For the same reason Latin plays on Old Testament subjects are rare, and there are none on the three main cycle subjects, Cain and Abel, the Flood and the Sacrifice of Isaac. There was also no Latin liturgical play of the Last Judgment, an allegorical representation of this subject through the parable of the Wise and Foolish Virgins being preferred. The possibilities of influence are therefore restricted to the Prophets' Play, the Visits of the Shepherds and the Magi, and the Visit to the Tomb and the Resurrection Appearances.

A consideration of this question is necessarily hampered by the lack of Anglo-Latin texts: one can only look for the presence either of elements highly characteristic of liturgical drama in general or of those distinctive of the Rouen tradition. A further problem is that so much of liturgical drama consisted of the adaptation of biblical dialogue: therefore, when this dialogue is absent from a vernacular play, one can safely say that there was no liturgical influence, but the argument cannot be reversed: it is only when non-biblical dialogue is imitated that the influence of liturgical drama can be certainly inferred.

The absence of liturgical influence can be most clearly demonstrated in the shepherds' plays. The *Officium pastorum*, as we have already seen, had as its kernel a non-biblical scene, namely the dialogue between the shepherds and the midwives. But this had not been an apt invention, being dictated by the Easter model: it was therefore appropriately ignored in the vernacular cycles. The only exception is York, which probably embodied some form of this dialogue at an earlier stage, for Burton's list of characters records the presence of an *obstetrix* in the shepherds' play known to him in 1415 (and also in The Purification), whilst a relic of this figure and of the *Quem quaeritis* dialogue still survive in the revised play of the Adoration of the Magi.[82] The influence of the *Visitatio* was probably equally negligible, but because of the preponderance of biblical dialogue in it, this issue is less readily determinable. The *Ludus Coventriae* can alone be said to be entirely independent in that it does not even contain the *Quem quaeritis*. The Resurrection plays of York and Towneley (which share the same text) and of Chester, however, include both this dialogue and the preliminary question often added, *Quis revolvet*:[83] in all probability the authors knew both the *Visitatio* and its source in Mark, and it is pointless to ask which was the decisive influence. Chester alone includes the race between Peter and John, but this is so ineptly linked to the preceding Visit of the Marys to the Tomb that it is reasonable to infer that the author was not heeding a liturgical model, but, as was his custom, was following the gospels very closely (in Chester Mary Magdalene, though she has heard the angel's revelation, bewails to the apostles that Christ's body had vanished, whereas in the *Visitatio* she announces the Resurrection to them in the words of the *Victimae paschali*).

There is rather more evidence for the influence of the *Officium stellae* and the *Ordo prophetarum*. Whilst the characterisation of Herod in the vernacular cycles cannot be reduced to the simple influence of liturgical drama, it would be perverse not to allow that the indications of Herod's rage in the twelfth-century versions of the *Officium stellae* might have provided the germ of the idea. It is also possible that the dramatists learnt something about the management of the material in the Nativity sequence from liturgical models. There is, for instance, nothing in the gospels to suggest that the unspecified person (or people) of whom the

Magi ask the way, was an emissary of Herod. But in York and Towneley, as in the texts of the *Officium stellae*, they address themselves to a messenger of Herod, who already has instructions to bring them or any suspicious persons to Herod's court. Again in York and Towneley the idea of the Massacre is proposed to Herod by his councillors, and, as we have already seen, it was a characteristic of the Rouen play of the twelfth century that Herod did not devise this plan for himself, but had it suggested to him either by his son or by the soldiers.

It might be thought that any dependence of the vernacular cycles upon liturgical drama would most clearly be seen in the prophets' plays, where the opportunity for fresh dramatic invention would be slight. But, whilst three of the cycles (the exception is York) present a prophets' play as a convenient link between the Old and New Testaments, in at least two instances (the *Ludus Coventriae* and Chester) the dramatists have modelled their work, not upon the *Ordo prophetarum*, but upon variations of the theme which had taken place in the iconographic tradition.[84]

Some of these points will be discussed more fully in the later analyses of the plays themselves. But it will be clear from this rapid summary that the dramatists never followed liturgical drama uncritically: they ignored what was not useful but took occasional hints from it. Even these hints are largely confined to York and to the Towneley cycle which was dependent on it. The influence of liturgical drama must not of course be confused with the influence of the liturgy itself: as we shall see later, the dramatists sometimes drew upon the liturgy for the creation of special effects or as the source for some felicitous line. This briefly is the situation as it was at the time of the writing of the plays in the last quarter of the fourteenth century and the first half of the fifteenth. The dramatic offices of the liturgy had, however, influenced the non-liturgical drama, whether Latin or vernacular, of the twelfth century, and some of this drama can reasonably be considered the remote ancestor of the mystery plays. It is therefore the emergence of non-liturgical drama in the twelfth century that must next be considered.

Twelfth-Century Knowledge of
Plays and Acting

Christian literature in western Europe, with the possible exception of the hymn, has no forms peculiar to itself: Christian epic, lyric and drama have been written in deliberate imitation of classical models. Liturgical drama, however, did not spring initially from the adoption of secular forms that had literary prestige, but, as we saw in the previous chapter, arose through a complex series of chances and decisions remote from literary thought. Nevertheless the fragmentary dramatic episodes of the tenth century became transformed in the twelfth century into literary pieces, which, though comparatively tiny, bore all the lineaments of a play. To what extent this development was itself stimulated by conscious knowledge of and reflection upon the art of drama, and to what extent liturgical plays were understood to be of the same genre as secular drama, is nowadays a matter of dispute. It is, however, worth briefly considering whether the first writers of substantial plays, either in Latin or the vernacular, inherited not only the dramatic elaborations of the liturgy but also a concept of the imitation of life upon the stage which had roots in the classical tradition of Rome.

Whilst this question may seem a direct and straightforward one, even a tentative answer to it can only be arrived at by collecting a ragbag of scraps of evidence of widely different kinds. These pieces of evidence consist of matters as diverse as the knowledge and understanding of Roman comedy in the twelfth century; the professed imitation of it in the Latin works known as *comoediae*; the use of traditional metaphors drawn from the stage; the work of professional entertainers, both its origins and its nature; the non-religious terminology used in reference to religious plays; and finally, outside the classical tradition, the possible existence of folk-drama with its roots in fertility rituals. Whilst all this material has been the source of controversy, and whilst the reasonable inferences to be drawn from it do not tend invariably in the same direction, it is nevertheless worth investigating, for a circumstantial case can be built up from it to support the view that the art of drama was understood and valued in the twelfth century.

The only classical dramatist whose plays continued to be well-known in the Middle Ages was Terence. From the Carolingian period onwards his plays were copied in splendid manuscripts with lively illustrations and ample commentary.[1] In England there were copies in at least six religious houses, including St Albans.[2] In contrast to the very large number of surviving manuscripts of the plays of Terence, medieval manuscripts of Plautus are rare: two twelfth-century manuscripts from Bamberg and Halberstadt are extant, and there is known to have been a manuscript at Bury St Edmunds.[3] The plays of Plautus were, however, better known in learned circles of the twelfth century than this meagre count would suggest. In particular the authors of the Latin *comoediae* claim to be imitating him:[4] Vitalis of Blois cites the *Aulularia* and the *Amphitryo* as the sources respectively of his *Geta* and *Amphitryo*, though in the first instance he was certainly following the *Querolus* (a fifth-century re-working of the *Aulularia*)[5] and may have had a similar late Latin version of the *Amphitryo*, though the arguments for postulating the existence of this are not conclusive. It is clear anyway that the reputation of Plautus was high in the twelfth century – Vitalis would not otherwise have used it to enhance the dignity of his own works – and that his name was linked with that of Terence; that there was some confusion between Plautus's genuine works and later redactions of them under the same title is scarcely relevant to the present argument. It is interesting also to notice the use of the name of Menander in a similar context: another writer of *comoediae* from Blois, William, claims a play of Menander as the source of his *Alda* or *Mascula virgo*. Whilst at first sight a reference to a Greek writer looks like a second-hand reference to another great name,[6] it has been plausibly suggested that William of Blois may have come across a Latin translation of Menander's lost *Androgenos* when in Sicily.[7]

There is in fact sufficient evidence to show that Roman comedies were known in the twelfth century in the centres of learning, which were often themselves the home of liturgical drama. However, a connection between the two (even of the vaguest kind) cannot be immediately assumed as a reasonable probability, as it is often held that the Middle Ages did not understand that the plays of Terence and Plautus were written for acting upon the stage. Although the ninth- or tenth-century dialogue between Terence and his *delusor* may have served as a prologue to an actual performance of a play,[8] it is safe to assume that in general Roman comedies were read and studied rather than acted. Those who would have been capable of acting them, namely clerics, would have been forbidden to do so, and those who would have been free to do so, namely professional entertainers, would have been unable to perform a play in Latin. It would not, however, follow from this that the learned did not understand the distinction between drama and narrative.

There was admittedly a recurrent misconception that the manner of performance of classical plays had been that one man read the text aloud, whilst others mimed the action.[9] Whilst this belief appears in the earliest of the medieval Lives of Terence,[10] it does not seem to have gained general currency until popularised at the end of the twelfth century by Hugutio in his *Magnae derivationes*.[11] But the less bizarre notion, namely that Calliopus, who was thought to have been a friend of Terence instead of a later editor, recited the plays himself (but not with accompanying mime) appears in even the less fanciful of the *vitae*,[12] though the notes themselves usually give the impression that Calliopus's part was to speak in his own person the prologues and valedictory *Plaudite*, as if he were in fact a medieval *meneur du jeu*. It is this conception of Calliopus's role that seems to be reflected in the illustrated manuscripts of Terence, in which Calliopus appears in the position normally reserved for the author's portrait. The general impression given is that whilst the occasional description of Calliopus as *fabulae recitator* might mislead the unwary, the manuscripts were not organised to illustrate this assumption nor did they consistently emphasise it.

The inference to be drawn from the professed imitation of Plautus and Menander in the *comoediae* is equally uncertain. The *comoediae* (some of which are of English origin)[13] are not strictly dramatic in form, for, though they contain a high proportion of dialogue (far higher than would an ordinary narrative poem), nearly all have narrative links. The presence of such links in religious drama, however, shows that this is not certain evidence against the theory that they might be acted: a *lector* would then read the narrative passages.[14] The contemporary description of these works as *comoediae* might imply not only an imitation but also an understanding of the classical form, but again the term was sometimes applied to any story with a happy ending. Isidore of Seville had introduced this mistake into one of the definitions in his *Etymologiae*, though at another point he recognised tragedy and comedy as dramatic forms.[15] His mistake, however, was repeated by later lexicographers and from the thirteenth century onwards it became universally accepted.

In weighing this conflicting evidence it is essential not to regard the Middle Ages as one undefined and unvaried whole and also not to assume a steady progress towards accurate historical knowledge. In the twelfth century, which has often been given the title of a period of renaissance, classical drama may well have been better understood than in the thirteenth century. As has often been pointed out, John of Salisbury shows in the *Policraticus* an informed understanding of classical comedy.[16] He had certainly read the plays of Terence and knew that they had been acted, and he knew that the plays of Plautus and Menander were of the same genre. Though it is possible that he knew of the latter two only by repute, it is equally likely that he had read some of Plautus's work, as had his contemporary Osbern of Gloucester,[17] and that, as de Ghellinck has suggested, he knew the Sicilian translation of the *Androgenos*, used, as it is thought, by William of Blois.[18] If this latter suggestion is true, it is most improbable that John of Salisbury recognised the translation of the *Androgenos* as a play, whilst William of Blois did not: they belonged to the same humanist circles, had both been in Sicily, and William's brother, Peter of Blois, was a close friend of John of Salisbury. It is in fact a reasonable probability that John of Salisbury's knowledge of classical drama was shared with other scholars of the learned schools of Chartres and Orleans. The mistakes about the Roman stage were made by men who, though learned, were in this instance repeating information uncritically from earlier and respected sources. On the rare occasions when a twelfth-century humanist speaks independently and thoughtfully of the Roman stage, he is not misled by the errors of the encyclopaedic tradition.

The now famous medieval misconception about classical drama has in every way been over-emphasised. Today the difference between quietly and privately reading a play of Shakespeare and seeing it performed seems a radical one. But in the Middle Ages, when all literature was read aloud and dialogue often given vocal impersonation, the distinction must have seemed more blurred. It is therefore likely that the learned in the twelfth century understood the dramatic form, but did not think of it as exclusive to the stage and therefore inappropriate for reading, particularly for reading aloud, either by one reader with a change of voice or by a number of different readers. It is interesting to note that the earliest Italian humanists, who very ostentatiously modelled their plays on those of Seneca, Terence and Plautus, nevertheless wrote for public recitation and not for performance on the stage.[19]

It seems very likely that the *comoediae* too were written for public recitation.[20] There is nothing in the texts to suggest a full-scale dramatic representation and indeed the obscenity of some of the action is a clear indication to the contrary. Yet, as others have pointed out, the *comoediae* include dramatic effects, such as the changing of voice for the purpose of deception, which would lose their point unless heard. The performance of the *comoediae* must therefore have been something like the concert performance of an opera, which may even include a slight degree of mime. Nevertheless it can be assumed that at least some of their authors recognised that they were imitating a classical form for a typically medieval style of performance.

Some of the main developments in liturgical drama took place in the period when Roman comedy was known and imitated, and it is tempting to suppose that it was an understanding of Latin drama that led learned clerics to recognise the nature of the rudimentary plays that had grown up in the liturgy, and therefore to undertake something more self-conscious and substantial.[21] The resemblance in general cannot have been closer for the stock plots and characters of Plautus and Terence could not serve as precise models. A distinction here, however, has to be made between biblical drama and plays on saints' lives, for in the latter situations analogous with those in Roman comedy could arise. The pagan's passion for his treasure in the *Iconia Sancti Nicholai*, for instance, is of the same kind as that of the miserly Euclio in the *Aulularia*, and it has been plausibly suggested that the pagan's lament for the loss of his treasure in the version of the Fleury Play-book, a lament which is unusually written in hexameters,[22] was influenced by that of Euclio when he finds that the slave has made off with his carefully hidden gold.[23]

There was also a more theoretical parallel to be made. Hrotsvitha, who claimed in the preface to her plays, to be producing a pious substitute for the too enticing work of Terence, had an ingenious argument, namely, that she would 'glorify . . . the laudable chastity of Christian virgins in that self-same form of composition, which has been used to describe the shameless acts of licentious women'.[24] She chose for her plays the stories of the virgin martyrs whose chastity has been threatened by evil pagans, and was thus able to preserve the theme of love, though morally reversed. The same kind of comparison was made by William Fitzstephen in the twelfth century. His Life of Thomas à Becket is introduced by a rhetorical eulogy of London, studded with classical quotations, and purporting to show London as then superior to Rome at the height of its glory. Amongst the many ways in which it surpasses its great fore-runner is that 'Lundonia pro spectaculis theatralibus, pro ludis scenicis, ludos habet sanctiores, representationes miraculorum quae sancti confessores operati sunt, seu representationes passionum quibus claruit constantia martyrum.'[25] William Fitzstephen praises London's plays on the subject of the miracles and martyrdoms of saints as a holier equivalent to the theatre of Rome. Whether his omission of any reference to plays on biblical subjects is determined by theory or fact remains unclear. It is possible that his vague and general statement reflects knowledge of a more precise and ingenious antithesis of the kind made by Hrotsvitha, and that he would therefore have hesitated to include biblical plays such as the *Mystère d'Adam*. It was not until the sixteenth century that the ancient argument of the superiority of Christian subject-matter to pagan was applied to plays based on Old Testament subjects and the life of Christ, and a corresponding change then took place in style and treatment of material.[26]

There are possible approaches to the question of what dramatic traditions survived in the twelfth century very different from the investigation of the knowledge and understanding of Roman comedy amongst the learned. At that time educated men could become aware of the idea of theatrical imitation from sources of widely varying kinds, works of information, metaphorical usages, and contemporary practice. Typical of the informative kind was the much-studied *Etymologiae* of Isidore of Seville, a work which is in modern terms a cross between a dictionary and encyclopaedia. In his exposition of the words *theatrum* and *scena*, Isidore showed an accurate understanding of the nature of the Roman stage,[27] apart from the minor mistake of supposing that the audience stood rather than sat, an error of venerable scholarly ancestry (it had begun with Valerius Maximus, and was repeated by many including Augustine).[28] This work was well known throughout the Middle Ages, and Isidore's information was repeated in another much-read work, the *Speculum doctrinale* of Vincent of Beauvais.[29] It may be noted incidentally that, whilst Roman theatres in western Europe had fallen into ruin, and if serviceable at all were used as forts or barracks, some learned travellers recognised them for what they were: Gerald of Wales, for instance, understood the ruins at Caerleon-on-Usk as *loca theatralia*[30] and an Englishman, Alexander Neckham, mourned in an elegy the ruined amphitheatre at Paris.[31] In more common thought, however, the idea of a theatre was distinct from that of a building, and the word was loosely used for any place in which plays might be performed, and in context therefore even of a marketplace.[32]

The idea of a theatre was also deeply embedded in traditional metaphors. The idea that 'All the world's a stage' is of very ancient origin, and, as Curtius has described, it reached the Middle Ages from both pagan and Christian antiquity.[33] According to Curtius, the phrase *mimus vitae* was proverbial in classical times: Cicero, Horace, Seneca, Suetonius and Boethius all used variations upon it. In the Middle Ages this metaphor received its most subtle elaboration in the *Policraticus* of

John of Salisbury,[34] but it is also found as a casual image in a poem to the Virgin in one of the *Cambridge Songs*.[35] Whilst in origin the image implied man's dependence upon the gods, it acquired also more reverberant connotations of the impermanence and insubstantiality of life. In the work of early Christian authors, however, the image was given a much more precise and polemical reference. In their use of the image the point of the comparison is that the life of Christian virtue and the eschatological culminations will provide a more important and awe-inspiring spectacle than that provided by the stage.

The starting-point for the Christian usage – and one often thereafter quoted – was St Paul's description of the martyrdoms of the apostles as a divinely appointed spectacle for men and angels (1 Corinthians iv. 9). A series of ingenious variations upon this are to be found in the concluding chapters of Tertullian's famous denunciation of the Roman stage, the *De spectaculis*.[36] The grace-given gifts of the Christian are the *spectacula Christianorum*, which far surpass worldly entertainments; the conflict between virtue and vice is better than the wrestling of athletes; and then at the last will come the greatest of all spectacles, that of the Day of Judgment, in which the damned will serve as tragic actors: 'Quae tunc spectaculi latitudo!'[37]

From this tradition, begun by Paul and extended by Tertullian, there were two lines of descent. One kept close to Paul in finding the point of comparison in the virtuous life: according to St Bernard, for instance, the *bonus ludus* is that which provides a pleasing spectacle to the heavenly audience; most undeserving of the title of *ludus* are the contortions of the contemporary entertainers, the *ioculatores* and *saltatores*.[38] The other followed Tertullian in finding the source of the spectacle in the torments of the damned: Rabanus Maurus, for instance, in the *De universo* (a work which condenses and allegorises Isidore's *Etymologiae*) says of the theatre, 'Mystice autem theatrum praesentem mundum significare potest', but he reduces this classical generalisation to a precise point of comparison, that the follies and punishments of the wicked give entertainment to the servants of God.[39]

A very remarkable development from this tradition was that of the vision of hell, in which the damned are seen to put on a theatrical entertainment for the pleasure of their devilish masters. A very detailed account of such a display is related in the Vision of Thurkill, a work written in the early thirteenth century, and incorporated in an abridged form in the Chronicles of Matthew Paris and Roger of Wendover.[40] According to this narrative, Thurkill (who was an Essex peasant) was conducted in his vision to hell, where he saw a large circular theatre:

around the iron walls sat the devils, whilst the other seats were filled with the damned. At the command of the prince of the devils, representatives of the wicked were seized from their seats and compelled to act out their former sins: the *superbus* mimed the gestures and expression of a haughty man and spoke arrogant words; a *placitator* repeated his *actus vitae* in a little sketch that showed him taking bribes; whilst, perhaps in the decadent tradition of the Roman theatre, a pair of adulterers repeated their crime upon the stage.

Of a similar literary kind is the portrayal of some of the Seven Deadly Sins in the *Ancrene Wisse*. In this the setting for the entertainment is not a theatre, but, as it would so often have been in the Middle Ages, a court. At the devil's court, Pride, Envy and Anger are respectively trumpeters, jesters (*ioculatores*) and jugglers, who practice their skills to amuse the devil.[41] The allegorical relationship between the sins and their representations differentiates this carefully contrived allegorical scene from the revelation given to Thurkill, but there is in both the same underlying image of contemporary entertainment transferred to the theatre or court of hell.

It will be seen from this, as it could from many other passages, that the image of the *mimus vitae* very often became an occasion, not merely for an illuminating and probing analogy, but also for an attack upon all kinds of contemporary stage performances. Many passages embodying it, therefore, not only illustrate the continuance of the image, but also cast light upon what kind of dramatic impersonation might be found in the twelfth century outside liturgical drama. They therefore lead to the third possible link of continuity with the classical past, namely a continuity at sub-literary level of the profession of the *mimus* and his traditional sketches.[42]

The possibility that successive generations of actors (of however primitive a kind) provided a continuous chain between the late Roman stage and the secular entertainments of western Europe in the twelfth century makes an attractive theory. The stumbling block to its acceptance is that one is in effect postulating the influence of a lost body of literature upon another body of literature, which is itself hypothetical. All that can be done is to estimate whether there are sufficient coincidences in the scanty accounts of the performances of the Roman and medieval *mimi* for this connection to be a likelihood. A judgment on this issue must to a large extent depend upon one's own private sense of the probable. Grimace and gesticulation, for instance, seem to have been an important part of the Roman mimic actor's style just as they were of twelfth-century entertainers. Whether this seems a significant correspondence or whether it may be thought the type of comedy that could be reborn over and over again is an issue not to be settled objectively. Again there is evidence that one of the commonest subjects of mimic drama was a plot that involved adultery. One, which has been reconstructed from a passing reference in one of Juvenal's satires, turns upon a situation in which a wife hides her lover from her husband, unexpectedly returned, in a small and uncomfortable chest.[43] The theme is anticipatory of that of many fabliaux, but if there is, for instance, a continuous path to be traced from the Roman mime to the *Interludium de clerico et puella*,[44] it is an obscure and devious one, and such stories could well have passed from drama to narrative and back to drama again.

It is, however, worth briefly considering what can be reasonably inferred about the dramatic arts of the medieval entertainer, for, whilst we may feel that the issue of historical continuity has to be left an open question, twelfth-century writers probably assumed that when they condemned the *mimi* and *histriones* they were condemning what had offended the Fathers eight hundred years earlier. The interesting point that emerges from the attempt to piece together the scattered scraps of evidence about medieval entertainments is that the skills of the twelfth-century *mimus* or *ioculator* included the impersonation of recognisable character types or recognisable moods. Some of the evidence for this occurs in works already mentioned, the Vision of Thurkill and the *Ancrene Wisse*. In the latter the description of the face-pulling of the envious *ioculator* may well be a belittling reference to satirical impersonation: one might associate it, for instance, with the character-sketch in the same work of the back-biter, who 'pulls a long face' before beginning his malicious gossip, though the author of the *Ancrene Wisse* borrowed this immediately from one of St Bernard's sermons on the Song of Songs.[45] This kind of imitativeness is implied by the common comparison of *jongleurs* to apes,[46] and it is alluded to more specifically in a fabliau which refers to *jongleurs* of which 'l'uns fet l'ivre, l'autres le sot'.[47] It might even be thought that the common representation of Gluttony amongst the Seven Deadly Sins as a rolling drunkard instead of a more abstract personification was influenced by acting traditions. The description of the lawyer in the Vision of Thurkill, who accepts bribes, is particularly interesting in that it suggests the sketch of a primitive Ruth Draper, who could suggest by his manner and tone of voice that there were other actors with him upon the stage.

This interpretation of the medieval mimic arts is to some extent confirmed by the scenes of exaggerated and stylised gestures found on misericords or other unobtrusive places in church or in the margins of manuscripts. The work of popular entertainers, musicians, animal-trainers, acrobats, trumpet-blowers, knife-throwers, fools, tumblers and contortionists, is often represented in these small and insignificant positions: so too are the grimaces (such as sticking out the tongue) of the *ioculatores*. Particularly noticeable in some of the scenes, which are usually taken to relate to fabliaux and exempla, is the use of mimic gesture, gesture so expressive that words are unnecessary. In one marginal scene, for instance, a hermit kneels with hands extended in an imploring gesture; opposite him is a young woman with hands out-stretched in a gesture of horrified denial.[48] Speaking gestures of this kind are common and are not described in the narrative counterparts to these episodes: it is tempting to suppose that they represent the acting style of the *mimi*.

The common use in the twelfth century of the terms *mimi* and *histriones* is therefore interesting, not because it establishes a direct, historical link between late Roman and medieval dramatic entertain-ments, but because it may cast light on what medieval scholars thought had been the nature of the Roman *ludi*, so often uninformatively referred to; and in particular because dramatic impersonation would then appear to have been part of the Roman entertainers' repertoire, just as it was in the twelfth century. This conclusion, drawn from the terminology for professional entertainers, is necessarily speculative and peripheral, contributing at most to defining a little the relevant intellec-tual and literary ambience in which religious drama first flourished. More central and more precise are the inferences to be drawn from the terminology used for the plays themselves.

The word used for the plays of Terence and Plautus was *comoediae*. It is therefore striking that a religious play staged in Riga in 1204 should be described by an almost contemporary chronicler as 'ludus prophetarum ordinatissimus, quem Latini comoediam vocant'.[49] This application of the term *comoedia* to a religious play appears to be unique, though it has been rightly associated with a twelfth-century *scholium* on Horace's *Art of Poetry*, 1.179, which illustrates Horace's point by reference to a play of Herod, and with another *scholium* of the same period on Ovid's *Fasti*, 1, 47, which again draws a parallel between Roman dramatic spectacles and the plays of the Massacre of the Innocents.[50] Creizenach also quotes examples from fourteenth-century *scholia*,[51] and it seems likely that a thorough investigation of medieval commentaries upon relevant passages in classical authors would reveal a tradition of this type to have been both widespread and continuous.

The word *ludus*, also used by the Riga chronicler, is much better documented, and in the twelfth century sometimes came to supplant the liturgical words that had hitherto been used, *ordo, officium, processio*, etc.[52] It is employed three times for the plays from Benediktbeuern (for the plays of the Passion and Resurrection and in a rubric for the Nativity Play);[53] the Beauvais *Daniel* is called a *ludus*,[54] and so also is Hilarius's play of St Nicholas.[55] Most important of all, when in the mid-twelfth century, Gerhoh of Reichersberg needed a precise term to describe what he condemned (*ordines* or *officia* obviously would not serve), he referred to the religious plays as *ludi*.[56]

The Latin word *ludus* or *ludi* had in classical times been extended from the games to associated spectacles, and hence had become very general in meaning. Isidore in his article *De spectaculis* defines four kinds of *ludus* the fourth of which is *ludus scenicus*,[57] and it is obviously in this sense that it is sometimes used of the more substantial religious plays. It shows of course a clear sense of a play as opposed to a dramatic passage in the liturgy; but it is a word of less dignified associations than *comoedia*, and would tend to link the religious plays on account of their form with the dramatic impersonations of the *mimi*, whether Roman or medieval, rather than with plays of literary prestige. The equivalents of *ludus, jeu, spiel, pley* (less often *gamen*) became the accepted terms for later vernacular drama.

Miraculum or *miracula* (the plural is often used in a singular meaning) is a word of similar type, though its semantic history is unclear, and it is not certain whether like *ludus* it is a word of secular origin, which then became applied to religious plays, or whether it travelled in the opposite direction.[58] It first appears with reference to a play in the Fleury Play-book where the play on the subject of the *Iconia Sancti Nicholai* is introduced as *Aliud miraculum*, and at its end is written *Finitur miraculum*.[59] There is of course some ambiguity here, in that *miraculum* could refer to either form or subject-matter or both, and it is possible to find in this usage the starting-point of the semantic development of the word. In the same century, however, the *Ludus de S. Katerina* from Dunstable, which was fairly certainly a Passion, is said to be of a kind that in the common tongue (*vulgariter*) is called *miracula*.[60] This suggests that *miracula* then seemed a popular word in contrast to the learned word *ludus*. In the second quarter of the thirteenth century *miracula* was again used with a slight tone of apology for its popularity by Robert Grosseteste in his condemnation of the satirical and dramatic ceremonies of the Feast of Fools,[61] in which the clergy seem to have introduced into the church some of the styles of acting of the *mimi*. In this sense, though perhaps also extended to popular dramatic ceremonies, it is used a little later by Robert Mannyng.[62] The clearest use of it with reference to popular dramatic spectacles occurs in an illuminating little story preserved in a series of religious tales in MS. Sloane 2478: two friars travelling through the country hear sounds of laughter and applause from a nearby meadow, and 'estimabant ibi spectacula celebrare, quae nos miracula appellare consuevimus', and they go there to preach.[63] The impression therefore given is that *miracula* is a word of popular and secular origin (the miracles being originally conjuring tricks rather than the wonders worked by saints), but that at an early stage it became applied to religious plays, the transference perhaps being encouraged by the subject-matter of many of the saints' plays. Its implications would therefore be of the same kind as those of *ludus*, but it would reflect popular rather than learned usage.

In this chapter some twelfth- and early thirteenth-century evidence has been assembled to indicate a propitious secular environment for the development of liturgical drama into genuine plays, works that were conceived as plays by their authors and recognised as plays by their audience. In doing this it has been necessary to consider both the learned tradition of the comedies of Plautus and Terence, and the unlearned tradition of the dramatic performances of popular entertainers, which twelfth-century scholars, whether correctly or not, associated again with the Roman stage. There remains the possibility, to be finally considered, of a secular dramatic tradition outside the classical tradition, that of the folk-play.

These plays often consist of a combat, in which the hero is usually, though not invariably, St George; the hero is then killed but revived by a doctor. Like many of the ballads, the folk-plays survive only in texts written down by folklorists in comparatively recent times, but unlike the ballads, there is nothing in their style that suggests the Middle Ages as the original time of composition. The folk-poem is always a difficult thing to detect since, by definition, none can survive that has not been open to contamination by a contemporaneous literary culture. But if, for the sake of argument, we accept the theory that we can instinctively recognise a folk-poem, it is clear that the qualities which we are tempted to identify as those of folk-poetry do not appear in the style of the folk-plays. R. J. E. Tiddy, an early exponent of the folk-play, cited as instances of the folk imagination two remarks that had been made to him by labourers: one said of Portland Castle that it was 'Like the clouds when they be low', the other compared a clumsy dancer to 'a great toad putting his feet down one after the other on the floor'.[64]

It is precisely the unexpectedness, and freshness of these similes, that are lacking in the surviving texts of the folk-plays, which are written more in the manner of the urban hack-writers of later periods with their tedium and flatness, than with the supposed untutored spontaneity of the unlettered.[65]

It is therefore the content of the plays, with their primitive enactment of death and rebirth (reflecting the natural seasons of the year) that is indicative of village ceremonies; and the most recent students of the plays (who are interested in them entirely from the folklorist and anthropological point of view) maintain that 'the basis of the Play is an action around which texts have grown in an effort to rationalise what had become inexplicable with the passage of time'.[66] The authors do not speculate on when these texts were written; the probability is that the plays, as opposed to the action, are very late indeed, and show a crude attempt to impose upon a village mime (itself a relic of an early fertility ritual) a plot and dialogue influenced by miracle plays, which might seem analogous in their recurring theme of the miraculous and seemingly dramatically casual restoration of the dead to life,[67] and which provided a historical identity for the hero, namely St George, and for his antagonist, the Turk.[68] On present evidence it would therefore be safe to say that it was the religious drama of the church that influenced the folk-play and suggested the usefulness of dialogue and not vice versa.

Whilst the folk-play itself is probably late, the village ceremonies that preceded it are referred to from the beginning of the thirteenth century, when amongst the various *ludi* condemned by Robert Grosseteste are the *Inductio Maii sive Autumni*;[69] a little later the *Constitutions* of Walter de Cantilupe prohibit clerics from taking part in the *ludos . . . de Rege et Regina*,[70] presumably a reference to the same type of seasonal mimetic ceremony. Such ceremonies may tentatively be added to the list of medieval entertainments that provided the right ambience in which religious drama could flourish and be esteemed even by the most ignorant members of the audience. The account of the play put on in Riga (already referred to)[71] describes how some of the pagan audience (namely the Lettish inhabitants of Riga and the surrounding country) took fright at the representation of the fight between David and Goliath and fled for their lives. This story of the inability to distinguish between life and its imitation upon the stage is one in a recurring pattern: the most famous literary example is Partridge's fear of the ghost in Hamlet, when Tom Jones took him to the theatre. The fact therefore that in England in the Middle Ages even simple villagers were accustomed to a ceremony that involved dressing up, and to a familiar person feigning for the occasion to represent somebody else, can well have contributed to a simple enjoyment and understanding of religious drama when first performed in the vernacular and in a public place. It is very unlikely that the ritual acting of the 'folk' contributed anything more than this.

Drama in the Twelfth Century

The reasonable conclusion to be drawn from the scattered and some-times ambivalent pieces of evidence surveyed in the previous chapter is that in the twelfth century there was some understanding of drama as a secular literary form. The importance of this conclusion is that it may well account for the remarkable developments in religious drama at this period, and in particular for the creation of semi-vernacular or entirely vernacular plays. If vernacular drama had not been written before the fourteenth century, its appearance then could have been explained solely in terms of the widespread movement for the instruc-tion of the laity, a movement which undoubtedly contributed to the sudden efflorescence of vernacular drama two centuries after its first appearance. The earlier developments, however, were rather of a learned and humanistic origin, and the partial or total use of the verna-cular seems often (though not invariably) to have been determined by aesthetic considerations rather than by the spiritual needs of the unlettered.

While all scholars would agree that in the discussion of twelfth-century drama a distinction has to be made between genuine plays and dramatic embellishments of the liturgy (however lengthy), most dispute what criteria should be applied and to which classification any given work belongs. A very common system of classification takes language as its chief criterion and distinguishes three categories: plays entirely in Latin which are liturgical; plays part-Latin and part-vernacular which are called transitional; and plays entirely in the vernacular which alone are said to have outgrown and discarded their liturgical origins. This system is tendentious and over-rigid, and leads to groupings of plays that in literary terms are ludicrously inept. Not all Latin plays are confined within the formal limits imposed by a liturgical context. For the learned in the twelfth century Latin was not only the language of the liturgy and of philosophy and theology, but also of the literature of entertainment: it is for them that the plays in the Benediktbeuern manuscript were probably written. Some plays, in which a mixture of Latin and the vernacular is used, do not represent a stage in evolutionary progress, but in their subtlety and inventiveness rival the finest of the later religious plays: of this kind is the Anglo-Norman *Mystère d'Adam*. Finally, some plays, though written entirely in a vernacular, are very stiff and cautious pieces.

A less common, but perhaps more soundly based, distinction is that between plays set to music and plays spoken. The setting of Gregorian chant would intentionally and inevitably suggest the liturgy and would impose a formal solemnity entirely at odds with dramatic realism. The music would not even, as in opera, serve to heighten emotion and underline the dramatic, for, as John Stevens has pointed out, music in the twelfth century was not used in this naturalistic way.[1] In assessing the literary impression made by a text it is therefore important to remember whether the words have a musical setting, but a division of works along these lines would nevertheless yield odd results. The *Sponsus*, for instance, despite its vernacular passages and literary power, would be relegated to the conventional liturgical category, and the short Passion Play from the Benediktbeuern manuscript,[2] which is formed by the piecing together of dramatic utterances from a harmony of the gospels, would be given greater literary importance than the much more impressive Christmas and Easter plays from the same manuscript.

A third criterion is that of time and place of performance, and this indeed would be very helpful were this extra-textual information regularly ascertainable. While one would not expect a perfect correspondence between liturgical plays and literary formality and non-liturgical plays and dramatic expressiveness, this distinction would make a firm and satisfactory base on which to rest further analysis. Plays performed in the monastic refectory, in the schoolroom, in the church but not as part of the liturgy, and in the churchyard would obviously need their own substance and weight: they could not be simple, mimetic pieces, given meaning and solemnity by their liturgical context. Unfortunately, however, manuscript rubrics rarely make plain the place and occasion of the performance, and there is therefore a tendency nowadays to infer these from the nature of the work, a reasonable procedure but one that can readily lead to a circular argument.

In the last resort, therefore, the distinction between play and liturgical office rests upon literary judgment alone: a play is a work that repays literary analysis because the author brought to bear upon it a literary imagination and a sense of the dramatic. The activity of these powers can be inferred from the way in which the subject-matter is handled. The playwright has to impose a pattern upon his material, whereas in liturgical drama the pattern is imposed by the surrounding framework of the liturgy and by the character of the feast upon which the drama is acted. Therefore the characteristic of liturgical drama, even at its most ample, is the simple accretion of episode and the filling in of detail: there is no interpretative pattern to determine the principles of selection and invention. The playwright has also to consider his audience, and therefore potentially undramatic material must be made dramatic and there must be a sufficient degree of characterisation for the attention of the audience to be held. The author of liturgical drama, however, did not have to consider, except in a minimal way, how to engage his audience's interest (in some instances there might not even be an audience). Though there are early references to the intention of exciting devotion and conveying instruction, this aim would be contained by the idea of liturgical embellishment: an analogy would be the composing of a hymn rather than writing a play for the theatre. For in the audience of liturgical drama a consistent attempt at concentration, an open willingness to heed and to be moved, could be presupposed.

The differences between liturgical drama and genuine plays in the handling of these literary issues may be illustrated from the Benedikt-beuern Christmas Play. In the historical sweep of this play, which extends from the prophets to the death of Herod, the events that centre on Herod himself have their own inherent dramatic tension, but the sequence of the prophecies is highly undramatic, and the annunciation to the shepherds and their visit to the Christ-Child is more pageant and spectacle than play. The author of this work is unique in finding a method of giving the episode of the prophets a dramatic interest: this is done by introducing the figure of Archisynagogus, who argues against Augustine, mocking the notion that a virgin should bear a child in intellectual and verbal jokes: the *Laetabundus* sung by Augustine, for instance, is parodied by Archisynagogus always replying to the refrain, 'Res miranda' with the words 'Res neganda'.[3] This ingenious introduction of conflict was no doubt suggested to the author by the debate form that flourished in the twelfth century,[4] but it is precisely this skilful borrowing from other and often secular forms to give life to the undramatic that is the hallmark of successful religious plays throughout the Middle Ages. The treatment of the shepherds' scene is similarly inventive: other ways were later found of making this placid scene yield a dramatic clash, but again the Benediktbeuern treatment is unique in introducing the angels' traditional enemy at this point, the devil, who repeatedly urges the shepherds not to be deceived by the angels' announcement that a virgin has borne a child, subtly suggesting that such a belief could only spring from ignorance and simple-minded credulity. These two inventions are not only dramatically satisfying in themselves, but also contribute to a moral and doctrinal pattern that is carefully worked out, namely that at every stage there is an attempt to thwart God's redemptive plan.

The date of the Benediktbeuern Christmas Play is not known: it cannot be later than the early thirteenth century, which is the date of the manuscript,[5] and it could have been written any time in the preceding fifty to eighty years. In thought and style it has some affinity with the Tegernsee *Antichristus*, which has fairly plausibly been dated about 1160.[6] The elaborateness of the staging and the large acting area required make it very improbable that it was performed as part of the liturgy, though like its liturgical predecessors it is set to music; and, despite the minor detachment from liturgical time shown by the inclusion of the Annunciation, its general compass seems to be determined by the feasts celebrated during the twelve days of Christmas, the Nativity, the Holy Innocents and the Epiphany. Whether the play was performed outside the church or within the nave is uncertain: on grounds of general probability an indoor performance seems the more likely, as to put on a play of this scale out of doors in late December or early January seems an unlikely undertaking even in an area a little more southerly than England.[7]

The Benediktbeuern Christmas Play is an interesting example of a work that is a genuine play and not a dramatic office, although it is still set to liturgical music, tied to a liturgical season, and written entirely in Latin. It can therefore be seen safely as part of the twelfth-century movement of play-writing, of which the works are more often characterised by a partial or total use of the vernacular. Plays of this kind are found in every western European language, French, German, Spanish, Italian and Anglo-Norman. Before discussing these, however, it is necessary to consider briefly the possibility, so far relegated to one side, that the vernacular was sometimes specifically used as an aid to the unlearned.

There survives from the concluding decades of the fourteenth century a very elaborate description of a sumptuous dramatisation of the office of lauds on the feast of the Presentation of the Virgin, as it was performed at Avignon. At the end it is said that the *carmina de Laudibus* are very moving and intended to arouse the greatest devotion amongst those who understand Latin; since, however, many people do not understand Latin, it is permissible to translate them into the vernacular and then to perform them in some dramatic way.[8] This passage is important in the history of liturgical drama, for in it is stated explicitly for the first time that the vernacular may be used in order to make the office intelligible to the unlettered laity. But, though permission to use the vernacular in a dramatic office is never before stated, the reason for its use, namely that the congregation shall be aroused to devotion by the drama, is (as we shall see in chapter V) an ancient one, and found regularly from the twelfth century onwards.[9] It follows from this that the liturgical drama was seen, not solely as part of the liturgy in which the congregation unite with the clergy in worshipping God and doing honour to Him, but partly at least as a sermon, in which the priest faces the congregation and expounds Christian doctrine to them in the style and language that they can understand. When from the twelfth century onwards priests came increasingly to preach in the vernacular, a situation arose in which vernacular liturgical drama might come to be tolerated. The possibility therefore of a vernacular religious play having formed part of the liturgy can never be ruled out, though surviving evidence suggests that it remained a rare practice. An unmistakable example is the fragment of *Les Trois Maries*, preserved in a mid-thirteenth-century manuscript, though quite possibly of earlier origin.[10] There is nothing in this that is not or could not be a direct translation from a Latin liturgical play: part of it, for instance, consists of a rendering of the *Victimae paschali*. This disorganised fragment has been written into a blank page of a manuscript containing an abbreviated version of the Old Testament. Its rather chancy preservation here may indicate that the likelihood of vernacular liturgical plays surviving was slight. As in the office of the Presentation of the Virgin, the official version would always be in Latin, and it is this that would be preserved in ordinals or other service-books, whilst any vernacular version would be a lowly alternative, undeserving of a permanent method of preservation. No plays written entirely in the vernacular survive in their correct liturgical position in regular service-books.

Latin plays containing a few lines, or even substantial passages in the vernacular, are of a different kind. In most of them the use of the vernacular seems to have little to do with a desire for comprehensibility, but corresponds rather to a deliberate change from high to low style. In particular it is clear that the vernacular was considered the language of lament: the Blessed Virgin makes her *planctus* at the foot of the Cross in German (Benediktbeuern Passion Play)[11] or in Italian (the Montecassino Passion Play);[12] Mary Magdalene sorrowfully repents her sin in German (Benediktbeuern Passion Play)[13] and in French expresses her desolation before Christ appears to her (the Easter Play from Origny-sur-Loire);[14] Martha and Mary grieve for the death of Lazarus in French (Hilarius's *Suscitacio Lazari*)[15] and in French too the pagan merchant rages over the loss of his treasure in Hilarius's *Ludus super iconia Sancti Nicolai*;[16] and finally the foolish virgins mourn their sleep of sin in the Provençal refrain, 'Dolentas, chaitivas, trop i avem dormit' (*Sponsus*).[17]

That the use of the vernacular is determined by a purely literary decision can be seen from a comparison between the two surviving plays on the Raising of Lazarus, the one by Hilarius, the other from the Fleury Play-book. Both authors have given a dramatic focus to the subject by inventing a long dialogue between the grieving sisters and their comforters. Hilarius has aimed at a lyrical effect by giving to each of the sisters a vernacular refrain that catches a poignant simplicity possible only in the language of common speech:[18]

> Hor ai dolor,
> hor est mis frere morz;
> por que gei plor.

In contrast the anonymous author of the Fleury Play has been more interested in the nature of the comfort offered and has ingeniously given to the comforters a very moving but non-Christian consolation:[19]

> Moriemur et nos similiter;
> omnes gentes aduncat pariter
> mortis hamus.
> Tali lege intramus seculum,
> ut quandoque carnis ergastulum
> exeamus.
>
> Pro dilecti fratris interitu
> ne ploretis; in eius exitu
> est gaudendum.
> Liberatus multis sup(p)liciis
> iam evasit quod restat aliis
> paciendum.

Both scenes are touching and both prepare equally well for Christ's demonstration of His power to raise the dead. But the resigned gravity of the comforters is best expressed in Latin, the immediacy of sorrow in the unelevated vernacular.

The most striking and unusual of this group of plays is the *Sponsus*, in which Latin and French dialogue is combined to give the impression of a linguistically hybrid play. It is an early work, written scarcely later than the beginning of the twelfth century, and it is preserved in a *troparium* from Limoges.[20] The unmistakable power of this play derives from the tension between literal and allegorical levels. On the surface the story seems to be a simple one about thrifty forethought and gay imprudence, not unlike the fable of the ant and the grasshopper, but in the Bible it is told as one of the series of eschatological parables in Matthew xxiv and xxv.

It is not known for certain at what season in the year the play was acted, but the theme and treatment suggest the first Sunday in Advent, when it is Christ's second coming that is heralded. If this were so, it would explain the emphasis in the play on the sleep of the foolish virgins instead of on their lack of oil, a divergence from the parable that has often been discussed. Both of course have the same allegorical significance. In a preceding parable, that of the thief in the night, it is sleep – the failure to keep watch – that permitted the entry of the devil,[21] whereas in that of the wise and foolish virgins, it is the failure of the foolish virgins to supply themselves with oil, that is with good deeds, that is the nub of the allegory, and not the sleep that prevented them from doing so.[22] But the shift of allegorical emphasis seems excellently related to the epistle of the mass for this Sunday, which begins 'Et hoc scientes tempus, quia hora est iam nos de somno surgere'.[23]

This parable, even as told in Matthew, is disconcerting, for the wise virgins, who signify the blessed, seem ungenerous in their refusal to share their oil with the foolish. This springs from the difference in time between the literal and the allegorical levels; the action on the literal level takes place in the present world, in which mercy is still freely given, whilst that of the allegorical level takes place on the Last Day, when the time for mercy is passed and only justice will be seen. In the *Sponsus* this disquieting clash is heightened through the naturalism of the vernacular passages. The refrain of the foolish virgins (already quoted) is touching in its simple self-reproach, whilst the wise virgins' refusal to help is expressed in a tone of colloquial and sharp rebuke: [24]

> De nostr' oli queret nos a doner
> N'on auret pont alet en achapter
> Deus merchaans que lai veet ester.
> Dolentas, chaitivas, trop i avet dormit!

45

The vernacular here is used to make the literal level of the play more lively and immediate, but it is also used for the non-literal level at the beginning of the play, when Gabriel describes the sufferings of Christ in a speech which echoes the complaints of Christ at the Last Judgment.[25] It has been suggested that during this speech the foolish virgins were shown sleeping, but as the play has no stage-directions, this can only be a guess: certainly it would have been a very effective way of driving home the folly of their sleep. But, even without this mimetic emphasis, the use of the vernacular in Gabriel's speech (for which one would have expected Latin) is doctrinally and dramatically effective, for it indicates that in the ordinary simple world of the surface of the story, in which the foolish virgins pathetically beg for help, Christ also suffered.

The plot of the *Sponsus*, as has already been pointed out, resembles that of *Everyman*,[26] the difference being that it takes place at a moment later in time, when it is too late for repentance. This interpretation is borne out by the commentaries, which see in the virgins' lack of oil the lack of the good deeds which must accompany all those who will be saved.[27] The allegory for this reason works in a peculiarly powerful and disturbing way: for the effect of the plot here, as in *Everyman*, is to build up sympathy for those who can find no help when they need it, and the threefold rejection (by the wise virgins, by the oil-merchant, and by Christ) gathers a terrifying momentum. On a tiny scale it resembles the rejection of Falstaff.

The *Sponsus* brings home the Advent call to repentance in a specially powerful way. In didactic terms it may be considered an exemplum to illustrate the summons to awake in the opening words of the epistle for the first Sunday in Advent which in its light seem more menacing, and yet consoling in their assurance to the congregation that for them at least it was not too late to awake from the sleep of sin and to acquire the oil of good deeds. But in literary terms it brings home the fate of the damned in an elusively moving and poignant way. Every literary depiction of Christ's rejection of the damned engages the audience's sympathy for those condemned. But the author of the *Sponsus*, who combined the formality of the Latin dialogue with the simplicity and homeliness of the Provençal, seems to have been sensitively aware of this inevitable response and to have deliberately manipulated it. The precise subtleties of the *Sponsus* depend upon the bilingual mode. Our sympathies go unreservedly to the foolish virgins because the use of the vernacular confers a touching realism upon the literal level of the parable, whilst the use of Latin with its theological and liturgical associations drives home the point that our sympathies have gone to the justly damned. Without the vernacular the *Sponsus* would be a lifeless versification of the parable, without the Latin it would be a pointless and rather disagreeable little story of some people who frantically sought for help and were meanly refused it. The *Sponsus* is a superb illustration of the particular potentialities of the macaronic play.

There is oddly enough only one entirely vernacular play surviving on the Continent from this period, and its circumstances are mysterious: it was written in Spain in the mid-twelfth century and had no successors for three hundred years. This fragmentary work, the *Auto de los Reyes Magos*, is copied with musical notation at the end of a manuscript belonging to the Cathedral chapter of Toledo, the main contents of the manuscript being commentaries on the Song of Songs and the Lamentations of Jeremiah.[28] From this it would be reasonable to infer that the play was acted by the Cathedral clergy but not any other circumstance of its performance. It contains, as has often been pointed out, a rare apocryphal motif, that of the Magi bringing their symbolic gifts, not as a tribute of faith and adoration, but as a test of the Christ-Child's divinity. This unusual idea seems to have been sporadically current in France in the twelfth century, and, as Winifred Sturdevant has shown, the Spanish play is directly or indirectly indebted to French Infancy narratives containing this theme, a debt indicated by verbal echoes (the languages were sufficiently alike for this argument to be convincing).[29] The question that remains, however, is whether this is a Spanish composition directly influenced by the French poems or whether it is a close translation of a lost French play. Either is possible and the question seems unanswerable.[30]

Whilst this point is obviously very important for the literary history of the two countries, in terms of our present consideration of the methods and style of twelfth-century religious plays, it scarcely matters. For the interesting point here is that the dramatist, whether French or Spanish, has made an original and entirely dramatic transformation of the borrowed motif. The Visit of the Three Kings, like the Annunciation to the Shepherds, was an undramatic subject: it made a splendid procession but hardly a play. Even in the later mystery cycles it is one of the most unexciting scenes, and one of the few that the authors have been content to leave bare without imposing some dramatic pattern upon it. The author of the Benediktbeuern Christmas Play, who was so ingenious with the prophets and the shepherds, dealt simply with the Three Kings by giving little space to them. In the Spanish

play, however, a conflict has been introduced by the alternations between belief and scepticism expressed in the opening monologues of the
Three Kings (a conflict that would have been resolved in the lost conclusion to the play, in which the Child would have manifested His
divinity by His acceptance of the gifts). This dramatic pattern was not
borrowed from the Infancy poems, for in them the apocryphal motif is
used carelessly: although the Kings announce that they will offer their
gifts as a test, this decision is psychologically unmotivated, since they
have already expressed with equanimity their faith and confidence.[31]
The first king in the *Auto* begins as follows:[32]

> Dios criador, qual maravila
> no se qual es achesta strela!
> Agora primas la e veida,
> poco timpo a qua es nacida.
> Nacido es el Criador
> que es de la gentes senior?
> Non es verdad non se que digo,
> todo esto non vale uno figo.

This dramatic use of scepticism is reminiscent of the Benediktbeuern
Play, but there are two differences. Firstly, faith and scepticism are not
externalised through the introduction of new characters, Archisynagogus or the devil, but are expressed in a naturalistic way through
interior monologue: the meaning is the same as that of the devil's
urging of the shepherds to recognise that the angel's message is nonsense, but the effect is different. Secondly, doubt is not made amusing
through intellectual jokes and puns, but through the exploitation of the
colloquial and rhythmical resources of the vernacular: the king in effect
says that the belief that the new-born child is the Creator of all men is
not worth a fig, not worth tuppence, to use a corresponding modern
idiom; whilst the repetition with inversion between ll. 4–5 of the
quotation compels the speaker's voice to assume an inflection of
unbelieving astonishment.

When the vernacular is used as skilfully as this, and when nothing is
known of the conditions of performance, it is impossible to tell whether
the author rejected Latin for the sake of comprehensibility or because
it was too formal a language to suit his literary intentions. Occasional
use of the vernacular in works nevertheless intended for a clerical
audience cannot be ruled out: the *Auto* may be a fugitive and
experimental piece acted some year on the Epiphany, but in the
refectory rather than the church. It is certainly unwise to infer from

this solitary piece that vernacular drama was an established form in Spain at this period, taking the place of Latin liturgical drama.

England was by no means behindhand in its production of religious plays in the twelfth century. The very earliest reference to a play on a saint's life comes from England: it is the famous story of Geoffrey of Le Mans, who organised a play about St Catherine, while a school-master at Dunstable; the year must have been about 1110.[33] The play, which would have been acted by the schoolboys, was probably in Latin, though the possibility that it was in Anglo-Norman cannot be ruled out. By the end of the thirteenth century miracle plays are mentioned among the glories of London in the passage already quoted from William Fitzstephen:[34] the martyrdoms presumably included that of St Catherine, and the miracles those of St Nicholas, which had been dramatised in France at least from the time of Hilarius (who had been a pupil of Abelard) and perhaps earlier.[35] The language of these plays, acted for a public audience in the capital, was probably Anglo-Norman: the time corresponds roughly to the first known appearance of a vernacular miracle play in France, the *Jeu de S. Nicolas* of Jean Bodel,[36] which is a very ample and in parts lively adaptation of the story of the pagan merchant (transformed into a Saracen king) and his treasure. By the mid-thirteenth century there were plays on the miracles of St Nicholas in English, as the verse sermon from MS. Trinity 323 testifies.[37] Unfortunately the history of the miracle play, which in the early period cannot be divorced from dramatic develop-ments in general, can only be sketchily reconstructed from a series of references (even of the many fifteenth-century plays only a couple survive). Twelfth-century Biblical drama, however, is represented by two important texts, the *Mystère d'Adam* and *La Seinte Resureccion*.

The *Mystère d'Adam*, which on linguistic evidence is dated in the mid-twelfth century,[38] has often been called a transitional or semi-liturgical play; the grounds for this are the passages in Latin, which are taken to show strong liturgical attachments. The label 'transitional', however, is misleading, for, far from marking an intermediate stage between the formality of liturgical drama and the freedom and vivacity of later vernacular drama, the parts of the *Adam* that survive rival or surpass the finest that was to come. The Fall of Man is treated in a more subtle and dramatically thoughtful way than in any of the later cycles; the portrayal of Cain as a miserly and disgruntled farmer compares well with all later versions except that of the Wakefield Master, whilst the sequence of the prophets shows a rare attempt at dramatic effect by the introduction of Judaeus to argue (though he has not the wit and impertinence of Archisynagogus in the Benediktbeuern Christmas Play) and of the devils to carry off each prophet to hell after he has spoken his prophecy.[39]

The initial rubric makes it plain that this play was staged outside a church, with a scaffold for paradise, a hell-mouth, and a variety of other playing areas. Elaborate stage directions indicate costume, positioning and gesture: the author is aware of the rhetorical tradition of suiting the action to the word ('et gestum faciant convenientem rei, de qua loquuntur').[40] Like all the plays that we have been discussing it would have been acted by clerics. It is superficial features such as these, that the actors were clerics, that the place of performance was the churchyard, that have given the illusion that the play is transitional, whilst the scattering of Latin in the text has suggested that it was semi-liturgical.[41]

The play probably opened with a prologue in which the *Figura* spoke the first twenty-seven verses of Genesis.[42] There follow at various points eight choral antiphons, of which seven occur in the Fall (forming clusters on either side) and one in Cain and Abel: these are taken from the responses first found in the Gregorian *Liber responsalis* and come ultimately from Genesis itself.[43] These are sung as narrative comments by the choir, who might well, as Mr Stevens has recently suggested, seem to stand for the heavenly host:[44] some of the same responses are specifically given to a choir of angels in two fifteenth-century German cycles, *Der Sündenfall*[45] and Eger;[46] this might, however, have been a late rationalisation of an earlier, ambiguous practice. Some of them refer to action that is past, the more dramatic and momentous anticipate what is to come, liturgical impersonation mysteriously preceding dramatic impersonation. In one instance the key words from the response *Dum deambularet* (which paraphrases Genesis iii. 8–10), are strikingly repeated in the play in the first words of the *Figura* after the Fall, 'Adam, ubi es?'. The effect of the chorus's part is to add solemnity and dramatic gravity to the less realistic parts of the play: they strikingly arrest the stylistic naturalism, so that one is suddenly aware of the action, not in terms of psychological verisimilitude, but *sub specie aeternitatis*.[47] It is only in the Prophets' Play (which, as we have seen, always remained close to its liturgical predecessors) that Latin is used as an ordinary part of the dialogue within the play, and, as far as one can see, through straightforward liturgical imitation, rather than through deliberate literary choice.

La Seinte Resureccion[48] may be of slightly later date, the earlier of its two manuscripts being of the late twelfth century. It is a long play: the end is missing but in all it must have amounted to at least a thousand lines and perhaps considerably more. This compares with the leisure-liness of development of Bodel's *Jeu de S. Nicolas* as opposed, for instance, to the succinct Benediktbeuern Easter play with its 129 lines (though the latter begins at a slightly later point in time). Length, of course, cannot be equated with literary inventiveness in its best sense, but it does reflect dramatic self-consciousness and literary freedom, the author's confidence that it is proper for him to fill in scenes that are only tersely mentioned in the Bible. Indeed, this play has the kind of conversational solidity that is not found again in drama of English origin until the work of the so-called York Realist about two hundred and fifty years later.

The staging of the play is also elaborate, requiring the simultaneous scenic display that has been shown to be characteristic of French drama throughout the Middle Ages. Like the *Adam*, it may well have been composed for performance outside a church. This supposition rests upon a miracle story related in the thirteenth-century continuation of the Life of St John of Beverley, which tells of the death and miraculous restoration to life of a boy who climbed into the triforium of Beverley Minster in order to have a better view of the Resurrection play that was being performed down below.[49] This story is informative in that it tells us that the play was acted 'intra saepta polyandri . . . ex parte aquilonari' (between the buttresses on the north side), and that it was put on *tempore quodam aestivo* (at a certain time in summer). It is attractive, but perhaps excessively tidy, to assume that this play performed at Beverley is the one Anglo-Norman Resurrection play extant; it remains, how-ever, reasonable to allow the play and the Beverley record to cast light upon each other, namely to suppose that the Beverley play may have been in French, and that the *Resureccion* was performed against what-ever side of a church provided the most suitable architectural back-ground and on occasions other than Easter.

La Seinte Resureccion has not the brilliance of the *Mystère d'Adam* and it is easy therefore to underestimate it: it is the more difficult to judge because at least half, and that the more important half, is lost (the frag-ment ends before the Resurrection). Nevertheless the play is well organised and there are many felicitous touches, sometimes comic, sometimes moving, notably in the opening interview between Pilate and Joseph of Arimathaea, in the sceptical speeches of the men who disbelieve in Longinus's faith in the crucified figure, and in the boasts of the soldiers set to guard the tomb. There is, for instance, a feeling thoughtfulness in the following lines spoken by Joseph as he ponders the death of Christ:[50]

Ohy, Jesu! ohy bel sire!
En tun vivant esteies bon mire,
Ke Lazere de mort resuscitas:
E ke fras meimes? dunc ne relveras?
Dunt ne releveras tu de mort?

Liturgical drama is not recalled in the *Resureccion* by the use of anti-phons or other quotations from the liturgy, though it could well be that, like many later dramatists, the author turned to liturgical chant to convey the mysterious solemnity of the Resurrection itself.[51] The presence, however, of narrative links, spoken presumably by a *lector*, suggests the conventions of liturgical drama, where dramatic action could be interrupted by narrative antiphons sung by the choir, such as the description of the race between Peter and John, 'Currebant duo simul'.[52] Liturgical custom may also be reflected in the fact that the figure on the Cross was a statue, not a live actor: the object of the visits of the shepherds and the Magi, for instance, were often wooden figures of the type still familiar to us in Christmas cribs. But these are only tiny traits that betray an ultimate ancestry: in its freedom and confidence the *Resureccion* is as remote from the liturgical plays of the Resurrection as were plays of the fourteenth or fifteenth century.

This brief survey of twelfth-century religious drama in England and on the Continent shows that the drama of this period is distinguished from that of the later Middle Ages by its rarity, but not by its quality. On the one hand it is clear that, even when allowance has been made for a high proportion of lost plays, fully developed texts were isolated phenomena, and were not a regular part of literary and dramatic life, as they were later to become. On the other hand, in quality and dramatic ambitiousness these plays are not timid and stilted forerunners of late medieval works. If one takes a bird's eye view of the religious drama of western Europe up to the end of the fifteenth century, it is arguable that the best treatment of the Fall of Man is in the *Mystère d'Adam*, the best *Ordo prophetarum* is in the Benediktbeuern Christmas play, the best presentation of the Visit of the Magi is in the *Auto de los Reyes Magos*; whilst the *Sponsus* has no parallel until *Everyman*. It is of course true that the early dramatists put their imaginative energy into subjects that later authors were content to leave undeveloped, and had available amongst their sources some useful apocryphal motifs that were later shunned and forgotten. In contrast the authors of the mystery cycles made the Nativity and Passion the heart of the cycles and drew for their sources of amplification upon works of meditation rather than eccentric apocryphal traditions. Nevertheless, it can be clearly seen that when religious plays came to be acted in the marketplace by laymen instead of in church or churchyard by the clergy, this did not confer new freedoms nor represent an evolutionary advance. In pursuing the history of religious drama in England, therefore, it is change rather than progress that has to be described, and the explanation has to be of a less prejudiced and dogmatic kind than that current until a few years ago.

IV

The Development of the Cycle Form

The last stage to be described in the history of the religious drama of the Middle Ages is the emergence of the English cycle, which stretches from the Fall of the Angels to the Last Judgment. This is not a development that can be closely charted, though there are enough hints to suggest that the cycles were not born full-grown and parentless at a time close to their first appearance (*c.* 1375).[1] In the attempt to reconstruct some of their antecedent history it is again valuable to look in part at continental analogues.

From the point of view of later developments one of the most important characteristics of twelfth-century plays is their partial detachment from liturgical time. There were two kinds of detachment, the one determined by the demands of literary structure, the other by practical convenience. A play had obviously to be self-sufficient in narrative terms, and would therefore tend to gather within itself events which were liturgically commemorated on different days. This had happened even in the liturgical *Officium stellae*, but the Christmas season is so unified in mood and theme that the enactment of the Visit of the Shepherds on the Epiphany did not constitute a major break with liturgical time. Much more remarkable is the combined Passion and Resurrection play of southern Germany and Italy in the latter half of the twelfth century.[2] This type of play encompasses events belonging liturgically to the four days from Maundy Thursday to Easter Sunday. With hindsight it can be seen as an inevitable development, since in terms of plot the Resurrection is the dénouement of a story that began at least with the Arrest of Christ. Though no plays of this kind are known in England, *La Seinte Resureccion* begins with a scene of the Deposition which properly belongs to Good Friday.

The tendency to overleap the narrow confines of liturgical time was probably encouraged by the practical difficulties of performing religious plays on the correct liturgical occasion but not in church. The Middle Ages, insofar as they knew of theatrical traditions, inherited these from the sunny countries of southern Europe. The theatres of Greece and Rome were unroofed: in countries with a stable climate the advantage of daylight thus gained far outweighed the disadvantage of the lack of protection from wind and rain. This lack of a classical tradition of a roofed theatre meant that even the learned, who had seen and recognised the ruins of Greece and Rome or who had read Vitruvius,[3] knew nothing of what we nowadays think of as the main benefit of a theatre-building, namely the comfort for both actors and audience of being indoors. Thus even London, with its continuous traditions of acting and its many resources, had as its *theatrum* the Clerkenwell Fields. From this there arose a dilemma: plays in England could only be satisfactorily performed in the summer months when the chances of fine weather were good and long hours of daylight were certain, whilst the two great festivals commemorated by liturgical drama fell in winter or early spring.

Recorded references to the performance of plays from about 1200 to 1500 suggest an intermittent but sometimes ingenious search for a warm but liturgically proper day on which to perform an already existing play. A simple example of what could be done was the Scottish adoption of the feast of the Translation of the body of St Nicholas (9 May) for the occasion of acting a play about the saint instead of the anniversary of his martyrdom (6 December).[4] Nativity plays might be transferred to Candlemas (2 February and perhaps scarcely an improvement) or in the later Middle Ages to St Anne's Day (26 July). But the easiest solution and the one most ready to hand was the performance of plays on the recurring festival of Sunday. In the later Middle Ages this seems to have been a common practice. *Dives and Pauper* (a fifteenth-century treatise on the Ten Commandments) discusses the legitimacy of performing plays on *grete festes and in Sundayes*, whilst the Lollard sermon against mystery plays speaks of men wishing to see or act plays on *the haliday* (a term which in context may refer exclusively to Sundays).[5] The production of the *Ludus Coventriae* described in the extant banns was also to be given on a Sunday. The solution of using a Sunday as a suitable day for the performance of religious drama had, however, been found much earlier than the fifteenth century, for the summer occasion on which the Beverley Resurrection play was performed may be safely inferred to be a Sunday.[6]

The partial detachment of short plays from liturgical time has some bearing upon the development of the cycle play, which appeared at about the same time as the combined Passion and Resurrection play. The characteristic of the cycle play is that (like a series of narrative wall-paintings) it sets forth a number of different episodes, which are doctrinally and thematically related, but which do not fuse into one extensive plot as does the matter of the Passion and Resurrection play.

The earliest known example of cyclical drama is the *Mystère d'Adam* and the occasion of its performance was probably Septuagesima. The association of the *Adam* with Septuagesima through the use made in it of the responses for the Sunday and Monday of Septuagesima has often been noticed[7] and so has its resemblance to a lost play from Regensburg, which is briefly noted in the *Annales Ratisponenses* for the year 1194.[8] Fortunately the *Annales* record the exact date on which the play was performed, namely 7 February, which in that year was the Monday following Septuagesima Sunday. Whilst we therefore know the occasion of the performance of the Regensburg play and through it can infer the occasion for which the *Mystère d'Adam* was composed, the exact compass of each play unfortunately cannot be determined. As was fitting to a Septuagesima play, both make the Fall of Man their starting point (though the Regensburg play had a fall of the angels as a preface to this) and both had an *Ordo prophetarum*, but whether, or to what extent, the cycles extended to the New Testament is in both cases, though for different reasons, uncertain.[9]

There are three possible structures for a Septuagesima cycle. It could, as it were, be a two-part play with the lenten season intervening between the parts. The first part would depict the Fall of Man, perhaps some further Old Testament material, and a kind of prophets' play in which the prophets would not only speak their prophecies but also be carried off to hell, thus demonstrating at once the consequences of the Fall and the promises of its reparation. The subject of the second half would be the Passion and Resurrection, which might be dramatised or might receive only liturgical enactment. The second possibility is that the cycle dramatised these subjects in one continuous play, the events remembered in the whole lenten season being for propagandist purposes set out initially in one instructive work. Later German passion plays, which begin either with an *Ordo prophetarum* or a Fall of Man, show that this kind of arrangement was accepted as fitting by medieval dramatists.[10] Finally there is the possibility that, for the sake of doctrinal completeness, but with disregard to the liturgical season, the Nativity was also included.[11]

It is unlikely that Septuagesima cycles were all identical in structure, but the supposition that such a cycle could relate the whole history of the Redemption, including the Nativity, is given fairly strong support by the recorded reference to another lost cycle of 1204. Though this play was performed in Riga, it most probably represents a north German dramatic tradition (of slightly earlier date) transplanted there by the missionary bishop, Albert of Riga, and his fellow clergy. The

Life of Albert, which contains this reference, says only that the play was acted in winter, but in view of its cyclical character it is most likely that it was performed at Septuagesima rather than at Christmas or the Epiphany. The description of the play is allusive and its exact scope can therefore not be known, but in that its intention was to instruct the native inhabitants through a dramatisation of the doctrine of the Old and New Testaments, it must at least have begun with the Fall of Man and have extended to the Resurrection.[12] It also had a fairly large number of Old Testament episodes (David and Gideon are named)[13] and it included the Nativity (Herod too is specifically referred to). Any further comment must be pure speculation, but the description of the Riga play conveys so many hints of an ambitious and comprehensive design that it seems reminiscent of the kind of iconographic scheme represented by the *Hortus deliciarum*, the encyclopaedic work compiled by Herrad of Landsberg for the instruction of her nuns some decades earlier.[14]

It would be particularly interesting to know whether, like the *Hortus deliciarum*, the Riga play pursued its visual presentation of doctrinal history as far as the Coming of the Antichrist and the Last Judgment. Whilst strict liturgical propriety would of course require that the Resurrection or the Resurrection Appearances should provide the climax of a Septuagesima play, the missionary aim of expressing Christian doctrine in attractive and comprehensible form would be better fulfilled if it continued to the end of the world; the emphasis upon wars and strife in the description would be especially fitting if the cycle included the story of the Antichrist. All that one knows for certain, however, is that the next recorded play, that of Cividale nearly a hundred years later, extended to the Antichrist and the Last Judgment and that on the second occasion of its performance (1303) it began with the Creation and Fall of Man.[15] The occasion of the performance of the Cividale play, however, was not Septuagesima but Whitsun: it would seem that just as the earlier cycles were liturgically connected to Septuagesima by the dramatisation of the Fall of Man, so this later cycle was attached to Whitsun by the inclusion of the Coming of the Holy Ghost. It was, however, less fittingly linked to this festival than the later French *Passions*, which were also acted at Whitsun, in that the Coming of the Holy Ghost did not provide the climax and close of the play. The looseness of the attachment in fact strongly suggests that in the strict sense cyclical plays were considered non-liturgical: approximately the same type of play could be acted at Septuagesima or Pentecost, but for practical reasons the great summer festival came to be preferred. Whitsun remained a favourite occasion for plays throughout the Middle Ages, whereas in later documents Septuagesima is not mentioned.

It is tempting to believe that England had an uninterrupted tradition of cyclical drama from the time of the *Mystère d'Adam* until the sudden efflorescence of this type of play towards the close of the fourteenth century. There are, however, such areas of uncertainty in our knowledge of this period and the positive evidence is so tenuous that it can only be considered a pleasing hypothesis. In the first place we do not know the original extent of the *Mystère d'Adam* and, even if we make the assumption that it was a Septuagesima play extending to the Resurrection,[16] we know nothing of its currency after the mid-thirteenth century when a defective copy was made of it in a French manuscript from Tours. Round about 1300 the Abbess of Clerkenwell complained of the damage done by crowds who assembled to see the plays in the Clerkenwell Fields.[17] The plays which the crowds had come to see could have been the ancestors or even substantially the same as the vast cycle of plays acted in the same place in the closing decades of the fourteenth century;[18] but the fact that the Clerkenwell Fields remained London's theatre throughout this period is not evidence against the possibility that different types of play were acted there at different times. Nevertheless London probably had a cyclical play by about 1320–30, the date when the *Holkham Bible Picture Book* was probably composed, though like the *Mystère d'Adam* and the text in this manuscript it might possibly have been in French.[19] The existence, however, of a cycle in English of about this date is suggested by a few lines of verse preserved in a manuscript of Latin sermons associated with Bishop Sheppey of Rochester. They are part or the whole of a speech in which the devil tempted Eve. Whilst the content is not so dramatically developed that they could not have formed part of a narrative poem, it is more likely that they are a quotation from a play, as Carleton Brown supposed.[20] They may therefore tentatively be taken to indicate the existence of an English cycle beginning with the Fall round about the year 1340. These scraps of evidence that suggest the existence of a London cycle in the middle of the fourteenth century seem to corroborate each other, but that this was a direct descendant of the *Mystère d'Adam* remains an unsupported hypothesis: the London plays could have lacked a native ancestor and have been born afresh under the influence of some Continental cycle such as that of Cividale.

If there were London plays from about the middle of the fourteenth century onwards, the northern cycles could not have escaped their influence. Because the plays have been lost this influence cannot be investigated; but it is reasonable to suppose that the northern dramatists did not slavishly imitate the drama of the metropolis, that they were aware of the complex traditions that lay behind it, and that working within these traditions they designed their own form of cyclical play. It is necessary to consider the traditions available to them in order to understand the choice that they made.

The records of the Septuagesima play from Riga and the Whitsun play from Cividale indicate slightly different approaches to the historical play of the Redemption. The first had a substantial Old Testament sequence for it extended as far as David and Gideon (the latest possible Old Testament episode, as we shall see). The second had a different balance: its main substance was the New Testament sequence from the Annunciation to the Last Judgment, with the Creation and the Fall of Man as the sole necessary introduction. These two introduce the main possible variables in the contents of a historical cycle: one, how many Old Testament plays to present; the other, at what point to end. For the ending there were four possible events: the Resurrection or Resurrection Appearances, the Ascension, the Coming of the Holy Ghost or the Last Judgment. Medieval drama presents examples of all of them. The work of Redemption could be said to stop with the Resurrection, though a play for the sake of completeness might well continue to the Ascension or Pentecost. In contrast the Last Judgment takes the cycle out of historical time and introduces a different and more disturbing note. There are no separate twelfth-century plays of the Last Judgment, except insofar as it is allegorically referred to in the *Sponsus*: unlike later plays of the Antichrist, the famous play from Tegernsee ends with a thanksgiving for his defeat and proceeds no further.[21] While it is possible to postulate a number of reasons for the decision to extend the cycle to the Last Judgment, the most simple and obvious one is that the scope of the New Testament sequence was determined by the Creed. The Apostles' Creed divides into three parts for the three persons of the Trinity: its largest section refers to Christ. The following table shows the main episodes of the cycles alongside the corresponding item from the Creed:

Annunciation:	'. . . Who was conceived by the Holy Ghost'
Nativity:	'born of the Virgin Mary'
Passion:	'suffered under Pontius Pilate'
Crucifixion:	'was crucified'

Deposition & Entombment:	'dead, and buried'
Harrowing of Hell:	'He descended into hell'
Resurrection:	'the third day he rose again from the dead'
Ascension:	'He ascended into heaven and sitteth on the right hand of God the Father Almighty'
Last Judgment:	'from thence he shall come to judge the quick and the dead'

In addition God the Father could be represented by a play of the Creation ('Maker of heaven and earth') and the Holy Ghost by the Descent of the Holy Ghost, though strictly this would have to be played out of its order in the Creed.

The Cividale play was no doubt not an explicit dramatisation of the Creed as was the much later play of the Creed at York. This lost play was performed every ten years, and on one occasion was allowed to replace the Corpus Christi cycle.[22] It was of moderate length (the manuscript containing it had eighty-eight leaves, which, depending upon the size of the page, would make it about one-third to a half of any of the existing cycles). It has often been conjectured that the subject of the play was the apostles (each of whom was thought to have contributed one article to the Creed), but the theory that it was a dramatised Fates of the Apostles is unconvincing.[23] This play of the Creed was probably a sleeker version of an Old and New Testament cycle. It would have no Old Testament plays after the Creation and Fall of Man and would have a New Testament sequence uncluttered by plays relating to Christ's ministry or specifically to the Blessed Virgin. In general structure, therefore, the play would have been indistinguishable from some of the ordinary historical cycles, though minor devices, such as perhaps individual prologues by the apostles, might have been used to emphasise its special character.[24]

There is no reason to think that anything was done in the Cividale play or its successors to indicate a particular relationship with the Creed. It is rather that the subjects enumerated in the chronicle account correspond exactly to the summary of the Creed, and that there is no reason to think of this as chance coincidence, as a clerical author seeking for the salient events in the work of Redemption could hardly have escaped recalling those repeated in the Creed day after day. It is also worth recalling that the Cividale play belongs to the era after the Fourth Lateran Council of 1215, which required that priests should regularly instruct their parishioners in the Creed. That priests saw in such plays a useful popular exposition of the Creed and directed their congregations to understand them in that light is a reasonable supposition. There is a much later story – now often quoted – in *A Hundred Merry Tales*, in which a parish priest preached on the articles of the Creed to his congregation one Sunday, and then advised those who did not believe him to go 'for a more sure and sufficient authority' to Coventry, where they would see them all played.[25] The crux of this joke is fairly certainly not that the priest naïvely observed a relationship between the plays and the Creed, but that he muffed the point of fairly standard homiletic advice.

Though the English cycles, like the Cividale play, contain very markedly the sequence from the Annunciation to the Last Judgment, they also have affinities with the Riga type of Septuagesima play which included a substantial part of Old Testament history. The amount of Old Testament history to be dramatised would obviously be determined by time: the northern English cycles usually lasted a day, but performances in some places were allowed to extend to two or three days,[26] and a particularly magnificent one in London lasted for seven.[27] For a cycle which had to be presented in one day only the Old Testament subjects would have to be rigorously selected. Before this selection can be understood in perspective it is necessary to consider what the range of possibility was. It is clear that the main principle was historical, not typological: that is the events were chosen for their importance in a historical sequence, and not in the first place because they foreshadowed the Redemption. The minimum was therefore the Creation and Fall of Man and the maximum the whole range of the Old Testament including the books which, in the Protestant tradition, have been relegated to the Apocrypha. Not all the books of the Old Testament, however, lend themselves to dramatic or artistic presentation. Genesis and Exodus provide a continuous narrative, but the remaining three books of the Pentateuch contain the exposition of the law and are without important incident apart from the story of Balaam and Balak and the death of Moses at the very end of Deuteronomy. The historical line is then again emphasised in nine books from Joshua to 2 Chronicles: these contain the stories of Joshua, Gideon, Samson, Ruth, Samuel, David and Solomon; thereafter the structure ceases to be primarily historical, though scattered amongst the prophetic books are the stories of Esther, Job, Daniel, Jonah and Tobit.

This narrative pattern of the Old Testament can be seen very faithfully mirrored in the works of writers and artists who were not constrained by the exigencies of time or space. Amongst plays the most ambitious and comprehensive sequence is the fifteenth-century *Mystère du viel testament*, which runs to 49,386 lines. It covers, though not in equal detail, the multifarious events from the Creation of Man to the Visit of the Queen of Sheba, and continues with separate plays on five subjects taken from the later books, Job, Tobit, Daniel, Judith, and Esther.[28] Though for part of the work the episodes are connected by a continuing debate between the Four Daughters of God,[29] it is unlikely that so unwieldy a cycle was ever performed as a whole: when it was combined with a Passion play, extracts only are known to have been used.[30]

The same system can be seen in the first part of the *Byzantine Guide to Painting*, which describes 'How the wonders of the ancient law are represented'.[31] This proceeds in its enumeration of subjects continuously from the Fall of the Angels to the Building of the Temple (2 Chronicles), and then continues with selected incidents, which include the stories of Elijah and Elisha, Daniel, Jonah, Job and Judith. This enumeration was presumably permissive rather than prescriptive: there is no known Old Testament iconographic cycle in east or west that is quite so comprehensive. However, cycles which extend to Kings or Chronicles are not uncommon: in these the emphasis is usually upon the Octateuch and the story of David.[32] In England, for instance, the roundels in the south porch at Malmesbury range selectively from the Creation of Adam to David and Goliath,[33] the 400 or so Norwich roof-bosses extend from the Creation to the crowning of Solomon,[34] and the very ample Old Testament illustrations in *Queen Mary's Psalter* continue to the death of Solomon.[35]

It is clear that so massive a presentation of Old Testament history was only rarely feasible, even when the design did not extend beyond the Old Testament; when the Old Testament itself was only portrayed as a prelude to the New Testament, it was obviously impossible. The method that was adopted to reduce the proportions of Old Testament history can be best illustrated from a consideration of shorter Old Testament sequences in art and in particular from an examination of the iconography of some English and French psalters of the twelfth and thirteenth centuries: the latter are particularly relevant because a custom had grown up of incorporating in them, after the calendar and before the text of the psalms, a series of pictures illustrating the history of the Redemption: the designers of this series obviously had a problem corresponding to that of the dramatists, for one the limitation of space, for the other the limitation of time.

Our consideration of the Bible showed that there was a convenient natural stopping place at the end of 2 Chronicles, at which point continuous narrative ceased. But there was also a much earlier break in the narrative at the end of Exodus, where the codification of the law superseded narrative for three books. It was therefore at this point that short Old Testament sequences normally ended. The earliest occurrence of this arrangement noted by M. R. James was in the now vanished paintings (probably of the fifth century) in the Roman Church of San Paolo fuori le Mura;[36] later and more relevant examples may be seen in the thirteenth-century carving in the chapterhouse at Salisbury[37] and in the fifteenth-century glass at Malvern.[38] Amongst psalters MS. Arsenal 1186[39] and the *Ingeborg Psalter*[40] end their Old Testament illustrations with the Golden Calf, but more often in psalter illustrations the sequence is not quite the standard one in that one or more scenes from the life of David follow the Exodus illustrations, the explanation of course being that David was thought of as the author of the psalms. Within this category come MSS. Cotton Nero C IV (the Psalter of Henry of Blois),[41] B.N. lat. 8846,[42] and the *Huntingfield Psalter*.[43] That Genesis and Exodus were thought of as a narrative unit can be seen from the Middle English poem which paraphrases them as though they were one.[44] The relevance of this religious and iconographic tradition to the English mystery cycles is self-evident, for, with the exception of the lost Norwich cycle, which included a play of David and Goliath, no extant cycle and no recorded list of the contents of lost cycles proceeds beyond some episode in the life of Moses.

Old Testament history, even when reduced to the portion narrated in Genesis and Exodus, was still very substantial. The fifty chapters of Genesis are particularly crowded: they cover the Creation of the World and Fall of Man, Cain and Abel, the Flood, the Sacrifice of Isaac, Jacob and Esau, Jacob's Ladder, and the episodic story of Joseph. Reference to the psalters and other manuscripts shows that again a selection was often made from within Genesis. The following sequences are found: the Fall of the Angels, Fall of Man, the Flood, the Sacrifice of Isaac (MS. Arsenal 1186); Creation of Adam, Expulsion, Sacrifice of Isaac (York Psalter);[45] the Creation of Eve, the Flood, Sacrifice of Isaac (Winchester Bible).[46] It will be seen that, whilst these series are varied in content, they have one important point in common, that is that they all end at Genesis xxii with the Sacrifice of Isaac. Their unanimity on this point confirms the existence of the tradition (to which Professor Geoffrey Shepherd has already drawn attention)[47] of finding a stopping place in Genesis at chapter xxii: it is at this point that the Old English poem, *Genesis*, comes to an end, and Bede's commentary on Genesis does not extend beyond this point. The propriety of this stopping place is self-evident: the effects of the Fall have by then been fully displayed and the Redemption has been fully foreshadowed.

The influence of this tradition upon the English cycles is clear: all the extant cycles and the Norwich and Beverley lists show a fairly continuous dramatic paraphrase of Genesis up to chapter xxii.[48] The only cycle to include events from the later chapters of Genesis is the Towneley cycle, which includes a fragmentary play of Jacob and Esau and a short play of Jacob's dream and wrestling with the angel. They are both written in the uncommon dramatic metre of couplets and, though quite touching, have a stiffness uncharacteristic of extant mystery plays. Their history is obscure.

It may seem that against this background the selection of Old Testament plays in the English mystery plays is explained. The four extant cycles have a sequence of Genesis i–xxii and part of Exodus; but the Beverley cycle did not proceed beyond Genesis xxii, a stopping point which is perhaps confirmed by the *Holkham Bible Picture Book*.[49] There are, however, some kinds of tradition that may cast further light upon the cycles and their predecessors in art. The relevance of one of these traditions has recently been suggested by V. A. Kolve, who has argued that the principle of selection in the Old Testament sequences of the English cycles was the allocation of one play to each of the figures representing one of the Seven Ages of the World: Adam, Noah, Abraham, Moses and David (the last two ages belong to the new dispensation).[50] This widely known patterning of history was explicitly referred to by the author of the *Ludus Coventriae*, when he made Noah say, 'In me Noe þe secund age / in dede begynnyth . . .',[51] and the list of Old Testament plays belonging to the lost Norwich cycle conforms so perfectly, in that it includes a play of Moses and (exceptionally in the English dramatic tradition) of David and Goliath, that it is unlikely to have been a coincidence:[52] one wonders whether here the characters or an expositor drew the audience's attention to the pattern. The other cycles depart from this pattern, however, by not invariably having a play of Moses (as we have already seen), and by not having a play of David. Kolve's suggestion that the Prophets' Play was equivalent to a play of David is not quite happy in that this play timelessly spans the ages,[53] and anyway two cycles, those of York and Beverley, seem not to have had one.[54]

There were, however, two other possible series of a related kind. One was that of equating the various stages at which the labourers entered the vineyard with Old Testament figures. This produced a series of five: Adam to Noah, Noah to Abraham, Abraham to Moses, Moses to the birth of Christ, and the birth of Christ to the Last Judgment. This series was set out in a homily of Gregory the Great, of which the relevant passage was one of the readings in the breviary for Septuagesima.[55] The other series consists of the allegorisation of the seven office hours, found in the work of medieval commentators on the liturgy. As each office hour is an act of praise, this was a list of those who praise God: Adam and Eve, Abel, Noah, Abraham, the prophets, the apostles, and the just on the last day.[56] None of these lists correspond exactly to the cycles, but it is worth noticing that there are no Old Testament subjects in the cycles (with the exception of Towneley noted above) that are not found in one or more of these lists. It would seem, therefore, that the accumulated effect of such patternings of history upon the dramatists was to confirm the iconographic tradition and to sharpen their understanding of it: they thus guided but did not bind the authors in their selection of Old Testament subjects.

A consideration of the sequence of Old Testament plays in the English cycles against the background of the iconographic tradition of the psalters shows that the authors in general chose the minimum number of subjects for a historical sweep. Anything less than a presentation of the first twenty-two chapters of Genesis would not be history. The subjects dramatised were obviously far fewer in number than those of the Riga play of 1204 which (since it included plays about Gideon and David)[57] stretched at least as far as 1 Samuel probably without omitting Judges. It may be conjectured that in the Riga play the balance between Old and New Testament subjects was different from that of later cycles, the Passion sequence not being given the disproportionate amount of time, which, if we speak in purely narrative terms, it is given in the later cycles. Some idea of early proportions may be gained from the Benediktbeuern Passion Play, in which the Passion sequence proper, i.e. from the appearance of Christ before the high priests to the Crucifixion, occupies only one-third of the surviving text, the first two-thirds being given to preliminary material, the summoning of Peter and Andrew, the entry into Jerusalem, the repentance of Mary Magdalene, and the raising of Lazarus. Whether or not Hardin Craig is right in saying that this play 'seems to have been generated from the already established office of the *Conversion of Mary Magdalen* and *Raising of Lazarus*'[58] it is clear that the striking emphasis upon these must be explained by the liturgical antecedents. By contrast in the York cycle, to take an extreme example, the proportions are almost exactly reversed, one-third of the corresponding narrative sequence being given to the preliminary material, and two-thirds to the Passion. This intensity of treatment and dramatic focusing upon the Passion so that it towers over the surrounding episodes is first found in the earliest vernacular Passion plays in France, such as the *Palatine Passion*.[59] Though this begins with the preparations for the Last Supper, it deals briskly with preliminaries, and then drawing upon the many meditative expansions of the Passion, which had been written by the mid-fourteenth century, it lingers movingly and dramatically upon the sufferings of Christ and the Blessed Virgin.

This emotional concentration upon the Passion, which was characteristic of Christian popular devotion from the thirteenth century onwards, inevitably affected the proportions of the historically designed cycles. Its culmination may be seen in the massive plays of the mid-fifteenth century in France in which the sweep of historical time is almost forgotten. The vast Passion play of Arnoul Greban, for instance, begins with some introductory Old Testament scenes covering the Creation and Fall of Man and Cain and Abel, but they form such a minute part of the whole (about 1,700 lines out of more than 30,000) that they can have made little dramatic impression;[60] whilst in the slightly later tripartite play of Jean Michel, which borrowed from Greban's work, there are no Old Testament scenes at all, and of the three sections, Nativity, Passion, and Resurrection, the Passion is longer than the other two put together.[61] In these late French plays a new form has undoubtedly emerged: it is neither a play on the history of the Redemption, nor a Passion play of the traditional kind (which, as we have seen, should begin at some point in the ministry of Christ), but a play on the life of Christ. It is possible to understand the emergence of this shape in a variety of ways; one might see it as a historical play in which the Old Testament parts have become dislodged or at least shrivelled up, or one could see it as a new sequence made up of three earlier types, Nativity, Passion and Resurrection. Whatever its historical development, however, it is clear that the idea of a play on the life of Christ received definition and authoritative confirmation from the famous meditative lives of Christ, such as the *Meditationes vitae Christi* ascribed to Bonaventura[62] and the later *Vita Jesu Christi* of Ludolf the Carthusian.[63] It may be noted that, like the *Meditationes*, the late French plays begin with a debate between the Four Daughters of God, which serves the same doctrinal and narrative purpose as a play of the Creation and Fall in that it establishes the need for the Redemption.

Whilst a play on the life of Christ is undoubtedly the typical late

French form of religious drama, just as the historical play from the Fall of the Angels to the Last Judgment is the typical English form, it is clear that not all French authors and organising towns preferred it to the older type. Some cycles were designed on the principle of presenting the history of the Redemption from the Fall to the Resurrection Appearances: of this kind is the *Passion de Semur*,[64] the *Passion de Valenciennes*,[65] and the *Passion* in MS. B.N. 904;[66] all of these contain an Old Testament sequence corresponding closely in subjects chosen and in length to the English cycles. The records of the Passion Play from Lucerne show a yet more ample Old Testament cycle, including the stories from the second half of Genesis (Jacob and Esau and Joseph) and David and Goliath.[67] An alternative to possessing a cycle of this kind was the construction of a composite cycle: Troyes, for instance, at the end of the fifteenth century acted a four-day cycle made up roughly of part of the *Mystère du viel testament* and part of Greban's *Passion*.[68]

The same kind of variety may be noted in the German-speaking lands of the Middle Ages. In these the Passion play, in its correct sense, was the dominant form: famous examples are those from Frankfurt, Alsfeld and Donaueschingen.[69] But there were also works of another kind, such as those from Eger and Kunzelsau, which begin with the Fall of the Angels and continue with Old Testament plays extending as far as David and Goliath. Of these two the *Künzelsauer Fronleichnamsspiel*, as its medieval title indicates, belonged to the feast of Corpus Christi,[70] but the Eger play, though now called a *Fronleichnamsspiel*, is not known to have been acted on any regular occasion.[71]

In contrast to the Continent, in England the commonest type of religious drama was the cycle play extending from the Fall of the Angels to the Last Judgment. All four extant cycles are of this kind, and so also was the lost Beverley cycle. The evidence for the plays at Coventry, Newcastle and Norwich is less certain, since the surviving lists are incomplete. Coventry may not have had any Old Testament plays, or at least none except for the Fall;[72] Newcastle may have ended with the Assumption of the Virgin (the last play recorded is the Burial of the Virgin);[73] and the Norwich cycle with Pentecost.[74] It has been customarily assumed that these lost cycles must have conformed to the structural model of those extant, but the diversity of practice on the Continent suggests that this assumption may not be well founded. It may be noted that, whilst at first sight we may appear to have the testimony of five different cycles in favour of uniformity, Chester, York, Towneley, the *Ludus Coventriae* and Beverley, the Towneley cycle from Wakefield was influenced by York, and in all probability so was the Beverley cycle; in fact we only have the evidence of three independent witnesses, evidence which is therefore suggestive but by no means conclusive.

There is, however, a further argument put forward to support the theory of uniformity, which is that all these cycles were Corpus Christi plays, and that the liturgical feast had determined the precise form. The English plays in the Middle Ages were almost invariably described as Corpus Christi plays, but this appellation could just as well have arisen from the customary date of performance as from the propriety of subject-matter to the feast.[75] Indeed by analogy with the similar collocation, Christmas carols, this is the more probable explanation, for many of the carols are not about the Nativity, and evidently merited their title only because they were customarily sung during the festivities of the Christmas season.[76] The term 'Corpus Christi play' therefore at most leaves the question open, but obviously the very custom of performing the cycles at Corpus Christi suggests a doctrinal relationship. This relationship, if at all close, could be of three kinds. First, a dramatist-theologian, pondering the spiritual nature of the feast, might have devised the cycle as being pre-eminently fitting to it. Second, these could be plays which, though they might be performed at times other than Corpus Christi, were fitting to the feast: if it were to be celebrated by the performance of plays, then this was the only type of play that was liturgically apt. Third, the cycle play might be connected to the feast of Corpus Christi because, though it was only one of several types of play that might then be performed, it was itself never performed at any other time. None of these propositions is true.

That plays of this type could be acted on occasions other than that of Corpus Christi we have already seen. The plays of Riga and Cividale were devised long before the institution of the feast (and so too were the corresponding iconographic cycles of the psalters). Though France seems never to have adopted the custom of acting plays at Corpus Christi, it had corresponding cycles acted at different times. In England the lost London plays, which dramatised the Old and New Testaments, were acted on some neutral date in the summer,[77] and the evidence of the *Holkham Bible Picture Book* is that the London cycle in the mid-fourteenth century was identical in scope and contents to the northern Corpus Christi cycles. It is not even certain that all the northern cycles were composed for performance on the feast of Corpus Christi: in the second half of the fifteenth century, the Chester and Norwich cycles were being acted at Whitsun (and a Lincoln cycle on St Anne's Day, 26 July). The common assumption that all these were originally acted at

Corpus Christi rests upon reference to them as Corpus Christi plays: when such references are early (as they are, for instance, for Beverley), they can be trusted to indicate the date of performance; but, when they are late, as they are for Chester, Norwich and Lincoln, they cannot be taken uncritically at their face value.[78]

'There are two other types of play, which were acted at the feast of Corpus Christi. One was a play dramatising a eucharistic miracle.[79] The much-mentioned Holy Blood play from Aberdeen must have been of this kind[80] (probably a miracle of the bleeding host, such as that of Bolsena, now famous from Raphael's fresco) and by the sixteenth century at least a play of this kind was acted at Chester on Corpus Christi day in association with the procession.[81] Plays of this kind survive in England with the *Croxton Play of the Sacrament*[82] (though the banns to this refer to a performance of this play on a Monday), and in the Netherlands, France and Italy.[83] The French play on one recorded occasion was acted in Paris after a smaller procession of the Blessed Sacrament on a Friday in May:[84] it is very likely that the Aberdeen and Chester plays were also performed in this position.

The other kind of play was one that was typological rather than historical in arrangement. The only clear record of this in England is Lydgate's 'A Procession of Corpus Christi', which is a meditative description of what was probably a series of tableaux rather than of plays. The procession began with a Crucifixion, then followed an Old Testament sequence, and after that a roll-call of prophets, evangelists and Fathers of the church. The Old Testament sequence consists of a chronological series: Melchisedek, Abraham entertaining the three angels, the sacrifice of Isaac, Jacob's ladder, the manna in the wilderness, Aaron, and David and Goliath, all ancient types of the eucharist and Christ's sacrificial priesthood, save for the last which is a type of the Redemption.[85] The same attention to typology is found in a Corpus Christi play from Zerbst,[86] a town, admittedly far from England, where Corpus Christi drama flourished. The Zerbst *Prozessionsspiel* has the same compass as the English cycles and proceeds in what appears to be a straightforward historical way up to the sacrifice of Isaac; but then comes what is from the point of view of mystery cycles an odd list: Jonah and the whale, David harping, the spies bringing back the grapes, Solomon crowning his mother, and the enclosed garden, a series that is both unusual and also careless of historical chronology, the latter always being a sure sign of a typological rather than a historical approach. Even more obviously typological is the *Ingolstädter Fronleichnamsspiel*, which, beginning with the Creation and ending with the Last

Judgment, includes a long sequence of Old Testament types, including Gideon's fleece, Aaron's rod, the burning bush, the grapes of Engaddi, etc.[87] The series is again historically unchronological, but is chronological in relation to the events prefigured, which extend from the Annunciation (Gideon's fleece) to the Last Judgment (Judgment of Solomon). As N. C. Brooks has pointed out, the series is borrowed from one of the most famous medieval typological works, the *Biblia pauperum*.[88] All these works of course are tableaux not plays, and it is undoubtedly true that it is easier to present types in art, and therefore in tableaux, than in drama. Nevertheless the *Heidelberger Passionsspiel*, which consists of pairs of types and antitypes,[89] shows that typological plays are possible, and the English Old Testament plays could be transformed into a typological sequence by some comparatively minor alterations: for instance, if the play of Noah were excluded, and the story of Melchisedek were invariably included (it occurs only in Chester), the sequence of Cain and Abel, the offering of Melchisedek and the sacrifice of Isaac, would stand out as a clear and well-defined set of types, corresponding to the three great typological sacrifices which are enumerated in the priest's eucharistic prayer in the canon of the mass.[90] It is certain therefore that the dramatists deliberately eschewed this quite obvious approach.

Though these two types of Corpus Christi drama appear to be rare, they are important in showing the possibility of variety, and particularly interesting in casting light on the question of the propriety of the mystery cycles to the feast. No contemporary documents discuss this issue and therefore a modern judgment only can be made. But whilst it would be impossible nowadays to theorise in the abstract about what would be appropriate, to make a comparison between three existent types is not so speculative an undertaking. Since one of the purposes of the feast was to celebrate and popularly affirm the doctrine of transubstantiation, to act a play about an incident which miraculously demonstrated the truth of this would obviously be highly appropriate. Nevertheless such plays would focus on only one aspect of the feast, would be small in scope, and would be outside the main traditions of drama. It is therefore not surprising that these did not become the dominant type. A cycle celebrating the history of the Redemption would be more magnificent, more in keeping with tradition, and, as Kolve has already pointed out, equally, if not more appropriate to the meaning of the feast.[91] But, within this more limited range of possibility, the Zerbst *Prozessionsspiel* seems far more thoughtfully designed than the mystery cycles. For both the bull and the Corpus Christi office emphasise over and over again that the age of types is over and that what was shadowily prefigured is now come.[92] It seems inconceivable that any author, accustomed to the office, even if he did not know the bull, should not have thought it more appropriate to present his Old Testament plays as a typological rather than as a historical series.

There is one further curious point about the mystery cycles and, because it does not arise from this comparison of medieval ways of celebrating Corpus Christi in drama, it is more conjectural. This point is the oddity of Corpus Christi cycles ending with the Last Judgment. The keynote of Corpus Christi is triumph and rejoicing. A medieval verse sums it up: 'Quantum potes, tantum gaude'.[93] But the Last Judgment is a penitential theme which arouses fear not delight. As sermons and hymns emphasised over and over again, the Day of Judgment will be a day of terror, on which even the just man will scarcely be saved. All must therefore dread that they will find themselves amongst the rejected on Christ's left hand.[94] Christians were expected to meditate upon the Last Judgment in Advent according to liturgical time, and, as an aid to penitence, upon any day outside liturgical time. There are, however, a few days in the church's calendar in which the Christian is allowed to think only of what is joyful: Christmas Day and Easter Sunday are obvious examples, but Corpus Christi is undoubtedly a third. To be liturgically apt therefore the cycles should have ended with the Resurrection or the Ascension; the English cycles surely end with the Last Judgment because, long before the feast of Corpus Christi was instituted, dramatic and iconographic sequences had established that this was the correct place to end.

We have already seen that the series of subjects in the Corpus Christi plays had probably occurred in drama and had certainly occurred in art more than a hundred years before the institution of the feast. It is therefore now clear that the authors of the cycles took over this tradition without making to it the fairly minor, though nevertheless crucial, adaptations that would have made the traditional sequence peculiarly fitting to the feast. It remains certain, however, that these cycles were for a period at least closely related to the feast: on this issue the English evidence is confirmed by the cycles of southern Europe, such as that from Kunzelsau. The question of the nature of this relationship therefore remains to be answered.

It is possible that the connection was primarily a negative one, namely that the plays were performed at Corpus Christi, not because they were appropriate, but because they were not inappropriate.

Cycles of plays already existed; what was required was a great summer feast on which they might be acted: the French chose Whitsun, the English Corpus Christi. Whilst this interpretation of events may be true, it is also probably less than the truth. In doctrinal terms, for instance, England surely made the better choice. Whitsun, like Christmas or Easter, commemorates a definite historical event according to liturgical time. But Corpus Christi was unique in the church's calendar in being outside the commemoration of historical events, since the actual event celebrated, the Last Supper, had already been commemorated on Maundy Thursday.[95] Both plays and feast therefore had the peculiar characteristic of not being tied to historical commemoration.

There is, however, a more positive reason why Corpus Christi may at least temporarily have attracted a cycle of plays to itself, or, to put it more exactly, why the Corpus Christi procession did so, for it is important that the plays became attached, not to the office, but to the procession. The procession, but not its nature, had been prescribed by the bull instituting the feast. It was clearly a propagandist ceremony, and, whilst the organisers would obviously be concerned with the honour due to the Host, their chief object would be the devotional education of the bystanders. Anything that conduced to this was therefore potentially suited to the occasion. An interesting example of this principle at work may be seen in the *Fronleichnamsspiel* from Innsbruck, which, being dated 1391, is the oldest of the Continental Corpus Christi plays.[96] A rubric describes it as follows: 'Incipit ludus utilis pro devotione simplicium intimandus et peragendus die corporis Christi, vel infra octavas, de fide katholica'.[97] What follows is a dramatisation of the illustrations of the creed which had earlier appeared in art (and which M. D. Anderson has associated with the 'creed play' of York).[98] The opening of the Innsbruck play presents the Fall, but thereafter come in pairs twelve apostles and twelve prophets: the prophets speak the prophecies familiar from the Prophets' Play, whilst each of the apostles delivers one of the twelve articles of the creed. The exactness of the rubric should be noted for it is instructive: it is a play *about* the catholic faith to be performed *at* Corpus Christi: Corpus Christi plays therefore do not have to be about Corpus Christi.

The example of the Innsbruck play brings the argument full circle. The early Septuagesima plays had obviously diverged far from the celebratory mimesis of liturgical drama: unlike Christmas and Easter, Septuagesima is not an occasion for rejoicing. What the lections of Septuagesima recall must be remembered with penitence and sorrow, and dramatic re-enactment, which must always contain an element of pleasure, would at first sight seem extraordinarily unsuitable. But traditionally the lenten season was an occasion for instruction and in particular for instruction of new converts to Christianity: from this point of view the Riga play performed for the edification of the Lettish neophytes was highly suited to Septuagesima. The plays acted at this season were therefore designed to present Christian history, and in particular the events narrated in the Creed, to the uneducated laity. But, whether for practical or doctrinal reasons, Septuagesima lapsed as an occasion for cyclical plays and the makeshift attachment to Whitsun was devised. Later again, however, there arose a feast of which the chief phenomenon was a procession intended for the edification of the laity, the adornment of the procession being left to local initiative. In some places, notably the north of England, the type of play which had originated at Septuagesima was at least temporarily adopted for Corpus Christi, this feast providing the needed occasion rather than the subject-matter of the plays.

Whilst the feast had little effect upon the subject-matter of the plays, it had considerable influence upon the manner of their presentation, for it can only have been the style of the Corpus Christi procession itself that can account for the unusual system of using moving pageant-carts instead of the traditional fixed acting area with various scaffolds to indicate different geographical locations. This had important dramatic consequences, such as the framelike effect given by a small stage, the closeness of actors to audience, the frequent need for one character to be impersonated by a number of different people, and the suggestion of the passing of time. This system also led to the practical advantage of each play being acted anything from eight to twelve times on the same day, so that the audience could spread themselves more thinly and consequently see better what was happening. Nevertheless this arrangement is so extraordinary, and so unlike earlier acting traditions that it must surely have emerged from the fusion of plays with procession. There is no known record of plays being performed in this way when they did not belong to the Corpus Christi tradition.

Whilst from the dramatic point of view the processional performance of plays developed numerous advantages, from the point of view of the religious procession it must have proved disastrous.[99] Even if we were to assume that in the original arrangement the cycles were briefer, and, though the procession halted at different stations,[100] each play was only acted once, the time that elapsed between the procession setting off from the church and its return must have been intolerably long.

Furthermore, the disputes about the number of stations at which plays should be acted, which are recorded in York documents from the end of the fourteenth century, seem to indicate that by that time each play was being acted at each station.[101] In this situation, if the procession of the Sacrament came last, it would have passed at nightfall when the bystanders were exhausted, or if it came first, it would have returned to the church long before the conclusion of the plays, and therefore without a congregation to honour it. In either instance, it would only have been natural if the bystanders were distracted from the basic devotion of the day, which consisted of gazing at the Host as it was carried past in splendour, either by fatigue at long standing, or by an impatient eagerness for the plays that were to follow. It is therefore not surprising that, as we know, the assimilation of plays to procession was rarely permanent, the cycles either being acted at some other season, as happened at Chester and Lincoln, or at least separated from the procession as at York and Beverley and Newcastle.[102] It also seems likely that this divorce is reflected in our extant texts of the plays (which are all of the fifteenth century or later): had it not already occurred, one would have expected some device to link the plays to the sacrament, such as is invariably found in the Corpus Christi plays of southern Europe. For instance, at the beginning of the *Künzelsauer Fronleichnamsspiel* (a play corresponding very closely in structure to the English cycles), two angels call for attention, the *rector processionis* (i.e. the expositor always present in German plays), addresses the sacrament in vernacular speech, and a choir sings 'O vere digna hostia': it is only after this that the plays of the Creation and Fall of the Angels begin.[103]

The dissociation of the cycles from the Corpus Christi procession during the course of the first half of the fifteenth century no doubt reflects ecclesiastical dissatisfaction with an experiment that was only partially successful. By severing the plays, but not suppressing them, however, religious authorities were able to have the best of both worlds: the Procession of the Sacrament would regain its dignity and importance and the plays would continue to edify the laity. It is interesting to notice that insofar as Corpus Christi processions in the later fifteenth century were used to display the history of the world, this was done through tableaux, occasionally consisting of wooden statues, but more often of live actors. Processions of this kind are recorded from all over western Europe: Dublin, Hereford, Draguignan, Béthune, Valencia, Bologna, Freiburg-im-Breisgau, etc.[104] Sometimes only the existence of such a procession is known, sometimes a list of pageants has survived. Whilst there is considerable overlap between the subjects presented in the mystery cycles and the tableau-pageants, the differences are significant. The tableaux often do not present either the Fall of the Angels or the Last Judgment; they tend to end their New Testament scenes at the Crucifixion, none having in completeness the vital sequence of the Harrowing of Hell, the Resurrection and the Ascension; they all to a greater or lesser extent have a concluding section made up of apostles, saints, doctors of the church, and sometimes eminent figures drawn from other historical fields, King Arthur or the Nine Worthies.[105] The impression given is therefore of a jubilant presentation of the history of the world rather than a doctrinal history of the Redemption. There has been much dispute over whether Corpus Christi tableaux led to plays or whether the plays became attenuated to the form of tableaux. The issue seems irresolvable since the documentary records for any town are too incomplete to furnish historical evidence, and on *a priori* reasoning either development is possible, for there could have been pressures to expand tableaux into plays or to reduce plays to tableaux.[106] It is, however, probably a mistake to assume that of these two, plays and tableaux, one was invariably the parent, the other the child. Coincidences of subject-matter might indicate a common indebtedness to iconographic tradition and, insofar as there was a direct influence of one on another, the direction of this influence may have varied from country to country. In England, for instance, what evidence there is suggests that the plays came first; in Spain, where the only surviving vernacular drama (apart from the *Auto de los Reyes Magos*) is very late indeed, the adoption of the custom of presenting tableaux seems to have come first and may well then have encouraged the adoption of plays as well. It is, however, more interesting to note that religious tableaux and religious plays co-existed for a time than to speculate about their historical relationship.

The development of the cycle form has formerly been explained in liturgical terms: it has been thought of either as an unconsidered conjunction of plays originally distinct and closely attached to liturgical seasons or as a dramatic form specially constructed for the feast of Corpus Christi. Whilst any attempt to reconstruct the historical development of the form is necessarily speculative, it seems more likely in view of the evidence set out in this chapter that, whilst the cycles were consciously designed, the authors were not primarily moved by liturgical considerations. Far more important was the intention of instructing the unlearned, and far more influential, possibly at an early date, and certainly at a later date, were the iconographic cycles, whether on church walls or in manuscripts, which also for the sake of instruction set out the history of the redemption in pictorial form. These inferences, made from a consideration of the plays themselves or from extant records of lost plays, are confirmed by a study of medieval comments upon the plays themselves.

V

Attitudes to Drama and Dramatic Theory

The Roman stage was morally and artistically degenerate for many centuries before the fall of Rome: this is by now a historical truism. Its degree of decadence, however, is not known with any precision, for knowledge of it comes largely from polemical attacks, which clearly use the licence to exaggerate permitted to satiric indignation. It may, however, be conjectured that the situation was roughly comparable to what it would be nowadays if the plays of Shakespeare and other former dramatists were never acted, if there were no plays being written by contemporary dramatists of serious intentions, and therefore all that was left was pantomime and variety sketches of the now disreputable kind. There were thus in Rome from the first to the fourth century no theatrical performances that literary taste could admire, and Christian writers therefore attacked the stage with whole-hearted abhorrence, undisturbed by the ambivalent feeling that marked their attitude to pagan literature, such as the *Aeneid*.

The violent rejection of all theatrical spectacles as a display and occasion of vice continued down the centuries: local church councils repeated the vehemence of Tertullian in their condemnation of performed entertainment, even though it can only have been the fairly innocent minstrel troops with jugglers and performing animals that were the object of their hostility: in particular they stressed that clerics must never have anything to do with such displays.[1] The repugnance that the Roman stage had justifiably aroused thus persisted long after the lavish but debased spectacles, which had provoked it, had vanished. Whilst the full-throated attacks of Tertullian are not heard again until the sixteenth century, when there was once again a flourishing secular theatre to denounce, echoes of them reverberate throughout the Middle Ages. The dramatic offices of the liturgy, when they came to be recognised as drama, provoked indignation, at least amongst the religious; the clerical acting of vernacular religious plays seems to have aroused more widespread and more effective hostility; whilst the lay performance of mystery plays led to the most bitter attack of all, but from the Lollards, not from the Church. Attacks by individuals must of course be distinguished from the central and authoritative voice of the Church. The first attack on liturgical drama was met by an official statement of reserved toleration; the second seems to have accorded more with official opinion; whilst the third, since it came from a heretical source, generated in the Church a warm approval and a serious defence of religious drama; in England from about 1375 until the Reformation there seems to have been a fortunate period in which mystery plays could be written and acted without those involved having cause to fear that the long shadow of Tertullian's disapproval would fall across them.

Two of the early antagonists of liturgical drama now known by name, were Gerhoh of Reichersberg (1093–1169) and Herrad of Landsberg, abbess of Hohenburg (1167–95). Gerhoh, a militant reformer and supporter of Gregory VII, was by far the more vehement of the two, and twice added an attack on liturgical drama to his denunciations of contemporary licence. The first attack occurred in his commentary on Psalm cxxxiii. 3, where the injunction to bless the Lord leads to an indignant examination of the negligence and licentiousness of monks, who do not sleep in their dormitories, nor eat in their refectories unless some theatrical entertainment, perhaps the play of Herod, attracts them there.[2] Gerhoh returned to the subject in a much later work, the *De investigatione Antichristi* (which deals primarily with the conflict between papal and imperial power), and there gave a whole chapter to it:[3] in this attack upon priests who turn churches into theatres the tones of Tertullian seem to be echoed in the deliberate rhetoric and the emotional vocabulary with the pattern of recurring words and phrases, *abominatio, vanitates, insaniae falsae*. More interesting than the style is the reasoning, for Gerhoh here uses the arguments that recur in antitheatrical treatises from Tertullian's *De spectaculis* to Prynne's *Histriomastix*: stage impersonation and theatrical feigning are hypocrisy and lies (a view that Plutarch had attributed to Solon,[4] this Platonic notion of deceit being re-enforced for Christians by the prohibition in Deuteronomy on men putting on women's clothing). Furthermore to portray something good is to treat it with derision, to portray something bad is to share in its wickedness. These two passages from Gerhoh's works, taken together, suggest that Gerhoh at first condemned Latin drama as part of the widespread degeneration of the monastic life, and that many years later he returned with a more serious and considered attack, fortified by a knowledge of patristic anti-theatrical arguments.

The objections to theatrical drama endorsed by Herrad of Landsberg were more moderate and less learned. Towards the end of the vast encyclopaedic work that she compiled for her nuns, the *Hortus deliciarum*, she included a short treatise on the religious life containing a measured attack on liturgical plays.[5] Unlike Gerhoh, this treatise both states and admits the force of the traditional justification of the plays, that they are to be permitted *pro augenda fide*,[6] but nevertheless forbids them for bad things can come of good, and the performance of liturgical drama has led to drunkenness, revelling, licentious speaking and other similar vices; finally it argues that liturgical impersonation, such as is found in the ceremonies of Maundy Thursday, is sufficient for devotional purposes.

Both Gerhoh and Herrad speak for religious orders, and their disapproval of religious drama must be understood in the light of what was considered fitting in a monastery or convent. To what extent they furthermore speak as isolated figures it is difficult to say, but the historical fact (which we have already noted) that liturgical drama, once it had gained substance, flourished in secular rather than monastic churches, suggests that their views within context were shared by other religions, though perhaps in a more temperate and less combative way. A continuing hostility to drama is also suggested by the mid-thirteenth-century gloss on a decree of Innocent III condemning the buffoonery and masquerades of the Feast of Fools (a decretal which had become part of Gregory IX's codification of canon law). The gloss is as follows:[7]

Non tamen hinc prohibetur repraesentare praesepe Domini, Herodem, Magos et qualiter Rachel plorabat filios suos, etc., quae tangunt festivitates illas, de quibus hic fit mentio, cum talia potius inducant homines ad compunctionem, quam ad lasciviam, vel voluptatem: sicut in Pascha sepulchrum Domini, et alia repraesentantur ad devotionem excitandam.

The implication of this gloss is that some people had attempted to argue that the *ludi theatrales* of the Christmas season condemned by the decretal included also the *Officum stellae*. The refusal to distinguish between the Christmas play and the Feast of Fools had been part of the polemical techniques of Gerhoh and Herrad, but it would seem that their successors went too far when they sought to find what was essentially a debating point enshrined in canon law: the gloss provided an answer to them, the Christmas play must be classified not with the indecencies of the Feast of Fools but with the solemn ceremonies associated with the Easter sepulchre. The gloss was of course only permissive: no church was compelled to make a Christmas play part of its liturgy. But it silenced those who would have wished to suppress the custom in churches within their own jurisdiction or to have denounced it in others. No further misgivings about liturgical drama or hostility to it were expressed until about 1500, when they came among the early reverberations of the Reformation.[8]

The gloss to Innocent III's decretal had amplified a little the reasons for classifying the Christmas play with the Easter ceremonies rather than with the dramatic activities on the Feast of Fools: the Christmas play conduced to devotion, rather than to lasciviousness and sensuous pleasure as did the Feast of Fools, just as the Easter ceremonies were performed *ad devotionem excitandam*. This justification of the plays is a recurring theme in the Middle Ages, the emphasis being sometimes on the exciting of devotion, sometimes on the strengthening of faith. The first known occurrence of the argument is in the *Regularis concordia*, where the purpose of the ceremony of the Burial of the Cross is said to be 'ad fidem indocti vulgi ac neophytorum corroborandam';[9] it seems likely, therefore, that the idea of liturgical mimeticism as an aid to the unlearned was first applied to ritual dramatic action and then by a natural progression extended to liturgical drama. The authoritative extension of the argument is of course in the gloss, but it had occurred much earlier. For, as we have already seen, Herrad had initially conceded that liturgical drama served the purpose for which it had been allowed, namely *pro augenda fide*. From the thirteenth century onwards this argument is heard repeatedly throughout western Europe, though usually, as fitted the spiritual emphasis of the times, in the form of a stimulus to devotion rather than a strengthening or increasing of faith. It is, however, interesting to note that Robert Mannyng in his discussion of acting in the *Handlyng Synne* (to which we shall be returning), altered the motive given in his Anglo-Norman source, 'Pur plus aver devociun' into 'To make men be yn beleve gode' and 'To make men beleve stedfastly'.[10] The idea of the stimulus to devotion, however, is found in England in the story of the Beverley miracle at the play of the Resurrection, to which, we are told, a large crowd had come out of a variety of motives, some in search of entertainment, some out of curiosity, and some for the awakening of devotion;[11] and Katherine of Sutton introduced the plays at Barking with the deliberate intention of countering the lassitude and indifference of the nuns by a custom that would move them to devotion.[12]

The Beverley story might be taken to imply that when religious plays came to be acted out of doors, the traditional apology for liturgical drama was simply extended to them. Commentary upon clerical acting, however, in two slightly later works, the Anglo-Norman *Manuel des péchés* of William of Waddington and the *Handlyng Synne* of Robert Mannyng of Brunne, which is a free English translation of it, suggest that such a placid acceptance of the value and propriety of vernacular drama was by no means general. It would seem rather from these works that when the decrees of canon law were applied to the recent dramatic developments, they were judged, not in the light of the decretal and gloss already quoted, but in that of the adjoining article, which repeated the ancient prohibition on priests being present at or taking any part in dramatic spectacles. This interpretation is tentative because both authors seem to follow a method common amongst legislators and commentators upon legislation, which is to be exact and explicit about what might or should be done, but general and allusive about what should not be done, for fear of putting ideas into people's heads and to prevent some local abuse from slipping through the net of comprehensiveness. Unfortunately William of Waddington and Robert Mannyng have been fairly successful in their object of not allowing the reader to know what was being prohibited unless he could recognise it from his own experience. Nevertheless a close examination of what is said about clerical acting may enable us to penetrate the evasiveness and obscurities of style and to make some inferences about what was being forbidden to clerics.

The discussions of clerical acting come under the heading of sloth, for a neglect of rules or duties is always a branch of this sin. Both in their context and in themselves they keep close to the structure of canon law: they fall into three parts. The first consists of a condemnation of the Feast of Fools, here as often referred to as *miracles*, and the decree of Gregory IX is cited as authority.[13] There follows a paraphrase of the gloss, sanctioning the performance of liturgical drama at Christmas and Easter. Finally come the allusive lines, which forbid some kind of acting that took place out-of-doors in churchyards, city streets or village greens. Here it seems clear that the authors take as their starting-point the prohibition upon priests having anything to do with plays and then interpret it in the light of contemporary practices. The precise question is therefore whether these practices were religious or secular. If they were religious, they might be a vernacular Christmas or Easter play; if they were secular, they were probably the May Day festivities and other popular spectacles which had already specifically been forbidden to clergy by the thirteenth-century diocesan constitutions of Walter de Cantilupe and by Robert Grosseteste in both his Constitutions and letters to officials in his diocese[14] (for works written in Lincolnshire one would particularly look to the latter).[15] The *Manuel* gives the fuller account:[16]

> Mes, fere foles assemblez
> En les rues des citez,
> Ou en cymiters apres mangers,
> Quant venent les fols volunters, –
> Tut dient qe il le funt pur bien, –
> Crere ne les devez pur rien
> Qe fet seit pur le honur de Dée,
> Einz del deable, pur verité.

In the English version these lines are reduced to a single couplet: 'Ʒef þou do hyt yn weyys or grenis/A syght of synne truly hit semys.'[17] The Anglo-Norman account is the more illuminating because it suggests very strongly that what is being forbidden is not clerical indulgence in dubious secular pastimes, for the clerics are able to make a defence for their actions: they say that what they do serves a good purpose and is to the honour of God. While recollection of William of Malmesbury's famous story about Aldhelm, who sang secular songs to attract an audience, may cause us a moment's hesitation,[18] it nevertheless seems most unlikely that partaking in May Day ceremonies, however much this was done in a missionary spirit, could be justified in such terms.

The contrast between what is allowed and what is forbidden is much more starkly expressed, though with some verbal obscurity that may not be entirely intentional. The ambiguity lies in the phrase 'do hyt', verb and pronoun, which seem to substitute for 'pley þe resurreccyun' and 'pleye . . . howe God was bore yn ʒole nyght', though the alternative that it is used rather loosely and means simply 'act' remains a possibility. The supposition that the former is the correct meaning is slightly borne out by an apparent contrast between the phrases 'yn þe cherche' and 'yn weyys and grevis', the former being the place in which priests may act plays of the Nativity and Resurrection. The insistence that these should be acted in church is considerably more marked in the *Manuel*:

> Fere poent representement, –
> Mes qe ceo seit chastement
> En office de seint eglise.

This emphasis upon the church and the liturgy as the proper place and the proper occasion for drama is not found in the gloss, which is other-

wise here being paraphrased, and is only readily explicable if we assume
that the authors knew of performances of religious plays in other
places and at other times.[19]

The fairly clear tendency of this internal evidence is supported by a
more general consideration of external probability. That there was
some clerical acting of vernacular plays in the thirteenth century is
certain, and it would perhaps be odd if such local but comprehensive
statements of the permissible and impermissible ignored this. Furthermore the supposition that there was strong ecclesiastical opposition to
priests acting in religious plays, except insofar as they were integrated
in the liturgy, is supported by the known historical facts: the emergence
of vernacular drama in the twelfth century as an apparently vigorous
growth; its fitful and tenuous continuance in the thirteenth and first
half of the fourteenth centuries, and then the sudden profusion of plays
when their performance had been taken over by the craft gilds.

If this historical reconstruction is correct, then the allocation of the
plays to the gilds for performance in the Corpus Christi procession can
be seen to have provided a solution to a long-standing dilemma. On
the one hand the theory that the plays were useful as a stimulus to
devotion was likely to encourage extra-liturgical performance, for
obviously the more understandable they were (and sung Latin cannot
have been readily understood) and the more naturalistically the subjects
were treated, the more moving they would be. A comparison between
any *Officium stellae* and any vernacular nativity sequence would illustrate this point. Yet on the other hand the better the plays were designed
to fulfil their purpose, the more unsuitable they became for performance by the clergy. The abhorrence that Gerhoh and Herrad expressed
for the practice of priests taking the parts of soldiers or women must
not be thought to reflect special pleading or the scruples of purists.
There is a serious and widespread belief that a person should not act the
part of a character wholly alien to his nature: it is, for instance, said in
Plato's *Laws* that freemen should not impersonate slaves. In liturgical
drama, however, the identification of impersonator with impersonated
was never complete, for a cleric would emerge from his liturgical role
momentarily to act and then be subsumed back into the performance of
the office, and furthermore, as we have already seen, the liturgical
context was also part of the total dramatic effect.

A performance out-of-doors and detached from the liturgy will have
appeared very different. There would no longer be the liturgy itself to
remind the audience that the actors were in fact priests engaged in part
of their religious duties, nor the Latin language and chant to indicate

that this was a natural extension of the liturgy. The greater realism that resulted will have created a far stronger theatrical illusion, and probably the clothing became correspondingly more naturalistic, and costume no longer a matter of selecting the most suitable of the available ecclesiastical vestments. Under these circumstances it would be little wonder that those who were more concerned with decorum in clerical conduct than with the spiritual benefiting of the laity decided that such performances should be classed with the *ludi* long forbidden to clerics rather than with the dramatic adornments of the liturgy.

Looking back at the situation now, we may wonder why it did not occur to people for more than a hundred years that if vernacular religious plays were good in themselves, but it was unsuitable for priests to act them, then the help of the laity should be sought: the problem seems so closely defined that it compels the discovery of its own solution. But this is certainly to be wise after the event. Firstly, the long liturgical associations would have suggested that if religious plays were to be performed, then priests should be the performers: the undertaking will thus have seemed too solemn for the laity, too frivolous for the clergy. Secondly, and more importantly, the solution when it came was made possible in its precise form by two new developments. The occasion was there, namely the feast of Corpus Christi with its proper emphasis upon popular edification. Moreover the actors were there, namely the trade gilds, who in the second half of the fourteenth century had emerged as prosperous and responsible bodies,[20] who were both willing to expend time and money on religious duties (such duties are written in their ordinances),[21] who had the necessary talent and resources,[22] and who could be trusted to carry out activities that potentially might lead to disrepute with appropriate seriousness and decorum. The new feast and the new secular organisations, brought together by a fortunate conjunction in time, thus provided a situation in which religious drama could again flourish without opposition from the Church.

A fresh attack came, however: not this time in terms of breaches in clerical decorum, but in terms of the impropriety of the plays themselves. The attackers were the Lollards, who like their Puritan descendants in the sixteenth century saw in the stage a source of viciousness, and in religious plays the bringing of religion into contempt. This attack, being of heretical origin, was taken seriously by the Church, which then formulated a carefully reasoned and ingenious defence. As again in the sixteenth century, literary theory was born out of the need for self-justification. Unfortunately no sermon or treatise in defence of mystery plays survives, though one hears of such defences being made. The learned Franciscan, who preached on the plays in York in 1426, commending the play to the people, 'affirmando quod bonus erat in se et laudabilis valde',[23] was fairly certainly responding to Lollard attacks; the propriety of drama as an aid to the unlearned was one of the many issues on which Lollards and Franciscans particularly opposed one another. About a hundred and fifty years later the Protestant presbytery at Stirling made a schoolmaster named John Brown argue the following thesis: 'Is it lesum to play clark playis on þe sabboth day or nocht And qwethir gif it be lesum or nocht to mak clark playis on ony part of þe scriptur.'[24] Again nothing is known of the arguments used by John Brown to defend the 'clark play' acted by his school-children.

While no apology for the plays survives, a summary of the arguments advanced in their defence is provided by the famous Lollard treatise condemning the plays: the author quotes his opponents' arguments in order to refute them. The manuscript preserving this work consists of a collection of Lollard treatises, of which another is an attack on images.[25] The latter is obviously a reply to works in defence of images, such as the Latin treatise of Walter Hilton.[26] It may be reasonably conjectured that the Lollard author of *A Tretise of Miraclis Pleyinge* was replying to some corresponding Latin treatise in defence of mystery plays. Six arguments in defence of plays are enumerated:

1 Mystery plays are acted in honour of God.
2 Men are converted to virtuous living by seeing the mystery plays, for they learn from them the folly of pride and the wiliness of the devils in their attempts to ensnare pople.
3 By seeing the sufferings of Christ people are moved to compassion and devotion, and they weep bitter tears.
4 There are some people who can only be converted through the device of entertainment.
5 People must be given some entertainment for refreshment after their work, and religious plays are far better than the frivolous pastimes with which they would otherwise occupy themselves.
6 Since it is permissible to portray the work of the Redemption in art, it must be permissible to portray it also in drama, the latter being yet more memorable and effective than art, for the one 'is a deed bok, the tother a quick'.[27]

Three of these arguments, those here numbered 1, 4 and 5, are of only passing interest since they do not have any literary bearing on the texts.

Number 1 is a ringing asseveration rather than a reasoned defence: it is not new, for William of Waddington had quoted it as an attempt at self-justification that was not to be heeded.[28] Numbers 4 and 5 are a part of the recurring controversial issues that divided the Lollards from the orthodox tradition and are only incidentally applied to the plays: the legitimacy of using some entertaining device, such as verse or exempla in sermons, in order to catch people's interest had often been attacked by Wycliffe and his followers, and so also had the Thomist view that entertainment was permissible so long as it was decorous, since men need recreation for the spirit just as they need rest for the body.[29] The other three arguments, however, which are all interrelated, are extremely important. The key to their interpretation lies in the sixth:

> Also, sithen it is leveful to han the myraclis of God peyntid, why is not as wel leveful to han the myraclis of God pleyed, sythen men mowen bettere reden the wille of God and his mervelous werkis in the pleyinge of hem than in the peyntynge, and betere thei ben holden in mennus mynde, and oftere rehersid by the pleyinge of hem than by the peyntynge, for this is a deed bok, the tother a quick.

When mystery plays were first attacked by the Lollards, the novelty of the genre must have caused embarrassment to the apologists, who were accustomed to support all arguments by an appeal to patristic or other ecclesiastical authority. The author of the fifteenth-century treatise *Dives and Pauper* tried to meet this point by assuming that the gloss could cover vernacular plays as well as liturgical drama, and that he could therefore rest his case upon canon law. He thus provided himself with an authority, but with an interpretation of authority that might well be questioned, and therefore hardly satisfactory or available in every circumstance:[30] it is probably not accidental that no imitation of his defence of plays is now known. The method of defence found by the apologists quoted in the *Tretise* was far more ingenious and resourceful for, by equating plays with pictures, they gained for themselves, almost by a stroke of the pen, a set of well-tried arguments and a solid phalanx of authorities. In order to understand the nature of this defence, which was not only brilliant polemically, but also rich in aesthetic implications, it is necessary to consider briefly the history of the attack on images and their defence.[31]

The earliest statement in the west of the justification of the use of images occurs in the writings of Gregory the Great, and in particular in the second letter that Gregory sent to Serenus, Bishop of Marseilles, who appears to have been the first of the western iconoclasts. When Gregory heard that Serenus had caused all the images in Marseilles to be destroyed, he wrote to him twice, the second letter being the more important because it is the fuller and also the one to be thereafter repeatedly cited. The crucial passage in it is the following:[32]

> Aliud enim est picturam adorare, aliud per picturae historiam quid sit adorandum addiscere. Nam quod legentibus scriptura, hoc idiotis praestat pictura cernentibus, quia in ipsa etiam ignorantes vident quid sequi debeant, in ipsa legunt qui litteras nesciunt. Unde et praecipue gentibus pro lectione pictura est.

In this argument that pictures served as books to the unlettered, Gregory was echoing a theory that had been formulated two centuries earlier by the Cappadocian Fathers, St Basil the Great and St Gregory of Nyssa.[33] In their works, however, as in Gregory's, references to images are only passing and incidental, and it was not until the iconoclastic controversy of the eighth century that full-scale apologies were written. Of these the most famous was the *De imaginibus* of John Damascene[34] and, whilst this treatise was not known in the west, its thought was echoed in the deliberations of the Second Council of Nicaea in 767, which, though they took place in Greek, were translated into Latin in the west.[35] John Damascene also included a briefer defence of images in the *De fide orthodoxa*, a work that was translated into Latin in the twelfth century, and became one of the authorities most commonly cited by the scholastic theologians.[36] In particular the section on images in Book IV of the *De fide orthodoxa* is quoted by St Thomas in his *quaestio*, 'Utrum imago Christi sit adoranda adoratione latriae' in the *Summa theologica*,[37] and in England by some of the more learned defenders of images at the time of the Wycliffite attack.[38]

Through the record of the proceedings of the Second Council of Nicaea and through the translation of the *De fide orthodoxa* the very fully formulated eastern theory of images reached the west, and western theologians drew upon it to counter spasmodic outbreaks of iconoclasm or at least of antipathy to religious representational art. It formed a method of adding to the briefer defence of Gregory the Great, which itself came to be incorporated in Gratian's *Decretum*, a compilation which by the mid-twelfth century formed part of the official body of canon law, the *Corpus juri canonici*.[39] From the early twelfth century onwards the view that images served as *libri laicorum* became so widespread that it would be impossible to enumerate all those who expound it. It is found, for instance, in the work of the great scholastic theologians, Albert the Great and Thomas Aquinas, and in the commentaries on the liturgy of Honorius of Autun, Sicard of Cremona and Durandus;[40] the statutes of a painters' gild quote it casually.[41] When images came under attack in England through Wycliffite influences, it was repeated by Walter Hilton and Roger Dymmok and by many preachers, including Robert Rypon, Thomas Brinton and John Mirk;[42] and it is found in many treatises on the Ten Commandments (the second commandment was of course the key authority used by iconoclasts) including the well-known *Dives and Pauper*.[43] The theory eventually re-appeared in Counter-Reformation treatises regulating and defending the veneration of images, such as the *De historia SS. imaginum* of Molanus.[44]

Whilst some of the references here listed are fleeting, many form part of a fairly substantial defence of images. In these fuller discussions the theory of *libri laicorum* is one of three traditional arguments for the esteeming of images, the other two being that images aid the memory and that they are especially moving since what is seen is more immediately vivid than what is heard. Though Gregory the Great had known and stated the theory that images excited devotion,[45] these twin arguments in their medieval form had been transmitted by the eastern sources already noted.[46] The following quotation from St Thomas's *Commentary on the Sentences* is a typical early western statement of this triad:[47]

> Fuit autem triplex ratio institutionis imaginum in Ecclesia. Primo ad instructionem rudium, qui eis quasi quibusdam libris edocentur. Secundo ut incarnationis mysterium et sanctorum exempla magis in memoria nostra essent, dum quotidie oculis repraesentantur. Tertio ad excitandum devotionis affectum qui ex visis efficacius incitatur quam ex auditis.

That images recall to the memory what they represent is a proposition that does not need to be expounded. In late medieval works it is usually stated rather barely, though often given a colouring that derives from the devotional temper of the period. Honorius of Autun, for instance, had said that images were placed in churches 'ut priorum vita in memoriam revocetur',[48] whereas in *Dives and Pauper* it is said that images 'be ordeyned to stere mans mynde [i.e. memory] to thynke on Christis incarnation and on his passion, and his lyvynge';[49] here the exclusive reference to the life of Christ and the specific mention of the Passion show that the ancient argument in defence of images has merged with the medieval theory of the value of meditating upon the life of Christ and in particular upon His Passion. Within this frame of reference the very act of calling to mind was in itself a work of devotion. Mirk in his defence of images says:[50]

> Saynt Austyn sayde: 'þe mynde of Cristis passion is þe best defence aȝens temptacions of þe fende'. Herefor ben roodes sett on hey in holy chirch, and so by syȝt þerof have mynd of Cristis passion. And þerfor roodes and oþyr ymages ben necessary in holy chirch, whatever þes Lollardes sayn.

And much earlier this thought had been movingly and succinctly expressed in the first line of the famous Latin hymn 'Dulcis Iesu memoria' and in the rather jingly English verse:[51]

> Þe minde of þi passiun swete Ihesu,
> þe teres it tollid,
> þe heine it bolled,
> þe neb it wetth,
> in herte sweteth.

In this way the original argument that images recalled to the memory what was important in the history of salvation changed into the idea that images by their presentation of Christ's Passion aroused in the beholder feelings of compassion and love. It thus became closely allied to the last argument, which praised images because they quicken the heart and the imagination more readily than words. This argument depended upon the supposition that the sight is the highest of the cognitive senses, a theory inherited from Aristotle and expounded by St Thomas. When this theory was applied to the defence of art, it conferred upon images a pre-eminence in the realm of devotional communication, since, by a practical extension, what was heard was understood to include also what was read. The implications of this theory for religious experience had already been very skilfully explored in a now much-quoted passage from the records of the Second Council of Nicaea. During the fourth session, biblical and patristic authorities were read and deliberated upon, one of these being a passage from St Gregory of Nyssa, describing how he had wept at the sight of a painting of the Sacrifice of Isaac.[52] The bishops then commented as follows:[53]

> See how our father grieved at the depicted history, even so that he wept.

Basil: Many times the father had read the story, but perchance he had not wept; but when once he saw it painted he wept.

John: If to such a doctor the picture was helpful and drew forth tears, how much more in the case of the ignorant and simple will it bring forth compunction and benefit.

Theodore: If the holy Gregory, vigilant in divine cogitation, was moved to tears at the sight of the story of Abraham, how much more shall a painting of the Incarnation of Our Lord Christ, who for us was made man, move the beholders to their profit and tears.

This point is explained carefully and clearly by Durandus:[54]

> Pictura namque plus videtur movere animum, quam scriptura.
> Per picturam quidem res gesta ante oculos ponitur; sed per
> scripturam res gesta quasi per auditum, qui minus movet animum,
> ad memoriam revocatur. Hinc etiam est, quod in Ecclesia non
> tantam reverentiam exhibemus libris, quantam imaginibus et
> picturis.

It is unnecessary to stress how important this argument would have seemed in an age when the supreme devotional activity was considered to be a loving meditation upon Christ in His sufferings.

Traditional apologies for images had thus set out three arguments in their defence: they recalled what they represented to the memory; they moved the beholder to compassion and compunction more effectively than what was heard or read; they were books for the unlettered. All these three arguments, which were constantly repeated in the late fourteenth century when Wycliffites were rejecting images as idolatrous, were transferred and given a fresh application in the defence of mystery plays. Though the numerical division is different, three of the six arguments which we have already summarised repeat them. The important argument that images provide a more effective emotional stimulus than the written or spoken word is divided between arguments 2 and 3 so that it better reflects the meditative theory of the Middle Ages, which saw the contrasting emotions of fear and love as appropriate to different spiritual conditions and to different stages in the life of devotion. This distinction had already been noted by some exponents of the value of images, though not in such a way as to disturb the traditional numbering. Durandus, for instance, had pointed out the different purposes served by paintings of heaven and hell: 'Rursus

quandoque in Ecclesiis paradisus depingitur, ut aspicientes ad delecta-
tionem praemiorum alliciat, et quandoque infernus, ut eos formidine
poenarum a vitiis deterreat.'[55]

According to the *Tretise*, one argument in defence of images was
bifurcated when applied to plays, whilst the two other arguments are
run together in number 6 in which it is said that plays are even better
than paintings in that they present God's works in such a way that they
are better retained in the memory, and can be yet more vividly
apprehended for plays make a living book but pictures a dead one. In
this way it is ingeniously argued that the traditional apology for
images when applied to mystery plays provides a yet stouter weapon
in their defence, for the purposes served by images are served even
more effectively by plays.

Before we examine the justice and aesthetic value of this transference
of the arguments in defence of images to the defence of plays, it is
worth noting that there is evidence that this apologetic method, once
devised, was known in countries other than England and was remembered for more than a hundred and fifty years. It is probable that it was
known in France near the beginning of the fifteenth century:[56] it
certainly was by the middle for Eustache Mercadé alludes to it in one
of the epilogues in his long play, the *Vengeance de Nostre Seigneur
Jhesucrist sur les Juifs par Vespasien et Titus:*[57]

> A plusiers gens ont moult valu
> Qui n'entendent les escriptures,
> Exemples, histoires, pointures,
> Faictes ès moustiers et palais,
> Ce sont les livres des gens lais.
> En espécial l'exemplaire
> Des personnages leur doit plaire
> Qui sont des fais de Jhesucris,
> Selonc que mettent les escrips
> Et les livres de saincte église.

In more polemic form this theory re-appeared in the works of some of
the Counter-Reformation writers on iconography. The most famous of
these, Molanus, discusses religious plays in a sub-section of his treatise
on images and justifies them in the same terms, citing as authorities
Conradus Brunus, *De imaginibus* (Augsburg, 1548), and Guillielmus
Lindanus (Wilhelm von Lindt), *Apologeticum ad Germanos* (1580). In the
latter, plays are defended as follows:[58]

Haec enim Dei optima beneficia si docendo et legendo, adeo et pingendo, pium est Christianis saepe in memoriam revocare, quis nisi Iudaico Christi odio excaecatus, aut Turcica potius Christi invidia rabidus, neget prodesse summopere illa ipsa vivis exemplis refricare, et quantum res patitur, ad vivum repraesentare. Quid enim aliud sunt ista spectacula, quam vivae Laicorum Historiae, quibus multo efficacius humanus movetur animus, quam si idem privatim legat, aut ab alio etiam lectum publice audiat.

The last sentence in this quotation, which is repeated word for word by Molanus,[59] is especially striking in its resemblance to the arguments summarised in the *Tretise of Miraclis Pleyinge*.

In England in the sixteenth century a different facet of this tradition is recalled. At this time Puritan attacks upon the general licentiousness of the stage were met by reasoned defences founded on classical theory. The attackers, however, sometimes included in passing a denunciation of religious plays, and cited as a kind of insolence the people who said that they learnt more from seeing a religious play than from hearing a sermon.[60] The frequency with which this remark is quoted suggests that it was a standard defence, made perhaps by sympathetic clergy, or handed down by word of mouth, at a time when mystery plays were not only condemned by Puritans, but were also appearing increasingly repugnant to ecclesiastical authority in the Church of England. The theory that plays were better than sermons is evidently an ingenious variation in the traditional defence made, or at least commonly used, at a time when it was useless to justify drama by analogy with art, since paintings, stained glass and carvings were being fanatically destroyed all over England. Behind this argument of course lies the doctrine of the superiority of the sense of sight over the sense of hearing, and also a definition of images as *muta praedicatio*, a phrase found in the *De imaginibus* of John Damascene,[61] and repeated in a less aphoristic way by the second Council of Nicaea.[62] It is easy to see how with these theories as a starting point, and by analogy with the theory that plays were like pictures but more effective, it was possible to argue that plays were also like sermons but more effective.

It is clear even from a brief historical survey that the arguments used in defence of images were extremely well known and firmly established, and that the apologists for the mystery plays depended upon an informed recognition of the analogy which they had so skilfully constructed. The defence of mystery plays was obviously very late and comparatively much rarer, but it is well diffused in both time and geographical area, and this dispersal can only be accounted for if we assume that many intermediaries have been lost. While it would be pleasant to have further documentation for the prevalence of this theory, it is reasonable to assume that whenever plays were attacked, this defence was both available and used. From the literary point of view, however, the interesting issue is not the existence in itself of this theory, but that of its aesthetic implications. An examination of this issue must proceed in several stages, with a consideration of the relationship of painting to literature and to drama in particular, then with the reverse of this in a reconstruction of the probable relationship of the plays to art, and finally with some observations upon the usefulness of this theory to the critic nowadays.

It is worth noting first of all that the eastern defence of images, though normally couched in purely religious terms, had antecedents in the aesthetics of antiquity. When the Byzantine Fathers said aphoristically that painting was a silent sermon or books for the unlettered, they were echoing the aphorism, attributed to Simonides by Plutarch (the aphorism that was to be so often quoted during the Renaissance), that a picture was silent poetry and poetry a speaking picture.[63] The point of this aphorism is of course that both poet and painter aim to externalise the visual images in the mind, the one using words as his medium, the other line and colour. This comparison had been already made in the fourth century by St Basil who in his Sermon on the Forty Martyrs wrote as follows:[64]

Nam et res in bello fortiter gestas saepe tum oratores, tum pictores exprimunt, illi quidem eas sermone ornantes, hi vero ipsas depingentes in tabellis, et utrique non paucos ad fortitudinem excitarunt. Quae enim historiae sermo per auditum exhibet, ea ob oculos ponit silens pictura per imitationem.

The last sentence of this quotation was repeated by the bishops at the Second Council of Nicaea: 'For that which words by description present to the hearing, a silent painting displays by imitation.'[65]

When this idea passed to the west with the record of the Council, its origins in the *Moralia* could not have been recognised, as Plutarch's works were not translated until the sixteenth century. There was, however, in Horace's *De arte poetica* the passage beginning 'Ut pictura poesis', which made the same comparison though in a more limited way.[66] That Horace's lines, which were to become so famous in the Renaissance,[67] were associated with the traditional defence of images is suggested by the fact that Durandus in his discussion of images, quoting from the *De arte poetica*, after giving precise rules for the representation of Christ, angels, martyrs, etc. says: 'Sed et diversae historiae tam novi, quam veteris testamenti pro voluntate pictorum depinguntur, nam *pictoribus, atque poetis quaelibet audendi semper fuit aequa potestas.*'[68] This argument for the freedom of the artist in his treatment at least of lesser religious subjects, based on lines from Horace that associate poets with painters, is unexpected, and tantalising in its hint of some larger aesthetic awareness, a hint that can no longer be followed up.

This classical equation between art and literature was not repeated in the Middle Ages through mere lip-service, as a convenient theory to ward off the attacks of at least tentative iconoclasts. On the contrary it bears closely on the subject-matter and style of both literature and art, and remains helpful to the critic nowadays even though he has no wish to approach the arts through the theories generated by ancient controversies.

It would be irrelevant here to explore the highly visual qualities of medieval narrative, sermons and lyrics. The attempt in them to re-create a visual picture is well known, though such passages have the disadvantage, which the bishops at Nicaea had noted: a person or scene has to be described by a listing of separate items, and therefore cannot so readily present a sense of the whole as can painting or sculpture. In particular meditative poetry from the thirteenth century onwards had precisely the same aim as representations of the Crucifixion traditionally had, namely that of presenting to the reader or hearer a meditative picture which would serve to arouse his compassion and move him to tears.[69]

The relationship of painting to literature in the Middle Ages is yet more apparent. Whilst some religious art might be said to correspond to portrait painting in later periods, since the aim is to represent a person outside the narrative context of his life, most could, to use later terminology again, more properly be called history paintings. The aim is to tell a story by illustrating a crucial scene, the beholder supplying the rest: in such instances ignorance of the story will be a major impediment to enjoyment and understanding of the work. It is usually said that this exclusive concentration upon one moment in time is a distinguishing characteristic of art as against literature: the medium of words allows for narrative development, the medium of art does not. Medieval religious art, however, in defiance of its inherent limitation, contrived to provide for the uninstructed beholder by presenting the whole story. One method was the very common form of a sequence of frescoes, each one in its own square compartment, and in the centuries when the walls of churches were covered with frescoes, most churches must have presented the whole narrative of the Redemption visually to the congregation. The designers of such series undoubtedly took very seriously indeed the doctrine that painting was the *libri laicorum*. An alternative to the presentation of successive stages of the narrative in separate compartments was the combination of them in one picture, events that took place at different times being related to one another in a single composition. A well-known example of this very common type of composition is Gozzoli's *Adoration of the Magi* in which the kings in the forefront offer their gifts, but in the background the procession is seen over and over again winding its way down through the mountains.

Another way in which art attempted to achieve the effects of the verbal was in the selection for illustration, not of some moment of important action, but of some moment of important dialogue. The representation of dialogue in art has an ancestry in the antique.[70] But, though Greek and Roman art used a convention of gesture to indicate something of what was said, it normally indicated conversation in general rather than precise speech: perhaps the discourse of philosophers, such as one sees in the much later and well-known fresco by Raphael, *The School of Athens*. Medieval art, however, perhaps initially through the influence of drama, attempted to indicate the precise words, if need be by inserting the dialogue or a narrative explanation in the top margin, or by inscribing it on scrolls which undulate from the mouths of the speakers. A very early example of this has been noted by Professor Pächt in an eleventh-century Emmaus scene from Salzburg, in which Christ and the disciples carry scrolls on which their speeches are written.[71] Illuminated manuscripts influenced by drama, such as the *St Albans Psalter* and the *Holkham Bible Picture Book*, abundantly illustrate this principle. By the fourteenth and fifteenth centuries, however, the combination of pictures with words was widespread: the Dance of Death is a well-known example, and in this neither words nor painting is complete without the other. Against the background of such paintings the doctrine that drama is more effective than art, since in it the visual and the verbal can be combined (they are living books not dead ones), loses its first appearance of being a clever debating point and seems rather a self-evident truth.

The dependence of art on drama can finally be seen in the slavish imitation of features entirely unrealistic and necessitated by the conditions of theatrical performance. From the eleventh century onwards the Marys visiting the sepulchre are shown carrying their spices in what are manifestly censers, and, to quote a more curious example, in eleventh-century manuscripts from Beaucaire and Modena, the holy women who visit the spice-merchant are obviously men.[72] Less marked, but more immediately relevant, is the picture of Adam and Eve in the Garden of Eden in the *Holkham Bible Picture Book*,[73] where the wall is so low that no intruder would have to leap over it: he could step across it by lifting one foot very slightly (when Paradise was presented on a scaffold, the wall would have to be unrealistically low if the actors were to be visible to the audience). More spectacular examples are provided by the fifteenth-century alabasters in which, as Hildburgh has pointed out, the Christ-Child can be seen to be a wooden doll and in the Ascension the figure of Christ is also obviously an effigy (suitable for raising on a pulley).[74] These strange echoes of stage-performance, spanning the eleventh to the fifteenth century, are interesting and important in showing the work of artists, who so traditionally turned to drama for their models that they ceased to exercise discrimination in what they imitated.

That much medieval art was influenced by the drama is a proposition that modern art-historians would readily accept. The much more ticklish question is that which is our chief concern, namely to what extent drama was influenced by art. It seems likely, however, that from the beginnings of liturgical drama a parallelism between the two was observed: The imitation of the properties or conventions of theatrical performance, which we have just noted in eleventh-century manuscripts, demonstrates this recognition on the part of the artist; whilst the justification of liturgical drama as a stimulus to devotion,[75] which we can now see to relate to the defence of images, suggests a similar recognition on the part of the promoters of liturgical plays. It is, however, a mistake to mention artists and promoters of drama as though they were entirely different and unrelated people: both religious art and drama came from centres of monastic learning, and the people responsible for them, even if they were not the same would usually have been men in close touch with one another. That artists imitated drama but that the authors and organisers of plays took their own wayward course without reference to iconographic tradition is beyond the bounds of credibility.

Nevertheless it is obviously impossible to prove the influence of art on drama, and particularly upon the more diversified scenes of the mystery plays, in the way that it is possible to prove the reverse: the evidence has vanished with the medieval performances. Whilst stage directions may sometimes indicate a correspondence (though even these might often equally well derive from a common ancestry in meditative literature), they are comparatively scanty, and much must have been left to the decision of the producer. But again, that he could determine dress or position the actors without the conscious or unconscious influence of representational art is a hypothesis too unlikely to be taken seriously. There are furthermore two passages in the *Journal d'un bourgeois de Paris,* which are suggestive. In both of these the anonymous author is describing religious spectacles which were put on to honour a royal visit. The second of these, which took place in 1424, consisted of a series of tableaux: 'devant le Chastellet avoit ung moult [bel] mistere du Vieilz Testament et du Nouvel, que les enfens de Paris firent, et fut fait sans parler ne sans signer, comme se ce feussent ymaiges eslevez contre ung mur'.[76] The earlier display was in 1420, and insofar as the author does not comment on the absence of words and gesture, as he was later to do, it may have been a genuine play: 'Et fut fait en la rue de la Kalende devant le Palais, ung [moult] piteux mystere de la passion de Nostre Seigneur au vif, selon que elle es figurée autour du cueur de Nostre-Dame de Paris . . . et n'estoit homme qui veist le mistere à qui le cueur n'apiteast.'[77]

It is likely that the author of the *Journal* knew the traditional defence of drama. Whilst there is no reason to doubt that people were moved to pity by presentations of the Passion (even the Lollard polemicist concedes this),[78] the insistence that there was not a single person whose heart was not moved to compassion suggests an understanding of the theory of the form rather than a literary or empirical observation. The comparison with art also recalls the idea of speaking pictures, but here it is likely that understanding of theory has been given body by recognition of practice. In both passages the dramatic spectacles are compared to or said to imitate the very full set of bas-reliefs on biblical subjects which once surrounded the apse of Notre Dame; whilst this could have been a perceptive comment on the part of a writer who perceived a general resemblance, it is more likely to be the accurate observation of an effect deliberately contrived by the producer.

Whichever of these explanations now seems the more acceptable, it remains that the comparison of the tableaux, silent and motionless, to religious art helpfully suggests the intermediary point which made the theoretical relationship between art and drama imaginatively convincing. For if one postulates the following series, religious painting, tableau of the same subject, mime, play, it is unclear at what point one would want to cry halt and draw the line between a difference in degree and a difference in kind. It is moreover historically plausible that the tableau did provide such a transition, for while, as we saw before, there is no evidence that in England at least Corpus Christi tableaux preceded Corpus Christi plays, there is evidence of lesser religious tableaux and mimes acted by the gilds in the mid-fourteenth century.

The most interesting of these is the Pageant of the Purification performed by the Gild of St Mary in Beverley,[79] a gild formed in 1355. Members of the Gild were dressed to impersonate the Blessed Virgin (who carried a doll to represent the Christ-child), Joseph, Simeon and two angels. With the rest of the gild they went in procession to the church, and when they had entered, it is directed that 'the pageant Virgin shall offer her son to Simeon at the high altar'.[80] Whilst there is nothing so striking as this in any other of the gild records so far published, the evidence for gild customs in the middle of the fourteenth century is not very sure, and it is perhaps noteworthy that this record comes from Beverley, the home of one of the earliest cycles of mystery plays. The important issue here, however, is not to insist upon mime as a stepping stone in the progress of dramatic development, but as an instance in which play and picture could very readily seem to merge. If dramatic paintings with words on rouleaux seem to be straining the natural bounds of the form in order to achieve the effects of drama, in the Beverley custom and the Paris tableau one can see human impersonation striving hard to achieve the effects of art.

The argument that drama was not different in kind from painting or sculpture met, perhaps by chance, some of the more serious criticisms that could be made of its propriety. It answered, for instance, the traditional and ancient objection (which we noted in Gerhoh) that acting involved lying and hypocrisy, for according to this theory an actor would no more impersonate or claim to be what he represented than would a statue. This particular point would have been particularly clear in that all discussions of images differentiated very sharply indeed between the image and its prototype in order to distinguish the veneration of images from idolatry. Present preconceptions may suggest that this distinction breaks down when the image is not inanimate. But the modern view, so much stressed by the Method school, that an actor must think himself into his part, so that his personality temporarily fuses with that created by the dramatist, is entirely alien to medieval style. Firstly, as we shall see, there are no rounded characters in the mystery plays: no use is made of the specific virtues for which literature was later judged to be superior to painting, namely the ability to display psychological conflicts, development and ambiguities;[81] when there is no inwardness of characterisation, any temptation for an actor to identify himself with his role must largely disappear. Secondly, the indifference to a psychological relationship between actor and character can be seen in the willingness to adopt the processional method of presenting the plays; for the inevitable consequence of this was that whenever a character appeared in more than one play, as all the important New Testament characters do, this character would be impersonated by a number of different actors. Under these circumstances any personal mannerisms or gestures, any individual modulations of the voice, even the personality conveyed by individual physiognomy, will have been inappropriate or irrelevant. Continuity between one play and another can have been indicated only by dress, and no doubt the dress that iconography had long made instantly recognisable. One has only to try to imagine a production of Hamlet in which the prince in each act was impersonated by a different actor, to realise that the dividing line between mystery plays and the plays of Shakespeare is as marked as the dividing line between tableaux and mystery plays.

This argument is also helpful in meeting the problem, which perhaps aroused disquiet in the Middle Ages and which nowadays provokes patronising smiles, namely that of presenting God the Father upon the stage. Some hesitation over the representation of the Trinity and of God the Father in art had early been expressed, for the most convincing reply to the Mosaic prohibition against graven images was that this did not apply to the world of the New Dispensation, in which God had taken visible human form.[82] But this argument could not be used in defence of images of God Himself, God who is invisible, incomprehensible, incorporeal and uncircumscribed. The Lollards, therefore, whilst denouncing all images, considered the representation of the Trinity to be especially an abomination.[83] Nevertheless the Bible had used anthropomorphic symbols for God. He has a voice and a hand, and it thus became customary to represent God the Father, who according to Daniel is the 'ancient of days', as an aged and reverend man, even though all educated people understood that God was unknowable and invisible. There may have been ignorant people who were misled by painting and drama into believing God to be corporeal, but as Roger Dymmok maintained, 'si laici ex pictura illa aliquam concipiant falsitatem, eis imputandum est, non ymagini',[84] and the plays were not designed for them. For the authors show a careful awareness of the problems involved in transferring the visual symbol to the stage, while relying on art for their initial authority: if one dismisses the enterprise at the outset as naïve and primitive, one will miss the pleasure of seeing a religious and aesthetic problem sensitively and decorously resolved. In this issue, as in so many others, the notion of speaking pictures provides the boundaries within which modern critical examination can operate.

One final conclusion emerges, and that is that the mystery plays, more than many other kinds of drama, are meant to be seen. The dialogue has not the richness of texture that would make a constant re-reading of the words rewarding. It is not coincidence that the present recognition that the plays are both moving and powerful began with their widespread revival on the stage, following the success of the first York production at the Festival in 1950. Whilst modern productions, however, have revealed the literary value of the texts, they have necessarily not been able to recapture the very close resemblance to painting, although producers have rightly borrowed freely from medieval art. For a modern stage, whether out-of-doors, as against the background of the ruins of St Mary's Abbey at York, or on the stage of the Mermaid Theatre, is too large and produces too unconcentrated an effect for close resemblance to a painting: but the effect of actors dramatically grouped in a medieval wagon must have resembled that of a compartment in a series of frescoes. Not much is known for certain about the wagons,[85] neither their structure nor their size, but one crucial point is clear: the wagons were roofed, and the roof must have rested upon pillars at each corner.[86] Such an arrangement must have given an effect of a picture-frame just as did the later proscenium arch. In all probability a curtain was hung across the back, thus providing the necessary backdrop, and also at the sides.[87] The wagons judged as stages will have been comparatively small (they had to be pulled through the narrow streets of a medieval town),[88] and were sometimes perhaps no more than fifteen feet in length.[89] When, therefore, there were quite a number of actors on stage at one time, as for instance in the Crucifixion scene, the arrangement must have been cramped, but of course Gothic, as opposed to Renaissance, art is also lacking in spaciousness. Some scenes require quite a lot of movement on more than one level, and for these an additional scaffold might be provided or conceivably the ground in front of the wagon might be used as the lower *locus*; but many scenes, and amongst them the most dramatically important ones, could be confined within one wagon, providing the opposite ends represented different geographical areas (this, as described above, would also be familiar from art). There must, however, have been considerable stillness, with none of the unfunctional restlessness that is common in modern productions for purposes of realism: it may be assumed that characters stood still unless the plot demanded that they should move. A scene, therefore, such as the Annunciation must have appeared exactly as a speaking picture.

The conception of the plays as speaking pictures is therefore useful in enabling us to reconstruct the medieval understanding of biblical drama, and is helpful to us nowadays as is any definition of a genre to which a given work belongs. It cannot of course replace the critic's investigation of the literary skill of the authors, but it defines expectation, the expectation of what to find, and, even more importantly, of what not to find.

The Plays

VI

Plays of the Fall

The Fall of the Angels
The Fall of Man
Cain and Abel

The mystery cycles begin and end in the heavens, the opening play of the Fall of the Angels being on a subject never dramatised before and rarely since.[1] The story was reconstructed by the Fathers by the piecing together of a number of biblical texts: of these the most important were the apostrophes addressed to the Prince of Babylon (Isaiah xiv. 12–15) and to the King of Tyre (Ezekiel xxviii. 2–19), which were understood in the light of Christ's words in Luke x. 18, 'I beheld Satan as lightning fall from heaven', and applied figuratively to the devil; to these was sometimes added the account of the war in heaven (Revelation xii. 3–9). The account of Satan's Fall, first amply and consistently expounded in *The City of God*,[2] is now best known from the elaborate narrative in *Paradise Lost*, and present-day criticism of Milton has made everyone highly conscious of the pitfalls that await those who venture to treat this theme in literary rather than theological form. Medieval authors largely evade these pitfalls by a concise and symbolic treatment of the subject, the most symbolic of the plays, that in the York cycle, being also the most successful.

The characters, God with the good and bad angels, are all supernatural, and might therefore seem to present the dramatist with even more perilous and intractable material than the narrative poet. Iconography, however, provided a straightforward solution to the appearance of angels, for, though they were held to be immaterial and therefore invisible, the Bible recorded many scenes in which they had adopted a visible, human form, and some of these such as the Annunciation were represented in art over and over again. However, even with the help of traditional iconography, the portrayal of God presented difficulties, for in the heavens He is not any one person of the Trinity but the Trinity itself. Pictorial representations dealt with the mystery in a variety of ways,[3] ranging from the depiction of three identical human figures to the more abstract and intellectual symbol of geometrical patterns, interlaced triangles or circles of different colours such as Dante imagined at the end of the *Paradiso*. But such representations were disturbing in narrative art though theologically exact when the subject was the work of Creation, since it had been accepted from the time of Augustine that the plural forms in Genesis i. 26, 'And God said, Let us make man in our image, after our likeness', indicated the work of the Trinity. Artists occasionally showed the world or Adam being created by three identical figures or by a somewhat Janus-like figure with three faces,[4] but more often at the cost of theological precision, scenes of the Creation depicted the creator as though He were God the Father alone, a reverend, white-bearded figure. The authors of the plays adopted the latter tradition; within the greater realism of the plays the adoption of the former seems inconceivable and would certainly have passed the boundary which divides the strange or mysterious from the grotesque.

The authors of the plays therefore had a twofold problem: the one, earlier described, that though God appeared in human form, He was incorporeal and uncircumscribed; the other, that though He appeared as God the Father, He was yet the three persons of the Trinity. In all the plays this problem is solved by an opening speech in which God defines Himself, His eternal and unique self-understanding being deftly implied by the fact that He speaks without directly addressing the angels within the play or the audience without. He is alpha and omega, the first and the last, God without beginning or end, maker unmade, the true Trinity, Father, Son and Holy Ghost. In the York play, in particular, the splendour of the thought is sustained by the measured stanza form made weighty by alliteration:

> I am gracyus and grete, god withoutyn begynnyng,
> I am maker unmade, all mighte es in me,
> I am lyfe and way unto welth wynnyng,
> I am formaste and fyrste, als I byd sall it be.

The York author does not quite succeed in sustaining this opening dignity throughout, and the other writers are perhaps altogether less successful; the aureate diction of the later Chester play nowadays sounds mannered rather than magnificent. Nevertheless it is clear that all aim at and largely achieve the same effect. In particular all are careful not to give God any words that would suggest that His corporeal appearance was other than symbolic: with one tiny exception in the *Ludus Coventriae*,[5] God never speaks of Himself as having a body, and in the York play He does not even move, but stands throughout with symbolic stillness.

The second and yet more difficult problem consists of how to depict the Fall itself. To this problem the authors adopted different solutions reflecting divergent theological traditions about the nature of Satan's sin and the moment of its commission. In his commentary on Genesis, St Augustine in a sentence that was to be much quoted later said that the devil had sinned 'ab initio temporis'.[6] This theory, while excellent in cutting the Gordian knot in regard to the question of how an angel, created perfect, could have sinned, laid itself open to a Manichaean interpretation, and therefore proved unacceptable to the orthodox. In the Middle Ages the question, 'An aliqua mora fuerit inter [angelorum] creationem et lapsum' was asked by Peter Lombard in the *Sentences*, and all subsequent theologians therefore commented upon it, amplifying Peter Lombard's own answer that 'fuit ibi aliqua morula, licet brevissima'.[7] St Thomas gives as the more probable view 'quod statim post primum instans suae creationis diabolus peccaverit',[8] the point being that the good angels in the first instant after their creation in their free will 'by one meritorious act came to beatitude', and the devil, conversely exercising his free will, fell. From the dramatists' point of view the theory that Satan sinned after the first moment of his creation was as convenient as the belief that he had sinned instantly, for it enabled them to show Satan as fallen from the moment that he spoke. The author of the Chester cycle who alone does not follow the scholastic theologians on this issue is much the least convincing, since he inevitably raises in his diffuse play a moral and psychological problem that it was well beyond his capacity and intention to answer: he therefore has to show an abrupt and unmotivated change of heart in Satan, and his treatment seems mechanical, even crude.

A related question was that of the precise form that Satan's pride took, in other words what was meant by his ambition to be like to the most high (Isaiah xiv. 14). Some eleventh-century theologians, Rupert of Deutz in his *De Victoria verbi Dei*[9] and Honorius of Autun in his *Elucidarium* (a work which continued to be well known throughout the Middle Ages)[10] understood this in its fullest sense: according to them Satan wished to rule as a tyrant over the other angels, desiring to be adored and worshipped by the angelic hosts 'tanquam Deus et Dominus ipsorum'. The scholastic theologians, however, expounded a more subtle view. According to St Thomas Satan did not wish to be as God 'per aequiparantiam . . . quia scivit hoc esse impossibile naturali cognitione'[11] (for nothing can desire to belong to a higher order of being, since one could not achieve this without losing one's identity); rather he wished to be as God *per similitudinem*, that is he wished to have what he would anyway have attained had he remained unfallen, but 'quasi propria virtute, et non ex virtute Dei':[12] to put it simply he wanted to be the source of his own happiness, to derive his beatitude, not from God, but from himself. In the mystery cycles the York author follows the latter tradition, the other three the earlier.

The best of these three is the play of the Fall in the *Ludus Coventriae*, in that it is the most lively and economic, and the weakest is the Chester play in that it is the most ample in narrative content and the most unsmiling (the Chester cycle is alone in not putting wit to the service of theology). After God's opening monologue in the *Ludus Coventriae*, the angels sing the three verses from the *Te Deum* describing how the angels unceasingly cry 'Sanctus, Sanctus, Sanctus, Dominus Deus sabaoth'. Whereupon Lucifer, speaking for the first time, asks with impudent bravado: 'To whos wurchipe synge ȝe þis songe, / To wurchip god or reverens me?' But of course what is impudence in Lucifer is inventive audacity on the part of the poet. After his rejection by the good angels, Lucifer then completes his blasphemy visually by sitting upon God's throne (God having presumably withdrawn during the singing of the *Sanctus*). At the corresponding point in the Towneley cycle the author catches well a tone of coarse and blustering self-assertiveness:

> Say, felows, how semys now me
> To sit in seyte of trynyte?
> I am so bright of ich a lym,
> I trow me seme as well as hym.

In these two plays the authors do not attempt to imagine the quality of angelic pride: instead they show an already fallen angel who is a boastful and crude impostor, and the jingly brashness of his speech in context reflects the monstrous indecorum of his action.

The theological doctrine here followed has led naturally to a fairly flamboyant treatment, whereas the theory that Satan rejected his status as creature leads in the York play to a more subdued and subtler style. In this play after the good angels have again sung the *Sanctus*, the first good angel begins his speech in praise of God and in gratitude for his creation:

A! mercyfull maker, full mekill es þi mighte,
Þat all this warke at a worde worthely has wroghte,
Ay loved be þat lufly lorde of his lighte,
That us thus mighty has made, þat nowe was righte noghte.

And Lucifer, joining in as it were antiphonally, replies with praise of himself:

All the myrth þat es made es markide in me,
Þe bemes of my brighthode ar byrnande so bryghte,
And I so semely in syghte my selfe now I se,
For lyke a lorde am I lefte to lende in þis lighte,
More fayrear be far þan my feres,
In me is no poynte þat may payre,
I fele me fetys and fayre,
My powar es passande my peres.

There follow four further stanzas in which the good angels adore God as the source of their being, while Satan with increasing confidence and rapture praises his own beauty and excellence and rashly asserts his immutability. Then as Lucifer works himself up to the epitomisation of his rebellion, 'I sall be lyke unto hym þat es hyeste on heghte', he falls within the space of one extended metrical line, 'Owe! what I am derworthe and defte. – Owe! dewes! all goes downe!' In the other plays Satan falls at God's command,[13] but here he is shown to fall not as a penalty or judgment imposed by God, but as the inevitable consequence of what he himself says: God is present but silent. Up to this point the York author has deliberately excluded all action and all dramatic dialogue (Satan and the good angels do not address each other). Whereas the other authors used a theological tradition that provided them with a plot (Satan usurps God's throne, demands adoration from the angels, which is granted by some, refused by others), the York author follows a tradition which deliberately excluded a narrative of the Fall, yet contrary to normal assumptions he is for this very reason the more successful. What is so acutely presented in logical argument by St Thomas is here most deftly and imaginatively translated into literature.

All the plays end with the lament of the devils in hell. There was a long tradition, going back to the sermons of the eastern Fathers, of the plaints of the devil (the first part of the Old English *Christ and Satan* is founded upon it). This tradition confers upon the devil the human dignity of one who grieves for intolerable loss. The effect of this within the framework of drama can be seen in German plays, and particularly in the *Egerer Fronleichnamsspiel*, where Lucifer in a moving lyric lament calls upon all created things to intercede for him, the beauty of the natural world thus invoked contrasting poignantly with his own dark dungeon:[14]

> Ich klag dirs paide windt und lüfft,
> Ich klag dirs regen, tau und tüfft,
> Ich klag dirs hiz, kelt und auch schne,
> Ich klags den plümen und grünen klee, . . .
> Ich klag dirs suess vogelgeschall,
> Ich klag dirs perg und tieffe tall,
> Ich klag dirs fells und allen stain,
> Ich klags auch aller welt gemain:
> Das got ie von seinnen gnaden schüeff,
> Zu den thu ich heut meinen rueff,
> Das si fur mich mit guttem sitten
> Den almechtigen noch wolten pitten.

This approach, however, is not compatible with the degradation of the devil in the English plays into a brutish and contemptible figure, a conception which seems to have its origins in iconography rather than patristic tradition.

Milton's conception of Satan as 'not less than archangel ruined' had its origins in the Fathers and particularly in the writings of Gregory the Great, which stressed that Satan was a fallen angel with the stress as it were as much upon the second word as upon the first. However, while devils like angels were thought to be immaterial and invisible, hagiographic narratives required that the tempter should take visible form, sometimes that of an animal in order to terrify or of an angel of light in order to deceive. Most commonly, however, he appears as a black man – he is sometimes called an Ethiopian – and this form is obviously a symbol of his character through the primitive association of darkness with evil. When from the twelfth century onwards wall-paintings of hell with the Last Judgment became frequent in churches, it became customary to represent the devil by a far more striking moral symbol, the evil of his nature being indicated by the repulsive ugliness of his appearance. In giving shape to this ugliness artists seem to have been influenced by the deformed creatures found in antique art. In medieval iconography, therefore, the devil may be shown half man, half beast, erect like a man, but with claws, horns, bat's wings, tail and perhaps with an animal face. He is often hairy like an animal, and may have more than one head, the others being placed in grotesque or obscene positions.[15] Some of these details will have been actually represented on the stage: the inventory for the Drapers' Pageant of the Last Judgment at Coventry includes masks for the devils and coats of canvas covered with hair.[16]

The important point at the moment, however, is not the relevance of iconography to stage presentation but to the dramatists' imaginative understanding of the fallen angels, for they evidently seek to arouse in their audience the contempt and disgust which were the normal responses to the devil in art. The very brief eight-line lament of Lucifer in the *Ludus Coventriae*, of which the following is the second verse, illustrates this point:

> Now to helle þe way I take,
> In endeles peyn þer to be pyht.
> Ffor fere of fyre a fart I crake
> In helle donjoon myn dene is dyth.

The satirising of evil in terms of lavatorial humour is especially characteristic of the morality plays, *Mankind* in particular, and anal emphases in the depiction of hell are found in works as disparate as the poems of Dunbar and the paintings of Bosch. The force of this passage, however, is that the devil is shown to acquire a body by falling, for words here grossly indicate a real body as opposed to a corporeal symbol, and a body which, like human bodies after the Fall, alarmingly no longer obeys the will.

The same effect is achieved by the York playwright but more delicately. Here the debasement and deformity of the devils is indicated by the shattering of the hitherto shapely stanza into little scraps of raucous ejaculation, screamed by the devils as they attack each other in the turmoil of hell:

Lucifer   Walaway! wa! es me now, nowe es it war thane it was.
            Unthryvandly threpe ʒhe, I sayde but a thoghte.
2nd devil   We! lurdane, þu lost us.
Lucifer   ʒhe ly, owte! allas!
            I wyste noghte þis wo sculde be wroghte.
            Owte on ʒhow! lurdans, ʒhe smore me in smoke.
2nd devil   This wo has þu wroghte us.
Lucifer   ʒhe ly, ʒhe ly!
2nd devil   Thou lyes, and þat sall þu by,
            We lurdans have at ʒowe, lat loke.

It is only on the page that this passage can be recognised as metrical. Similar effects of stridency are found in the other cycles but less ingeniously contrived.

In the plays of the Fall of the Angels patterns are begun which are to recur throughout the cycles. God and the good angels are necessarily characterless, but Satan's hollow displays of power and his delight in his own existence and beauty are later echoed in the speeches of Herod and Pilate. Similarly the contrast between the dignity and tranquillity of heaven and the noise and agitation of hell, all visually, verbally, and metrically emphasised, begin one of the most important recurring themes in the cycles, which again will receive its climax at the Crucifixion. Whilst of course none of the plays should be judged solely as a self-sufficient unit without relation to its position within the larger pattern, this is particularly true of the Fall of the Angels, of which the reverberations will not be exhausted until the play of the Last Judgment. It is the fact that the authors are dispensed from the need to provide narrative self-sufficiency that enables them to treat the subject so symbolically and therefore so effectively. For there seems to be no successful middle path between an ambitious and thoroughly anthropomorphic presentation such as Milton's and the impressionistic brevity of the English mystery plays. Comparison of the English plays with their French and German analogues draws attention to their authors' sense of timing and contrast and their economy of design. There is an attempt in the *Mystère du viel testament* to make the action more naturalistically ample by a long episode in which Lucifer appeals to his followers and they promise obedience and worship; but this makes the play neither more dramatically nor more theologically impressive.[17] The Chester play, which was probably influenced by Continental models,[18] equally illustrates the futility of employing normal dramatic methods in the treatment of this subject and, despite some skill in Satan's speeches, is the weakest of the English plays. The York play which is at the opposite pole from it is the best.

The plays of the Fall of the Angels, in keeping with the traditional exegesis of Genesis i. 1, had presented the creation of the angels as God's work on the first day: the work of the next five days succeeds the Fall. This is the construction of all the cycles save Towneley which, contrary to normal tradition but with considerable gain in convenience, extends God's initial creation speech to the creation of the animals on the fifth day, and can therefore begin the scene of the Fall of Man with the creation of Adam. The subject of the Creation is one of the few that the techniques of medieval drama were inadequate to mould into effective form, for in this reliance upon iconographic parallels would not solve aesthetic difficulties. Medieval art, though it does not rival the grandeur of Michelangelo's scenes of creation, is often able to suggest something of creative energy and of the beauty of the newly created world. The opening folios of the *Holkham Bible Picture Book* are a good example of what art could achieve and may also indicate what the stage attempted. When in the plays the creating Trinity spoke the monologues of Creation, He may well have held such a pair of gigantic compasses[19] and behind Him there may well have been a backdrop with birds and animals painted upon it (alternatively painted cloths or boards may have been held up in turn to show the work of each day, as the stage directions require in the *Mystère du viel testament*).[20] But this can only have been a crude imitation of art, and the splendour of poetry could alone have compensated for the missing beauty of painting or sculpture. Imaginative intensity, however, or sublimity of style are not within the compass of the authors of the mystery cycles.

These monologues, however, should not be dismissed as a running commentary ineptly attributed to God: for God created by His word, and His speeches therefore do not simply describe the act of creation but represent that act itself. Furthermore, whilst one may regret the absence of a noble style to correspond to the majesty of the idea, the dramatic relaxation that results comes usefully between the more compelling scenes of the successive falls. Throughout the cycles the authors deliberately allow some poetically humdrum scenes to provide links between scenes of heightened comedy or horror. It might, however, be thought that it was still too early in the cycles for relaxation to be needed, and, if so, the author of the *Ludus Coventriae*, who despatches the five days of creation in twelve lines, may seem the most successful.

None of the plays of the Fall of Man is as elegant and well contrived as the York Play of the Fall of the Angels: the multifarious problems of representing the subject upon the stage are met with varying degrees of skill; now one cycle shows an especially felicitous touch, now another. The opening difficulty of showing the garden, in which Adam and Eve are set, as a place of abundance and delight is tackled only by the author of the *Ludus Coventriae*. The initial rubric of the *Mystère d'Adam* had specified that the scaffold for paradise should contain trees of various kinds with fruit hanging from them 'ut amoenissimus locus videatur'.[21] The authors of the York and Chester cycles presumably also assumed stage properties of this kind, but they cannot have been sufficient to convince the imagination that Eden was a place of supreme pleasantness and charm. Within the *Adam* Eden is described in the kind of negative statements that had already been applied to it by Augustine: it is a place where man will feel neither hunger nor thirst, cold nor heat,[22] but its physical abundance is only once alluded to when the Figura says to Adam, 'De nul delit n'i troverez falture'.[23] In contrast to this brevity, God speaks as follows in the *Ludus Coventriae:*

> Now come Fforth Adam to paradys,
> ther xalt þou have all maner thynge,
> bothe flesch and ffysch and frute of prys,
> all xal be buxum at þi byddyng.
> Here is pepyr, pyan, and swete lycorys,
> take hem all at þi lykyng,
> both appel and pere and gentyl rys.

In this passage the dramatist has evocatively drawn upon the alliterative catalogues of spices and fruits from other literary gardens, that of Mirth in the *Romance of the Rose* or the earthly paradise visited by King Alexander.[24] By poetically recalling the exotic and sensuous delights of the idealised medieval garden the poet is able to establish that Eden is truly *locus amoenissimus*.

In the *Ludus Coventriae* the dramatist neatly returns to the theme of the delightful abundance of the garden in order to motivate the separation of Adam and Eve which, in accordance with the impressionistic narrative style of the Bible, is left unaccounted for Adam praises the fruits as *woundyr dowcet*, adding:

> In þis gardeyn I wyl go se
> all þe fflourys of fayr bewte
> and tastyn þe frutys of gret plente
> þat be in paradyse.

Whilst neither art nor any authoritative source could have helped with this transition, earlier vernacular narratives such as the *Cursor mundi* had made a functional link, however brief, 'Adam ʒode walkand in þat welth',[25] and the author of the Towneley cycle uses the same explanation: the skill of the author of the *Ludus Coventriae* therefore lies not in invention but in relating this necessary transition to a larger pattern. In the York cycle the Temptation forms a separate play, and there is thus no need to motivate Adam's departure: he is simply not on stage when the play begins. But the Chester author, who is the least talented in dramatic craftsmanship, seems unaware of the problem: presumably the producer directed Adam to leave the stage inconspicuously, unless (and more awkwardly) Adam, as in the mosaics of San Marco, stood with his back turned as though not a part of the scene.[26]

At this point with the appearance of the devil, the central episode of the Temptation begins, and problems of theology, psychology and stage-craft come thick and fast. According to the usual theological tradition the tempter was the devil who had entered into the serpent of Genesis: a legend of rabbinic origin, however, told that the species of serpent used by the devil had a woman's head, and this bizarre variation was included in the *Historia scholastica* of Peter Comestor, thus acquiring authority and becoming thereafter almost invariable in art and literature.[27] The construction of the York and Chester plays requires that the devil first appear in his own form, in which he explains his fall and his envy of mankind, and then change into a snake, a double appearance also found sometimes in English art.[28] In the Chester play it is untheologically, but for obvious stage convenience, a matter of disguise rather than transformation, and the devil announces that he will put on his 'adders coate', words no doubt accompanied by action. In the York play, however, it is conceived as a genuine change (Satan says, 'In a worme liknes wille y wende'), and how this was contrived is indicated neither by text nor stage direction. The adoption of serpent form also posed a problem in plausibility, which theologians had recognised and thereby emphasised. Scholastic commentators, following Augustine, had argued that God had restricted the devil's choice of form: Peter Lombard suggested that he might have preferred the form of a dove, Bonaventura said that he might have preferred human form as being *affabilior*, and St Thomas that he would have preferred 'formam boni persuasoris scilicet angeli' but this was prohibited by God.[29] In some artistic traditions, however, such as the illustrations of the *Speculum humanae salvationis*, the tempter appears in a strange but magnificent shape—a winged dragon, rather than a snake,[30] and the reference in the Chester plays to an 'adder' which has 'wynges like a byrd' indicates that it was this tradition that the author had chosen to follow (in the York cycle the presentation of the animal must have been at the producer's discretion).

In all the plays save that of the *Ludus Coventriae*, which is eccentric, the tempter explains himself in an opening speech. In Towneley this appears to be spoken in hell (it is addressed to other devils): unfortunately the rest of the play is lost so that the author's further disposition of the action is not known. In Chester the tempter arrives in paradise, and in a place apart laments his fall, that pride had cast him down, and now moved by envy he grieves and grudges that Adam 'a Caytife, made of claye' should take his place in heaven. The same situation occurs in the York, except that Satan gives a new and extraordinary motive for his rebellion in heaven, namely that God had purposed to take upon him man's nature:

> And we were faire and bright,
> Þerfore me thoght þat he
> The kynde of us tane myght,
> And þer-at dedeyned me.

In an apocryphal tradition, repeated by some of the early Fathers, it had been held that Satan had resented God's decision to create men in His own image,[31] but Satan's base fancies of favouritism towards man here take what must be a late shape in that they depend upon the theory of Duns Scotus and other Franciscan theologians that the Incarnation would have taken place irrespective of the Fall. This motive reappears in the seventeenth-century play of the Fall, Vondel's *Lucifer*, where the wicked angel's determination to fight against God is aroused by Gabriel's announcement: 'Ye shall behold the everlasting Word,/ Clothed in the flesh and blood of human kind.'[32] In the York play, however, this motive is introduced with an unusual disregard for consistency, and whether the relic of an older version, or introduced by the injudicious vagary of a later redactor, it remains a startling blemish, in which one may suspect the hand of a polemical Franciscan.

The temptation of Eve and her consequent persuasion of Adam is managed rather formally in the York and Chester cycles: where they can the authors keep close to their source in Genesis, though the Chester author is a little more daring in allowing the tempter's malice to be blatantly revealed, when he says to Eve, 'yow may well wyt he [God] was your foe'; where they have no source, as for the nature of Eve's persuasions of Adam, they are brief. Dramatists could have found sanctions for invention even in so momentous an episode in Augustine's comment that Eve gave the apple to Adam, 'fortassis cum verbo suasorio, quod Scriptura tacens intelligendum relinquit',[33] but little guidance from theologians on Eve's motives, whether amiable or base. There had, however, been detailed analysis of the nature of Adam's sin: theologians, following 1 Timothy ii. 14, held that Adam, unlike Eve, had not been deceived by the serpent's promise that they would be as gods, and, following Augustine, that Adam had consented out of

'amicabili quadam benevolentia',[34] the good will of one creature towards another. The York playwright, however, entirely ignores this
interpretation and adopts the mechanical course of showing Adam
deceived by the serpent's promise which Eve repeats. The author of the
Chester plays is more subtle and more theologically correct. In this
work Adam appears overtly to be merely pleased by the fruit (he
says, 'the fruite is sweete and fayre in feere'), but, though gluttony was
considered an element in the Fall, dramatically it seems insufficient
in this context, and we are therefore more aware of Adam responding
to the affection in Eve's speech:

> Adam, husband, life and deere,
> eate some of this apple here;
> it is fayre, my leeif fere,
> it may thou not forsake.

These loving endearments suggest that it is Eve rather than the apple
that Adam cannot bring himself to reject. This interpretation of the
episode, which Milton later was so movingly and magnificently to
adopt, is found also in the Cornish plays, where Eve threatens, 'Since
thou wilt not believe/Thou shalt lose my love.'[35] But whereas the
Cornish author depicts crude blackmail, the Chester dramatist in his
treatment is gentle and elusive: at what point, if any, innocent affection
merges with feminine wiles, it is impossible to detect.

Whilst the Chester author by this slight touch succeeds in suggesting
the mood in which Adam slipped to sin, the author of the *Ludus
Coventriae* is more adept in indicating the insidiousness of the tempter's
speech to Eve. He, like the authors of the late Norwich plays of the
Fall, follows an apocryphal tradition, which had earlier appeared in
the *Mystère d'Adam* and *Genesis B*, and which ultimately derived from
the apocryphal Book of Enoch, namely that the devil when tempting
took the form, not of a serpent but of an angel of light.[36] That in later
times the devil tempted in this form (his appearance being thus as
deceptive as his words) was established by tradition based on 2 Corinthians xi. 14, but to suppose that he thus tempted Eve goes bluntly
against the text of Genesis, and, as we saw above, had been obliquely
but specifically denied by St Thomas. From the dramatic point of view
the value of this apocryphal fantasy is that it allows the tempter to
proceed in a more elevated and therefore deceptive manner; he does not
have to approach the issue by cunning questioning, but, knowing
already the best point of attack, he greets Eve as though she were a
noble lady from the world of romance:[37]

Tu es fieblette e tendre chose,
E es plus fresche que n'est rose;
Tu es plus blanche que cristal,
Que neif que chiet sor glace en val;
Mal cuple em fist li criator:
Tu es trop tendre e il trop dur;
Mais neporquant tu es plus sage,
En grant sens as mis tun corrage.

The opening words of the tempter in the *Ludus Coventriae*, 'Heyl Ffayr Wyff and comely dame', are not so poetically beautiful (and of course do not so subtlely attempt to awaken in Eve a desire to be superior to Adam), but they show the same strategem of winning Eve's interest through flattery. Similarly in the earlier of the two Norwich plays the tempter's first words are 'O gemme of felicyté and femynyne love', and in the later, 'Oh lady of felicité'. In contrast in the York play the serpent simply addresses Eve by her name and in the Chester play yet more bluntly as 'woman'. St Thomas, again following Augustine, had said that Eve at the tempter's earliest promptings had felt an *elatio* that laid her open to his subsequent and more concrete proposal of evil:[38] in these plays it is skilfully demonstrated that Eve's initial responsiveness springs from an awakening of feminine self-esteem, an interpretation that is more closely defined than was perhaps theologically orthodox but is dramatically very convincing.

So advantageous is this approach in terms of at least momentary psychological realism that it probably accounts for the English dramatists' adoption of this apocryphal theme; for, unlike the Cornish playwright, who shows a constant preference for apocryphal legends with their weird narrative solidity, they normally proceed in paths central to theological and literary traditions. However, while in narrative the serpent could splendidly flatter Eve as he does in poems which stretch in time from Avitus's *Poematum de Mosaicae historiae gestis* to *Paradise Lost*, on the stage high-flown compliments from an actor in some snake-like costume would have seemed incongruous: in drama dignified words to be convincing have to be spoken by a dignified figure. It could only be a serious dramatic reason of this kind that could have led the author of the *Ludus Coventriae*, who is the most theologically alert of the English dramatists, to choose or tolerate in his source a highly eccentric and unorthodox motif.

In their handling of Adam and Eve's remorse and their expulsion from the garden, the plays again vary in style and quality. The dialogue outlines for this episode in Genesis iii. 9–19 are unusually complete and consistent, and provided a firm structure for the plays. The dramatists in their amplifications, however, provide two imaginative insights into the condition of the fallen world and fallen man that are rewarding. On the question of unfallen man's knowledge of God, theologians held that they did not behold God face to face as do those who in heaven enjoy the beatific vision but they beheld Him more clearly than fallen man: Adam and Eve saw in a glass but not darkly.[39] This is reflected in the York play, where Adam replies to God's question, 'Where art thou?', not with a paraphrase of Genesis iii. 10, 'I heard thy voice in the garden, and I was afraid, because I was naked; and I hid myself', but with a statement far more movingly evocative of his changed condition, 'I here þe lorde and seys the noзt'; and this change is expressed yet more poignantly in the *Ludus Coventriae*: 'A lord for synne oure flourys do ffade/I here þi voys but I se þe nought.' The conjoining of the idea of man's diminished apprehension of God with the beautiful and perennial symbol of transience is especially effective: the poetry conveys a nostalgic sense of loss rare in medieval literature, the withered flowers seeming rather to anticipate Herbert's posy and Herrick's daffodils, or, to take a more relevant example, the garland of roses in *Paradise Lost* which, after Eve's first base speech of persuasion, drops already faded from Adam's hands.

In their treatment of Adam and Eve's relationship after the Fall— their recriminations and repentance—the authors of the York cycle and the *Ludus Coventriae* again illuminate our understanding of the scene. The Chester author is alone in simply paraphrasing the Genesis text, and thus shows Adam willing only to shift the blame to Eve and Eve to shift the blame to the serpent: neither gives a dignified impression by acceptance of responsibility and neither expresses contrition whether towards God or each other. The author of the *Ludus Coventriae*, however, has taken pains to minimise the unpleasant impression left by the Genesis accusations by enclosing them in two pairs of less self-exculpatory speeches. Instantly upon eating the apple Adam blames Eve, 'Alas, Alas ffor þis fals dede/my flesly frend my fo I fynde', but continues by making an equal confession of guilt, 'oure lordys wurd wold we not drede/þerfore we be now caytyvys unkynde'; and Eve similarly, whilst first lamenting the speech of the 'fals Aungel' continues, 'Alas oure makers byddyng is brokyn/Ffor I have towchyd his owyn dere tre'. Whilst at this point Adam and Eve fittingly think of their relationship towards God, after the biblical accusations, Eve thinks of the harm she has done Adam, 'my husbond is lost because of me', and invites him therefore to kill her; and, whilst Adam rejects this invitation to murder with some colloquial anger, his tone suggests shared responsibility for sinning, 'our wytt was nesch', and of shared companionship in the hardships to follow.

In the York cycle the recriminations of Adam and Eve are amplified at length, an expansion to some extent necessitated by the division here, as elsewhere, of single subjects into distinct scenes acted by different gilds: the expulsion from Eden thus has to be full enough to stand on its own, and this is achieved by making the angel of the banishment repeat God's condemnations, which are interspersed with further excuses and reproaches from Adam and Eve. Eve here enlarges upon her self-exculpatory accusations by hitting back at Adam's anti-feminist reproach, 'Allas! what womans witte was light!', with the rebuke that he should therefore have ruled her, 'Mans maistrie shulde have bene more', the traditional moral allegorisation of Adam and Eve as reason and senses or soul and body[40] thus providing the material for what in human terms is spirited but profitless wrangling. Nevertheless in this final episode there occur some beautiful lines of lyric lament in which Adam and Eve cease recriminating and think only of the nature of their loss and their sin. Adam is given an exceptionally long complaint, of which the following stanza is a part:

> Gone ar my games with-owten glee,
> Allas! in blisse kouthe we noʒt bee,
> For putte we were to grete plente
> > at prime of þe day;
> Be tyme of none alle lost had wee,
> > sa welawaye.

The idea of the short space of time from prime to noon (from early morning until midday) which elapsed between Creation and Fall was in accordance with theological speculation, but it has been transformed in this stanza into a nostalgic sense of the brevity of happiness, awareness of responsibility for its loss intensifying regret. And whilst Adam follows this with further reproaches of Eve (which will be later considered from another point of view), Eve at last meets and checks them with a counsel of resignation and a grieving confession of fault:

> Be stille Adam, and nemen it na mare,
> > it may not mende.
> For wele I wate I have done wrange,
> And therfore evere I morne emange,
> Allas! the whille I leve so lange,
> > ded wolde I be!

This speech Adam matches with an expression of resignation to God's will and a prayer for His help: on this muted note the play ends.

Up to this point we have considered the plays as though they were independent works, the authors' problem being to present a theological understanding of the Genesis text with sufficient narrative consistency and psychological plausibility to make it alive upon the stage. But in traditional thought the Fall of Man was only half the story, it was an event to be reversed and repaired at the Redemption, and the plays must therefore be considered in relation to the later parts of the cycles. It was not of course necessary to state the Redemption at length or explicitly in cyclic plays of the Fall: it is only in the second Norwich play, which could be acted apart from the parent cycle, that the hope of salvation is strongly emphasised, and the work can thus fittingly end with a song of praise.[41] But in all plays some brief allusion or some symbolic adumbration was needed.

It is possible that intimations of future redemption were sometimes supplied visually in the plays, as they were also in art. In the *Holkham Bible Picture Book*, for instance, there is a nest at the top of the tree in which a pelican feeds her young from her wounded breast (a common bestiary type of the Redemption). In the Caedmon manuscript there had already been a little cross at the top of the tree in the scene of the Creation,[42] and in later Continental manuscripts one even finds a crucifix set within the branches.[43] This type of iconography was not, however, so common that we should assume that it was regularly imitated in the mystery plays: it is in fact only in the *Ludus Coventriae* that such a visual foreshadowing would correspond admirably with the text, since it is in this cycle alone that the Crucifixion is specifically mentioned – in the seraph's dismissal of Adam and Eve to misery,

> Tyl a chylde of a mayd be born
> And upon þe rode rent and torn
> To save all þat ʒe have forlorn
> ʒour welth for to restore.

Whilst Adam's disobedience to God's command by taking the fruit of the forbidden tree was only fully reversed when Christ in obedience hung upon the tree of the Cross, the reversals that were equally stressed were Mary's obedience at the Annunciation in contrast to Eve's disobedience, and Christ's rejection in the wilderness of Satan's temptations to pride, avarice and gluttony, which reversed the Fall in which, according to Gregory the Great and many subsequent writers, Adam and Eve had manifested these very sins.[44] The authors of the cycles seem in general to have been uninterested in the latter parallelism. In their plays of the Temptation in the Wilderness the authors of the York cycle and the *Ludus Coventriae* make no mention of Adam, whilst the Towneley cycle as preserved does not even include a play on this subject. The Chester author, who is particularly interested in typological correspondences, is therefore alone in making Christ expressly draw a parallel between his own temptation and that of Adam. There is, however, nothing in the play of the Fall to indicate that at this point he already had the parallelism in mind and was laying the foundations for subsequent recapitulation.

By far the most important parallel, and the one that most interested the authors of the plays, was that between Eve and Mary:[45] it was a comparison expounded from the time of the early Fathers, and the potentialities of this symmetrical antithesis were gradually explored with astonishing ingenuity. During the Middle Ages the conjunction of the Fall and the Annunciation is frequently demonstrated in art: in the *Bible moralisée*, the *Biblia pauperum* and the *Speculum humanae salvationis*, type and antitype, the Annunciation and Eve tempted by the serpent, invariably accompany one another. Even in non-typological art, the banishment from the garden is often found in some subordinate position in representations of the Annunciation: over and over again on the closed panels of triptychs, as the subject of medallions or other decorative carvings in the Virgins' chamber, or as distant figures in a landscape, Adam and Eve are shown leaving the gates of paradise, whilst inside the shutters or in the forefront of the painting the Blessed Virgin receives in obedience and humility the angel's message.[46]

In literature the parallelism between Eve and the Blessed Virgin was worked out in a different way, the two figures corresponding to two literary styles, the satiric literature in denigration of women and the formal, ornate poetry in praise of women. In satiric attacks upon women they are possessed of every vice, they are faithless, avaricious, lecherous, vain, obstinate and disobedient, and a source of disaster to their husbands:[47] a list of wicked women from the Bible became a commonplace in the literary form of the dissuasion from marriage and in other more serious treatises, and this catalogue was headed by Eve.[48] In the complementary poems written in praise of women (such pairs might be written by the same author), women were seen as the source of every virtue, they were gentle, loving, gracious and faithful, and Mary was their prototype. In the Middle English debate between the Thrush and the Nightingale on the subject of women, their defender, the nightingale, at last triumphs in argument by quoting the example of the Blessed Virgin.[49]

In the plays of the Fall an attack upon women grows naturally out of Adam's biblically based accusation of Eve, but becomes far more heavily accentuated than the narrative and psychological context could warrant. In Chester Satan in his opening monologue explains his decision to approach Eve in a flagrantly anachronistic generalisation, 'That woman is forbyd to doe,/for any thinge therto will shooe': Eve's sin is thus reduced to the level of sheer obstinate perversity, a common theme, as we shall see, of anti-feminist satire. The theme in one of its many variations is resumed by Adam in a direct address to the audience later in the same play:

> Now all my kinde by me is kent,
> to flee womans intisement;
> whoe trustes them in anye intent,
> truly he is decayved.
>
> My licorous wife hath bene my foe,
> the devilles envye shent me also,
> they twayne together well may goe,
> the sister and the brother!

A similar warning is given in the York play, where Adam, after reproaching Eve for her disobedience and evil counsel, adds, 'Nowe god late never man aftir me/triste woman tale'.

This theme is repeated on a large scale in the play of Noah, where the authors are free to depict a woman who by her speech and conduct exemplifies these vices. Eve, however, could not be characterised with mocking derision: contempt is displayed in what is said about her but not in the presentation of her as a debased and comic figure. There is therefore a discrepancy between Eve herself and the comments made upon her by the devil and Adam, a discrepancy that would jar if understood in terms of psychological realism. But anachronism and discrepancy are used ostentatiously to draw attention to the beginnings of a pattern: the unexpected satiric tone heard in Adam's speeches serves obliquely as a promise of Redemption, not of course within the play, but to the audience. The heavy emphasis upon Eve as the prototype of foolish, obstinate, disobedient women, very obviously begins a pattern which is incomplete, and thus signals that only half the story has been told: Eve thus derided can only be the *first* Eve and the *second* Eve is yet to come.

When parallelisms between the Fall and the Redemption were worked out, they might be extended to Cain and Abel. Tertullian makes a comparison between Eve the mother of the first murderer and Mary the mother of the Redeemer.[50] This extension of the Fall to include the murder of Abel is sometimes reflected in iconographic schemes, as, for instance, on the eleventh-century bronze doors of Hildesheim, where eight scenes of the Fall are adjoined to eight scenes of the Redemption, the last two scenes of the Fall being taken from the story of Cain and Abel.[51] Reasons for this extension are easily understandable. Whilst the sin of Adam and Eve was pride, an inordinate wish to be as God, and thus the greatest of the seven deadly sins, the actual form that it took was obviously not an example of monstrous depravity. The prohibition upon eating the apple was understood as a minute obligation imposed by God as a reminder of His sovereignty; the tree was not supposed to have any special properties in itself, being called the tree of the knowledge of good and evil only because of its effect. Medieval literature often stresses the triviality of the action itself: the famous lyric, 'Adam lay I-bowndyn' does so by a touch of rollicking style, 'And al was for an appil, an appil þat he tok',[52] and Langland by a characteristically laconic expression 'Tho Adam and Eve eten apples unrosted'.[53] Origen in a passage later cited by St Thomas had stated that someone placed in the highest state of perfection could not suddenly drop to the lowest grade of wickedness, 'sed paulatim et per partes defluere eum necesse est'.[54] The distinction is made clearly in the *Ludus Coventriae*, where Adam recoils from Eve's suggestion that he should kill her in retribution, 'Ffor yf I xulde sle my wyff/I sclow my self with-owten knyff'. In terms of ordinary reckoning man has obviously still a long way to fall, and the Fall is therefore in a sense not complete until Cain has slain his brother Abel.

The dramatists' interest in showing a continuation of the Fall can be seen by omission in their treatment of Abel. Abel had a double typological significance: his offering of the lamb was a type of the eucharistic sacrifice, his death a type of the Crucifixion. That the evil consequences of the Fall are arrested in Abel is of course made clear: his obedience, to God, to his father, and to his brother are everywhere stressed; and his virtuous offering of the best of his flock is made important, though it is only in the *Ludus Coventriae* that the parallelism between Abel's lamb and Christ who will suffer on the Cross 'in a lombys lyknes' is made explicit.[55] There is, however, no dramatic concentration upon Abel at his death, the attention is solely upon Cain.

Abel never speaks before his death; though in the Towneley cycle he makes one powerful cry as he lies slain (the author has given a daring twist to Genesis iv. 10): 'Veniance, veniance, lord, I cry!/ for I am slayn, and not gilty.'⁵⁶ But, though the second line here undoubtedly anticipates the Crucifixion it is from the point of view of man's wickedness rather than God's love. How the authors might have presented the murder of Abel, had they wished to stress its typological significance, can be seen from the *Mystère d'Adam*, where Cain's statement of murder, 'Jo t'occirai', is followed by a substantial dialogue: during the course of this Abel expresses his obedience to God's will, 'Del tut me met a son plaisir', and dies, as is fitting, with a prayer, 'Deu pri qu'il ait de mei merci'; at this point the stage directions instruct that Abel shall fall upon his knees, facing to the east. Abel, like Christ, therefore dies a willing sacrifice.⁵⁷ This treatment of the victim the authors of the mystery plays reserve until the Sacrifice of Isaac.

A more positive method of showing the pattern of descent into evil was by overtly relating the story of Cain and Abel to that of Adam and Eve, so that in the one episode the fallen but soberly virtuous Adam is contrasted with the fallen and unequivocally evil Cain. There is an element of this in the *Ludus Coventriae*, in which Adam, now a dignified patriarch, gives grave advice to his sons on the duty of sacrifice (an incident deriving from the *Historia scholastica*)⁵⁸ and sends them forth with a prayer for God's blessing. It is, however, in the Chester plays that the management of the episodes is self-evidently organised to display this pattern. The Chester author firmly embeds the murder of Abel in the life-history of Adam and Eve, the Fall and the murder in fact forming one play. There comes, however, a large jump in time after the expulsion for, when Adam speaks next, his sons are grown men; one misses here the journey of each succeeding pageant-wagon which must have served well to indicate the passage of time, progress in space being a common symbol for progress in time. The play, unusually, begins with a long monologue in which Adam relates the vision granted to him during the creation of Eve, in which, according to common exegesis, the Redemption and Last Judgment were revealed to him.⁵⁹ After he has given the instructions on sacrifice, Eve echoes him with a shorter speech, describing the penalties of the Fall and the importance of doing God's will. Against this background Cain and Abel depart to the sacrifice and the murder, and to this background Cain returns to relate his crime, and the play ends with the laments of Adam and Eve. The incident of Cain's return is implausible, but may have been imposed upon the author by his decision to excise from his play the apocryphal character of Cain's sister, Delbora, who in the *Mystère du viel testament* is the bearer of the news.[60] But Eve's lament for Abel is essential to the pattern, since it begins a series that will be resumed when the mothers of the Holy Innocents mourn their children and will reach its climax in the *planctus* of the Blessed Virgin at the foot of the Cross. When in the sixteenth and seventeenth centuries this scene was illustrated in art, the disposition of the figures was modelled upon that of a *Pietà*, Eve contrary to any tradition holding the body of Abel in her lap.[61] In his treatment of the murder of Abel the Chester author showed evil in its most monstrously human forms, and related this to Adam and Eve, who are both its begetters and partially its victims (a point more didactically emphasised in the Cornish *Origo mundi*).[62] This position of Eve, however, has been partially redressed, for, whilst she is the mother of the first murderer, she is also the mother of Abel, the first type of Christ; in this concluding episode the dignity thus obliquely conferred upon her is revealed through her *planctus*, which, though poetically more subdued than that later spoken by the Virgin, unmistakably anticipates it.

It is, however, in the character of Cain himself that the full abysses of the Fall are horrifyingly shown, superbly of course in the work of the Wakefield Master in the Towneley plays,[63] but pointedly and skilfully in all of them. Though the Chester dramatist is more interested in revealing religious significance through the patterning of episodes, his Cain is far less woodenly and perfunctorily treated than in most Continental versions of the story. Even in his very first speech there is a hint of base self-interest in his declaration that he will offer a sacrifice of corn to God and then 'will make to looke if he [God] will send me any more'. Churlish avariciousness is even plainer when he comes to select the corn for the sacrifice: here he explains in realistic detail how he will keep the 'eared corne' for himself, and offer only sheaves of the corn from which animals have nibbled away the grain, a decision accompanied by the significant oath 'the divill hang me'. The same type of Cain is presented in the *Ludus Coventriae* but intensified. Whilst Adam is less important here, Abel's speeches of grave virtue throw into relief Cain's avariciousness and lack of natural feeling. Cain not only hates Abel, resenting his virtue, as Ambrose had early described,[64] but also feels contemptuous indifference towards his father, replying to Abel's insistence that they should visit him with the words, 'thow my fadyr I nevyr se/I ȝyf not þer of An hawe', and he agrees to Adam's counsel to do sacrifice grudgingly and insolently, 'and ȝitt I say now to ȝow both too/I had levyr gon hom well ffor to dyne'. Cain's contempt and antagonism extend also to God. His resolve to 'tythe þe werst' is shown not to spring from simple miserliness but from a furious contempt for God:

> What were god þe bettyr, þou sey me tyll,
> to ȝevyn hym awey my best sheff
> and kepe my self þe wers:
> he wyll neyther ete nor drynke
> Ffor he doth neyther swete nor swynke;
> þou shewyst a ffebyl reson me thynke,
> what, þou fonnyst as a best I gesse.

In Cain's base thought the fact that God is incorporeal and uncircumscribed evokes not awe but jeering.

This lively sketch of Cain as a grotesque, half comic, half ugly, is overshadowed by the characterisation of Cain in the Towneley plays, in which this style is developed with extraordinary freedom and lack of reserve. In this play Cain's role of the surly, avaricious farmer, fiercely grudging of the tithes that he must pay, is given unaccustomed solidity. Other dramatists seem to use the concept of tithes for the practical purpose of making the unfamiliar notion of a burnt offering recognisable in contemporary terms, thus removing a possible barrier between play and audience. But the Wakefield Master with his ostentatious reference to a priest who has Cain's farthing,[65] and his adaptation of traditional excuses – Cain maintains that he is too poor, his last crops were bad, it is better to be thrifty than to be driven to beggary, etc. – excuses similar to those cited in sermons against false tithers, gives to the figure a sharply contemporary ring.[66] Whilst no doubt some satirisation of contemporary false tithers was intended, this conception of Cain forms part of a more complex pattern. Cain's laborious counting of his sheaves with his miserly reluctance to part with any is built up into a focus of sheer farce,[67] but this theme, as in the *Ludus Coventriae*, is subordinated to the larger one of Cain's alienation from God.

As elsewhere this is expressed in Cain's abusive speech, his swearing by the devil, and the contemptuous replies which he gives to any suggestion that is against his narrowly conceived self-interest. But this style is greatly heightened in the Towneley play. Cain here is extraordinarily foul-mouthed: his opening dialogue with Abel consists of little but scatalogical abuse. He begins with a coarse but no doubt current greeting, 'Com kis myne ars!', and responds to Abel's injunctions to sacrifice with an obscener variant: 'Hold thi tong, yit I say/

Even ther the good wife strokid the hay.' These verbal violations of decency reach a blasphemous climax in Cain's determination to offer no more than two mean sheaves to God, 'Not as mekill, grete ne small/As he myght wipe his ars with all'. Earlier Cain had twice told Abel to kiss the devil's arse, and one can therefore see how violently Cain has obliterated the distinction that for stage purposes dramatists had skilfully and decorously drawn between the apparent corporality of God and the devil. When God has entered and reproached Cain, he answers with further extravagant blasphemy, reducing God to the level of the hobgoblin of folklore:[68]

> Whi, who is that hob-over-the-wall?
> We! who was that that piped so small?
> Com, go we hens, for perels all;
> God is out of hys wit.

But in its very exuberance and verbal jocularity (God has presumably spoken in a deep and solemn voice), this passage seems less sinisterly evil than Cain's earlier abuse. In sum, however, Cain in the Towneley plays comes close to being a serious study in damnation, not a state of damnation that is magnificent in its anguish and apprehension of loss, but one that is mean, ugly and churlish. Such a study, however, might have upset the balance of the cycle by giving excessive imaginative weight to one play, and for this reason the author seems to have contrived an ending which is formal and comic, thus distancing Cain and exploding the scene in farce.

This ending depends upon the presence of a third character, Cain's servant, who had opened the play with lively and obscene abuse of the audience. The provision of a servant at a point in historical time when there could not have been one is in itself striking, and strongly suggests the adaptation of established convention: indeed the *garcio* here oddly anticipates the many comic servants of sixteenth-century biblical plays, both English and foreign, who were regularly invented upon the model of Plautus. Cain's *garcio* appears in fact to be a diminished descendant of the stock figure of the witty, intriguing slave of Roman comedy,[69] who in turn was adopted in the twelfth-century Latin *comoediae*, such as the *Amphitryo*, and who re-appeared in French farces including the earliest of them, *Le garçon et l'aveugle*.[70] This farce, as Gustave Cohen has pointed out,[71] was imitated by the authors of the *Passions* who often provided the man born blind and Longinus with a rascally boy to lead them about.

The grumbling abusive servant is a familiar figure in French farces

and farces also provide some striking stylistic analogues to the concluding set piece of the Wakefield Cain and Abel, in which Cain proclaims
for himself and Garcio a king's pardon, using the appropriate legal
formulas.[72] This mock pardon is only tenuously related to the substance
of the play, being immediately provoked by Garcio, who, like his
forbear, Byrria, is an amusing coward. One can of course see it as a
comic transformation of the mark which God set upon Cain to protect
him from human vengeance (Genesis iv. 15) or, more fancifully, as
recalling the legal pardon which elsewhere Christ conferred upon man
at the Crucifixion[73] (it would then imply Cain's exclusion from the
Redemption since the only pardon that he can have is one delivered by
himself). But the elaborate contrivance of the episode, including
Garcio's comic asides, suggests that it should primarily be taken at its
face value of stylised farce. The pardon proceeds in alternate lines of
dialogue (being the first example of stichomythia in an English play):

Caym	I commaund you in the kyngis nayme,
Garcio	And in my masteres, fals Cayme,
Caym	That no man at thame fynd fawt ne blame.
Garcio	Yey, cold rost is at my masteres hame.
Caym	Nowther with hym nor with his knafe,
Garcio	What, I hope my master rafe.
Caym	ffor thay ar trew, full many fold;
Garcio	My master suppys no coyle bot cold.
Caym	The kyng wrytis you untill.
Garcio	Yit ete I never half my fill.
Caym	The kyng will that thay be safe,
Garcio	Yey, a draght of drynke fayne wold I hayfe.
Caym	At thare awne will let tham wafe;
Garcio	My stomak is redy to receyfe.

The joke of this passage is obviously that whilst Cain announces the
pardon in a stylistically serious proclamation, Garcio consistently undercuts this, either with colloquial asides about food and drink or with a
line which completes Cain's sentence in a way manifestly unintended
by the speaker. The process of deflation is in general reminiscent of
much medieval parody, in which, for instance, lines of famous hymns
were used to lead into the praise of drink, money or love. A typical
example is: 'Jam lucis orto sidere/statim oportet bibere.'[74] More interestingly perhaps the dramatic outline is reminiscent of the opening of the
Miles gloriosus of Plautus, in which the parasite undercuts the high-
flown boastings of the braggart soldier with asides to the audience about

the quality of his food, '. . . his cook makes a marvellous olive salad' or 'Oh dear, what I have to suffer for my stomach's sake'.[75] It would be imprudent, however, to assume that the Wakefield Master could have known the plays of Plautus, and in fact one can more safely find yet closer parallels in French farces of the fifteenth century. On one of these Petit de Julleville commented: 'Ce procédé par lequel un personnage bouffon se fait l'écho d'un personnage sérieux, est fréquent dans nos farces et traditionnel au Moyen Age.'[76] The farce of which he speaks is *La Présentation des joyaux*, in which a messenger brings to a lady various gifts from her prospective bridegroom and offers them to her in a complimentary and courtly monologue. This monologue is constantly interrupted by the base or bawdy comments of the *sot* who observes the scene. The following is a typical passage:[77]

> Dame, d'honneur le parement,
> Dieu vous doint honneur et liesse
> Et maintienne cette noblesse,
> En vivant tresjoyeusement . . .
> Tenez ce chappeau gracieux
> Qui est honneste, riche et gent.
>
> Il a bien cousté de l'argent;
> Pleust a Dieu qu'il fust en ma bource!

Another example is the *Cris de Paris*, in which the dialogue of the two young gallants about the evils of marriage is punctuated by the street-cries of the fool, such as mustard, pickled herring, old iron, etc., cries which metrically complete the couplet and also often complete the speaker's sentence with unexpected aptness.[78] In yet another farce, that of the *Gaudisseur et le sot*, the *gaudisseur* boasts in high-flown terms of his military or amatory achievements, whilst the fool interrupts sardonically with the base truth: the *gaudisseur*, for instance, vaunts of his prowess in a certain battle, whilst the fool comments that he in fact spent the time hidden in a ditch, and came out only when the fighting was over in order to go pillaging.[79] The joke of these farces is invariably that of serious or bombastic speech continuously undercut by fool or servant, and it is very probable that some farce of this kind was known to the Wakefield Master. His adaptation, however, is unique in its ingenuity, far surpassing in its complex subtleties any extant analogue in French secular drama.[80]

As in all the plays of the Wakefield Master, the *Mactacio Abel* partly keeps close to convention, is partly entirely distinctive. Its comedy is grimmer, its moral understanding darker, its literary manners more self-consciously artful. The underlying religious pattern, however, is never forgotten, and often intensified. In the *Ludus Coventriae* the theme of the continuing fall reaches its conclusion in Cain's banishment: as Adam and Eve became exiles from paradise, so Cain becomes an exile from all the dwellings of men; but Adam and Eve still awaited 'sum comforth', whereas Cain will 'nevyr make merthis mo'. But in the Towneley cycle Cain takes his leave of the audience as follows:

> Now fayre well, felows all, ffor I must nedis weynd,
> And to the dwill be thrall, warld withoutten end:
> Ordand ther is my stall, with Sathanas the feynd.

In this cycle therefore the Fall reaches its final end in the eternal damnation of hell.

VII

Types and Prophecies of the Redemption

Noah
Abraham and Isaac
Moses and the Prophets

The biblical story of the Flood shows a continuation of the Fall with the world become so wicked that God repents that He has made man (Genesis vi. 6). Amongst medieval cycles, however, it is only the *Mystère du viel testament* that introduces representatives of this wicked world into the play: here representative offspring of Seth and Cain speak bluntly, though not obscenely, of their physical desire for one another, and make the morally unnatural marriages, which, according to Genesis vi, aroused God's wrath.[1] This not entirely comprehensible episode the authors of the English plays avoid, and we hear only of the sinful world by report, a world infected by evil in general or more specifically by the seven deadly sins which the Towneley Noah enumerates in due order. The resulting impression is therefore of sin more abundant in quantity but not greater in degree than that of Cain; and, since it is only Noah and his family who appear upon the stage, it is of them that we are immediately aware, and the reported wickedness of the rest of the world does not become part of the pattern of the plays.[2]

Like the story of the Creation the biblical narrative of the Flood lent itself better to portrayal in art than drama. It is true that the ship-wrights who normally acted the play must have been able to do some convincing mime with genuine tools during the building of the ark; that at the embarkation animals *depicta in cartis*, as in the Chester play, might be introduced; and that the waters of the flood might be simulated by a painted cloth waved in front of the ark. None of this, how-ever, could have amounted to a serious imaginative reconstruction of the story, such as one finds in the *Holkham Bible Picture Book*, where the waters around the ark are horribly filled with the corpses of the drowned, both men and animals. With all that was exciting and terrifying in the story precluded by the exigencies of stage performance the authors were compelled to focus exclusively upon a historically narrower, but typologically appropriate, understanding of the narrative, the relationships of Noah and his family, their relief at the entry into the ark and their joy at arrival upon dry land or at least the promise of it with the return of the dove (God's covenant and the rainbow have vanished from the story in all the cycles save Chester). This exclusive concentration was justified by typological interpretations of the story, which saw in Noah a type of Christ, in the ark a type of the Cross and more importantly of the church, and occasionally in Noah's wife a type of the Virgin.[3] On this interpretation conflict between virtue and vice is absent, and the story is solely a foreshadowing of the Redemption. Medieval plays divide into the Continental branch which follow this typological pattern exactly and which appears in English in the *Ludus Coventriae*, and the characteristically English branch, which, whilst preserving the main typological outlines and indeed in some ways accentuating them, sees in Noah's wife not a figure harmoniously in the scheme of salvation but one who initially repeats the pattern of the Fall.[4]

According to the Bible Noah was a just man who walked with God: since, however, the moral theme of the plays is that paradise was lost through disobedience and regained through obedience, Noah's virtue is concentrated in obedience to God's will. An extreme example of this treatment can be seen in the *Künzelsauer Fronleichnamsspiel* where the vast subject is reduced to a tiny episode in which God commands Noah to build the ark and Noah instantly and obediently agrees to do so.[5] That this scene could be chosen to represent the whole is a warning that we should not approach the plays too realistically. One's first thought is that Noah is being instructed to his own advantage and in a way that he could readily see to be to his own advantage; and, since obedience therefore seems scarcely meritorious, one may pass too lightly over the very explicit professions of obedience to God's will which Noah makes in all the plays. It is necessary, therefore, to have the pattern in mind and to remember that the last time God had made a specific command He had been disobeyed. It is also permissible in some of the plays to bear in mind that God's command did not seem immediately attractive: the flood was not an apparent danger, the building of the ark was a long and burdensome duty. The former point is explored in some eastern versions of the tale in which Noah's wife and one of his sons mock him for building a ship when living far inland. In the same way the *Cursor mundi* shows people jeering at Noah for his building of the ark, saying, 'quy ys þis carle so ferde'.[6] It is, however, the latter point that is commonly emphasised in the plays. The Wakefield Master, influenced a little perhaps by the traditional satiric descriptions of old age, has skilfully indicated that God's command was not an easy one for an old man to execute:

> Ah! my bak, I traw, will brast! this is a sory note!
> Hit is wonder that I last sich an old dote
>   All dold,
> To begyn sich a wark!
> My bons ar so stark,
> No wonder if thay wark,
>   ffor I am full old.

Whereas in the Towneley play the idea that the building of the ark will be a back-breaking labour is introduced only when Noah is at work, and thus casts retrospective light upon his earlier obedience, in the York plays and the *Ludus Coventriae* Noah's first thought on hearing God's command is that he is far too old for such a task: 'I am full olde and oute of qwarte' (York) and 'It is not for me þis werk to undyr-take/ Ffor ffeynnesse [faintness] of Age my leggys gyn folde' (*Ludus Coventriae*). Against this plausible human reaction the York Noah's slightly later expression of unstinted submission, 'A! lorde, þi wille sall ever be wrought' is impressive and fittingly forms a moral climax to the play.

In the *Ludus Coventriae* Noah's actual acceptance of God's command is far less moving; 'I am full redy as god doth me bydde/a shypp for to make be myght of his grace'; though the reference to God's grace makes the submission theologically exact, the style is too perfunctory for it to carry poetical weight. This, however, scarcely matters, since in this cycle Noah's profession of obedience at this point is only a small part of the theme which is reflected in a larger lyrical pattern. The play opens with a long speech in which Noah prays that he and his family may do God's will, this speech is then echoed at some length by Noah' wife and more briefly by Noah's three sons and their wives, each having an individual quatrain. Balancing this set passage is a similar series of speeches spoken by Noah and his family in the ark, in which they mourn the sin that led to the destruction of the flood and thank God for saving them. The play ends in triumphant gratitude, for, after the crow and the dove have been successively sent forth and the dove (sometimes thought of as a type of the Holy Ghost) returns, Noah and his family sing Psalm cxv, the psalm of thanksgiving, 'Non nobis, Domine non nobis, sed nomini tuo da gloriam'.[7] The weight of the play therefore lies in these two harmonious and symmetrically arranged set passages and in the liturgical conclusion.

The middle of this very formal play is rather curiously given to the episode of Lamech's slaying of Cain. The story of Lamech, the blind archer, who shoots Cain, mistakenly guided by his young son, and then in turn kills the child in horror at having disobeyed God's command, was common in the Middle Ages, being found in both the *Historia scholastica* and the *Glossa ordinaria*.[8] It is dramatised in some of the Continental cycles, including the *Mystère du viel testament*, and is represented fairly frequently in art, including the *Holkham Bible Picture Book*.[9] The odd thing about the *Ludus Coventriae* is therefore not primarily its inclusion, though the author tends to be highly selective in the material he chooses, but its position, which is not in correct chronological order immediately after Cain's banishment, but comes as an intrusion in the narrative of the Flood. The explanation seems to lie in the problems of dramatic craftsmanship. The thematic pattern adopted by the author was entirely static: it is possible that the agreeable symmetry of the design would have proved tedious had it not been interrupted by some exciting action, and the effect is startling even though the high drama of the Lamech story is treated in a cool and muted way. Without it the play might also have seemed broken-backed, for the author had evidently decided to omit the scene of the building of the ark, presumably because it could not be done without some bustling hither and thither, which would have marred the serenity of the main theme. The Lamech episode therefore stands in place of the building of the ark and may be seen as an example of a dramatic device, rarely used in the plays, namely the indication of the passage of time essential to some off-stage action by substituting for it on stage some other action that fills in the intervening gap.

The omission of the construction of the ark is peculiar to the *Ludus Coventriae*: the other plays give considerable attention to it, both in the speech of God which paraphrases the very detailed instructions of Genesis vi. 14–16, and in the corresponding monologue spoken by Noah whilst he is at work. Noah's own descriptions, which to the ignorant at least suggest verisimilitude in their use of technical terms, may perhaps have had the practical function of serving to cover the time required for the assembling of the ark in front of the audience,[10] and also serve to illustrate Noah's obedience in action. God's speech is at first sight more puzzling, for, since the dramatists do not adopt as a regular principle that all dialogue in the biblical sources must be paraphrased within the plays, one may wonder why they regularly chose to paraphrase the disconcertingly precise instructions for the construction of the ark, instructions which cannot in fact have been executed in the stage ark. The explanation probably lies in the fact that for them at least the measurements and structure of the ark were replete with symbolical meaning. Many different allegories were found in the ark, all of them related to salvation.[11] A chapter from the *De arca Noe morali* of Hugh of St Victor may be taken as typical of the method: the length of three hundred cubits denotes the three periods of history, those of the natural law, the written law and of grace: the fifty cubits in breadth denotes all believers with Christ as their head; the height of thirty cubits the thirty books of the Old and New Testaments; the three storeys of the ark the three grades in the Christian life, whilst the hundred years that the art took to build represent the period of grace.[12] The latter point is particularly interesting, for the dramatists sometimes show themselves aware of it by making Noah feel an influx of grace which strengthens him in his labour;[13] furthermore the awkward insistence in the plays on the passing of a hundred years can only be accounted for if this implausible passage of time had for the dramatists a significance too august for it to be ignored. This episode is one of the rare examples of an allegory that determined the author's handling of his material but was probably only recognised by the small number of learned amongst the audience.

The author of the *Ludus Coventriae* demonstrates obedience through a lyrical iteration of the theme: from the dramatic point of view the most effective way of treating submission to God's will (unless the command was of a spectacularly harsh kind as in the story of Abraham and Isaac) was to contrast it with disobedience, thus showing how easy the refusal to submit one's own will might be. This is one of the many purposes served by the characterisation in the other plays of Noah's wife as a shrewish and obstinate woman. The suggestion for this seems to have derived from eastern legend and folktale that reached England through some unidentified intermediary.[14] The legend falls into two parts. In the first part the devil, eager to discover and thwart the divine plan (which is concealed from him since God has instructed Noah to keep the building of the ark secret), approaches Noah's wife and advises her to offer Noah a potion, whereby he will be induced to tell her what the secret is: this she successfully does. In the second part the devil seeks a means to enter the ark and hovers by Noah's wife: he is able to enter when Noah, made impatient by his wife's hesitations, is driven to swearing and says something like, 'Come on board, you devil': the devil is similarly expelled from the ark when Noah, on the dove's return, exclaims 'Benedicite'. This legend was known in England by the mid-fourteenth century when *Queen Mary's Psalter* was composed. In this the devil's temptation of Noah's wife is fully illustrated whilst the accompanying French narrative text mentions God's injunction to secrecy. Rather curiously Noah's wife's hesitation to enter is not shown, but in the illustration of the return of the dove the devil is seen leaving the ark so that some story of the devil's entry must have been known to the designer of the illuminations.

The only surviving play to dramatise the first episode is the Shipwrights' play from Newcastle, which is the sole survivor of that lost cycle.[15] In this work the devil, angered that the just Noah with his family will escape the destruction of the world, seeks to bring about his downfall. As in the Garden of Eden he attempts this by approaching the woman, explaining, 'In faith she is my friend/She is both whunt [wise] and slee'. Though the devil appears in his own ugly shape (he swears by his crooked snout) Noah's wife welcomes him and accepts without contradiction a speech in which he inflames her suspicions of Noah and advises that she should give him the magic potion. This she in due course does with hypocritical words of affection:

> Welcome, Noah, as might I thee,
> Welcome to thine own wayns!
> Sit down here beside me,
> Thou hast full weary baynes.

Unfortunately the second half of the play is lost (as at York the subject of the Flood must have been divided between two gilds);[16] but the devil's assurance to Noah's wife that when she goes on board the ark, 'I shall be *by* thy side', suggests that the author continued to dramatise the eastern legend in the second half of the work.

The Newcastle play is a rather confused and mechanical handling of the subject. The theme of secrecy is inconsistently treated, since the devil knows of God's plan before he approaches Noah's wife, and the purpose of the potion therefore becomes unclear; furthermore though Noah is overcome by it, breaks God's command and reveals the secret, it leads to no disaster and the building of the ark continues as before. The importance of this play therefore does not lie in its own literary quality but in its exemplification of an English adaptation of the eastern legend. From it we can understand how Noah's wife could be seen to stand midway between Eve and Delilah: her openness to the devil's temptation recalling the former, her false blandishments of her husband to win his secret the latter. It is this suggestion, not the bizarre legend itself, that the other dramatists adopted.

The only substantial detail which the dramatists borrowed was that of Noah's wife's reluctance to enter the ark, a detail at the heart of their interpretation, but only of subsidiary importance in the eastern legend, where it served primarily to motivate Noah's impatient swearing. But in the imagination of the dramatists it acquired, as we shall see, a crucial and different significance, and considerable care was then taken to give it at least superficially a psychological plausibility. This was the common method of the dramatists: events, which in their biblical source happened without psychological preparation, such as the murder of Abel, were made dramatically comprehensible by previous dialogue: on the rare occasions when this was not done, as in the *Passion de Semur*,[17] the effect is at once tedious and disconcerting. The dramatists, however, had to invent fairly freely for Cain, for the *avarus agricola*, as Vincent of Beauvais called him, was not a recognised character type in medieval literature. The refusal of Noah's wife to enter the ark, however, immediately suggested the stock figure of the shrewish wife common to all misogynistic literature, Latin satire, sermons, comic poems and fabliaux.[18]

Literature of this kind was so common and so widely current throughout the Middle Ages that there can be no question of trying to identify particular sources. It can, however, be conveniently illustrated by two works: the dissuasion from love with which Andreas Capellanus concludes the *Art of Courtly Love*, for it is exceptionally comprehensive, and the *De conjuge non ducenda*, since it was a poem well known in England, being copied in manuscripts continuously from the thirteenth to the fifteenth century and translated into English by Lydgate.[19] Andreas gives a list of the characteristics of woman (the *proprietates mulierum* which, as a commonplace, circulated independently):[20]

> Furthermore, not only is every woman by nature a miser, but she is also envious and a slanderer of other women, greedy, a slave to her belly, inconstant, fickle in her speech, disobedient and impatient of restraint, spotted with the sin of pride and desirous of vain glory, a liar, a drunkard, a babbler, no keeper of secrets, too much given to wantonness, prone to every evil, and never loving any man in her heart.

Not all of these apply to Noah's wife: in particular the favourite fabliau theme that women are insatiably lascivious and invariably adulteresses is irrelevant, though it is part of anti-feminist satire that the dramatists ingeniously reverted to later in the cycles. But that women are greedy, deceiving, disobedient, angry and evil-tongued is a proposition well exemplified by Noah's wife. In the *De conjuge non ducenda* the theme that wedlock is *longa miseria*, a hell or purgatory, is brilliantly and wittily argued by the angelic visitors divinely sent to protect Golias from the catastrophe of his proposed marriage:[21]

> Nam omnis mulier est irascibilis,
>   fallax et invida et nunquam humilis;
>   maritus factus est asello similis,
>   qui est ad onera semper passibilis.

This view of the miseries of marriage is that presupposed by the fabliaux, and, though many of these deal with triangular situations with many obscene variations upon the lecherous nature of women, a number deal solely with the subject of the malicious, shrewish wife and the suffering husband,[22] and it is the latter who, in the battle as to who shall wear the breeches (as the Middle Ages already put it), is exceptionally allowed the victory.

It was to this stock figure that the dramatists turned in their need to motivate a highly implausible action, namely the refusal of Noah's wife to come on board the ark. To understand the English authors' decision to borrow this detail from the eastern legend and to organise a large part of the plays round it, one has to remember the allegorical significance of the ark, namely the church. 'Extra ecclesiam nulla salus' (there is no salvation outside the church), and, as Jerome says commenting on this doctrine, 'Si quis in Noe Arca non fuerit, peribit regnante diluvio.'[23] Noah's wife therefore, who does not wish to be in the ark when the flood comes, represents the recalcitrant sinner, perhaps even the sinner on his deathbed, who refuses to repent and enter the church. The dramatists draw attention to this allegorical pattern by their treatment of Noah's wife once she is on board the ark. Had they wished solely to treat her in a realistic way, they would surely have shown her continuing to grumble fiercely or at least have shown her evil-will gradually subsiding. But in fact the moment on board she becomes meek and submissive both to Noah and to God's will: a psychologically unmotivated change of heart signals the allegorical meaning.

It is in the light of this allegory that the various excuses given by Noah's wife for her refusal to enter the ark (or to delay until it is too late) must be interpreted. The excuses vary from play to play: in York she wants to go back to collect her belongings and she insists that her friends and relations must come too; in Chester she wants to stay drinking with her *gossips*; in Towneley she wants to finish her spinning. These excuses are on a par with those in the parable made by the guests invited to the marriage feast, and it is important to interpret them in this way, as otherwise the attachment of Noah's wife to her friends might be taken as a sympathetic sign of human feeling, which the authors manifestly do not intend.

The lively and colloquial treatment of Noah's wife has largely concealed how implausible her behaviour is on the realistic level: for with the waters rising and the ark the only hope of safety, Noah's wife will still not obey her husband and enter it. But in real life the instinct for self-preservation is stronger than any other, certainly stronger than any base instincts however habitual. Noah's wife therefore has to be shown preferring perverse and obstinate disobedience to escaping death. A favourite story in satire and fabliaux had fortunately provided a precise model for such unrealistic conduct. An entertaining version of it occurs in the *Art of Courtly Love*: it is the story of a 'wise man' who found marriage to his disobedient wife no longer bearable but shunned the thought of killing her with his own hand; he therefore put a mixture of wine and poison into a valuable flask, and said to his wife, 'My sweetest wife be careful not to touch this vessel, and don't venture to taste any of this liquor, because it is poisonous to human beings.' The wife of course drank from the flask the moment that her husband's back was turned.[24] The variations upon the basic pattern of this story are almost numberless: sometimes the wife brings death upon herself as a result of her husband's stratagem: in a sermon exemplum, for instance, the wife of a knight deliberately ate from a poisoned box of sweetmeats which her husband had warned her against, spurning the innocuous one which he had recommended.[25] Sometimes, however, it is only grave physical harm, as in the exemplum in the *Summa praedicantium*, where the wife, contrary to her husband's command, climbed a rickety ladder and broke both her legs,[26] or, as in the fabliau of *Dame Jouenne*, where the wife presses her hand into a hole full of sharp nails, which her husband had told her to avoid.[27] It is worth noting that if we refer to Andreas again the wheel of our argument can be brought full circle, for, just as we have compared Noah's wife with Eve, so also did Andreas compare the wife of his salutary tale to Eve who 'destroyed herself by the sin of disobedience'.

The author of the Chester plays, who, as we have seen, always preferred a lucid pattern to exuberant detail, designed this pattern clearly though at one point inconsistently. When Noah, after hearing God's command, calls to his family for help, his wife with the others co-operates benevolently in the labour: obviously here the author was unwilling to disturb the litany of obedient assent. But when a little later the ark is built and Noah summons his family in, Noah's wife has turned into the perverse shrew:

> In faith, noe, I had as lief thou sleppit;
> for all thy frankish fare
> I will not doe after thy red.

In a manner typical of the wicked characters in the mystery plays Noah's wife has here inverted the nature of the person she describes: the grave and obedient Noah has become a man of affected arrogance who deserves no respect. After all have entered the ark save Noah's wife she becomes more vehement in her churlish obstinacy:

> Yea, Sir, set up your sayle
> And rowe forth with evill heale!
> for, without any fayle,
> I will not out of this towne.

And the scene continues in this vein until Shem at last drags her forcibly up to the ark and she, having given Noah a box on the ears, vanishes inside. During this scene, the Chester author obliquely but unmistakably hints at the religious allegory through religious asseverations; Noah urges his wife to come in 'on gods half'; he replies to Ham's suggestion that they should drag his mother on board, 'yea, sonnes, in Christs blessinge and myne';[28] and Japhet beseeches his mother to enter 'for his love that you boughte'. Whilst we should not always attempt to extract a deep significance from oaths in medieval literature, this triple anachronistic reference to the redemption is too conspicuous in context to be dismissed as thoughtless colloquialism.

Though the love of Noah's wife for irrational obduracy is expressed in this play by touches of lively abuse and colloquial contempt, the theme is equally clearly expressed through Noah's comments upon her and women in general: 'Lord, that women be crabbed aye', 'Thou art ever froward', and '. . . thy mother is wraw,/for sooth such another I do not know': her character is thus established as much by what is said about her as by what she herself says. In contrast the author of the York plays does not rely at all on satirical anti-feminist generalisations, but has taken some trouble to build up a convincing scene containing about seventy lines of spirited dialogue and some action in which Noah attempts to seize his wife and she responds with blows. Whereas the Chester author seemed only aware of the learned tradition of anti-feminism, the York scene is reminiscent of the abuse and fisticuffs found in some fabliaux such as *Sire Hain*.[29] It is tempting to posit the influence here of fabliaux as opposed to general misogynistic traditions, for fabliaux and plays share in common the literary arrangement of preparing for the shrewish wife's demonstration of flamboyant obstinacy by carefully contrived dialogue. However, our knowledge of the circulation of fabliaux in England is so uncertain that it would be dangerous to insist on a direct influence: it is possible that dramatists, starting from the same generalisations about the horrors of marriage and woman's reckless passion for disobedience, hit upon a similar style for expressing these ideas comically in verse. The most that can therefore safely be said is that to anyone of any period who knows both plays and fabliaux the resemblance would come immediately to mind.

It is, however, in the Towneley play of Noah that the fabliau style is most marked, perhaps even to the extent of surfeit: one physical battle between husband and wife is perhaps enough: little is gained by repeating the effect. The Wakefield Master is well aware of the character pattern of the shrewish wife, and as so often, he develops a traditional element with such inventiveness and verve that the harmonious distribution of the parts becomes unbalanced. At the beginning the author has kept to the spirit of the eastern legend but not the letter: unlike the York playwright who preserved the detail of the secret building of the ark in order to give Noah's wife further material for resentment and rage, the Wakefield Master has Noah tell her instantly of God's command, and she as instantly rages at him for his folly. At God's vanishing, Noah speaks a brief monologue of alarm about how his wife will take the news:

> My [wife] will I frast what she will say,
> And I am agast that we get som fray
> > Betwixt us both;
> ffor she is full tethee,
> ffor litill oft angre,
> If any thing wrang be,
> > Soyne is she wroth.

His fears are immediately borne out, as his wife meets his formal and friendly greeting, 'God spede, dere wife, how fayre ye?' with the tart answer, 'Now, as ever myght I thryfe the wars I thee see', and within moments they are launched into an exchange of abuse and blows. Abuse and brawling continue for two hundred lines except for the stylised inset of the description of the building of the ark. At the end, just before his wife's final submission, Noah, like Adam in the York play of the Fall, gives advice to the audience: 'Yee men that has wifis whyls they ar yong,/If ye luf youre lifis chastice thare tong.' This is typical homiletic advice that seems well founded in the previous action. It is possible that this warning repeated one earlier given by Adam, but since most of the Towneley play of the Fall of Man is lost, one cannot be certain. But it is noticeable that it is only in the *Ludus Coventriae* that the theme of feminine depravity is not introduced at the time of the Fall, and that correspondingly in this cycle alone Noah's wife is treated as a meek and virtuous woman.

The Wakefield Master has, however, developed the character pattern of Noah's wife at the cost of obscuring the allegorical significance of Noah. In order to display both verbal and physical cut and thrust between husband and wife he has dispensed with the patience of Noah, which in the York play controlled his replies to his wife's assaults: the pattern of Christ summoning the sinner into the church is therefore obscured. The most recent edition of the play, that by Professor Cawley, has also raised the more disconcerting possibility that the author also missed the significance of the sharp change that Noah's wife should undergo on entering the ark, and put it at too late a point for it to have allegorical meaning. The issue turns upon the locality at which the last of the three battles takes place: the first is before the building of the ark, the second when Noah's wife will not enter, the third either at the door of the ark or inside it. It is reasonable to conjecture that it is at the door and that the wife's obstinate statement, 'I will not, for thi bydyng,/Go from doore to mydyng'[30] is just an abusive way of saying that she will not go one step beyond the entrance. The Chester author, who in his understanding of religious allegory is above suspicion, had similarly, though far more briefly, made Noah's wife give Noah a last cuff and a last word of abuse before passing through the door of the ark. On this reading it is possible to praise with Professor Kolve the very moving expression of the restoration of order, when Noah's wife says, 'I se on the firmament/Me thynk, the seven starnes', which reverses Noah's earlier omen of disaster, 'the planettis seven left has thare stall'.[31]

The treatment of Noah's wife in the Towneley play and to a lesser extent in the York and Chester plays raises the interesting question of the nature of the realism in the plays and incidentally in medieval literature in general. These plays of the Flood undoubtedly give the impression of realism that always derives from the exaggeration of vice and from the use of colloquial and low diction. There always seems to be an earthy reality about sin – even spiritual sins – which is lacking to virtue. The idealised conduct of characters in courtly romance and the gross and vicious behaviour of characters in fabliaux are both equidistant from the mean of normal behaviour, but fabliaux seem more 'real' than romances. For heightening of vice leads to a more realistic effect than heightening of virtue, though both, at least in the Middle Ages, were equally achieved by conscious selection and the application of well-defined conventions. The same is true of insult as against compliments; the exclamation of the Towneley Noah's wife, 'Hold thy tong ramskyt [ramshit]', sounds more realistic than the devil's flattering salutation of Eve in the *Ludus Coventriae*, 'Heyl Ffayr Wyff and comely dame', though a further explanation is probably that the imagery of abuse has remained more constant in the last five hundred years than the language of compliment.

Various qualifications about the much-praised realism in the portrayal of Noah's wife have to be made. It is firstly, as we have said, a style of characterisation adopted for a religious purpose; and, whilst no doubt the dramatists to a greater or lesser extent took an artist's delight in the depiction of such a figure, to understand Noah's wife as a comic diversion would be to read the plays far more shallowly than the authors intended. Furthermore this portrayal derived from a style of characterisation that was itself intended to be comically and satirically unrealistic though giving an illusion of realism in a special sense. It was borrowed from a body of literature in which truth to life was achieved by an exaggeration of extremes: fabliaux fall into place as the reverse of romance. and in France had been copied in manuscripts also containing romances, long before Chaucer found a more subtle balance by combining them in one framework. The fabliau in its reflection of life is an incomplete and dependent form; the Miller's and Merchant's Tales complement those of the Knight and Franklin. Similarly the treatment of Noah's wife emphasises the one-sidedness begun in the comments about Eve. To see Noah's wife as a realistic character sketch is to distort the pattern of the cycles, for the more her irascible disobedience is dramatically exaggerated the more incomplete she seems, and the more necessary is the reversal in the meek obedience of the Virgin. It can thus finally be seen that the dramatists understood the doctrine that Noah's wife signified the Virgin in an idiosyncratic way, for in her the redemption is adumbrated, but the relationship is not that of Noah to Christ but of Eve to the Virgin.

The Flood is followed by Abraham's sacrifice in all the cycles save Chester where a brief representation of Melchisedek's offering intervenes. In Genesis this is an insignificant detail: Melchisedek, King of Salem, offers bread and wine to Abraham on his return from victory over the four kings who had taken Lot captive. In Christian thought, however, this action was a type of the eucharist, and in the canon of the mass Melchisedek's offering was linked to those of Abel and of Abraham. This ceremonial episode was therefore included for typological reasons, and its meaning was made plain firstly by the fact that Melchisedek carries eucharistic vessels, a chalice and paten,[32] for his offering, and secondly by the commentary of the expositor, a figure common in Continental drama, but one rarely introduced into the more naturalistic sequences of the English cycles.

In the other cycles Abraham's sacrifice is juxtaposed to the Flood and in it the prefiguration of the redemption through dramatic art is brought to a final unclouded explicitness. In the plays of the Flood, with the exception of the *Ludus Coventriae*, the pattern of redemption was flawed by the disobedience of Noah's wife. This disobedience, however, not only failed but was treated by the dramatists in a light-hearted way. Wickedness no longer has the substantiality of virtue and, though Noah's wife is dramatically the more interesting character, Noah alone has moral solidity. In the plays of Abraham and Isaac, however, there is no echo of the Fall whatsoever, and through the characterisation of Isaac obedience becomes for the first time dramatically interesting.

The action itself, the decision to kill a near kinsman, recalls that of Cain and reverses it: the monstrous deed formerly done easily is now undertaken with agonised distress. The violation of nature involved is excellently stressed in the *Mystère du viel testament*, where on this theme the style moves from its normal arid elevation to genuine eloquence, as, for instance, when Isaac says how fearful it will be for Abraham to kill 'Son sang, son enfant, son semblable'. The English plays all touch upon the unnaturalness of the action, and in the *Ludus Coventriae* it becomes almost a refrain: 'but ʒitt þe fadyr to scle þe sone' (ll. 91, 163), 'now must þe fadyr his swete son schende' (l. 99), 'thyn owyn fadyr þi deth must be' (l. 139), 'þi careful fadyr must be þi ffo' (l. 144), 'myn owyn sybb blood now xal I spylle' (l. 172). But, while Abraham's moral understanding of the action contrasts with Cain's evil incomprehension, his willingness to offer his son foreshadows the divine plan of the Redemption.

The doctrine that in the work of redemption God the Father gave the Son was firmly established in medieval Christian thought. St Thomas in the article, 'Utrum Deus Pater tradiderit Christum passioni', quotes the key text from Romans viii. 32, 'Proprio Filio suo non pepercit Deus, sed pro nobis omnibus tradidit illum' (which itself seems to echo Genesis xxii. 16),[33] and then sets out three ways in which God the Father gave the Son, of which the first is that He ordained the Passion as the means of man's redemption. The traditional way of relating this doctrine to Abraham's sacrifice can best be illustrated from the *Mystère du viel testament*, in which the point is explicitly made in the episode of the debate between the Four Daughters of God which precedes the play. God first proclaims the Passion as His will:[34]

> Bref, je ne pardonneray point
> A mon filz Jhesus qu'il ne meure;
> Je le condampne de cest heure
> Par jugement irrevocable.

and then in God's further speech the relationship of the divine pattern to the human is expounded:[35]

> Sus Abraham le monstreray
> Et dessus je figureray
> Mon vouloir comme, sans doubter,
> Luy mesme encor vouldra bouter
> Son seul filz de propre lignaige.

Amongst English plays it is the Chester cycle alone that makes this pattern explicit, when at the end the expositor says, 'By Abraham I may understand/the father of heaven . . .', but it lies behind the treatment of Abraham in all the plays. For the awkward questions that would otherwise arise in any amplification of the spare biblical narrative, of how God could command so cruel a thing or Abraham accept it so unhesitatingly, are answered by the understanding that this pattern lies in the Divinity itself. The authors therefore are able to treat the matter serenely, giving no explanation and making no apology. It may be conjectured that we should remember this even when considering the Northampton (more commonly called the Dublin) play, in which, as Professor Kolve has pointed out, there is within the play some questioning of divine justice:[36] for questions asked within a play that by common consent between author and audience have an acceptable answer, do not have the ring of passionate scepticism that they would have in a different social context.

The dramatists therefore show in Abraham reasoned obedience tempered by natural human feeling. Since he is a type of God the Father he can feel no conflict nor judge the situation as a tragic dilemma. The dramatists are concerned only to show what the cost of obedience can be. Just as Noah had done, though in far less testing circumstances, Abraham instantly expresses obedience to God's will. Examples may be picked at random: 'And sertis, I sall noght say hym nay,/If God commaunde my self to sloo' (York), 'Now goddys comaundement must nedys be done/All his wyl is wourthy to be wrought' (*Ludus Coventriae*), or most movingly and amply in Towneley:

> A, lovyd be thou, lord in throne!
> hold over me, lord, thy holy hand,
> ffor certis thi bidyng shall be done.
> Blissyd be that lord in every land
> wold viset his servand thus so soyn.

The words here glow with transcendent love and trust. To find comparable passages in which man had seemed to see God so plainly and to respond with such devotion to his commands, one would have to look back to the speeches of Adam before the Fall.

The prefiguration in Abraham of God the Father giving the Son was, however, only half, and perhaps the lesser half, of the typological significance of the story, for in theological and iconographic traditions it was even more commonly emphasised that Isaac at the moment of the sacrifice was a type of Christ. St Thomas in the article, 'Utrum Christus fuerit ex obedientia mortuus' (which immediately precedes the one quoted above), quotes Philippians ii. 8, in the form 'Factus est obediens Patri usque ad mortem' and Romans v. 19, 'sicut per unius hominis inobedientiam peccatores constituti sunt multi, ita per unius hominis obedientiam iusti constituantur multi'.[37] This second text relates Christ's obedient self-offering to the whole pattern of Fall and Redemption. In His temptation initially, but supremely in His death, Christ, the second Adam, reversed the disobedience of the first. The implications of this for the interpretation of the story of Isaac are again set out by the author of the *Mystère du viel testament* in the speech of God the Father immediately following that about Abraham quoted above (Mercy had briefly intervened with the exclamation, 'Ce sera terrible couraige'):[38]

> Ainsi le fera, puis après
> Je figureray par exprès
> De Jhesu Crist l'obedience
> Sus Ysaac plain de innocence,
> Qui, quant son pére le vouldra
> Mettre a mort, a gré le prendra,
> Sans contredire ne douloir.

Again amongst the English plays it is only in Chester that the allegory is openly expounded, the expositor explaining at the end:

> By Isaac understand I may
> Jhesu that was obedyent aye,
> his fathers will to worke alway,
> his death to underfonge.

But in all the plays the dramatists have unmistakably been guided by this allegory in their handling of Isaac, whose obedience to death at his father's hands is made yet more dramatically important than Abraham's submission to God's will.

The necessity to make Isaac willingly obedient might seem at first sight to be impossibly at odds with any naturalistic treatment of his character: one could expect either a stiff unfeeling display of obedience or a realistic portrayal of a frightened child, but not a combination of typological sense with lively characterisation. These two extremes are occasionally found. The Towneley play is a unique example of the latter. Isaac's uncomprehending terror is prepared for in the journey to the sacrifice when Abraham is anguished to the point of twice lying to him with the promise that he will bring him home safely (in the other plays Abraham is reservedly evasive); and, when Abraham is at last compelled to tell him the truth, Isaac alternately pleads pathetically and seeks persuasive arguments to save his life: he asks what Abraham will do for a son when he is dead, begs to be spared for his mother's sake, and so on. The effect is touching but not impressive. At the opposite pole is the play of Isaac in the *Heidelberger Passionsspiel*, which is a work ordered on a typological pattern, the play of Isaac being paired with that of Christ carrying the Cross.[39] In this the author is concerned with the typological significance alone: Isaac speaks only twice, once to express his willingness to carry the wood of the sacrifice (a type of Christ carrying the Cross), and once to express his willingness to die. The speeches are formal and there is no attempt at characterisation.

The best of the English plays, however, those of the *Ludus Coventriae*, Chester, and the separate Brome play, find a most satisfying and ingenious way of reconciling the two. The method adopted is the same as in the plays of the Flood: an action, psychologically implausible in itself, namely Isaac's childish willingness to die, is made dramatically convincing by recourse to a character type in other literary genres, in this instance that of the innocent child who shows a virtuous simplicity in the face of hardship, physical pain and death. The finest and nowadays the most well-known example of this type of character is the little boy in the Prioress's Tale: this 'innocent' in simple devotion to the Virgin insists upon learning the 'Alma redemptoris mater' without regard to danger, though the danger that he as a seven-year-old child conceives, is that of being beaten for not having properly studied his primer: Chaucer seems deliberately to have modified his sources in order to achieve this effect.[40] Less conspicuously but no less subtly Chaucer made the children of Hugolino in the Monk's Tale innocently generous in the face of death. The detail, horrible in itself, of their inviting their father to eat them to assuage his hunger, derives from Dante,[41] but Chaucer has altered the tone by putting it into a context of simple acquiescence in death: one three-year-old says, 'Farewel, fader I moot dye!', kisses Hugolino and dies the same day, and the others after offering their flesh just lie down in their father's lap to die. Whilst Chaucer's effects of pathos are unrivalled, the figure of the innocent child recurs in sermon literature. There is the exemplum in the *Gesta Romanorum* of the innocent child born in prison who accepts the constrictions of the dark dungeon with innocent sweetness,[42] or that in the *Summa praedicantium* of the children so innocent of death's meaning that they play with the pall which covers the dead bodies of their parents; the sermon illustration of the child who quickly forgets the beating that he has received, and on being offered a flower or an apple rushes affectionately into his mother's arms, or the many stories of children who happily offer a share of their food to other children, to animals or to a statue of the Christ-Child.[43] From such stories there emerges a picture of a child as instinctively loving and generous, more concerned for the cares of others than for self-protection, innocently free of resentment or of the complex adult demands upon life, and too innocent to have the heavy knowledge of death that weighs upon those who have lived longer.

Upon this pattern Isaac is modelled. In the *Ludus Coventriae* Isaac's reactions consist solely of tender concern for his parents. When he first notices Abraham's distress, he tries to cheer him:

> Lat be good fadyr ʒour sad wepynge,
> ʒour hevy cher agrevyth me sore:
> tell me fadyr ʒour grett mornyng
> and I xal seke sum help þer-fore.

and when Abraham has told him that he must die, he replies;

> Al-myghty god of his grett mercye
> Fful hertyly I thanke þe sertayne,
> At goddys byddyng here for to dye
> I obeye me here for to be sclayne.
> I pray ʒow fadyr be glad and fayne
> trewly to werke goddys wyll;
> take good comforte to ʒow agayne
> and have no dowte ʒour childe to kyll.

In this way Isaac's typological statement of obedience is caught up in a moving pattern of loving anxiety for his father, a pattern that is elaborated in the rest of the dialogue in which Isaac seeks ways of comforting Abraham, suggesting, for instance, that he should turn his head away at the moment of the blow so that he may not have the pain of seeing it. In the fifty lines of dialogue Isaac does not once say that he is frightened, but the scene is conducted with such sweetness and charm that this omission is as fitting aesthetically as it is typologically.

The author of the *Ludus Coventriae* is alone in making Isaac entirely unafraid and entirely willing to die. In the two other plays of this group, Chester and Brome (which in the scene of the sacrifice are closely related), Isaac is both frightened and reluctant until he understands that his death is God's will, whereupon his fears lessen and reluctance fades into obedience. In the Chester play, as in the *Ludus Coventriae*, Isaac is moved by his father's evident unhappiness to question him, 'but why make you so heavie cheare?', but then draws his own inferences and asks four times in terror and distress whether he must be the victim. When Abraham at last admits this, Isaac's first reaction is the childish one that this must be some parental punishment, and he begs pathetically that he may instead be given a beating and wishes that his mother were there to intercede for him. But when Isaac fully understands that the sacrifice is God's will, his response changes to, 'Mary! father, God forbydd/but you doe your offringe'. Thereafter, as in the *Ludus Coventriae*, Isaac's concern is for his parents' grief, and he tries to comfort Abraham with the thought that he has other sons at home and will soon forget him, and to protect his mother asks Abraham not to tell her what has happened; and though Isaac again feels impulses of fear, his willingness to die does not waver, the climax of his obedience being a committal of his soul into God's hands, which, like Abel's in the *Adam*, anticipates Christ's Word from the Cross.

The Brome play is a little more ample, Isaac's compassion for his parents being yet more intensified, and his willingness to die being yet more movingly expressed. The amplifications are felicitous, but the general effect of the accumulation comes close to excess. It is not inconceivable that the Chester author pared down a version of the Brome play to fit his own preference for a severer style; alternatively, and more probably if the Brome play was never part of a cycle, the Brome author may have embellished the Chester text with sentimental variations on the basic pattern in order to give it more solid existence as an independent work. Either answer to the question of priority is possible, and fortunately it matters little from the literary point of view which is historically correct.[44]

The York and Northampton plays require separate comment, though for different reasons. Amongst English plays York is the most formal, though if it were not overshadowed by other plays, one might easily be pleased by its sustained gravity of tone, occasionally broken by little chinks of human feeling. The author does not make use of the character of the innocent child, since he has preferred to follow the tradition established by Peter Comestor that Isaac was a man of twenty-five to thirty years at the time of the sacrifice.[45] This gives him one advantage only, that of being able to show a more adult acceptance of death, in which an instinctive delight in life is controlled by a reasoned submissiveness to God's will. Amongst the plays observant of typological meaning York is the most emphatic about the fear of death, which recurs in Isaac's speeches: 'I knaw myselfe be cours of kynde,/My flessche for dede will be dredande' (ll. 209–10); 'Now fare wele, all medilerth,/My flesshe waxis faynte for ferde' (ll. 269–70), 'A! dere fadir, lyff is full swete,/The dred of dede dose all my dere'. In these laments an elegiac sense of loss mingles with an exact expression of the type of fear permissible (because natural) to the virtuous man, and the last paraphrases the much-used Latin words from the Office for the Dead, 'Timor mortis conturbat me', which in fifteenth-century poetry were even ascribed to Christ Himself.[46] It was accepted by theologians that fear of death was as natural to man as hunger or thirst: therefore though Christ was obedient to the Passion and to death, they were repugnant to His natural will, and He expressed His fear of death when he said, 'Tristis est anima mea usque ad mortem'.[47]

Fear of death was only wrong if it led a man to deny Christ, as it did St Peter. This of course is an idea that it would have been dangerous to explore in the Passion sequences; but in the Sacrifice of Isaac the York author shows himself theologically and imaginatively aware of the issue, and treats it with some sensitivity in what may at first sight seem a stiff and unfeeling dramatisation of the subject.

Fear of death is also emphasised in the Northampton play but at the cost of dramatic and typological consistency. In this work Isaac is a child, as Sarah's homely concern for him makes clear: she is afraid that if he accompanies Abraham on his expedition Isaac will catch cold or get his clothes dirty. However, though the impression of childishness thus conveyed to some extent rubs off on Isaac, his own speeches lack any childish quality, except insofar as he recalls how his mother kissed and fondled him and petted him with endearments. But outside his remembered relationship with his mother, Isaac speaks as an adult with an eloquence and a kind of angry despair that no child could have. Isaac's unwillingness to die is thus too convincingly established, so that when for manifestly typological reasons he at last consents to the sacrifice, 'With al my hert I assent þerto', this comes too late and is too unprepared for to be moving. The construction of the Northampton play and in particular the presence of Sarah, who appears in no other English play, has led scholars to assume the influence of some version of the Isaac play in the *Mystère du viel testament*.[48] Whilst it is indeed likely that the author derived the idea of introducing the figure of Sarah from the French, his purpose is plainly his own, namely the characterisation of Isaac as a child by showing him to us through his mother's eyes; and he has pursued his own eccentric aim by stripping away the typological elements in the characterisation of Isaac until he is left with the bare minimum of one line. If, however, the Northampton play was originally part of a cycle, then it is possible that the author had in mind a different typological emphasis, and that his concentration upon Sarah's maternal tenderness and grief might have formed part of a pattern begun by Eve's lament for Abel and resumed in the treatment of the Virgin at the Passion. But this suggestion is at best tentative.

The plays of Abraham and Isaac are the most moving and compact of all those in the cycles and, unlike any others, their dramatic impressiveness does not derive from a contrast between the serenity of good and the harshness of evil. Other plays, such as the Annunciation, that similarly celebrate only goodness, could not be praised for dramatic power outside their context in the cycles. These exceptional qualities seem to have marked them out for special treatment in that two, the Brome and Northampton plays, have been copied independently in fifteenth-century commonplace books.[49] These two plays are usually grouped today with the two other single plays which we have already referred to, the Norwich Fall and the Newcastle Noah, and classified as non-cyclic, but this practice is primarily for editorial convenience. For the latter two are only non-cyclic in the sense that by chance they have been preserved when the rest of their respective cycles has been lost; the Brome and Northampton plays are genuinely non-cyclic, in the sense that, whether or not originally composed as part of full cycles, in their extant form they have been deliberately recorded as self-sufficient pieces.[50] Furthermore, whilst there is nothing in the text to suggest that they were not composed for performance on the stage, it is possible that they were copied for private reading, since they seem to be preserved on equal terms with other kinds of poetry, some religious, some secular.[51]

There is one small peculiarity about the Brome play which may finally be noted: it is the epilogue of the doctor, written in different metre, which turns the play into an exemplum for parents who grieve excessively for the death of their children. Unlike a typological exposition, this moral is disconcertingly constrictive, and from the purely literary point of view even more infelicitous than the fairly common moral that the play demonstrates how children should be obedient to their parents. The Brome *moralitas* turns the play into a complement to *The Pearl*, and it is possible that these parallel studies in rebelliousness and obedient acquiescence in loss may have been occasional works, the occasion being some bereavement, which of necessity can no longer be identified.[52]

The cycles treat the next subject, that of Moses, in a variety of ways, and therefore, with the exception of Towneley which has borrowed the York play, each must be considered separately. The York play is the most successful, since, with the important, didactic matter of the Ten Commandments reserved until the play of Christ with the doctors in the Temple, the dramatist was able to concentrate upon the Exodus itself, a rather dispersed narrative which he shapes by making the scene between Moses and Pharaoh (in which Moses demands the release of the Israelites) the focal point of the play. This scene is most carefully modelled to foreshadow the dialogue between Christ and Satan in the Harrowing of Hell. In seeing the Exodus as a type of the Harrowing the author was of course following tradition: in the *Speculum humanae salvationis*, for instance, the illustration of Christ leading the patriarchs from Limbo is accompanied by one of Moses leading the Israelites from Egypt.[53] But the indication of this type through the creation of a verbal duel between Moses and Pharaoh seems to have been a felicitous invention of the York dramatist: it is certainly not an allegory inherent in the biblical story, where Aaron as well as Moses is present in the scene, and it thus fails to provide the basis of the one for one correspondence characteristic of the typological method; nor did dramatists normally impose this pattern upon the episode: the author of the *Viel testament*, though, as we have seen, very concerned with typology, ignores this possibility altogether, since he not only retains the biblical Aaron, but also introduces two *médecins*, who comment upon the miracle of the rod.[54]

Whilst the foundations for the figurative meaning are laid by the omission of Aaron, it is through style that it is conveyed to the audience. Whilst at first sight Pharaoh through the speeches to his officers appears merely as a wicked and ranting ruler, seemingly a pale anticipation of Herod and Pilate, it gradually becomes clear that more than this is intended. Pharaoh's connection with Satan in the Harrowing of Hell is displayed, not merely by the extraordinary frequency with which he swears by the devil, but also by a small nexus of vocabulary which is conspicuously used in both plays: *lads, lurdans, boyes* (as terms of contempt),[55] *gaudis* (to refer to the supposed trickery of the good), and *maistris* (as a derogatory term for God's power). In the scene with Moses there are also larger stylistic resemblances. Pharaoh's dismissal of the claims of Moses, 'Nay, nay, þat daunce is done,/þat lordan leryd overe late' and 'But þis boyes sall byde here in oure bayle,/For all þair gaudis sall noght þam gayne', have precisely the jeering tone that Satan was later to use in rejecting the idea that Christ would release the souls from hell; and the calm asseverations of power with which Christ then responded are similarly anticipated in the speeches of Moses to Pharaoh. The York author thus ended his Old Testament series with an adumbration, not of the Redemption, but of its first fruits, and, as the cycles were acted year after year, this foreshadowing by stylistic means would have become remarkably plain to the audience.

The Moses play of the *Ludus Coventriae* is entirely different: the author has chosen two distinct episodes from Exodus, God's appearance to Moses in the burning bush and the Ten Commandments, and has run them together in an unhistorical way by making God deliver the tables of the law to Moses from the burning bush instead of at a far later point in time from Mount Sinai. The explanation for this treatment is probably that, whilst not wishing to dramatise the Exodus, the author did not want to omit the episode of the bush that burnt without being consumed, as it was such a beautiful and important type of the virgin birth. Whilst this typological significance is not expounded, Moses's comment upon the marvel, 'It figuryth sum thynge of ryght gret fame', would call the audience's attention to a hidden meaning. There follows what is in effect a versified sermon on the Ten Commandments, in which Moses preaches directly to the audience, expounding them with reference to contemporary society. Poems of this kind were quite common throughout the Middle Ages and there is nothing in Moses's sermon to distinguish it from any other competent version. The author's treatment of the Ten Commandments here is far more ample than the contrast between the old law and the new requires, and his intention therefore must have been primarily didactic, that of refreshing the audience's attention to a common piece of pulpit teaching by putting it into a new context.

The Exodus play of the *Ludus Coventriae*, though dramatically unexciting, is lucidly and economically organised. In contrast the Chester play, though containing passages of interest, is more dispersed and sprawling. If for the moment we leave on one side the episode of the prophets, which in the text printed by Deimling is awkwardly inserted in this play, the work falls into two disconnected parts, the divine delivery of the Ten Commandments to Moses on Mount Sinai, a difficult subject rather cursorily treated, and the more elaborate episode of Balaam and Balak. The latter is a strange subject to have treated at length. The author certainly found a model for his play in the *Mystère du viel testament*,[56] but his indebtedness to the French cycle would not account for his choosing to dramatise this particular episode, since it is there only a part of a methodical dramatisation of the whole of biblical history. A possible explanation is that the Chester author decided to leave on one side the undramatic prophets' play and in its place to dramatise one detail of it very fully; for this purpose he chose one of the rare prophecies spoken in the context of a dramatic situation and not merely forming part of prophetic discourse; for this reason there had occasionally been brief passages of dialogue in the episode of Balaam in the liturgical prophets' plays.[57] Since such passages in liturgical drama, however, were extremely brief, Balaam's prophecy was combined with the episode of the ass; whereas the Chester author, with the help of his French source, makes a correct historical arrangement of the plot. The author took some trouble with the characterisation. Balaam, who like Jonah, was one of God's reluctant prophets, he seems deliberately to have given no personality to: in contrast to the

Balaam of the *Viel testament*, who is represented as a fraudulent and money-seeking magician, the Chester Balaam remains a dignified but uncharacterised figure. But Balak, the Moabite king, who wished Balaam to curse his enemies the Israelites, is turned into an embodiment of anger, which expresses itself in abusive speech. Like the York Pharaoh he swears continuously by the devil, and each time that Balaam, in accordance with God's will, blesses the Israelites, he turns upon him with abusive colloquialisms, such as 'What the Devilles! eyles the poplart?/Thy speach is not worth a fart'. It is, however, the characterisation of the ass that is the most interesting, for here the author has turned the formal scene of Numbers xxii. 23–20 into a lively and touching episode. When the ass halts at the sight of the angel, the oblivious Balaam swears at it in a realistic way, 'Goe forth, Burnell! goe forth, goe,/what the dyvell! my Asse will not goe'; and the ass replies in the reproachful tone of a faithful, loving and obedient animal: 'Maister, thou dost evell witterly,/so good an ass as me to nye,' and again:

> Am I not, Master, thyne owne Ass,
> that ever before ready was
> to beare the whether thou woldest pas?
> to smyte me now yt is shame.

> Thou wottest well, Master, pardy:
> thou haddest never Ass like to me,
> ne never yet thus served I thee;
> now I am not to blame.

The Chester author has understood the episode of Balaam and his ass in the light of the many medieval stories, found in bestiaries and elsewhere, of the unwavering devotion of domesticated animals, especially dogs, and more particularly in the light of stories, such as that of the faithful greyhound in *The Seven Sages of Rome*, where the master has ill-treated (or in this instance killed) the animal through unjustified mistrust of its obedience and loyalty.[58] Through recourse to this characterisation, the author has given sentimental realism to a strange, miraculous episode, and has touchingly fitted the ass into the pattern of innocent obedience.

Some reviser of the Chester plays seems to have been dissatisfied that only one prophecy should be heard, and therefore after Balaam's 'Orietur stella ex Iacob', he has, without regard to narrative consistency, inserted seven more. This insertion is modelled upon the prophets' part of a Creed play rather than a liturgical prophets' play (though the series is an uncommon one).[59] As the expositor himself explains, the prophets are so arranged that they prophesy in due order the Nativity, the Passion, Resurrection, Ascension and Descent of the Dove. This sequence would therefore in itself form an admirable doctrinal introduction to the New Testament part of the cycles, but placed as it is in the extant manuscripts, before Balak's dismissal of Balaam, it is extremely unsatisfactory.

The prophets' play of the *Ludus Coventriae* is equally a departure from liturgical tradition. Whilst in one iconographic development the prophets were paired with the apostles as authors of the Creed, in another, that of the Tree of Jesse, they were set alongside the kings in the genealogy of Christ. It is this arrangement that the author of the *Ludus Coventriae* follows, prophets and kings alternating with each other symmetrically. One curiosity that arises from this dramatisation of an iconographic pattern is that the first speaker in the genealogical line is apparently an allegorical one, 'Radix Jesse'. Though this work is commonly described as a prophets' play, in the manuscript it is called a play of Jesse, which is the more appropriate title.[60] It is a work that cannot appropriately be assessed in literary terms. On the page at least it seems monotonously long, the theme that could be splendidly decorative in the simultaneous display of art (and in particular in the luminosity of stained glass), seeming merely repetitive when set out successively in time (the speeches of the kings are scarcely differentiated). It is possible, however, that when acted, with each speaker distinguished by his dress, and presumably imposing in appearance, the unrelenting accumulation may have seemed more impressive, as each of the prophets and forbears of Christ revealed himself to the audience.

The remaining prophets' play to consider is that of the Towneley cycle (York is without one, though some of the prophecies are alluded to in the prologue to the Annunciation).[61] The method adopted by the author is that of presenting a small number of prophets (there are four only in the play as it is preserved, but the end is missing). This gets over the necessity for perfunctory versifying as in the corresponding play of the *Ludus Coventriae* where no less than twenty-seven characters speak, and permits either a didactic amplification, as in the monologue of Moses, or devotional extensions that have some of the emotive touches characteristic of medieval English lyric style.[62] The portrayal of David as a minstrel singing a romance of the Incarnation and of the sibyl as a seer with full foreknowledge of the Last Judgment and some of its antecedent signs is in itself well done, but even as it stands

the play has a discontenting diffuseness which, one may fear, would
have seemed yet more accentuated in the complete form of the play.

A prophets' play, however, is necessarily static and repetitious: its
dramatic virtue lies in the provision of a smooth transition between
the Old and New Testaments. Though the doctor's prologue to the
Annunciation in York has a theological pointedness and vivacity,
necessarily lacking in the prophets' plays, it follows too abruptly upon
the drowning of the Egyptians in the Red Sea. Again the Chester
conjunction of the play of Balaam with the Annunciation does not
work quite satisfactorily on the theoretical level since the prophecy
applies primarily to the Visit of the Three Kings,[63] and in practice the
prophecy is dramatically submerged in the lively events of the play.[64]
Towneley may be presumed to have supplied a satisfactory link,
though since the play, as it survives, is out of order and incomplete,
its structural value is difficult to judge. Best of all is the Jesse play of the
Ludus Coventriae: this dramatisation of the Tree of Jesse stops short of
the familiar apex of the tree, the Virgin herself. Its effect is therefore
propellant and we pass without sense of awkward interruption into
the subsequent plays of which the Virgin herself is the subject.

VIII

Nativity Plays, I

Caesar Augustus,
The Early Life of the Virgin
Joseph's Doubts
The Visit to Elizabeth
The Trial of Joseph and Mary
The Nativity

Prophecies of Christ did not end with the Old Testament prophets, but extend into the biblical world of the New Testament with those of Elizabeth, Simeon and John the Baptist, and out into the gentile world with those of Virgil and the sibyl. The cycles deal with the continuation of the theme in a variety of ways. The York plays bring the prophecies into immediate conjunction with the Annunciation by a prologue, in which some of the most important prophecies, including that of John the Baptist, are enumerated. In two other cycles, Towneley and Chester, the Annunciation is accompanied by a scene of further prophecy, that made to Caesar Octavian or Caesar Augustus (the tradition varied). In Chester this scene, which more commonly accompanied the Nativity, follows immediately upon the Annunciation. It is based upon the legend of the Tiburtine sibyl, which grew up in connection with the church of the Ara Coeli in Rome, and was disseminated by the *Legenda aurea* and the *Speculum humanae salvationis:*[1] according to this tradition the emperor Octavian temporised when his councillors wished him to be worshipped as a god, and asked the prophetess whether one greater than he would be born, and the sibyl replied with a prophecy of the birth of Christ. In Chester this story combines with that of the emperor's decision that all his subjects should pay tribute and homage to him by the offering of a penny bearing his likeness, an amplification upon Luke ii. 1–2, first recorded in the *Historia scholastica.*[2] Octavian in this play is a wise man, who recoils from the attribution of divinity through an awareness of his own mortality, which he expresses in traditional reflections upon transience: 'I must die wot not what daye' and 'and of my life most parte is gone,/age shewes hym so, I see'.³

The Towneley play of Caesar Augustus, which precedes the Annunciation, consists of a coherent but nevertheless garbled version of this story. In this work the prophecy is made, not by the sibyl, but by a councillor, and the decision to demand the homage of a penny (which is consequent upon the prophecy) is accompanied by an order to seek out the Christ-Child and kill him, this being Augustus's two-pronged method of re-establishing his sovereignty in the face of the prophecy. The story of Octavian and the sibyl has here obviously been re-modelled upon that of Herod and the Magi, and so has the character of Augustus, who in his arrogance, fury, and cruelty, resembles Herod.⁴ Unlike the Chester Octavian, who in a later episode expresses delight and faith in the Christ-Child, the Towneley Augustus reacts in the manner typical of the evil. His first response to the prophecy is to swear by the devil, the next to take refuge in blustering and colloquial abuse, the child is a 'snoke horne' and a 'gadlyng'. All his speeches are peppered with oaths: most often he swears by 'mahowne', the mystery plays following the example of romances in seeing Mahomet as an agent of the devil.⁵ The pattern that the Towneley author had in mind in the creation of this Augustus is plain: the emperor repeats Pharaoh and anticipates Herod. But it is possible to feel that the author had an indiscriminate liking for this theme and lacked an imaginative sense of when it could fittingly recur.

These three cycles link the New Testament to the Old by a repetition of prophecy: in the *Ludus Coventriae* this is done much more amply and solidly by three plays on the Conception and early life of the Virgin, which follow fittingly upon the play of Jesse with its genealogical theme and numerous prophecies of the Virgin: indeed the plays on the Virgin seem to emerge as fittingly from that of Jesse as does the Virgin from the tree of kings and prophets in iconographic representations. The subject-matter of these three plays on the Conception of the Virgin, the presentation in the Temple, and her betrothal, derives ultimately from three apocryphal gospels, the *Protevangelium*, the Gospel of the Pseudo-Matthew and the *Evangelium de nativitate Mariae*.⁶ These works continued to be known throughout the Middle Ages, but their content was also available to the author of the *Ludus Coventriae* through almost countless intermediaries. Though the legendary material was not included by Peter Comestor in the *Historia scholastica*, it is found in the only slightly less influential work, the *Speculum historiale* of Vincent of Beauvais,⁷ and it forms the substance of the sermon for the Nativity of the Virgin in the *Legenda aurea*:⁸ from these two sources respectively it passed into other chronicles and sermon collections. In the fourteenth and fifteenth centuries many vernacular narratives of the life of the Virgin were composed: in England the three stanzaic versions of the Life of St Anne[9] and Lydgate's *Life of our Lady*.[10] The life of the Virgin was represented in art as early as the famous frescoes of Giotto in the Arena Chapel at Padua, and is found in England in the carvings of the Lady Chapel at Ely, in the frescoes of Croughton Church, Northamptonshire and of Chalgrove, and the stained glass at Malvern.[11]

Whilst the representation of the life of the Virgin is common in art and literature as a distinct subject from the twelfth century onwards, it is only by the mid-fifteenth century that we find it firmly established that the history of salvation must begin, not with the Annunciation as had previously been done, but with the story of Joachim and Anna. This integration is of course found earlier: the *Meditationes vitae Christi* begins slightly tentatively with the presentation of the Virgin in the Temple (but omits the less spiritually edifying betrothal) and the *Speculum humanae salvationis* provides the full series. In England the incorporation of the legendary material into a biblical history occurs first in the *Cursor mundi*.[12] The most illuminating parallels to the structure of the *Ludus Coventriae* are, however, provided by Continental plays. The early life of the Virgin is dramatised in France and Germany not only in independent sequences which have their climax in the Nativity, such as the *Mystère de la Conception de la Vierge*,[13] but also in plays of the life of Christ, the *Mystère de la Passion* of Jean Michel and the *Passion de Valenciennes*, and in full Old and New Testament cycles such as the *Egerer Fronleichnamsspiel*. Consideration of Continental drama written between 1450 and 1500 shows that the early life of the Virgin was included far more often than not, and therefore, whilst the presence of plays on this subject in the *Ludus Coventriae* usually arouses a flurry of excited speculation in scholars, it would perhaps be more noteworthy if a mid-fifteenth-century composition excluded this material. Indeed one could go so far as to say that the absence of plays on this subject in the other English cycles is an indication that their structure was fixed before the fifteenth-century flourishing of the cult of St Anne.

The apocryphal account of the Conception of the Virgin is intended to foreshadow the more wonderful birth of her Son, and is modelled upon the conception of Isaac, whom Sarah, contrary to nature, bore in her old age.[14] According to the three apocryphal gospels, Joachim and Anna grieve for their barrenness, which is seen as a sign of God's rejection. When on these grounds Joachim's offering in the Temple is refused, he withdraws in shame to his sheep and shepherds in the country. During this time an angel announces the future birth of Mary to Joachim and Anna in turn, and their grave and passionless union is symbolised by their embrace at the Golden Gate. This story, first told in the *Protevangelium*, reflects Hebraic values in its stress upon barrenness as a curse. This was not an easy idea to transfer to a medieval setting: the fate of Jephtha's daughter, for instance, who before her death retired to the hills to mourn her childlessness (thus illustrating the sin of sloth), strikes a discordant note in the *Confessio amantis*.[15]

The author of the *Ludus Coventriae* uses much literary artifice to make this unfamiliar idea convincing, giving to both Anna and Joachim a series of impassioned laments. The elevation and anguish that one might have expected in the speeches of Abraham are sustained in those of Joachim. In contrast to the Old Testament plays, however, the tone seems a little forced and some of the rhetorical devices are used too unsparingly. The threefold repetition of a word to convey distress (ploce) is at first moving, 'A Anne, Anne, Anne, god scheeld us fro shame', but the imitation thirty lines later, 'A, Anne, Anne, Anne, Al our joye is turned to grame', comes a little too soon, and detracts from the third occasion when Anne questions God's will, 'Why do ȝe thus to myn husbond, lord, why, why why'. Rhetorical questions (erotema) to express despair, as in Joachim's '. . . what is this lyff/What have I do lorde to have þis blame' and later 'What art þou lord, what am I wrecche . . .' are another device, as is also the great generalisation (*sententia*), such as 'Aftere grett sorwe evyr grett gladnes is had'. One could of course make a list of rhetorical figures in, for instance, some of Chaucer's poetry, but whereas this method would not there bring one to the heart of the matter, with this play it does.

The next play is entirely formal: Mary at the age of three is offered by her parents and offers herself to the Temple, which in the fiction of the *Protevangelium* has acquired Vestal Virgins. Deliberately and in keeping with tradition no attempt is made to characterise Mary as a child, the adult gravity of her speeches reflecting her miraculous power to ascend the fifteen steps of the Temple unaided.[16] The core of the play is Mary's meditative monologue as she makes the ascent, each step symbolising one of the gradual psalms (the only comparable monologue appears to be in the *Passion de Valenciennes*);[17] the description of the five allegorical maidens which follows, and Mary's petition for seven graces belong to the traditional substance of this theme, as does also the visit of the angel, but the angel's praise of Mary through an ornate acrostic of her name, appears to be the author's own embellishment of the topic.[18]

The play of the Betrothal which follows is episodic and diffuse. The author covers the high priest's edict that all girls of fourteen must take a husband, Mary's refusal since she has taken a vow of virginity, the revelation to the high priest of the method of choosing a suitor, Joseph's dialogue with the other descendants of David, the miracle of his flowering rod, the marriage which includes the exchange of vows of the medieval ceremony, a farewell to Joachim and Anna, Mary's sojourn in the Temple studying the psalter whilst Joseph leaves to prepare a house for her, and finally Mary's departure from the Temple accompanied by three maidens. In order to produce such an all-embracing treatment of the subject, the author seems to have drawn on a variety of sources, sometimes welding them together at the cost of pointless inconsistency in narrative and characterisation. The opening scene in which Mary leaves her parents' home although she had been presented to the Temple (ll. 66–7) is illogically placed, since it should succeed, not precede, the high priest's edict.[19] Similarly Mary's sojourn in the Temple appears inconsequential since it follows a scene that presupposes her immediate departure.

A comparable lack of sureness is shown in the treatment of Joseph in this play. The author on the one hand has chosen to follow the *Protevangelium* in contemptuously stressing Joseph's old age and extreme reluctance to marry. He is so old that he can scarcely walk, 'I am old and also cold, walkyng doth me wo' or 'But I am so Agyd and so olde /þat both myn leggys gyn to folde'. His cynicism also makes him apprehensive of the dangers of marrying a young wife, as when he says to the bishop:

> An old man may nevyr thryff
> With a ȝonge wyff so god me save
> nay, nay, sere, lett bene;
> xuld I now in age begynne to dote
> If I here chyde she wolde clowte my cote
> blere myn ey and pyke out a mote
> and þus oftyn tymes it is sene.

The author is obviously laying the foundations for the play of Joseph's suspicions of Mary, but unnecessarily. At the same time he evidently wished to preserve the solemnity of the divinely decreed marriage of Our Lady by showing Joseph accept her in a reverent and obedient spirit: 'Aȝens my God not do I may,/here wardeyn and kepere wyl I evyr be.' This tone is more in keeping with the other two apocryphal gospels and with common medieval treatments of the theme. It has been conjectured that this play is a re-working of an older one: if this were so, it would satisfactorily account for its lack of sureness of touch which is in general so unexpected and unaccustomed in the writing of the *Ludus Coventriae*.[20]

The *Ludus Coventriae* not only differs from the other cycles in including plays on the early life of the Virgin but also in its introduction to the scene of the Annunciation; and whereas we may doubt the literary advantage of including the three plays so far discussed – the material was perhaps intractable – the following sequence is impressive. The play of the Annunciation, like the preceding ones, is heralded by a prologue spoken by a figure called Contemplacio. Up to this point Contemplacio, despite the august title given him in the manuscript, had seemed indistinguishable from the doctor, expositor, or whatever he may be called, who regularly in Continental drama spoke prologues, epilogues and perhaps linking speeches, which made clear to the audience what they were about to see or what they had seen. Not only was Contemplacio identical in function with this Continental figure, but so also was he in appearance, for a rubric in the later Passion sequence specifically describes him as an 'exposytour in doctorys wede'. But in the prologue to the Annunciation this functional and unpoetic figure, suddenly and with mysterious force momentarily turns into a personification of the human power of contemplation, whether of God or of the scriptures,[21] and speaking partly in the person of the souls in hell and partly in the person of man on earth, he pleads with God for mercy and implores Him to come.

For this theme there are again analogues in a form of prophets' play found in Continental sequences either as a preface to the debate between the Four Daughters of God or directly to the Annunciation. Unlike a liturgical prophets' play, it is not unlocated in time and space, but takes place in the Limbo of the Fathers, where the patriarchs and prophets of the Old Testament rehearse their prophecies and implore their fulfilment. This procedure occurs in Greban's *Passion*, the *Mystère de l'Incarnation*, the *Passion de Valenciennes* and the *Sündenfall*.[22] It is only, however, in the late *Passion de Valenciennes*, that an allegorical figure is introduced at this point, namely *Oraison* (a personification of the patriarchs' prayers) who makes her way to heaven to plead with *Misericorde*.[23] Greban's version of this scene, in which the longing pleas of the souls in hell are lyrically expressed, is especially moving. Adam, for instance, asks:[24]

Quand vendras tu, sauveur du monde
qui des prophetes es promis,
visiter tes povres amis
qui tant ta venue desirent.

and Isaiah, addressing Christ in the beautiful images of his prophecies, implores:[25]

Vien donc, rosee souveraine,
vien tendre fleur et amyable,
secourir la perte dampnable
qui sans toy ne se peust reffaire.

But, while the main pleas come in this scene, the *acteur* begins his prologue at the very opening of the cycle with a responsory used in the Advent office, 'Veni ad liberandum nos, Domine Deus virtutum'.[26]

It is reasonably certain that some work such as this gave the author of the *Ludus Coventriae* the idea for Contemplacio's prologue. He did not, however, need to retain the element of prophecy, which had already been expressed in the play of Jesse, but could concentrate rather upon the other traditional strand in the Continental scenes, namely the echoes of the many Advent antiphons, and in particular the seven great O-antiphons, in which during the week before Christmas the church at vespers implores Christ's coming and in particular impersonates the patriarchs in hell and the world under the old dispensation.[27] The direct influence of the Advent O's can be seen firstly in the ambivalence of the speaker: there is in Contemplacio's invocations a timeless, almost mythic cry, which makes it suitable that the speaker should not be a historical person: the effect is of liturgical rather than of dramatic impersonation. Secondly the pleas of Contemplacio are exceptionally direct. The church's repeated cries, 'Veni et salva hominem', 'Veni et educ vinctum de domo carceris', etc.,[28] are echoed in Contemplacio's 'Com down here in to erth', 'Cum vesyte us in þis tyme of nede' and most magnificently in the concluding line, 'Gracyous lord, Gracyous lord, Gracyous lord, come down', in which the effect of the threefold repetition is superb.

The pleas of Contemplacio are far more urgent and impassioned than those of the prophets in Continental drama:

I prey þe, lord, þi sowlys com se
How þei ly and sobbe ffor syknes and sorwe,
With þi blyssyd blood ffrom balys hem borwe,
thy careful creaturys cryenge in captyvyte:

> A tary not, gracyous lord, tyl it be to-morwe;
> The devyl hath dysceyved hem be hys iniquite.

and again:

> As gret as þe se, lord, was Adamys contryssyon ryght,
> Ffrom oure hed is falle þe crowne,
> Man is comeryd in synne, I crye to þi syght
> Gracyous lord, Gracyous lord, Gracyous lord come down.

Sources can be found for some of the most striking of the individual
lines in these passages (the first line of the second quotation, for instance,
derives from an antiphon sung on Holy Thursday),[29] but as a whole
Contemplacio's prologue in its majesty and subtlety eludes scholarly
analysis: it is more reminiscent of *Piers Plowman* than of the normal
limpid style of the mystery plays.

Following Contemplacio's prologue, the angels add their prayers on
man's behalf, an intercession described in the *Meditationes vitae Christi*,[30]
whereupon God, moved by 'þe porys lamentacion', by the supplica-
tions of his prophets, and by his 'contryte creaturys' who 'crye all for
comforte', announces the time of reconciliation; whereupon, again
as in the *Meditationes*, the debate between the Four Daughters begins.
In origins this famous debate was theological in purpose, being an
allegorical method of displaying how, as in Anselm's analysis of the
nature of the Redemption, God's justice was reconciled with His
mercy. The placing of this debate, however, in the context of a
dramatised history of man from the creation of the world, and immediately after the prayers of Contemplacio and of the angels, leads to a
different emphasis. Since the redemption has already been prophesied,
the issue is not primarily whether man should be redeemed but when.
Therefore, though Justice continues to insist that man should not be
redeemed, 'xulde he be savyd, nay, nay, nay', Mercy's pleas are not
chiefly grounded in theologically based arguments, but are an immediate response to man's desperate recognition of his own misery and
cry for help, 'All hefne and erthe crye ffor mercy'. They thus relate
to the theological analysis of whether God became man at the most
fitting time: for St Thomas in reply to the proposition that God
should have become incarnate from the beginning, quoted the *Glossa
ordinaria* on Galatians iii. 19, where it is said that God delayed so that
man 'cognita sua infirmitate, clamaret ad medicum, et gratiae quaereret
auxilium'.[31]

The debate between the Four Daughters of God had undoubtedly been a very successful literary method of attributing the reasoning of scholastic theologians to the godhead without indecorum: Milton by rejecting the device laid himself open to the well-known charge of making God turn school divine. But we may wonder how prudent it was to go a step further and present these figures upon the stage, even though morality plays and the portrayal of these personifications in art had prepared the way.[32] There was also the further problem in this play that the Trinity was also represented, most probably in the shape of three identical figures (the presence of the Trinity was not inescapable for in Greban's *Passion* it is God the Father alone who resolves the Daughters' arguments).[33] There would seem to be only two ways of dealing with all these hazards: one, that adopted by the French dramatists, was to present the scene with such learned formality that it did not spring to dramatic life; the other to make it so poetically moving that the abstract question of propriety could not relevantly come to mind: this is what the author of the *Ludus Coventriae* has done.

Whilst structurally the substance of the episode is the traditional debate, the author has made his poetic theme the encounter between man's wretchedness and God's burning love, a theme which illumines the play with flickers of sublimity. Justice says of the hypothetical redeemer, 'Hes love nedyth to be ful Ardent/that for man to helle wolde gon'; the Holy Ghost, who is the love of the Father and the Son,[34] says to Christ, 'I love to ʒour lover xal ʒow lede'; and the Son urges speed upon Gabriel in his mission to the Virgin, 'I have so grett hast to be man thore'. Man's urgent need, God's burning love, Christ's loving delight in the Virgin, the Virgin's love for Christ, all unite in one large web of reciprocal charity. As in the prologue of Contemplacio, the author writes with grandeur, freedom and imaginative confidence, and one feels again that he had learned of poetic possibilities from Langland.

The scene of the Annunciation which follows Gabriel's despatch to earth is not so splendidly written but continues the grandeur of the thought. The author resumes the theme of the anxious and expectant universe with the help of a passage from one of St Bernard's homilies on the *Missus est*, in which he himself dramatically intervenes to beg the Virgin to consent to the Incarnation:[35]

Exspectat angelus responsum: tempus est enim ut revertatur ad Deum qui misit illum. Exspectamus et nos, o Domina, verbum miserationis, quos miserabiliter premit sententia damnationis. Et ecce offertur tibi pretium salutis nostrae: statim liberabimur si consentis. In sempiterno Dei Verbo facti sumus omnes, et ecce morimur: in tuo brevi responso sumus reficiendi, ut ad vitam revocemur. Hoc supplicat a te, o pia Virgo, flebilis Adam cum misera sobole sua exsul de paradiso, hoc Abraham, hoc David. Hoc caeteri flagitant sancti Patres, patres scilicet tui, qui et ipsi habitant in regione umbrae mortis. Hoc totus mundus tuis genibus provolutus exspectat. Nec immerito quando ex ore tuo pendet consolatio miserorum, redemptio captivorum, liberatio damnatorum: salus denique universorum filiorum Adam, totius generis tui. Da, Virgo, responsum festinanter. O Domina, responde verbum, quod terra, quod inferi, quod exspectant et superi.

This passage is closely paraphrased in Gabriel's speech to the Virgin:

> Mary, come of and haste the
> And take hede in thyn entent
> Whow þe holy gost, blyssyd he be,
> A-bydyth þin answere and þin assent . . .
>
> Fferther more take hede þis space
> Whow all þe blyssyd spyrytys of vertu
> Þat are in hefne by-ffore goddys face
> And all þe gode levers and trew
> That Are here in þis ertheley place,
> thyn owyn kynrede þe sothe ho knew,
> And þe chosyn sowlys þis tyme of grace
> Þat Are in helle and byde rescu,
>
> As Adam, Abraham, and davyd in fere
> And many othere of good reputacion
> Þat þin Answere desyre to here
> and þin Assent to þe incarnacion.

To this plea (in which the theme of Contemplacio's Prologue is resumed) Mary gives the simple biblical answer, 'Se here þe hand-mayden of oure lorde'. The play then ends with Gabriel's jewelled farewells in which by anticipation he addresses the Virgin by the eulogistic titles with which the Church later honoured her, 'trone of þe trinyte', 'qwen of hefne', 'empres of helle' and 'modyr of mercy', and with the angelic singing of a hymn based on the *Ave*.[36] All the other cycles treat the Annunciation simply and unremarkably. The author of the *Ludus Coventriae* alone by a brilliant combination of different sources has succeeded in transposing it into a cosmic setting and preserving some of the mysterious grandeur that great devotional writers had seen in the event.

The order of the next two scenes, those of Joseph's Doubts and the Visit to Elizabeth, is variable in the cycles. The traditional order, established by the gospel harmonies and the *Protevangelium* and generally followed in medieval art and literature, was that the Visit to Elizabeth immediately succeeded the Annunciation (as it seems to in Luke), and after this came the episode of Joseph's Doubts (which in historical time must have occurred some months later).[37] The Towneley cycle and the *Ludus Coventriae*, however, reverse this order (in the latter the arrangement seems to be the result of revision). The reason for the departure from tradition is clearly to allow the boisterous and ironic treatment of Joseph's Doubts to be followed by a more overtly pious and solemn recognition of Mary's sanctity in her encounter with Elizabeth. From the literary and doctrinal point of view this unhistorical arrangement makes the better pattern.

According to this pattern the serenity and gravity of the scene of the Annunciation are fractured by the episode of Joseph's Doubts, in which Joseph seems to turn into the stock character of the aged cuckold. This interpretation has appeared gross and irreverent to many people nowadays, and the *Ludus Coventriae* play, in which this idea is developed in a most spirited way, has seemed especially repugnant. This cannot in itself be called an anachronism in modern taste, for the same hesitancy is found in many medieval writings. Even the plain meaning of the gospel text then aroused scruples, and it was said that Joseph determined to leave his wife, not because he doubted her virtue, but because he believed himself unworthy to be her companion.[38]

The implications of Matthew i. 19 were first developed in the *Protevangelium*, in which Joseph's reluctance to marry a young wife at the time of the Betrothal prepared the way for his later conviction that he had been deceived. This is the only one of the apocryphal gospels to treat the theme with cynical realism and also to present an actual conversation between Joseph and Mary. In the Gospel of the Pseudo-Matthew Mary is sheltered from accusation in that the dialogue takes place only between Joseph and her attendants, and in the *De nativitate* the theme is reduced to Joseph's one rather cautious monologue. The narrative of the *Protevangelium* had, however, been further amplified and enlivened in the dramatic dialogues embedded in eastern sermons on the Annunciation.[39] The most striking of these is the long dialogue in one of Germanus's sermons for the Annunciation in which much is made of the fact that Joseph's mortification at seeing his wife with child is aggravated by the malicious gossip that surrounds him. It is likely that, as La Piana has suggested, this treatment of Joseph was influenced by the traditions of the mime, which continued to flourish in Constantinople long after the fall of Rome.[40] Eastern dialogues of this kind became known to the west through colonies of Greek monks in central and southern Italy, and were undoubtedly available to the authors of the mystery plays, as they had been much earlier to the poet of the Old English *Advent*.

Just as the eastern Fathers understood St Joseph's predicament in the light of the contemporary adultery mime, so the English medieval dramatists developed the scene with the help of the large complex of secular literature that dealt with the wretchedness of marriage (which we have already mentioned in connection with Noah and his wife). In accordance with these satiric or burlesque traditions, Joseph sees himself in the contemptible role of an old man, feeble and impotent, married to a wanton young wife who has taken an equally young lover in his place. The plays all begin with Joseph's return after several months' absence and his seeing that Mary is pregnant; and the immediate vitality of the plays lies in Joseph's spirited disbelief in the explanations given him of Mary's virtue. For instance, in the *Ludus Coventriae*, when Mary replies to Joseph's questioning with the riddling answer that the child is God's son and his, he objects, 'God dede nevyr jape so with may', thus taking her words in their crudest sense, as though she were saying that the Christian God had adopted the habits of Jove. Again, when one of the attendants (whom Mary had brought with her from the Temple) tries to defend her mistress by referring to the angel's visit, Joseph's mind leaps to what one might call a fabliau-style interpretation:

> An aungel! allas, alas, fy for schame,
> Ʒe syn now in þat Ʒe to say,
> to puttyn an Aungel in so gret blame.
> Alas, alas, let be, do way,
> It was sum boy be-gan þis game
> þat clothyd was clene and gay,
> And Ʒe Ʒeve hym now an Aungel name.

Though the source for this is the Gospel of the Pseudo-Matthew, where Joseph replies, 'Potest enim fieri ut quisquam se finxerit angelum domini et deceperit eam',[41] it acquires in the *Ludus Coventriae* a fabliau aura: one is reminded, for instance, of the story in the *Decameron* of a friar with evil designs who deceived a vain and gullible woman by telling her that the angel Gabriel wished to visit her at night, and came himself disguised with some finery.[42]

The other important element in the plays is the monologue of Joseph in which he generalises about the untrustworthiness of women and mourns his old age, often giving warning to the audience from his supposed experience. Abundant examples can be found in all the plays of this generalising of the situation: in Towneley Joseph says:

> She is with chyld, I wote never how,
> Now, who wold any woman trow?
> Certys no man that can any goode.

in Chester:

> God let never an old man
> take him a yonge woman,
> ne set his hart her upon,
> lest he beguiled be!

whilst in the *Ludus Coventriae* Joseph gives a savage warning in which, as in late medieval complaints of old men, images drawn from archery are used with obscene meaning:[43]

> ȝa ȝa all Olde men to me take tent,
> and weddyth no wyff in no kynnys wyse;
> þat is a ȝonge wench be myn a-sent
> ffor doute and drede and swych servyce.
> Alas, Alas, my name is shent,
> all men may me now dyspyse
> and seyn, 'olde cokwold þi bow is bent
> newly now after þe frensche gyse'.

It is clear from these speeches that Joseph sees himself as standing in the long tradition of men who have been deceived by women: the phrase 'I am begiled' echoes through all the plays and becomes almost a refrain in York. Joseph as it were imagines himself married to the type of character whom we have already seen in Noah's wife, and of whom the ancestor and archetype was Eve. By the style therefore the dramatists have obliquely expressed the point that was made explicitly in the *Protevangelium*, where Joseph says: 'Who hath done this evil in mine house and hath defiled the virgin? Is not the story of Adam repeated in me? for as at the hour of his giving thanks the serpent came and found Eve alone and deceived her, so hath it befallen me also.' With the light cast upon the plays by this quotation it is possible to be yet more precise about the nature of Joseph's misconception: his suspicions are an ironic mirror image of the truth, for he thinks that he is married to the first Eve, whereas in fact he is married to the second.

That Mary was the second Eve was such an ancient and traditional commonplace of religious thought that it would be scarcely necessary for the dramatists to formulate it within the plays. Nevertheless, as we have seen, the York and Chester authors indicate the first half of the antithesis in the plays of the Fall of Man; the other cycles state it more plainly in the plays of the Annunciation. In the *Ludus Coventriae* Gabriel addressed the Virgin in a famous pun which epitomised this reversal, 'here þis name Eva is turnyd Ave',[44] whilst in God's doctrinal prologue to the Towneley Annunciation the beautiful symmetry of the divine plan of redemption is set out succinctly:

> Ffor reson wyll that ther be thre,
> A man, a madyn, and a tre.
> Man for man, tre for tre,
> Madyn for madyn; thus shal it be.

Whilst theologically the pattern of the first and second Eve is made complete at the Annunciation, the dramatists have contrived that the climax should be extended to the plays of Joseph's Doubts: this they have achieved by bringing the two worlds of Fall and Redemption into a dramatic collision. Doctrinally Joseph's doubts serve by ironic reversal to emphasise that the Virgin is the second Eve, and for this reason the *Ludus Coventriae*, which had most exalted the role of the Blessed Virgin, also most elaborates (even to the point of obscenity) Joseph's conviction that he has been deceived.

It is finally worth noting that the dramatic dialogues in the eastern sermons served exactly the same purpose, though the idea is there less subtly executed. These dialogues are always embedded in sermons which eloquently glorify the Virgin, and Germanus, the author of one of the dialogues most apparently influenced by the conventions of the mime, is famed as one of the great eastern promoters of the cult of the Virgin. It is therefore reasonable to look for religious significance in what at first sight seems a tasteless imitation of burlesque, and it is in fact easy to find. In the dialogue of Germanus, for instance, Joseph's threats of vengeance against Mary's supposed lover have an entirely secular ring, but the religious point is made explicit in Joseph's condemnation of Mary: 'Now will I say, Mary, that thou dost follow in the footsteps of thy mother Eve. Just as she was sent forth from Paradise because she opened her ears to a whisperer, so shalt thou, guilty as thou art, be thrust out of my house.'[45] The important literary difference between eastern dialogues and medieval plays, however, is that in the former Mary as well as Joseph thinks of the surrounding world as that of the adultery mime. It is not just that Joseph reacts with angry suspicion but Mary too behaves as though a jealous husband were the norm: on one occasion she warns Gabriel that Joseph will not like her to talk alone to a stranger,[46] on another she dismisses him with contemptuous words: 'Before the aged man come, depart from my house; leave here, lest he seize thee, for he is of jealous mood.'[47] By contrast in the mystery plays the fabliau world exists only in Joseph's imagination, while Mary still lives in the spotless and serene world of the Annunciation. This discrepancy between Mary's real world and Joseph's cynical fantasies makes the religious pattern much more pointed: as Mary says in the York play, where she turns Joseph's refrain upon himself, 'yhe ar begiled'. With the help of this standard of comparison it can therefore be seen that the plays of Joseph's Doubts, which at first sight seem dramatically and aesthetically crude, are on a more careful reading amongst the most delicate and masterly works in the cycles.

The two cycles to place the Visitation after the episode of Joseph's Doubts conclude the latter with a brief scene of forgiveness and reconciliation (in York this is too perfunctorily done to deserve mention and in Chester it does not occur at all). This subject is ritually treated as befits the previous patterned treatment of the offence, but it catches a little of the tenderness and delight that sometimes accompany similar scenes at the end of a Breton Lay. In Towneley Mary's unwavering affection expressed in her reply to Joseph's conventional 'what chere' with 'The better, sir, that ye ar here' is well done, as is also Joseph's excited pleasure after Mary's solemn act of forgiveness, 'A, what I am light as lynde!' In the *Ludus Coventriae* Joseph's delight in being forgiven is more gravely but no less touchingly conveyed: 'Gramercy myn owyn swete wyff,/gramercy myn hert, my love, my lyff', and these terms of affection follow fittingly upon the little action of reconciliation in which Mary refuses to let Joseph kiss her feet, offering her mouth instead: in this way the full significance of their chaste but loving marriage is restored.

The tone of joyfulness in the Towneley reconciliation is continued in the Visitation, in which Elizabeth receives her kinswoman's visit with a warmth that expresses itself in recurrent terms of endearment: 'blyssed blome', 'dere hart', 'dere derlyng' and 'freely foode'; whilst

Elizabeth's statement in Luke i. 44, 'the babe leaped in my womb for joy', turns into 'The chyld makys Ioy, as any byrd', a simile which, like 'light as lynde', is not in itself original but is made particularly evocative by the new context. Whereas Towneley in this scene sustains the mood of the reconciliation, the *Ludus Coventriae* reverts to the manner of the Annunciation: here Elizabeth addresses Mary, not with human endearments, but with some of the most august of her later typological titles, such as 'trone and tabernakyl of þe hyȝ trinite', and by the significant adaptation of the biblical phrase *mater domini* to the supreme theological title of the Virgin, *modyr of god*, which is three times repeated. Above all the sense of the Annunciation is daringly recapitulated in one fine line, 'Ther I conceyvid god At my consent-ynge'. The *Ludus Coventriae* is also the most successful in dealing with the *Magnificat*. Mary's song of praise, which the Church repeated every day at vespers, is included in all the cycles, whether in translation, as in Towneley and Chester, or in Latin as in York. The *Ludus Coventriae* finds an effective compromise between naturalism and liturgical associations by an antiphonal arrangement of quatrains, in which Mary speaks the first two lines in Latin, and Elizabeth then chimes in for the next two lines with an English paraphrase. The result of this small literary *tour de force* is dignified and moving.

This theological elevation in the play of the *Ludus Coventriae* is necessary since it stands between Joseph's Doubts and another play of similar type, the Trial of Joseph and Mary. The *Ludus Coventriae* is unique in dramatising this apocryphal subject, which is found in the *Protevangelium* and the Gospel of the Pseudo-Matthew, and in medieval narratives founded upon the latter, such as, in England, the stanzaic Lives of the Virgin and Lydgate's *Life of our Lady*.[48] Outside these narratives, this was an uncommon subject: though frequent in eastern art, it is extremely rare in the art of the west, and none of the Continental cycles, however ample, include it. According to the Pseudo-Matthew, the priests of the Temple heard a rumour that Mary was with child, and, since both she and Joseph had taken vows of virginity, they were brought before the high priest that it might be seen whether Joseph had broken his vow or Mary was guilty of adultery. The method of proof was that both should drink a special bitter water (as described in Numbers v) and walk seven times round the altar: a guilty person would not emerge from this test without some discoloration or disfigurement of face. The English vernacular narratives follow this account closely, except that in accordance with standard principles of adaptation the high priest is called a bishop.

However, in one of the most striking examples of the deliberate dissolving of historical time in the plays, the author of the *Ludus Coventriae* has transformed the scene. The setting has become a medieval ecclesiastical court and the characters have been increased in number to conform to the demands of this transformation (in contrast to the dramatic method of French dramatists, English writers rarely present additional characters). There is the bishop who presides over the court, two learned clerics (*legis doctores*) who sit with him as assessors, a summoner to bring the accused before the court, and, as in all cases of alleged adultery, two witnesses to give evidence that the accusation is a matter of common knowledge. So firmly is the contemporary legal setting established that the actual nature of the test, which is more reminiscent of the magic chastity tests common in romances of fabliau type,[49] oddly does not seem to jar with the realistic legal procedures.

The play opens with a prologue of the Summoner who, no doubt addressing the audience, summons a long list of people with comic alliterative names to attend the court, Malkyn milkduck, Lucy liar, Laetitia little trust, Meg merry widow, and many more. At the same time he characterises himself in traditional satiric fashion as an adept in bribery, at a later point asking openly for *mede*[50] and here, more obliquely, urging those summoned to make their coins jingle effectively in their purse: 'And loke ʒe rynge wele in ʒour purs/Ffor ellys ʒour cawse may spede þe wurs.' Jests about purses are a commonplace of anti-clerical satire of the Middle Ages: Chaucer's Summoner who warned his victims not to worry about the penalty of excommunication, 'But if a mannes soule were in his purs;/For in his purs he sholde ypunysshed be', stands with the Summoner of the *Ludus Coventriae* in the long line of tradition. Such passages of contemporary satire are used with reserve in the mystery plays, but, unless over-expanded as in the Towneley Last Judgment, fall satisfactorily into place.

The Summoner in his address to those accused of sexual faults is also coarsely familiar and obscene, but by no means as consistently obscene as the two remarkable characters in the play, the first and second detractor. These are both witnesses and backbiters in one, their legal function being that of witnesses, but their character being understood in the light of the stock sermon type of the backbiter, for they show an agile tongue and malicious delight in the spreading of malicious rumour, though they lack the backbiter's traditional cloak of hypocrisy.[51] To them the report that Mary is with child is a piece of juicy scandal, and they mull over it with open relish and obscene repartee, the one favouring the view that Joseph is a lecherous old man unable to resist the delights of a young bride, the other preferring the view that Mary, like all young women, is lecherous by nature and has taken a handsome young lover. The author in the creation of this dialogue showed spirited inventiveness and considerable ingenuity, particularly in the following jeering speeches addressed to Mary in the course of the trial:

1us *detractor* In Ffeyth I suppose þat þis woman slepte
                With-owtyn all coverte whyll þat it dede snowe,
                And a flake þer of in to hyre mowthe crepte
                And þer of þe chylde in hyre wombe doth growe.

2us *detractor* Than beware, dame, for this is wel i-knowe,
                whan it is borne, yf þat þe sunne shyne,
                it wyl turne to watyr ageyn, as I trowe,
                for snow on to watyr doth evyr more reclyne.

This sceptical scoffing is based upon the story of the snow-child, current in Latin poetry between the tenth and twelfth centuries (including the wittily written *Modus Liebinc* amongst the *Cambridge Songs*) and later in French fabliaux.[52] It is the story of a merchant who, returning to his wife after a long absence, finds her with a small baby. His wife, frightened by his anger, then makes the excuse that one day when she was thirsty she drank some snow and thus conceived. Five years later the merchant took the child on a voyage with him and gave him as a surety to another merchant. Returning alone, he explained to his wife that the snow-child (*nivis-natus*) simply melted away when sitting in a hot sun. The author of the *Ludus Coventriae* has moulded this fabliau plot to provide the detractors with insolent, taunting fantasies.

Though the author has drawn upon fabliau traditions in the depiction of the detractors, they have not been given fabliau personalities as had Noah's wife or Joseph. Rather, they seem inhuman figures, like the vice or other evil characters in the morality plays: they show the same enormous zest, witty inventiveness, cold glee, and unmotivated delight in malice. There is here the first adumbration of a pattern later to become fully revealed, namely that when Christ or His family or His representatives (for instance, the Holy Innocents) encounter wickedness, it is in the form of a delight in malignity, which is communicated through the vivacity and unchecked abundance of what the wicked say. But always this viciousness, even if obscenely expressed, fails to leave any stain upon the victims, but rather increases their stature. In the Trial Mary, who in the preceding play had been addressed as *modyr of god*, endures such obscenities as the Summoner's leering jibe, 'Ffayre mayde . . . dede not þe Archere plese ȝow ryght well?'[53] From the dramatic point of view the audience, appalled by such horrific blasphemy, is made more imaginatively aware of Mary's purity than by the more formal praise of her virginity that had preceded. As in the play of Joseph's Doubts, the author has taken the opportunity of pointing the doctrinal significance of the Virgin and of enhancing her virtue by placing her in sharp contrast to the satirical fabliau style of the fallen world.

The sequence of events begun by the prophecies reaches its climax in the Nativity; but this event, so stupendous in religious significance, was extremely difficult to present upon the stage. A consideration of the plays shows the dramatists struggling with intractable material and only the York dramatist successful. There were two possible approaches to the birth of Christ. One was through the apocryphal gospels and the *Legenda aurea*, which seek to convey the magnitude of the event by surrounding it with a crowd of strange happenings and marvellous portents. The other was through the *Meditationes vitae Christi*, which by concentration upon the realistic circumstances of the birth itself, aims to arouse a love for the Christ-Child and compassion for Him, born as He was into poverty and hardship. The *Ludus Coventriae* and the Chester cycle adopt the former method, York the latter.

The bolder of the two plays based upon the apocryphal gospels is that of the *Ludus Coventriae*, in which the theme of scepticism rebuked is pursued. The first example is the miracle of the cherry tree which bows down to the Virgin's hands, a miracle now well-known from the Cherry Tree Carol.[54] In origin this miracle is one of those which, according to the Pseudo-Matthew, occurred during the flight into Egypt, and in this context its purpose was to demonstrate the divine power of the Christ-Child.[55] How it became transferred to the journey to Bethlehem with the new purpose of demonstrating Mary's virgin innocence is not known. The re-modelling, however, may show some eastern influence, for Joseph's bitter retort to the Virgin's request for some of the cherries growing high upon a tree, 'lete hym pluk ȝow cheryes [þat] begatt ȝow with childe' (or in the carol, 'Let him pluck thee a cherry/that brought thee with child) recalls similarly designed rebukes in the eastern dialogues.[56] This brief episode in the *Ludus Coventriae* is quite well done and serves to provide dramatic dialogue to accompany the journey to Bethlehem, but it would of course only be fitting in a cycle that did not contain either the play of Joseph's Doubts or the Trial of Joseph and Mary.[57]

The second and much more substantial illustration of scepticism rebuked is the episode of the midwives, which takes up almost two-thirds of the play. This story, found in variant forms in both the *Protevangelium* and the Gospel of the Pseudo-Matthew, seems to be designed upon the pattern of the two thieves crucified with Christ, the one who believes and the other who does not; whilst the conduct of the sceptical midwife who will not believe in Mary's perpetual virginity until she has touched is clearly modelled on that of Thomas and the resurrected Christ. Doctrinally the point of the presence of the midwives is to emphasise that Mary in her miraculously painless childbirth did not need the help necessary to all other women. In the *Ludus Coventriae* Joseph goes off to search for midwives, troubled by the thought of the pains of labour, 'Travelynge women in care be bownde/ with grete throwys whan thei do grone', but returns with them to find the child already born and encompassed with light. In accordance with the version of the Pseudo-Matthew, Zelomy, the faithful midwife, then examines the Virgin but in a spirit of reverence and in eagerness to help; and afterwards in humility she describes the miracle:

> O myghtfull god, have mercy on me,
> A merveyle þat nevyr was herd be-forn
> Here opynly I fele and se,
> A fayr chylde of a maydon is born,
> and nedyth no waschynge as other don,
> Fful clene and pure for soth is he,
> with-outyn spot or ony polucyon,
> his modyr nott hurte of virgynite.

Zelomy here announces a twofold marvel: Mary has borne a child without the seal of her virginity being broken, the Child having left her body as the sun passes through glass (to quote a common persuasive image for the doctrine of *virginitas in partu*); but the Child also is spotless, without need for the bath which in iconography the midwives were often depicted as giving Him.[58] This spotlessness had already been stressed by St Bridget in her *Revelations*: 'Carnes ejus mundissimae erant ab omni sorde.'[59] The Christ-Child was thus born free from the squalid physical circumstances that attend normal birth, of which Innocent III had said, 'Turpe dictu, turpius auditu, turpissimum visu',[60] and which he had seen as the first in a long chain of disgusting phenomena that culminate in the decay of the grave. The devotional significance of the idea stands out most plainly against the background of the *De contemptu mundi* literature.

In contrast to Zelomy, Salome is sceptical of the miracle, and because she touches in this spirit of doubt, her hand when she withdraws it is withered. But she is cured of this punishment for doubt by touching the clothes of the Christ-Child, whereupon she makes the affirmation of faith which is the poetic climax of the play:

> In every place I xal telle þis
> Of a clene mayd þat god is born
> And in oure lyknes god now clad is
> Mankend to save þat was for-lorn.
> His modyr a mayde as sche was be-forn
> natt fowle polutyd as other women be
> but fayr and fresch as rose on thorn
> Lely wyte clene with pure virginyte.

The speech parallels that of Zelomy, and by means of these two devout proclamations the author evidently sought to impose a poetic pattern upon the material, just as he had contrived a thematic pattern by beginning with the miracle of the cherry tree. But, though he was not lacking in poetic awareness, nothing can make his apocryphal subject-matter aesthetically pleasing. It is not merely that nowadays it is difficult to avoid some perhaps prudish reaction to the representation of Mary undergoing a test for virginity upon the stage (however discretely this might be done), but far more importantly that the method of the apocryphal gospels, which is to discredit incredulity by a prolification of sensational miracles, seems aesthetically inadequate to the subject-matter. When accompanying the sublime miracle of God made man, trivial miracles such as that of the withered hand seem random and tasteless.

The same objections apply to the Chester play of the Nativity, in which the author has rather timidly followed the narrative in the *Stanzaic Life of Christ*, which itself combines material from the apocryphal gospels as related in Higden's *Polychronicon* and the *Legenda aurea*.[61] The play opens with the strange happening on the journey to Bethlehem, when Mary sees two kinds of people, some rejoicing, some mourning, who signify church and synagogue; the middle is the story of the midwives, here following the more pointed version of the *Protevangelium*, according to which only the sceptical midwife touched the Virgin; and the concluding section is the expositor's narrative of the wonders that accompanied the birth of Christ throughout the world, the author here having necessarily abandoned dramatisation of the narrative and keeping very close to the *Stanzaic Life of Christ*. Two charming verses in which Joseph and Mary in turn give loving reverence to the Christ-Child show that the author knew of the more imaginative approach of the *Meditationes*, but he evidently did not trust himself to conceive a whole play in this style. Fortunately the York author did.

The York play is very economically and compactly organised: there is no setting save that of the stable, no characters save Mary and Joseph. The author has dispensed with the journey to Bethlehem and with the search for lodgings, the situation being made plain through Joseph's opening prayer for God's help. So movingly is this done, however, that it is only on reflection that one becomes aware that this speech has a narrative as well as an emotional purpose. Joseph throughout is the distressed observer of the scene: he stresses the cold and dark and the ruined stable, the lack of bed and bedclothes, their great weariness; but this is not spoken in a tone of grumbling but of lament for Mary. Whilst he goes out to search for fuel the Child is born. It is only in this cycle that the author clearly intends the audience's attention to be focused upon Mary at the moment of the birth, and no doubt this was achieved, as in modern York productions, by the Blessed Virgin parting her cloak to show the Child (a wooden doll) lying upon the ground. Immediately Mary adores the Child,

> Hayle my lord God! hayle prince of pees!
> Hayle my fadir, and hayle my sone!
> Hayle sovereyne sege all synnes to sesse!
> Hayle God and man in erth to wonne!

and then, when Joseph has returned, after asking, 'O Marie! what swete thyng is þat on thy kne?', he too worships the Child.

After this very beautiful demonstration of the Virgin's painless and effortless childbirth, the author returns to the opening theme of the hard world into which Christ is born by dramatising the tender fantasy of the ox and the ass warming the Christ-Child with their breath:

> *Jos.* O Marie! beholde þes beestis mylde,
> they make lovyng in ther manere
> as þei were men.
> For-sothe it semes wele be ther chere
> þare lord þei ken.

Mar. Ther lorde þai kenne, þat wate I wele,
    they worshippe hym with myght and mayne;
    the wedir is colde, as ye may feele,
    To halde hym warme þei are full fayne
                  with þare warme breth,
    And oondis on hym, is noght to layne,
              to warm hym with.

The presence of the ox and the ass, who know their master, is a fulfilment of prophecies recited in prophets' plays and the liturgy,[62] but
their touching animal concern for the shivering baby was an invention
of the *Meditationes vitae Christi*, which one finds imitated even in
medieval art where the animals sometimes appear to be nuzzling the
Christ-Child.

The author of the York play in his lyrical treatment of the theme is
indebted partly to the *Meditationes* with its Bernardine stress upon
the poverty of the Christ-Child and the harsh circumstances of his
birth, partly to the *Revelations* of St Bridget, who had described how
the Child had been born whilst the Virgin knelt in prayer.[63] But it
would not be right to attribute the success of the York play solely to the
author's wiser choice of sources. Most Continental plays also follow
this double tradition, but are far less daring in design.[64] They produce a
cluttered effect: there will be a long scene with an inn-keeper, then a
diversion to an initial scene with the shepherds, then a return to the
birth of the Christ-Child with angels present to sing the *Gloria in
excelsis*.[65] This incessant switching no doubt reflects the possibilities of
a fixed stage and perhaps also the French liking for *entrelacement*, so
characteristic of French romances, though the same arrangement is
found in the Coventry play.[66] The unwillingness, however, to concentrate on the Nativity itself for more than a short space at a time
suggests some nervousness in the handling of the subject. In contrast
the York author, probably with the help of iconography and literature, has presented the scene with the stillness of a painting and the
gentle charm of the Nativity lyrics:[67] the result is a play which is
elegant, tranquil and moving.

Nativity Plays, II

The Adoration of the Shepherds
The Adoration of the Magi
The Purification
The Massacre of the Innocents

The dramatists in their treatment of the Nativity and of the events preceding it had a wealth of apocryphal or meditative amplifications to draw upon. The story of the shepherds, however, had gained no accretions of this kind. The basis therefore remained Luke ii. 8, 'And there were in the same country shepherds abiding in the field, keeping watch over their flock by night'. Though the idea of rustic innocence has acquired for us the many overtones of a pastoral convention unknown to the Middle Ages, there would seem to be some idyllic quality inherent in Luke's narrative, and patristic and medieval glosses, which explained that the Christ-Child was first revealed to the shepherds because they too were poor, humble and innocent,[1] confirmed these implications. The mystery plays, however, drew surprisingly little upon this idealisation of simple virtue.

The only shepherds to conform to it entirely are, not those of the Nativity sequence, but the three who guard Joachim's sheep in the *Ludus Coventriae*. After his disgrace in the Temple, Joachim withdraws to his flocks in the country and to his shepherds of 'lytel pryde'. They greet him gravely and warmly, assuring him of the welfare of his sheep: 'A welcome hedyr blyssyd mayster: we pasture hem ful wyde,/ they be lusty and fayr and grettly multyply.' When they realise Joachim's distress they are compassionate and devout, 'Sympyl as we kan, we xal for ȝow pray', and, after they have heard of the angel's message, they rejoice with Joachim in their simple way: 'We xal make us so mery now þis is be-stad/þat a myle on ȝour wey ȝe xal her us synge.' This brief scene provides an illuminating background to the treatment of the later shepherds, for it shows that medieval writers were quite capable of combining simplicity with dignity and of not confounding innocence with rude ignorance. There are no other plays that preserve this balance.

The English shepherds' plays divide roughly into two groups: those that are brief and comparatively formal though sometimes with passages of feeling simplicity and those that are large, elaborate and grotesque containing long stretches of invented comic action. The most severe and reserved is the play in the *Ludus Coventriae*, which opens immediately with the angels singing the *Gloria in excelsis*, and continues with a series of speeches in which the shepherds explain their understanding of the revelation in terms of the Old Testament prophecies. The author is evidently influenced by allegorical expositions in which the shepherds (*pastores*) mystically signified the clergy who also watch over their flocks and can penetrate to a spiritual meaning beneath the letter of the text.[2] In realistic terms the shepherds are thus incongruously learned, though there is a possibility that the eclogues of Virgil which were known throughout the Middle Ages provided for the poet at least a literary context in which the shepherd as a man of learning would not seem out of place.[3] The shepherds on their way to Bethlehem then sing a well-known hymn to the Virgin, 'Stella caeli exstirpavit',[4] and on arrival salute the Child in apostrophes which again show considerable theological understanding. The shepherds are thus entirely uncharacterised and the sole point of the play is to show the meeting point between prophecy and fulfilment.[5]

The York play opens equally formally with the shepherds rehearsing Old Testament prophecies but progresses to a more imaginative and tender conclusion. Unlike those in the *Ludus Coventriae*, the prophecies here precede the angelic revelation, and this the shepherds greet, not with instant understanding, but with colloquial shouts of astonishment; moreover, while the author is too concerned with the dignity of simple virtue to use the favourite English joke of the shepherds being puzzled by the Latin of the *Gloria* and their grotesque attempts at imitation, there is a hint of this theme when the first shepherd boasts that he could sing as well as the angel. In the climax of the play, which corresponds to the *Shrewsbury Fragments*, the shepherds offer gifts that reflect their simplicity and poverty, a brooch with a tin bell, two cobnuts on a ribbon and a hornspoon. This theme, which is common to all western European drama and is particularly frequent in late French Nativity poems, is obviously modelled upon the offerings of the three Kings; but, whereas they offer gifts that reflect their riches and Christ's divinity, the shepherds offer presents that reflect their poverty and

Christ's humanity.[6] Three themes are intertwined in the shepherds' speeches of adoration: regret for their poverty and simplicity, an affectionate delight in the Christ-Child as a baby, and a faith in His power: like the penitent thief on the Cross they can see through the humble circumstances and the suffering to God Himself:

> ii. *Pas.* þou sonne! þat shall save boþe see and sande,
> Se to me sen I have þe soght,
> I am ovir poure to make presande
> Als myn harte wolde, and I had ought.
> Two cobill notis uppon a bande,
> Loo! litill babe, what I have broght,
> And when ȝe shall be lorde in lande,
> Dose good agayne, forgete me noght.

This conclusion to the York play is infused with the devotional understanding of the annunciation to the shepherds expressed in the *Meditationes*:[7]

> Wherefore cristes innocens and childhode conforteth not
> iangeleres and grete spekeres; cristes wepynges and teris conforteth
> noȝt dissolute lawheres; his symple clothinge conforteth not hem
> that gone in proude clothynge; and his stable and cracche
> conforteth noȝt hem that loven first seetes and worldes
> worschippes. And also the aungels in cristes Nativite apperynge
> to the wakynge scheephirdes conforten non othere but the povere
> travailloures; and to hem tellen they the ioye of newe liȝt and
> noȝt to the riche men that haven her conforte here.

The end of the York play therefore perfectly matches the tone of the preceding Nativity.

While the meditative tone of the conclusion of the York play resumes that of the Nativity, in the Coventry play a meditative interpretation of the Nativity is achieved largely through the treatment of the shepherds.[8] The actual Nativity dialogue here consists of only fifteen lines sandwiched between two comparatively long shepherds' scenes: and, whilst these lines contain a brief adoration of the Child by Mary and Joseph, some emphasis upon the cold and a reference to the animals warming the Christ-Child with their breath, the episode is far too short to carry the necessary weight. But Mary's lament, 'A! Josoff, husebond, my chyld waxith cold,/ And we have noo fyre to warme hym with', is given intensity of meaning by the shepherds' previous complaints (three times made) about the bitterly cold night.

This theme of hardship is resumed in the nature of two of the gifts: one shepherd offers his hat, another his mittens. These gifts to clothe the naked are accompanied by speeches of naïve charm:

> Now, hayle be thow, chyld, and thy dame!
>   For in a pore loggyn here art thow leyde,
> Soo the angell seyde and tolde us thy name;
>   Holde, take thow here my hat on thy hedde!
> And now off won thyng thow art well sped,
> For weddur thow hast noo nede to complayne,
> For wynd, ne sun, hayle, snoo and rayne.

Between the shepherds' first remarks about the coldness of the night and the offering of the gifts of covering for the child there occur some of the traditional elements of the shepherds' plays. Prophecies are quoted, though there is perhaps a faint suggestion that these prophecies are not so much learned information as the kind of traditional folk wisdom that is passed down from father to son. The shepherds are also ignorant of Latin and misrepeat the words of the *Gloria*, though the author refrains from introducing the embellishment of the ludicrous quarrelling born of self-assertive ignorance. Nevertheless, despite the predominantly meditative tone, elements of the allegorically learned and comically grotesque lurk in this play. The gift of the shepherd's hat, for instance, is obviously very different in tone from the detail in the *Meditationes* of the Virgin removing her veil in order to provide a covering for the Child. Therefore, whilst the episodes of the shepherds are undoubtedly meditative in function, they teeter on the border between the sweetly comic and the grotesque.

The other three plays, Chester and the alternatives in Towneley, are entirely different in tone and design. In these the authors have given a large part of each play to establishing the shepherds before the story of the annunciation begins: the construction resembles that of some of the *Canterbury Tales*, such as the Merchant's or Pardoner's, in which the borrowed plot provides a sequence of rapid and important action in about the last third of the tale. The chronological position of the shepherds' plays is unusual in the cycles, for the action that takes place before the angelic annunciation belongs to the old world before Christ is born, and the cycle has therefore moved back in time (Coventry and French plays of course preserve correct chronological order by dividing the subject of the shepherds into two parts with the Nativity inter-vening). It is important to remember this regression in time, as it is clearly the intention of the dramatists to show something of the old world before Christ is born; but the methods by which this is done are unusual in the cycles.

The plays all begin with long explanatory monologues. In the Chester play the first shepherd begins with a self-congratulatory monologue in which he sets out his skills in curing sheep-diseases, and he is followed by the second shepherd who describes how he uses his wife's cooking utensils for brewing medicaments when her back is turned. In the *Prima pastorum* the first shepherd begins the play by lamenting that all his sheep have died of *rot* (a specific disease). It has already been well pointed out by Professor Kolve that this theme has religious associations, those of Christ as physician and Christ as the good shepherd.[9] The reference to *rot*, however, also has a realistic and topical appearance, since outbreaks of murrain throughout the Middle Ages had accompanied the successive outbreaks of plague. There could also be hints of a further meaning in this topicality. In a satirical approach, now more familiar to us from the *Shepherds' Calendar* and *Lycidas*, Petrarch in his sixth and seventh eclogues had drawn upon the details of the contemporary murrain to satirise the corruption of the Church.[10] If this type of allegory were in the mind of the dramatists, the sheep dying of *rot* would be mankind before the Incarnation. It may seem more likely that there are hints of this in the *Prima pastorum*, in which the first shepherd has lost all his flock, than in Chester, where the shepherds are confident of their pharmaceutical skills. But the moral position of the Chester shepherds is also, as we shall see, ambivalent.

The shepherds talk about their excellence in this craft but with suspiciously boastful exaggerations: the first shepherd, for instance, announces immediately that there is no better shepherd than he 'from comelie Conway unto Clyde' (i.e. anywhere). The only things that they actually do, however, are to eat and take part in the sport of wrestling. What Wilmotte called an extraordinary gastronomic interest is displayed in the shepherds' plays and in the Nativity poetry of many places.[11] Wilmotte suggested an association with the Roman Saturnalia,[12] but Professor Kolve's theory of a connection with the Christmas feasting after the Advent fast is far more plausible.[13] The use made of eating or of the gastronomic list varies from work to work:[14] in general it evidently serves to root the shepherds very firmly in realistic material enjoyments, corresponding perhaps to Jean Michel's shepherds' scene, in which the shepherds linger over, not the delights of food, but of nights spent with shepherdesses. Within the harsher, satirical tone of Towneley and Chester, however, the shepherds' feast has perhaps further overtones. For it becomes clear that the shepherds are more interested in feeding themselves than in feeding their flocks, a duty semantically indicated by the Latin word *pastor*, and within religious allegory by Christ's command to St Peter, 'Pasce oves meas'.[15] The mood of the Towneley and Chester shepherds' scenes reminds one of Breughel's *Land of Cokayne*, in which the peasants are stretched out in lazy sleep around a table laden with food. Breughel has imposed an atmosphere of coarse repulsiveness upon the traditional never-never-land of abundant food.[16]

If there is a similar atmosphere in the Chester play, it would follow that the dramatist intended a contrast between the three shepherds and Gartius, who alone is actively caring for the sheep. It is not quite clear whether the Chester author, like the Wakefield Master, has conceived the *pastores* as small farmers, who have in their joint employ a boy to guard their sheep, or whether they are all employees of a lord, the boy then being a groom who would work with them and under their supervision: the boy's hint that he has difficulty in getting his wages out of them (cf. l. 232) suggests the former. At any rate it is clear that it is not the *pastores* who are keeping watch by night,[17] but the boy; and he, though impudent, is conscientious in his care for the sheep and satisfied with his lot. The boy's contempt for the shepherds and their dirty food ('the grubbs thereon do creepe') and his abusive dismissal of them, 'To the devill I all you betake', seems in the play to be dramatically well-founded in their lazy self-indulgence. This understanding of the relationship of Garcius to the shepherds would accord well with the interpretation of Professor Kolve, who sees in the wrestling-match, in which the boy overthrows each of the shepherds in turn, the allegorical pattern of Christ's victory,[18] a victory which, one might add, had already been foreshadowed in the defeat of Goliath by David, 'that Shephard with his Sling', as Herod calls him in the next play.

The moral distinctiveness of the shepherds' boy is further indicated in the second half of the play which deals with the angels' message and the visit to the Christ-Child: here the symmetrical arrangement makes the boy the leader, a privilege more often given, as in Coventry, to the third shepherd. In Chester each step forward in religious understanding is taken first by the boy. When the star first appears, the shepherds speaking in turn express fear and surprise: it is Gartius who instantly dedicates his life to it and recognises 'Gods might' (ll. 329–38); then, when after the angelic singing, the shepherds embark upon their comic misunderstandings of the Latin, Gartius does not at first join in, but speaks only of the feeling of delight that the words gave him.

Admittedly after that Gartius joins equally in the stupid misunderstandings, but it is again Gartius who first speaks the words that biblically
belong to the shepherds, 'Now wend we forth to Bethlem' (cf. Luke ii.
15), and again after the angel's reassurance, 'To Bedlem take we the
waye'. By the end of the play the shepherds and Gartius are of course
all equal in proclaiming their devotion to the Christ-Child and in their
resolution to lead the life of secular priests and religious, though it
may not be chance that it is the boy, who in resolving to adopt the life
of an anchorite, chooses the most contemplative form of life.

It would of course be a mistake to read the Chester shepherds' play as
though it were similar in design to the plays of Flood where the
surface realism is founded on solid religious allegory. It is immediately
clear that there is no typological characterisation in the shepherds'
play: the shepherds are not Cain nor the boy Isaac. Whilst there are
hints at religious allegory that cannot be ignored, the dramatist's main
purpose is obviously to depart from the previous stylisation of character, which might seem to show the Christ-Child born into a world
aesthetically removed from the contemporary and familiar. Sin and
virtue are reduced to size; Gartius is a dutiful shepherd, but his attitude
to life, which resembles Autolycus's 'I care for nobody no, not I',
is as indicative of an unredeemed world as is the lazy shepherds' preoccupation with food and stupid self-esteem. All therefore equally need
the unrealistic conversion to priestly orders that is brought about by
their recognition of the Christ-Child.

Insofar as there is any plot in the Chester shepherds' play before the
biblical story begins it lies in the wrestling-match: in other words the
author has invented action by drawing upon the common sports of the
peasant community. The Wakefield Master proceeds differently in
that briefly in the *Prima pastorum* and lengthily in the *Secunda pastorum*
he dramatises the type of plot that in France was the subject of independent farces. The secular plot of the *Prima pastorum* is that of the
Three Wise Men of Gotham, which now survives only as a story in jest-
books.[19] Within it, however, as a short inset, is the story of Moll and
her pitcher, which is the subject of a lost French farce,[20] and which a
little later Gil Vicente, the Portuguese dramatist, incorporated in a
Nativity play composed for performance on Christmas Day.[21] The
plot of the *Secunda pastorum* now has only a close parallel in a late
eighteenth-century ballad,[22] but in type it resembles the plot-type
involving ingenious trickery which is used in many French farces,
including the most famous of them all, *Maître Pathelin*.[23] Plots of this
kind were evidently floating ones, appearing in exempla, novellae,

jest and farces.[24] There is thus no way of telling precisely from what source or genre the Wakefield Master borrowed his plots, but, as we have already seen, he in all likelihood knew the genre of the French farces,[25] and must therefore have been conscious that he was adapting the material of farce to a religious context.

The interesting point is of course the manner in which these plots are adapted to their new context. The theme of the Wise Men of Gotham as also of Moll and her pitcher is foolishness and make-believe. These elements the Wakefield Master heavily underlines, using the second of the plots to illuminate the first. According to the jest, two shepherds quarrel over the issue of whether one of them may bring back the flock of sheep that he is about to buy over a certain bridge, part of the foolishness consisting in the fact that these sheep are as yet unbought. In the *Prima pastorum* this is elaborated: the first shepherd who has lost his sheep through *rot*, has scarcely any money to buy more sheep at the fair to replace them, yet in the quarrel he asserts that he will bring back a hundred sheep – a provocatively large number – and, further to enrage the other, acts the part of driving them on, 'Go now, bell weder'. The entire illusoriness of the situation is emphasised by the third shepherd, who sets himself up as a wise man and tells the story of Moll and her pitcher to illustrate their folly: the shepherd's hundred sheep are thus as much in the imagination as Moll's dreams of wealth, all lost when she dropped the pitcher. The third shepherd, however, is just as foolish, for to make a more telling illustration, as in the jest, he empties his sack of meal, which he then demonstrates to be as empty of meal as the heads of the other shepherds are empty of wits. At this point the author of *A Hundred Merry Tales* draws a moral: 'This tale showeth you that some man taketh upon him to show other men wisdom when he is but a fool himself.' The Wakefield Master at the same point introduces the character of Garcio to draw the same moral:[26]

> Now god gyf you care, foles all sam;
> Sagh I never none so fare, bot the foles of gotham.
> Wo is hir that yow bare, youre syre and youre dam,
> had she broght furth an hare, a shepe, or a lam,
>   had bene well.
> Of all the foles I can tell,
> ffrom heven unto hell,
> ye thre bere the bell;
>   God gyf you unceyll.

Like the Chester Gartius, Garcio is in the employ of the' shepherds, and his attitude to them is yet more pointedly contemptuous. It is again he who is looking after the sheep, and when he invites the shepherds to come and see for themselves how flourishing they are, the shepherds prefer to sit down and eat the grotesque abundance of provisions that they have brought with them. After that they are weary, and when the angel appears, far from watching their sheep they are fast asleep. The turning point in the *Prima pastorum*, however, comes much sooner than in Chester, for, once the angel has announced the Nativity, the shepherds become learned men, as they are in the *Ludus Coventriae*, and they interpret the angel's message in the light of the prophecies. The third shepherd is even able to quote the prophecy of Virgil's shepherd in the fourth eclogue in Latin. Their salutations of the Christ-Child and their offering of simple gifts mark the climax of their devotioṇ. As in Chester, there is no psychological continuity between the foolish, lazy, grumbling shepherds of the first part and the devout worshippers of Christ in the second.

More than half of the long *Secunda pastorum* is taken up by the plot of the sheep-stealing, which is contrived as a burlesque of the Nativity and antecedent themes.[27] It is as though the world before the Incarnation contained not types of the Redemption but deformed adumbrations, or, to put the matter with less seriousness, the whole episode could be considered a witty pretence at typology. There are, to begin with, clear equivalences between the plot and characters of the sheep-stealing episode and the sequence of the annunciation to the shepherds and the visit to the Christ-Child which follows. Mak (the sheep-stealer) tells the shepherds when they wake up of the supposed birth of his child; in the cottage when the shepherds arrive are Mak, the hen-pecked husband and ostensible father, his wife who has been feigning the pains of childbirth, and a lamb in the cradle. Then in the unmasking episode (which the dramatist must have invented since it is the nature of the plot that the trickster should be successful),[28] the fraud is discovered through the third shepherd's kindly wish to give the child a present: the affectionate term, 'Lytyll day starne' by which he refers to him, is of course later used of the Christ-Child and is a title proper only to Him.

The Mak episode has been compared to the sub-plot of Elizabethan drama or the anti-masque.[29] The parallel with *The Midsummer Night's Dream*, for instance, is interesting but there is the important difference that, whereas the antics of Bottom and his companions follow upon the serious love story, the sheep-stealing in the *Secunda pastorum* precedes the religious matter that it buffoons. The placing of the Mak episode is in fact important, for, whilst in one way it provides a type or rather, like the Fall of Man, an antitype of part of the Redemption, it also pretends to be in itself a fulfilment of earlier typological patterns. This is particularly clear in the relationship of Mak and his wife. Mak in his cottage is obviously a debased version of St Joseph, and like St Joseph he sees himself in the role of the unhappily married man. But his wife, who is the leading partner in the fraud, to some extent casts herself as the second Eve. Thus whilst Mak complains about the sufferings in an evil marriage, his wife is given to *sententiae* about the virtues of women: 'Yit a woman avyse helpys at the last' (her comment upon the good advice that she has given about the trick) or 'Ffull wofull is the householde/That wantys a woman.' Other figures should similarly be seen in a twofold relationship: for instance, the sheep purporting to be a baby anticipates the baby who was symbolically a lamb, but it is also a grotesque fulfilment of the lamb offered by Abel and the sheep offered in place of Isaac.

The Wakefield Master has set the story of Mak within a fairly straightforward treatment of the three shepherds. In contrast to the other plays these shepherds are genuinely suffering from oppression, truly poor and actually looking after their sheep: they are not feasting, wrestling or quarrelling. It is not that their complaints are to be taken entirely straight. The second shepherd who has a monstrously ugly wife ('She is browyd lyke a brystyll, with a sowre loten chere') and who warns the young men in the audience against marriage, is the undignified husband of anti-matrimonial satire; whilst the first shepherd who complains that taxes and the oppression of the *gentlery-men* have made him too poor to cultivate his land is speaking no more than a half-truth. But, while the shepherds' explanations of their predicament are slightly comic and rebound upon themselves, that they live a life of hardship is plain, and their sufferings cast light upon the sufferings of the Christ-Child. At the end of the play the second shepherd says compassionately of the Christ-Child, 'he lygys full cold'; but earlier in the play the effects of cold had been described in realistic detail: the shepherds complain that their feet are numb in their boots, their eyes water, and their hands are chapped. To emphasise the Christ-Child's sufferings through cold was, as we have seen, part of the meditative tradition, but it is only in this play that the actual sensations of cold are made alive to the imagination by describing them with such unelevated precision. Since the shepherds in this play deserve through their sufferings the comfort of the revelation of the Nativity, it is fitting that their speeches of adoration should be the most moving; and, whilst this is partly through their poetic quality, it is also partly because they are rooted in the earlier presentation of the shepherds: they do not have to become entirely new and different men before they worship the Christ-Child.

Whilst the shepherds in the *Secunda pastorum* are treated with more evident devotional purpose than in the *Prima pastorum* or Chester, the play is undoubtedly dominated by the Mak episode, and it is therefore not surprising that the author only supplied it as an alternative.[30] For, though the episode has a religious orientation lacking in the comic sequences of, for instance, the Rouen *Nativité*,[31] it could easily be missed by the unsophisticated, who would then understand it only as simple farce. To understand it this way would of course be great impoverishment: though quite well done, the dramatisation of the fraud is much inferior to the urbane *Maître Pathelin*, and of course crude beside Chaucer's narrative comedies. But, when understood within a religious framework its subtlety and literary self-awareness are reminiscent of Chaucer's manner and one wonders whether it may have been written for performance on some special occasion when it would have a fitting audience.

The dramatist's tone in his treatment of the shepherds in the *Secunda pastorum* is less ambiguous than in the *Prima pastorum* or in Chester, though at the point at which the third shepherd appears to accuse the others of being niggardly employers, it is less certain, and, as in the *Prima pastorum*, the shepherds are not guarding their sheep but asleep when the angel appears. In general it can be said that the authors of these three plays have put the shepherds into a morally intolerable position. In historical terms they are small farmers rather than shepherds, and their employment of a boy or groom to look after the sheep on their behalf is a practical arrangement since it leaves them with the necessary time to cultivate the arable land which they would own or hold on lease. But within the play this customary and sensible arrangement becomes morally odd, for it is necessary that the men should be called shepherds and that they should be abroad at night. But since their night wanderings serve no practical purpose, it gives them a vagabondish air and leaves them with time for senseless quarrels and feastings.[32] It is now very difficult to recapture how this would have seemed or exactly what the authors' intentions were. In Wakefield, which had grown prosperous on the cloth industry, many of the audience must also have been small farmers, and the fact that the shepherds are unnamed (or have *ad hoc* names), in contrast to Cain, who is the historical Cain first and a farmer second, must have increased their appearance of contemporaneity. Furthermore, whilst some of their grumblings about the oppression of the rich must be taken with a certain reserve (they have a slightly archaic air in that they would fit the social conditions of the late fourteenth century more appositely than those of the mid-fifteenth) and they perhaps reflect equally upon the grumbler and the rich, the complaints about maintained men are evidently genuine satire of contemporary abuse. It is clear, however, that there is no idealisation of poverty as the meditative tradition would have required: the dramatists had as sharp an eye as Langland for the portrayal of the grumbling and lazy poor. All the elements of social satire, fantasy and farce yield in every play to the idealised picture of the adoration of the Christ-Child, and this contrast is evidently the primary purpose of the design of the plays. But nowadays it is impossible to recapture the precise mood of the first part of the contrast, for whereas in other plays the key to their understanding lies in other forms of literature, in these it fairly certainly lies in life.

The Adoration of the Shepherds is followed in all the cycles by a long interwoven sequence which begins with the meeting between the Three Kings and ends with the Massacre of the Innocents. The figure of Herod dominates this sequence, but, before considering his part, it is worth briefly touching on the action which intervenes, the Adoration of the Magi, the Purification and the Flight into Egypt (the latter in York and Towneley only).

For the Adoration of the Magi it is convenient to begin with the Chester play, which provides the most learned and elaborate treatment of the subject. Since we are leaving on one side for the moment the Kings' encounter with Herod, there remain two episodes, the opening one with the appearance of the Kings and their later offering of gifts to the Child. The Chester author has here reverted to his sources for the Nativity, the *Legenda aurea* and the *Stanzaic Life of Christ*. The author begins with the fairly common tradition that the Three Kings were in the line of Balaam, whose descendants had successively kept watch for the star which their ancestor had foretold, and to whom the star appears as an answer to their prayers. The *Stanzaic Life* at this point includes an account of Balaam: the Chester author had prepared the way for this legend by his play of Balaam,[33] which is recalled not only through the extensive discussion of the prophecy but also in the Second King's reference to 'Balaak, that king so wood' (l. 19), which serves to bring to mind the whole story (in the other plays Balak is not mentioned). The star, which then appears to guide the Kings, has a Child in

193

it (l. 79), again a detail deriving from the *Legenda aurea* though not uncommon in iconography. In this cycle the form of the star obviously links it to the star of the sibyl's vision which was its type.[34] The star itself is carried by an angel, which appears to be the Chester author's variation upon an alternative tradition expounded by the *Legenda aurea*, namely that the star was in fact an angel, who had assumed this abstract form in order to be intelligible to the pagan astronomer-kings. The angel carrying the star is, however, also found in iconography, though the star does not usually then contain the Child.[35] The Kings follow the star until (again in accordance with the *Legenda aurea*), they lose sight of it, and for this reason allow themselves to be led to Herod's court.

A large part of the actual scene of the Adoration is given to exposition of the mystical significance of the gifts. According to the main tradition, which is followed in all the plays, the gold symbolises Christ's kingship, the frankincense His priestly office, and the myrrh His death. The Chester author, however, still faithfully following the *Legenda aurea*, includes two other sets of significances. One, attribted to St Bernard, and emphasised by Nicholas of Lyra,[36] was that the gifts all had a simple practical value: the gold to meet Christ's poverty, the frankincense to dispel the stench of the stable, and the myrrh as a health-giving ointment for children. The other is the fairly common moral interpretation, that the gifts in order signify love, devotion to God, and mortification of the flesh.[37] In the Chester play all this exposition is set out in plain didactic style, and the Kings seem to speak in turn as preachers unfolding the inner meaning of a text. The scene has therefore little literary merit, though it is likely that the splendid costuming of the Kings would have pleased the eye, whilst the ear listened to the doctrinal significances of the scene.

None of the other plays is so preoccupied with doctrine or with the stranger accretions to the legend. The Kings recognise the star as the fulfilment of Balaam's prophecy but, with the exception of Digby, are not his descendants; the star, in accordance with tradition, is said to be more brilliant than any other, more radiant 'Then any son that ever shone,/Or mone' as one of the Towneley Kings says, but there is no Child in it; the offerings have their standard significances as the Kings of the *Ludus Coventriae* describe: gold 'Ffor he . . . is kynge of hevyn holde', frankincense because 'of all prestys he xal be rote', and myrrh 'Ffor he xal th[o]lyn byttyr dent'. Since there is less learned discussion of the gifts, the emphasis falls rather upon the speeches of adoration, which are more formal and elevated than those of the shepherds, thus making a poetically satisfying complement to them.

In two of the cycles (Towneley and *Ludus Coventriae*) the Kings according to tradition understand and salute in the Child the mystery of the
Trinity, 'Hayll, oonefold god in persons thre!'[38] The plays vary
considerably in manner and length; by a paradox common to the
mystery plays, the Towneley play which attempts a rounded treatment
of the meeting between the Three Kings with genuine conversation,
seems dull and verbose, whilst the *Ludus Coventriae*, which gives the
Kings only short monologues appropriate to speaking pictures, is the
most effective.

The treatment of the Kings in the York cycle is unremarkable except
for one point of literary-historical interest. When the Kings arrive at the
'house' over which the star is standing, they are greeted by an *ancilla*,
who asks them, 'Whame seke ʒe syrs . . .', and, after they have explained, replies, 'Come nere, gud syris and see,/Youre way to ende is
broght'. This episode, peculiar to York, recalls the part played by the
obstetrices in the *Officium stellae*, though the initial question is evidently
modelled upon the *Quem quaeritis* addressed to the shepherds in the
Officium pastorum.[39] It is very likely that the *ancilla*, who has so mysteriously appeared here in the York cycle, was originally the *obstetrix*,
who, according to Burton's list, had played a part in the earlier version
of the Nativity. The transformation of the *obstetrix* into the more
neutral figure of an *ancilla* was then made by a reviser after the adoption
of the later Nativity play.

The subject which should follow the Adoration of the Magi according to harmonisations of the gospels is the Purification. The narrative of
Matthew ii, which gives the Adoration of the Magi and the Massacre
of the Innocents as an uninterrupted sequence, had to be reconciled
with that of Luke ii, which gives the Purification as the next event after
the Adoration of the Shepherds. The standard method of harmonising
the two accounts was to assume some delay between the departure
of the Kings and Herod's recognition that he had been deceived by them
and consequent decision to order the Massacre. During this time Mary
remained in the stable and, at the end of the forty days prescribed by the
law, went to the Temple for the ceremony of purification. Thereafter
Herod ordered the Massacre, and, warned by an angel, Mary with
Joseph and the Child fled to Egypt, returning only six years later after
the death of Herod.[40] From the purely dramatic point of view this
chronological placing of the Pucarifition disturbs the consistent
development of the story of Herod's machinations, and some of the
dramatists seem therefore to have been reluctant to follow it.

The *Ludus Coventriae* is in fact the only cycle incontrovertibly to follow the harmonisation, though two others very probably did. In the York cycle the Purification, which appears to be a late play, is out of order in the manuscript (it comes after Emmaus); but in Burton's list its place is after the Three Kings, and the reference in the play to its being forty days since Jesus was born (ll. 191–2) makes plain that this was the position intended for it by the author. In the surviving version of the Towneley cycle the Purification comes after the Massacre, but a similar reference to the passage of forty days since the Child was born shows that this cannot have been the position envisaged for it by the dramatist. This inconsistent rearrangement has obviously been influenced by the type of order found in Chester and Coventry where the Purification and the Doctors are combined in one play,[41] and Digby where the Purification also follows the Massacre (though the Prologue had outlined the events to follow in reverse order). Both Coventry and Digby deal with the chronological problems resulting from this arrangement by eliminating from the subject the idea of the purification, which was, as we shall see, only one of its three elements. With this gone there was no reason why the event should not have taken place after the return from Egypt. The Chester author, however, has not dared to make so drastic an alteration in his material, but seems rather to have chosen to be evasive. The elapse of forty days is mentioned and so also is the law of Moses, but that it is forty days from the birth of Christ is not made explicit. Moreover, since Chester is one of the cycles to show Herod's death as coming immediately upon the Massacre, that play ending with the angel's recall of Mary, the impression is left that the duration of the sojourn in Egypt could have been extremely short. Nevertheless this timid method of dealing with chronological inconsistency by blurring the issue is not very satisfactory.

Three themes combine in the plays of the Purification. The first from which the plays take their title is the ceremony prescribed in Leviticus xii for all women who have given birth. The nature of this Jewish ceremony is fully explained in the priest's opening monologue in York, but more usually it is briefly explained in dialogue between Joseph and Mary. The tone of this dialogue, however, usually derives from meditative literature, which stressed how needless purification was for Mary, since she, who bore a child in her virginity, could not be considered unclean. In her humility, however, the Virgin chose to obey the law, just as Christ had needlessly suffered the Circumcision (an event for obvious reasons omitted in the English cycles).[42] The second aspect is the offering of the first-born child to God in obedience to God's command in Exodus xiii. 2, an offering that had to be redeemed by the payment of five shekels.[43] In Christian thought the Offering of the Christ-Child upon the altar in the Temple became an anticipation of the offering upon the Cross. The third aspect was the manifestation of the Christ-Child to Symeon in his old age, this being a revelation that he had long desired.

All three themes are presented very delicately and deftly in the treatment of this subject in the *Ludus Coventriae*. The opening monologue expresses the aged Symeon's eagerness to be rid of life but yet greater longing to see the Christ-Child; a brief dialogue between Joseph and Mary briefly gives the facts and emphasises their humility; and the antiphonal salutations of Symeon and Anna to the Child are long enough to be moving but not so long (as for instance in the York play) as to seem ornate, and even the ceremony is filled with devotional feeling. The author has successfully imposed upon this scene some of the liturgical forms of Candlemas: the prayer 'Suscepimus deus misericordiam tuam',[44] the singing of the *Nunc dimittis*, and the procession with candles, which, though found only here and in Digby, had long formed part of iconographic representations of the scene.[45] But the episode is chiefly made poetically moving through its associations with the Crucifixion, which are only fully brought out in this play. The author has transferred Symeon's allusive prophecy, which in Luke follows the *Nunc dimittis*, to the beginning of the scene and has made it explicit:

> In þe temple of god, who undyrstod,
> þis day xal be offeryd with mylde mood
> which þat is kynge of Alle.
> þat xal be skorgyd and shedde his blood
> And Aftyr dyen on þe rood
> With-owtyn cawse to calle;
> Ffor whos passyon þer xal be-ffalle
> Swych a sorwe bothe sharpe and smerte
> þat as a swerd perce it xalle
> ȝevene thorwe his moderys herte.

Though the gift of myrrh foreshadowed Christ's death – the Third King had said, 'and byttyr deth xall be þy endyng' – this is the first full statement of the Passion and the emphasis upon Mary's grief establishes the devotional mood. The theme is subtly resumed in the Virgin's solemn offering of the Child upon the altar, accompanied by the prayer which ends:

But þow I offre hym ʒow be-forn,
good lord, ʒit ʒyf me hym A-ʒen
Ffor my comforte were fully lorn
If we xuld longe A-sondyr ben.

The Virgin's words ironically remind one that at the later and full
sacrificial offering her Son would not be returned to her.[46]

The *Ludus Coventriae* is the only cycle to make the Temple scene
interesting and moving and to make the Virgin the focus of interest.
Others, in particular York and Towneley, concentrate rather upon
the figure of Symeon, giving him at the outset a substantial monologue
which draws upon the traditional themes of old age. The York Symeon,
in a long speech which proceeds from complaint to a meditation upon
the prophecies, laments:

> For I ame wayke and all unwelde,
> My welth ay wayns and passeth away,
> Where so I fayre in fyrth or feylde
> I fall ay downe, for febyll, in fay;
> In fay I fall where so I fayre,
> In hayre and hewe and hyde, I say.
> Owte of this worlde I wolde I were!

and the Towneley Symeon is more explicitly detailed, drawing upon
the traditional list of the signs of old age:

> No wonder if I go on held:
> The fevyrs, the flyx, make me unweld;
> Myn armes, my lymmes, ar stark for eld,
> And all gray is my berd.
>
> Myn ees are woren both marke and blynd;
> Myn and is short, I want wynd;
> Thus has age dystroed my kynd,
> And reft myghtis all.

The contents and form of this, though not the tone, recall such lyrics as
'Le regret de Maximian'.[47] But of course these Symeons are not, like
the old men of the lyrics, figures of derision: they have the physical
weaknesses of the satiric tradition, but not the characteristic vices, such
as avarice and irascibility. On the contrary they are firm and dignified
in faith and stand in the tradition of the prophets upon whose fate the
Towneley Symeon so movingly reflects:

Bot yit I mervell, both evyn and morne,
Of old eldres that were beforne,
wheder thay be safe or lorne,
.where thay may be;
Abell, noye, and abraham,
David, daniell, and balaam,
And all othere mo by name,
Of sere degre.

The recurring association of Symeon with the Old Testament prophets derives from and is a reminder of the fact that Symeon in the traditional list of the *Ordo prophetarum* is also a prophet, and the dramatists are concerned to show here not the meeting point between prophecy and fulfilment as with the shepherds or the kings, but the actual meeting between prophet and the prophesied. The expectation and long weary waiting of the prophets and the world under the old dispensation seem to be summed up in the aged Symeon,[48] and whilst the idea of waiting and longing are not nearly so movingly expressed in his monologues as in the speech of Contemplacio, they serve something of the same purpose.

In the Chester cycle the attention is also upon Symeon but not in so illuminating a way. The author is here once again following the *Stanzaic Life of Christ*, and this accounts for the play's most startling and disconcerting features, namely the long episode of Symeon's twofold and ineffectual attempt to expunge the word 'virgin' from Isaiah's prophecy and to replace it by 'good woman'. This story, which recalls the more malicious attempt of Caesar Augustus to have the prophecy of Christ's birth erased from the statue of Jupiter upon which it had miraculously appeared,[49] is ultimately of unknown origin: it is not found in any of the usual sources of the *Stanzaic Life*.[50] It is certainly an infelicitous invention since it destroys the dignity of Symeon, and the Chester author was unwise to adopt it. The play, however, improves with the Temple scene: the offerings, which include a wax candle (here signifying, not as more commonly the 'lumen ad revelationem gentium'[51] but Mary's virginity),[52] are made with solemn clarity, and dignity is further restored by Symeon's monologue of welcome, which contains one of the better translations of the *Nunc dimittis*, and a neat rendering of the famous paradox in one of the responsories in the office for the Purification: 'Though I beare thee nowe, sweete wighte,/ thou ruleste me, as it is righte.'[53] Even this scene, however, is unimpressive when compared with that of the *Ludus Coventriae*.

The Coventry episode of the Purification is extraordinary: it extends for 550 lines, thus exceeding by a hundred the longest of the other plays on this subject, that of York. Most of this unusual length is taken up by a comic episode in which Joseph, once more imagining himself as an ill-used husband, angrily and obstinately refuses to provide the doves for the offering: according to the whim of this version the doves have to be snared not bought. Joseph therefore complains that he is too old to go hunting for birds' nests and grumbles about the hardships of being married to a young wife (the characteristic of her youth being that she is so demanding). As in the plays of Joseph's Doubts he has to be brought to his senses by an angel, and even then his tetchy recalcitrance is not quite at an end. This episode is written with humour and liveliness[54] but is indecorous in its position. For, as we have seen, the pattern of anti-matrimonial satire ends with the second Eve, and in the other cycles the last of the unhappily married men are the shepherds. To re-introduce this theme after the Nativity is therefore to disrupt one of the most important patterns of the cycles. It also puts Mary into an unsuitable position. Since she is the second Eve, she is normally obedient and humble, not only towards God but also to her husband, and her submissiveness to Joseph's judgment is particularly demonstrated at this point in the other cycles: moreover she never spoke to him harshly even in the plays of the Doubts. But, since in the Coventry play Joseph behaves like a foolish, irritable old man, the Virgin necessarily has to address him in a fairly tart manner and to give him sharp commands. This obliteration of the religious pattern took place in the sixteenth century and it is of historical interest to observe that there was then an author at work who was sensitive to the literary style of the cycles but blind to the relationship of this to the underlying theological and devotional design.

It is worth comparing the treatment of Joseph in the Coventry Purification with that in the York and Towneley plays of the Flight into Egypt. Though these plays are referred to as the Flight, they in fact deal only with the preparations: there is no dramatisation in extant English cycles of the Flight itself with the various apocryphal miracles which happened on the way,[55] except that Chester introduces as an isolated symbol the idol which fell as the Holy Family entered Egypt, this being the least random of the apocryphal wonders since it was invented as a fulfilment of Isaiah xix. 1, and became accepted by the learned.[56] The preparatory scene, however, in which Joseph is warned by an angel to flee to Egypt with Mary and the Child, gave an opportunity for further characterisation of Joseph, and in some German plays, for instance, for a comic display of Joseph's apprehensive and fussy preoccupation with assembling utensils and food for the journey.[57] The general situation of course resembles that invented by the author of the Coventry Purification, in fact it is so close that he may have been influenced by it: for in both Joseph is ordered to do something for which he feels he is too old and weak and yet grumblingly consents.

In York, however, Joseph's alarm and irritability are limited by the author's devotional intention. Joseph is in the first place the good and protective husband upon whom Mary depends; nevertheless he is complainingly anxious about the journey, fearing that he will die before they reach its end,[58] and, when Mary, forgetting in her alarm that Joseph has said that they must flee to Egypt (l. 131), laments that she does not know where they can go, Joseph replies rather sharply, 'To Egipte talde I þe lang are'. But Joseph's irritable anxiety is controlled throughout by his sense of duty to God and his wife, and at the end, like Noah and Symeon, he finds as he obeys God's will a sudden access of strength;[59] and, as he finally carries the Christ-Child in his arms to relieve Mary of the weight, he confesses his faith in one beautiful line, 'I have oure helpe here in myn arme'.

The Towneley play, which is less devotionally conceived, provides therefore the better comparison with the Coventry Purification. Here, for instance, Joseph's reply to the angel is not one of devout obedience as in York, but of grumbling hostility, a reaction which is not diminished by the angel's rebuke, but more touchingly by the sight of Mary, to whom he says, 'Mary, my darling dere,/I am full wo for the'. This movement from grievance crossly expressed to compassion for Mary in her plight is several times repeated: at one moment Joseph even resumes the theme of the evils of marriage with his address to the audience, 'Yong men, bewar, red I:/wedyng makys me all wan', but this passes quickly again into grave expressions of comfort and sober protectiveness. There are two important differences between the Joseph of this play and that of the Coventry Purification. Firstly Joseph's grumbling dismay fits the facts, for meditative literature saw in the Flight a further example of affliction to be endured:[60]

In hoc etiam tribulatio erat, quod terram longinquam quam ignorabant, et per vias asperas eos ire oportebat, cum essent inhabiles ad eundum, Domina propter juventutem, Joseph vero propter senectutem, ipse etiam Puer quem portare habebant, adhuc tenerrimus erat.

Joseph's reactions can therefore be considered those of the good natural man (to borrow Professor Kolve's description of the Coventry Joseph): they represent a psychologically realistic lapse from devout patience in the face of the great hardship (itself biblically based) rather than the response of aged petulance to a ludicrous situation deliberately contrived by the dramatist. The second important difference follows from this: since Joseph retains his dignity, Mary can fittingly remain a submissive wife: in fact she leans upon him in her distress and depends upon him for advice, as when she asks, 'Dere Ioseph, what red ye?'. The picture therefore remains of an idealised marriage with its mutuality of affection and sharing of responsibility.

The three plays so far discussed, the Adoration of the Kings, the Purification and the Flight into Egypt, are all muted in tone, and to discuss them in succession may have been to obscure the fact that they provide restful passages of ceremonial and solemn quiet between the scenes dominated by the emphatically sketched fury of Herod. The raging of Herod has been made proverbial by Shakespeare's famous phrase, 'to out-herod Herod'; but the characterisation of Herod seems to have been already fixed for Chaucer and his audience, since the point of the reference to Absalom's having played the part of Herod must depend upon the discrepancy between the dandyish, love-lorn clerk who sang like a nightingale and the strident character whom he impersonated. Moreover the Coventry stage-direction, 'Here Erode ragis in the pagond and in the strete also',[61] gives the impression of prescribing a bit of burlesque action designed to meet popular taste and expectation. Unfortunately this now much-quoted stage-direction together with Shakespeare's coinage has given an impression of mindless rage and bombastic ranting, and has obscured the fact that much careful and subtle thought went into the creation of the character of Herod.

It would have been possible to present Herod as an egoistic political figure, moved to anger at hearing of a contender to his throne, and to violence in defence of it. The Herod of Arnoul Greban is of this kind and so also on a much smaller scale is the Herod of the *Ludus Coventriae*. It would also have been possible to conceive Herod as the more malign pagan ruler of the saints' lives, who is an oppressive tyrant eager to retain his power, furious when thwarted, and willing to indulge in barbarous cruelty for the sake of vengeance or his own advantage. There are in fact some hints of this stock figure in Towneley, where Herod is determined to impose the worship of his own heathen god, Mahowne, upon the people; and in German plays, where Herod has the devil as his adviser, there may also be echoes of the pattern of the saint's life.[62] But in the English cycles Herod is usually far more than either of these: his rage springs not from political fears that another king will take his throne or from an overbearing response to defiance, but from the intense hatred of one who believes himself a god and now finds that the true God has come. A long self-descriptive monologue spoken by Herod opens all the sequences, save that of Chester where the monologue is more implausibly deferred until the arrival of the Kings at Herod's court. In these monologues Herod attributes to himself fantastic and godlike powers.[63] In York Herod is 'prince of planetis', the winds and the thunder are at his bidding, and Saturn is his subject; in Coventry too he is 'the cawse of this grett lyght and thunder', and in Chester he says, 'the Sonne it dare not shyne on me/if I byd hym goe downe'. Herod is the ruler, not just of Judaea, but of the whole world: 'Lord am I of every land' he says in Towneley, 'All erthly thyng bowes to my hand', and in Chester, 'I am king of all mankinde'. Sometimes Herod's powers extend further: in the *Ludus Coventriae* he claims: 'I dynge with my dowtynes þe devyl down to helle/ffor bothe of hevyn and of herthe I am kyng sertayn', and in Coventry he asserts, 'And prynce am I of purgatorre and cheff capten of hell'. Whilst Herod's claims to rule hell may at first sight seem to indicate his devilish affiliations, and may indeed be double-edged, the more important meaning is that of a usurpation of the Virgin's title of empress of hell. Once Herod even maintains that he has created the whole universe and sustains it in being: 'For I am evyn he thatt made bothe hevin and hell,/And of my myghte powar holdith up this world rownd.'

Mingled with this blasphemous boasting is the recurrent theme of Herod's praise of his own beauty. In the *Ludus Coventriae*, for instance, he is 'þe comelyeste kynge in gleterynge golde/ʒa and þe semelyeste syre þat may be-stryde a stede', in Towneley he is 'Clenly shapen, hyde and hare,/withoutten lake', whilst the Coventry Herod makes the most extravagant claims of all:

> Beholde my contenance and my colur,
> Bryghtur then the sun in the meddis of the dey.
> Where can you have a more grettur succur
> Then to behold my person that ys soo gaye?
> My fawcun and my fassion, with my gorgis araye, –
> He thatt had the grace all-wey ther-on to thynke,
> Lyve he myght all-wey with-owt othur meyte or drynke.

The rewards of seeing Herod are here said to be those of the contemplation of the Godhead, but the more general significance of these rather surprising claims to supreme beauty is their echoing of Satan's biblically based praise of his own loveliness.[64] Perhaps no specific signal was necessary to make clear to the audience that Herod in his claims to be like God was an express image of the devil, but, if one were needed, his praise of his own beauty would certainly provide it. The dramatists have thus resumed the theme of the Fall of the Angels by making Herod repeat the sin of Satan, and the ambition to be as God is shown in its full emptiness and folly.

This unrealistic treatment continues in the scenes between Herod and the Kings. The point of these plays should be Herod's duplicity, his concealment of an evil design behind fair words; but in fact, in all the plays save the *Ludus Coventriae* and Coventry, Herod reveals himself as so envious and arrogant that in realistic terms the Kings could not have needed the angel's warning to return home by another way; for after his abuse of his councillors and sometimes of the Kings themselves, anyone could have seen through his final words of false benevolence. Only the York author seems sufficiently troubled by this inconsistency to indicate that Herod's insults and threats are made in asides which the Kings cannot hear. But realism and dramatic impressiveness do not coincide: the best of these scenes is in Chester where the author is indifferent to psychological plausibility.

In Chester Herod's consultation with his *doctores* (Matthew ii. 4–5) concerning the Old Testament prophecies is very fully set out, indeed the doctors' solemn recitation of prophecies is in effect a substitute for a prophets' play; whilst Herod in his interruptions seems a coarser and more stupid version of the Archisynagogus of Benediktbeuern, his sceptical comments consisting more of blustering insult than of intellectual mockery. The prophecy of Jacob (Genesis xlix. 10) made in his old age as he lay dying is dismissed with a jeer, 'that olde villard Iacob, all doted for age'; so also is the revelation given to Daniel in a dream (cf. Daniel ix. 24, 26) for he was a 'sleeping slogard', and as for David's prophecy (Psalms lxxi. 10), he was just a 'Shephard with his Sling'. This verbal violence extends to the Christ-Child: He is a 'peevish page', an 'elvish gedling', an 'Elfe and vile congeown', or (to quote from a later scene) a 'rocked ribald' and a 'misbegotten marmoset'.[65] Chester is not alone in including abusive references to the Christ-Child (though not all the dramatists are so talented in the invention of alliterative insults), but it is only Chester which extends this common technique to the prophets.[66] In this play, whilst

Herod in his boastings repeats the pattern of Satan, in his intellectual destructiveness expressed in violent sneering he recalls the manners of Cain.

This establishment of Herod's imaginative murderousness through jeering contempt for anything that threatens him is dramatically necessary, for at the time of the massacre it is the soldiers who carry it out that are important, not Herod himself. Indeed, though in Chester Herod threatens wholesale slaughter in one of his furious outbursts (grandiosely comparing the intended massacre to its type, Athaliah's murder of all the children of the blood royal),[67] more often, as in liturgical drama, the idea of the massacre is suggested to Herod by a councillor, thereby diminishing Herod's part. The conception of the men who perform the massacre varies from cycle to cycle. In some, the *Ludus Coventriae*, Chester and Coventry, they are characterised by having a specific rank in society. Affinities with the contemporary satire of 'carpet-knights' have been noted by Owst[68] in the extravagant boasting of the Chester knight who claims to have killed a hundred thousand men in one engagement and in the Towneley knights whose reaction to the message that Herod wants them to appear fully armed is one of cowardly alarm. But the dramatists are also aware of the romance ideals of chivalry and of the monstrous inappropriateness of killing babies as an activity for knights. This idea is treated in a straight-forward way in Coventry, where though the scruples of the *milites* are initially political, since they fear that the massacre will cause an uprising, they later see the cries of the bereaved mothers as 'grettly rebukyng to chevaldry'. In Chester and Digby the same idea is treated satirically. The Chester knights at first complain that it would be a *vyllany* for 'knightes of good degree' to take on the killing of 'a shitten-arsed shrew' (the vileness of their speech of course instantly belying their care for the standards of chivalry). It is therefore not surprising that they should be reassured of the dignity of the enterprise when told that it is not just one or two babies that they must kill but more than a thousand. This farcical inversion of the romance ideal is more broadly marked in Digby where the low-born Watkin, who wishes to be dubbed a knight in virtue of his heroism in baby-killing, but who is terrified of the mothers and at last thrashed by them, is a cousin of Sir Thopas, however gross and remote.[69]

More interesting, however, than the plays which attempt some social and satirical characterisation are those in which the soldiers are characterised only through a malign and psychologically unexplained relish in evil (in Chester the two conceptions are combined). In the *Ludus*

Coventriae this horrible and unmotivated delight is shown in the soldiers' response to Herod's order:

> Ffor swerdys sharpe,
> as An harpe,
> quenys xul karpe
> and of sorwe synge;
> barnys ʒonge,
> they xul be stunge,
> thurwe levyr and lunge
> we xal hem stynge.

This lingering over the details of brutality in a metre distinctive for its lyricism suggests a cold, inhuman glee. In Chester and Towneley, however, the relish in evil is shown rather in the vicious speeches of the soldiers as they engage in the massacre. In Towneley these are characterised by the coarse abuse of the mothers: the second soldier, for instance, advances upon one saying, 'Com hedyr, thou old stry!/ that lad of thyne shall dy', and variations upon *stry*, such as *hoore* and *bawd*, are repeated. But more icily sinister are the Chester soldiers who, like their counterparts in the later Passion sequences, pretend that they are playing a game. The second soldier, for instance, tackles one of the mothers with the following words:

> Dame, thy sonne, in good fay,
> he must of me learne a play:
> he must hop, or I goe away,
> upon my speare ende.

The game metaphor here very horribly conveys enjoyment in the savagery.[70]

Much care in all the cycles has gone into the treatment of the soldiers, and it is through them that the deaths of the children and the sufferings of Christ in the Passion are worked into a continuous pattern, the children in their deaths being types of Christ.[71] There could obviously be no characterisation of the babies of two years and under: in liturgical drama, which specifically celebrated them, the parts of the Innocents might be taken by child actors;[72] but this unrealistic method of impersonation would have been impossible in the plays, where the mothers obviously carry rag dolls, which the soldiers could hoist upon their spears, as they so often do in iconographic representations of the scene.[73] It is only in the Coventry play, in which the mothers sing the beautiful lullaby lament, 'O sisters too', before the arrival of the soldiers, that the pathos of innocent babies so randomly slaughtered is touchingly brought out.

Whilst, however, one could not expect the dramatists to do other than show the babies as passive objects of the soldiers' savagery, the treatment of the mothers is surprising. According to Matthew there was fulfilled at this time Jeremiah's prophecy of Rachel weeping for her children, and in the Fleury *Ordo Rachelis*, for instance, Rachel as the representative mother speaks three stylised but moving *planctus*.[74] In the exegetic tradition Rachel is the type of the Church, and within the patterning of the action in the mystery plays one might have supposed that the mothers in their grief would anticipate the Virgin at the Cross. Often, however, the mothers are shown as women of spirit, who in their encounters with the soldiers give almost as good as they get, meeting the sword strokes with blows from distaff or cooking pan and matching abuse with abuse. The Towneley mothers, for instance, address the soldiers as 'harlot and holard' and a Chester mother says of one 'stibbon, stallon, stickt tode' and 'scabbed bitch [cur]'. Though the mothers of course grieve, in Chester their laments mingle with threats even within individual quatrains, and in Towneley the third mother's cry, 'Thy body is all to-rent', which verbally echoes the Crucifixion complaints, is almost lost in the prevailing ferocity of tone. It is only in the *Ludus Coventriae* and York that lyric laments stand out unmuffled by colloquial outbursts of anger. The complaint of the first mother in the *Ludus Coventriae*, 'Longe lullynge have I lorn', is quite effective, whilst the two mothers' brief laments in York are extremely touching:[75]

> *ii Mul.* Allas! þis lothly striffe!
> No blisse may be my bette,
> þe knyght uppon his knyffe
> Hath slayne my sone so swette;
> And I hadde but hym allone.
> *i Mul.* Allas! I lose my liffe,
> Was nevere so wofull a wyffe,
> Ne halffe so wille of wone!

These laments deliberately echo the Virgin's distress in the Flight into Egypt:

> I ware full wille of wane
> My son and he shulde dye,
> And I have but hym allone.

and in tone anticipate the Virgin's mourning speeches to Christ upon the Cross. This tone of intense but subdued grief is, however, rare amongst the cycles, and the noisy screaming of the mothers seems to have become almost as much a commonplace as the raging of Herod. Chaucer alludes to it in an outrageously funny simile when describing January's reaction to the shocking sight within the tree:[76]

> And up he yaf a roryng and a cry,
> As dooth the mooder whan the child shal dye:
> 'Out! help; allas! harrow!' he gan to crye.

and much later Shakespeare made Henry V refer to this theme when grandiloquently threatening the citizens of Harfleur with the carnage that they will see if they do not yield:

> Your naked infants spitted upon pikes,
> Whiles the mad mothers with their howls confus'd
> Do break the clouds, as did the wives of Jewry
> At Herod's bloody-hunting slaughtermen.

After the massacre the soldiers return to Herod boastfully to report their success, and occasionally, as in the *Ludus Coventriae*, one still carries a child transfixed upon his spear. At this point the focus is once more upon Herod. It is only in Towneley that Herod remains deluded to the end. The Wakefield Master has contrived a nicely satiric little scene, in which Herod rewards his greedy men with money, lands and women, and then bloodthirstily congratulates himself on his peace of mind:

> I sett by no good now my hart is at easse,
> That I shed so mekyll blode. Pes all my ryches!
> ffor to se this flode from the fote to the nese
> Mefys nothyng my mode – I lagh that I whese.

But after this Herod's comic farewell, 'bot adew! to the devyll!/I can no more fraunch',[77] though presumably intended to lighten the tone, in fact comes as an anticlimax; and, though it is likely that Herod's asseverations, 'Were I dede and rotyn' (l. 494) and 'Begyn I to rokyn' (l. 508), are grimly ironic hints of his horrible death (to which we shall return),[78] they are too fleeting and elusive to carry poetic weight and diminish the impression of jocular dismissal.

The York and Coventry plays have rather abrupt endings in which Herod either fearing that the Christ-Child may nevertheless have

escaped (York) or being told by a messenger that the Child has fled to
Egypt (Coventry), decides in wrath to set out in pursuit himself. This
is a rather rare invention of eastern origin,[79] and according to the full
story Herod's armed chase of the Child is halted by an angel. As so
briefly stated in these plays, however, Herod's pursuit of the Child
recalls Pharaoh's vain and fatal pursuit of the children of Israel, an
association which, though not immediately founded in typology,
would extend to many parallels already observed between the stories
of Pharaoh and Moses and of Herod and Christ with the Innocents.[80]
Therefore, whilst these plays seems to end on an inconclusive note,
in York at least Herod's last words, 'Comes aftir as yhe canne,/For we
will wende be-fore', must have seemed fatefully to echo Pharaoh's
injunction, 'Do charge oure charyottis swithe,/And frekly folowes
me', words spoken only moments before the drowning in the Red Sea.

This hint of future disaster, however, seems insubstantial when
compared with the full display of the death of Herod in the other three
plays. This non-biblical episode is found first in Josephus, who gave a
detailed and gruesome account of the symptoms of Herod's mortal
disease, and was made widely known to the Middle Ages through the
Historia scholastica of Peter Comestor, who saw in the vileness of
Herod's death God's vengeance for the massacre.[81] Since the Massacre
and the death were thus thematically related, dramatists, beginning
with the author of the Benediktbeuern Christmas play, often disregarded the historical time scheme, and had Herod die instantly after
the return of the soldiers. Both Digby and Chester make this conjunction almost perfunctorily close. In Digby, after Watkin has
repeated to Herod the cries of the women, 'A vengeaunce take kyng
herode for he hath our children sloon', Herod instantly feels himself
overtaken by madness and terror, and dies upon the stage. In Chester
the scene is a little more elaborated but with some uncertainty of time.
The author follows the tradition that one of Herod's sons was amongst
the slain,[82] and the dialogue in which the foster-mother announces
this to Herod, and Herod, whilst abusing her, understands it as a
vengeance, is skilfully written. There is also some horror in Herod's
description of his putrefying flesh and of the devils come to snatch his
soul:

> My legges rotten and my armes;
> I have done so many harmes,
> That now I see of feendes swarmes
> from hell cominge for me.

Herod then accepts his damnation by bequeathing his soul to Satan (in Digby it was Mahowne), a travesty of the opening formula of medieval wills in which the testator committed his soul to God,[83] and the play then ends on a semi-comic, semi-minatory note, with the devil telling the audience how he will carry Herod off to hell and then come back as fast as he can to 'fetch moe'. A satirically designed warning to tapsters who give false measure contributes to the concluding mood of boisterous irony.

Neither of these episodes is of much literary merit: in contrast the scene of the death of Herod in the *Ludus Coventriae* is exceptionally powerful. In this Herod in his delight at the massacre orders a banquet and sits down to feast with his knights; and as Herod expresses his pleasure, 'I was nevyr meryer here be-forn', Death appears and stands at one side. In a strong speech Death denounces Herod's pride and the futility of the massacre, for 'goddys sone doth lyve, þer is no lorde but he', and he, Death, as God's messenger, rules all, and he mocks Herod, for in his feasting, 'of deth hath he no dowte, he wenyth to leve evyrmore'. There follows some small talk between Herod and his knights, Herod still ironically boasting, 'Ffor now my fo is ded . . . above me is no kynge', and the knights commenting in conversational tones about the 'good game' of killing the children. And then, whilst the festive trumpets sound, Death strikes them all with his spear,[84] and the devil, who now also appears, carries them off. The play then ends with Death's address to the audience, of which the following is the third and last stanza:

> Thow I be nakyd and pore of array
> and wurmys knawe me al a-bowte,
> ȝit loke ȝe drede me nyth and day
> Ffor whan deth comyth ȝe stande in dowte.
> Evyn lyke to me as I ȝow say
> shull all ȝe be here in þis rowte.
> Whan I ȝow chalange at my day
> I xal ȝow make ryght lowe to lowth
>   and nakyd for to be.
> Amonges wormys as I ȝow telle
> Undyr þe erth xul ȝe dwelle
> and thei xul Etyn both flesch and felle
>   as þei have don me.

This scene has been compared with the *Pride of Life*, in which Death also appears with a spear and strikes down the over-confident and vainglorious king of life.[85] Certainly the design is that of a morality play, and its adoption reflects the late medieval tendency to introduce allegorical figures into the mystery plays, a tendency particularly marked in Continental drama.[86] But in these it often seems no more than a piece of ornamental elaboration, whereas the actual appearance of Death in the *Ludus Coventriae* is essential and effective. The structural advantage is that the recourse to personification obviates the need for the weak and implausible monologues with which Herod dies in the other plays. But more importantly it enables the meaning of Herod's death to be extended in a way which is both morally and dramatically effective. For the audience is jolted out of the comfortable feeling that Herod's death was a special punishment for his specially monstrous wickedness, and are reminded that they too must die and they too must rot in the grave (it is interesting that it is the figure of Death rather than Herod who here appears worm-eaten). In Death's warning are used many of the themes traditional in the lyrics on death,[87] but it was a stroke of brilliance to present them in this context to an unsuspecting audience; and, while it might be thought that this imposing of the themes of morality plays and lyrics upon the death of Herod might diminish his grotesque and gigantic figure to the ordinary size of the emperor who leads off the Dance of Death, in effect this sudden rooting of Herod in the familiar world of mortality does not diminish, but rather confers a horrifying solidity upon him.

X

The Life of Christ between the Nativity and the Passion

The Doctors in the Temple
The Plays of the Ministry
The Entry into Jerusalem
The Last Supper
The Agony in the Garden

The plays to be considered in this chapter are primarily those of the ministry but included also are a few which, though properly belonging either to the Nativity or Passion sequences, resemble in treatment the plays of the ministry in that in them Christ verbally dominates the drama. The play of Christ with the doctors was traditionally associated with the sequence of Christ's birth and childhood rather than with the ministry. The three great French *Passions* of Mercadé, Greban and Michel, for instance, bring the events of the first day to a close with this subject; some German cycles take as their starting point the next subject, that of the Baptism;[1] as we have already seen, the authors of two English cycles thought it not inappropriate to present the Purification and the Doctors in one play. The theoretical and liturgical connection is that in this play (as of course also in the Baptism) the epiphany continues, whilst the historical connection is that Christ is still a child in his parents' household, and there is therefore some dramatic continuity in the treatment of Mary and Joseph (the latter appearing here for the last time). Nevertheless in its didacticism and in the fact that Christ in it for the first time appears as the central and speaking character (before he will have been represented by a doll),[2] this play more obviously resembles those of the ministry. It can therefore best be described as transitional and for convenience we link it with later plays.

The curious feature of the five surviving plays of the doctors is that four of them are closely related, Towneley, Chester and Coventry all being variants of the play first recorded in the York cycle. Why this dull and infelicitous version should have had such a diffusion is unclear.

Its central point is Christ's summary of the Ten Commandments (in York and Towneley the versification of these from the *Speculum Christiani* is borrowed),[3] and it is this skill which rather unconvincingly arouses in the doctors the amazement at His understanding, which Luke had described without giving any detail. Admittedly invention was here compelled upon the dramatists in a slightly unusual way, but the solution found by Continental dramatists that Christ joined in the doctors' discussion of the Old Testament prophecies of the Messiah, and demonstrated how many of them had already been fulfilled, seems straightforward and readily devisable. The English dramatists evidently therefore preferred simple didacticism to plausibility, for in the Middle Ages it cannot have been a feat for a twelve-year-old boy to be able to rehearse such a standard piece of Christian teaching. This insistence on didacticism is nevertheless understandable in York and Towneley, where the play of Moses had not included the Ten Commandments, but puzzling in Chester where the Ten Commandments had already been set out once before.[4]

This play in its four variants is very muted in tone. There are touches of liveliness in the doctors' initial annoyance and contempt for the Child who would join in their learned discussion, emotions expressed in their attempted dismissal of him with the sentiment that they have better things to do 'þan now with barnes bordand to be' and in their jibe after his first assertion of authority, 'he wenes he kennes more than he knowes'.[5] There is also a hint of characterisation in Joseph's reluctance to go in and claim the Child from the 'men of myght' who 'are so gay in furres fyne' and also in Joseph's common-sense confidence that the Child is not lost but will overtake them. And there is in York at least a little feeling in Mary's lament to Joseph when she realises that the Child is not with them:

> A! sir, where is oure semely sone?
> I trowe oure wittis be waste as wynde,
> Allas! in bale þus am I boone,
> What ayleth us both to be so blynde.
> To go overe fast we have be-gonne,
> And late þat lovely leve be-hynde.

This subdued tone, however, provides the right environment for Christ's claims to divinity, which are made powerfully but differently in the various versions: 'Certis I was or ȝe,/And schall be aftir ȝou' (York), 'My father and I together be/in one godhead withoutten dreed' (Chester), and finest of all in Coventry where Christ asserts

His knowledge of the law, 'For in those placis have I be/Where all owre lawis furst were wroght'. In this play most strikingly begins a series of resounding affirmations of divinity, which serve as an important doctrinal and dramatic background to Christ's later silence in the Passion sequence.

The mediocrity of the York play and its variants is most marked if it is compared with the distinctive version of the *Ludus Coventriae*. This play opens with an entertaining satirical presentation of the doctors, whose claims to learning are proud, self-satisfied and fantastic in their inclusiveness. They begin their magniloquent self-praise with a simile absurd in its context: 'Velud rosa omnium florum flos'[6] so are they unique amongst learned men. Then comes a comically topical and exhaustive list of the subjects in which they are pre-eminent, these including the seven liberal arts, medicine, and canon and civil law. This boasting leads to Christ's first words, 'Omnis sciencia a domino deo est',[7] a rebuke met by antiphonal jeers, which in their mocking inventiveness recall the style of the detractors:

1st doctor Goo hom lytyl babe and sytt on þi moderys lappe,
and put a mokador a-forn þi brest,
and pray þi modyr to fede þe with þe pappe:
of þe for to lerne we desyre not to lest.

2nd doctor Go to þi dyner for þat be-hovyth the best,
whan þou art a-threste þan take þe A sowke,
Aftyr go to cradyl þer-in to take þi rest,
Ffor þat canst þou do bettyr þan for to loke on book.

After this begins the disputation proper, in which the marvellousness of Christ's understanding is shown in the fact that he can expound the doctrines of the Trinity and of the Redemption with the subtlety of a scholastic theologian. The dramatist is undoubtedly taking the opportunity here to instruct the audience: some of the intellectual images used, that of the sun with its brilliance, heat and light as a simile for the three persons in one Godhead, or that of the sun passing through glass as a persuasive image for the Virgin Birth, are clearly incorporated to teach the audience as well as to amaze the doctors. But this is the lesser part and purpose of the play. More important is that part in which Christ's unfolding of divine mysteries is designed to provide a doctrinal heart to the cycle, resuming earlier patterns and beginning new ones. The need for the Incarnation of the Son as the redemptive remedy for the Fall is set out in the following way. The doctors who by this time serve as the questing and subservient interlocutor of theological dialogue, ask why it was the Second Person of the Trinity who became man, to which Christ answers:

> To þe sone connynge doth longe expres
> ther with þe serpent dyd Adam A-say:
> Ete of þis Appyl he seyd no lesse
> and þou xalt have connynge as god verray.

This reply expresses a traditional theological argument, found for instance in the *Summa theologica*,[8] but verbally it echoes the tempter's speech to Eve in the Play of the Fall (ll. 182–5) in a way that cannot be coincidental.

Whilst the exposition of the work of the Trinity looks backwards, the interpretation of Christ's life hitherto looks forward. In particular Christ's explanation of why it was necessary for the Virgin to marry begins a strand of soteriological doctrine that is woven through the cycle:

> To blynde þe devyl of his knowlache
> and my byrth from hym to hyde
> þat holy wedlok was grett stopage
> þe devyl in dowte to do A-byde.

The doctrine is here introduced elusively and might well puzzle the audience; it was, however, to be resumed much more fully and explicitly in the play of the Temptation,[9] and thereafter accounts for the importance given to the devil in the Passion sequence, in which he is presented as an incessant adversary of Christ, a treatment peculiar to the *Ludus Coventriae* amongst English cycles, though extremely common on the Continent. The later importance accorded to the devil is heralded here by the use of martial imagery for the Crucifixion:

> That maydonys childe xal do grett cure
> convicte þe devyl in þe opyn felde
> and with his bolde berst fecch hom his creature
> mankende to save his brest xal be þe shelde.

Whilst the image of Christ as a knight fighting to rescue man from the devil's rape is extremely common in medieval literature, it was used with a variety of emphases:[10] here the word *creature* rather than lady, as, for instance, in the exemplum in the *Ancrene Wisse*, dispels courtly associations, and gets the stress on to the Redemption as primarily an issue between God and the devil, a stress characteristic of the image when associated with the soteriological doctrine of the devil's rights, of which the theme of Christ's concealment of His Divinity is an inseparable part.

The dramatist's theological concerns in this play extend to the Blessed Virgin. According to a more extended list of the sorrows of the Virgin the fifth was her losing of Christ in Jerusalem.[11] Greban draws attention to this devotional understanding of the episode by giving the Virgin a long, lyrical *planctus*.[12] The English dramatists in general, however, seem not to have accentuated the Virgin's distress more than the gospel text would demand. Indeed insofar as they show any interest in developing the dialogue outside the Temple, they concentrate rather on Joseph, the Coventry author in particular continuing the characterisation of Joseph in the Purification, though his grumblings about old age and weariness on the journey to Jerusalem are more serious and decorous than in the preceding episode. It would, however, have been remarkable if the *Ludus Coventriae*, which had already so much emphasised the role of the Virgin, had not included a touch at least of dramatic concentration upon her distress. This occurs in the following lines:

> Alas! Alas! myn hert is wo,
> My blyssyd babe a-wey is went.
> I wott nevyr whedyr þat he is go,
> Alas, for sorwe myn hert is rent.

Whilst this passage is extraordinarily brief as compared with Greban's elaborate set-piece, it is in form a *planctus*, unlike, for instance, the lines quoted above from York, which are Mary's naturalistic expression of anxiety to her husband. Through the form therefore Mary's grief here is shown to anticipate her later and deeper grief at the Crucifixion.

The next subject in all the cycles save Chester is the Baptism of Christ. It too can be called a transitional play, for, whilst it marks the beginning of Christ's ministry, it also brings to a close the complementary themes of epiphany and prophecy. Though it was only in the east that the feast of the Epiphany celebrated the Baptism (instead of the Visit of the Kings), in the west, gospel readings and antiphons in the office for the octave of the Epiphany preserved this earlier association.[13] At the same time, according to the tradition of the *Ordo prophetarum*, John the Baptist was the last in the long line of the prophets. The idea of the meeting between prophet and prophesied, already expressed in the plays of the Purification, here reaches its culmination. The *Ludus Coventriae* in fact makes John's recognition of Christ the high point of

the play, and his revelatory greeting, 'Ecce agnus Dei qui tollit pec-
cata mundi' (John i. 29), is expanded into a long stanza foretelling the
sufferings of the Passion, which takes up and amplifies Symeon's
earlier prophecy.

In Towneley the point is treated twice, once with heavy-handed
explicitness in the opening monologue and once more movingly and
obliquely in dialogue between Christ and John. In John's first speech
he explains who he is and his character as prophet, 'Emang prophetys
then am I oone', and continues with the prophecy that Christ shall shed
his blood upon the Cross, 'Not for his gylt bot for oure goode'. This
blunt undramatic exposition is, however, useful in making possible the
later more imaginative and elusive treatment. This occurs after the
Baptism, where the longings of Symeon are repeated in John's words
of thanksgiving, 'I have desyryd this sight ful lang,/ffor to dy now rek I
no dele'; whereupon Christ hands to him a lamb, and John testifies,
'ffor I have sene the lamb of god'. The treatment here is more pictorial
than verbal. The detail of Christ's handing the lamb to John was
presumably invented to account for iconographic representations in
which John the Baptist is shown holding a lamb, as his emblem; and in
the cycle the lamb (a symbolic *agnus Dei* with a cruciform nimbus)[14]
would visually recall and reinterpret Abel's offering and the cradled
lamb of the *Secunda pastorum*. Its presence is also important in giving an
additional overtone to John's stylised farewell to Christ, 'Ffarwell!
the frelyst that ever was fed!', for it would seem less of a decorative set-
piece when spoken by a figure holding the symbol of Christ's future
suffering.

The *Ludus Coventriae* is exceptional, not only in giving the prominence of centrality to John the Baptist as prophet but also in giving
emphasis to John the Baptist as preacher. This theme is of course
biblical in origin, but York and Towneley relegate the substance of
John's call to repentance to a subsidiary place in the opening explanatory monologues: John does not preach but recalls how he preached.
In contrast half of the Baptism in the *Ludus Coventriae* is given to
John's two sermons at the beginning and end of the play. The structural
difference between these two sermons is of interest. The first is historical: it is John's call to the Jews to repent and be baptised, with the
audience here functioning as the crowd within the play; in Continental
analogues there are two or three Jews upon the stage to listen to the
sermon. The second is devotional: John has become a timeless figure
urging the audience in their own persons to repent and make confession of their sins. Addresses to the audience become increasingly

important as the cycles develop, but often the relationship between speaker and audience is more elusive than here, and it is therefore useful to have at such an early stage two clear-cut examples in close proximity.

The Baptism in the *Ludus Coventriae* is otherwise only remarkable for its adherence to the gospel narrative. It includes the descent of the dove and the Father's proclamation of the Son, 'This is my welbelovyd chylde', a momentous event curiously omitted in York and Towneley. It also presents the actual baptism historically: it is a baptism of water as in the gospels, not the baptism instituted by Christ in the name of the Trinity, as described in the other plays. The contemporary liturgical associations are made especially plain in York where the two angels sing the *Veni creator spiritus*, and the Towneley baptism includes an anointing with oil, also part of the liturgical act. For practical reasons, however, the baptism in all of them was no doubt performed, not by immersion as in the gospels and early representations of the scene in art, but by infusion as in the familiar ceremony, and later iconography where John pours the water on Christ's head from saucer, cup or jug.

Whilst the author of the *Ludus Coventriae* is concerned with the theme of sin and repentance (a concern to be justified in dramatic terms by its more subtle resumption in the play of the Woman taken in Adultery), the York and Towneley dramatists have a warmer and more devotional understanding of the scene. In both plays John's opening monologue is followed by a dialogue with two angels, whose presence in the scene had long been established by iconographic tradition. The purpose of this dialogue is to introduce the complementary themes of John's fearful reluctance to baptise his Lord and Christ's humility in subjecting Himself to a ceremony of purification, which, like Mary's in the Temple, was unnecessary. These themes were fully explored in meditative literature, and in the *Vita Jesu Christi*, for instance, can be found the source or analogues of all the detail included in York and Towneley. In Towneley, John's unwillingness to obey the divine command, which seems to deprive him of fitting self-abasement before his divine master, is first expressed in his refusal to obey the angel's order to await Christ's coming where he is, 'Shuld I abyde to he come to me? . . . I shall go meyt that lord so fre', and later in his plea to Christ to be spared a duty so repellent to natural feeling:[15]

> This bewteose lord to bryng to me,
>   his awne servande, this is no skyll,
> A knyght to baptyse his lord kyng,
>   My pauste may it not fulfyll . . .

And therfor, lord, I ask mercy;
　　hald me excusyd as I have ment;
　　I dar not towche thi blyssyd body,
　　My hart will never to it assent.

It is only after further insistence from both Christ and the angels that John accepts the paradoxical act of humility imposed upon him and, though he trembles and shakes with fear, calls with dignity for Christ's submission, 'Abyde, my lord, and by me stand'. The same feeling of devout unwillingness is expressed in York through the rhetoric of paradox, 'What riche man gose from dore to dore/To begge at hym þat has right noght?', and more movingly in:

Þat place þat I yarne moste of all,
Fro thens come þou, lorde, as I gesse,
How schulde I þan, þat is a thrall,
Giffe þe baptyme, þat rightwis is,
　　　　And has ben evere?
For þou arte roote of rightwissenesse,
　　Þat forfette nevere.

Though far less subtly and magnificently conceived, John's unwilling-ness in these plays to co-operate in Christ's work of redemption is reminiscent of the Cross's appalled obedience to the divine will in the *Dream of the Rood*.

This presentation of John is not only touching in itself but also provides a human response against which Christ's speeches of authority and instruction can sound out clearly. Much of Christ's speeches con-sists of the exposition of the reasons for His baptism as defined by biblical commentaries: Christ explains that He is baptised in order to sanctify baptismal water for ever after and to be a *mirroure*, an example to man of what he must do (York, ll. 92–105). This treat-ment is typical of the speeches given to Christ throughout the plays of the ministry: He speaks either the words of the Bible or of the Church's interpretation of biblical action. Christ is an uncharacterised teacher and man of authority in the plays, but here at least the emotions of John give human shape to this necessarily impersonal figure.

According to the gospels the Baptism of Christ was immediately succeeded by the Temptation in the Wilderness: the cycles therefore proceed next to this subject, except for Towneley, which jumps directly from the Baptism to the Raising of Lazarus. There were two traditional ways of imposing on the Temptation a deeper significance than the surface one of Christ enduring and withstanding temptation. One was that this was an essential part of the pattern of redemption: just as Christ on the Cross overcame death, so in the Temptation he drew the sting of man's fall, for as Adam had sinned in gluttony, vainglory and pride, so Christ in the three temptations conquered sin in precisely these forms: for this reason Milton was later to call his poem on the Temptation in the wilderness *Paradise Regained*.[16] The alternative (though in doctrinal terms they were not mutually exclusive) was to see in this event Satan's attempt to thwart the redemption. According to this theory Christ's plan of redemption depended for its success on His keeping His identity secret from the devil: for according to the theory of the devil's rights, the nature of the redemption was that the devil laid claim to Christ at His death, but unjustly since Christ was perfect man, and through this abuse of his power the devil forfeited his right to keep mankind in hell. This legalistic and less than sublime interpretation of the Redemption had been held by the early western Fathers, but had been thoroughly demolished by Anselm in the *Cur Deus homo*, and thereafter it never formed any serious part of soteriological doctrine. Nevertheless the theory must have remained well known to the learned throughout the Middle Ages since it had been set out in the *Sentences* of Peter Lombard,[17] and though it was not expounded afresh in the abstract, it remained part of the traditional commentary upon specific biblical episodes, appearing in explanations such as that Christ wept as a baby in order to conceal His divinity, that the devil tempted Him in order to test His identity, and that in the dream of Pilate's wife the devil, having by now recognised the divine trap prepared for him, attempted at the last moment to prevent the Crucifixion. This theory seems to have been echoed in the Middle Ages whenever it would be poetically useful, and, as we have already noted, it recurs noticeably in the *Ludus Coventriae*, though it is an exaggeration to maintain that it constitutes the organising principle of this cycle.[18]

The Temptation in the *Ludus Coventriae* opens with a council of the devils, in this resembling Continental analogues with a similar doctrinal emphasis, but differing from the two other English plays, which begin only with Satan's explanatory monologue: the serious deliberations of Satan, Beelzebub and Belial establish the weight of their anxiety and the significance of the test to come. The folly and uselessness of the enterprise is made explicit at the end when Satan flees with a confession of failure accompanied by the recurrent sign of his debasement:

What þat he is I kan no se,
Whether god or man what þat he be,
I kan not telle in no degre
Ffor sorwe I lete a crakke.

The actual development of the theme in the Temptation itself, however, is not clearly done: it compares poorly, for instance, with that of Greban, who with unusual economy has made the matter plain with scarcely longer space.[19] It is therefore with the help of learned commentaries that one can best come to understand how Satan's plot was designed to work and how Christ was able to escape the trap. The point is that each temptation is two-pronged though in different ways. In the first temptation Satan hopes that Christ will either confess Himself unable to turn the stones to bread (thus showing himself mere man), or perform the miracle thus revealing His divine powers whilst at the same time misusing them; in the second that Christ will drop from the pinnacle of the Temple, and either be killed (again mere man) or be miraculously saved, again using divine powers in a magical, wonder-working way; in the third that Christ will either accept the kingdoms offered to Him by Satan, or as maker and ruler of the world will refuse this offering of what is already His own. The verbal skill with which Christ eludes Satan's attempt to ensnare Him in the first and third temptations is self-evident, but His escape from the second needs comment. Here one must imagine that, insofar as stage properties permitted it, Christ was shown standing upon the topmost tower of the Temple, and that, after refusing Satan's taunting invitation to reveal His divinity by throwing Himself down unscathed, He walked calmly down some steps, as Ludolf, for instance, describes, and returned to the ground in the natural, human way.[20] The obscurity of the text at this point would of course have been made clear in the production, but in general it is surprising that the author of the *Ludus Coventriae* who is normally so doctrinally articulate, failed to execute with clarity the design of his play. One may suspect that, while as a dramatist he preferred this interpretation of the Temptation, as a teacher he wanted simply to show Christ's exemplary rejection of the temptations to gluttony, vainglory and avarice (it is this moral that is emphasised in Christ's concluding address to the audience), and thereby was led to fudge the outlines of the intellectual issues that he had raised.

Whilst the author of the *Ludus Coventriae* was primarily concerned with the theme of the devil's quest for Christ's identity, the Chester author adopted as his central theme Christ's reversal of Adam's three sins. This interpretation, which derived from a much-quoted sermon of Gregory the Great, was extremely common in the Middle Ages, but it is reasonable to assume that the dramatist was encouraged to give it prominence by the emphasis upon it in his regularly used source, the *Stanzaic Life of Christ*.[21] Frequent references to Adam's Fall in the speeches of both Christ and Satan draw attention to the parallelism, which is explicated in direct sermon-fashion by the expositor at the end. With the theme of the reversal of Adam's Fall goes the imagery of conflict, and each time that Christ rejects a temptation, Satan laments in terms of defeat in battle: 'but ever he wynnes the victory', 'Was I never rowted in such aray', and finally, 'though I to threpe be never so thro,/I am overcome thrye'; and in his last lament Satan foresees that paradise regained will be the outcome of Christ's victory, 'Now sone out of sorrow he [Adam] must be shut,/and I pyned in hell pitt'. Whilst Satan in this play speaks largely in the dismal complaining voice of the vanquished, there are touches in his opening monologue of lively contempt for virtue, particularly in his favourite denigratory reference to Christ as 'Doseberd',[22] and as his parting shot his contempt for all is expressed in his testamentary bequest of *the shitte* to the audience.[23]

Whilst the author of the York play is evidently aware of the two interpretations of the Temptation which had been given pride of place, respectively, by the dramatists of Chester and the *Ludus Coventriae*, he is more simply concerned with the nature of temptation and the example set by Christ in rejecting it: as in the Baptism Christ at the end instructs mankind to make him their *myrroure*. The author has therefore put some life into Satan's speeches of temptation, in particular making the first familiar and insidious:

> For þou hast fastid longe, I wene,
> I wolde now som mete wer sene,
> For olde acqueyntaunce us by-twene,
> Thy-selve wote howe.
> Ther sall noman witte what I mene
> but I and þou.

Though the ugliness of Satan's appearance must have seemed an unequivocal symbol of his wickedness,[24] his insinuating manner here and his delicate unwillingness to call a spade a spade, catches well the speciousness of the devil's traditional manner of temptation. Outside his temptations Satan is a comic figure. He begins his opening monologue in a bustling way, 'Make rome be-lyve, and late me gang', and goes on confidently to dismiss the rumour that he has heard that some-one has come to redeem those in hell, 'But certis þis tale is but a trayne,/ I trowe it noȝt'. Such traces of irony recur in the devil's speeches which give the appearance of rattling on, and his last cursing of Christ, 'hye mote he hang', brings the ironic strain to a climax. The York author's disregard for major doctrinal patterns seems to have left him time for attention to smaller dramatic effects, which give this play a certain vitality lacking in the more sustained formality of the other two.

The dramatists necessarily exercised selection in their adoption of subjects between the Temptation and the Entry into Jerusalem. A comparison with French and German cycles shows that whilst those that begin either with the Nativity or the Baptism had the leisure to be fairly inclusive in the events dramatised, those beginning with the Fall show fairly rigorous selection. The miracle almost invariably included was the Raising of Lazarus: but Christ's power, here demonstrated, to raise the dead from the grave itself is so obviously a proof and type of the Resurrection that there is no reason to search further for its presence. But the reason that all the English cycles save Towneley include the episode of the Woman taken in Adultery is not so immedi-ately clear and cannot be accepted as part of an invariable tradition: the *Egerer Fronleichnamsspiel*, for instance, omits it.[25]

A consideration of the plays themselves suggests that the subject pleased the dramatists because it was so potentially rich in patterns already recurring in the cycles. Firstly, it has a penitential meaning: the fact that the woman did not try to exculpate herself when questioned by Christ was understood as a free admission of sin, in response to which Christ showed mercy. It could thus provide an exemplary climax to the themes of temptation, sin and repentance developed in the two preceding plays. Secondly, it can form a parallel to the Temptation when interpreted as a test of Christ's identity, for just as Satan was thought then to attempt to catch Christ upon the horns of a dilemma, so also according to tradition did the Jews do here, in that they sought to manœuvre Christ into a position where He would have to exercise either justice or mercy, the one at the expense of the other. Thirdly, the woman taken in adultery is obviously related to the Virgin for she has committed the crime of which the Virgin was falsely suspected and she is therefore in a sense her anti-type as were Eve and her descendants in the Old Testament plays. But the occurrence of a fabliau-type situation at this point in time enables the dramatists to look at it in a new way, and to show the woman not only as an anti-type of the Virgin but also as a descendant of the second Eve in that she is not fixed

by characterisation in her sin, and is therefore a figure accorded
dignity and conceived with compassion: in other words the treatment
of an old theme in a new way signals the age of the redemption. Whilst
all three patterns are inherent in the subject the dramatists of course
vary in the extent to which they develop them.

The Chester author, who deals with the subject in a brief and
reserved way, is concerned solely with the theme of temptation or
testing: for this reason he makes the episode part of the play of the
Temptation, one action succeeding immediately upon the other: an
explanatory narrative link, presumably intended for the producer,
stresses the connection, 'tunc venient duo Iudeorum cum muliere
deprehensa in adulterio, ut Iesum tentarent',[26] whilst for the audience
the first Jew immediately announces his plan, 'for to tempte him I have
tight'. The whole play is therefore appropriately headed, 'De tentatione
salvatoris'.[27] The exact nature of the trap which Christ's adversaries
lay for Him is clearly set out in the Second Jew's speech:

> Hit is good redd, by my fay,
> so we may catch him by some way,
> for if he doe her grace to-day,
> he dothe against the law.
>
> And if he bydd punishe her sore,
> he dothe against his owne lore,
> that he hath preached here before:
> to mercy man shall draw.

The wise biblical answer with which Christ eluded his adversaries'
wiles is well known, 'he that is without sin amongst you, let him first
cast a stone at her'; but Chester, both in the action itself and in the
expositor's commentary at the end, lays considerable stress upon a
traditional amplification of this, namely that Christ's writing on the
ground, which is so enigmatically referred to in the gospel, consisted
of the listing of the sins of his Jewish accusers. This makes the dis-
comfiture of the Jews in this trial of wits the more marked, and
motivates their cries of lament and flight from the stage. Whether by
chance or not the vanquished exclamation of the Second Jew, 'Out!
alas! that wo is me!' almost precisely repeats that of Satan, 'Out! alas!
now me is woe!' only a hundred lines before.

The York author by contrast seems to have been comparatively
uninterested in the theme of temptation but concentrates strongly on
the other two. The play is unfortunately incomplete—about sixty lines

from the middle are lost[28] – but it is clear that the emphasis was not upon the verbal ensnaring of Christ, for at the beginning of the play the Jews are not conspiring to catch Him out, as in Chester, but are simply bent upon bringing the adulteress before two lawyers that she might be punished in accordance with the law of Moses. These two Jews are reminiscent of the detractors in the Trial of Joseph and Mary in the *Ludus Coventriae* for they both revile the woman with coarse abuse, 'A! ffalse stodmere and stynkand stroye',[29] and also intend to act as witnesses in the case, 'We will bere witnesse and warande/How we hir raysed all unarayed'. The conduct of the lawyers who hear the witnesses' accusations is not certain, as the gap in the manuscript occurs soon after their entry, but the 'new mater' which strikes one of the lawyers at this point was no doubt the device of using the case of the adulteress to tempt Christ. The positioning of this element would therefore have made it subordinate to the theme of vindictive relish in fulfilling the law expressed through the Jewish witnesses. When the play resumes the emphasis is upon the theme of repentance and for-giveness, the latter being expressed not obliquely and negatively as in the other plays which here follow the words of the Bible, 'Neither do I condemn thee' (John, viii. 11), but as an explicit act of pardon, 'Of all thy mys I make þe free', which is an exact translation of the formula of absolution after confession, 'Te absolvo ab omnibus peccatis tuis'. The combination in one play of this subject with the raising of Lazarus also seems to direct attention to the parallelism between Christ's power to forgive sins and His power to raise the dead, but this may be an acci-dental enrichment of meaning since the dramatisations were originally distinct.[30]

The finest and most complex of the plays on this subject is in the *Ludus Coventriae*, and in it all three themes are developed and inter-twined. The author here has, to begin with, heightened the fabliau element in the situation by dramatising the actual scene of the discovery including the detail of the frightened and angry lover escaping so hastily that he still carries his breeches in his hands, an invention that has been much praised by recent critics for its comic realism. As in York, a distinction is made between an *accusator* who enjoys the 'ryght good sporte' of breaking in on the lovers, and the learned men, the scribe and pharisee, who are more interested in the enterprise as a means of outwitting Christ, though the two motivations are not here chronologically distinguished. All three moreover take part in the scurrilous and obscene vilification of the woman, the scribe and pharisee in particular joining in the kind of antiphonal abusiveness which we have already noticed in the detractors and in the doctors in the Temple:[31]

Scribe   Come forth þou stotte, com forth þou scowte,
com forth þou bysmare and brothel bolde,
com forth þou hore and stynking bych clowte;
How longe hast þou such harlotry holde?

Pharisee   Com forth þou quene, com forth þou scolde,
com forth þou sloveyn, com forth þou slutte;
We xal the tecche with carys colde
A lytyl bettyr to kepe þi kutte.

Both style and arrangement here emphasise the parallelism between this incident and the accusations against Mary in the Trial.

But just as in the Trial the vileness of the detractors served only to intensify the virtue of Mary, so also here the ugly speeches of the accusers throw into relief the dignity of the woman in her humility and contrition. Penitence, which had sounded an arid duty in the sermon of John the Baptist, is here made beautiful to the imagination. Over and over again the woman asks for mercy, uselessly at first from the scribe and the pharisee and perhaps then with a touch of self-seekingness, but feelingly and devoutly with Christ, 'O holy prophete graunt me mercy . . . With all myn hert I am sory'. The importance of the theme of contrition had been established in the complaint of Christ with which the play opens: in style this complaint, which is half devotional in its appeal for love and half didactic in its demand for repentance, is reminiscent of the style of lyric complaints of Christ in the fifteenth century:[32]

In to þe erth ffrom hevyn A-bove
þi sorwe to ses and joye to restore,
man, I cam downe all ffor þi love,
Love me ageyn I aske no more.
þow þou mys-happe and synne ful sore
ʒit turne Aʒen and mercy crave,
it is þi fawte and þou be lore:
haske þou mercy and þou xalt have.

and the theme is resumed again at the end of the play, where the moral given is not the immediately applicable one that as sinners we have no right to condemn others (cf. York, xxiv, 83–6), but the more moving and general one, 'God of mercy is so habundawnt/þat what man haske it he xal it have'.

This play has been seen as a sermon on the text of the opening line, 'Nolo mortem peccatoris', with the story serving as exemplum.[33] But, whilst this theory is illuminating, the theme of mercy is perhaps more subtly interwoven with the progress of the action than it allows for. The Jews in this play, as in the others, seek to manœuvre Christ into a position in which justice and mercy must conflict, and Christ, again as in the other plays, outwits them by turning their call for justice back upon themselves. Christ's method here of dealing with his antagonists is that which He had used with the devil, namely He enunciates a true moral or religious principle which is sufficient to defeat them, but conceals from them the majesty of the divine plan which alone would give the full and splendid answer. But in the *Ludus Coventriae* this full answer is given to the audience. The very mention in this cycle of a conflict between justice and mercy would of course recall the debate between the Four Daughters of God, and the solution to this debate is re-stated in Christ's opening complaint, 'My ffadyr me sent the, man, to bye,/All þi Raunsom my-sylfe must pay': in other words the strategem of the Jews fails, not merely because they cannot justly inflict upon her the punishment of stoning, but more importantly because the woman can be justly forgiven since Christ has come to pay the penalty for her sin. A further resonance to the theme of justice and mercy is perhaps heard in the speeches of the Jews as they read their sins inscribed upon the ground: for in this scene there are faint echoes of the Last Judgment when all men's sins will be revealed, and the cry of the *Accusator*, 'I wolde I wore hyd sum-where out of syght', is reminiscent of the lamentations of the damned at Doomsday. This suggestion of the Last Judgment therefore hints at the idea that, though Christ here shows mercy, there will come a time (as we have seen in the *Sponsus*) when justice alone will prevail.

The Raising of Lazarus which follows (except in Chester) is a splendid subject but one difficult to present with matching majesty upon the stage: no medieval dramatisation rivals the magnificence of the passionate, lyrical treatment of the subject in the *Philomena* of John of Howden, which concentrates upon the moment of sublimity in Christ's command, *Veni foras*.[34] Whilst the plays naturally include these words, insofar as they amplify the gospel narrative, it is by invention either at the beginning or the end. The *Ludus Coventriae*, like many Continental plays, adopts the former method. The death of Lazarus is the only natural death within the cycles, and the dramatist here takes the opportunity to present a death-bed scene in the *Ars moriendi* tradition, and to investigate the grief of the sisters and the comfort offered by the *consolatores*, just as the twelfth-century dramatists had done. Lazarus's death is a model one: he is not fearful, grumbling or rebellious, but acquiescent in his sickness, and dies, as he should, bequeathing his soul to God, 'to god in hevyn my sowle I queth'.[35] The moral position of the four *consolatores*, however, at this point is uncertain, for they are bent upon persuading Lazarus that his acceptance of the imminence of death springs not from resignation but depression, 'Pluk up ʒour herte with myght and mayn/and chere ʒour sylf with all ʒour wyll': their hearty cheerfulness would appear to be a piece of naturalism that deliberately flies in the face of the advice given in the *Visitatio infirmorum* about fostering patience in the sick.[36]

A similar moral probing into the correct attitudes to death may be detected in the subsequent scene between the grieving sisters and the *consolatores*. The sisters, as in all the plays, are eloquent in their wish that they too might have died, and the *consolatores* use the traditional consolatory topics about the inevitability of death, 'Ffor deth is dew to every man', and the uselessness of tears, 'All ʒour wepynge may not amende itt'. Christ's weeping for the death of Lazarus had been a proof of the propriety of grieving for the dead, providing that the grief was not immoderate, and the distinction between controlled and rebellious grief was clearly in the mind of the dramatist, since a *consolator* at one point accuses Martha of the latter, 'þus for to grugge agens godys myght/Aʒens hyʒ god ʒe do offens'. The human propriety of tears, however, is demonstrated only through the sisters, since the author of the *Ludus Coventriae*, like the other dramatists, is too reticent to show Christ Himself grieving.[37] The author in his treatment of these scenes is thoughtful, but not as feeling as the situation requires. The arguments of the *consolatores*, though similar in substance, lack the moving gravity of tone of their analogues in the Fleury play, whilst the sisters' expressions of loss are less touching, not only than those in Hilarius's play, but also than those in York and Towneley.

Whilst the *Ludus Coventriae* puts its emphasis upon the beginning of the story of Lazarus, Towneley very powerfully embellishes the end by giving to Lazarus a long monologue. The idea that the risen Lazarus on his return to life could remember the sufferings that he had seen and endured in his four days' death and related them to his friends and family is first found in one of the pseudo-Augustinian sermons and was made current by its inclusion in the *Historia scholastica*.[38] The brief statement made in these works, that Lazarus related the pains of hell during the supper at the house of Simon the Leper, was in due course expanded in the apocryphal *Visio Lazari*, a work modelled upon the many stories of visionaries who, while their bodies lay in a coma, were shown the torments of hell, and returned to this world to amend their lives and warn others to repentance. Knowledge of this *Visio* is attested for Marseilles (the centre of a cult of Lazarus) in the middle of the fourteenth century, and thereafter it became widely known.[39] In England the author of *The Pricke of Conscience* borrowed from it in his section on hell.

The important point for the Towneley play of Lazarus, however, is that most of the French *Passions* drew either directly or indirectly upon the *Visio Lazari*.[40] In the *Passion Ste Geneviève* and the *Passion de Semur*, for instance, Lazarus gives an account of the nine pains of hell, whilst in Greban's *Passion*, Lazarus describes the four parts of hell, beginning with a more general account of its terrors:[41]

> Marthe, seur, c'est ung lieu sans plaire;
> et a vous deviser les peines
> dures, horribles et villaines
> dont ce malheureux lieu habonde,
> toutes les langues de ce monde
> ne le sçaroient recenser
> et parlassent eulx sans cesser.
> C'est ung abisme de destresse,
> ung hideux gouffre de tristesse
> ou toute misere survient.

This kind of description is in the same tradition as Fearlac's account of hell in *Sawles Warde* and many other sermon evocations of its torments, but the new context gives it an unexpected force. The traditional portrayal of Lazarus's agony of mind is neatly summarised in *The Pricke of Conscience*:[42]

> Yhit lyfed he after fyften yhere,
> Bot he lughe never, ne made blythe chere,
> For drede of ded þat he most efte dreghe,
> And of þe paynes þat he saw with eghe.

Whilst in the French plays Lazarus's monologue is never more than a formal set-piece, which if detached could be spoken by anyone, it is usually introduced by some dramatic touch which conveys the mood of recollected pain: in Semur, for instance, the monologue is prompted by Barnabas's reproach to Lazarus for not eating the good food on the table, whilst in Greban's *Passion*, it becomes Lazarus's reply to Martha's concern for his unfestive melancholy.

Whilst these French scenes are effective, the Towneley play provides a superb variation upon the common tradition, in that the dramatist has changed the immediate dramatic context and the content of the speech. With the exception of the late *Mystères provençaux*,[43] the French *Passions*, as we have seen, conservatively defer Lazarus's warning monologue until the supper at the house of Simon the Leper; but in Towneley it follows immediately upon Lazarus's rising from the tomb, and this unusual placing conveys the startling effect of a man so appalled by the horrors that he has experienced and so impelled by the need to warn others, that he must speak instantly; and not only does he speak instantly, but he speaks, not to his sisters and friends on the stage, but directly to the audience. Equally striking is the difference in content, for Lazarus does not give a numbered, mnemonic list of the pains of hell, but passionately and in disordered fashion describes the horrors of the decaying body in the tomb.

The idea of the body already beginning to decay is of course in the Bible narrative, where Martha protests at Christ's command that the stone should be removed, 'Lord by this time he stinketh'; and in art Martha's apprehensiveness is often shown, by her holding her nose. That Lazarus, however, could know from personal experience of the horrors of decay of the tomb is of course a poetic fancy without theological basis, though in meditative literature the squalidness of the grave and the pains of hell seem to merge as though they were both part of one appalling torment. The Towneley dramatist is deft and elusive for he does not explicitly state that Lazarus speaks from his own knowledge; but the context makes this inference inescapable, whilst if Lazarus delivered his speech still wrapped in his grave-clothes the point would also be made visually.[44] The dramatist has constructed for Lazarus the kind of warning that in lyrics is normally spoken from the grave: in it are assembled most of the traditional themes of the lyrics on death, but the monologue far surpasses in its power any of those that survive:[45]

> Under the erthe ye shall thus carefully then cowche;
> The royfe of youre hall, youre nakyd nose shall towche;
> Nawther great ne small To you will knele ne crowche;
> A shete shall be youre pall, sich todys shall be youre nowche,
> Todys shall you dere,
> ffeyndys will you fere,
> youre flesh that fare was here
>   Thus rufully shall rote;
> In stede of fare colore
>   sich bandys shall bynde youre throte.

Youre rud that was so red, youre lyre the lylly lyke,
Then shall be wan as led and stynke as dog in dyke;
Wormes shall in you brede as bees dos in the byke,
And ees out of youre hede Thus-gate shall paddokys pyke;
To pike you ar preste
Many uncomly beest,
Thus thai shall make a feste
Of youre flesh and of youre blode.
ffor you then sorows leste
The moste has of youre goode.

There is no doubt that the dramatist knew of the tradition of Lazarus describing the pains of hell (indeed at the end of his monologue Lazarus says that if there were time he could relate much of 'the paynes of hell/There as I have bene'), but with a touch of brilliance he saw how to give this a more profound and disturbing resonance by drawing upon the themes of the English lyrics on death.

The Raising of Lazarus was, as the Proclamation to the *Ludus Coventriae* states, 'The grettest meracle þat evyr jhesus/In erthe wrouth be-forn his passyon' (ll. 195–6): it surpasses in strangeness and power the healing of the blind and the lame, and touches the imagination more forcibly than the other miraculous restorations to life which took place more instantly after death. It could therefore be taken to stand for all Christ's miracles and Towneley in fact represents no other. The authors of York and the *Ludus Coventriae* appear, however, to have been uneasy at omitting the other miracles altogether, though unwilling to devote a whole play to them; they therefore found the neat but slightly unhistorical compromise of including the healing of a blind and a lame man (York) or two blind men (*Ludus Coventriae*) during the formal Entry into Jerusalem.[46] Chester is alone in dramatising the healing of the man born blind (though York, according to Burton's list originally included it). As far as one can tell, this subject did not find favour in England as it did in France, where, as we observed before, it provided the opportunity for the introduction of a comic servant. Though the blind man in Chester has a boy to lead him the situation does not give rise to comic inventiveness, and the dramatist keeps close to the text of John ix, which is already fully provided with dialogue. The only point of interest is that Christ's exposition of Himself as the Good Shepherd, which occurs in John x, is incorporated into the play both in Christ's opening prologue and in a later speech: the effect is to cast retrospective light upon the shepherds' play and this may well have been the dramatist's intention.[47]

The last three subjects to be considered in this chapter, the Entry into Jerusalem, the Last Supper and the Agony in the Garden, in terms of narrative begin the Passion sequence (no Passion play begins later than this point). They are also structurally integrated to the Passion sequence in all the cycles, since interwoven with them is the conspiracy of Judas, in which some of Christ's enemies appear for the first time. This interweaving is dramatically important, and especially so in the *Ludus Coventriae*, where the Passion sequence is designed for performance on a fixed stage and, as in Continental drama, it is therefore possible to make rapid switches from one *locus* to another and thus to achieve startling contrasts between morally disparate events such as Christ's giving of Himself in the Last Supper and Judas's selling of Him to the high priests which are shown to occur simultaneously in time. Nevertheless for the sake of analysis it is necessary to unravel the interlacing and to consider these three subjects in isolation, just as we did some of the later episodes of the Nativity sequence: for these plays are still written in the style characteristic of the plays of the Ministry and the dramatic focus is still upon the speeches of Christ with much paraphrase of the wording of the New Testament. They are therefore distinct from the Passion plays proper of which the substance is the malignant verbosity of Christ's enemies and their varied characterisation.

The Entry into Jerusalem was an especially difficult subject to dramatise, partly because of its total lack of plot, partly because the mood depends upon the movement of triumphal progress. Though Christ enters Jerusalem humbly, not upon the back of a horse but of an ass,[48] He is greeted by the crowds as a great prophet. Both the *Ludus Coventriae* and Chester seem to have got round the problems of staging by using the *platea* around or across which Christ rode possibly mounted on a live animal. However, even with this degree of realism, the idea of triumph had necessarily to be conveyed verbally rather than representationally, and it is worth noting that the York dramatist, who did not impose such verisimilitude upon actor and producer, was the most successful in catching the tone of celebration. In this play there is much eulogistic rehearsal of the past: citizens relate Old Testament prophecies now fulfilled and some of Christ's healing and life-giving miracles including the apocryphal one of the field miraculously filled with corn during the Flight into Egypt.[49] The impression of a new era of wholeness and abundance is effectively suggested, and confirmed by Christ's healing of the blind and the lame man who then add their praises to those of the citizens. The theme of the celebration of Christ's power culminates in the formal eulogistic welcome of the citizens at the end of the play, the long series of hail anaphoras recalling the speeches of the kings in the Adoration, though here the imagery, which includes flowers and precious stones, conveys delight as well as theological understanding. The play is thus a fine verbal encomium of Christ, lyrical rather than dramatic.

The York author boldly built up this unpromising subject into a substantial play: the other two dramatists to deal with it evaded the problems by making the episode as brief as possible. In the *Ludus Coventriae* the bulk of the scene is taken up by the sermon of Peter who expounds a traditional moral allegory, finding in the blind, the lame and the dumb apt (and common) symbols of a spiritual condition,[50] and by a didactic speech of John heralding Christ's Entry. The Entry itself is very brief and consists of the short obeisances of the citizens and their singing of the Palm Sunday hymn, 'Gloria laus et honor tibi sit rex christe redemptor'.[51] In Chester the citizens sing their biblical and liturgical greetings, 'Hosanna filio David' and 'Benedictus qui venit in nomine Domini', and in individual quatrains the six citizens and two boys honour Christ by expressions of faith. The Chester author demonstrates his characteristic adherence to the full biblical narrative by ending the episode with the cleansing of the Temple, an event omitted in the other cycles. At this stretch of the gospel narrative there is an obvious danger that fidelity to biblical completeness will lead to the disintegration of the cycle into tiny scenes, and this is the effect of the Chester's author's unwillingness to select or rearrange. A simple contrast may be made between the methods of Chester and the *Ludus Coventriae*. It is only in these two cycles that the repentance of Mary Magdalene is dramatised (other cycles perhaps omitted it because its significance had been anticipated by the Woman taken in Adultery). Chester correctly follows a long-established tradition by placing it at the house of Simon the Leper and makes this a distinct episode before the Entry into Jerusalem.[52] The *Ludus Coventriae* with structural economy transfers it to the beginning of the Last Supper, an arrangement which is dramatically much more satisfactory.[53]

While the Chester author is especially timid in his moulding of the gospel text into dramatic form, nearly all the dramatists lack poetic confidence in their treatment of the Last Supper. Towneley here bases itself very closely on John, thus startlingly omitting the institution of the eucharist.[54] It proceeds briskly through Christ's recognition of Judas's betrayal, His washing of the disciples' feet, and then with greater leisure paraphrases in quatrains some of Christ's address to the disciples in John xiv. One has the impression of a dramatist cautiously doing his duty but eager to get past a subject so beset by problems of theology and reverence. The York play is difficult to judge because about sixty-five lines are missing from the middle. As it stands it does not contain the institution of the eucharist, but Christ's words, that a new meal and a new law are to supersede the old law and the eating of the lamb of the Passover, indicate clearly that it must have been included (an inference confirmed by Burton's list). But though the play is fragmentary, it is fairly clear that, whilst it did not display inventiveness, it dealt with all the important material with a fitting gravity of tone. Its design was probably close to Chester, where Christ initially explains that 'the tyme is come/that signes and shadows be all done', and after that follows the New Testament fairly closely in Christ's words over the bread and wine, Judas and the sop, Christ washing the disciples' feet, and His address to them based on John.

It is in the *Ludus Coventriae* alone that a dramatic pattern is imposed upon the scene. The incident of Christ's announcement that one of the disciples will betray Him is excellently done, each disciple in an individual stanza in turn condemning the traitor with horror and dismay; Matthew, for instance, says, 'He þat þe doth selle ffor golde or for other good/with his grett Coveytyse hym-self he doth kylle'. When eleven disciples have spoken, Christ intervenes, putting thereby a close to the crescendo of appalled denunciation, and then at last Judas speaks, in cool and unemotional terms asking the question of who the traitor is. This episode was of course suggested to the dramatist by the gospel description of each disciple asking of Christ concerning his betrayer, 'is it I?', though this precise detail is actually represented later in the play.[55] But by this well-designed elaboration with its imaginative sensitivity, the author has transformed the familiar detail into an exciting dramatic passage. There follows a fine theological speech in which Christ expounds Himself as the true paschal lamb which in future they will eat (the author is here following traditional commentaries),[56] and then offers communion to each of the disciples. The action here must have resembled the somewhat unusual iconography that we see in the fresco of the Last Supper of Fra Angelico in the Convent of San Marco. Here the disciples are not seated at a meal, but standing or kneeling they await the Host which Christ is putting into each disciple's mouth in turn. This in fact is not the historical Last Supper but a liturgical act of communion.[57] In the *Ludus Coventriae* also it is a Host (*oble*) that was used, and the Host probably had an *Agnus Dei* stamped upon it, thus associating it with Christ's description of Himself as the new lamb without spot or stain,[58] though admittedly not all the audience would have perceived the connection.

In the *Ludus Coventriae* also, the Last Supper is fitted into the theme of man's sin and Christ's redemptive love which had been begun in the plays of the ministry. This theme is expressed through the imitation of the style of the lyric complaint (just as in the opening monologue of the Woman taken in Adultery). After the scene of communion, for instance, Christ begins His exposition of the eucharist as follows:

> Takyth hed now bretheryn what I have do;
> With my flesch and blood I have ʒow fed,
> Ffor mannys love I may do no mo
> Þan for love of man to be ded.

And Christ's last words before the beginning of the next scene of the Agony in the Garden are:

> Man for my brother may I not forsake
> Nor shewe hym un-kendenesse be no wey
> In peynis for hym my body schal schake
> And for love of man man xal dey.

In these stanzas Christ is speaking to his disciples, not directly to man, and they therefore do not have the exact structure of the complaint form, but with their slightly persistent emphasis upon what Christ has done for love of man and with the image in the second of man as Christ's brother, they are typical in tone and content of the lyric complaints of the fifteenth century.

Whilst Passion plays begin no later than the Entry into Jerusalem, meditations on the Passion often begin with the Agony in the Garden (or at the arrest of Christ).[59] Whether a devotional and compassionate pondering upon Christ's sufferings should begin at this point or not until the Arrest depends upon the interpretation put upon the compressed and slightly enigmatic accounts in the New Testament, and also upon the extent to which the more emotional account in Luke was harmonised with that of Matthew and Mark (John does not include the scene). The issues are as follows. In Matthew and Mark Christ says, 'Tristis est anima mea usque ad mortem', which gives a minimal suggestion of suffering. But if one extends this by taking Christ's words, 'Spiritus quidem promptus est, caro autem infirma', to apply not to the unwatchful disciples but to Christ Himself, if the cup which He prays should pass from Him is the chalice of His blood expended in the

Passion, and if the detail of the bloody sweat from Luke is included, then there emerges a picture of a crisis of interior suffering which is as appalling as the physical suffering to follow.

Chester, which perhaps may represent an early version of this subject, dramatises it austerely and briefly. The only hint of apprehensive suffering is in the translation of 'Tristis est anima . . .', 'My hart is in great mislyking/for death that is to me cominge'. There is no mention of the cup or the sweat, whilst the contrast between the flesh and the spirit is part of a sharp rebuke to the disciples for failing to keep watch. The versions of the other three cycles, all probably written in the mid-fifteenth century, reflect the more emotional temper of the period and in particular perhaps the devotion to the seven blood-sheddings of Christ of which the second was the bloody sweat.[60] In these three plays the text about the flesh and the spirit is referred to Christ, an interpretation not usually found in medieval commentaries though it had the sanction of some of the Fathers such as Bede. By associating this text with Matthew xxvi. 38, it was possible to stress a fear of death in Christ as a natural symptom of His human nature. York and the *Ludus Coventriae* express this idea both emphatically and movingly: 'My flesshe dyderis and daris for doute of my dede' (York, xxviii, 2), 'My flesshe is full ferde and fayne wolde defende' (ibid., 105), 'My flessh is full dredand for drede . . . I swete now both watir and bloode.' In the York play at least a very solid impression is given of the intense human fear of pain and death which Christ chose to endure.

In all three cycles the resolution of the agony comes through divine comfort, in two of them offered by an angel as in Luke xx. 43, but in Towneley by the *Trinitas*.[61] Luke does not specify the nature of the comfort but it was taken to be a reassertion of the necessity of Christ's death for the salvation of man. In Towneley the speech of *Trinitas* is especially long and dogmatic, thereby exceeding its dramatic function and being quite evidently designed to instruct the audience. The best treatment of this conclusion of the Agony in the Garden is that of the *Ludus Coventriae*. In this, as the rubric specifies, the angel, in accordance with late iconography, appears carrying a chalice and the Host.[62] In the text the angel expounds these as Christ's body and blood which for ever after will be offered to the Father in priestly sacrifice. In this way the eucharistic emphasis of the Last Supper is resumed and at the same time the blood which Christ at that moment sheds in agony is seen as part of the eternal redemptive sacrifice. It may finally be noted that the angel affirms the necessity for this sacrifice by recalling the decree of 'þe parlement of hefne'. The speech thus fittingly brings to a close the life of Christ before the Passion by turning the wheel full circle to the moment of the Annunciation. Though this is done less subtly in the other cycles, all versions (save Chester) make a pause at this point in the cycle for dogmatic reflection on what is to follow.

XI

The Passion

The Trial before Annas and Caiaphas
The Trials before Pilate and Herod
The Buffeting and Scourging
The Crucifixion and Burial

The Passion sequence in the *Meditationes vitae Christi* begins with a
striking passage which emphasises how from the Arrest to the sixth
hour of the Crucifixion Christ was given no respite from cross-
questioning, insult, manhandling and torture:[1]

> One of them seizes Him, (this sweet, mild and pious Jesus,)
> another one binds Him, another attacks Him, another scolds
> Him, another pushes Him, another blasphemes Him, another spits
> on Him, another beats Him, another walks around Him, another
> questions Him, another looks for false witnesses against Him. . . .
> He is led back and forth, scorned and reproved, turned and
> shaken here and there like a fool and an imbecile; like a thief and
> a most evil malefactor He is led now to Annas, now to Caiaphas,
> now to Pilate, now to Herod, and again to Pilate, now in, now
> out.

The incessancy so skilfully expressed here through quick, accumulated
detail, is powerfully indicated in the plays by the unremitting torrent of
boasting, insult and scheming which surrounds the silent figure of
Christ during the long scenes of the Trial. It is not until Calvary that the
voices of divine authority and of human compassion reassert themselves: until Christ takes up His Cross and meets the women on the
road to Calvary, almost the entire substance of the plays consists of the
speeches of the evil characters with their malignant verbosity. These
characters fall into three groups: the sinister instigators of the actions,
namely the devil and Judas; the aristocratic villains, Pilate, Herod, and

Annas and Caiaphas, who assault Christ with words, and the base figures, soldiers or Jews, who maltreat him.

The biblical statement that 'the devil entered into Judas' led gradually to Satan being given an increasingly large role in the popular expansions of the biblical narrative. The culmination of this tendency can be seen in Continental drama, in which the devil not only inspires Judas, but tempts Mary Magdalene, tries to thwart the Redemption through Pilate's wife, assists in Judas's suicide, and finally at the Crucifixion hovers by the Cross to seize Christ's soul and to encourage the unrepentant thief in his obduracy. In part this treatment of the devil is moral rather than doctrinal: Satan is the devil of the morality plays rather than of the Fall of the Angels, and in England the logical end of this style is the hybrid Digby play of Mary Magdalene, in which the devil is supported by the seven deadly sins.[2] The authors of the English mystery cycles, however, who rarely amplified their material by the adoption of themes from the morality plays, used the devil sparingly or not at all. In Towneley and Chester Satan has no part in the Passion sequence, in York he necessarily appears in the episode of Procula's dream (but, though the subject is extensively elaborated, the devil's part is small), and it is only in the *Ludus Coventriae* that Satan is established as the arch-conspirator, speaking an initial prologue, meeting Judas with affectionate endearments after the Last Supper, and manipulating Procula to serve his ends. The importance here given to the devil, together with other features peculiar to this cycle, may be taken as clear evidence of Continental influence upon the Passion sequence. Since the devil's relationship to Judas and Procula belongs to the doctrinal tradition, they can best be examined in the scenes devoted primarily to these other figures, but Satan's prologue, which is partly in the morality play tradition, deserves separate consideration.

The first part of the prologue serves a narrative and doctrinal purpose. Satan passes in it from relishing the thought of the swarms of souls that he has won from hell to apprehensiveness at the recollection of Christ's miracles, at last comforting himself with an authoritative text, 'quia in inferno nulla est redempcio', a quotation from the Office for the Dead and ultimately from Job, which the York Satan also cites in the Harrowing of Hell, but there only to be confounded by Christ's correct exposition of its meaning.[3] This part of the prologue therefore lays the foundations for Satan's mood and methods of argument at later points in the cycle. The second half of the prologue, however, serves to establish a relationship between the devil and the audience in the manner of a morality play. At the outset of the speech the devil had announced himself to the audience, 'I am ʒour lord, Lucifer' – a self-identification made especially necessary by the fact that, like the devil in *Wisdom*, he is disguised as a young gallant[4] – and in this second part of the prologue he addresses the audience in the jaunty, persuasive style normally used by the devil to the representative of mankind in the morality plays. He exhorts the audience to love of fine clothing, such as he wears, and to other sins, contempt for the poor, swearing, lechery and bribery. His reassurance that he has brought the audience *newe namys*, so that in future pride shall be called honesty, lechery *naterall kend*, avarice wisdom, and so on, is especially reminiscent of a common morality theme.[5] The dramatist, however, skilfully abandons this morality style, by obliquely bringing the prologue back to its point in chronological time with Satan's promise, 'I am with ʒow at all tymes', the comfort which Christ in accordance with John, was shortly afterwards to offer to the disciples at the Last Supper.

The characterisation of Judas in the plays is exceptional: though so pre-eminently a collaborator with the devil in his betrayal of Christ, and placed by Dante in the mouth of Satan himself in the deepest circle of hell, yet in the plays he is not modelled upon the devil, and is unique amongst the villains in being neither arrogantly boastful nor coarse-tongued. All the other villains are conceived as reflections of the devil, and therefore, though often lively, they are always stereotyped figures of evil; but Judas is shown as a human being moving along the path to damnation, and does once writ large, what everyone else does often in miniature, and the treatment of him is for this reason deliberately designed not to distance him from the audience. People can relax with the comfortable feeling that they are not Cain or Herod, but they cannot be so certain that they are not Judas, and therefore he is portrayed in such a way that his fate, unlike, for instance, that of Herod, arouses a mixture of horror and compassion.

Within the compass of this generalisation the treatment of Judas varies from cycle to cycle. The York author begins in an especially subtle and unusual way with Judas's arrival at Pilate's hall where he encounters a porter. His summons to be given leave to enter by stylistic parody inverts Christ's summons to enter hell, based on Psalm xxiv: 'Do open, porter þe porte of þis prowde place,/That I may passe to youre princes.' The porter replies in the grumbling, abusive style fitting to the porter of hell-gate,[6] but lurking in his ready-tongued insults are terms pregnant with prophetic meaning: to him Judas is an 'onhanged harlott' with a face 'uncomely to kys'.[7] Even the striking line, 'For Mars he hath morteysed his mark', in which the astrological ornament most immediately catches the eye,[8] perhaps contains also a farther meaning in the figurative use of the verb *morteyse*, since the corresponding noun was so regularly used in the mystery plays of the socket into which Christ's Cross was fixed. Combined with these hints is the skilful characterisation of Judas through the eyes of the porter: Judas's speeches are mild and rather colourless, contrasting therefore the more strongly with the porter's horrified apprehension of him as an evil man and one already lost. This method is the more effective for being so rarely used.

This first scene, which seems to have no analogue, provides a sure foundation for the briefer reappearances of Judas, and in particular for his greeting of Christ at Gethsemane. For the falsity of Judas's kiss the dramatist of course followed the gospels, but Judas's hypocritical words of affection have a chilling effect against the background of the earlier scene. It is rare in the cycles for a character to say one thing and mean another.

In the scene of Judas's remorse the York author follows the tradition that Judas, grieving for his sin, attempted to persuade Pilate and the Jews to take back the money and set Christ free. After Judas's initial and moving monologue of repentance, there follows a powerful scene in which his pleas for Christ's release are rejected with cold rationality:

> Thyne is þe wronge, þou wroughte it,
> Þou hight us full trewlye to take hym,
> And oures is þe bargayne, we boughte it.

In these lines the unusual feminine rhymes drive home the iron simplicity of the situation as Caiaphas sees it. Equally striking is the passage in which Judas attempts to bribe the Jews to set Christ free by offering to make himself their bondsman, assuring them of faithful service, an offer rejected by Pilate with the exclamation, 'For by mahoundes bloode, þou wolde selle us all'. This scene has an unusual complexity in that Judas's touching speeches of self-reproach arouse in us a perhaps sentimental readiness to believe in his repentance, whilst the long-standing tradition of remembering Judas as the arch-traitor, compels us to accept that it is Pilate's cold-blooded assessment of the situation that is right. Judas's suicide is fittingly omitted (it had been represented in an earlier stage of the cycle):[9] he leaves the stage with a short despairing monologue and with Pilate's last words of abuse resounding in our minds, 'þe devill mot þe hange'.

In both Chester and in Towneley (as it now stands) Judas's part is very small. The Chester author has taken a little trouble to make Judas's anger at the loss of the money convincing, but otherwise keeps Judas's speeches as brief as the plot permits and ignores him after the Arrest. In Towneley the scene of the betrayal is conducted in a fairly lively manner and Judas is necessarily given a long monologue of self-explanation since the episode of the ointment had not been dramatised. But thereafter his part is tiny and likewise ends with the Arrest of Christ. There is, however, at the end of the Towneley manuscript part of a long narrative monologue spoken by Judas under the heading *Suspencio Iude*. It therefore seems likely that in an earlier version of the cycle Judas had had a substantial part, and that his remorse and suicide were written out by the Wakefield Master in his later version of the various stages of the Trial.[10] The monologue is a narrative summary of the fanciful details of Judas's birth and early life put together from various romance elements, including the themes of patricide and incest, now most familiar from the story of Oedipus.[11] From this fragment it is not possible to reconstruct what the whole play was like, but in all probability it was static and undramatic. The many Continental versions of the *Suspencio* are given dramatic substance by methods not normally used by the English dramatists. Commonly one or more devils take part, to whom Judas can speak, and who wind up the play by carrying his soul off to hell. More ambitiously Greban introduces the allegorical figure of Despair, a daughter of Satan come from the depths of hell.[12] *Desesperaunce* has not the insidious sweetness of Spenser's Despair, but argues forcefully that Judas's crime exceeds the bounds of Christ's mercy. The recourse to personification allegory is here very successful in enabling Greban to present a convincing psychological study of Judas at the point of suicide, but it is extremely unlikely that an English author would have so boldly borrowed from morality play conventions. The dramatist's problem in giving body to this scene is probably indicated by his placing the legendary narrative at this point: in Continental drama it usually occurs much earlier, for instance at the Summoning of the Apostles (Greban), after the effusion of the ointment (*Didot Passion*), or after the Betrayal and Last Supper (*Semur*).[13] Nevertheless though this monologue was perhaps too undramatic to be successful on the stage, it is well written and effectively presents a figure doomed to evil from the moment of his conception, when his mother felt within her 'a lothly lumpe of fleshly syn', the latter apparently a felicitous borrowing of the famous image from *The Cloud of Unknowing*.[14]

The part played by Judas in the *Ludus Coventriae* is small in quantity of lines but nevertheless conceived with some intensity. This intensity is achieved by compression and unusual juxtaposition. Since, as we have said before, the dramatist placed the repentant Magdalene's effusion of the precious ointment at the beginning of the Last Supper, Judas's consequential decision to betray Christ is necessarily delayed until the course of the Last Supper itself, and indeed until after Christ's prophecy of a betrayer. This arrangement provides a context in which Judas's rejection of his master can be seen to be a blasphemous enormity. It also enables the dramatist to follow the tradition that Judas actually took communion from Christ, it being stressed that Judas ate to his damnation. The unnaturalness of the action is, however, best brought out by the devil who, though he had not appeared to incite Judas to treachery, now appears to commend Judas as he leaves the Last Supper, and to welcome him as his darling, summing up gleefully and epigram-matically what Judas has done, 'Thow hast solde þi maystyr and etyn hym also'. The scene of Judas's remorse is exceptionally brief but still pointed. Judas appears before Caiaphas to throw down the unwanted money, and Annas dismisses him contemptuously, 'þou soldyst hym us as hors or kow'. Here again, as in York, the evil characters penetrate to and reveal the vileness of Judas's crime. A rubric finally states 'þan judas castyth down þe mony and goth and hangyth hym-self'. Whilst this kind of narrative rubric, repeating a biblical text, and lacking any precise reference to the *place* or the scaffold on which the action was to be depicted, is slightly suspect as a stage-direction, it remains possible that there was a brief dumb show in which Judas mimed his suicide or, more probably, in which an image of Judas was at this point strung up.[15] One may speculate that if this was so, the devil also took part in it, and seized Judas's soul (which would be represented by a little doll concealed in the belly of the image), as he does so often in Conti-nental drama and art, and in England in the *Holkham Bible Picture Book*.[16]

The last episode in the Passion sequence to portray the devil is that of Pilate's wife. In the *Ludus Coventriae* this is heralded by the re-entrance of the devil upon the stage after the Trial before Herod, and, according to the stage-direction, he comes *in þe most orrible wyse* and disports himself in the *platea* whilst Christ is being re-clothed after the scourging. The positions are then reversed: Christ is humiliatingly led round the *platea*, whilst Satan – presumably now mounted upon a scaffold – makes his first speech. Satan begins in a style of ranting self-congratulation about those within his power and continues by explain-ing the vengeance which he has prepared for Christ: the Cross, nails and sharp spear. When, however, his narrative leads him to envisage the precise moment at which Christ will enter hell, he becomes a little alarmed and calls upon hell to make ready to receive so formidable a visitor. Thereupon an anonymous devil is heard to speak from hell warning in terror that if Christ enters hell it will be to destroy the devil's authority. At this Satan hits upon the plan of giving Pilate's wife a warning dream.[17] This episode is awkwardly treated: the dramatist seems to have wished to keep the design found in works such as Greban's *Passion*, but to reduce it to a fraction of the size. Greban's elaborate scene makes much more convincing sense. In it the fears of the devils are first aroused by the anticipatory rejoicing of the patriarchs, a council follows, and a contrast is made between the uneasy devils in hell and the jubilant Satan newly returned from earth to describe the brilliance of his machinations against Christ. The sudden apprehensions of the devils in hell are thus properly motivated,[18] while the device of the warning dream emerges as part of the considered resourcefulness of Lucifer who has presided over the anxious consultations of the other devils. The remainder of the episode in the *Ludus Coventriae* is equally brief: Satan's warning to the sleeping Procula is given in dumb show (but the stage-directions for it are clear and precise), and the contents of the terrifying dream are revealed only in Procula's speech to Pilate. Though very brief, this part of the episode is effectively done, whereas the impression left by the earlier part is that the dramatist's overall design compelled him to include it, but that he felt far less interest in the scene than he did in the earlier interventions of the devil.

Unlike the author of the *Ludus Coventriae*, the York dramatist in this episode puts the emphasis not upon the devil and his intention to thwart the Redemption,[19] but upon Procula, and the result is much more successful. The construction of the episode is different in that the prelude to the dream is not a portrayal of Satan but a scene between Pilate and his wife. Pilate's opening speech of self-praise is echoed by the extravagant compliments of Procula, who proceeds from eulogistic adulation of her husband to delight in herself:

> All welle of all womanhede I am, wittie and wise,
> Consayve nowe my countenaunce so comly and clere.
> The coloure of my corse is full clere,
> And in richesse of robis I am rayed.

It is safe to imagine here that Procula's fine clothing was as ludicrously sumptuous as was her praise of herself comically flamboyant. These introductory speeches are followed by a short scene of conjugal embrace—unique in the mystery plays—in which Pilate ostentatiously relishes their kiss and calls to mind the greater pleasure of kissing in bed, to which Procula assents with a coyly frank statement about what women enjoy, in which there seems to be a faint echo of the Wife of Bath. This ludicrously amorous little scene is followed by one in which Procula rails at the beadle like a miniature Cleopatra and is at last appeased by the festive drink which Pilate offers her before she leaves for her dwelling place. This scene as it progresses gives the appearance of being a tiny comedy of manners developed for its own sake. But the farther significance is made plain by the opening line of the devil's speech, 'O woman! be wise and ware, and wonne in þi witte', which recalls Procula's praise of herself as 'wittie and wise'. The devil's exhortation has thus the ring of a temptation, and the York dramatist obviously had in mind the parallelism between Eve and Procula noted in the *Glossa ordinaria,* namely that just as the devil through a woman brought death to man, so he sought by a woman to retain the *imperium mortis,* of which he might be deprived by Christ's death.[20] Furthermore, while the devil in the *Ludus Coventriae* is reported to have warned Procula that she and Pilate would go to hell unless Christ was set free, in York the devil causes alarm by warning that they will lose their power and their riches. The threat therefore is psychologically well-grounded in the earlier portrayal of Pilate and his wife. There is also a further subtlety, probably intentional. The devil's advice to Procula is morally ambivalent: in his eagerness to frustrate the Redemption he has to advise an action which is in itself right. But by establishing Pilate and Procula as an arrogant and luxurious couple he is able to make clear that Procula advises Pilate to do the right thing for the wrong reason. The scene between Pilate and his wife, like the scene between Judas and the janitor, appears to be the invention of the reviser of the York cycle, now referred to as the York Realist. Whilst he has been justly praised for his realistic dialogue, his skill in constructing original scenes, which put the subsequent and traditional action in a different light, has not been adequately noticed.[21]

Though the devil and Judas are Christ's primary enemies, in terms of dramatic construction they move on the periphery, the devil at this stage never directly encountering Christ, and Judas meeting Him only at the moment of the kiss, an action momentous in itself but treated in the plays in a muted way. Of those who confront Christ directly the next group to be considered are the aristocratic villains, Pilate, Herod, and Caiaphas and Annas, who retain a preposterous sense of rank unlike the nameless plebeian torturers who lack all semblance of

dignity. With the exception of Towneley the cycles present an ambivalent treatment of Pilate. This ambivalence has been explained by the
dual and contradictory traditions of a good and bad Pilate, but it may
also have been conditioned by the doctrinal ambivalence which itself
led to the dual tradition, namely that on the one hand Pilate decreed
the Crucifixion and could therefore be considered the arch-enemy of
Christ and a type of the devil, on the other he gave the decree necessary
for the redemption of the world. Therefore, while one tradition
ascribed to Pilate a vicious youth (during which, like Judas, he
murdered his brother) and a horrible end, another gave him a
saintly death accompanied by a voice from heaven, which applied
to Pilate the words of the *Magnificat*, 'All generations shall call thee
blessed'.[22]

None of the English cycles go as far as the Continental plays, which
often describe Pilate outright as *guter mann* or *sant homs*, and may build
up a picture of a just and honest man struggling to reconcile justice
towards Christ with his obligations towards Caesar and the Jews.
Greban's Pilate, for instance, is shown to try at every turn to escape
the dilemma: he sends Christ to Herod for this reason, he offers the
choice between Christ and Barabbas, he has Christ beaten and mocked
to show the destruction of Christ's claims to royalty, he even unbiblically offers to banish him. When all these stratagems fail he makes
a moving speech to the Jews, compassionately pleading Christ's common humanity in order to persuade them to cease pressing their
accusations against him. Pilate's sympathy towards Christ, repeatedly
expressed, is here used as an effective foil to the vindictiveness and
implacability of the other characters.

The English dramatists never so positively establish Pilate as a
pleasing character, but with the exception of the Towneley author they
make Pilate uncharacteristic of Christ's enemies in general in that he
takes no relish in what he does. The two cycles, however, which most
clearly present Pilate as unvillainous, do so chiefly by the negative
method of giving little space to him. In the *Ludus Coventriae* the part of
Pilate, as compared with that of the vicious Herod, is small: when he
speaks he is mild, and over and over again he repeats in various ways his
biblical words, 'I can find no fault in this just man': 'ffor no defawth
in hym I fynde' (l. 554), or more positively, 'I can fynde in hym but
good'. His depiction of Pilate is not only brief but also stylised and
therefore allows for the long speech (ll. 654–75) in which with extraordinarily precise detail he gives instructions for the Crucifixion. If this
speech is understood literally, Pilate has obviously changed into a

sadistic ruler who commands sufferings far in excess of legal necessity. But more probably it should be taken as a set-piece of prophecy describing what Christ himself has chosen to endure. This interpretation is suggested both by the formality of tone and the curious change in the course of it from commands to the executioners to direct address to Christ:

> Whan he is betyn crowne hym for ʒour kyng
> and þan to þe cros ʒe xal hym bryng.
> And to þe crosse þou xalt be fest
> And on thre naylys þi body xal rest.

The Chester dramatist seems to have begun with the same conception of Pilate but to have executed it with less mastery. Though Pilate's intention is to elude the necessity to condemn Christ, he nevertheless in the course of his brief part swears by the devil (l. 257) and refers insultingly to Christ as a *losenger* (a lying rascal). Against this the decorum of Pilate's speeches in the *Ludus Coventriae* is particularly noticeable.

In contrast to these two cycles York and Towneley give Pilate a substantial part, in both instances this being the result of fifteenth-century rewriting. Pilate's part in York is exceptionally elaborate and not by modern standards consistent. Scattered through Pilate's many speeches are the stylistic devices which had previously signalled a devilish affiliation. Nearly all of his appearances are heralded by a bombastic monologue in which Pilate asserts his pre-eminence and savagely threatens anyone who thwarts him. One of these, in which Pilate – strangely for a ruler – arrogantly rejoices in his own beauty, is particularly reminiscent of Satan:

> For I ame þe luffeliest lappid and laide,
> With feetour full faire in my face,
> My forhed both brente is and brade,
> And myne eyne þei glittir like þe gleme in þe glasse.
> And þe hore þat hillis my heed
> Is even like to þe golde wyre,
> My chekis are bothe ruddy and reede,
> And my coloure as cristall is cleere.

Consistent with these monologues are the many occasions on which Pilate swears by the devil, Lucifer and Mahoune, his abusive references to Christ, his happy acceptance of Judas's treachery, his own undisguised robbery when he defrauds the Squire of his land,[23] and his fury

in the apocryphal incident of the standard-bearers.[24] Nevertheless
intertwined with this presentation of Pilate as an agent of the devil is
the theme of Pilate as a just ruler, since he is by no means acquiescent
in the vindictiveness of Annas and Caiaphas and often insists upon a
fair trial. The dramatist seems to have hit upon a fairly straightforward
distinction, namely that Pilate is reasonable, even sympathetic, whenever Christ is represented only as a threat to the Jews, but raging and
furious when his own power seems to be threatened. It is difficult to
know what further conclusions should be drawn. Obviously Pilate's
delaying tactics are essential to the length of the sequence, and if the
author wished to give weight to this part by making a different ratio
between narrative length and importance of subject-matter, this would
be a sufficient explanation. This relationship between cause and effect
could, however, be reversed, and one could maintain that this sequence
was long at least partly for the reason that the dramatist was interested
in making a study of Pilate as a vacillating character. The latter view,
however, seems unlikely. The depiction of a ruler who administers
justice composedly when personally unaffected by the issues, but flies
into a fury when his own position is at stake, does not reveal any
unusual insight into human vagary; it would seem to be a conception
satisfactory enough if it serves some farther purpose, but poor if there
is no literary justification for it save its own interest. Furthermore the
interpretation of Pilate as a vacillating character is a misreading of the
text. Admittedly the dramatist shows Pilate proceeding four times
from an indifferent benevolence to anger against Christ, but these
psychological movements should not be understood cumulatively:
each play stands as a separate unit. If this were not so, the dramatist
would have shown at least once, if not more often, what it was that
appeased Pilate after his fit of anger. But, whilst he shows quite carefully why Pilate moves from friendliness to rage, he never shows the
reversal of this: that Pilate is once more benevolent has to be accepted
at the beginning of each play.

Unlike the morally parti-coloured Pilate of the York cycle, the
Wakefield Pilate is a gigantic personification of evil. In part, as has
often been pointed out, he is the unjust judge of medieval satire: his
interest in any case lies in which party will bribe him to give them a
favourable verdict. He happily welcomes to his court plaintiffs, quest-
mongers, jurors and outriders providing they are all false. But this list
also suggests that Pilate is far more than a corrupt judge who uses the
administration of the law to line his own pocket: for, whereas a corrupt
plaintiff would obviously be of practical benefit, a corrupt outrider

(i.e. summoner) would most certainly not be, since, through his own acceptance of bribes, he would in fact bring less business to Pilate's court. This hint of a love of evil for its own sake is openly developed some lines farther on, in which Pilate proclaims that backbiters and slanderers are his *dere darlyngys*, a phrase which would more readily be used by the devil or some personification of evil, the former affinity being confirmed by Pilate's description of himself as *auctor malis*.

The most striking way, however, in which Pilate far exceeds the role of unjust judge is in his unexplained hostility to Christ:

> ffor no thyng in this warld dos me more grefe
> Then for to here of crist and of his new lawes;
> To trow that he is godys son my hart wold all to-clefe,
> Though he be never so trew both in dedys and in sawes
> Therfor shall he suffre mekill myschefe.

It is part of the morally inverted world of the Trial scenes that what before had been presented as Christ's great glory, namely that he healed the sick and raised the dead to life, become instead accusations. Occasionally some explanation for this is given – he performed his miracles through witchcraft or for bribes – but more often these matters are stated baldly as proof of his wickedness. But Pilate in this speech goes even further than this in perverted judgment, and his heartbreak at the thought that Christ may be God's Son can only be understood as the reaction of pure evil towards the divine.

Towneley is unusual in presenting so evil a figure of Pilate: on the Continent, even when allusion was made to his suicide, he was still shown to conduct himself during the Trial in the neutral manner of the gospel accounts. By common tradition it is Herod, not Pilate, who treats Christ with callous contempt; this interpretation is based upon his behaviour in Luke, where Christ's unwillingness to speak provokes Herod and his court to mock Christ and to dress him in a white robe, which commentators took to be the dress of a fool (a gloss repeated by the dramatists, though this can scarcely have been apparent on the fifteenth-century stage, since by that time motley clothing seems already to have become the mark of the court fool).[25] Towneley does not present the trial before Herod, though from references within the text it seems that an earlier Herod play was cut out at the time of the Wakefield Master's revision (the building up of the character of Pilate would account for this excision). All the other cycles, however, contain a fairly developed figure of a raging and menacing ruler. Chester's Herod is portrayed in a rare passage of lively speech. Herod begins quietly but is shown to work himself into a fury on account of Christ's silence; his understanding of the matter is that Christ is mad, obdurate and useless, a fit object only for insult: he is a staniel, 'dumbe and deafe as a doted doe'. The same pattern occurs in the *Ludus Coventriae*, but more intensified in that Herod has already characterised himself in a monologue in which he rejoices in the thought that it was he who brought John the Baptist to death (a subject often included in Continental drama but not in English plays), and boasts of his delight in savagery: 'To kylle a thowsand crystyn I gyf not An hawe,/to se hem hangyn or brent to me is very plesauns.' The depiction of Herod as a persecutor of Christians appears to be a motif drawn from hagiography.

The only Herod to be given elaborate treatment is that of York, where the dramatist has distinguished him from Pilate by making him grotesquely savage and sadistic. His opening monologue establishes his ferocity: he is a subduer of giants and dragons, and those who oppose him will have their brains bashed in, their bones broken, or be clapped into chains. Like most monologues of its type, this creates a mood rather than a psychological foundation for what is to follow, though the threatening tone continues in Herod's recurrent swearing by the devil and in the abusive language applied to Christ, the latter being echoed in the speeches of Herod's two sons. This play confirms one's earlier impression that Middle English was especially rich in terms of contempt and that the unit of the alliterative phrase was very adaptable to insult. Especially striking in this play is the use of the insulting diminutive, such as *myting* (Christ is a *mummeland myghtyng* when he will not speak), and *sauterell*, which appears to mean a tiny saint. Striking too are some of the ironies which emerge from the mockery of Christ. Herod, for instance, at one point says to his son: 'No sone, þe rebalde seis us so richely arayed,/He wenys we be aungelis evere ilkone.' It is quite possible that there was a common joke that rich clothes led the naïve to believe their wearers to be angelic or divine: its most famous literary expression is the mistake of the youthful Parsifal. The dramatist's inventiveness in applying this jest to Christ is a superb example of literary audacity. It is this kind of pattern that is most satisfying in the play rather than sustained characterisation; and, whilst the author has rightly been praised for a new kind of realism (as, for instance, in the servant's invitation to Pilate to wash his hands whilst the water is still warm), his skilful elaborations of the more traditional style deserve equal attention.

Of the aristocratic villains there remain only Annas and Caiaphas.

In the cycles they are subsidiary figures in the sense that they are rarely given their own arrogant, boastful prologues. They therefore do not tower over the action as giant figures of evil, but in a less flamboyant way plot the seizing of Christ and encourage Pilate to his verdict. The Chester pair waver between politically motivated animosity towards Christ – they fear that he will provoke the wrath of Rome – and the sheer malevolence which they display when Christ is actually before them, though, as in most of the cycles, one of them – it varies which – is made more cunningly prudent than the other. In Chester it is Caiaphas who cautiously restrains the Jews from the excesses of savagery, whilst Annas vilely eggs them on, 'Despyse him! spurne and spitt!'. The Annas and Caiaphas of the *Ludus Coventriae* are characterised initially by short monologues, in which they pride themselves on their powers as upholders and administrators of the law, the piled up aureate diction suggesting the emptiness of their self-congratulation. In later scenes, however, their tone is more neutral and they seem in fact pale schemers beside the savagery of Herod.

Towneley and York make much more of Annas and Caiaphas. In Towneley on their first appearance they seem quietly characterless, but the scene derives horror from the apparently sweetly reasonable way in which they cite Christ's miracles of healing as evidence of his villainy. But in the Wakefield Master's play of the Buffeting a sharp and effective distinction is made between the two: Caiaphas is raging and brutal, Annas quiet and fair-minded, though apparently only from a sense of public decorum. Caiaphas is violent both in intention and language. He would like to kill Christ with his own hands, to put out his eyes or to break his neck and, when restrained by Annas, urges on the torturers. Whilst Caiaphas, unlike Cain, cannot commit the murder that would please him, he is reminiscent of the Towneley Cain in the violent breaches of decorum in his speech. Excremental imagery recurs, as when he says to Christ, 'weme! the dwillys durt in thi berd,/vyle fals tratur'. His insults include distastefully oblique accusations against Christ's mother, 'where was thy syre at bord/when he met with thi dame', this being followed by the more blunt corollary that Christ is a bastard (*fundlyng*).[26] This Caiaphas is perhaps the most horrifying of all the villains: in the others their pride, modelled upon the devil's, is emphasised through mock-heroic style; but in Caiaphas there is a cold human villainy which makes him seriously frightening.

There is a small point of interest in the manner in which Annas persuades Caiaphas neither to kill Christ himself, nor to impose a sentence of death, but to send him to Pilate. On this issue the New

Testament simply has Annas say that it is not legal for them to impose a death sentence, the historical explanation being that the Jews under Roman rule had not this power. Two cycles, in which the matter is not important, assign to Annas the biblical explanation without elucidating it. But Towneley and York offer an ingenious and more readily understandable reason. Annas and Caiaphas as bishops are forbidden by canon law to sentence a man to death:[27] this can only be done by Pilate as a judge in the civil courts. This anachronism is of course of the same order as the understanding of Cain's sacrificial offering as tithes, and like many of the anachronisms dispels any tendency to think of the action happening in a strange country long ago; but in its unexpected appositeness it reveals a literary intelligence at work in a way that is very satisfying.

The Annas and Caiaphas of the York cycle are introduced in a more muted way, since Pilate from the first presides over the conspiracy and dominates the scene. Gradually, however, they acquire a sinister personality. This is effected partly through the usual method of coarse, colloquial diction, but also, more subtly, in the way in which they refer to others. The usual kind of abuse is applied to Christ, but more unusually Judas is referred to by them as *gentill Judas*, and Pilate as a lord, *most lofsom of lyre*, an alliterative, eulogistic phrase which anticipates Beelzebub's description of Lucifer as *lovely of lyre* in the Harrowing of Hell. A perverse use of insult is common in the cycles, but a perverse use of compliment rare, and therefore the more telling in effect. Ironic anticipation of the Harrowing of Hell becomes more marked in the subsequent plays attributed to the York Realist, and in these some of Satan's misunderstandings, which were to be so majestically refuted, here pass in silence. One of the most striking parallelisms is Annas's reply to Caiaphas's accusation of Christ that he called himself 'God sone of hevene':

> I have goode knowlache of þat knafe,
> Marie me menys, his moder highte;
> and Joseph his fadir, as god me safe,
> Was kidde and knowen wele for a wrighte.

These lines are verbally echoed in Satan's later taunting rejoinder:[28]

> Thy fadir knewe I wele be sight,
> He was a write his mette to wynne,
> And Marie me menys þi modir hight,
> Þe uttiremeste ende of all þi kynne.

This is a kind of stylistic subtlety that performance year after year would enable the audience to become alert to.

Mingled with the episodes in which the aristocratic villains engage in verbal assaults upon Christ are those in which various plebeian and nameless men physically torture and manhandle Him. Meditative elaborations of the gospels, based upon gospel harmonies, provide four scenes of this kind: the buffeting at the house of Annas and Caiaphas, the humiliation of Christ after the Trial before Herod, the scourging commanded by Pilate, and finally the nailing to the Cross. Dialogue was normally provided to accompany the action in all these scenes, and occasionally elsewhere as, for instance, in the Arrest in the *Ludus Coventriae*, where these usually anonymous figures are given names as they were in Continental drama, in York where the soldiers roughly abuse Christ as they lead him back from Herod to Pilate, and recurrently in Towneley, where the men insult Christ both on this occasion and also earlier when they lead Christ from Annas and Caiaphas to Pilate. These men are referred to by various generic titles: in Chester and the *Ludus Coventriae* as Jews, in York as *milites*, and in Towneley as *tortores*. These differences in classification are not reflected in the dialogue, but probably would have been in dress. If the men were represented as soldiers they would wear coats of mail; if as Jews, the actors would probably wear the distinctive Jewish cap, familiar from iconography, and perhaps also masks, in which the characteristic Jewish traits of physiognomy, such as the hooked nose, would be accentuated as in caricature. Historical sense indicates that the emissaries of the high priests who arrested Christ would be distinct from the followers of Pilate who carried out his orders. Some distinction is often made in art: in the *Luttrel Psalter*, for instance, Christ's persecutors are sometimes ugly peasant figures, sometimes mailed soldiers.[20] In the English plays, where this historical distinction appears to be ignored, all the figures are equally grotesque, characterised through their speech and action; and whilst the use made in Nazi Germany of the medieval iconographic tradition of Jewish caricature has nowadays made it offensive to all sensibilities, the dramatic, visual use of this tradition was probably almost as innocent of immediate malice as the convention of symbolising an evil soul by a black skin.

The traditional theological and meditative emphasis upon the sufferings of Christ required that the scenes of the buffeting and scourging should be made as extensive as possible. If these were performed in dumb show as are two of the three in the *Ludus Coventriae*, their duration would presumably have to be short. It was therefore in general necessary to invent lengthy passages of dialogue. The obvious type of invention – one much used on the Continent – was that the blows should be accompanied by brutal description of the torment, so that words should make vivid to the imagination the sufferings which could only be enacted symbolically upon the stage.[30] This is the method used to some extent in all the cycles, and in particular at Chester, where the buffeting and scourging are commented upon in the short, facile quatrains of the Jews, each of whom describes the blow that he gives minutely and with savage relish, frequently referring to disgusting physical detail: in the second scene in particular the emphasis upon spittle and mucous is hideously repellent. Less physically ugly, but in another way at least as horrifying, is the Scourging in Towneley, in which the *tortores* instead enumerate Christ's miracles, and one must suppose that each miracle cited, Christ healing the leper, giving sight to the blind, or raising the dead, is accompanied by a blow: the scene thus presents a bafflingly evil inversion of normal values.

The gospel text suggested other ironic possibilities. The mock arraying of Christ as a king with a thorn-circlet for a crown and a reed for sceptre is verbally paralleled in York, where this scene culminates in a series of jeering hails (which ironically repeat the citizen's greetings to Christ as he entered Jerusalem):

> Ave! riall roy and rex judeorum!
> Hayle! comely kyng, þat no kyngdom has kende,
> Hayle! undughty duke, þi dedis ere dom,
> Hayle! man, unmyghty þi menȝe to mende.

More importantly the blindfolding of Christ with the question, 'Prophesy who smote thee?', led to the recurring ironic elaboration that the men were pretending to play a game of blind man's buff.[31] A hint of this ancient game perhaps lurks in the gospel text itself, and this hint was detected by medieval dramatists who took it up and invented variations upon it. In Semur one of the buffeters says that he wants to play at *chappel fol* (l. 6439), and in a longer and livelier scene in Greban one devises *ung tres bon jeu* (l. 20952), an episode repeated with some colloquial additions by Michel. An unusual variation of this occurs in Eger (ll. 4315–35), where the buffeters propose to play *puczpirn* with Christ (a game which they say to be common amongst children), and in which apparently one player represents the pear tree whilst the others pretend to knock fruit off it. Less remarkable are versions of the Scourging in some French plays, in which the scourgers engage in a contest of strength, the winner to be given a cup of wine. The theme of the game of blind man's buff is elaborately worked out in three out of the four English cycles (Chester is the exception), and the speech of the buffeters interestingly preserves the kind of rhyming nonsense (such as 'whele and pille') and the simple incantatory questions (e.g. 'ho was þat?'), which are characteristic of children's games throughout the centuries. The same kind of chilling recourse to children's rhymes at moments of intense brutality is found in some Continental scenes of the Crucifixion, in which the executioners enumerate their hammer blows on the nails in the kind of nursery rhyme counting still familiar in England from verses such as 'One, two, buckle my shoe'.[32]

Whilst the zestful inventiveness with which the theme of the game is elaborated in the plays seems to be peculiar to the medieval dramatists, and in particular to the English writers, the idea itself is found much earlier in hagiographical accounts of the passions of the martyrs. In Abbo's *Passio sancti Edmundi*, for instance, the Danes shoot arrows at Edmund *quasi ludendo*, in other words as though they were engaged in a game of archery.[33] In scenes such as this, one finds also the pattern of evil, which upon the stage becomes so startling, namely that amongst the crowd of brutal executioners there is not a single sympathetic figure. The simple dramatic device of contrast would not of itself have been out of keeping with the dramatists' method of working. In the episode of the Scourging in Greban, for instance, there is one reluctant participant named Estonné, who from time to time recoils from the savagery:[34]

> Il est tant gasté
> de cracher amont et aval
> que le cueur me fait tres grant mal
> a le regarder en la face.

Estonné is successfully egged on by the others to join in, but such occasional touches of ordinary human feeling provide an outlet within the play for the distress of the spectators, and at the same time confer a touch of naturalism, for by the standards of general probability there would be at least one man in such a group who co-operated in the horror as minimally as possible. The presence of Estonné makes the reading of the scene in Greban more tolerable, but the stylised English scenes are the more powerful for excluding any representation of the sensibilities of the spectators upon the stage. In the English plays the game metaphor represents the turn of the screw in the accentuation of horror, for through it is conveyed a naked enjoyment in the activity of evil which is hellish in its reverberations.[35]

At the quiet centre of so much boasting, plotting, insults and violence stands the still figure of Christ. Where in the plays of the ministry Christ dominates the stage by his magisterial speeches, in the scenes of the Trial he does so largely by his silence. This impressive conception of Christ's part derives ultimately from the gospel account of the trial before Herod, in which Christ meets Herod's inquisition with a contained silence. In the gospels, however, this silence only partially extends to the earlier and later stages of the Trial: according to all four Christ replied to the questions and charges of the high priests, while John records a continuous passage of dialogue between Christ and Pilate. For medieval authors who represented this sequence in narrative or drama there were two possible ways of clarifying the ambivalence of the gospels with their fluctuations between silence and authoritative rejoinder. One way is that adopted in the *Meditationes*, in which the author describes only the words and actions of Christ's judges, accusers and torturers, whilst of Christ he says, 'See the Lord shamefacedly and patiently remaining silent to all . . .' or 'He holds His peace and most patiently remains silent . . .'.[36] At the other extreme from the presentation of a consistently silent Christ is the portrayal of a Christ who consistently answers his accusers. This second way was made possible by the following of a gospel harmony, for if authors included all Christ's words in all four gospels they would inevitably provide him with a substantial speaking part. This is the method used, for instance, by the author of the Cornish cycle.[37]

The English dramatists on the whole chose to portray a silent Christ, though they evidently did not feel that they could treat the gospels quite so boldly as did the author of the *Meditationes*, and therefore they did not entirely omit all Christ's gospel words. The only dramatist, however, who manifestly did not aim to achieve the doctrinal and dramatic effectiveness of Christ's silence is the author of the *Ludus Coventriae*, who once again shows his Continental affiliations, not only by attributing to Christ many of the texts from Matthew and John for the trial scenes, but also by transferring to this place texts spoken by Him at other times in the gospels. Chester, despite its normal cautious adherence to the gospels, unwaveringly depicts Christ's silence until the last episode (the final appearance of Christ before Pilate), in which the dialogue of John xviii. 34–7 is amply paraphrased; here by contrast, the scene momentarily acquires the tone of trial scenes in the lives of saints, in which the saint triumphs in a battle of wits against his or her persecutor. York shows Christ speaking twice, once, as recorded in Matthew, to the high priests, and once, unbiblically, to Pilate. On

account of the extraordinary length of the Trial scenes in York, however, these brief speeches appear insignificant lapses from a long silence.
It is Towneley, however, which is most impressive in its consistent
presentation of the silent Christ. Here Christ speaks only once, just
before the Flagellation, where in lines based on John xix 10 he tells
Pilate that it is only through the Father that he has power over him.
Even this, however, may be considered a failure of nerve in the dramatist, who at last felt it necessary to remind the audience of the true
doctrinal position. His earlier treatment of the silence has been particularly powerful, it being especially accentuated through the means of
jeers, such as that of Caiaphas, 'Though thi lyppis be stokyn/yit myght
thou say, mom'.

The author of the *Meditationes* conceives Christ's silence as a sign of
his patience and humility: though the gospels record Christ speaking,
yet for the purpose of devising a devout meditation the author felt
free to rely upon Isaiah liii. 7: 'He was oppressed, and he was afflicted,
yet he opened not his mouth: he is brought as a lamb to the slaughter,
and as a sheep before her shearers is dumb, so he openeth not his
mouth.' In the mystery cycles this idea is part of the effect but not the
whole. Far from Christ's silence being solely a manifestation of his
unquestioned submission to human suffering, it becomes rather a sublime expression of his divinity; where elevated language could only
fail, silence becomes a magnificent symbol of the inexpressible. Even
from the printed page the reader can sense the intensity of the omission.
Continental texts draw attention to the silence before Herod by the
recurring rubric, 'Ihesus tacet',[38] but the English plays are so designed
that this reminder is not necessary: it is clear that the pattern of contrast
between noise and stillness, begun in the plays of the Fall of the Angels,
reaches its climax in the plays of the Trial where verbal raucousness and
violence enclose but do not overcloud the heavenly silence at their
centre.

After the Trial scenes the dramatic pattern of the Passion sequence
changes. Whilst Pilate and Caiaphas and Annas continue in their malice
and boasting, and the soldiers persist in their savagery, finding new
variations upon their former themes of insult, Christ casts away his
silence; and a mood of involved compassion is no longer severely
excluded, but introduced and emphasised through the laments of the
Virgin and the other Marys. These three strains are woven together in
harmonious and pungent contrasts.

The soldiers continue their exuberant relish in the work of torture
and the taunting of their supposed victims as they nail Christ to the Cross

and when he hangs upon it. Meditations had stressed the manner of the nailing and described it as an agonising, long-drawn-out torture.[39] All the cycles preserve the traditional detail that the Cross with the holes bored in it was too large for Christ's body and that his limbs had to be wrenched in order to make them fit the holes. In the brief *Ludus Coventriae* episode the Jews speak only of this difficulty and there is no ironic comment from the soldiers: but their derision, as in some German plays, is expressed in the horrifying action of their dancing round the Cross as though it were a maypole.[40] In Chester the short quatrains effectively convey the Jews' busy pride in their role of executioners as also their brutal contempt: 'As ever have I wynne,/his Arme is but a fynne', one says, when finding Christ's arm too short to reach the borehole. The York soldiers keep up a lively flow of insult and of complaining about the difficulty of the job, and in their speeches, more than in the other cycles, there is much blunt description of actual suffering for the understanding of the audience. There is, for instance, a mention of the common meditative detail of how Christ's garments have stuck to the wounds of his body so that they have to be stripped off violently. It is Towneley, however, which is the most remarkable in its handling of the jibes of the *tortores*, and in particular in its adaptation of the much-used image of the Christ-knight to the purposes of ironic insult.[41]

The ironic method employed can be illuminated by reference to passages in two French plays which manipulate ideas in the same way for a similar purpose. One occurs in the *Passion de Semur*, where Annas taunts Christ as follows as he hangs on the Cross:[42]

> Raby, le grant Dieu vous redresse!
> Bien ressanblés homme de festes
> Au chappel dessus vostre teste.
> Il sanble que danser veullés
> A vous bras cy esparpillez,
> Fy, Jhesu, je dix de toy fy.

The raw material for this taunt is found in a medieval commonplace, occurring, for instance, in the *Legenda aurea*, in which the same ironic parallelism is made between Christ on the Cross and some gay young man on a festive occasion, between the crown of thorns and the garland of flowers and the arms outstretched on the Cross and the arms outstretched to dance.[43] But the play makes a startling reversal of tradition: an analogy invented to give point to Christ's loving reproach to man has been transferred to a context in which it conveys the speaker's sense of derision for Christ. The other illuminating passage occurs in

Greban, where one of the executioners named Malcuidant makes a verbal play upon Christ's promise to rebuild the Temple within three days:[44]

> Jhesus, fay ung temple nouveau
> acoup, car au lieu de marteau
> tu as trois clous a grosses pointes
> au travers de tes membres pointes,
> et en lieu de bois pour ouvrer
> tu peuz d'ung gibet recouvrer
> qui t'estend les nerfz et les vaines.

Here also Christ's words are turned back upon Himself, and the conceit, which consists in the mason's hammer becoming the nails and the wood of the Cross serving for building materials, resembles the similar conceits developed from the Christ-knight image, in which the instruments of the Crucifixion by a witty but savage conjunction are seen as part of the accoutrements of a knight.[45]

In Towneley the *tortores* goad and mock Christ by pretending to see their task of nailing him to the Cross and of standing the Cross in its socket as that of serving men horsing a knight before a tournament. The fourth *tortor*, for instance, says as he helps to raise the Cross:

> Let me go therto, if I shall;
> I hope that I be the best mershall
> ffor [to] clynke it right.
> do rase hym up now when we may,
> ffor I hope he and his palfray
> Shall not twyn this nyght.

In theme this is the same, but in tone the exact reverse of the lyric complaint in which Christ says:[46]

> My palefrey is of tre,
> wiht nayles naylede þurh me.
> Ne is more sorwe to se –
> certes noon more no may be.

Whilst this lyric is unusual in its moving manipulation of the image for pathetic effect, the Christ-knight image normally serves as a demonstration of the humiliation and suffering that Christ endured for love of man. Therefore to put an ample expansion of it into the mouths of the *tortores* would startle and horrify those familiar with medieval devotional traditions, and is a stroke of inventiveness comparable to that of giving Lazarus a speech of warning from the dead.

The second strain to be considered is the speeches of Christ Himself. According to the gospels, Christ spoke once on the way to Calvary when he ominously rebuked the daughters of Jerusalem, and upon the Cross he spoke the Seven Words honoured throughout the Middle Ages in various devotional forms.[47] In addition various other biblical texts were ascribed to Christ on the Cross in the liturgy of Holy Week: of these some of the most important or recurrent were, 'O vos omnes qui transitis per viam, attendite et videte si est dolor sicut dolor meus' (Lamentations i. 12); 'Populus meus, quid feci tibi?' (Micah vi. 3); 'Quid est quod debui ultra facere . . .' (Isaiah v. 4); and 'Vulpes foveas habent et volucres caeli nidos, Filius autem hominis non habet ubi caput suum reclinet' (Luke ix. 58).[48] The English cycles divide into two kinds: those which keep closely to the gospels (Chester and the *Ludus Coventriae*), and those which, taking the liturgy as their starting point, ascribe a series of complaints to Christ (York and Towneley). In Chester the adherence to the gospel record must again reflect its general caution in the treatment of Christ, and indeed, despite the passage of lively jesting and a moving complaint of the Virgin, the whole Crucifixion scene is handled with brevity and reserve. It is the cycle to use the least non-biblical material at this point and, unlike any of the others, contains not a single one of the following episodes: John's announcement of the Crucifixion to the Virgin, Veronica and the handkerchief, and the story of Longinus. By contrast the *Ludus Coventriae* includes all three, and this particular combination of apocryphal incident with reliance upon the Seven Words again suggests a Continental model. The two cycles, however, resemble each other in that in both the Seven Words are unimpressively presented: padded to fit the metrical forms they lack the lapidary quality of their biblical originals.

York and Towneley, which, though they include the Seven Words, put the chief emotional weight upon a series of speeches (largely in the form of complaints), are far more dignified and striking. Though the liturgy largely provides the authority for these, the main source is a literary one, namely the vernacular lyric complaints of Christ.[49] The influence of the native literary tradition fairly certainly accounts for the differences here between English and Continental drama. French authors, lacking a comparable lyric heritage, only once dramatised a complaint and then not from the Cross.[50] German authors, however, who often made a skeleton for their plays from liturgical texts, sometimes included the *Improperia*, the sung Latin being followed by a versified translation. The *Improperia* were not, however, given central prominence: the position was variable but usually was either on the road to Calvary (Alsfeld and Sterzing) or at Calvary but before the nailing to the Cross (Eger and Frankfurt).[51] Alsfeld is exceptional in that it includes also two liturgical texts sung from the Cross ('O vos omnes' and 'Vulpes foveas habent'), followed again by a vernacular paraphrase.[52]

The use of the complaint form in York and Towneley is markedly different from these German parallels: firstly because the force of the complaints depends upon their being spoken by the crucified figure in the middle or after the savage comment of the crucifiers and secondly because, though they echo liturgical texts, they do not embody the paradoxical antitheses of the *Improperia*, but are written in the freer and more moving style of the vernacular form. Whilst the Towneley complaints contain many of the traditionally evocative themes,[53] they are metrically and structurally disordered, and are also overshadowed by the more poetically moving laments of the Virgin. It is therefore easiest to illustrate how the composed and magisterial address of Christ can be made to interweave significantly with the base and malign talk of the soldiers from the York plays of the Crucifixion and the Burial. In the York Crucifixion Christ speaks twice. On the first occasion it is after the soldiers have busily assembled their tools and are about to begin their work with relish. At this moment, Christ, as in the *Meditationes*, makes a solemn offering of himself to the Father in a sacrificial speech which suddenly puts the action into its divine perspective:

> Almyghty god, my Fadir free,
> Late þis materes be made in mynde,
> Þou badde þat I schulde buxsome be,
> For Adam plyght for to be pyned.
> Here to dede I obblisshe me
> Fro þat synne for to save mankynde,
> And soveraynely be-seke I þe,
> That þai for me may favoure fynde,
> And fro þe fende þame fende,
> So þat þer saules be saffe,
> In welthe withouten ende;
> I kepe nought ellis to crave.

Christ's free offering of Himself (he suffered *quia ipse voluit*) is then confirmed by Christ's action of laying himself upon the Cross, an action dramatically prompted by a soldier's jeering invitation to him to do so.

The meditative emphasis upon the extremity of Christ's sufferings, which led to the invention that Christ was forcibly thrown to the ground and brutally nailed to the Cross where it lay, had caused the abandonment of the earlier symbolic expression of Christ's willingness to die through his unconstrained ascent of the upright Cross.[54] The dramatist here with a spark of inventive brilliance has found a way of reconciling the two ideas in one splendid dramatic moment.

The second time that Christ speaks is nearly two hundred lines later when he hangs upon the Cross, and ignoring the taunts and insults of the soldiers, he addresses the audience in a complaint based upon the 'O vos omnes' combined with the first word from the Cross:

i Mil.	Say, sir, howe likis þou nowe,
	Þis werk þat we have wrought?
iv Mil.	We praye youe sais us howe,
	ȝe fele, or faynte ȝe ought?
Jesus	Al men þat walkis by waye or strete,
	Takes tente ȝe schalle no travayle tyne,
	By-holdes myn heede, myn handis, and my feete,
	And fully feele nowe or ȝe fyne,
	Yf any mournyng may be meete
	Or myscheve mesured unto myne.
	My Fadir, þat alle bales may bete,
	For-giffis þes men þat dois me pyne.
	What þai wirke wotte þai noght,
	Therfore my Fadir I crave
	Latte nevere þer synnis be sought,
	But see þer saules to save.
i Mil.	We! harke! he jangelis like a jay.
ii Mil.	Me thynke he patris like a py.

This serene and magisterial speech which directly involves the audience in the action of the play, since it is they who pass by way or street, contrasts with the contemptuous insults of the soldiers, which ironically rebound upon themselves: for it is they, whose little scraps of raucous speech have sounded so harsh and jarring, who could most aptly be said to have jangled like a jay or chattered like a magpie.

In the second Crucifixion play Christ's farther complaints intertwine harmoniously with the laments of the Virgin. There is also a sensitive arrangement of the Words. One of these, 'Woman behold thy son', is allowed to stand on its own because of its importance as a compassionate response to the Virgin's sorrow; but the remaining five are divided into two groups and spoken continuously, filling two whole stanzas. The dramatist is thus able to preserve the pattern (which we noticed in the Fall of the Angels) that while for the evil characters the stanzas are fragmented into life-like segments of jerky dialogue, for the good the stanza is undivided and thus retains its metrical shapeliness. The dramatist has ingeniously adapted his material to achieve this impressive effect.

The third strand in the Crucifixion sequence is that of the distress and compassion of the Virgin and of her companion mourners, St John and the three Marys. The gospels say nothing of the Virgin until the tragic moment when she stood by the Cross, but this historical blank was amply filled in by the author of the *Meditationes* and similar meditative works. Influenced by this tradition, the authors of the French cycles introduce the theme of the Virgin's sorrow at an early point of the Passion sequence. They borrowed, for instance, from the *Meditationes* the incident of Christ's leave-taking of his mother before setting out for Jerusalem,[55] giving to the Virgin at this moment the first of her anguished speeches. Since the *Meditationes* also narrated how the news of Christ's arrest was brought to the Virgin and how she was unobtrusively at hand throughout the progress of the Trial, Continental dramatists were also able to repeat the motif of lament during the long scenes of interrogation and brutality. The only English cycle, however, to draw upon the meditative treatment of the Virgin for the first part of the Passion sequence is the *Ludus Coventriae*. In this the first half of the Passion play is brought to a close by a scene in which Mary Magdalene comes to the Virgin to tell her of Christ's arrest.[56] The Virgin's response is in the shape of a formal and highly wrought lament. The style of this monologue, in which the Virgin moves from passionate outcry to the questioning of the divine will to sad acceptance, recalls that of some of the Contemplacio plays. The resemblance does not lie merely in the trick of threefold repetition to indicate distress, as in 'A, jhesu, jhesu, jhesu', but, more imposingly, in the sense of sustained theological thoughtfulness. The lines, for instance, in which the Virgin suddenly and painfully sees that she too may be in need of the Redemption, are both theologically and psychologically fine:

> Where-fore þan xuld ȝe sofer þis gret peyn?
> I suppoce veryly it is for þe tresspace of me,
> And I wyst þat myn hert xuld cleve on tweyn.

In a much earlier dialogue-lyric between the Virgin and Christ on the Cross, Christ had said with what was in human terms a disconcerting theological bluntness, 'If ich ne deye þou gost to helle'.[57] It is probable that the fifteenth-century dramatist, unlike the earlier poet, accepted the doctrine of the Immaculate Conception, according to which the Virgin was conceived free of original sin (though this was a unique privilege and was made possible only by Christ's Passion). The Virgin's frightened insight is therefore the exaggeration of anguish, but she is not entirely wrong in perceiving that the work of the Redemption must extend to her as well.

Midway between the *Ludus Coventriae*, which introduces the Virgin immediately after Christ's arrest, and Chester, which with biblical fidelity defers the entrance of the Virgin until Christ is on the Cross, stand York and Towneley, which in a related scene show the news of the Crucifixion brought to the Virgin by St John and their hastening to meet Christ on the way to Calvary. In both the daughters of Jerusalem are not an anonymous company of women, but are identified with the Marys.[58] This identification leads to a certain awkwardness: Christ's biblically based reproof that the women should weep rather for themselves and for their children sounds jarringly even in Chester and the *Ludus Coventriae* where it is addressed only to grieving *mulieres*;[59] when addressed to the Marys (and in York perhaps even the Virgin herself), it is truly infelicitous. Towneley, however, to some extent diminishes the impact of this impropriety, by inserting between the Marys' lament and Christ's rebuke the elaboration popular in the fifteenth century, that the Virgin attempted to help Christ carry the heavy Cross until persuaded by him that it was beyond her strength. Towneley is the only English cycle to dramatise this meditative embellishment, but the *Ludus Coventriae* at this point has another apocryphal episode, that of Veronica who with her handkerchief wiped the face of Christ, whose likeness became miraculously imprinted upon the cloth.[60] York also has this incident but curiously Veronica (who is mentioned in Burton's list), has been superseded by one of the Marys. It is only Chester which deals briefly with this pause on the way to Calvary; all the others develop it, and in York and Towneley in particular the way in which the Virgin and her companions are driven back with insults by the soldiers recalls the pattern of the Massacre of the Innocents.

The pause for lament on the way to Calvary provides a satisfying outlet upon the stage for the instinctive feelings of the audience, but the attempt to match the enormity of the action by a corresponding intensity of anguish is reserved until Christ is on the Cross. The *planctus* of the Virgin spoken during the Crucifixion itself has its origins in the very earliest stages of the Passion play. The long Passion play from Benediktbeuern provides for the singing of two Latin *planctus*, the 'Planctus ante nescia' and 'Flete, fideles animae' as well as including a vernacular lament, whilst the short Passion play (though otherwise consisting almost entirely of biblical texts) directs that the Virgin shall make a lament. The Montecassino Passion play seems also to have included a *planctus*. The lament of the Virgin thereafter became an invariable element in dramatisations of the Passion, whilst the Latin dialogue hymns, such as the 'Qui per viam pergitis' in which the Virgin, St John and Christ all speak, were imitated in the vernaculars of many countries including England.[61] Both in the lyrics and the plays the *planctus* is usually integrated in the scene by making the Virgin's sorrow the stimulus for Christ's word committing the Virgin to St John.

The cycles vary in whether the Virgin is given a *planctus* as a formal set-piece or whether her lamentation is brief and naturalistically integrated to the rest of the dialogue. Despite its customary rejection of all unbiblical matter, Chester gives the Virgin a substantial monologue upon her entrance: it is moving in content and carefully placed immediately after the insults of the soldiers and before Christ Himself has spoken. It thus serves the same function as the complaints of Christ in York and Towneley. The *Ludus Coventriae*, though also lacking a complaint, gives to the Virgin only brief snatches of impassioned outcry. These outbursts are dominated by the Virgin's appeal to death to take her, 'A deth, deth, deth, why wylt þou not me kylle', to be hung upon the Cross with Christ, 'for þer he is þer wold I be', and for her heart to break, 'A hert, hert, why whylt þou not breke'. These laments vary from the rhetorically chill to the touching; visually they are matched by the two occasions upon which the Virgin swoons (as so often in fifteenth-century art) and by her hysterical embrace of the Cross.

The arrangement of the laments in York is generally similar to that of the *Ludus Coventriae* but they are more pleasing in style. The author allows the elaborate and harmonious stanza form to impose a shape upon the content of distress, so that the Virgin does not appear distracted and uncontrolled but has rather the reserves of dignity befitting to her pre-eminence. The most substantial and the most moving lament of the Virgin occurs, however, in Towneley. The first part is written in the style of many meditative lyrics, grief for Christ's sufferings being expressed through detailed compassionate description:

ffestynd both handys and feete
With nalys full unmete,
his woundes wrynyng wete,
　　Alas, my childe, for care!
ffor all rent is thi hyde;
I se on aythere syde
Teres of blode downe glide
　　Over all thi body bare.
Alas! that ever I shuld byde
And se my feyr thus fare.

The second part expresses the traditional themes of the Virgin's *planctus*, such as the apostrophes to other women to weep with her, to death to take her, and the reproach to Gabriel who had once announced joy to her.[62] But despite shifts in metrical form the effect of the whole is homogeneous and nearly all is worthy of quotation.

The plays of the Crucifixion all end on a quiet note with the Burial performed by Joseph of Arimathaea and Nicodemus. After the Virgin's passionate expressions of sorrow, there is here only a subdued tone of grief. Even in the *Ludus Coventriae* where the Virgin is exceptionally given a lament as she holds the dead body of her son in her lap, her *planctus* (contrary to tradition) is brief and restrained. In the other cycles she is not present at all. The intention of the dramatists is evidently to bring the long Crucifixion sequence to a muted close before the assertion of victory in the Harrowing of Hell.

One cycle departs from this pattern, namely Towneley, which interposes the strange *Processus talentorum*[63] between the Burial and the Harrowing of Hell. No precise source is known for this play, which is evidently an addition, since in the Crucifixion the soldiers had already disposed of the seamless garment by drawing lots for it as in the Bible. The starting point for the plot is clearly the narratives of the wicked Pilate, which show Pilate some time after the Crucifixion in possession of this garment in Rome, but without giving any explanation of how he obtained it.[64] The Towneley play fills in this narrative lacuna by depicting an avaricious Pilate who tyrannically wrests it from the dice-playing soldiers. The only surviving medieval play besides Towneley to reconstruct this incident is Donaueschingen: it does so briefly and neatly by making one of the executioners give the coat to Pilate when he comes to inspect the Crucifixion.[65] For a brief period, however, York had a short play in which 'Pilatus et alii milites ludebant ad talos pro vestimentis Jesu . . .'[66] It is reasonable to assume that this lost York play

was known to the Towneley dramatist;[67] but this assumption does not
explain why a reviser of the Towneley cycle (probably the Wakefield
Master) chose to introduce so substantial a treatment of a rather
unimportant episode into the cycle nor why he placed it at so odd a
point in time (if he had adopted the order of the York cycle, the play
would have followed the *Flagellacio*).

Two reasons may be suggested, one fairly obvious, the other less
obvious but, if true, more important. The obvious reason is that it
provided an opportunity for moralisation about the evils of dicing,
itself a favourite pulpit theme.[68] From an early date the biblical description of the soldiers casting lots had been transformed into a game of
dice. The villainy of this was sometimes emphasised by French dramatists. Mercadé and Greban, for instance, included an episode according
to which one of the soldiers was taught the game of dice by the devil,
who gave him a particularly blasphemous version of it.[69] This aspect
was undoubtedly in the mind of the Towneley writer when, unrealistically but with effective dramatic surprise, he has the three soldiers at
the end, turn about and warn the audience against the folly and disastrous consequences of games of dice.

The second explanation is more elusive but more resonant in its
implications, and it emerges from the coalescence of four different
strands of tradition. According to a meditative elaboration found, for
instance, in the *Vita Jesu Christi*, Christ's seamless robe had been made
by the Virgin herself (and it miraculously grew in size as he did).[70] But
according to an allegory associated with the theme of Christ as lover-
knight, Christ's *aketoun* was the human flesh which the Virgin gave him
in her womb.[71] In Towneley itself these two ideas are fused in the play
of the Crucifixion, where the Virgin laments:

> To deth my dere is dryffen,
> his robe is all to-ryffen,
> That of me was hym gyffen,
> And shapen with my sydys.

The robe therefore might in the Talents be taken to signify Christ's
body, and the continued use of the image in this way could have been
aided by the not uncommon allegorisation of the soldiers who cast lots
for the single garment as the evildoers throughout the ages who rend
the Church (an unstated link here being the idea of the Church as
Christ's body).[72] Not entirely dissimilar in thought and allegorical
method is the common denunciation of blasphemous swearing as a
fresh tearing of Christ's body;[73] and swearing was associated with

dicing and the anger that it generates. This homiletic nexus is found, for instance, at the beginning of *The Pardoner's Tale* which (whether by coincidence or not) is verbally linked to the Talents by the description of the dice as *byched bones*.

It would be unwise to insist that the play of the Talents is allegorically designed in the sense that there is a clear and steadily worked out equivalence between on the one hand the soldiers and Pilate quarrelling, swearing and dicing over the garment, and on the other hand evildoers or in particular gamesters who rend Christ's body, the Church, or crucify him anew. Nevertheless it is reasonable to think that most or all of these ideas were in the mind of the dramatist as he wrote and that he intended that they should peep through his elaborate and otherwise almost inexplicable invention.

This interpretation does not turn the Talents into a successful play. Its position remains disturbing, and its contents tiresome in their repetitiousness, even if the repeating of Pilate's boasting and the soldiers' low jests was designed to carry special significance. But it may explain what the dramatist was aiming at; and therefore we can see that the play is not just the ill-judged effort of a dramatist who did not know when to stop, but rather an ambitious attempt at a *tour de force* which was not quite successful.

XII

Triumphal and Eschatological Plays

The Harrowing of Hell
The Resurrection and Resurrection Appearances
The Ascension
The Coming of the Holy Ghost
The Death and Assumption of the Virgin
The Antichrist
The Last Judgment

The last plays provide the resolution and winding up of the complex story that reached its climax in the Crucifixion. The history of Adam comes to a close when in the Harrowing of Hell Christ leads the patriarchs, with Adam at their head, from the grasp of the devil. In Chester, when Christ says as he takes Adam by the hand, 'Peace to the, Adam, my Darlinge', the effect is of a healing restoration after long scenes of dissension and suffering. The history of Christ (founded in the New Testament), however, continues then with the Resurrection, some of the Appearances to the apostles, the Ascension, and with the fulfilment of Christ's promise in the Coming of the Holy Ghost. The life of the Virgin had also to be completed and, though plays on the subject of her death and Assumption survive only in York and in the *Ludus Coventriae*, most cycles at one time included them.[1] But the wheel does not quite come full circle until the Last Judgment, the subject with which all the cycles end (Chester prefaces it with a play of the Antichrist): then, with the scene set once more in the heavens, the story which opened with the Fall of the Angels is at last finished, and the disorder begun by Satan is finally repaired.

The most obvious characteristic of this last sequence is that its subject-matter is to a greater or lesser extent supernatural, and the plays therefore adhere especially closely to the familiar visual symbolism long established by iconography. There are therefore two necessary starting points for a discussion of the Harrowing of Hell: on the one hand, the original source for the subject, the *Gesta Pilati* (or *Gospel of Nicodemus*), well-known in the Middle Ages and translated into many vernaculars;[2] on the other, contemporary iconography, of which f. 34r of the

Holkham Bible Picture Book may be taken as representative. In this the
Limbo of the Fathers is depicted as a small, battlemented building: its
doors, with their heavy locks, have already crashed to the ground at
the touch of Christ's Resurrection Cross, whilst perched upon its roof,
or lurking beneath, comic little devils uselessly brandish their weapons.
Christ has already released Adam and Eve who stand behind him, and
now draws a third patriarch through the doorway. At the extreme right
is shown the hell of the damned from which there is no release. It is
conceived as a smoking cauldron, from which emerge the heads of the
damned souls: beneath it long flames surge from the mouth of leviathan.[3] It is this kind of visual arrangement that must be imagined for all
the plays, for, though the *Gospel of Nicodemus* provided the themes and
some of the dialogue, its conception of the scene was visionary with a
magnificent contrast between light and dark. But, though in Chester
and York Isaiah recalls his prophecy that the people that sat in darkness
shall see a great light (Isaiah ix. 2), and Adam in York celebrates the
glorious gleme which brings them hope, it is unlikely that this effect
could be achieved upon the medieval stage (as it can in modern performances), and the lack of contrast between light and dark in contemporary artistic representations of the scene – chiaroscuro being as yet
unknown – no doubt obviated the need for producers to try some
token effect with torches or candles.[4] With a touch of sublimity Langland described Christ's approach (through the mouth of a devil): 'And
now I se where a soule cometh hiderward seyllynge/With glorie and
with grete liȝte, god it is, I wote wel.'[5] The mystical splendour, conveyed by these lines, was necessarily outside the range of both dramatists and artists in the Middle Ages.

The English play to keep closest to the design and dialogue of the
Gospel of Nicodemus is Chester, presumably through the intermediaries
of the *Legenda aurea* and the *Stanzaic Life of Christ*. The play opens with
the rejoicings of the patriarchs who rehearse their prophecies as they
see them fulfilled. After a passage of alarmed dialogue from the devils,
Christ speaks his splendid summons to hell gates to open (the summons
based on Psalm xxiii), and then after a scrap of devilish comedy (of
course a medieval feature), St Michael, at Christ's command, leads the
patriarchs from hell. On their journey they meet Enoch and Elijah
(who, according to tradition had been rapt to the earthly paradise) and
also the penitent thief: this encounter with the Old Testament prophets
who had been assumed was often omitted by dramatists, but the
Chester author no doubt chose to include it for its relevance to his later
play of the Antichrist. After this digression the play regathers momen-

tum with the singing of the *Te Deum*. At this point some manuscripts add a brief, satiric episode of the fraudulent ale-wife who remains in hell to marry one of the devils. Some German plays, such as Alsfeld and Eger, introduced one or more souls of the damned at some point in the Harrowing of Hell in order to point the distinction (which we have already seen visually made in the *Holkham Bible Picture Book*) between the hell of the damned and the Limbo of the Fathers which alone was visited by Christ.[6] But the style is usually of a Last Judgment type, with the souls speaking an agonised plaint for joy lost for ever and perpetual torment. But, though the Chester *mulier* begins in this manner, her monologue quickly changes into a piece of homiletic social satire, and the verses in which the devil welcomes her continue this tone. The light tone is an anticlimax after the *Te Deum*, but less disturbing than the grave style of the damned soul's plea for mercy in Eger, which of theological necessity meets with no divine response.

The York play of the Harrowing of Hell (borrowed by Towneley) is the finest of the three English versions, and it too retains the disposition of events established by the *Gospel of Nicodemus*, though with a more classic structure than Chester, in that it includes neither the more random marvel of the meeting with Enoch and Elijah nor any satiric excrescences about the sins of the damned. The dramatic weight of the play rests upon two finely constructed episodes. One is the heralding of Christ by the prophets which is balanced by their speeches of thanksgiving at the end. It was stressed by theologians that the chief pain of the Limbo of the Fathers was the absence of God: in a sense then Christ did not release the Fathers so that they might proceed to the glory of heaven but already brought the glory of heaven to them there. The York dramatist is able to convey something of the joy and splendour of this theological doctrine by his serene and measured poetry, which, without poetic flourish, quietly suggests paradise regained. More spectacular is the lively debate between Christ and Satan which lies at the heart of the play. In this debate about the nature and justice of the Redemption, Christ's magisterial assertion of the divine plan of redemption meets Satan's impudent misunderstandings of scripture and theology. It is possible that the author learnt from Langland how the ceremonial subject of the Harrowing of Hell could be made dramatic through theological argument.[7] But the argumentative style of the York play, with Satan shown as an excellent debater, endowed with quick-witted agility in verbal attack and repartee, is perhaps more reminiscent of *The Pearl*, and certainly owes much to the tradition of vernacular debate. In the York play Christ's verbal defeat of the devil is a far more impressive symbol of the victory of the redemption than his token destruction of the gates of hell.

Prefaced to the York play is a short prologue spoken by Christ, which serves to make the subsequent action clear in doctrinal terms. One point in it requires comment, namely Christ's statement, 'My bodie bidis in grave', which is recalled at the end of the play, where Christ announces, 'Mi grave I woll go till,/Redy to rise uppe-right'. The dramatist's intention was clearly to stress the theological point that it was Christ's soul alone which descended into hell, while His body lay in the tomb. The York dramatist thus deals easily and obviously with the danger that to the audience of the play it might well seem that Christ descended in His own human body. On the Continent, however, and in England in the *Ludus Coventriae*, this potential misconception was eliminated by much more drastic methods.

Iconography, which could base itself upon the statement in the *Gospel of Nicodemus* that in the Harrowing of Hell Christ appeared 'in the form of a man', traditionally portrayed Christ in His human shape. In the *Holkham Bible Picture Book* the symbolic body of Christ at the Harrowing of Hell is differentiated from his real body at the Resurrection by the fact that one is physically perfect whilst the other bears the marks of the wounds in hands, feet and side: this ingenious distinction, however, seems to have been rare. But, though iconography provided a model for the actor playing Christ, Continental writers were apparently uneasy, and for this reason placed the Harrowing of Hell after, instead of before, the Resurrection. This is the order in the earliest Continental drama to include the subject, the Easter play from Klosterneuburg, and thereafter in most German vernacular plays.[8] In France this order is found in all the earlier plays, the *Passion d'Autun* and the related *Sion* fragment and in the Ste Geneviève *Resurrection*.[9] This sequence of events, of which the origin is obscure,[10] solved one theological difficulty only by introducing another, namely the reversal of the order of events fixed by the apostles' creed, a reversal which to the learned at least must have looked like an uncomfortable flouting of St Thomas's analysis of the Harrowing of Hell in the *Summa theologica*. An alternative and less disconcerting structural solution was that of the *Palatine Passion*: in this the Harrowing of Hell is placed between the Crucifixion and the Burial, and it can thus be clearly understood that Christ's soul alone descended into hell, since his real, human body remains to be taken from the Cross at the deposition.[11]

It is this kind of arrangement that must have influenced the author of the *Ludus Coventriae*, who divides the Harrowing of Hell into two parts, one immediately following the Crucifixion, the other (about three hundred lines later) immediately preceding the Resurrection. In the first part, immediately after Mary has withdrawn from the Cross (and before the Deposition), the *anima Christi* addresses the audience as in York, making an explicit self-identification, 'I am þe sowle of cryst jhesu'. Upon this there follows instantly Christ's summons, 'Attollite portas', and after Belial has spoken a brief lament, Christ casts down the gates ('þi derke dore down I throwe'). The emphasis is entirely upon Christ, and he is shown to fulfil what he had spoken between the sixth and seventh word from the Cross, 'I xal go sle þe fende þat freke'. It would seem to be the exigencies of this dramatic arrangement that prevented the dramatist from including the episode of the prophets' anticipatory joy at Christ's coming, an episode both moving in itself and necessary if the scene of their release is to carry full emotional weight. Without it, the second part of the Harrowing of Hell, the thanksgivings of the prophets, seems merely a formal tribute, and the fact that at this stage they have to introduce themselves to Christ (so that the audience may know who they are) shows a kind of dramatic clumsiness exceptionally rare in the cycles.

This division of the Harrowing of Hell was made possible by the performance on a fixed stage, which permitted the rapid switching from one scene to another and back again. Dramatically the effect of this switching is to indicate the passage of time (a great deal happens between the first and second parts of the Harrowing) and coincidence in time (one is aware of events in hell and events on earth taking place simultaneously). The first of these effects serves only a theological purpose: St Thomas and other theologians held that Christ stayed in hell for the two nights and a day that His body was in the tomb, and the arrangement in the *Ludus Coventriae* makes this point admirably clear. The second, however, is dramatically important, for the events thus juxtaposed should reflect upon one another. To the extent that this happens in this part of the *Ludus Coventriae* the result is unhappy. Though in strict theological terms Christ's victory over hell begins at the moment of His death, in Passion meditation the human grief lasts until the Burial. Thus, whereas in the Last Supper Judas's protest at the communion, 'Lord þi body I wyl not forsake' resonates the more appallingly because a scene of the betrayal has been presented simultaneously in time with the Last Supper, in the close of the Passion sequence the Virgin's maternal distress as she holds Christ's body in her lap, 'þi blody face now I must kysse', would be emptied of emotional impact if we remembered the irrelevance of it since Christ has already

273

destroyed the gates of hell. The treatment of the Harrowing of Hell in the *Ludus Coventriae* is typical of the daring experimentation of the dramatist, but, unlike his other experiments, it is not dramatically successful.

After the Harrowing of Hell, with its potentialities for debate, comedy and lyrical expression of joy and reconciliation, there remained a series of subjects awkward to dramatise. In these it was difficult and often impossible to translate the doctrinally important into dramatically effective scenes, or indeed sometimes to provide any dialogue at all. The presentation of the actual Resurrection was particularly intractable, for, though iconography established the appearance of the scene, there was scarcely any possibility for dialogue. In the twelfth century the Latin Easter plays had mostly evaded this problem by beginning only after the Resurrection, and the three which open with the setting of the guard (Klosterneuburg, Benediktbeuern and Tours), follow the account given by the soldiers to the rulers of the synagogue in the *Gesta Pilati*, which relates how they observed an earthquake and an angel who rolled away the stone and sat upon it, and how they themselves then lay as if dead. In the plays the stage-directions prescribe the sound of thunder, the arrival of the angel, and the collapse of the guards *velut mortui*. In the two German plays the angel sings some verses in celebration of the Resurrection, but in none does Christ Himself appear.[12]

It was probably the influence of art, in which Christ's emergence from the tomb came to be regularly depicted from the twelfth century onwards, which led to the inclusion of this difficult moment in the later vernacular drama. The earlier French plays of the Resurrection and many German plays solved the problem of dialogue by recourse to the liturgy. Adapting or paraphrasing the introit for Sexagesima, 'Exsurge, quare obdormis, domine', they showed one or more angels summoning Christ from the tomb with words such as, 'Lieve toy sus, Jhesu . . .' or 'Stant uff, herre Jhesu Crist . . .'.[13] At this call the risen Christ may speak a brief prayer to the Father (characteristic of French drama) or some address amplifying upon the Easter introit, 'Resurrexi et adhuc tecum' (common in German plays): in either case the form of the speech does little more than provide a frame for explanatory narrative. On the Continent the only alternative to this design is that found in three late French *Passions*, where the Resurrection takes place in mime. Greban, for instance, provides the following stage-directions: 'Icy les chevaliers s'endorment, puis les angles ostent la pierre de l'huis du monument; lors Jhesus ressuscite portant une croix vermeille, et les angles demeurent assis sur la pierre du dit monument.'[14] Christ thus rises in total silence, a well-judged effect in that it would excellently convey the mysterious and unearthly nature of the action.

Amongst the English cycles York is alone in adopting the method of the early Latin plays. Though the stage-direction, 'Tunc Iesu resurgente', is laconic and incomplete, the description of the scene later given by the soldiers to Pilate (ll. 360–400), shows that Christ's rising was preceded by the sound of thunder (imitated by the rattling of stones) and the frightened stupor of the soldiers, and followed by the angelic singing of the Easter antiphon, 'Christus resurgens'.[15] In contrast the other three cycles mould the scene in a typically native way, by drawing once more upon the tradition of vernacular complaint. Either silently, as in the *Ludus Coventriae*, or to the singing of the 'Christus resurgens' as in Chester and Towneley, Christ rises, and standing still within or beside the tomb, he appeals to man directly by his sufferings. It was the medieval iconographic form of the Resurrection, according to which Christ, with his wounds strongly marked, motionlessly confronts the beholder as if demanding a devotional response, that must have suggested both the propriety and the possibility of placing a complaint at this point.[16] The vernacular lyric, however, supplied the literary source. Both the *Ludus Coventriae* and Towneley at this point incorporate, with some adaptation, already existing lyrics. The *Ludus Coventriae* has two stanzas beginning 'Harde gatys have I gon', of which the first is closely related to a complaint spoken by Christ at the beginning of the Middle English *Harrowing of Hell* and less closely to a four-line verse (unprinted) in John of Grimestone's preaching book.[17] Much more ambitiously Towneley departs from the York Resurrection by inserting at this point a long complaint of which the largest part is the independent lyric, 'Thou synfull man that by me gais'.[18] Only the complaint in Chester may be a new composition, though Christ's description in it of how he released his *deere Lemmon* from a deep dungeon derives from the common lyric theme of Christ the lover-knight.[19] To give Christ at the very instant of his Resurrection such an address was a bold and felicitous invention, and it seems likely that here one dramatist borrowed from another. It gives the scene a dramatic weight and impact lacking in other versions.

While the English dramatists find a new way for presenting the moment of the Resurrection, the method by which they imposed dramatic realism upon the divine mystery is within convention: it is to treat the soldiers who guard the tomb half comically, half satirically. There was a dual tradition about the state of the soldiers during the Resurrection: according to the naturalistic view they simply neglected their duty and went to sleep; according to the other, which goes back to the *Gesta Pilati*, they were struck into an astonished trance so that, though aware of what was happening, they could not move or intervene.[20] Either interpretation permitted an ironic contrast to be made between their initial flamboyant boasting and their actual conduct at the crucial moment. The most highly developed treatment of the soldiers is in Chester and the *Ludus Coventriae*, particularly the latter. In Chester each of the soldiers responds to Pilate's summons and instructions with protestations of bravery and boastful menaces of how they will deal with Christ if 'he once heave up his head'.[21] In the *Ludus Coventriae* this theme is repeated twice: in the presence of Pilate the soldiers vie with one another in asserting the fantastic numbers of enemies that they are prepared to take on, while at the sepulchre, in the gliding stanza form earlier used for the soldiers in the Massacre of the Innocents, they describe with bombastic threats the fearful deaths that they will mete out to anyone who comes near them.[22] This portrayal of the soldiers, which is reminiscent of the Plautine *miles gloriosus* and of the *soldat fanfaron* of fifteenth-century French farce,[23] occurs as early as the Anglo-Norman *Seinte Resureccion*, and is very common in French and German drama.[24] It provides an opportunity for dramatic inventiveness in the heightening of the theme: in Alsfeld, for instance, one of the soldiers boasts that he will take on any opponent, though it were Dietrich von Bern himself.[25] It is a type of characterisation, however, which is typically Continental, rather than English; whilst it gives life to the plays, it has no relevance to their serious doctrinal meaning.[26]

The characterisation of the soldiers in the mystery play does, however, serve one minor purpose. The appropriate corollary of their bragging is of course that they are cowardly and lazy, and this prepares the way for their ready acceptance of Pilate's orders and bribes. The soldiers' willingness to conceal the Resurrection offered many opportunities for satiric development. Again as early as the Klosterneuburg Easter play, for instance, the soldiers directly address the audience or congregation in blatant lies, telling them how the Jews stole the body away. This strikingly dramatic device recurs in some later German plays.[27] In the mystery cycles the about-turn of the soldiers is commented upon by Pilate or Annas in the ironic style of vernacular satires on the corruption of the times.[28] In the *Ludus Coventriae* Annas, after a whispered conference with Pilate about what is best to do, speaks publicly: 'Ffor mede doth most in every qwest/and mede is mayster bothe est and west.' Whilst in York, after the soldiers have accepted the offer of a bribe, Pilate sums up: 'Thus schall þe sothe be bought and solde,/And tresoune schall for trewthe be tolde.' The bribing of the soldiers is a biblical fact (Matthew xxviii. 12–15), but such echoes of contemporary satire have the effect of making the theme of venality timeless, whilst at the same time giving a fresh twist to the theme, since here the denunciatory generalisation of the satirist becomes the satisfied observation of the villain.

This depiction of the guard as men who could have borne witness to the Resurrection, but were suborned through avarice, follows established tradition. Contrasting with them in the plays are the faithful witnesses, who testify to the truth. Chief of these are the three Marys, but to them must be added the centurion, who, at the beginning of the York play of the Resurrection, describes the wonders that accompanied the Crucifixion:

> *Anna.* We praye þe telle us of what thyng.
> *Cent.* All elementis, both olde and ȝing,
> In ther maneres þai made mornyng,
> In ilke a stede;
> And knewe be countenaunce þat þer kyng
> Was done to dede.
>
> Þe sonne for woo he waxed all wanne,
> Þe mone and sterres of schynyng blanne,
> Þe erthe tremeled, and also manne
> be-gan to speke;
> Þe stones þat never was stered or þanne
> gune a-sondir breke.

This passage goes back to a beautiful patristic tradition which saw in the eclipse and the earthquake a sign of nature mourning the death of her creator.[29] The York author does not express the thought as succinctly as had done the author of the *Dream of the Rood*, 'Weop eal gesceaft,/ Cwiþdon cyninges fyll', but there is an elegiac lyricism in his stanzas beyond the reach of Old English poetry. The York centurion speaks out of character: the corresponding but more prosaic speech of the centurion in the Cornish plays has greater psychological probability.[30] But the figure serves as a voice to speak a probing and poetic insight, which fittingly here mingles with the political and narrow-minded machinations of Pilate and the high priests.

Even in the simplest forms of liturgical drama the devotional duty of the Marys was to obey the angel's command, 'Ite et nunciate quia surrexit'. In the York Resurrection their willingness to give true testimony is stated in one simple line, 'As we have herde, so schall we saie', whilst in Chester and the *Ludus Coventriae* their announcement to Peter and John that Christ is risen is dramatised. The difference in treatment of this important theme reflects larger differences in design. Chester includes all the separable segments of the longer Latin liturgical plays. Within the space of little more than two hundred lines the author covers the Marys' laments as they approach the sepulchre, the *Quis revolvet* and *Quem quaeritis* dialogues, the return to the two apostles and their running to the tomb, the dialogue between Mary Magdalene and the angel and the *Hortulanus* episode, and in addition two further appearances of Christ (to the Marys and to Peter) as listed by the *Legenda aurea* and the *Stanzaic Life*.[31] The *Ludus Coventriae* includes almost the same range of episodes in scarcely longer space. Such comprehensiveness within short compass does not allow for the imposition of a dramatic pattern, the lingering over some especially moving or significant moment, and the treatment is therefore necessarily perfunctory.

In contrast York omits the episode of Peter and John and defers the Appearance to Mary Magdalene until a separate play (Towneley appends a briefer version of the latter to the York Resurrection). This arrangement permits a leisurely and tender treatment of the subject, the laments of the three Marys at the beginning and of Mary Magdalene alone at the end being very touchingly done. The *Quem quaeritis* dialogue is also deftly fitted into the lyric stanza form:

> *Ang.* ʒe mournand women in youre þought,
>   Here in þis place whome have ʒe sought?
> *i Mar.* Jesu, þat to dede is brought,
>   Oure lorde so free.
> *Ang.* Women, certayne here is he noght,
>   Come nere and see.

The easiness of the style is deceptive: economically and feelingly the formal Latin dialogue has been translated into one poised vernacular stanza. The lucidity of the stanza is characteristic of the whole episode which, uncluttered by excessive narrative detail, stands out with a classic prominence fitting to the importance of the subject.

Whereas theologians, harmonising and occasionally amplifying the gospels listed between ten and thirteen Resurrection appearances (and in this were followed by the three great *Passions*),[32] the English cycles more selectively concentrate upon three devotionally and dramatically important ones, namely those to Mary Magdalene, to the two disciples at Emmaus and to Thomas with the assembled apostles. Three out of the four cycles, the exception being the *Ludus Coventriae*, prepare for the latter by beginning the play with Christ's appearance to the apostles when Thomas was not present. To these, Chester, as we have already noted, briefly adds two further appearances, which took place on Easter Sunday, those to Mary Jacobus and to Mary Salome. The *Ludus Coventriae* with dramatic fittingness includes also the greatest and most moving of the apocryphal appearances, that of Christ to the Blessed Virgin. From these appearances, which are, according to the time-scheme of the plays, all clustered together soon after the Resurrection, the cycles leap to Christ's last appearance to the apostles, which, according to Acts, immediately preceded the Ascension.

Though Christ's appearance to His mother was commonly accepted in the devotional thought of the Middle Ages, amongst French dramatists Greban alone includes it; in Germany it is commoner – Alsfeld and Donaueschingen, for instance, include it – but its presence is by no means the rule.[33] It is also dramatised in the Cornish plays.[34] One reason for its rarity was perhaps the technical problem of where to place it, since the closely interlocking narrative, based upon the gospels and fixed by liturgical drama, hardly allowed the insertion of another important scene. Like Greban and the Cornish dramatist, the author of the *Ludus Coventriae* boldy puts the scene immediately after the Resurrection, before the waking of the guard and the visit of the Marys to the tomb, and this decision to give it startling centrality is poetically and dramatically justified. Within the scene the right point of balance between doctrinal statement and personal feeling is also sensitively found. Though Christ's speeches serve for theological exposition they are not unfeelingly frigid, whilst Mary's replies movingly express reverence for Christ as God and human tenderness for Him as her son. There is a sense of joyful reunion in the scene and a precise recapturing of the marvel that Christ who was buried deep has now risen from 'þe cley so colde'. The Virgin's last address is especially fine:

> Ffare wel my sone, fare wel my childe,
> Ffare wel my lorde, my god so mylde:
> myn hert is wele þat ffyrst was whylde,
> Ffare wel myn owyn dere love.
> Now all mankynde beth glad with gle
> Ffor deth is deed as ʒe may se,
> and lyff is reysed endles to be
> In hevyn dwellynge Above.

In the sixth line of this stanza (when the Virgin has turned to proclaiming the Resurrection to the audience), she echoes a line from Christ's preceding speech, 'Ffor deth is deed and lyff doth wake', which nimbly and movingly adapts the Easter antiphon based on Hosea xiii. 14, 'O mors ero mors tua'. The idea is not here stated with the trumpet tone of Donne's 'Death thou shalt die', but the paradox is not the less reverberant for being formulated in the gayer style of lyric celebration.

Worthy to be compared with this scene is the York play of the Appearance to Mary Magdalene, which is a beautiful lyric handling of the themes of loss, recognition and recovery. The York play follows upon the episode of Pilate and the high priests and the soldiers, and in contrast to the noisy activity of this, and indeed of most of the Passion sequence, there is an aesthetically satisfying stillness in this play in which only two characters appear. The sole movement required by the text is that Christ at the moment of self-revelation should show his wounds and that Mary Magdalene should twice extend her hands in some gesture of affection (though it is possible that she should kneel when she says 'A! Rabony', as she so often does in art). The poetry is sustainedly fine: only Christ's speech in which he describes the armour of the lover-knight which Mary must inscribe upon her heart is a little jarring in its transplantation of a traditional theme to an unsuitable context.[35] Otherwise it is a moving and tranquil idyll, which in its serenity is reminiscent of Fra Angelico's painting of the same subject.

All four cycles continue next with a play of the *Peregrini*, a subject difficult to invest with dramatic life. On the Continent attempts to force it into realistic mould tended to go beyond the bounds of decorum: in France dramatists would introduce comic business turning upon the additional characters of the host and his wife at the inn;[36] in Germany the disciples eat and drink with a gross relish far exceeding that of the English shepherds at the Nativity.[37] The more sober method on the Continent of giving substance to the *Peregrini* was that of illustrating the statement in Luke xxiv. 27 that Christ expounded the Old Testament prophecies to the two disciples. Greban allots a hundred lines to this. Much more briefly Chester has Christ cite the type of the burning bush and the promise of consolation in Isaiah lxvi. 13. In contrast to Greban's excessive sermon and Chester's perfunctory enumeration, the *Ludus Coventriae* turns the idea into a well-designed debate between Christ and disciples, between instruction and scepticism. Christ begins by quoting the type of Jonah emerging from the whale's belly as a proof of the Resurrection; Cleophas, answering with the voice of unbelieving common sense, puts his finger on the difference: Jonah did not die when imprisoned in the whale's belly, whereas Christ died on the Cross. Christ then continues with the miracle of Aaron's rod (more commonly a type of the virgin birth than of the Resurrection); to this Luke replies that, though it is a marvel that a dry rod should burst into flower, that a dead man should rise again is a much greater marvel, and one that he cannot believe. It is only when Christ recalls the raising of Lazarus, 'þat deed lay undyr þe duste/And stynkyd ryght foule', that the disciples feel great delight in his words and urge him to lodge in their company that night.

This biblically based offer of companionable hospitality is given a felicitous twist in the *Ludus Coventriae*, where the disciples urge Christ to stay with exceptionally emphatic entreaties and, when these fail, keep him with them by physical compulsion:

> 3a, brothyr cleophas, be myn Assent
> lete us hym kepe with strenth and myght.
> Sett on 3oure hand with good entent
> And pulle hym with us þe wey well ryght.

To this use of main force Christ yields 'with herty wyll'. It is for allegorical purposes that the conventional friendly gesture of one traveller to another has been turned into apparently so rough and rude a treatment. For the violence of the disciples is that used by Jacob when he wrestled with the angel. According to the common exegetic tradition (which much later Wesley drew upon for his beautiful hymn, 'Come, O thou Traveller unknown'), Jacob in this mysterious combat held on to God and would not let Him go until He had revealed Himself. Typological applications were found for this story in the Middle Ages. Sometimes, as in the *Biblia pauperum*, it was associated with Doubting Thomas who knew Christ by touching Him; elsewhere, as in the *Meditatio in Passionem et Resurrectionem Domini*, with the individual Christian, who, keeping watch by the sepulchre, wrestles with the angel of the Resurrection until he knows his name.[38] The fittingness of this allegory to the encounter at Emmaus is obvious[39] and it is likely that the dramatist had an authoritative source. But the decision to adapt the idea dramatically is another instance of the working of the author's subtle and devotional imagination.

In the *Ludus Coventriae* the episode of the *Peregrini* is immediately followed by that of Doubting Thomas, with Thomas refusing to believe the testimony of Luke and Cleophas, since a dead man cannot rise again in living flesh and blood. In effect Thomas's common sense disbelief in such a miracle repeats the earlier theme of the *Peregrini*, and the author therefore does not linger over it, but moves speedily to the climax in which Thomas's scepticism is reversed in a concluding monologue of faith. This monologue, a lyric of five stanzas with the refrain, 'Quod mortuus et sepultus nunc resurrexit', is directly addressed to the audience, and herein lies its dramatic strength. To the audience Thomas proposes himself as an example of doubt dispelled and rebuked, and to them he raises up his hand, wet with the blood from Christ's side, as he says, 'Þou man þat seyst þis, from ffeyth nevyr þou ffade'.

The *Ludus Coventriae* has conveniently but unhistorically telescoped the Appearances to the pilgrims and to Thomas, making the latter dependent on the former. All the other three cycles interpose the Appearance of Christ to the assembled apostles, when He ate broiled fish and a honeycomb to convince them that He was not a ghost. The treatment of this subject in York and Chester is unremarkable. In York the play is written in the same agreeable lyric metre as the Resurrection and it has a certain pleasantness and literary composure. By comparison Chester is dull and prosaic, though, as in the *Ludus Coventriae*, the audience at the end are directly addressed. Here, however, it is Christ who speaks, and the style is anticipatory of that of the Last Judgment: those who believe shall be Christ's *Darlinges*, those who do not shall be eternally in hell. The naked and threatening didacticism at this point is disconcerting. The author of the *Ludus Coventriae* had achieved the same homiletic purpose in a more persuasive and dramatically satisfying way.

The Towneley play of Thomas is conceived to a far more ambitious design. It begins with some lively dialogue between Mary Magdalene and the apostles, who refuse to believe her announcement that she has seen the risen Christ. Here, as in the French *Passions*, the incredulity of the apostles (which is biblically based) is expressed in terms of misogynistic ironic comment on women, who are 'fekyll in word and thoght' and like apples, fair to look at but rotten at the core.[40] Some commentators put Eve and Mary Magdalene into a significant antithesis: Eve as messenger of death, Mary Magdalene as the messenger of life.[41] The touch of anti-feminist satire here therefore momentarily serves the same purpose as the more elaborately developed satire in the plays of Joseph's Doubts. After this passage of spirited and colloquial dialogue, there is an abrupt change of style; with the complaint spoken by Christ when He appears, we find ourselves, as it were, transported from the world of the fabliaux to that of Richard Rolle. The following two stanzas, for instance, with their emphasis upon Christ as lover-knight and on the compelling power of love, are reminiscent in thought and feeling of some of the poems of Rolle, as well as being identical in metre:[42]

> Ffor oon so swete a thyng my self so lefe had wroght,
> Man sawll, my dere derlyng to batell was I brought;
> ffor it thay can me dyng to bryng out of my thoght,
> On roode can thay me hyng yit luf forgate I noght.

> Luf makys me, as ye may se, strenkyllid with blood so red;
> Luf gars me have hart so fre, it opyns every sted;
> Luf so fre so dampnyd me, it drofe me to the ded;
> Luf rasid me thrug his pauste, it is swetter than med.

The next part of the play consists of dialogue between Thomas and the apostles. The latter, each in turn, urge him to faith in the Resurrection, and Thomas expresses his scepticism, partly once more in antifeminist comment, but more often in some splendid poetic statements of despairing resignation and unbelief of the kind that poetry so readily lends itself to: 'His cors that dyed on rood for ever hath deth embraced' or 'Sen he was god and ded lay from ded who myght hym call?' Thomas responds to Christ's appearance with a very fine penitential prayer for mercy: this prayer is a lyric of six stanzas, through which the word *mercy* runs as an anaphora, and the name Jesus is lovingly repeated. Except in the first two lines, there is nothing in it that links the verses to their speaker rather than to every man: it is in fact an intimate and ecstatic appeal to Christ, in which recollection of the Passion and of the Holy Name intertwine with the speaker's resolve to discard his fine clothing as a sign of contrition. This monologue is again influenced by Rolle or his school and successfully so. Whereas in the complaint of Christ the echoes of Rolle seemed more like pastiche than imaginative imitation, here the style is feelingly adapted. Christ's reply, which ends the play, is, as in Chester, a Last Judgment warning, but the strain of didacticism is more easily absorbed by the intense and eloquent style.

All the cycles preface the Ascension with a final Appearance of Christ to the apostles, at the cost of repetition, but with the advantage of beginning this difficult subject with a familiar scene. The problems inherent in dramatising the Ascension are self-evident: it is clear that no ingenious stagecraft with pulleys and images could catch the majesty or mystery of the event. The English dramatists, like their Continental counterparts, wisely fell back upon liturgical chant, described as *angelsong*, to convey the solemn and celebratory joy of the occasion, the voices probably being those of invisible singers. The sudden intrusion of invisible voices is a very effective stage device, and would be the more striking here for its novelty; whilst the idea of angelic singing itself would recall the heavenly chant of the *Sanctus* in the opening play (only Towneley had not included this).[43] In the York and Towneley Ascension it is the antiphon, 'Ascendo ad patrem meum', that is sung: in the *Ludus Coventriae* the song is not specified and any of the splendid antiphons for the feast of the Ascension might have been used. To this simple design of the image drawn aloft to the accompaniment of singing, Chester provides an exception: aided by the *Stanzaic Life*, but with unusual daring, it treats the scene far more ambitiously. In this play, as He is gradually raised above the level of the apostles, Christ Himself sings, 'Ascendo ad patrem meum', and then as Christ stands between two angels, *quasi supra nubes*,[44] there follows the dialogue beginning, 'Quis est iste qui venit de Edom' between the angels and Christ, at first in Latin and then in an amplified English translation. This dialogue, deriving from Isaiah lxiii, formed part of the Holy Week liturgy, but elsewhere was associated with the Ascension, the angels being mystified by the blood-stained figure who ascends to the heavens.[45] The imagery of Christ as the treader of the winepress and with the bloody drops upon him is esoteric and therefore unlike the normal style of the mystery plays, but in context it suggests well the numinous quality of the event.

Equally difficult to dramatise was the descent of the Holy Ghost. The experience of the apostles, recorded in Acts, that tongues of flames descended upon them, was impossible to reproduce upon the stage. Only Chester has a stage-direction specifying *ignem*, which was presumably represented by red ribbons. In all the plays singing again indicates the mysterious solemnity of the event, either the famous hymn 'Veni creator spiritus' or other liturgical pieces appropriate to the occasion, such as 'Accipite spiritum sanctum' (the latter sung by angels in Chester). Strangely none of the English plays seem to use the simple device – sanctioned by iconography – of using a dove as the symbol of the Holy Ghost.[46] It was also difficult to provide a solid foundation of dialogue which could contain the moment of marvel. The author of the *Ludus Coventriae* prudently does not try to reconstruct a realistic historical scene but compresses into forty lines a doxology of the apostles, the Jews' contemptuous scepticism, and Peter's sermon. Less courageously, but with more regard for conventional dramatic form, the York author contrived a normal-length play. He built up the event by merging with it the earlier assembly (Acts i. 15–26) in which the apostles cast lots for the successor to Judas, made much of the Jews' mockery (inventing a preliminary episode), and devised for the Virgin (who by tradition was present) some pleasing speeches of devotion.

Only Chester attempts an ambitious and lengthy treatment of the subject. Some of the methods used to extend the subject-matter are unremarkable: the representation, as in York, of the assembly in Acts i; the composition of the apostles' creed; and a translation of the great Pentecost hymn 'Veni creator spiritus', each verse being contributed by a different apostle. Startling, however, is the interruption of the apostles' gathering by a scene in the heavens, in which at the plea of the Son and the command of the Father, the Holy Ghost descends upon the apostles. This scene has developed from two different starting points, the one liturgical and literary, the other theological and iconographic. The first consists of Christ's words in John xiv. 16, 'Et ego rogabo Patrem, et alium Paraclitum dabit vobis . . .', which were part of a *lectio* and provided a response in the liturgy for the vigil of Pentecost.[47] In the chapter on the Coming of the Holy Ghost in the *Meditationes* this text is developed into a brief scene, in which Christ asks that his promise to the apostles may now be fulfilled, and the Father agrees.[48] Mercadé and Greban, who both very readily bring heavenly matters upon the stage, amplify the dialogue of the *Meditationes* yet further in the latter part of a long scene which concludes the Ascension with a representation of Christ taking his seat in glory on the right hand of the Father.[49]

The theological issue may be illustrated from the sermon for Pentecost in the *Legenda aurea*. Here it is emphasised at the beginning that the sending of the Holy Ghost was the work of the whole Trinity, the Father and the Son sending the Spirit, the Spirit sending and giving Himself.[50] An iconographic expression of this theological point occurs in medieval art. An illuminated initial, S, from a fifteenth-century German choirbook, for instance, depicts in the upper half the Father and Son, seated side by side upon an architecturally designed platform, and linked together by an open book which rests equally upon their laps: in the lower half of the S appear the assembled apostles upon whom the dove descends.[51] How the scene could be represented upon the stage can easily be inferred from this.

The Chester treatment of this scene is not close to that of any known analogue.[52] In design it is impressive, for the divine decision is shown as an instant response to the apostles' appeal, 'Veni creator spiritus', and during the divine dialogue they remain upon the lower stage, frozen in attitudes of ecstasy or prayer. But while there is an unexpected touch of sublimity in the design, the execution is clumsy. Some of its inadequacy is admittedly the result of textual corruption. Christ's initial prayer to the Father would be pleasingly clear if there were not a lacuna in it.[53] But the Father's long monologue of reply, as it now stands, confuses the voices of the Father and the Son, and, even without this disconcerting blemish, too manifestly serves a narrative and didactic function in its resumé of the Fall and Redemption.[54] Possibly there has been some botched rewriting but, certainly as we read it now, the scene presents a piece of theological and literary fumbling, which serves chiefly to throw into relief the accomplishment of the Parliament of Heaven in the *Ludi s Coventriae*.

With the coming of the Holy Ghost the dramatisation of the New Testament narrative in the cycles ends. Occasionally Continental plays pursue the subject-matter of Acts a little further and show the apostles preaching and baptising, but none extends to the apocryphal matter of the fates of the apostles (though there are separate plays on this subject). In the English cycles the play of Pentecost serves excellently to round off the history of the apostles. But there remained the Virgin, whose life in the plays had been so closely entwined with Christ's, and whose Death and Assumption were by tradition made a part of those portrayals of the Redemption that extended to the Last Judgment: well-known examples are the *Vita Jesu Christi* and the *Speculum humanae salvationis*. It is this tradition that is followed in the four English cycles,[55] for, though plays of the Assumption survive only in York and the *Ludus Coventriae*, Chester in the fifteenth century had one, and so probably did Towneley (there are leaves missing at this point in the manuscript).

The cycles vary, however, in the extent to which they prepare for the play of the Assumption by observing the tradition that the Virgin was among the apostles both at the time of the Ascension and at Pentecost.[56] York in this is the most consistent in that it gives the Virgin an important role in both of the plays; Towneley probably proceeded in the same way, for the Virgin is prominent in the Ascension; but, since the plays between this and the Last Judgment are lost, one can tell no more.[57] The *Ludus Coventriae* had maintained its unusual emphasis upon the Virgin by including Christ's Resurrection appearance to her, but rather oddly does not show her present at Pentecost, and, though the initial rubric lists her amongst the characters in the play of the Ascension, she does not have a speaking part and the summary of the play in the proclamation does not include her.[58] The only cycle, however, which seems deliberately to allow the Virgin to fade unnoticed from our attention is Chester, where nothing more is heard of the Virgin after John leads her grieving from Calvary. Whilst the play of the Assumption would have tied up a loose narrative thread, its excision has not disturbed a dramatic pattern.[59]

The main source for the Death and the Assumption of the Virgin was the *Transitus Mariae*, an apocryphal work incorporated in the *Legenda aurea* for the feast of the Assumption.[60] Whereas the gospels, on account of their impressionistic narrative method, permitted or demanded ample meditative or dramatic invention, this apocryphal work with its consistently detailed narrative and abundant dialogue, forbade or at least discouraged the exercise of the literary imagination. All medieval plays follow its narrative closely, and dramatise successively the angel's appearance to Mary to announce her death, the miraculous assembling of the apostles, Christ's appearance to receive the Virgin's soul, the Jews' malicious interception of the funeral procession, the strange miracle of Fergus's hand and the subsequent conversion of many of the Jews, the burial with the apostles waiting by the tomb, and the corporeal assumption of the Virgin three days later: only the Coronation of the Virgin, common in art from the twelfth century onwards, does not derive from this source.

The play of the Death and Assumption of the Virgin in the *Ludus Coventriae* is stylistically at variance with the rest of the cycle: it is wooden, stilted and lifelessly aureate in diction. It is easy to dismiss it as the work of an inferior writer.[61] Nevertheless it is almost as unfair to criticise this text on the basis of the printed page, as it would be to judge an opera libretto, similarly presented, naked of its musical setting. The impact of this play was clearly to the eye and to the musical ear: spectacle and music are essential to it.

In considering the play as spectacle some readjustment in taste has to be made, for nowadays, the difference between painting and poetry (which we discussed earlier), namely that the one depicts a single moment, the other the passing of time, seems to bear crucially upon the suitability of the Assumption for representation. With a painting such as the famous *Assunta* of Titian, it is easy to believe that the artist has caught the Virgin for a moment on some glorious journey to celestial infinity; but on the stage it would surely seem too obvious that an actor or an image was being hauled up to a platform in the roof. Medieval audiences, however, cannot have reacted in this way for civic organisers would go out of their way to stage the Assumption on occasions of especial importance. To take an example at random:

Siena in 1458 produced an Assumption in the piazza to celebrate the election of Aeneas Sylvius Piccolomini, the famous humanist scholar, to the papacy; a chronicler stresses the magnificence of the representation, the spectacular effects that astonished the audience and the delightfulness of the music.[62] Nearer home, Chester in 1488 staged an Assumption to honour a visiting nobleman, and York in 1486 similarly honoured Henry VII.[63] Obviously the splendour of the spectacle was intended to match the dignity of the occasion.

More particularly when discussing the play in terms of spectacle and music, we have to bear in mind that a successful execution of the stage-directions would at least require performance in a fixed place with multiple staging, and preferably performance in the nave of a church, which would provide a better setting than the open air for the music and singing, and than a wagon for the contrivance of the large and elaborate descents and ascents, which the text unsparingly envisages.[64] In Spain vernacular plays of the Dormition and Assumption are known to have been performed on 14–15 August (i.e. the vigil and day of the feast) as appendages to the liturgy.[65] Records show that Lincoln Cathedral in the fifteenth century also had a play of the Assumption,[66] and to suggest that sometimes it was given in English would not be an unduly bold hypothesis. It is certainly reasonable to take the Assumption of the *Ludus Coventriae* as a play of this type, for then the formal style and the reliance upon music and spectacle all become appropriate to the occasion. To go further and postulate that this Assumption is the lost Lincoln play is tempting but exceeds what is warranted by the available evidence.

The use of music to signify sublime mysteries is yet more marked in the Assumption of the *Ludus Coventriae* than in any of the plays of the Ascension. On three occasions instrumental music accompanies the marvellous: lutes (*cithares*) are played when the angel descends to announce the Virgin's death, and it is probably organ music that is prescribed at the two most solemn and supernatural moments, those when Christ returns to earth to fetch the Virgin's soul and when the Virgin herself is assumed into the heavens.[67] While organs in the Middle Ages were sometimes used on secular occasions, they were especially associated with ecclesiastical splendour (great cathedrals normally possessed one), and would therefore carry the right associations of solemn and sacred celebration.[68] Choral singing is also effectively used. When Christ ascends bearing the Virgin's soul, choirs of angels and martyrs answer one another in the liturgical dialogue, 'Que est ista que assendit de deserto',[69] whilst at the beginning of the funeral procession a choir of angels *in celo* sing 'Alleluia'. *In celo* as a stage-direction will signify 'from an upper place', and, if we assume that this Assumption was originally composed for performance in church, then voices at this point would be heard from a high gallery, and the unexpectedness and the distance would confer a sense of the elusive and the beautiful. Music and spectacle in this play happily combine, and especially so at the end, when an image of the Virgin was raised by some machinery to the sound of the organ with its 'heavenly harmony' and the Coronation was applauded with the angels' resounding song 'Deo gracias'.

Though many plays of the Assumption keep uncritically close to the *Legenda aurea*, and depend for their aesthetic effectiveness on spectacle and music, not all are lacking in literary interest: in Italy, for instance, the *rappresentazione sacra* of the Assumption at Orvieto has a pleasing lyrical grace,[70] while the York handling of the Assumption reveals a sensitive imagination at work in the recasting of this difficult subject. The first of the three plays in the York group is that of the Dormition. In accordance with a tradition different from that of the *Legenda aurea* (but found also at Orvieto), the celestial messenger is not a mysteriously anonymous angel, but Gabriel, and in the first line of the play, he greets the Virgin with an *Ave*, just as he had earlier done at the Annunciation. The parallelism between the two scenes derives from the apocryphal source, but the York dramatist draws attention to it and also hints at a plangent contrast between the two occasions. This contrast is movingly and majestically made by Orcagna in his famous tabernacle in the church of Orsammichele in Florence: in the earlier scene the Virgin has the charm and gracefulness of youth, and the angel, carrying the lily of the Annunciation, is alert and joyful; in the later scene the Virgin has the dignity and wearied composure of age, whilst the angel, carrying the palm divinely sent for her funeral, has a matching gravity and air of understanding compassion. The York dramatist's achievement does not rival Orcagna's, but he shows a similar sensibility, and conveys a touch of the same poignancy.

This mood is continued in the second scene of the Virgin's Dormition. The author, unafraid that grief at the parting imposed by death may be taken to signify lack of faith, gives touching expression to the sadness of the Virgin's friends and the apostles at her impending death. Unlike the *Ludus Coventriae*, where there is only one stilted line of regret, 'Youre peynful absence schal make me doloure', the maidens here lament with genuine distress, whilst the grief of St John is movingly expressed, 'A! with þy leve, lady, þou nevene it me noght,

Ne telle me no tydingis to twynne us in two!' Equally agreeable in human terms is the treatment of the reunion between Christ and the Virgin. One of the arguments adduced in support of the fittingness of the Assumption was that it was not credible that He who had said, 'Honour thy father and thy mother', would not Himself attend upon His mother at the hour of her death. The York play conveys the feeling of this argument. The Virgin prays directly to her child that He will have mercy on those close to her and that in future the prayers of those who appeal to her for help may avail. At this Christ Himself appears to comfort His mother and to answer her prayer in person, and there is thus a genuine human interchange. The play ends with the Virgin's dying prayer (which is that fitting to all Christians) instantly followed by angelic celebration and their singing of the 'Ave regina celorum': the transition from sadness to joy is beautifully done.

The York cycle, as it survives, does not include a play of the Burial of Mary, though whether or not through chance omission remains uncertain. Towards the end of the fifteenth century the gild of the linen-weavers asked and received permission to cease producing this play.[71] One of the arguments by which they justified their request was that the subject provoked unseemly laughter amongst the audience, an argument that is convincing if we recall the paintings in which the hand of the wicked Fergus is shown detached and grotesquely adhering to the coffin. Certainly the York cycle appears the more dignified without it. Burton's list records that the two plays after the Burial were the Assumption, including the miraculous episode of Thomas and the girdle, and the Coronation. As the plays stand, however, the Assumption is dramatised twice, first in the play of Thomas[72] and again as a prelude to the Coronation. It would be possible to infer from this duplication that in any performance of the cycle only one or other of the two plays was given. Nevertheless the dramatisations are complementary, the Assumption being related once from the point of view of Thomas who sees the vision of the Virgin borne aloft in a company of angels, and once from the divine point of view with the angels commanded by Christ to fetch the Virgin's body from the tomb. Whilst the method of depicting the same incident from different points of view seems more modern than medieval, it remains that the two plays could be acted successively without disconcerting repetition.[73]

In the first of the two plays the dramatic emphasis is upon Thomas, who as a character is in the line of Noah, Joseph and Symeon: old, weary, and slightly grumbling, but with a mind still open to divine revelation. The play is written in thirteen-line stanzas of which the first eight lines are long and made weighty by alliteration, whilst the remaining five are short and lyrical. This slightly unusual metre is an excellent vehicle for the changes of tone within the play. The weighty lines are emphasised for Thomas's long monologue, in which he grievingly recalls the events of the Crucifixion, at the start of the play, and for the dialogue at the end in which Thomas convinces the other apostles (whose turn it is this time to doubt) that Mary has been corporeally assumed. Their disbelief is well expressed in lines such as, 'In a depe dene dede is scho, dolven þis day,/Marie, þat maiden and modir so milde'. In contrast, the short lines set the tone of lyrical lightness in the central episode, where the angels summon the Virgin to rise and Thomas addresses her in a series of 'hails'. This presentation of the Assumption through the eyes of Thomas is a very satisfactory way of rooting the supernatural glory in a realistic world.

In the last play of the group there is a sustained tone of lyrical sweetness. Again the human relationship and the reunion of son and mother is formally but feelingly suggested. In the *Ludus Coventriae* an image was fairly certainly used for the Virgin; in York, however, she has a speaking part, and we may assume that the Virgin, when she had arrived in the heavens, seated herself beside Christ with arms folded across her breast and head inclined, as she does in so many paintings of the Coronation, of which the fresco of Fra Angelico is the most beautiful and famous.[74] At the close of the play, Christ's long monologue, in which he recapitulates the five joys of the Virgin,[75] provides a decorous and pleasing solution to the problem of finding words to fit the iconographic symbolism of the ineffable.

All four cycles leap from past historical time to the future time of the end of the world. Chester is exceptional in that it devotes three plays to the last things, prefacing the Last Judgment with two related plays which present eschatological prophecies and the story of Antichrist. Whilst there were many plays of the Antichrist in the Middle Ages (the majority from Germany and Italy), like their famous forerunner the twelfth-century *Ludus de Antichristo* from Tegernsee, they are independent works, not part of a narrative cycle.[76] Apart from Chester the only cycles known to have included this subject are the lost cycle from Cividale and the *Künzelsauer Fronleichnamsspiel*. Many separate plays of the Last Judgment, however, began with the Antichrist, such as the *Jour de jugement* in France, and it may have been commonly so in England, for, according to the Lollard polemicist, people would say, 'Pley we a pley of Anti-crist and of the day of dome, that sum man may be convertid therby'.[77] The Chester dramatist's decision to adopt the design of heralding the Last Judgment with the Fifteen Signs and the Antichrist may well have been influenced by the Advent sermon in his much-used source, the *Legenda aurea*,[78] though the latter did not furnish him with an exact source for the Antichrist nor for the prophets' sequence.

The prophets' sequence with which the Chester eschatological group opens is clearly modelled upon a prophets' play. Four prophets, Ezekiel, Zacharias, Daniel and St John (as author of the Apocalypse) speak prophecies, Ezekiel of the Resurrection,[79] and the other three of the Antichrist, the passages chosen being some of the key texts upon which the weird legend was founded.[80] As in the earlier Chester prophets' sequence, each prophecy in turn is interpreted by an expositor, who amplifies them in such a way as to narrate most of the story before it is dramatised. The expositor then concludes the play with an enumeration of the Fifteen Signs of the Last Judgment. The only other known Antichrist play to begin in this way is the later and massive play from Lucerne,[81] which gives about a thousand of its five thousand lines to a succession of prophets; a German play of the Last Judgment also begins with a sequence of prophets and Fathers of the church, including Jerome who, being traditionally thought of as the author of the Signs, appropriately narrates them.[82] This arrangement is more dramatically satisfactory than that of Chester where the play, with the expositor's list of the Signs, lapses into straight narrative, any attempt at dramatic form being abandoned.

Whilst the Chester dramatist's source for his prophets' sequence remains unknown and beyond the boundaries of fruitful hypothesis, there are many works that can be suggested as sources or analogues to the Fifteen Signs: the *Holkham Bible Picture Book*, for instance, includes them in the section on the last things, and the signs are versified in long narrative poems, such as the *Cursor mundi* and *The Pricke of Conscience*; there are also many independent lyrics on the subject.[83] The theme of the Signs is the violent and unnatural phenomena which will herald the end of the world: the stars will fall, water burn, fields will be covered by a bloody dew. It has a horrific splendour which makes it unsuited to containment within the brief stanzas or couplets of medieval literature or visually into small compartments, as in the *Holkham Bible Picture Book* or the stained-glass illustrations to *The Pricke of Conscience* in the church of All Saints, York.[84] To represent them upon the stage would presumably have exceeded the ingenuity of medieval producers, though in the sixteenth century Coventry contrived to burn a painted world as the prelude to the Last Judgment[85] and in a late French *Juge-*

ment de Dieu the prologue seems to promise that the marvels of the Fifteen Signs will be performed upon the stage.[86] Chester's summary of the Signs (one or two quatrains being allotted to each) is a workman-like treatment of a difficult subject: it is less feeling perhaps than the earlier version in the Kildare manuscript, but much better than, for instance, Lydgate's attempt at the same subject.[87]

The play of the Antichrist itself is a fairly capable handling of a subject to which people in the Middle Ages responded imaginatively in a way that it is now difficult to understand. The play opens crisply with an example of the false preaching of the Antichrist, who by his proclamation of himself as the messiah succeeds in converting four representative kings. There follows an enumeration of the miracles that the Antichrist can perform, some of them unnatural and associated with the Signs of the Last Judgment, such as that of trees growing upside down, others blasphemous imitations of Christ's miracles, such as the raising of the dead, which is represented upon the stage. The culmination of the latter strain is the Antichrist's own resurrection from the dead and his granting of the holy spirit. After such displays of power the kings submit entirely to him and he rewards them with large kingdoms. The second part of the play deals with the denunciation of the Antichrist by Enoch and Elijah and their verbal contest with him, and their deaths at the hands of the Antichrist, who is himself then slain by St Michael and carried off by two devils to hell. The play ends with the resurrection of Enoch and Elijah who ascend to heaven with St Michael to the chant of the communion anthem for the feast of All Saints, 'Gaudete iusti in domino'.[88]

The subject of the Antichrist was often used in drama for political or satirical purposes.[89] It could also be made more rambling and bizarre by beginning with a dramatisation of his birth, which according to one tradition resulted from the union of a devil and a prostitute (this story has affinities with that of Merlin), and according to another resulted from an incestuous union of father and daughter (this story is of the same family as that of Judas and Pilate).[90] Though the Chester Antichrist may seem prolix, when compared with other versions it seems classically clear and controlled. The episodes included are chiefly those chosen for illustration in illuminated manuscripts of the Apocalypse: those, for instance, in the Apocalypse in the Bodleian Library (MS. Auct. D. IV. 17), are strikingly similar in range and tone to the Chester play.[91] The author has also imposed some coherence on the play by preserving unity of place: this was no doubt demanded by the wagon performance, but has literary advantages, for in contrast to surviving plays written for performance on a fixed stage with a variety of *loci*, it does not seem rambling or dispersed. The best moments in the play are those where the author exploits the theme of the Antichrist as *simia Christi* (the ape of Christ) and emphasises the many parallelisms between the work of Christ and its blasphemous parody. A play of the Antichrist embedded in a cycle unavoidably gains an additional ironic edge. But the dramatist, from time to time at least, consciously exploits the potentialities: sometimes by the selection or moulding of incident, as in the rare episode in which the Antichrist mimics Christ precisely in the bestowal of the holy spirit;[92] sometimes in a felicitous touch of style, as when a well-contrived pang of horror is delivered by the loving words of the kings as they set about the burial of the Antichrist, 'Take we the body of this sweet'.

Whereas with many of the post-Passion plays the dramatists were evidently labouring with unpromising subject-matter, for their last play they fortunately had highly dramatic material. Iconography was again helpful in the general organisation of the subject. With the exception of the *Ludus Coventriae*, the cycles, like the *Holkham Bible Picture Book*, divide the Judgment into two scenes, the first in which the last day is commanded, the second in which the judgment is given. In the first of the judgment illustrations in the *Holkham Bible*, Christ is depicted enthroned in the clouds of heaven; on either side of him stands an angel holding the instruments of the Passion, whilst beyond them are four more angels blowing trumpets;[93] well beneath Christ, on the earth, the dead emerge, casting aside their coffins.

In Chester, York (and no doubt Towneley, if the beginning of the play were not lost),[94] God orders the angels to summon the dead to arise: York takes the opportunity to provide a last recapitulation of the story of the creation, fall and salvation of man; Chester is more expeditious. There follows the angelic summons with which the *Ludus Coventriae* begins, 'Surgite! All men Aryse,/venite Ad judicium'. It is in the treatment of the response that the dead make to this call that the cycles diverge most from each other. The Last Judgment was traditionally thought of as a final and public ratification of the divine decision made for each man at the personal judgment (a scene sometimes dramatised at the close of the morality plays). The dead when they awaken therefore already know their fate. York portrays this with a lyrical symmetry reminiscent of the play of the Fall of the Angels: the damned arise lamenting and cursing their lot, but the saved, like the good angels at the moment of their creation, arise praising God, 'Loved be þou lorde, þat is so schene'. Though, for didactic purposes, York gives more space to the *animae malae*, it does not allow their wickedness to be reflected in disruption of metre or proportion. The Towneley reviser of the play, however, evidently found this scene too brief and harmonious: he therefore added to it another two damned souls, who lament at greater length and in a slightly different metre. The lament of the fourth soul, which is the only one to survive in full, is powerfully written and expresses well the anguish of the damned. There is a similar emphasis upon the feelings of the damned in Chester, but with the difference that here the risen souls are not socially un-identifiable, but are part of the cast of the Dance of Death: this is a variation in England peculiar to Chester, but quite common on the Continent.[95] As in Towneley, there is here no symmetry between good and bad, and the damned, pope, emperor, king, queen, judge and merchant, bewail at length the sins which, according to the satiric tradition, were characteristic of their rank or profession. Clusters of such representatives of society are sometimes seen in iconographic representations of the Last Judgment where, as no doubt in Chester, they are recognisable by their costume: normally of course the dead arise to the Judgment naked and sexless.[96]

In York and Chester devils are not yet present in this scene, and in the *Ludus Coventriae* their only part is to make a noise as the assembled damned groan and lament in one voice. The Towneley reviser, however, has added a digression of two hundred and fifty lines in which, as they make their way to the Judgment, the devils gloat over the manifold and various sins that will make so many of mankind theirs. The list of sins and sinners is an exhaustive piece of social satire written with wit and zest. The devils are jubilant: the world, they report, has become so wicked that the porter at hell-gate gets no rest, and indeed had the Day of Judgment been delayed any longer, the bounds of hell would have had to have been extended. The devils' initial alarm at the summons to judgment passes into avidity at the thought of the prey that will be eternally committed to them, and the first devil with sly and knowing relish anticipates the words to be spoken, 'Qui vero mala/ In ignem eternum'. Though this piece is a *tour de force*, it is jarring and inappropriate in context: with this and other additions the reviser has shattered the York play to pieces.

In the second scene Christ descends from the heavens to judge man-kind in a lower place, which theologians identified as the vale of Iosaphat.[97] According to common iconographic design this is a majestic-ally crowded scene. In the centre is Christ, who extends his hands so as to reveal his wounds, but with a difference of gesture, so that with his right he welcomes the blessed, with his left rejects the damned. Behind him angels again display the instruments of the Passion. Below and at his side is the Virgin, and beyond them, evenly divided, are the twelve apostles, who according to theological tradition would at the Judgment sit with Christ as assessors. The entry to heaven on Christ's right is an architecturally designed doorway, and it is guarded either by St Peter or an angel; near it are the saved. On Christ's left hand the entry to hell is symbolised by a cauldron or the mouth of Leviathan, and near or around it are a group of devils about to drag off the damned.[98] For a variety of reasons some of the mystery plays reduce this last cast.

The regular and most striking omission is that of the Virgin, who, in Continental plays, as in most iconographic representations, was shown to continue to intercede for sinners, sometimes both before and after the Judgment.[99] According to Burton's list, however, Mary appeared in an earlier version of the York Last Judgment, and it is reasonable to assume that she had a speaking part. Whilst it would probably be anachronistic to suppose that the Virgin was omitted out of theological scruples,[100] to the York dramatist at least can be attributed aesthetic considerations, for in the Continental plays the rejected pleas of the Virgin, like some of the poignant prayers for mercy from the damned, are disconcerting in their suggestion of a callous severity in Christ. The York dramatist shows himself far too sensitive to tone to have made such an artistic blunder.

The reason for the omission of the apostles or the angels carrying the instruments of the Passion was no doubt the purely practical one of the difficulty of providing enough actors. York seems to have been the only town capable of mustering so large a number of players from one gild. Burton's list enumerates twelve apostles and no less than eight angels carrying trumpets or the instruments of the Passion: the apostles are present in the new or revised play,[101] and one may conjecture that so also were the angels, as the instruments of the Passion would provide a satisfactory visual equivalent to Christ's long complaint (these angels of course never have a speaking part).[102] None of the other cycles, however, include the apostles (indeed the Towneley cycle has deliberately excised them) and only Chester makes plain that the instruments of the Passion are displayed.[103] The York play is therefore the only one to have the visual size and impressiveness of the Last Judgment in art.

Whilst dramatists were fairly free to invent dialogue for the resurrected souls or the devils, for Christ's speeches they necessarily kept close to the Bible or tradition. The plays usually begin with a complaint in which Christ for the last time recalls the sufferings that he endured for man: the exception here is the *Ludus Coventriae*, which perhaps again shows Continental affinities by this omission. The Last Judgment was a very ancient context for a complaint: indeed the earliest complaints are Last Judgment addresses. The complaint in York in particular effectively binds the Last Judgment to the Passion sequence. There follows the dialogue based on Matthew xxv, in which Christ divides the sheep from the goats in terms of whether or not they have performed the seven works of mercy. York has by far the finest version of this and Christ's welcome to the blessed is especially moving:[104]

> Mi blissid childre on my right hande,
> Youre dome þis day ʒe thar not drede,
> For all youre comforte is command,
> Youre liffe in likyng schall ʒe lede.
> Commes to þe kyngdome ay lastand,
> Þat ʒou is dight for youre goode dede,
> Full blithe may ʒe be where ʒe stande,
> For mekill in hevene schall be youre mede.
>
> Whenne I was hungery ʒe me fedde,
> To slake my thirste your harte was free,
> Whanne I was clothles ʒe me cledde,
> Ʒe wolde no sorowe uppon me see.
> In harde prison whan I was stedde,
> Of my paynes ʒe hadde pitee,
> Full seke whan I was brought in bedde,
> Kyndely ʒe come to coumforte me.
>
> Whanne I was wikke and werieste
> Ʒe herbered me full hartefully,
> Full gladde þanne were ʒe of youre geste,
> And pleyned my poverte piteously.
> Be-lyve ʒe brought me of þe beste,
> And made my bedde full esyly;
> Þerfore in hevene schall be youre reste,
> In joie and blisse to be me by.

Whilst the division of the saved from the damned is, to accord with Matthew, necessarily made in these terms, the rejection of the wicked because they had not performed the seven works of mercy conflicted with the commoner penitential classification of the seven deadly sins.

For homiletic reasons, therefore, Continental dramatists contrived to work in the theme of the seven deadly sins, as does also the author of the *Ludus Coventriae*, where the devils at the end seize the damned, accusing each one in turn of one of the deadly sins (at this point it becomes clear that the number of representative damned was precisely seven, so that each was an embodiment of one of the sins).[105] The indifference of the *Ludus Coventriae* to the seven works of mercy (the saved are not even praised for performing them and they are listed only in third person, homiletic form to the damned) is unfortunate; for the idea that Christ has given to man the privilege of seeing Him in the poor is a very moving and beautiful one, and whilst it would be an exaggeration to say that it had touched the imagination of the York dramatist as it had done Langland's, there is no doubt that, in marked contrast to other dramatists, he was aware of the imaginative power of the material that he was using.

The plays vary in the manner in which they bring the Judgment to a close. Chester allows to the devils a short passage of exultation as they lead away the damned; after this the four evangelists appear and announce how they had given warning to men in the gospels of the fate of the wicked at the Judgment. The final cry of 'Laus maxima omnipotenti' or 'Deo gratias' does little to mitigate the menacing tone of the conclusion. The Towneley reviser inserted a passage of satiric jubilation by the devils (as they lead off the damned) which in tone and metre matches their earlier comments. But a final stanza in which a saved soul gives glory to God and invites the singing of the *Te Deum* to some extent restores the balance. York alone with decorous reserve gives no speech to the devils after the Judgment, and what action they engage in must accompany Christ's final words of dismissal; and to Christ Himself is fittingly given the last stanzas of the play in which he proclaims the fulfilment of the divine plan. A final stage-direction prescribes that Christ with *melodia angelorum* return to the heavens (*a loco ad locum*), so that the very end is music and pageantry.[106]

Dramatists had a particular difficulty in their treatment of the Last Judgment, namely that it was a common topic in sermons designed to move people to penitence through fear of the *dies irae*; but this emphasis would not fit the close of the mystery cycles, which required rather a demonstration of God's work completed. As the foregoing analysis has shown, English dramatists did not on the whole avoid this pitfall, though they did not carry didacticism to the extreme of the Kunzelsau Last Judgment, which, following a well-established sermon tradition, incorporates a debate between Body and Soul.[107] Nevertheless a strong tendency to write as a homilist or satirist can be seen in all the English Last Judgment plays except for that of York: it alone movingly depicts the restoration of a serene relationship between Christ and the saved, which, in structural terms, is more important than the condemnation of the damned. The equipoise of York is perfect.

The English custom of ending cycles with the Last Judgment, instead of stopping at the Ascension or Pentecost, introduced an unexpected ambivalence in the finale. This ambivalence, inherent in the subject-matter, can be seen reflected in the divergent decisions of sixteenth-century dramatists, who, following the classical custom of giving a literary classification to their work, sometimes called their plays of the Last Judgment a tragedy, sometimes a comedy.[108] In medieval drama this ambivalence is reflected in the fact that for the first time the audience does not function as the crowd. John the Baptist had preached to them, Christ had appealed to them from the Cross, but at the Last Judgment Christ addresses characters on the stage, and the audience is outside the play. The effect is therefore that the audience must identify in turn with the blessed and the damned. The York dramatist is most skilfully aware of this. He displays Christ's redemptive work brought to a joyful and triumphant conclusion, but leaves to each beholder the disquieting doubt, that when he must in his own person take part in that great spectacle, he might be one of those whom Satan claims, and be excluded from the stage when Christ and the blessed return to the heavens to the accompaniment of angelic singing.

Conclusion

XIII

The Four Cycles

The oldest manuscript of the *Passion* of Arnoul Greban contains an initial rubric, stating that the work was written by 'maistre Arnoul Gresban, notable bachelier en theologie'. No manuscript of English mystery plays begins in this way. The evidence of the texts is that their authors were also learned theologians, but no care was taken to preserve their names. There is not even an attempt to provide for them some famed and respected author, except for the late sixteenth-century attribution of the Chester cycle to Randolf Higden, author of the *Polychronicon*.[1] It is certain that this impenetrable anonymity conceals in each instance more than one name. Even where authors were known, as in France, this did not prevent one dramatist from adopting and amplifying the work of a predecessor, as Greban did the *Passion* of Mercadé, and Michel the *Passion* of Greban. Such an accepted procedure would be yet more likely in the handling of anonymous works, where there could be no question of the poet retaining, as it were, some kind of copyright. Insofar as there was a concept of literary property applied to the plays, it would be that of the cycles as the possession of civic authorities.

Present knowledge that each cycle has had more than one poet at work upon it has proved an obstacle to literary appreciation. In particular it has led to a destructive approach, wherein an attempt is made to dissect the cycles, one level of revision being peeled off after another. Criteria commonly used in this process are changes in the paper used, varieties in metre, changes in style of rubrication, and discrepancies between existing plays and the enumeration of them in banns or other records. These things, however, can be no more than pointers, and they have usually been found to point to the presuppositions with which the scholar started. Subjectivity and circularity of argument are in fact inevitable in this approach, for, if one refuses to make any assumption about the probable date and development of a cycle and refrains from literary judgment, then this kind of evidence is usually too inconsistent and inconclusive to yield a definite pattern.

There are two disastrous aspects to this type of criticism. One is that it has naturally led to the corollary that many of the revisions were botched jobs, readily detectable by the modern eye. Examples of this are the arguments that in the *Ludus Coventriae* the plays of Joseph's Doubts (not mentioned in Contemplacio's enumeration of the following subject-matter) and of the Purification (not listed in the banns) are later insertions and highly unfitting, the first because it is low and jarring in tone, the second because it is unsuitably placed between the Nativity and the Three Kings: but, as we have seen, there are ample arguments for justifying both.[2] The second disadvantage is the more insidious because not so crudely misjudged. It arises from the minute examination of the texts with the aim of detecting almost imperceptible seams within a single play. The discovering of the seams becomes the critic's goal, and no attempt is made to admire the delicacy and skill with which a reviser may have enlarged the scope of an already existing play. But, with the notable exception of the Wakefield Master, poets who reworked the plays did not proceed without regard to the style and feeling of the already existing cycle, but, in typical medieval fashion, submerged individuality of style in adherence to a common pattern and tradition. Furthermore the structure of the cycles lent itself extraordinarily well to revision by different hands.

The construction of the cycles resembles that of *The Canterbury Tales*: small pieces are so juxtaposed that the whole work has a vitality and significance which abundantly overflow that of the sum of the individual parts. Similarly, varieties of style and metre co-exist equably so that the tone ranges among the lyrical, satiric, homiletic, comic, and narrative or functional, without conveying a disunified effect. The cohesion, which in *The Canterbury Tales* is provided by the framework, in the cycles is supplied by the unity of subject-matter, and in both the material is bound by recurring thematic patterns in situation and character, May and Dorigen, Eve and Mary. One of the most striking characteristics of this aesthetic method is that each small piece of the large whole seems to acquire an instinctive life through which it becomes happily knit to an adjoining part, even though this particular juxtaposition may not have been part of any author's contrived and conscious design. For this reason either of the now familiar arrangements of *The Canterbury Tales* seems to have an inherent rightness once one is familiar with it, and pieces of the cycles could be revised or entirely rewritten without disruptiveness. Within a design that depends upon variety, contrast and repetition, there is considerable licence for change, and some possibility at least for felicitous conjunctions that are haphazard beauties thrown up by the method.

The York cycle is an excellent illustration of this principle. York possessed a cycle by 1376, when a carriage-house was being leased for three Corpus Christi pageants, but no details are known of it. In 1415, however, an *ordo paginarum* was made of it by Roger Burton, the town clerk: his list shows that by this time the structure of the cycle was very similar to that of the extant text, copied as a register of the plays, about thirty years later. Burton's second list, made only a few years after the first, shows, however, that there was some fluctuation in between: separate plays on the subjects of Judas's death and the Casting of Lots appear newly in the second list, only to vanish again before the register was made.[3]

More importantly, a comparison of the extant cycle with Burton's first list (which for every play states the subject and enumerates the characters) shows that many of the plays were rewritten after 1415. Plays which appear to have been totally remodelled are those of Pharaoh, Joseph's Doubts, the Nativity, the Purification, the Passion sequence, the Harrowing of Hell, the Assumption and the Last Judgment. For other plays, such as that of Abraham and Isaac, there are minor discrepancies between the description in the list and the extant text: these could equally well be insignificant alterations or signs of extensive rewriting.[4] Other plays could of course have been rewritten without there being any divergence in the list of *dramatis personae* to tell the tale.

There is solid evidence that some of the most important parts of the York cycle were revised before the extant text was set down in about 1450, but the cycle is nevertheless exceptionally impressive, and at no point marred by disjointedness. In the plays known to have been rewritten there are marked varieties of style: the serene and lyrical mood of the Nativity and the Appearance to Mary Magdalene;[5] the dramatic dialogue and typological patterning of the Pharaoh and the Harrowing of Hell; the leisurely and 'realistic' fullness of the Passion scenes. These styles are entirely fitting to their subject-matter and therefore co-exist happily in one work. How much of the York cycle was rewritten, however, and how many poets worked upon it, are questions that must remain unanswered. But they are not questions that tantalise the mind, for, even if we had the answers, it seems unlikely that they would contribute to the appreciation or enjoyment of the cycle.

The York cycle, so dramatically fine, so various in style and metre, and so indisputably the product of multiple authorship, makes an interesting contrast with Chester, which appears the most homogeneous of the four cycles: for Chester illustrates the point that homogeneity is not of itself a virtue in this literary genre, since it is both the most uniform in style and metre and also the least imaginatively exciting. There are comparatively few records of the Chester cycle before the antiquarian documents of the late sixteenth century. The earliest reference to its existence is from 1422 when some gilds disputed their respective responsibilities for the plays of the Flagellation and Crucifixion, and continuance of the cycle thereafter is confirmed by fairly frequent but unilluminating references. It is, however, normally assumed that Chester, like York and Beverley, adopted a Corpus Christi play round about 1370-5, though the only evidence for this is the late attribution of the cycle to the authorship of Henry Francis, a monk in the monastery of St Werburgh in the latter half of the fourteenth century.[6]

Whatever the origin and date of the Chester cycle may be, it seems clear that the Old Testament sequence (and perhaps more) was re-written towards the end of the fifteenth century by an author who modelled his plays upon those in the *Mystère du viel testament*.[7] The peculiarity of this writer is not that he was influenced by French drama – on the contrary, the *Ludus Coventriae* has more characteristically Continental features than Chester – but that he worked consistently from one source, which he either knew very well or had open before him as he wrote. A similar consistent indebtedness to one source, namely the *Stanzaic Life of Christ* (and the corresponding parts of the *Legenda aurea*), is revealed by the New Testament plays:[8] it is an indebtedness of an entirely different kind from that of York to the *Northern Passion*. Whereas the authors of other cycles appear to write out of an awareness and understanding of the subject enriched from many sources, the Chester cycle bears a simple relationship to a few easily identifiable works.[9] This simplicity of method is reflected in the thinness of the imaginative texture of the cycle.

The impression of sameness given by the Chester cycle is accentuated by the almost consistent use of one metrical form, namely, eight-line stanzas throughout. In this adherence to one metrical form for the whole cycle, Chester shows a marked resemblance to the mid-fifteenth-century French *Passions*, which, with the exception of some lyrical set-pieces, were written entirely in octosyllabic couplets. It is true that the profusion of different metres in other cycles may have partially sprung from the work of revisers, but it is clear that if metrical consistency had been the norm or the ideal, English revisers would have continued the metre of their text, just as did French revisers. An interesting and deliberate use of various metres can be clearly seen in the late morality, *Mundus et Infans*, where the hero, as he passes through the seven ages of man, pauses at each to express his attitude to life in a style and stanza-form appropriate to his age.[10] Similarly in the mystery plays, but with less clearcut distinctions, a subtle use is made of metrical changes: different moods, whether devotional or psychological, or recurring patterns of characterisation, are quickly and nimbly indicated by changes in metre, either from play to play or within a single play. In their concepts of metrical propriety the writers who worked on York and Chester were poles apart, and York is by far the more successful.

The *Ludus Coventriae* presents again a different problem. In dramatic power this cycle rivals and perhaps even surpasses that of York, yet there are in it some oddities and discrepancies which suggest, not merely several stages of revision, as at York, but also at the last stage a thoughtless and inept piecing together of several different works.[11] It is beyond doubt that the Passion sequence had an existence independent of the cycle, being originally a Passion play, which, like the play of which the Digby Massacre of the Innocents is the only surviving part, was produced in sections over a period of years.[12] The main evidence for this play is the prologue of Contemplacio, which introduces Christ's trial and Crucifixion by summarising 'þe matere þat we lefte þe last ȝere', this matter extending from the Entry into Jerusalem to the arrest of Christ in the Garden of Gethsemane. In effect the play of the preceding year clearly began with the demon's prologue, which conveniently sets out the history of the Fall and Redemption up to this point, though, unlike that of Contemplacio, it merges imperceptibly into its new context. There is no precise indication of where the Passion play ended, since the text has been adjusted to obscure the dividing line, but it is reasonable to conjecture that it was a three-part play, with the Resurrection forming the central episode for the third year. A common stopping point for Passion plays was the Appearance to Mary Magdalene, and there are some indications in the lay-out and rubrication of the text to support this possibility.[13] Style and length, however, suggest that the play might have extended to the Appearance to Thomas: certainly Thomas's concluding monologue of faith would provide an excellent conclusion to an independent Passion play.

It is also very likely that the *Ludus Coventriae* incorporates what was once an independent Nativity play. This is suggested by the prologue of Contemplacio following the play of Jesse, in which he announces a group of plays to follow, the Conception, Presentation in the Temple, the Betrothal, Annunciation and Meeting with Elizabeth: this group is linked throughout by a prologue for each play and is brought to an end by Contemplacio's valedictory epilogue. That this sequence was not originally part of a full cycle is further indicated by the fact that the play of Joseph's Doubts is neither mentioned in Contemplacio's opening prologue nor possesses a prologue of its own. This subject, as we have seen, had a proper theological and aesthetic place in a cycle that began with the Fall of Man, but would lack this appropriateness in a self-contained Nativity sequence: Contemplacio's omission of it therefore seems significant. As in the Passion play, the occurrence of fairly elaborate stage-directions in English in this sequence confirms that it had a textual history different from that of the rest of the cycle.[14] For our supposition that this group of plays was followed in the next year by a sequence centring on the Nativity there is no manuscript or textual evidence, but the only satisfactory explanation for the Contemplacio group stopping short of the Nativity is that this subject was to be played the following year.[15] If this is so, the minor adjustments necessary to obscure its origins have been made, as they have also at the conclusion of the Passion play.

There is one other major discrepancy, namely that between the banns and the extant text. It is not, as we shall see, that the substantial differences between the description of the plays in the banns and the contents of the cycle itself are so significant or disconcerting, but that there is a manifest contradiction between the implications of the banns and the literary quality of the cycle. The banns clearly announce a play to be performed, like *The Castle of Perseverance*, by a company of itinerant players.[16] But the theological sophistication and the dramatic sumptuousness of the plays themselves have suggested rather that they were the cycle of some great town, and attempts have been made to prove that the *Ludus Coventriae* is the lost Lincoln or Norwich cycle.[17] Whilst it is interesting to learn from the banns that mystery cycles might be taken on tour, no doubt for the benefit of those who lived too far from a town to attend a performance there, it seems beyond belief that even the troupe which had *The Castle of Perseverance* in its repertory, could have successfully put on a work as long and ambitious as the *Ludus Coventriae*.

Nothing is known for certain about the place of origin of the *Ludus Coventriae*, and the evidence of external records can therefore not be brought to bear upon it. Any speculation about its history or development has therefore to be exceptionally tentative. It is not possible to theorise about the plays as though the banns could provide the same sure foundation for argument as Burton's list of plays or as though the extant manuscript was, like the manuscripts of York and Wakefield,[18] a municipality's official register of acting texts in the hands of the individual gilds. The text of banns must have been exceptionally volatile. Sometimes banns were completely rewritten: two different sets survive from Chester, and Beverley in the early fifteenth century paid for its banns to be revised.[19] But in between such full-scale rewritings there will have been a lot of *ad hoc* adaptation, with additions or excisions made almost from year to year. A set of banns are, as it were, the undated programme for a performance, and are thus more likely to yield hints about vagaries in the history of the performance of the plays than about the relationship of the extant cycle to its hypothetical origins.[20]

The large discrepancies between the banns and the text, like the lesser discrepant passages in the text itself, reflect the nature of the manuscript. It is clearly not an acting text. Inconsistencies, such as Contemplacio's reference to the previous year's performance, would be disastrous if spoken aloud to an audience, but to the reader they seem as trivial as the inconsistencies in reference to time and place between the links of *The Canterbury Tales*. Learned notes in the margins confirm that this was a manuscript made for private reading.[21] The copyist, for this reason, would be unconcerned that he was not providing a perfectly finished play, ready for acting. Instead we have what is manifestly a composite text: the banns are those which introduced a text related to this play, but not the same, and the larger part of the Passion sequence is a copy of the independent play, which (as the paper shows) the scribe had made at some other time.[22] The reasons why the scribe provided a composite text can no longer be ascertained; but the reason why it did not matter that he did so can be fairly certainly inferred.

The nature of the manuscript allows us to observe rough joins between different parts of the cycle, but it does not follow from this that the cycle is a rather crude piecing together of stretches of plays written by different hands. This would be an inevitable inference only if we held to the assumption that an author and reviser cannot be one and the same person. But if, instead, we postulate a poet, writing in the middle of the fifteenth century, who for different occasions composed a Passion play and a Nativity play and a full cycle of which these independent plays formed a part, the apparently conflicting evidence comes fairly happily together. It is then possible to explain why the cycle gives such a strong impression of a single controlling mind and individual sensibility and yet contains sections at least partially detachable. No doubt behind this poet's work there lies some more commonplace cycle or even cycles of which he retained some passages, and which (insofar as our present text shows) he did not rework beyond the Appearance to Thomas. Possibly, but less certainly, he drew upon some other source for the leisurely plays about the early life of the Virgin: but, as French plays also show, it would be extraordinary for a dramatist in the middle of the fifteenth century to start from scratch. The important point is that the subjective impression of the *Ludus Coventriae* as a cycle of striking imaginative unity does not clash irresolvably with the more objective evidence of discrepancies within the text.

The only cycle in which the different styles and stages of revision have not grown together into an organic whole is the Towneley cycle, convincingly identified as that of Wakefield. The cycle's lack of coherence is partly due to the defective state of the manuscript: through loss of leaves there is no Fall of Man, Pentecost or Assumption, and other plays are incomplete. A play of Lazarus at the end is out of order: like the York Purification, it presumably came into the copyist's hands too late to be given its proper place. A fragment of a *Suspencio Iude*, which follows Lazarus, but in a later hand, cannot be fitted into the Passion sequence, as it stands. A Nativity is also lacking. A cycle that has neither a Fall of Man nor a Nativity is necessarily broken-backed, but, even when allowances are made for the accidents of transmission, it is fair to judge Towneley an uneven and disjointed work.

The plays fall distinctively into groups: five plays borrowed outright, though sometimes with additions, from York, namely Pharaoh, the Doctors, the Harrowing of Hell, the Resurrection and the Last Judgment; five plays indisputably by the Wakefield Master, all written in his characteristic stanza form, namely Noah, the two Shepherds' plays, the Massacre of the Innocents, and the *Coliphizacio*; a group of plays, all of which have some striking dramatic individuality, which may be partly the work of the Wakefield Master, namely Cain and Abel, Lazarus, the *Fflagellacio*, the *Processus Talentorum*, and Thomas of India (the Last Judgment could also be included in this group); two plays about Jacob and Esau and Jacob's Ladder, which in their brevity and simplicity suggest some quite different origin; and, finally, the remaining fourteen plays, associated together largely for negative reasons, though many of them reveal very markedly the influence of York.[23]

Wakefield, a town about thirty miles from York, suddenly increased in size and prosperity during the first half of the fifteenth century, as a result of the wool trade.[24] The few surviving civic documents that refer to the plays are all of the sixteenth century, but it is reasonable to see in Wakefield's adoption of a cycle a reflection of its accomplished transition from village to flourishing town and a sign of its new civic importance. The Wakefield plays were undoubtedly composed under the shadow of York, and there are few of them that do not at some point reveal the influence of the more illustrious cycle. The many resemblances between the cycles (on which was based the earlier theory that both cycles had grown from one parent stem)[25] suggest that the author (or authors) who preceded the Wakefield Master had seen the York plays many times, so that when he came to write he imitated the York disposition of material and had many of the York rhymes lodged in his memory. How Wakefield came actually to possess some of the York plays cannot be known; it may, however, be of significance that the borrowed group consists entirely of plays revised or rewritten after 1415, three of them appearing to have been revised as a thematic series.[26] It is therefore possible that it was the author of this set of revised plays who himself gave a copy of his work to Wakefield, though whether he could have made such a gift without the consent of the York city council remains problematical.

The culmination of the Wakefield attempt to improve their cycle was the commissioning of the plays of the so-called Wakefield Master, a poet of wayward and individual talent who did not seek to accommodate the style of his plays to that of the existing cycle. They therefore stand out, splendid, eccentric and unfitting. The possibility must, however, be considered that the surviving register may not represent the completed intention of the Wakefield Master: in other words that his undertaking was to revise or rewrite the whole cycle. It would seem, however, that if this was the intention, it was never fulfilled, for the Towneley text was apparently still in use in the sixteenth century, when it was corrected for doctrinal reasons:[27] it is unlikely therefore that it was superseded.

XIV

The Decline of the Plays

The great period of dramatic creativity in the writing of mystery plays was approximately 1375–1450. After the close of the fourteenth century until the Renaissance there were no poets of stature in England, but amongst the lesser writers some of the finest were at work on the cycles: the Wakefield Master, the York Realist, and the poet of the *Ludus Coventriae* all wrote with a control and originality no longer to be found in lyric or romance. The form of the mystery play, which required a willing submissiveness to a communal tradition, would anyway have made it unsuitable for a poet of large talent, but it offered excellent opportunities for invention to a writer who could find his best effects by working within the secure confines of a shared literary genre. After this period of growth the cycles, with the exception of some passages here and there, appear to have become fixed, although they continued to be acted for more than another hundred years. The example of French drama and the rare instances of late rewriting in England suggest that, had the cycles continued to have been revised until the time of their suppression, it would have been to their literary detriment.

In France the *Passions* in the course of successive revisions became overblown: more and more invented incident was added to them, more ornate elaborations and irrelevant comic diversions. Only two of the characteristics of the French decadent style have any bearing upon English developments. One is the increasing intrusion of comic figures or episodes, unrelated to the main theme. In the late Digby *Massacre of the Innocents*, the cowardly Watkin with his heroic pretences has obvious French affinities. The other characteristic is the transference to biblical drama of personifications who belonged to the allegorical design of the morality plays. In the very late Norwich play of the Fall of Man (1565) the figures of *Dolor* and *Myserye* who lead man from the Garden of Eden are an ill-placed embellishment; whilst the Digby *Mary Magdalene* is a hybrid curiosity, part mystery play, part saint's life, part morality play with realistic low-life elements.[1]

The most sinister omen of potential decadence in the English plays, however, is the native feature of aureate diction. An opening fragment of a play of the Assumption, which has been copied at the end of the manuscript of the York plays in a later hand, illustrates the vapid magniloquence of this style, in which the Son addresses the Father by such titles as 'fulgent Phebus' and 'Parfite plasmator'. The intention must have been to replace Play xlvii of the cycle with this later version, but to exchange tender lucidity for frigid pomp would have been a sad change for the worse. The opening speech of God the Father in the Chester cycle is clearly another example of late revision and again shows the effect of the piling up of imposing words without the activity of exact thinking:

> I am greate god gracious which never had beginninge.
> The wholle foode of parente is set in my essencion;
> I am the tryall of the trynitie that never shall be twynninge;
> Peareles Patron Imperiall and Patris Sapientia.

This contrasts poorly with God's self-definitions at the beginning of the York play (quoted earlier), which are impressive in their clarity and precision.

The adoption of aureate diction for the speeches of the deity was ominous in its implications, for it showed a loss of confidence in the assumptions about style upon which the success of the mystery plays rested. These assumptions went back to the specifically Christian adaptation of classical theories about stylistic decorum, which allowed that the sublime matter of the Redemption might fittingly be treated in lowly style.[2] It was thus possible for God to speak in a plain but dignified style, and, with an interesting twist, elaborate, high-sounding diction was reserved for the evil characters, Herod or Pilate. Furthermore the late and deliberate preference for ornate language in the dialogues of heaven suggests literary self-consciousness in a disturbing way. The argument for the suitability of representing God upon the stage by analogy with His representation in art presupposed an unquestioning literary innocence. It may be conjectured that once poets reflected about propriety of style, the way had been opened to the conclusion that there was no style appropriate, and indeed the excision of the divine role was one of the most marked signs of the break-up of the medieval tradition: this happened commonly in France and seems to have been attempted at Chester, where a late version of the banns announces that God's presence shall be signified only by a voice heard from off-stage.[3]

In the Chester compromise of signifying the divine presence by

unseen voice and aureate diction it can be seen that hesitations about
the divine role were rooted not only in matters of stylistic decorum but
also in the more general Protestant distrust of the stage. Arguments
used by the earlier antagonists of the plays, Gerhoh or the Lollard
polemicist, were reiterated. Although Luther expressed qualified
approval of plays about the life of Christ at least in schools, 'propter rei
memoriam et affectum rudioribus augendum', in his sermons on the
Passion he nevertheless undercut the traditional devotional aim of the
Passion sequence by repeating the Protestant objection that Christians
should weep, not for Christ's sufferings, but for their own sins.[4]
Calvin, whose attitude to drama was ambivalent, but certainly less
lenient than Luther's, took the opportunity in his sermons on Deuteronomy to apply the prohibition upon men dressing in women's
clothing (and vice versa) to acting.[5] Even the Lollard writer's favourite
method of denouncing the blasphemy and levity of religious drama by
punning upon the word *pley* is used again: Jacques Grévin, for instance,
adopts this stylistic weapon in the *avant-jeu* to his secular comedy, *La
Trésorière*:[6]

> Aussi jamais les lettres sainctes
> Ne furent données de Dieu
> Pour en faire après quelque jeu.

Whilst the traditional arguments of the antagonists of the mystery
plays were thus re-voiced with new authority, the traditional apology
had lost its force. The argument that sacred matters might be represented upon the stage because plays were speaking pictures could
obviously not serve as a defence against Protestants who were themselves iconoclasts. But neither could it serve in humanist circles, whether
Catholic or Protestant, for there a quite different justification of
religious plays was formulated; it was of ancient Christian-Latin origin
and excellently fitted to the plays of which the humanists approved,
namely those designed upon classical models.

Humanist theory about religious drama took its inspiration from
authors, chiefly of the fifth and sixth centuries, who had adapted the
style of the *Aeneid* to biblical subject-matter. Prominent amongst these
was Juvencus, whose *Evangeliorum Libri IV* was a life of Christ based on
Matthew, Avitus, who wrote a poetical paraphrase of Genesis and
Exodus, and Sedulius, who in his *Carmen paschale* covered the whole
history of the Redemption from the Fall of Man to the Ascension.[7]
The aim of the Christian-Latin poets was to provide poetry of edifying
subject-matter for men whose literary taste had been formed by read-

ing Virgil. They justified their procedure by claiming the superiority of their subject-matter in terms of truth and dignity to that of the pagan poets. Profane subject-matter was false or fleeting, only Christian poets justly conferred poetic immortality upon what they sang, since it alone was both true and eternal. These ideas, which find a faint echo in some of the vernacular biblical narratives of the Middle Ages, such as the *Cursor Mundi*,[8] were ostentatiously repeated by the authors of biblical epics in the Renaissance.[9] At the same time they were applied by analogy to drama.

Some of the poetry of the Christian-Latin school was printed before the end of the fifteenth century: the *Evangeliorum Libri IV* of Juvencus, for instance, was first issued in 1490.[10] The largest and most famous collection, however, was that printed by Aldus Manutius in Venice between 1501 and 1504. It was to this edition that Quintianus Stoa was evidently indebted, when, in a letter published among his collected works in the Paris edition of 1514, he justified his *tragoediae* on the Passion and the Last Judgment by the examples of Juvencus, Sedulius, Prudentius and Proba Falconia.[11] Twenty years later Cornelius Crocus in the dedicatory epistle to his *Joseph* cited Prudentius, Sedulius, Juvencus, Arator and Gregory Nazianzenus.[12] Impulse was given to the argument of analogy between Christian epic and Christian tragedy or comedy by the rediscovery of two earlier practitioners of this genre. In 1501 an edition of the works of Hrotsvitha was published at Nürnberg by the German humanist scholar and poet, Conrad Celtes.[13] Later this example was re-enforced by the printing of the *Christos paschōn*, thought to be by Gregory Nazianzenus whose Christian poetry was already known: the Greek text appeared in 1542 and Latin translations in 1549 and 1550.[14]

It would be tedious and unnecessary to enumerate and discuss all the dramatists, whether strict humanists or not, who in prologues, dedicatory epistles or letters set out the theory of sacred comedy or tragedy, and affirmed the superiority of biblical subject-matter over that of classical authors: in France, for instance, Theodore Beza and Jean de la Taille, in Italy Stoa and Tibortio Sacco, in Germany Cornelius Crocus and Hieronymus Ziegler, and in England Nicholas Grimald and John Christopherson. The arguments of the latter two may be cited as typical. Christopherson in a dedicatory epistle to *Jephthae*, a tragedy written in Greek and modelled upon *Iphigenia in Aulis*, maintained that, though he was himself a poet far inferior to Euripides, this deficiency was made up for by the truth of his subject-matter (he had gone back to the *augustos veritatis fontes*).[15] Similarly Grimald in the dedicatory epistle to the *Christus Redivivus* quoted the opinions of his tutor, who had commended his subject-matter, saying that he had not used 'Ethnicarum fabularum portenta', but rather had chosen 'pro creaturis creatorem . . . ipsum autorem carminis Iesum Christum'.[16]

This theory is obviously not convincing since poetic truth and religious truth cannot so simply be equated, but its literary implications are interesting for it would obviously encourage a style radically opposed to that which was allied to the theory of religious drama as speaking pictures. It is worth briefly considering the propriety and success of the new style from a few examples of the plays, which became first the rivals and then the successors of the mystery plays.

A convenient starting point is Nicholas Grimald's play of the Resurrection, the *Christus Redivivus*, written in 1540 or 1541. In the dedicatory epistle, already quoted, Grimald acknowledges a debt only to Plautus, though in fact Plautine influences have here blended with medieval traditions and the influence of the contemporary French dramatist, Nicholaus Barptholomaeus, who had imitated Plautus in his Passion play.[17] The action of the play extends from the lamentations of the Marys at the sepulchre to the Appearance to Thomas and it is clear that Grimald has borrowed the shape and disposition of his material from the mystery plays which were still being acted at the time:[18] particularly close to the English tradition is his method of dramatising the moment of the Resurrection by making Christ directly address the audience. It is, however, Grimald's treatment of the soldiers who guard the tomb which is of note, for here all three influences have come together.

There were no historical characters in biblical narrative which could be remodelled on the character types of Plautine comedy. The only possible method of accommodating these was therefore to insert or develop minor anonymous figures, such as servants or messengers, who originally had served only a functional purpose. This had already to some extent been done in the French *Passions* on the model of similar figures in the farces and also in some of the plays of the Wakefield Master, but it was considerably developed in the sixteenth century. In the *Christus Xylonicus* of Nicholaus Barptholomaeus, for instance, the servant who brings to Pilate the warning message of his wife is turned into a jesting, grumbling figure, reminiscent of servants in classical comedy.[19] The Resurrection provided Grimald with a particularly good opportunity for this kind of approach, since, as we have already seen, the soldiers were already sometimes portrayed in miniature as types of the cowardly braggart. Grimald in his play therefore does not innovate, but fastened upon one of the rare comic excrescences of the mystery plays and developed it. Familiarity with Plautus has given solidity and variety to the boastful speeches: Dromo, for instance, had a herculean spirit from his cradle, and, being born under Mars, he drank warlike rage with his mother's milk. Each soldier has a different and well-turned vaunt to make.

The handling of the soldiers in the *Christus Redivivus* shows a rare but happy fusion of medieval and classical styles. More commonly there is no medieval precedent for the low-born comic characters who abound in sixteenth-century biblical comedies. Two further English illustrations of the method may be noted. One is *Jacob and Esau*, entered in the Stationers' Register for 1577–8.[20] This subject is an awkward one since in human terms Esau is unfairly treated and deceived by Jacob. Medieval renderings of it (Towneley and the *Mystère du viel testament*), however, are confident, even if reserved, since Jacob is a figure of the Church which in the divine plan supersedes the synagogue. The sixteenth-century author has struggled with the literal meaning of the story with moderate success, partly by making Esau a surly, misanthropic character, reminiscent of the medieval presentations of Cain. More substantially he has introduced four servants, of whom the most important is Esau's servant, Ragau, who dominates the play with his lively contempt for his master, his complaints of hunger and ill-treatment, and his quick ability to look after his own interests (whilst the famished Esau sells his birthright for food, the equally hungry Ragau gets it for nothing when Jacob's back is turned). Though the invention of the servants and the formal division into five acts are humanistic procedures, the play as a whole has a lively, engaging quality which suggests the influence of the mystery cycles; but, unlike the cycles, in this work dramatic vitality and religious meaning no longer coincide.

A less pleasing instance of the influence of classical comedy on biblical drama is the play of Naaman in the *Stonyhurst Pageants*. This fragmentary Old Testament series, written by an unknown Roman Catholic towards the end of the sixteenth century, was considerably influenced by Continental drama; *Naaman* itself, as Hardin Craig has pointed out, is based on the *Naaman* of Cornelius Schonaeus, the Dutch dramatist, who had given to his collection of biblical plays the title of *Terentius Christianus*.[21] Though the presence of servants in this play is authorised by its source in 2 Kings v, the lazy, grumbling Dorio and the sharp-tongued kitchen-maid, Bromia, are less well integrated into the main narrative than their counterparts in *Jacob and Esau*. This

English version of *Naaman*, written in fourteeners, is a tedious work, and the servants' quarrelling seems an irrelevant classical adornment. In classical comedy the prominence and emphatic characterisation given to the servants is necessary in that one at least was usually the manipulator of the plot: since this function could not be transferred to biblical drama, they inevitably remain on the periphery of the subject, and the use of them seems often to serve as an easy substitute for the more difficult undertaking of giving dramatic life to the main characters.

The same objection cannot be made to the imitation of classical tragedy, for in this Senecan influences bore directly upon the central matter. Nevertheless the application of Senecan principles to biblical subjects was not always equally apt, and in the treatment of the Passion this method worked far less well than the simpler approach of the mystery plays. One disadvantage was that it encouraged the accentuation of what was already in danger of being overdone in medieval drama, namely the lamentation of the Blessed Virgin and her companions. The first part of Quintianus Stoa's *Theoandrothanatos*, for instance, is dominated by the complaints of the Virgin.[22] An appropriate context for these is provided by the dramatisation of the mystery-play episodes of Christ's farewell to his mother and of St John bringing the news of Christ's arrest. But the style is Senecan, for to the humanist sense of propriety the Virgin cannot lament the approaching death of her Son in any less high eloquence than that of Hecuba for Polyxena or Andromache for Astyanax in the *Troades* (*The Trojan Women*). There had of course traditionally been some rhetorical figures in the Virgin's complaints, as, for instance, in her apostrophes to the Jews, to the Cross, to death, etc. But the finest parts had always been the simple expressions of grief, in which there was no high-pitched rhetoric, but only an elegiac and lyric grace.

The other marked disadvantage of Passion plays influenced by a classical sense of decorum was that all the most powerfully dramatic scenes, and in particular the Crucifixion itself, had to be excluded from the stage, upon which no violent action might be represented. In an early sixteenth-century work, the *Dialogus passionis* of Franciscus Bonadus, all the action is narrated by the Evangelist, an unclassical figure used to a classical end;[23] whilst considerably later, in the *Christus patiens* of Hugo Grotius, the Crucifixion is treated in formal classical manner, a first and second messenger narrating the events to a chorus of Jewish women.[24] The influence of this reborn sense of propriety can even be seen in the mid-sixteenth-century *Passionsspiel* of Sebastian

Wild, a work which does not emulate classical eloquence but, rather, is reminiscent in style of its earlier German predecessors: in this the absence of the Crucifixion makes a startling lacuna, which is inadequately filled by the description given by the *Hauptman* to Pilate and by the laments of the Marys at the Burial.[25] A classical shadow has here fallen across an unelevated vernacular play.

Passion plays were rare in the sixteenth century: none survives of English origin though there is a record of one being performed at Shrewsbury School in 1560,[26] and one of the many lost plays of John Bale was on this subject.[27] Whilst the Passion was the biblical subject most likely to arouse the deepest Protestant antipathy, this cannot be the only explanation, since plays on this subject are as markedly missing from countries of the Counter-Reformation as of the Reformation. It would seem, therefore, that on this issue, as so often, the doctrinal attitudes of the Protestants coincided with the literary judgments of the humanists, and that the universal preference for Old Testament subjects is equally explicable in religious or cultural terms.

Humanist dramatists who wished to emulate the plays of Seneca had a fairly restricted choice of subject-matter. They could, like the early Italian humanists, take classical subjects which Seneca had not used. Alternatives were to turn to native traditions, as did the English authors of *Gorboduc* or *The Misfortunes of Arthur*, or to the richer source of the Old Testament. The narrative of Genesis does not present so compact and intense a history of violence and horror as did the history of the House of Pelops, but, together with parts of Judges and Kings, it offered some extraordinarily close analogies. The most striking of these is the story of Jephtha's daughter, who, like Iphigenia, was doomed to die, as a divinely required sacrifice, at her father's hands, whilst the story of Isaac, though less close in some details, had, like that of Iphigenia, a happy dénouement. The accusation of Potiphar's wife against Joseph recalled that of Phaedra against Hippolytus, as did, somewhat less closely, the elders' accusation against Susanna. The madness of Saul suggested the madness of Hercules. Even when it offered plots less strikingly similar, the Old Testament was manifestly a storehouse of the kind of story that classical theorists approved, namely those which have the power to move even when related in brief summary, and which had themes fitting to the Senecan drama of passion and violence: rape, incest, murder, fratricide, madness, betrayal. According to Leicester Bradner the most popular Old Testament subjects among Renaissance Latin dramatists were: Joseph, with twelve plays written about him before 1650, and next Adam and

Eve, Abraham and Isaac, David, Esther and Susanna, each being dramatised about half a dozen times.[28] Four of these have clear Senecan affinities and the story of Esther is powerful though lacking in horror; only the story of Adam and Eve is entirely unviolent and has been chosen for theological rather than literary reasons. To these Old Testament subjects must be added one from the New Testament, that of the death of John the Baptist, since in its theme of forbidden sexual union leading to an unjust sentence of death, it had ample Senecan associations.

Plays written on these subjects were of course of widely varying quality and they were far more abundant on the Continent than in England. Some of the best, however, were either well known in England or were of English origin. Two of the most important Continental dramatists were George Buchanan and Theodore Beza. Buchanan's fame in England was considerable: many of the Elizabethan critics singled him out for praise.[29] His *Baptistes* was printed in England three times in quick succession in the years 1577 and 1578, and, though his *Jephthes* was not printed here until 1580, it was known before that time from its Continental editions (it was first published in Paris in 1554). The *Abraham sacrifiant* of Beza aroused immediate interest because it was written in the vernacular, and Arthur Golding made a translation of it into English which was printed in 1577.[30] Of English authorship the *Jephthae* of John Christopherson bears comparison with that of Buchanan on the same subject and so does Grimald's *Archipropheta* with Buchanan's *Baptistes*. An *Absalom* by Thomas Watson was highly praised by Elizabethan critics, Ascham coupling it with Buchanan's *Jephthes* as the only two contemporary tragedies 'able to abyde the trew touch of *Aristotles* preceptes and *Euripides* examples'.[31]

The contrast between medieval and Renaissance treatments of these subjects can be briefly made through a consideration of three characters, Jephtha's daughter, Isaac and Herod. To the Middle Ages the story of Jephtha's daughter served as an exemplum for the moral doctrine that bad vows should not be kept. Robert Mannyng tells it to this end. Gower also tells the story, but, manipulating the Jewish bent of the narrative in Judges, provides it as an exemplum against sloth in love. Both authors follow Judges in describing the obedient acquiescence of Jephtha's daughter and extract some pathos from it (the resemblance to Isaac had of course been noticed). In this period only Abelard, whose *planctus* show a remarkably imaginative probing into character, endowed Jephtha's daughter with heroic resolution.[32] In the sixteenth century Buchanan casts her in the mould of Iphigenia. He excises her biblical plea to be allowed time to mourn her barrenness which would blur her determination and constructs as the climax the messenger's description of her death, in which her heroic calm in the face of the lamentations of the crowd and her father's hesitations is impressive in its revelation of a spirit too noble to be beset by the fears and regrets of ordinary mankind.

Theodore Beza deliberately eschewed high style in his *Abraham sacrifiant* and for his treatment of the story drew in part upon the version in the *Mystère du viel testament*, which in the sixteenth century also circulated independently. Therefore, though like most sixteenth-century dramatists he did not care for typology, he had in his source an Isaac who freely offered himself. Beza also knew Buchanan's *Jephthes*, which no doubt suggested the propriety of an Isaac obedient and unafraid while at the same time encouraging a heroic enhancement of this response. The Isaac of medieval drama is touching and brave in a tiny, childish way, and appropriately so since the intention is to reflect a divine pattern of obedience which has nothing to do with the primacy of the human will. Beza's Isaac arouses admiration for the human capacity to rise above all base emotions and has the dramatic solidity necessary where there is no typological foundation.

None of the English cycles dramatise the death of John the Baptist but the long French *Passions* had included it. Herod, who is the ruler to whom Pilate is later to send Christ for judgment, falls naturally into the pattern of wicked rulers. Greban emphasises this pattern by making Salome's request for the head of John the Baptist part of a deliberate stratagem contrived by Herod and Herodias, who devise the rash promise as a means of condemning the Baptist to death without arousing the anger of the people. Grimald, however, in his *Archipropheta* has created the more dramatically interesting figure of a man caught in a dilemma posed by his illicit marriage to his brother's wife: on the one hand genuinely revering the religious zeal of John, on the other hand swayed by love for Herodias and her insidious, amorous pleading. Whilst none of these dramatists have the psychological refinement later shown by Racine in *Esther* and *Athalie*, they nevertheless create an imaginative world which is spacious and complex as compared with that of the mystery plays, whose authors had different aims and designed less bold effects.

The Christian epic of the fifth and sixth centuries, which provided the theoretical model for Christian comedy and tragedy in the sixteenth century, had not been poetically successful. It has been described by Curtius as a *genre faux*, a hybrid form created to meet the need to present Christianity in a shape pleasing to those of classical taste, but 'with an inner lack of truth'.[33] This could also be said of Christian tragedy or comedy about Christ's redemptive work. In Grimald's *Christus Redivivus*, for instance, one is chiefly aware (apart from the soldiers) of metre and form, the Plautine iambic senarius and the classical five-act structure,[34] and of a few other superficial transformations, such as hell called *orcus* and its emissary, who incites Caiaphas to conceal the Resurrection, Alecto (the fury).[35] But the application of classical methods to some Old Testament subjects was not restricted to such external matters, but encouraged a genuine imaginative illumination of the subject. It did so, however, at the cost of religious meaning and the clear patterns of moral judgment: in Buchanan's *Jephthes*, for instance, the dramatic impact is the stronger because the moral question of whether Jephtha should have carried out his vow, though debated at length, is left unresolved.[36]

Thus, by the time of the suppression of the mystery plays there had been established a clear and coherent theory of sacred drama, a theory which, though it sometimes led to a frigid and artificial application of classical style to Christian subject-matter, could more often lead to exciting innovations and could reveal many of the literary potentialities of the dramatic form which had been unknown in the Middle Ages. It is difficult to see how the mystery plays could in these circumstances retain prestige, and there is clear evidence that they did not. More striking and more insidious than any outright condemnation of the plays, whether religious or literary, are the disparaging stories about their production which circulated from the sixteenth century onwards. They are of various kinds. There is the story, for instance, of a mother who offered the producers a large sum of money if her son could have a part in the play of Cain and Abel: the play was already fully cast, but the bribe was so large that the child was given the part of the Blood of Abel.[37] Often the stories have to do with machinery that does not work: the dove of the Holy Ghost, for instance, fails to descend at the right moment.[38] But most often they are about actors who forget their parts. An English example is the story of Richard Carew about the Cornish plays, where the over-frequent need of the actors for the help of the prompter, led to 'a merry prank', whereby an actor repeated on stage instructions given to him privately.[39] The notable point about these stories is not that things went wrong (they can still do so nowadays in professional London productions and quite commonly in amateur productions which are otherwise admirable), but the sneering tone of the stories and their sudden prolification. In the period when the plays were esteemed, it is the members of the audience, who laugh when an actor muffs his lines, who are regarded as the boors; in the period of their disrepute, it is the actors who are the boors, the audience who laugh the men of intelligence and sense.

The long shadow of Renaissance contempt has lain across the mystery plays almost until the present day. In a well-known passage Boileau in his *Art poétique* described some pilgrims, a *troupe grossière*, who acted in Paris, 'Et sottement zelée en sa simplicité/Joüa les Saints, la Vierge et Dieu par piété.'[40] Had the mystery plays been known to Pope, one of his satires would no doubt have contained some equally lapidary sneer. But, though there is no such classic formulation in English literature, an unargued, patronising attitude to the plays lurks in the work of such great scholars as E. K. Chambers. It is easy to see how with a change in religious and cultural temper the plays ceased to be understood as serious works of literature. To any educated man in the second half of the sixteenth century they could only have seemed barbaric relics of an earlier, ignorant age, provincial, shapeless, and naïve. What the reformers destroyed was therefore productions of a moribund literary form, which, though still cherished by local townspeople,[41] no longer had any standing amongst the learned and the literary who formerly had written them, nor amongst the royal and aristocratic who had earlier been amongst their audience. It is only nowadays that it is possible to look at the plays with unbiased eyes and judge them in their own terms.[42]

Appendices

Appendix A

The Shrewsbury Fragments
The Plays of The Burial and Resurrection
(In MS. Bodley e Mus. 160)

The Shrewsbury Fragments survive in a liturgical manuscript written in an early fifteenth-century hand.[1] The manuscript is substantially a processional with the Fragments copied at the end as a group and out of liturgical order.[2] The manuscript was evidently made for the use of the man who took the part of the third shepherd in the *Officium pastorum*, of the third Mary (Mary Magdalene) in the *Visitatio sepulchri* and of the second disciple in the *Peregrini* (he also sang the part of the Jews in the Passion narratives of Palm Sunday and Holy Week). Whilst the date of the manuscript gives no indication of the date of the composition of the plays, its functional character does interestingly indicate that these pieces were actively in use at the beginning of the fifteenth century. The exact correspondence of the plays in subject-matter to those prescribed in the twelfth-century Lichfield Statutes of Hugh de Nonant[3] and the inclusion of a processional anthem for the feast of the Translation of St Chad, has reasonably suggested a connection with the Cathedral of St Chad at Lichfield, though it has been pointed out by Professor Davis that the linguistic character of the vernacular parts of the plays indicates that their author at least came from an area of the country to the north-west of Lichfield.[4]

Since the manuscript records only the part of one actor (with the last word or words of the preceding speaker to furnish the cue) and omits traditional Latin dialogue, too familiar to be forgotten, the scope of the plays can be only tentatively reconstructed and the degree of literary inventiveness only partially appraised. It is clear, however, that the most conservative was the *Officium resurrectionis*, a work that keeps carefully within the narrative confines of the traditional office, and that uses the vernacular with total lack of audacity. The play apparently began with the laments of the three Marys, each beginning 'Heu!', found also in the texts of the *Visitatio* from Barking and Dublin: conceivably, preceding these was some choral piece, such as 'Heu! nobis internas mentes', also from Barking.[5] The centre of the play was clearly the *Quem quaeritis* dialogue, though this is omitted in the manuscript, and at or near the close came the singing of the hymn, *Victimae paschali*, dramatically apportioned (possibly in the manner of Dublin):[6] whether this was followed by the race to the tomb, one cannot tell, though it seems a reasonable conjecture.

There is an ordered alternation in the play between sung Latin and spoken vernacular, a sequence of Latin dialogue being in general followed by vernacular paraphrase. The only clearly observable departure from this arrangement is that the Marys, having asked the traditional question, 'O Deus, quis revolvet nobis lapidem . . .' (which in itself gives the impression of helpless dismay), then give themselves the answer, Mary Magdalene at least resting her confidence in Christ:

> He þat þus kyndely us has kend
> unto þe hole where he was hid,
> Sum socoure sone he wil us send,
> At help to lift away þis lid.

This invention of a vernacular reply to the Latin question gives dramatic expression to the kind of comment found in the *Vita Jesu Christi*, where Ludolf observes that the women persisted with their journey to the tomb, 'credentes Domino esse possibile, quod humanae fragilitati videbatur impossibile'.[7]

This is the only instance in the *Officium resurrectionis* in which the meaning of the Latin is imaginatively extended in the English. By comparison the vernacular parts of the *Peregrini* are ampler and freer and even the Latin is less liturgically constrained. The most notable divergence from the traditional Latin office lies in the opening: whereas all other extant Latin texts begin with the disciples singing the hymn, 'Iesu, nostra redemptio', which then provides a theological and devotional frame of reference for what is to follow,[8] the Shrewsbury play opens with a Latin verse, in which the disciples express their fear of the people who crucified Christ and urge flight, *fugiamus* (the subsequent vernacular dialogue then seems to show one of the disciples to be more resolute than the other). The opening of the play is thus thoroughly realistic. A later and equally unexpected note of realism is struck in the conversation of the disciples on arrival at Emmaus, where the second disciple promises the other plenty of good wine, a comment which momentarily recalls the vernacular German plays,[9] and which contrasts sharply with the treatment of this episode in the English cycles, where the frugality of the meal is emphasised; it is a *poure pitaunce* (poor fare) as York describes it.

Two other dramatic touches of a different kind are oddly reminiscent of the *Ludus Coventriae*. One is the display of physical force with which the disciples prevent Christ from leaving them at Emmaus. In the *Ludus Coventriae*, as we have already seen, this motif was so highly developed that it recalled Jacob wrestling with the angel.[10] In the Shrewsbury *Peregrini* there is a less amplified statement of the same idea when the second disciple says to the other, 'Herk, broþer! help to hold him here', a suggestion of force which may have been corroborated by the other's reply. Nevertheless in terms of acting, the gestures accompanying these words must have been far more formal and stylised in the liturgical play than in the cycle – a restraining hand laid upon the shoulder rather than a struggle – and it might therefore be thought that the Shrewsbury dramatist intended no more than to give realistic expression to the coercion of love which commentators had seen in the biblical text from the time of Gregory the Great.[11] But the surprising fact remains that the depiction of physical as opposed to verbal compulsion seems to be peculiar to these two plays, and it therefore tantalisingly suggests both similarity of meaning and some irrecoverable historical connection.

The other dramatic touch is also noteworthy, though it associates the Shrewsbury play less exclusively with the *Ludus Coventriae* than did the first. It lies in the disciples' explanation to the apostles of how they recognised Christ in the breaking of the bread. Patristic commentators, when they explained this in a realistic way, understood Christ to repeat His eucharistic gesture and to give to the disciples the sacrament of His body.[12] In the Middle Ages, however, there arose a more eccentric and semi-miraculous interpretation, namely that when Christ broke bread with His hands, He divided it as cleanly and evenly as though He had used a knife. Ludolf, for instance, says in the *Vita Jesu Christi*, 'sic enim frangebat panem sola manu, ac si scinderetur cum cutello'.[13] In the *Ludus Coventriae* Luke expresses this point quite clearly:

> He brak þe loff As Evyn on tway
> as ony sharpe knyff xuld kytt breed:
> þer-by we knew þe trewth þat day
> þat cryst dede leve and was not deed.

and in the Shrewsbury play the second disciple expresses the same idea slightly more enigmatically: 'Þat hit was Crist ful wele we knewe,/ He cutt oure bred withouten knyfe.' Though the texts of religious plays in the Middle Ages do not as a general rule comment upon the nature of Christ's action (the eucharistic meaning was probably made clear by the manner of performance),[14] this curious explanation is not confined to the Shrewsbury play and the *Ludus Coventriae*. It occurs, for instance, in Towneley, not in the Emmaus play but in that of the Appearance to Thomas, where Peter cites as one of his proofs of the Resurrection of Christ that at Emmaus 'Ther bred he brake as even/ as it cutt had beyn', whilst in Greban's *Passion* a stage-direction specifies this manner of dividing the loaf.[15] Nevertheless this second coincidence between the Shrewsbury *Peregrini* and the Emmaus play in the *Ludus Coventriae* does seem to add weight to the first.

Quite a lot of the *Peregrini* is missing at the end since the second disciple took no part in it except to sing in the final chorus celebrating Thomas's recovered faith, and for this reason it is more difficult to get a literary impression of this play than of the other two. But there has perhaps been a tendency to underestimate its dramatic quality and to group it with the conservative *Officium resurrectionis* rather than with the very free *Officium pastorum* (which we are about to discuss). Its comparative stiffness, however, is inherent in the subject-matter and is therefore not necessarily indicative of the author's attitude to it. The *Peregrini* was a subject nearly always handled with a certain woodenness and reserve in the cycles, and, measured against its analogues, this play shows very clear flickerings of an independent dramatic imagination at work.

Whilst a connection between the Shrewsbury *Peregrini* and the *Ludus Coventriae* can only be tentatively suggested from unobtrusive hints in the play, the connection between the Shrewsbury *Officium pastorum* and the York shepherds' play is very clear indeed (and has often been discussed). Whilst the essential Latin elements of the office remain, they are in effect thinly distributed amongst the lively and lengthy vernacular parts which are close to or identical with much of the extant York play. The Shrewsbury play contains only four Latin pieces: an opening reading of Luke ii. 8–9 to provide the narrative setting, the angelic singing of *Gloria in excelsis* (not recorded in the manuscript), the shepherds' singing of the processional 'Transeamus usque Bethlem', and the Christmas *Quem quaeritis* dialogue: only the first and last of these are exclusively characteristic of liturgical drama.[16] In contrast the vernacular parts are substantial and contain the two main innovations of

English shepherds' plays, the misunderstanding of the angelic song and the simple gifts offered by the shepherds. Curiously enough the Shrewsbury play appears less reverent than the York analogue in that the shepherds do not, as in York, begin by speaking their prophecies of Christ, and more boisterously comic in that the stupid ignorance of the first two shepherds must have been heavily underlined in order to provoke the rebuke of the third:

> ʒe lye bothe, by þis liʒt,
> And raves as recheles royes!
> His was an angel briʒt
> Þat made þis nobull noyes.

It is particularly sad that this play cannot be acted, as it would only be in performance that one could judge whether the formal Latin and informal vernacular could fuse into a coherent and balanced whole.

The question of the relationship of these three plays to liturgical drama of the twelfth century and to vernacular cycles of the fourteenth is a fascinating one, though no sure answer can be given to it. The most plausible theory, however, is that these plays represent the reworking of earlier Latin offices under the influence of the cycles and that their date of composition was therefore close to the date of the extant copy. On the assumption that the author of the vernacular did not himself write any of the Latin parts, it would seem that he had available to him a traditionally brief version of the *Officium pastorum*, a *Visitatio* not unlike that of Barking, but without the Appearance to Mary Magdalene, and a *Peregrini* which seems fairly free in comparison with other extant Latin texts. It should be added that the case against an earlier date for these plays is not that they are too dramatically developed, since even the *Officium pastorum* is not as audaciously inventive as the *Mystère d'Adam*, but that it seems unlikely that liturgical plays would have been so free until a comparatively late date. It seems, however, that not only were these plays performed in a liturgical context in the early fifteenth century as the manuscript makes plain, but also that they were composed for liturgical use, since they are too short to be acted independently. The only alternative assumption is they were extracted from a full cycle written for independent performance, but this is an ambitious theory for which there is no evidence whatsoever.

Whilst the Shrewsbury Fragments survive in a liturgical manuscript, the plays of the Burial and Resurrection are preserved in a manuscript designed for private, devotional reading. A rubric nevertheless makes plain that these works could be acted instead of read, and that performance was to be on the correct liturgical occasions, the Burial on Good Friday and the Resurrection on Easter Sunday.[17] Whilst the plays are too long for performance as part of the liturgy, it seems clear that the place of performance was a church and the focus of them the Easter sepulchre. For the Burial there would be needed in addition a Crucifix (possibly that used for the *Adoratio*), with the figure of Christ detachable, as it was, for instance, for the *Depositio* at Barking.[18] In addition to the Easter sepulchre a subsidiary *locus* is necessary to represent the place where Peter, John and Andrew are assembled: in that they have a long stretch of dialogue amongst themselves this place is more solidly established than it would be in a *Visitatio*, but a side-chapel or some other fixed point in the church would nevertheless be all that was required: it may be noted that nothing realistic is said or done by the apostles that might jar with a formal and symbolic setting.

The action is in fact totally confined to that proper to liturgical ceremonies. The Burial is almost entirely static, save for the entrance and exit of the Virgin and St John and for the liturgical mime of the Deposition and Burial. Similarly in the Resurrection the action consists solely of entrances and exits and the traditional liturgical movement, the Marys' approach to the tomb, their seeking of the apostles and the race of Peter and John to the empty sepulchre. What particularly marks these plays as suitable only for meditative reading or for liturgical enactment is that when something potentially exciting has to take place on stage, it is performed only in mime, whereas in the mystery plays the dramatic nature of the action is pointed by accompanying dialogue. This is particularly clear in the Burial where we only know that Joseph and Nicodemus have removed the Body from the Cross when the Virgin speaks of Christ's body lying in her lap, whereas in the mystery plays Joseph and Nicodemus speak of the Deposition as they perform it. Though the plays are far longer than their cycle analogues, action and dialogue are almost totally divorced, except for the brief moments when liturgical precedent establishes their connection, as in the *Quem quaeritis* dialogue, where the vernacular is a fairly faithful translation of the Latin, or in the Marys' announcement of the Resurrection to Peter and John, where unexpectedly brisk English dialogue is preceded by the singing of the *Victimae paschali*.

The two plays are a curious hybrid in that whilst the action is liturgically determined, the leisurely speeches are reflective and meditative in style, having their origins in some of the famous Latin meditations of the Middle Ages. The first half of the Burial is oddly anticipatory of later classically influenced Passion plays in that the violent action, namely the Crucifixion, does not take place on stage but is minutely described in the speeches of eye-witnesses. Granted his purpose, the author has quite skilfully adapted traditional devotional material: a complaint from the Cross, for instance, has been moulded into a narrative address spoken by Joseph (ll. 274–321). While the meditative sources of the first half of the play are various, there is one clear source for the second half, the *Liber de passione Christi* attributed to St Bernard. From this come ultimately the long complaints of the Virgin, vernacular lyric complaints having served as intermediaries: this static *Pietà* scene forms almost half the work.[19]

The Resurrection is indebted to similar spiritual traditions, and it is notable in its emphasis upon the loving contribution of the two great penitents, Peter and Mary Magdalene, expressed in repetitive monologues. Historically this kind of emphasis is especially associated with the period of the Counter-Reformation, when the repentant Magdalene in particular became a favourite subject of painting and poetry. But Peter and Mary Magdalene were already important types of the forgiven sinner in the fifteenth century. In the early printed editions of the *Ars moriendi*, for instance, there is an illustration in which the dying man is consoled by a vision in which he sees St Peter, Mary Magdalene, St Paul and the penitent thief. The cock perches on his bedhead, whilst prominently beside him stand St Peter carrying the key and Mary Magdalene holding her vessel of precious ointment.[20] The theme of St Peter's remorse had already been amplified in the French *Passions*, which, in accordance with a tradition going back to Peter Comestor, represent St Peter's withdrawal to a pit for self-mortification after his denial of Christ.[21] Greban not only assigns to him a soliloquy of penitence upon entering the pit, as the authors of earlier *Passions* had done, but also a second and longer one on the Sunday morning before he seeks out his fellow apostles for consolation.[22] The author of the play of the Resurrection does not include the apocryphal motif of the pit, but he organises the theme of Peter's agonised remorse by showing Peter lament his treachery with tears to Andrew and John, who then comfort him by recalling Christ's promises of forgiveness.

The treatment of Mary Magdalene is most interesting both in terms of literary history and poetic effectiveness. Insofar as this play has power to move, it does so through the Magdalene's speeches of loving despair, and behind these lies the twelfth-century meditation upon Mary Magdalene at the sepulchre, commonly attributed to Origen, and in the early editions of Origen's Latin works entitled, *Homelia de Maria*

Magdalena.[23] This meditation is extant in large numbers of manuscripts and was known throughout Western Europe: several vernacular German religious poems of the thirteenth century were already influenced by it.[24] The earliest known adaptation of it in English is a lost work of Chaucer, which he describes in the Prologue to *The Legend of Good Women* as 'Origenes upon the Maudeleyne' and a fifteenth-century *planctus* of Mary Magdalene was included in the early printed editions of Chaucer on the supposition that it was his.[25]

The influence of this meditation upon the play of the Resurrection can be seen in general in the stress there laid upon the passionate lamentation of Mary Magdalene, and more precisely in two points that immediately strike the reader as unusual, one a detail of content, the other a matter of style and feeling. The first occurs in the speech (ll. 1070–98) in which Mary Magdalene reproaches herself for sloth and negligence in not having kept watch by the tomb, thereby missing the holy and glorious sight of Christ's Resurrection. This surprising self-accusation is a variation upon Mary's self-reproach in the *Homelia* that, had she kept watch, she could have prevented Christ's body from being stolen from the tomb.[26] The author's adherence to the dramatic outlines of the *Visitatio* necessitates the alteration. In the *Homelia* Mary Magdalene is too frantic in her grief to heed the appearance of the angels and she shows only distracted incomprehension when they ask her the traditional question, 'Quid ploras?'. She therefore persists in her despairing belief that the body has been stolen until Christ reveals Himself to her in the *Hortulanus* episode. In the play of the Resurrection, however, she inevitably knows at this point in time that Christ has risen and the author, while retaining her self-accusation of negligence, has had to modify her understanding of its consequences in order to fit the narrative outlines of the work.

The second point is the freedom and frequency with which Mary's love for Christ is expressed in the erotic language of the Song of Songs or in variations upon it. As in the *Homelia* Mary applies to herself the famous text, 'Quia amore langueo':

Filie Ierusalem, Wher-os ye goo,
Nunciate dilecto meo,
Quia amore langueo:
Of Ierusalem, ye virgyns clere,
Schew my best love that I was here!
Tell hym, os he may prove,
That I am dedly seke
And all is for his love.

Also deriving from the *Homelia* immediately and from the Song of Songs ultimately is the couplet with which Mary greets the risen Christ in the *Hortulanus* episode: 'O myn harte! wher hast thou bee?/ Com hom agayn, and leve with mee.' This is an adaptation of the Latin, 'Revertere dilecte mi: revertere dilecte votorum meorum',[27] a passionate plea which nevertheless sounds more formal, both because it is in Latin and because it is spoken in a rhetorical apostrophe and not addressed to the present Christ. In contrast the English lines have a simplicity and grace born of the native lyric tradition, but they perhaps come home to the heart with a poignancy inappropriate to their new dramatic context.[28] Their exquisite directness is moreover the more marked in contrast to the turgid aureate style in which the plays as a whole are written.

The long monologues and the lack of dramatic action show that the Burial and Resurrection were either not written for performance, or, if for performance, not in a situation that demanded that the author should have observed the primary obligation of the dramatist, namely to write in such a way as to hold his audience's attention. The plays are thus supremely liturgical in the sense that the devotion of the pious and the solemnity of the liturgical occasion are essential to their capacity to move. Despite the extravagant emotion expressed within the plays, only an audience which brought to them an alert devotional receptiveness could find them moving and unwearisome. It is reasonable therefore to suppose that, when the plays were performed, it was in the church of a convent, and that some of the nuns themselves acted. One would hesitate to assume that the men's parts were also played by women, as Gustave Cohen cautiously suggested in regard to the French Nativity plays in the Chantilly manuscript, which were also acted in a convent.[29] It would be sufficient that the nuns should have played the parts of the three Marys and the Virgin, since, in a large convent at least, the priests who would necessarily form part of the community could have taken the four male parts, Joseph, Nicodemus, St John and the risen Christ. The supposition that these plays belong to a convent is likely to remain incapable of either proof or disproof, but it is worth bearing in mind, since it alone seems to make sense of an actual performance of the plays.

Appendix B

French Influence on the Mystery Plays

It has been suggested at various points throughout this work that some of the English plays have been influenced by the French *Passions*. But this method of arrangement does not allow the plausibility of the theory to be sufficiently examined, and therefore the main arguments and assumptions will be set out in this appendix in order that they may be considered as a connected whole. The authors whom I have suggested were influenced by French drama are the Wakefield Master, the poet of the *Ludus Coventriae* and a late reviser of the New Testament sequence of the Chester cycle.[1] The things in the cycles that I have attributed to French influence are those that in the context of the English tradition look unusual, but to which there are close analogues in the *Passions*, these analogues themselves being amongst the most characteristic features of French drama. No extant French play would provide a model for everything attributed to French influence in the *Ludus Coventriae*, the English cycle in which French influence seems most pervasive. The absence of a single source to account for all the borrowings does not, however, tell decisively against the theory: firstly (as we shall note further in a moment) many French plays are lost; secondly, since the borrowings are of what is characteristic of many works rather than peculiar to one, they suggest familiarity with French dramatic conventions rather than a close adherence to a single exemplar.

French influences have only been detected in the work of men who were writing not earlier than 1440–50, and by 1450 all the great French *Passions* had been composed save that of Jean Michel. The only extant French *Passion* which can be dated with certainty in the fourteenth century is the *Passion du Palatinus*,[2] but already by 1380 a *Passion* was being acted annually in Paris,[3] and in 1402 the Confrèrie de la Passion was given the right thenceforward to perform religious plays regularly in Paris.[4] The plays in the manuscript from the Bibliothèque Ste Geneviève, which provide a connected sequence covering the Nativity, the Visit of the Three Kings, the Passion and the Resurrection, are usually thought to represent their initial repertory, though the manuscript itself belongs to the middle of the fifteenth century.[5] The earliest of the full-length *Passions* is the Burgundian *Passion de Semur*, which owes something to the Parisian plays: though it survives only in a manuscript of the late fifteenth century, it has been assigned by Roy on linguistic grounds to the first third of this century.[6] If the *Passion d'Arras* is by Mercadé, as has been plausibly suggested, it must have been written sometime before 1440, this being the year of Mercadé's death.[7] But even if it is not by Mercadé, Greban's dependence upon it shows that it cannot have been composed much later than this, for Greban's *Passion* had achieved fame by 1452, when the town of Abbeville asked for a copy of it.[8] In addition, records show that *Passions* were acted in many French towns besides Paris between 1395 and 1450: Nevers (1396), Chelles (1397), Amiens (1413, 1427, and 1445), Rennes (1430), Metz (1437), and Lyons (1447).[9] It is clear from these records (which must not be taken as complete) that *Passions* were acted in France with increasing frequency from about 1400 onwards, whilst the close family resemblances between the surviving plays suggest that they may be taken as fairly representative in style and range of the many *Passions* that must be lost.

In terms of dating there is thus no obstacle to the proposition that plays written in England *c.* 1440–50 were influenced by the French. It could, however, still be argued either that the resemblances are not so significantly close as to warrant this explanation or that, though notable, they arose through some historical process other than that of direct French influence upon the northern cycles. There is no need to repeat here the evidence for believing these resemblances to be so close that they cannot be a matter of chance, but it may be worth briefly investigating what other explanations for them there might be. There are three possibilities. One, that the resemblances are coincidental in that they arise simply from a common borrowing from the same learned Latin sources, such as the *Meditationes vitae Christi*. Two, that the connecting link between English and French plays was provided by religious narrative poetry of the fifteenth century, such as the narrative of the Resurrection in MS. Ashmole 61[10] or 'Þe Devilis Perlament' in MS. Lambeth 853.[11] Three, that some English cycle, now lost, provided a single dramatic intermediary between the northern cycles and France.

Neither of the first two possibilities seems to me adequate to explain either the quantity or the essentially dramatic nature of the resemblances: either would indeed go against the whole point of the argument which is that some English authors learnt of new dramatic possibilities by seeing how dramatists in another country had worked. But the third possibility is worth considering. If one of the many lost English cycles served as intermediary between the drama of France and the English cycles of the north, the most obvious candidate is the London cycle. As the play of the metropolis it may have possessed some particular prestige; it was performed on a fixed stage and could therefore have provided a model for some of the apparently French borrowings in the *Ludus Coventriae*, which depend upon this type of performance; finally, whilst one may hesitate over the assumption that three northern dramatists had all independently visited France, there is nothing extravagant about the supposition that a dramatist, writing in London, might have had some attachment to the court that would have taken him to France on official business during the period that part of France was an English possession. Unless the text of the London cycle were by some splendid chance recovered, this is a hypothesis that cannot be pursued further. But the supposition that the London cycle was influenced by the French and through it French influences were radiated to the north would certainly be sufficient to account for Chester and possibly sufficient for the *Ludus Coventriae*: only the eccentric Wakefield Master surely went to France.

Abbreviations

Books on drama and editions of plays referred to by abbreviated titles will be found in full in the bibliography.

A.H.   *Analecta hymnica*, ed. G. M. Dreves and C. Blume (Leipzig, 1886–1922).

Archiv   *Archiv für das Studium der neueren Sprachen und Literatur.*

E.E.T.S.   Early English Text Society.

  E.S.   Extra Series.

  S.S.   Supplementary Series.

J.E.G.Ph.   *Journal of English and Germanic Philology.*

M.E.D.   *Middle English Dictionary.*

M.L.R.   *Modern Language Review.*

M.P.   *Modern Philology.*

N.E.D.   *New English Dictionary.*

P.G.   Patrologiae cursus completus, series graeca, ed. J.-P. Migne.

P.L.   Patrologiae cursus completus, series latina, ed. J.-P. Migne.

P.M.L.A.   *Publications of the Modern Language Association of America.*

R.E.S.   *Review of English Studies.*

Sarum Breviary   *Breviarum ad usum insignis ecclesiae Sarum*, ed. F. Proctor and C. Wordsworth (Cambridge, 1879–86).

S.A.T.F.   Société des anciens textes français.

S.P.   *Studies in Philology.*

Warburg Journal   *Journal of the Warburg and Courtauld Institutes.*

Notes

I Latin Liturgical Drama

1 There is an excellent analysis of the fallacy of evolutionary growth in Essay I of O. B. Hardison, *Christian Rite and Christian Drama in the Middle Ages* (Baltimore, 1965), 1–34.

2 See, for instance, the account of the Rouen *Officium stellae* on p. 16 above. This tendency to retract rather than develop has been well emphasised by Hardison, op. cit., *passim*, though in reaction to Young's exaggerated insistence on growth he has perhaps too keenly sought for examples of contrary movement.

3 Statements about the function of liturgical drama and indications of literary self-consciousness are discussed in chapters II and V.

4 The medieval method of singing the Passion narratives from the four gospels in the course of Holy Week is described as follows by Willi Apel, *Gregorian Chant* (London, 1958), 207: 'the mediaeval practice was to sing them in a manner designed to bring out the contrast between the participants of the story: Christ, the Jews, and the Evangelist who narrates the events. This was done by providing for a recitation at three different pitch levels and speeds, low and slow for the words of Christ, high and fast for those of the Jews, and medium for those of the Evangelist.'

5 The most important allegorisation of the mass is that of Amalarius of Metz, *De ecclesiasticis officiis*, III, P.L. 105, 1102–64.

6 Ed. and trans. Dom Thomas Symons (London, 1953); for a discussion of Continental sources see xlv–lii and also the earlier and fuller article by the same author, 'Sources of the *Regularis Concordia*', *Downside Review*, lix (1941), 14–36, 143–70, 264–89.

7 Karl Young, *The Drama of the Medieval Church* (Oxford, 1933), I, 201, 210. For consideration of the relation of the trope of the Introit to the acted *Quem quaeritis* see below, p. 342, n. 24.

8 Whom do you seek in the sepulchre, O followers of Christ?

Jesus of Nazareth who was crucified, O celestial angel.

He is not here, but has risen as He foretold; go forth and announce that He has risen from the dead.

Alleluya. The Lord has risen; today, as a strong lion,

Christ the Son of God, has risen. Cry, thanks be to God.

Come and see the place where the Lord was buried, alleluya, alleluya.

The Lord who for our sake hung upon the tree has risen from the sepulchre, alleluya.

We praise thee O God.

I have expanded the Latin dialogue (the *Concordia* gives only the opening words of each speech) from the full text of the Winchester Troper (Young, I, 254–5).

9 Outside the *Concordia* the *Visitatio* is recorded in four other ordinals, either of the tenth century or thought to represent tenth-century usage. They are those of Metz (*Consuetudines monasticae*, ed. B. Albers, II [Montecassino, 1905], 104–6; cf. *Revue Bénédictine*, xx, 420–33); Trèves (Albers, op. cit., v, 39–41; cf. *Revue Bénédictine*, xxix, 366); Toul (E. Martène, *De antiquis monachorum ritibus*, III [Louvain, 1690], 446–7) and Verdun (Albers, op. cit., v, 123–4). Out of these five ordinals that of Verdun (which is related to tenth-century usage but not necessarily identical with it) alone contains a *Visitatio* without the preceding ceremonies. Under these circumstances the comment of Solange Corbin, *La Déposition liturgique du Christ au vendredi saint* (Paris, Lisbon, 1960), 200, that Young falsely associated the *Visitatio* with the other three ceremonies cannot apply to the earliest records of them, though it is true of later centuries when these came to be regarded as separable pieces, which could be adopted independently of one another.

10 The Adoration of the Cross in a Jerusalem ceremony of the fourth century is recorded by Etheria (cf. Éthérie, *Journal de voyage*, ed. and trans. H. Pétré [Paris, 1948], 234–5); by the seventh century it was incorporated in Roman service-books (cf. Hardison, op. cit., 131).

11 On early crosses and crucifixes cf. P. Thoby, *Le Crucifix des origines au Concile de Trente* (Nantes, 1959), 36–76, and *Supplément*, 11–18.

12 For the *Improperia* see L. Brow, 'Les Impropères du Vendredi-Saint', *Revue Grégorienne*, xx (1935), 161–79, xxi (1936), 8–16, xxii (1937), 44–51. They were in general use by the tenth century.

13 Cf. Symons, *Downside Review*, lix, 28–9.

14 Cf. N. C. Brooks, *The Sepulchre of Christ in Art and Liturgy* (University of Illinois Studies in Language and Literature, VII, 1921); Corbin, *La Déposition liturgique*, 42–69.

15 On the 'tower' as a eucharistic vessel and the symbolic significance given to it see Archdale King, *Eucharistic Reservation in the Western Church* (London, 1965), 40–2; for resemblances to the iconographic representation of Christ's tomb see Brooks, op. cit., 17–23. As Solange Corbin points out (op. cit., 235–6) both practical and symbolic necessity required that the sacrament reserved from Good Friday to Easter Sunday be placed somewhere well away from the altar (and therefore not in the usual place of reservation).

16 Young, I, 121.

17 Once the Host or Cross had been 'buried', it inevitably had to be removed from the sepulchre and it is inconceivable that this action could ever have been performed in a casual manner. Of the five tenth-century customaries which we are considering, however, only that from Metz specifies the manner of performing the *Elevatio*, and it may be conjectured that, when a *Visitatio* was to follow, the *Elevatio* was carried out reverently but without

symbolic elaboration. On the kinds of sepulchre used for the burial of the Cross see Brooks, op. cit., *passim*.

18 Solange Corbin (op. cit., 15) suggests that the *Depositio* of the Host arose in churches of Germany and Lorraine soon after the diffusion of the Mass of the Presanctified.

19 The symbolic implications of the terms used for the cloth, *pannus, sindon, linteamen* and *sudarium* are discussed by Corbin, op. cit., 190. Of these the only one that cannot bear the meaning, whether primarily or secondarily, of grave-clothes, is *pannus*. Though Corbin points out the relationship of *linteamen* and *sudarium* with John xx. 6–7, her insistence that these words only carry a symbolic meaning when used as a pair is over-rigid. Furthermore the choice of word may well depend upon whether the author is giving practical instructions or expounding an allegorical significance.

20 A. Wilmart, 'Le Samedi-Saint monastique', *Revue Bénédictine*, xxxiv (1922), 159–63.

21 The directions given in this ordinal are so brief that its silence about the *Quem quaeritis* is not conclusive evidence that this dialogue was not sung. But the statement that the cloth shall remain in the sepulchre *usque ad Te Deum* is fairly strong evidence that the *Quem quaeritis* was not used, as in all other tenth-century texts the *sudarium* is invariably displayed in the course of the dialogue. The ordinal is also explicit in its instructions about the *sudarium* and, if an acted *Quem quaeritis* were envisaged, it is odd that it gives no directions about this whatsoever. A procession of a normal kind would of course not have to be described.

22 For bibliographical references see above, p. 341, n. 9.

23 Cf. Young, I, 232–3.

24 There has been much discussion recently of the liturgical position for which the *Quem quaeritis* was originally composed. The possibility that it was devised to follow the third respond of matins has been disregarded because of the assumption that in this position it was always acted, whereas on grounds of general probability and its slightly illogical order it is clear that it was not specifically composed as a text for dramatic performance. If, however, the *Visitatio* was originally no more than a procession to the sepulchre, then the *Quem quaeritis* could have been written specifically for it. It is known, however, that a shorter version of this dialogue (the sentences relating to the discovery and display of the *sudarium* are not included) was already used as a trope of the Introit of the mass in Limoges before about 925. This is an appropriate position for it in that it dramatises the appointed gospel for the day, Mark xvi. 1–7 and leads smoothly into the beginning of the Introit, 'Resurrexi et adhuc tecum sum', which then comes as a Resurrection appearance, liturgically expressed. It may never be possible to resolve whether the *Quem quaeritis* was originally a trope of the Introit which was then extended for use during the *Visitatio*, or whether it was composed for the *Visitatio* and then shortened for use as a trope of the Introit. But certainly there is no clear evidence of its being used in any position except these two

in the tenth century: the manuscript of the Winchester Troper which places it before the *Benedictio cerei* is manifestly wrong. Hardison's view that the account of the *Visitatio* in the *Concordia* shows signs of its having been transferred from a different position is unconvincing (cf. *Theology*, lxx [1967], 318–21).

25 This arrangement occurs only in texts of a late date such as the fourteenth-century ordinal from Udine; Young, I, 298. It could represent the preservation or revival of archaic custom.

26 The opening procession was not everywhere abandoned: indeed in some places, and in particular in southern Germany, it was permanently retained; cf. Young, I, 321–4, 658, etc. For examples of the *Quem quaeritis* as part of a procession to the sepulchre made between terce and mass see ibid., 225–30.

27 Later commentators upon the liturgy, such as John Beleth in the twelfth century and the more famous Durandus a century later, explained the singing of the *Te Deum* at the end of the Easter dramatic office as follows: 'Tunc chorus, audita Christi resurrectione, prorumpit in altam vocem, inquiens: *Te Deum laudamus*.' When in the twelfth century the *Te Deum* followed plays on other subjects, it was integrated in other ingenious ways: at the end of Hilarius's play of the Raising of Lazarus, for instance, it is Lazarus himself who most appropriately begins this song of praise (cf. Young, II, 218).

28 The angelic summons to look in the tomb (which prompts the discovery of the discarded grave-clothes) and the triumphant response of the Marys are already absent from the text from Verdun, where there was also no *Depositio* (see above, p. 341, n. 9). Eleventh-century texts in which it is absent include those from Arras, Minden and Nevers (Young, I, 243–5, 579). The angel's words themselves derive from Matthew xxviii. 6; it is interesting to note that they had already been used in a dramatic way in a vespers ceremony cited by Hardison (op. cit., 174), whilst the Marys' 'Surrexit dominus' is used in association with the *Elevatio* in the ordinal printed by Wilmart (loc. cit., 162).

29 Examples will be found in Young under the headings of 'Visit to the Sepulchre: Third Stage' and '*The Ludus paschalis*': they are characteristic of the twelfth century.

30 Young, I, 678–81.

31 G. Gudiol, 'Cataleg dels manuscrits de Vich', *Bulleti de la Biblioteca de Catalunya*, vii (1923–7), 131, cited by R. Donovan, *The Liturgical Drama in Medieval Spain* (Toronto, 1958), 78–82.

32 Donovan, op. cit., 27–9. Young, I, 401–2, suggests that the origins of this development lay in the type of ceremonial detail described in the Toul *Visitatio*: in this the three clerics go to a side altar to collect the *vascula* already placed there, while at the same time the procession goes to the sepulchre singing the third respond (for a second time), which of course describes the buying of spices. This kind of semi-dramatic representation

was possible within the style of the Toul ceremony, but it was inevitably omitted in texts such as that of the *Concordia* as either too symbolical or, if re-cast in dramatic form, too realistic.

33 É. Mâle, *L'art religieux du xiie siècle en France* (Paris, 1953), 133-6.

34 Young, I, 310-11 (*Visitatio*) and 560 (*Elevatio*); the ceremony of the *Depositio* is not described but it is alluded to in the directions for the *Elevatio*, '. . . procedant ad locum ubi Crux et Corpus Domini in sexta feria fuerant tumulata'.

35 Young, I, 476-80; for the date of the manuscript, ibid., 476, n. 5.

36 Cf. Young, II, 4, 427.

37 Cf. Young, I, 7-8, for the text and comment upon the altar as symbol of the *praesepe*; in true dramatisations of the Visit of the Shepherds a Christmas Crib with wooden figures of the Virgin and Child was used.

38 To these can be added an allusion to a prophets' play at Tours (Young, II, 153) and a fragmentary play from Einsiedeln (ibid., 458-60). It should also be noted that the *Ordo prophetarum* was not necessarily acted on Christmas Day: the Rouen play (like that of Tours) was performed on the feast of the Circumcision (1 January); cf. Young, II, 168-9.

39 Young, II, 93-7.

40 See Young, II, 68, n. 1, and for other instances of the use of this quotation, ibid., 66 and 448.

41 Young, I, 438-47.

42 P.L. 147, 53-4. This work was presented to Maurille, archbishop of Rouen, for approval in 1167, and was perhaps commissioned by him. Modern scholars agree that it represents the customs of Rouen and it was so understood in the twelfth century, when a fragment preserved in a manuscript from Llanthony Priory was entitled *Consuetudinarium Ratimogensis* (cf. E. Bishop, *Liturgica historica* [Oxford, 1918], 299-300). See further R. Delamare, *Le De officiis ecclesiasticis de Jean d'Avranches, Archevêque de Rouen (1067-1079)*, Paris, 1923.

43 K. Young, 'A Contribution to the History of Liturgical Drama at Rouen', *M.P.*, vi (1908-9), 201-11.

44 Two small scraps of evidence suggest an early date for the original Rouen *Prophetae*. One is the presence of a semi-dramatic *Prophetae* in a sixteenth-century customary for Salerno (Young, II, 133), which might have its origins in the period when Salerno was part of the Norman kingdom of the two Sicilies and hence derive ultimately from Rouen. The other is the section on the prophets in the Anglo-Norman *Mystère d'Adam*, which suggests that an *Ordo prophetarum* was known in England in the first half of the twelfth century and this again would probably have been borrowed from Rouen.

45 Young, I, 269-70, 599.

46 Ibid., 660-1, 370-1.

47 Ibid., 476-80.

48 On this sequence and its use in liturgical drama see ibid., 273-88, 336-68.

49 Ibid., 459-62.

50 For the Rouen texts see ibid., II, 12-20. Elsewhere and occasionally one finds the Christmas trope transferred to the beginning or end of matins and performed with some degree of impersonation: at Padua (ibid., 9-10) there was a crib and some mimetic action and possibly also at Clermont-Ferrand (the texts from the latter are preserved in breviaries [ibid., 11-12] and therefore necessarily without 'stage-directions').

51 Ibid., 59-62, 68-72.

52 Ibid., 43-4, 435-9.

53 Ibid., 524-5; for further comment see, above, p. 78.

54 The Limoges text does not indicate impersonation (ibid., 138-42), but as it is preserved in a *troparium* this is not evidence that it was not acted.

55 Ibid., 154-65.

56 Dom David Knowles in *The Monastic Order in England* (Cambridge, 1950), 544, infers from the absence of the *Visitatio* in the *Constitutions*, 'that it was not known in the monasteries of Normandy'. The *Visitatio* was certainly known in the cathedral churches of Normandy (Rouen and Avranches) before the compiling of the *Constitutions*, but Lanfranc may have thought of it as a secular custom, unsuitable or unnecessary for monks. For the suggestion that the monastery at Mont St Michel had liturgical plays at an early date, see Edith Wright, *The Dissemination of the Liturgical Drama in France* (Bryn Mawr, 1936), 71-2.

57 See *The Monastic Constitutions of Lanfranc*, ed. Dom David Knowles (London, 1951), xxii.

58 O. Pächt, *The Rise of Pictorial Narrative in Twelfth-century England* (Oxford, 1962), 33-59; the *St Albans Psalter* with an introduction by O. Pächt, C. R. Dodwell, F. Wormald (London, 1960).

59 Pächt, *Pictorial Narrative*, pl. VII, 25.

60 *Visio monachi de Eynsham*, ed. P. M. Huber, *Romanische Forschungen*, xvi (1903), 653.

61 Cf. Knowles, *Monastic Order*, 402.

62 *Magna Vita Sancti Hugonis*, ed. D. Douie and Dom Hugh Farmer, II (London, 1961), 39-42.

63 *Register of St Osmund*, ed. W. H. Rich Jones (Rolls Series, 1884), II, 129. It is of course odd that only two crowns should be mentioned, unless the simple explanation is that one has been lost. R. M. Wilson, *The Lost Literature of Medieval England* (London, 1970), 210, incorrectly brings the number to three by associating with the latten crowns a crown of silver previously mentioned; but this with the dove and chains was *ad Eukaristiam*, that is for the reserved sacrament, which was suspended from the ceiling in a pyx in the shape of a dove, surmounted by a crown; for an illustration of such an arrangement, see Dom Gregory Dix, *A Detection of Aumbries* (London, 1942), pl. opposite p. 28.

64 C. Wordsworth, *Statutes of Lincoln Cathedral* (Cambridge, 1892-7), ii, 15, 23; Young, II, 522.

65 Wordsworth, op. cit., ii, 98; E. K. Chambers, *The Mediaeval Stage* (Oxford, 1903), II, 399.

66 'Dum legitur tercia lectio eant se preparare tres marie, cum magna reverencia in devocione. Finitoque responsorio intrent chorum. Peractisque omnibus iuxta consuetudinem devotissime incipiat episcopus *Te deum laudamus.' The Customary of the Cathedral Priory Church of Norwich*, ed. J. B. L. Tolhurst (Henry Bradshaw Society, lxxxii [1945], 94).

67 Virginia Shull, 'Clerical Drama in Lincoln Cathedral, 1318 to 1561', *P.M.L.A.*, lii (1937), 946–66.

68 Young, I, 164–6, 381–4.

69 Ibid., 170–2, 347–50.

70 In the thirteenth century the processional anthem *Cum rex gloriae* (ibid., 151), was sometimes sung on the way to the sepulchre for the *Elevatio*: two German manuscripts of this period record the custom. Before the Barking and Dublin texts, however, the only combination of this with the *Tollite portas* antiphons (commonly sung in Advent) was in the long Easter play from Klosterneuburg (ibid., 425). The singing of the *Cum rex gloriae* with perhaps one or two minor dramatic developments seems to have become more frequent in Germany in the fifteenth and sixteenth centuries (ibid., 152–77, 561–5); from the same period comes the only elaborate Harrowing of Hell, apart from those of Barking and Dublin: it is from Bamberg (ibid., 172–5). It is interesting to notice that a sixteenth-century printed breviary of Hereford contains a brief Harrowing of Hell (*The Hereford Breviary*, ed. W. H. Frere and L. Brown [Henry Bradshaw Society, xxvi, 1903], 324–5).

71 Cf. Young, I, 382 with 269–70.

72 For a more detailed comparison see Wright, *Liturgical Drama*, 57–8, 149–50.

73 See above, pp. 14–15.

74 See further Appendix A, p. 335.

75 It is interesting to note that this question occurs in the Dublin analogue (Young, I, 170), but the ceremony there is much less mimetic (it takes place at the Easter sepulchre) so that there is no question of apparently impersonating the devil, a practice which no doubt seemed dubious in the fourteenth century though recorded in a late Bamberg ceremony (ibid., 174).

76 Young (I, 166, n. 1) notes the occurrence of this antiphon in Hartker's Antiphonary; in England in the Middle Ages it was one of the antiphons used at lauds on the feast of All Souls (*Sarum Breviary*, III, 982). For the theme of the patriarchs' pleas for release in later drama see below, pp. 164–6.

77 Cf. Brooks, op. cit., 36, 39.

78 'Signifies by this how Christ after the Resurrection went to Galilee followed by the disciples.'

79 For an account of different types of liturgical manuscripts see F. Cabrol, *The Books of the Latin Liturgy*, trans. the Benedictines of Stanbrook (London, 1932), and C. Wordsworth and H. Littlehales, *The Old Service-Books of the English Church* (London, 1904). In the period up to the thirteenth century

the plays are largely found in ordinals, tropers, antiphonars and occasionally processionals (the latter when the *Visitatio* was preceded by a procession to the sepulchre). When from the fourteenth century onwards it became customary to gather all the different parts of the office together, instead of dispersing them amongst different service-books, the resulting book, namely the breviary, increasingly came to contain the *Visitatio* and other plays. The ordinal, which was the most suitable place for the stage-directions necessary for the performance of liturgical drama, continued alongside the breviary as a very common type of service-book to include liturgical drama. Large plays were of course unsuitable for inclusion in any service-book, even though the intention was to perform them in the traditional liturgical position: they would then be copied in a special manuscript, such as the famous Fleury Play-book. If the customs and ordinal of a church survive, and contain no reference to liturgical drama, it would be a fair, though not certain, inference that liturgical drama was, at least not regularly, used.

80 *Medieval Libraries of Great Britain. A List of Surviving Books*, ed. N. R. Ker (London, 1964), 62–76. Durham, however, differed from York and Lincoln in that it was served by Benedictines, not secular clergy.

81 For references to the Benediktbeuern and Montecassino Passion plays see below, p. 355, n. 2. For the occasional singing of a *planctus* at semi-dramatic ceremonies of the Adoration of the Cross on Good Friday in churches of Germany and southern Italy see Young, I, 503–13; see further Sandro Sticca, 'The literary genesis of the *Planctus Mariae*', *Classica et Medievalia*, xxvii (1966), 296–309.

82 See below, p. 195.

83 This question appears in one of the earliest versions of the *Visitatio*, that of Metz, and Young's association of it with the antecedent ceremonies of the *Depositio* and *Elevatio* is plausible (cf. Young, I, 259–66).

84 See above, pp. 156–7.

II Knowledge of Plays and Acting

1 L. W. Jones and C. R. Morey, *The Miniatures of the Manuscripts of Terence* (Princeton, 1931).

2 M. Manitius, *Handschriften antiker Autoren in mittelalterlichen Bibliotheks-katalogen* (Zentralblatt für Bibliothekswesen, 67, Leipzig, 1935), 15; M. D. Knowles, 'The Preservation of the Classics', *The English Library before 1700*, ed. F. Wormald and C. E. Wright (London, 1958), 144–5. For the St Albans manuscript see Jones and Morey, op. cit, 68–93.

3 Manitius, loc. cit., lists only these two manuscripts in the period preceding the humanistic revival; for the manuscript at Bury see R. A. B. Mynors, 'The Latin classics known to Boston of Bury', *Fritz Saxl, 1890–1948: A Volume of Memorial Essays from his Friends in England*, ed. D. J. Gordon (Edinburgh, 1957), 201.

4 La 'Comédie' latine en France au xiie siècle, ed. Gustave Cohen (Paris, 1931); for discussions see E. Faral, 'Le Fabliau latin au moyen âge', Romania, I (1924), 321–85; F. J. E. Raby, A History of Secular Latin Poetry in the Middle Ages II (Oxford, 1957), 54–69.

5 Ed. G. Ranstrand (Göteborg, 1951).

6 Menander was often mentioned in the 'Lives' of Terence, and a fictional reference to an authoritative source would not be out of keeping with medieval custom.

7 Cf. Cohen, op. cit., I, xviii, III, 114–16.

8 Chambers, The Medieval Stage, II, 326–8.

9 For the origins of this see Grace Frank, The Medieval French Drama (Oxford, 1954), 8. The more immediate source of the error was probably the definition of Mimi in the Etymologiae of Isidore of Seville (P.L. 82, 659). Isidore, however, shows a correct historical understanding of acting in his description of comic actors: 'Comoedi sunt qui privatorum hominum acta dictis atque gestu cantabant . . . ', loc. cit., 658.

10 This is the Life beginning 'Terentius comicus genere', of which a text is printed by C. E. Geppert, 'Zur Geschichte der Terentianischen Texteskritik', Neue Jahrbücher für Philologie und Pädagogik, supp. vol. XVIII (1852), 46. On the dating and classification of the Lives see E. K. Rand, 'Early Medieval Commentaries on Terence', Classical Philology, iv (1909), 359–89.

11 On this work see Mary H. Marshall, 'Theatre in the Middle Ages; Evidence from Dictionaries and Glosses', Symposium, iv (1950), 23–5.

12 E.g., the Life beginning, 'Legitur auctor iste', Scholia Terentiana, ed. F. Schlee (Leipzig, 1893), 163–73, commented upon by Rand, loc. cit.

13 Raby, op. cit., 126–32; quite a number of the manuscripts containing the comoediae are English.

14 See below, p. 355, n. 52.

15 In his definitions of tragoedi and comoedi (tragic and comic actors) Isidore was historically correct (see above, n. 9). In the earlier section, De poetis, however, Isidore divided comedy into the old and the new: Terence and Plautus illustrate the old, Persius and Juvenal the new; this was obviously a potential source of confusion.

16 Policraticus, ed. C. C. J. Webb (Oxford, 1909), I, 190.

17 J. de Ghellinck, L'Essor de la littérature latine au xiie siècle (Brussels, 1954), 296–7.

18 Ibid., 263–4.

19 L. Bradner, 'The Latin Drama of the Renaissance (1340–1640)', Studies in the Renaissance, iv (1957), 32–3.

20 For comment on the public recitation of other works in semi-dramatic form see Peter Dronke, Poetic Individuality in the Middle Ages. New Departures in Poetry 1000–1150 (Oxford, 1970), 84–7.

21 There may also have been from time to time a reverse influence, the dramatic passages in the liturgy showing clearly the nature of acting and therefore the possibility of performing the plays of Terence in the same way.

22 Young, II, 344–8.

23 Otto E. Albrecht, *Four Latin Plays of St. Nicholas from the 12th Century Fleury Play-book* (Philadelphia and London, 1935), 115.

24 *The Plays of Roswitha*, trans. Christopher St John (London, 1923), XXVI. On the question of whether these plays were acted see E. H. Zeydel, 'Were Hrotsvitha's dramas performed during her lifetime?', *Speculum*, XX (1945), 443–56.

25 Chambers, II, 379–80. 'London in place of shows in the theatre and stage-plays has holier plays, wherein are shown forth the miracles wrought by Holy Confessors or the sufferings which glorified the constancy of Martyrs'; F. M. Stenton, *Norman London*, with a Translation of William Fitz Stephen's Description by H. E. Butler, Historical Association Leaflets, 93–4, (London, 1934), 30.

26 For discussion of this point see above, pp. 314–21.

27 *De theatro*, P.L. 82, 657–8.

28 Pauly-Wissowa, s.v. *theatron*. Cf. W. Beare, *The Roman Stage*, 2nd ed., (London, 1955), 241–7.

29 *Speculum doctrinale* XII, XCV, 'de ludis scenicis'; cf. *Symposium*, iv, 11.

30 *Itinerarium Kambriae* (Rolls Series, 1868), 55; cf. *Symposium*, iv, 374.

31 'De laudibus divinae sapientiae', *De naturis rerum*, ed. T. Wright (Rolls Series, 1863), 454; cf. the elegy on the ruins of Rome by Hildebert of le Mans, *Carmina minora*, ed. A. Brian Scott (Leipzig, 1969), 25–7. These works are referred to by Marshall in *Symposium*, iv, 374.

32 For the argument that there were theatre-buildings in the Middle Ages, see R. S. Loomis, 'Were there Theatres in the Twelfth and Thirteenth Centuries?', *Speculum*, XX (1945), 92–5; 'Some Evidence for Secular Theatres in the Twelfth and Thirteenth Centuries', *Theatre Annual*, iii (1945), 33–43. Loomis's interpretation of the evidence is corrected by Dino Bigongiari, 'Were there Theatres in the Twelfth and Thirteenth Centuries?', *Romanic Review*, XXXVII (1946), 201–24.

33 E. R. Curtius, *European Literature and the Latin Middle Ages*, trans. W. R. Trask (London, 1953), 138–41; cf. also Jean Jaquot, 'Le Théâtre du monde de Shakespeare à Calderón', *Revue de littérature comparée*, XXXI (1957), 341–72.

34 *Policraticus*, ed. Webb, I, 190.

35 *Carmina Cantabrigiensia*, ed. Walther Bulst (Heidelberg, 1950), 66.

36 Tertullian, *De spectaculis*, trans. T. R. Glover (The Loeb Classical Library, 1960), 295–301.

37 'How vast will the spectacle on that day be!', loc cit., 296.

38 P.L. 182, 217.

39 P.L. III, 553.

40 H. L. D. Ward, 'The Vision of Thurkill', *Journal of the British Archaeological Association*, XXXI (1875), 420–59; Roger of Wendover, *Liber qui dicitur flores historiarum*, II (Rolls Series, 1887), 24–30; cf. H. L. D. Ward, *Catalogue of Romances in the Department of Manuscripts in the British Museum*, II (1893), 506–15.

41 E.E.T.S. 249, 109–10.

42 The arguments for this view are set out fully by Allardyce Nicoll, *Masks, Mimes and Miracles* (London, 1931), 135–74.

43 R. W. Reynolds, 'The Adultery Mime', *The Classical Quarterly*, xl (1946), 77–84.

44 *Early Middle English Verse and Prose*, ed. J. A. W. Bennett and G. V. Smithers (Oxford, 1968), 196–200.

45 E.E.T.S. 249, 47; cf. P.L. 183, 896 (Sermon, 24).

46 Cf. Curtius, *European Literature*, 538–40 and H. W. Janson, *Apes and Ape Lore in the Middle Ages and the Renaissance* (London, 1952), 287–95.

47 Cf. Nicoll, op. cit., 157–8.

48 Lilian M. C. Randall, *Images in the Margins of Gothic Manuscripts* (Berkeley and Los Angeles, 1966), figs 232–3.

49 Young, II, 542. This play was put on under the direction of Albert, the first bishop of Riga, and formerly a canon of Bremen. Whether it was in Latin or in German (the language of the settlers) is unknown. (The *interpretes* probably expounded the play in the language of the pagan natives).

50 For these references see Frank, op. cit., 16.

51 Wilhelm Creizenach, *Geschichte des neueren Dramas*, 2nd ed. (Halle, 1911), I, 8, n. 1.

52 Some helpful material on the use of these terms has been collected by Erwin Wolff, 'Die Terminologie des mittelalterlichen Dramas in bedeutungsgeschichtlicher Sicht', *Anglia*, lxxviii (1960), 1–27.

53 *Ludus breviter de Passione*, Young, I, 514; *Ludus, immo exemplum, Dominice Resurrectionis*, ibid., 432; '. . . propter honorem ludi', ibid., II, 180. The Tegernsee *Antichristus* is also referred to as a *ludus* in one of the stage-directions (ibid., 372).

54 *Danielis ludus*; ibid., 290.

55 *Ludus super Iconia Sancti Nicolai*; ibid., 338.

56 Ibid., 524.

57 P.L. 82, 651. The other three types are the *ludus gymnicus*, *ludus circensis* and *ludus gladiatorius*.

58 A useful list of occurrences of the word will be found in G. R. Coffman, 'The Miracle Play in England. Nomenclature', *P.M.L.A.*, xxxi (1916), 448–65.

59 Young, II, 344, 348.

60 Chambers, II, 366. The vernacular would of course be Anglo-Norman, not English.

61 Young, II, 503. For the Feast of Fools see Chambers, I, 274–335.

62 E.E.T.S., 119, 155. The meaning of this passage has been disputed, but the reference to the *decre* (for which see above, p. 79) shows that the distinction being made is between the irreverence of the Feast of Fools, here referred to as *miracles*, and the decorous performance of liturgical drama.

63 'They supposed that dramatic entertainments were being held there, which we by custom call miracles.' *Latin Stories*, ed. T. Wright (Percy Society, VIII), 99–100; cf. Coffman, loc. cit., 451, n. 7.

64 *The Mummers' Play* (Oxford, 1923), 65-6. The same point can be usefully illustrated by comparing the style of the folk-plays with that of the ballads.
65 Some texts are printed by E. K. Chambers, *The English Folk-Play* (Oxford, 1933).
66 *English Ritual Drama. A Geographical Index*, by E. C. Cawte, Alex Helm and N. Peacock (London, 1967), 13.
67 E.g. the very popular miracle of the Three Clerks, murdered by an avaricious inn-keeper and his wife, and brought to life again by St Nicholas.
68 For references to St George plays see Chambers, ii, 132.
69 Ibid., i, 91 and n. 2.
70 Ibid., 91 and n. 3.
71 See above, p. 34.

III Drama in the Twelfth Century

1 John Stevens, 'Music in some early Medieval Plays', *Studies in the Arts*, ed. Francis Warner (Oxford, 1968), 21-40; Apel, *Gregorian Chant*, 301-4.
2 Young i, 514-16.
3 Ibid., ii, 172-9. The presence of Augustine, the supposed author of the Christmas sermon on which the *Ordo prophetarum* is based, is rare but not unique to this play. An instance from Gerona is cited by R. B. Donovan, *The Liturgical Drama in Spain*, 121-2. The introduction of Augustine to preside and of Synagogus to mock and dispute is a characteristic of later German drama; cf. for instance the *Frankfurter Passionsspiel*, ed. Richard Froning in *Das Drama des Mittelalters* (Stuttgart 1891-2), 379-532, in which Augustine appears at the beginning, and Synagogus interrupts throughout the play.
4 Cf. H. Walther, *Das Streitgedicht in der lateinischen Literatur des Mittelalters*, Quellen und Untersuchungen zur lateinischen Philologie des Mittelalters, v, 2 (1920), and, for the debate between Church and Synagogue in particular, H. Pflaum, 'Der allegorische Streit zwischen Synagoge und Kirche in der europäischen Dichtung des Mittelalters', *Archivum Romanicum*, xviii (1934), 243-340.
5 Bernhard Bischoff in his introduction to the facsimile of the manuscript of the *Carmina Burana* (Munich, 1967), 27-31, states that on palaeographical grounds the manuscript cannot be later than the mid-thirteenth century and in all probability should be dated around 1230. This dating is borne out by the style of the miniatures, cf. A. Boccler, *Ars sacra, Kunst des frühen Mittelalters* (Munich, 1950), 104, and Otto Pächt, as quoted by Peter Dronke, 'A Critical Note on Schumann's dating of the Codex Buranus', *Beiträge zur Geschichte der deutschen Sprache und Literatur*, lxxxiv (1962), 173-83. The latter article convincingly shows that Schumann's literary arguments for a later dating of the manuscript are unfounded.
6 Young, ii, 371-96.

7 There is a tantalising reference to place in the opening rubric, where it is said that the *sedes* for Augustine shall be placed *in fronte ecclesiae*. This could mean 'in front of the church', but Young argues that it should be translated 'in the front part of the church', referring to the west end of the nave. (II, 196). The supposition that the congregation or audience stood with their backs to the altar has an anachronistic ring. It is conceivable that the *frons* was the east end of the nave, and just possible that *ecclesia* here refers not to the building, but to the congregation, in which case the phrase would designate no particular place, but mean 'to face the congregation'.

8 Young, II, 242.

9 See above, p. 80.

10 P. Meyer, 'Les Trois Maries', *Romania*, xxxiii (1904), 239–45.

11 Young, I, 530. The vernacular lament, beginning 'Awe, awe, mich hiut unde immer we!' (Woe, woe is me today and evermore) is followed by the Latin *planctus*, 'Flete, fideles animae' (for the text see Young, I, 498–9).

12 S. Sticca, 'The Priority of the Montecassino Passion Play', *Latomus*, xx (1961), 574. This unfinished play is dated in the second half of the twelfth century, though, according to some, the three lines of vernacular *planctus* are of a slightly later date. The text ends at this point, though it can be seen from the Sulmona Fragment (Young, I, 701–8), which consists of the part for one of the soldiers, that the whole play extended to the Resurrection.

13 'Tunc Maria surgat et vadat lamentando, cantans: "Awe, auve, daz ich ie wart geborn . . ." ' (Then Mary rises [from her knees] and goes [away from Christ] making this lamentation: 'Alas, alas, that I was ever born. . . .'); Young, I, 524.

14 This lament, beginning, 'Lasse dolante, que ferai/de mon Signour que perdu ai?' ('Alas, I grieve, what shall I do, now that I have lost my Lord') is embedded in a dialogue with the Resurrection angel; Young, I, 417.

15 Ibid., II, 213–14.

16 Ibid., 338–9.

17 'Miserable wretches, we have slept too long'; ibid., 362–4.

18 'Now I mourn, now is my brother dead, for whom I weep'; ibid., 213.

19 'We also shall die; Death's fish-hook catches all people alike. This is the law, when we enter the world we must sometime leave the prison-house of the flesh. Do not weep for the death of your dear brother; rather should you rejoice at it. He has been set free from many sufferings and has escaped what remains for others to endure'; ibid., 204.

20 The most recent and informative editions of the *Sponsus* are: *Le 'Sponsus'. Mystère des vierges sages et des vierges folles suivi des trois poèmes limousins et farcis*, ed. L.-P. Thomas (Paris, 1951), and *Sponsus. Dramma delle Vergini prudenti e delle Vergini stolte*, ed. d'Arco Silvio Avalle (Milan and Naples, 1965); but the earlier text of Young, II, 362–6, seems in retrospect to make a satisfactory compromise between the freely emended text of Thomas and the conservatism of Avalle. A translation into modern English is given by R. T. Hill, *Sponsus. Text and Translation* (New Haven, 1936).

21 This interpretation – fully explained in *Sawles Warde* – is patristic in origin; cf. *Catena aurea*, ed. P. A. Guarienti (Rome, 1953), I, 359.

22 Correctly in this parable the sleep is morally neutral since it signifies the sleep of death, from which all will awake at the Last Judgment; cf. Thomas, op. cit., 35, n. 1.

23 Romans xiii. 11. Cf. the comment on this in the *Glossa ordinaria*, P.L. 114, 513, 'Somnus est negligentia vel ignorantia'.

24 'Why should we give you our oil? You shan't have any, go and buy some from the merchants whom you see standing there. Miserable wretches, you have slept too long!' Young, II, 363–4.

25 Ibid., 362. Avalle, op. cit., 72, does not emend the manuscript rubric assigning this speech to the *Prudentes*. There is no doubt, however, as to the speaker, since he identifies himself saying 'Gabriels soi' (I am Gabriel).

26 Cf. Avalle, op. cit., 24.

27 St Thomas stresses this in his own observations on the parable in the *Catena aurea*, I, 363–6. It is suggested, however, by many of the patristic comments which he quotes.

28 The contents of the manuscripts are given by R. Menéndez Pidal in the introduction to his edition of the text, 'Misterio de los Reyes Magos', *Revista de archivos, bibliotecas y museos*, 3rd series, iv (1900), 453–63. The text of Menéndez Pidal is reprinted more accessibly in J. D. M. Ford, *Old Spanish Readings* (New York, 1911), 6–12. The most recent edition is that of Sebastião Pestana (Lisbon, 1965).

29 Winifred Sturdevant, *The Misterio de los Reyes Magos: Its Position in The Development of the Medieval Legend of the Three Kings*, Johns Hopkins Studies in Romance Literatures and Languages, x (1927).

30 For discussions of this work from the historical point of view and for a history of medieval Spanish religious drama in general see Donovan, *Liturgical Drama in Medieval Spain*, and N. D. Shergold, *A History of the Spanish Stage from Medieval Times until the end of the Seventeenth Century* (Oxford, 1967).

31 *Christi Leben von seiner Geburt bis zur Geschichte von der Samariterin*, ed. Emil Krappe (Greifswald, 1911), 4–5.

32 Ed. Pestana, 29. 'O God the Creator, what marvel is this! I do not know what this star is! Now, for the first time it has been seen: it is but a short time ago that it was born. Born, can it be that the Creator is born, who is the Lord of all men. It is not true, I do not know what I am saying; all this is not worth a fig'.

33 Chambers, II, 366.

34 See above, p. 29.

35 C. W. Jones, *The Saint Nicholas Liturgy and its Literary Relationships* (Berkeley and Los Angeles, 1963), argues that the earliest plays of St Nicholas were written c. 1100 in a north German centre, where the plays of Hrotsvitha were also known. His theories, however, must be corrected in the light of Christopher Hohler, 'The Proper Office of St Nicholas and

Related Matters with reference to a Recent Book', *Medium Aevum*, xxxvi (1967), 40–8.

36 Jean Bodel, *Le Jeu de saint Nicolas*, ed. F. J. Warne (Oxford, 1951).

37 Carleton Brown, 'An Early Mention of a St Nicholas Play in England', *S.P.*, xxviii (1931), 594–601; cf. Homer G. Pfander, *The Popular Sermon of the Medieval Friar in England* (New York, 1937), 32.

38 *Le Mystère d'Adam*, ed. Paul Studer (Manchester, 1918), xxxiv–lvi; the most recent French editions are those of Paul Aebischer (Geneva and Paris, 1963) and W. Noomen (Paris, 1971). All references are to Studer's edition.

39 The treatment of subject-matter in these plays is discussed more fully above, pp. 113–31, 156–8.

40 '. . . and let them make gestures fitting to what they speak', ed. cit., 1.

41 For a discussion of the liturgical occasion of the play, see above, p. 56.

42 That the initial words, 'In principio creavit Deus celum et terram', indicate a lesson from Genesis extending to verse 26 or 27 is argued by W. Noomen, 'Note sur l'élément liturgique du *Jeu d'Adam*', *Omagiu lui Alexandru Rosetti* (Bucharest, 1965), 635–8, and '*Le Jeu d'Adam*. Étude descriptive et analytique', *Romania*, lxxxix (1968), 145–93; it is more satisfactory than Hardison's view that this is a response used as a *lectio* (*Christian Rite and Christian Drama*, 260, n. 17).

43 The derivation from the *Liber responsalis* has been pointed out by both Hardison and Noomen (for references see preceding note).

44 *Studies in the Arts*, ed. Warner, 34.

45 *Der Sündenfall und Marienklage*, ed. Otto Schönemann (Hanover, 1855), 5, 26–7. The three responses sung are, 'In principio creavit Deus celum et terram', 'Formavit igitur Dominus hominem de limo terrae', and 'Plantaverat autem Dominus'. It may be noted that in this work the good angels had already sung their praises of God in Latin forms (the *Sanctus* and *Gloria in excelsis*), and therefore their singing of these responses is given a more natural appearance.

46 *Egerer Fronleichnamsspiel*, ed. Gustav Milchsack (Tübingen, 1881), 13, 17. Two responses are sung, 'Formavit igitur Dominus', and 'Dum deambularet'. They fit into the same pattern of angelic singing as those in the Innsbruck play.

47 For a different view see Noomen, *Romania*, lxxxix, 148–63, who sees the vernacular as *farciture*, that is comment and amplification upon the Latin. It should be noted that the normal purpose of responses was to comment upon and emphasise the accompanying lections, so that to use them in any other way would go against the liturgical grain.

48 *La Seinte Resureccion*, edition begun by T. A. Jenkins and J. M. Manly and completed by M. K. Pope and J. G. Wright, Anglo-Norman Text Society, IV (1943); for a clear, brief discussion see M. Dominica Legge, *Anglo-Norman Literature and its Background* (Oxford, 1963), 321–8.

49 Cf. Chambers, II, 338–9.

50 Ed. cit., 40. 'O Jesus, dear Lord, while you lived you were a good physician

and restored Lazarus to life from the dead: and what will you do for yourself? Will you not rise? Will you yourself not rise from death?'

51 See above, pp. 274–5.

52 Cf. Young, I, 309, 311, 312, etc. For narrative passages in vernacular drama, see W. Noomen, 'Passages narratifs dans les drames médiévaux français', *Revue belge de philologie et d'histoire*, xxxvi (1958), 761–85, and O. Jodogne, *Cahiers de civilisation médiévale*, viii (1965), 1–24, 179–89.

IV The Development of the Cycle Form

1 The earliest surviving references to the existence of mystery cycles before the end of the fourteenth century are 1376 for York, 1377 for Beverley, and 1392 for Coventry (Chambers, II, 109). Whilst these references only provide a *terminus post quem*, and the sudden crop of references to the cycles may only indicate that the last quarter of the fourteenth century is better documented than previous decades, it would nevertheless be hazardous to assume a substantially earlier date for the plays. The only hint of an earlier date is the record of two people making a payment in Cambridge c. 1350 on entrance of the gild of Corpus Christi *in ludo filiorum Israelis* (for a play of the Children of Israel); the title is ambiguous, as it could refer either to a play of Moses or a Massacre of the Innocents; if the latter, one could not infer from it the existence of a cycle (cf. p. 357, n. 19 below).

2 For the Benediktbeuern Passion play see Young, I, 518–36, and for the dating of the plays in this manuscript, p. 351, n. 5 above. The twelfth-century Montecassino Passion play is printed and discussed by Sandro Sticca, 'The Priority of the Montecassino Passion Play', *Latomus*, xx (1961), 381–91, 568–74, 827–39.

3 For a knowledge of ancient theatres see above, p. 30. Vitruvius, *De architectura*, was known in the twelfth century; cf. de Ghellinck, op. cit., 306.

4 Cf. Anna J. Mill, *Mediaeval Plays in Scotland* (Edinburgh, 1927), 283–4.

5 For further comment on these works see below, pp. 85–6.

6 See above, p. 51.

7 Noomen, *Romania*, LXXXIX, 150–4.

8 Young, II, 542.

9 The coincidence that the *Mystère d'Adam*, as it stands, ends in the middle of an *Ordo prophetarum* and that the last section of the Regensburg play is described as an *Ordo prophetarum* may seem to suggest that neither play extended beyond this point. But there is no way of knowing how much of the *Adam* is lost, whilst the term *Ordo prophetarum* could bear an unexpectedly inclusive meaning by the end of the twelfth century, since it is applied to the whole of the extensive Riga play, which we are about to describe.

10 The mid-fourteenth-century Frankfurt *Dirigierrolle* (scenario) opens with an *Ordo prophetarum* and begins the subsequent Passion sequence with the

Baptism of Christ (Froning, op. cit., 340–2); the earlier St Gall Passion play opens with a prologue spoken by Augustine (a figure sometimes preserved in the *Ordo prophetarum*) and then proceeds with the Marriage at Cana (F. J. Mone, *Schauspiele des Mittelalters*, 1 [Karlsruhe, 1846], 72–3). The *Wiener Passionsspiel* presents the Fall of the Angels, the Fall of Man and then starts the Passion sequence with the episode of Mary Magdalene (Froning, op. cit., 305–23). The association of the *Ordo prophetarum* with the Passion has already been noted by Craig, 'The Origin of the Old Testament Plays', *M.P.*, x (1912–13), 477.

11 The liturgical propriety of including the Nativity could be defended on the grounds that the period from Septuagesima to Easter symbolically recapitulates the whole history of the world; cf. Hardison, op. cit., 88, n. 6. This symbolism, however, would be more likely to confer a *post hoc* rationalisation than to prompt the initial choice of the design.

12 For the quotation of the whole relevant passage see Young, II, 542. Theo Stemmler, *Liturgische Feiern und geistliche Spiele* (Tübingen, 1970), 171, suggests that the subject of the Riga play was that of battles in which the good overcame the evil. To arrive at this implausible interpretation he ignores the emphasis upon *doctrinam Veteris et Novi Testamenti* and takes *bellum* to mean *Krieg*, though the context makes it plain that *bellum* must here bear the wider meaning of strife or conflict, since the Massacre of the Innocents is one of the instances cited. *Bellum* in this sense would cover almost anything that was doctrinally important in the Bible.

13 For further comment on the Old Testament subjects included in this play see above, pp. 61 ff. It may, however, be noted now that this work, which has the largest set of Old Testament subjects, does not confirm Craig's view that the Old Testament sequence developed from the gradual dramatisations of all the breviary lections for the lenten period (*M.P.*, x, 473–87). The argument that early cycles were composed for performance at Septuagesima shows why Craig found some resemblance between the Old Testament subjects chosen for dramatisation and the lenten liturgy (the authors would necessarily have these in mind) and also why the correspondence is not at all exact (the authors contriving a cycle from the outset were free to adopt any principle of selection that seemed appropriate).

14 For this manuscript, now destroyed, see the *Hortus deliciarum*, ed. A. Straub and G. Keller (Strasbourg, 1901). Amongst the Old Testament scenes are David and Goliath and portraits of the twelve prophets, but it does not include Gideon. It ends with the Antichrist and the Last Judgment, and it is interesting to note in relation to the Regensburg play that it begins with the Fall of the Angels.

15 Cf. Young, II, 540–1, and Alessandro d'Ancona, *Origini del teatro italiano* (Turin, 1891) 1, 91–4. Stemmler, op. cit., 169–70, maintains that the Fall of Man was not included since the chronicle does not mention it explicitly: the summary of the matter of the play begins: 'Imprimis de Creatione primorum parentum, deinde de Annunciatione Beatae Virginis . . .'. It

is perfectly clear that the play opened with the common juxtaposition of the Fall of Man and the Annunciation and that the title, *Creatio primorum parentum*, was understood to cover the whole and indivisible story. It would not mislead anyone familiar with medieval ways of thought.

16 There is support from contemporary iconographic sequences for this supposition: the *St Albans Psalter*, for instance, has illustrations extending from the Fall of Man to the Ascension, and the twelfth-century wall-paintings at Hardham in Sussex consist of three scenes of the Fall and a New Testament sequence beginning with the Annunciation (but omitting the Passion), and it ends with the Last Judgment; cf. *Twelfth Century Paintings at Hardham and Clayton*, with an Introductory Essay by Clive Bell (Lewes, Sussex, 1947).

17 W. O. Hassall, 'Plays at Clerkenwell', *M.L.R.*, xxxiii (1938), 564–7.

18 The first explicit reference to a Skinnerswell play, based on Old and New Testament matter, occurs in Malvern's Continuation of Higden's *Polychronicon*, where there is a brief reference for 1391. Malvern, however, had noted the performance of a five-day play in 1384, which one may reasonably assume to have been the same. In 1385, moreover, there had been a proclamation of the Mayor and Aldermen, forbidding 'the performance of the play that customarily took place at Skynnereswelle . . .' (Calendar of Letter-Books preserved amongst the Archives of the Corporation of the City of London, *Letter-Book H.*, ed. R. C. Sharpe [London, 1907], 272). A performance considered *customary* must presumably have occurred for at least fifteen to twenty years. For other references, including a number of later ones from the *London Chronicle*, see Chambers, II, 380–1. It is unfortunate that there are no town chronicles for London for the period c. 1345–1400.

19 *The Holkham Bible Picture Book*, ed. W. O. Hassall (London, 1954), 34–6, and *The Anglo-Norman Text of the Holkham Bible Picture Book*, ed. F. P. Pickering, Anglo-Norman Texts, xxiii (Oxford, 1971). Some bilingual fragments of the late thirteenth and early fourteenth centuries, however, suggest that plays were sometimes written in two parallel versions, English and French, and presumably acted in whichever language was appropriate to the occasion; cf. M. Dominica Legge, *Anglo-Norman Literature and its Background* (Oxford, 1963), 328–31. For the fragments themselves see E.E.T.S. S.S., I, 114–17. It seems likely that both fragments form part of prologues spoken by Herod to introduce a dramatisation of the Massacre of the Innocents.

20 Carleton Brown, 'Sermons and Miracle Plays: Merton College MS 248', *M.L.N.*, xlix (1934), 394–6. In terms of dramatic development the speech could come from works such as the *Cursor mundi* or *Genesis and Exodus* (E.E.T.S., 7), but the lyric metre is more suggestive of a play.

21 Young, II, 371–87. An example of the latter type is *Le Jour du jugement*, ed. E. Roy (Paris, 1902); cf. Frank, op. cit., 131–5.

22 Chambers, II, 405.

23 This theory is put forward by Hardin Craig, *English Religious Drama of the Middle Ages* (Oxford, 1955), 336–7.

24 What a framework of speeches by the apostles may have been like can be seen from the short Innsbruck play, described above, p. 72. The Innsbruck play corresponds exactly to the type of play that M. D. Anderson on iconographic evidence postulated as the lost York play (*Drama and Imagery in English Medieval Churches* [Cambridge, 1963], 37–40). From our knowledge of the approximate length of the York play, however, it is clear that it must have been a much more extensive work than the Innsbruck play, which is only 756 lines in length.

25 *A Hundred Merry Tales and Other Jestbooks of the Fifteenth and Sixteenth Centuries*, ed. P. M. Zall (Lincoln, 1963), 115–16. It may be just worth noting that the Coventry records do not refer to any Old Testament plays, and the Coventry cycle could therefore have been a genuine Creed cycle; but since the surviving list of plays is known to be incomplete, this suggestion can only be exceptionally tentative.

26 The Chester cycle extended over three days, at least in the sixteenth century; Chester Banns, ll. 32–3, E.E.T.S. E.S. 62, 3.

27 Chambers, II, 381.

28 Ed. J. de Rothschild, S.A.T.F., 6 vols (1878–91). The plays from Job onwards are presented as individual works, not as part of a continuous cycle, and the play of Esther, which is far longer than the others, obviously began as a self-contained unit.

29 For a history of this debate in medieval literature see Hope Traver, *The Four Daughters of God* (Philadelphia, 1907); in the *Mystère* the debate is not continued beyond the Exodus sequence, thus indicating some kind of stopping point there.

30 Cf. Frank, op. cit., 182.

31 A. N. Didron, *Christian Iconography*, trans. M. Stokes, II (London, 1891), 265–97.

32 Cf. *A Book of Old Testament Illustrations of the Middle of the Thirteenth Century* with an introduction by Sidney Cockerell and M. R. James (Cambridge, 1927), 10. James's introduction contains an excellent account of the history of Old Testament iconographic sequences from Catacomb art to the late Middle Ages.

33 F. Saxl, *English Sculptures of the Twelfth Century* (London, 1954), 60–2 and pls LXVIII–LXXXIII.

34 Anderson, *Drama and Imagery*, 87–104; cf. C. J. P. Cave, *Roof Bosses in Medieval Churches* (Cambridge, 1948), pls 146–57.

35 *Queen Mary's Psalter*, ed. G. Warner (London, 1912), 11–22, pls 1–118.

36 James, op. cit., 11–13.

37 Ibid., 20.

38 G. McN. Rushforth, *Medieval Christian Imagery* (Oxford, 1936), 148–89.

39 Abbé V. Leroquais, *Les Psautiers manuscrits latins des bibliothèques publiques de France* (Macon, 1940–1), II, 16.

40 Florens Deuchler, *Der Ingeborgpsalter* (Berlin, 1967). This sequence now begins with Abraham entertaining the angels, the earlier Genesis illustrations being lost.

41 James, op. cit., 26.

42 Leroquais, op. cit., 79.

43 *Catalogue of Manuscripts and Early Printed Books from the Library of William Morris, etc. now forming part of the Library of J. Pierpont Morgan* (London, 1906), no. 16.

44 E.E.T.S. 7.

45 T. S. R. Boase, *The York Psalter* (London, 1962).

46 James, op. cit., 22; Walter Oakeshott, *The Artists of the Winchester Bible* (London, 1945).

47 Geoffrey Shepherd, 'Scriptural Poetry', *Continuations and Beginnings*, ed. E. G. Stanley (London, 1966), 30.

48 The lists are given in Chambers, II, 425, 340.

49 The Old Testament sequence here in fact stops with Noah, but there is a blank leaf between the last Noah scene and the Tree of Jesse (which is the iconographic equivalent to the Prophets' Play): it may be conjectured that this should have contained one or two scenes of the Sacrifice of Isaac; that it was left blank to mark a division between the Old and New Testaments seems less probable.

50 V. A. Kolve, *The Play called Corpus Christi* (London, 1966), 86–100.

51 E.E.T.S. E.S. 120, 35.

52 Cf. Craig, op. cit., 300.

53 It is only in the prophets' play of the *Ludus Coventriae* that the prophets all belong to the fifth age (i.e. David's); the Towneley play begins with Moses, and in the Chester cycle the prophets are integrated in the stories of Moses and Balaam and Balak, which provide a framework.

54 In the York cycle the prophecies (which incidentally include that of Abraham, the initiator of the third age) are summarised in a prologue to the Annunciation.

55 *Sarum Breviary*, I, ccccxcii–ccccxciii.

56 Cf., for instance, Sicard of Cremona, *Mitrale*, P.L. 213, 159–60.

57 'Ubi autem armati Gedeonis cum Philistaeis pugnabant'; 'Nam in eodem ludo erant bella, utpote David, Gedeonis, Herodis.' The first subject was Gideon's battle with the Midianites (Judges vi–vii), which would include the episode of the fleece, an important type of the virgin birth; the subject of the David episode was probably his fight with Goliath (I Samuel. xvii).

58 Hardin Craig, 'The Origin of the Passion Play: Matters of Theory as well as Fact', *Studies in Honor of A. H. R. Fairchild*, ed. C. T. Prouty (Columbia, 1946), 88.

59 *La Passion du Palatinus, mystère du XIVe siècle*, ed. Grace Frank (Paris, 1922); cf. Frank, *Medieval French Drama*, 125–9. This play was indebted to a narrative poem, the *Passion des jongleurs*, on which a large part of the

Northern Passion is based (cf. *The Northern Passion*, ed. Frances Foster, E.E.T.S., 147, 49–65).

60 *Le Mystère de la Passion*, ed. G. Paris and G. Raynaud (Paris, 1878).

61 *Le Mystère de la Passion (Angers, 1486)*, ed. O. Jodogne (Gembloux, 1959).

62 *Meditations on the Life of Christ*, trans. Isa Ragusa and Rosalie Green (Princeton, 1961). The influence of this work on English mystery plays is discussed below in chapters viii–x, *passim*.

63 *Vita Jesu Christi*, ed. L. M. Rigollot (Paris, 1878).

64 Émile Roy, *Le Mystère de la Passion en France du XIVe au XVIe siècle* (Paris and Dijon, 1903–4), 3–189.

65 Cf. L. Petit de Julleville, *Les Mystères* (Paris, 1880), II, 418–21; this work, preserved in MS. Bibliothèque de Valenciennes 449 (*olim* 421), must be distinguished from the Valenciennes play described by H. Giese, *La Passion de Jésus-Christ jouée à Valenciennes, l'an 1547 (B.N. fr. 12536)* (Greifswald, 1905).

66 Petit de Julleville, II, 413–15.

67 M. Blakemore Evans, *The Passion Play of Lucerne* (New York and London, 1943).

68 Petit de Julleville, II, 411–13.

69 The *Frankfurter Passionsspiel* and the *Alsfelder Passionsspiel* are edited in R. Froning, *Das Drama des Mittelalters* (Stuttgart, 1891–2); the *Donaueschinger Passionsspiel* is edited by Eduard Hartl, *Das Drama des Mittelalters. Passionsspiele*, II (Leipzig, 1942).

70 *Das Künzelsauer Fronleichnamsspiel*, ed. Peter K. Liebenow (Berlin, 1969); a brief summary of the play is given by H. Werner, 'Künzelsauer Fronleichnamsspiel aus dem Jahre 1479', *Germania*, IV (1859), 338–61; cf. also W. F. Michael, *Die geistlichen Prozessionsspiele in Deutschland* (Baltimore and Göttingen, 1947), 33–42.

71 *Egerer Fronleichnamsspiel*, ed. Milchsack; this work is described as a three-day Passion Play by Neil C. Brooks, 'Processional Drama and Dramatic Procession in Germany in the late Middle Ages', *J.E.G.Ph.*, xxxii (1933), 167.

72 On the number of plays at Coventry see *Two Coventry Corpus Christi Plays*, ed. Hardin Craig, E.E.T.S. E.S. 87 (2nd ed. 1957), xi–xix, xl–xli, and Craig, *English Religious Drama*, 281–94. Craig retracted his original view that there were no Old Testament plays at Coventry on the assumption that a Corpus Christi cycle could not be complete without Old Testament plays. If one does not make this assumption, his earlier interpretation of the evidence is better in that it involves no special pleading. Craig's table of subjects (E.E.T.S. E.S. 87, xv) is convincing. There were ten plays, of which the subjects of six are known. There are therefore four plays in doubt. One was the Burial of Christ, which was performed by the Pinners and Needlers in 1414; a later rearrangement should not be conjectured here on the grounds that it was too short to remain an independent play (the corresponding play in the York cycle is slightly shorter than the

Last Judgment, which remained a separate play at Coventry), and it is easy to conjecture ways in which it might have been expanded. Of the other three, one must have dealt with the Ascension and Pentecost, and either one or two with a sequence ending with the Betrayal and beginning with either the Baptism or the Raising of Lazarus. There could therefore at most have been one Old Testament play (covering perhaps the Fall of the Angels and the Fall of Man), and conceivably not even this. This kind of reconstruction is of course speculative, but if pieces of evidence, such as that of the Pinners' Play in 1414, can be jettisoned as inconclusive, then it is better to abandon the whole enterprise as being too insecurely based.

73 Chambers, II, 424. This stopping point is found occasionally in art and drama, e.g. in the *York Psalter* (MS. Hunterian Mus. 229), and the *Passion de Valenciennes*.

74 Chambers, II, 425–6. Like the Assumption, this stopping point is occasionally found, e.g. in the *Ingeborg Psalter* and in the Passion Play performed at Valenciennes in 1547, Giese, op. cit., 61.

75 For examples of the use of this term, see Craig, op. cit., 140–2.

76 Cf. Woolf, *The English Religious Lyric in the Middle Ages* (Oxford, 1968), 384.

77 Chambers, II, 380–1.

78 Whilst, as we have argued, the term 'Corpus Christi play' originally referred to the date of performance, in due course it became a generic term in the north for biblical plays. A Chester record, for instance, speaks of a 'play of Corpus Christi' some decades after the plays, as other documents indicate, were being performed at Whitsun (Chambers, II, 353); much later the antiquary, John Weever, mentioning the London plays, noted that in his 'country' (i.e. Lancashire), a play on the Sacred Scriptures was called a 'Corpus Christi play' (Craig, op. cit., 141). Although certain evidence of this ambiguity is not found before the early sixteenth century, the possibility that it already occurred in the second half of the fifteenth century cannot be discounted.

79 Cf. Kolve, 47–8. Eucharistic miracles are amply discussed by Peter Browe, *Die eucharistischen Wunder des Mittelalters* (Breslau, 1938).

80 Chambers, II, 330–3; the fullest account of the Aberdeen records is in A. J. Mill, *Mediaeval Plays in Scotland*.

81 Glynne Wickham, *Early English Stages* (London, 1959), I, 347.

82 E.E.T.S. S.S. I, 58–89.

83 A play from its description very similar to the Croxton play ('La Rappresentazione di quel Giudeo che arrostì il Corpo di Cristo') was performed in Rome in 1473 (d'Ancona, op. cit., I, 288 and n. 2), and a *Miracolo del Corpo di Gesù Cristo* was acted in Florence on 29 May 1502 (ibid., 333); a printed text of a play of this kind survives, but it is not known whether it was this surviving play that was acted at Rome or Florence (ibid., 270, 288).

84 Petit de Julleville, II, 193–4, 574–6.
85 E.E.T.S. E.S. 107, 35–43. For a discussion of eucharistic types see M. Vloberg, *L'Eucharistie dans l'art* (Grenoble and Paris, 1946), 27–42.
86 Willm Reupke, *Das Zerbster Prozessionsspiel 1507* (Berlin and Leipzig, 1930); Fr. Sintenis, 'Beschreibung einer im Jahre 1507 zu Zerbst aufgeführten Prozession', *Zeitschrift für deutsches Altertum*, II (1842), 276–97.
87 Neil C. Brooks, 'An Ingolstadt Corpus Christi Procession and the *Biblia Pauperum*', *J.E.G.Ph.*, xxxv (1936), 1–16.
88 Ibid.
89 *Heidelberger Passionsspiel*, ed. Gustav Milchsack (Tübingen, 1880).
90 Cf. 'The Effect of Typology on the English Mediaeval Plays of Abraham and Isaac', *Speculum*, xxxii (1957), 807.
91 The arguments for the propriety of the cycles to the feast are strongly put by Kolve, op. cit., 44–9.
92 A translation of large parts of the bull will be found in Darwell Stone, *A History of the Doctrine of the Holy Eucharist* (London, 1909), I, 344–6; for the office see *Sarum Breviary*, I, mlxii–mlxxv. It has been conjectured that St Thomas contributed to both the bull and the office.
93 Cf. Peter Browe, *Die Verehrung der Eucharistie im Mittelalter* (Munich, 1932), III.
94 For further discussion of the Day of Judgment in the devotional tradition of the Middle Ages see 'The Tearing of the Pardon', *Piers Plowman: Critical Approaches*, ed. S. S. Hussey (London, 1969), 69.
95 The other great doctrinal feast was Trinity Sunday, but it celebrated a doctrine without such historical and physical roots and therefore did not lend itself to dramatic commemorations.
96 *Altteutsche Schauspiele* ed. F. J. Mone (Quedlinburg and Leipzig, 1841), 145–64.
97 'Here begins a play about the catholic faith, useful to the devotion of the simple, to be acted on the day of Corpus Christi or during its octave.' ed. cit., 145.
98 See above, p. 358, n. 24.
99 The problems of combining plays with procession are excellently discussed by N. C. Brooks, 'Processional Drama and Dramatic Procession in Germany in the late Middle Ages', *J.E.G.Ph.*, xxxii (1933), 141–71.
100 It was an ancient custom that religious processions stopped at various stations on their route to sing a hymn or anthem, the stations often being churches. During the fifteenth century this custom, as far as the plays were concerned, became fully secularised, wealthy citizens paying to have a station outside their house (M. L. Spencer, *Corpus Christi Pageants in England* [New York, 1911], 48).
101 Spencer, op. cit., 47.
102 For Chester and Lincoln see Craig, *Religious Drama*, 166, 268–9. A York ordinance of 1426, made in response to Franciscan disapproval, decreed that the plays should be on the vigil of Corpus Christi so as not to disturb

the feast; by 1477 the reverse had taken place, it being the procession that was postponed to the Friday (cf. R. Davies, *Extracts from the Municipal Records of the City of York during the Reigns of Edward IV, Edward V, and Richard III* [London, 1843], 243–4). For Beverley see Chambers, II, 341, and for Newcastle, Spencer, op. cit., 63.

103 Ed. Liebenow, 1–2; cf. Michael, op. cit., 34.

104 For Dublin and Hereford see Chambers, II, 363–6, 368–9; for Draguignan and Béthune (and French *mystères mimées* on other occasions), Petit de Julleville, II, 186–216; for Valencia, Shergold, op. cit., 53–6; for Bologna, d'Ancona, op. cit., I, 296–7; for Freiburg, etc., Michael, op. cit., 52–65.

105 E.g. Dublin, Chambers, II, 363–6.

106 Cf. Spencer, op. cit., 69–70 and M. Pierson, 'The Relation of the Corpus Christi Procession to the Corpus Christi Plays', *Transactions of the Wisconsin Academy of Sciences, Arts and Letters*, xviii (1915), 110–65.

V Attitudes to Drama and Dramatic Theory

1 Cf. J. Douhet, *Dictionnaire des mystères*; *Nouvelle encyclopédie théologique*, ed. J.-P. Migne, xliii (Paris, 1854), 15–32.

2 Young, II, 411.

3 Ibid., 524–5.

4 *Life of Solon*, xxix, Plutarch's *Lives* (Loeb Classical Library, 1959), I, 488–9.

5 For the quotation cf. Young, II, 412–14. I am very indebted to Mlle Christine Bischoff, who gave me the above information about the context of the quotation and allowed me to look at her as yet unpublished edition of the text of the *Hortus deliciarum*.

6 For further reference to this argument see above, p. 80.

7 'It is not, however, forbidden to represent the crib of the Lord, Herod and the Magi, how Rachel wept for her sons, etc. – subjects related to the feasts here mentioned – since such things conduce to devotion rather than to lasciviousness and delight of the senses, just as at Easter Christ's sepulchre and other things are represented in order to stimulate devotion.' *Decretales D. Gregorii papae IX cum glossis diversorum* (Lyons, 1624), 998–9; cf. Chambers, II, 100.

8 Harold Gardiner, *Mysteries' End*, Yale Studies in English, 103 (1946), 9, notes some evidently nervous legislation from the close of the Middle Ages.

9 'To strengthen the faith of the unlearned common people and of the neophytes', *Regularis concordia*, ed. Symons, 44.

10 E.E.T.S. 119, 155.

11 Chambers, II, 339.

12 Young, II, 411.

13 *Decretales*, ed. cit., 998.

14 The relevant references are given by Chambers, I, 91, nn. 2, 3. These diocesan Constitutions are discussed in general by R. Cheney, *English Synodalia of the Thirteenth Century* (Oxford, 1941).

15 Robert Mannyng came from Bourne in Lincolnshire and was a member of the nearby Gilbertine priory at Sempringham. It is not known where the *Manuel des péchés* was composed: E. Arnould has suggested Yorkshire or Lincolnshire (*Le Manuel des péchés* [Paris, 1940], 245–9).

16 'But to make foolish gatherings in city streets or in churchyards after people have eaten, a time when crowds will readily gather – though priests say they do it for good purpose and in honour of God – they should not be believed: truly it is rather in honour of the devil.' E.E.T.S. 119, 155.

17 Ibid. *Grevis* (i.e. grove, thicket) makes no sense and does not rhyme. In both manuscripts of the *Handlyng Synne* the letters u and n are often indistinguishably written, and this word should therefore be read as *grenis*, i.e. village greens. The resulting assonance would be acceptable for this poem.

18 William of Malmesbury in relating this episode claims to be following the lost *Handboc* of Alfred (*Gesta Pontificum* [Rolls Series, 1870], 336). There is thus no reason to assume the story to represent a common custom or to be connected with the post-Conquest church. Whilst medieval preachers used devices of secular entertainment to catch their audience's attention, there is no evidence that they actually joined in popular festivities in order to convert.

19 It is interesting to note that a similar distinction seems to be made in the twelfth-century *Siete Partidas* of Alfonso X. In the section on the proper conduct of the clergy, which is firmly based on canon law, there is under a section headed, 'Cómo los clérigos deben decir las horas et facer las cosas que son buenas et convenientes, et guardarse de las otras' (*Las Siete Partidas*, I [Madrid, 1807], 276–7), a paraphrase of the decree and gloss, which is very similar to those discussed above: after the enumeration of the permissible liturgical plays, it is said that they should only be performed in towns where there is a bishop or archbishop and with their permission, and not in small towns or villages and not in order to gain money (cf. Shergold, op. cit., 5); it seems likely that plays in villages would have been performed extra-liturgically and out-of-doors.

20 A brief and convenient account of the gilds is given by May McKisack, *The Fourteenth Century 1307–1399* (Oxford, 1959), 373–6.

21 Cf. *English Gilds*, ed. Lucy Toulmin Smith (E.E.T.S. 40). Their most common responsibilities were burials, requiem masses, a procession and attendance at church each year on the gild-day and the offering of candles in church.

22 The responsibility of the gilds for civic ceremonies is discussed by Glynne Wickham, *Early English Stages*, I (London, 1959), 53–5 and 132.

23 Ed. cit., xxxiv: 'affirming that [the play] was good in itself and highly praiseworthy'; cf. R. Davies, *Extracts from the Municipal Records of the City of York*, 243.

24 Anna J. Mill, *Mediaeval Plays in Scotland*, 290.

25 B.M. Add. MS. 24202, 26r–28r.

26 This treatise is unprinted; for a summary of some of its contents and for arguments in support of its attribution to Hilton see J. Russell-Smith, 'Walter Hilton and a Tract in Defence of the Veneration of Images', *Dominican Studies*, vii (1954), 180–214.

27 *Altenglische Sprachproben*, ii, ed. E. Mätzner (Berlin, 1869), 229; this treatise was first printed by T. Wright, *Reliquiae antiquae*, ii (London, 1843), 42–57, and was from there reprinted in *The English Drama and Stage under the Tudor and Stuart Princes 1543–1664* (Roxburgh Club, 1869), 73–95.

28 This justification is also sometimes found in civic records but in combination with a more practical motive, as in the *York Memorandum Book* for the year 1417, where the reason for the performances is said to be 'ad honorem precipue et reverenciam Domini nostri Jesu Christi et commodum civium predictorum' (especially for the honour and glory of God and the profit of the aforesaid citizens); cf. Arthur Brown, 'York and its Plays in the Middle Ages', *Chaucer und seine Zeit, Symposion für Walter F. Schirmer*, ed. Arno Esch (Tübingen, 1968), 407–18.

29 *Summa theologica*, ii, ii, 168, 2; for discussion see Rainer Hess, *Der romanische geistliche Schauspiel als profane und religiöse Komödie*, Freiburger Schriften zur romanischen Philologie, iv (1965), 153–62.

30 *Dives and Pauper* (London, 1534), 125. The supposition that the Gloss's approval of liturgical drama could be extended unquestioningly to extra-liturgical plays would have been difficult to defend; the author is even compelled to misrepresent his authority when he states that the Gloss approves plays at Easter, Christmas 'and other tymes also', the latter phrase being a deceptive little addition, no doubt needed to cover the Corpus Christi performances.

31 For a very useful account of attitudes towards images see the article by V. Grumel in the *Dictionnaire de théologie catholique*, ed. A. Vacant and E. Mangenot, vii (Paris, 1921), 766–844.

32 '. . . for it is one thing to adore a picture and quite another to learn from narrative paintings what should be adored. For what a book is to those who can read, a picture provides to even the unlearned who look at it carefully, for in it the unlearned see what they should follow, and those who cannot read books read it. Hence a picture especially serves as a book to the common people', P.L., 77, 1128.

33 For some account of early statements of the value of images in the east see E. Kitzinger, 'The Cult of Images before Iconoclasm', *Dumbarton Oaks Papers*, viii (1954), 85–150.

34 P.G., 94, 1231–420; cf. Gervase Mathew, *Byzantine Aesthetics* (London, 1963), 104.

35 According to C. J. Hefele, *Histoire des conciles*, iii, 2 (Paris, 1910), 798, an immediate translation into Latin was made on the orders of Pope Hadrian I; this translation was, however, superseded by that of Anastasius a century later.

36 J. de Ghellinck, *Le Mouvement théologique du XIIe siècle* (Brussels and Paris, 1948), 368–9, 374–412.

37 'Whether the image of Christ should be adored with the adoration of latria', III, xxv, 3.

38 Cf. G. R. Owst, *Literature and Pulpit in Mediaeval England* (Oxford, 1961), 140.

39 *Decretum Magistri Gratiani*, ed. Aemilius Friedberg (Leipzig, 1879), 1360.

40 References are given by L. Gougaud, 'Muta praedicatio', *Revue Bénédictine*, xlii (1930), 168–71.

41 Millard Meiss, *Painting in Florence and Siena after the Black Death* (Princeton, 1951), 106.

42 Many of these references and others are provided by Owst, *Literature and Pulpit*, 137–48; in addition see *The Sermons of Thomas Brinton*, ed. M.A. Devlin, II (Camden, 3rd Series, lxxxvi, 1954), 491, Mirk's *Festial* (E.E.T.S. E.S. 96), 171, and Roger Dymmok, *Liber contra XII errores et hereses Lollardorum*, ed. H. S. Cronin (Wyclif Soc. 1922), 198.

43 *Dives and Pauper* (London, 1534), 12; cf. A. Caiger-Smith, *English Medieval Mural Paintings* (Oxford, 1963), 107–8; Owst, op. cit., 141–3.

44 Ed. of Louvain, 1594, 189.

45 *Epistola ad Secundinum*, P.L. 77, 990.

46 That images recalled the past to the memory was an idea embodied in Gratian's *Decretum* (immediately following the quotation from Gregory the Great) upon the authority of the Second Council of Nicaea: 'Venerabiles imagines Christiani non deos appellant . . . sed ad memoriam et recordationem primitivorum venerantur eas et adorant . . .', *Decretum*, ed. Friedberg, 1360.

47 'There was a threefold reason for the institution of images in the church. Firstly, for the instruction of the simple who are taught by them as though by books; secondly, in order that the mystery of the Incarnation and the examples of the saints may be more firmly in our memory when they are daily made present to the sight; thirdly to excite the feeling of devotion, which is more effectually excited by what is seen than by what is heard.' *Scriptum super libros sententiarum*, III, ix, Solutio 2, ed. P. Mandonnet and M. F. Moos, III, (Paris, 1933), 312

48 P.L., 172, 586.

49 Ed. cit., 12.

50 E.E.T.S. E.S. 96, 171.

51 *English Lyrics of the XIIIth Century*, ed. Carleton Brown (Oxford, 1932), no. 56A. 'Sweet Jesus, the memory of thy passion, draws forth tears and makes the eyes swollen, it makes the cheeks wet, and brings sweetness to the heart.'

52 P.G., 46, 572.

53 The translation is taken from *The Seven Ecumenical Councils of the Church*, ed. H. R. Percival (*Library of the Fathers*, 1907), 539; J. D. Mansi, *Sacrorum conciliorum nova et amplissima collectio*, XIII (Florence, 1767), 9–12.

54 'For it is seen that a painting moves the imagination more than what is written. In a painting some action is placed before the eyes; but in literature the action is recalled to the memory as it were through the hearing, which touches the imagination less. Hence likewise in church we do not show as much reverence to books as we do to images and pictures', *Rationale de divinis officiis* (Naples, 1859), 24.

55 'Again sometimes heaven is painted in churches so that it may entice the beholders to a delight in the rewards of virtue, and sometimes hell so that by fear of torments it may frighten the beholders from sin.' ed. cit., 27.

56 See above, p. 97.

57 The play has not been printed, but this quotation is given by J. M. Richard in his introduction to *Le Mystère de la Passion* (Paris, 1893), xix.

58 'It is indeed a devout task to recall to the memory of Christians the wonderful gifts of God through teaching, reading aloud, and also through painting; who then, save one blinded by a Jewish hatred for Christ or rather enraged by a Moslem envy of Him, could deny it to be a work of great value to refresh these things through living examples, and in so far as the matter allows, to show them through live representation? For what are these dramatic spectacles but living histories for the unlearned, by which the human mind is much more effectively touched than if a man should read them privately or hear them read publicly by another', *Apologeticum*, III, 55, ed. cit., 331.

59 Ed. cit., IV, 18, p. 189.

60 'By the long suffering and permitting of these vaine plays, it hath stricken such a blinde zeale into the heartes of the people, that they shame not to say, and affirme openly, that playes are as good as sermons, and that they learne as much or more at a play, than they do at God's word preached', *John Northbrooke, A Treatise wherein Dicing, Dauncing, Vain playes, or Enterluds . . . are reproved*, E. K. Chambers, *The Elizabethan Stage*, IV (Oxford, 1923), 198; '. . . sacred Scripture is or may be acted by players on the stage, and thereby a man may learne more than at a Sermon', *A Shorte Treatise against Stage-Playes, The English Drama and Stage under the Tudor and Stuart Princes* (Roxburgh Club, 1869), 238.

61 Mathew, op. cit., 104.

62 Mansi, op. cit., 359–62.

63 *Bellone an pace clariores fuerint Athenienses, Moralia*, IV, 347a.

64 *Homelia xix. In sanctos 40 martyres*, P.G. 31, 507–10.

65 Mansi, op. cit., 299; cf. p. 114.

66 *De arte poetica*, ll. 361–5.

67 Cf. R. W. Lee, '*Ut pictura poesis*: The Humanistic Theory of Painting', *Art Bulletin*, xxii (1940), 197–263.

68 'But the various stories of the Old and of the New Testament may be represented according to the decision of the painters, for 'Poets and painters have always had an equal right to venture anything', *Rationale*, ed. cit., 27. The quotation is from the *De arte poetica*, ll. 9–10. This work

was fairly well known in the Middle Ages, but of course the possibility that the quotation was taken from a *Florilegium* cannot be entirely dismissed.

69 Cf. Woolf, *The English Religious Lyric in the Middle Ages* (Oxford, 1968), *passim*.

70 On this see F. Saxl, 'Fruhes Christentum und spätes Heidentum in ihren künstlerischen Ausdruckformem. I. Der Dialog als Thema der christlichen Kunst', *Wiener Jahrbuch für Kunstgeschichte*, n.s. 2, xvi (1923), 64–77; W. Artelt, *Die Quellen der mittelalterlichen Dialogdarstellung* (Berlin, 1934).

71 *The Rise of Pictorial Narrative*, 54.

72 G. Cohen, 'The Influence of the Mysteries on Art in the Middle Ages', *Gazette des beaux-arts*, 6th series, xxiv (1943), 329–30.

73 Facs. ed. Hassall, ff. 3v and 4.

74 W. L. Hildburgh, 'English Alabaster Carvings as Records of the Medieval Religious Drama', *Archaeologia*, xciii (1949), 62–3.

75 See above, p. 80.

76 *Journal d'un bourgeois de Paris 1405–1449*, ed. A. Tuetey (Paris, 1881), 200. 'In front of the Chatelet there was a very fine representation of the Old and New Testaments, made by the children of Paris. And they did it without words or movements, as though they were figures in a bas-relief.' There is a recent translation of the work by Janet Shirley, *A Parisian Journal 1405–1449* (Oxford, 1968).

77 'And in the Rue de la Calandre in front of the Palace there was a very touching representation of the Passion of Our Lord, done by live actors, just as it is depicted around the choir of Notre-Dame . . . and no man could see this representation without being moved to compassion'; op. cit., 144. The author was in some way connected with the Notre-Dame; cf. Shirley, op. cit., 17.

78 Mätzner, *Altenglische Sprachproben*, 232.

79 E.E.T.S. 40, 149.

80 Ibid.

81 Dryden, for instance, argued along these lines in the Preface to his translation of the *De Arte graphica* of du Fresnoy (*Essays*, ed. W. P. Ker [Oxford, 1900], II, 130–2. From the religious point of view, however, these virtues were not thought an advantage; St Nicephorus, for instance, in his contribution to the eastern controversy over images, the *Libri tres Antirrhetici*, had argued for the superiority of painting since it is free from the ambiguities and suggestions of conflict that are introduced by words (P.G. 100, 380–4); cf. *Dictionnaire de théologie catholique*, VII, 797.

82 E.g. *De fide orthodoxa*, IV, 16 (P.G. 94, 1169–72).

83 Cf. the 8th Error cited for refutation by Roger Dymmok, '. . . And þow þis forbodin ymagerie be a bok of errour to þe lewid puple, ȝet þe ymage usuel of Trinite is most abhominable.' (ed. cit., 180).

84 'If the common people conceive a false belief from a picture, the fault must be considered theirs and not that of the image', op. cit., 199.

85 For discussion of the scanty evidence see Craig, *English Religious Drama*, 122–5; F. M. Salter, *Mediaeval Drama in Chester* (Toronto, 1955), 54–64; Wickham, *Early English Stages*, I, 169–74.

86 There are various references in contemporary documents to a pageant roof (Salter, op. cit., 69); Thomas Sharp, *Dissertation on the Pageants or Dramatic Mysteries, Anciently performed at Coventry by the Trading Companies of the City* (Coventry, 1825), 19, points out that the Coventry Drapers' Pageant was embattled, and includes an engraving (opposite p. 22) which interestingly reconstructs its appearance. Pageants designed for plays involving miraculous ascents or descents are more likely to have had a pitched roof, in which the necessary machinery would be concealed.

87 Various documents refer to painted cloths or curtains. The inventory of the Norwich Grocers' Company includes the item, '3 paynted clothes to hang abowte ye Pageant', which would cover three sides. Craig's suggestion (op. cit., 125) that these served to obscure the nakedness of Adam and Eve, who would thus be seen only from the shoulders upwards, is unconvincing. If so, four cloths would surely be required; Adam and Eve would have been wearing the 'cote and hosen . . . steyned' mentioned in the inventory (i.e. flesh-coloured garments as in modern productions), and after the Fall put on fig-leaves (in the 1565 version of the play Eve says, 'With fygge-leavis lett us cover us', E.E.T.S. S.S. 1, 15). Wickham plausibly suggests (op. cit., 173) that space would be left behind the curtain at the back to serve as a 'green room' for the actors when not on stage. For curtains used to enclose scaffolds see the illuminating analysis of the Fouquet miniature in Richard Southern, *The Medieval Theatre in the Round* (London, 1957), 92–107.

88 This has already been pointed out by Wickham, op. cit., 50. It is obvious that the estimated size will depend upon the relationship of length to breadth; a vehicle with the proportions of a modern bus, for instance, can get round surprisingly narrow corners, but any increase in breadth would necessitate a compensating decrease in length.

89 Apart from the implications of narrow streets, the only evidence for size is the lease for the Chester Tailors' carriage house which specifies that it was five virgates long and three and a half virgates wide. Unfortunately the length of a virgate is not known for certain; it might have corresponded to the modern yard (Salter, op. cit., 62); the Chester Tailors' play was the Ascension, however, which would have required far more playing space than this. Salter's arguments here and throughout the chapter entitled 'A Day's Labour' are vitiated by the assumption, based on the parable of the Labourers in the Vineyard in the Authorised Version, that a penny was a fair wage for a day's work. In *The Pearl*, for instance, the payment is also said to be a penny, but the average labourer's wage at the end of the fourteenth century was far higher (see M. Postan, 'Some Economic Evidence of the Declining Population in the Later Middle Ages', *The Economic History Review*, 2nd series, II [1950], 221–46).

VI Plays of the Fall

1 The subject occurs occasionally in medieval Continental drama, as noted before (see above, p. 67). The only well-known Renaissance treatment is Vondel's *Lucifer*, often cited as a source of *Paradise Lost*; the comprehensive list of plays and poems on the same subject as *Paradise Lost* provided by W. Kirkconnell, *The Celestial Cycle* (Toronto, 1952), 483–682, includes only one other play, *La guerra angelica* (ibid., 595–6), a seventeenth-century work with personifications of a morality play type. Whilst the story of the Fall of Man presupposes that of the Angels, those who dramatised the former only dealt with the antecedent story in an explanatory monologue given to the tempter, a method early adopted in England by the author of the *Mystère d'Adam*. All the mystery plays except the *Ludus Coventriae* include such a speech, which might be taken to indicate imitation of a play or plays of the Fall which had not followed upon a play of the Fall of the Angels.

2 Books xi, xii. The earlier traditions, dependent upon the apocryphal Book of Enoch, which related the Fall solely or partially to Genesis vi. 2–4, ceased to be theologically acceptable after Augustine and are not relevant to the mystery plays. An excellent account of the whole subject is given by E. Mangenot in his article on *Démons* in the *Dictionnaire de théologie catholique*, IV, 322–409.

3 Cf. Didron, *Christian Iconography*, II, 1–82, Louis Réau, *Iconographie de l'art chrétien*, II, i (Paris, 1956), 14–29, and *Lexikon der christlichen Ikonographie*, s.v. *Dreifaltigkeit*.

4 On this see A. Heimann, 'Trinitas creator mundi', *Warburg Journal*, ii (1938–9), 42–52.

5 E.E.T.S. E.S. 120, 17, 'I am þe trewe trenyte/here walkyng in þis wone', probably a thoughtless use of a traditional alliterative collocation.

6 *De genesi ad litteram*, XI, xvi, P.L. 34, 437.

7 'Whether there was any interval between the creation of the angels and their fall'; 'there was some interval though a very brief one', *Libri IV sententiarum*, II, iii, 2 (Quaracchi, 1916), 319, 322; cf. Bonaventura, *Opera omnia*, II (Quaracchi, 1885), 115–17, Albertus Magnus, *Opera omnia*, ed. A. Borgnet, XXVII (Paris, 1894), 113–15, Thomas Aquinas, *Scriptum super libros sententiarum*, ed. Mandonnet, II, 134–6.

8 'That immediately after the first moment of his creation the devil sinned', *Summa theologica*, I, lxiii, 6.

9 P.L. 169, 1217–502. According to de Ghellinck (*L'Essor de la littérature latine*, 118) the work of Rupert of Deutz did not circulate widely outside Germany; the *De victoria verbi Dei* is therefore unlikely to have had a direct influence upon the English plays. It is, however, interesting to note that it was printed in the sixteenth century and, in view of its unusual emphasis

upon the war in heaven, might well have contributed to Milton's treatment of Satan's fall.

10 *P.L.* 172, 1109–76. Unlike the *De victoria verbi Dei*, this work was extremely well known in the Middle Ages; it presented a concise theological exposition in the form of a dialogue between master and pupil, and being therefore suitable for study by the less learned, it was translated into most vernacular languages, English, French, Provençal, German, Italian, etc. (cf. F. Schmitt, *Die mittelenglische Version des Elucidariums des Honorius Augustodunensis* [Burghausen, 1909], III–IV).

11 'by equality . . . for by his natural understanding he knew this to be impossible', *Summa theologica*, I, lxiii, 3.

12 'as from his own power and not through the power of God', ibid.

13 Unlike their German analogues, the English plays do not borrow at all from Revelation xii, and the intervention of St Michael is not shown.

14 *Egerer Fronleichnamsspiel*, ed. Milchsack, 8–9. 'I complain to you, both wind and air, I complain to you, rain, dew and mist, I complain to you, heat, cold and snow, I complain to you, flowers and green meadows . . . I complain to you, sweet song of birds, I complain to you hills and deep valleys, I complain to you rocks and all stones, I complain also to the whole world, which God in His mercy created: on these today I make my cry, that they should in kindness pray for me to the Almighty.'

15 Cf. Didron, op. cit., II, 109–46; on influences of the antique see Jurgis Baltrusaitis, *Le moyen Age fantastique* (Paris, 1955), 11–53.

16 Sharp, op. cit., 57 and 69.

17 *Le Mystère du viel testament*, ed. J. de Rothschild (S.A.T.F., 1878), I, 1–23.

18 On this issue see A. C. Baugh, 'The Chester Plays and French Influence', *Schelling Anniversary Papers* (New York, 1923), 35–63; Baugh's conclusion that the French influence is to be seen chiefly in the management of scenes and episodes applies very well to the Chester Fall of the Angels although he does not relate it specifically to this play.

19 The symbol of the compasses, which derives from Proverbs viii. 27, is not uncommon in medieval art, and there are many English examples of it, including the *Te Deum* window at York and one of the roof-bosses at Norwich (cf. G. McN. Rushforth, *Medieval Christian Imagery* [Oxford, 1936], 150–1) and *Queen Mary's Psalter*; cf. also A. Blunt, 'Blake's "Ancient of Days". The Symbolism of the Compasses', *Warburg Journal*, ii (1938–9), 53–63.

20 The following is typical of the stage-directions, 'Adoncques se doit monstrer ung ciel painct, tout semé d'estoilles et les noms des planettes', *Mystère du viel testament*, I, 26; others seem more ambitious, and one must remember the medieval love of strange stage contrivances, which sound almost as elaborate as those of the later masques.

21 'That it may appear as the most delightful place', ed. cit., I.

22 Ed. cit., 4; cf. *The City of God*, XIV, xxvi.

23 'In it no delights will be lacking to you', ed. cit., 6.

24 For reference to these gardens and others see *The Pearl*, ed. E. V. Gordon (Oxford, 1953), note to ll. 43–4.

25 E.E.T.S. 57, 52.

26 For an illustration of this scene and comment see Rosalie Green, 'The Adam and Eve Cycle in the *Hortus deliciarum*', *Late Classical and Medieval Studies in Honor of A. M. Friend Jr.* (Princeton, 1955), 340–7.

27 P.L. 198, 1072; cf. J. K. Bonnell, 'The Serpent with a Human Head in Art and in Mystery Play', *American Journal of Archaeology*, xxi (1917), 255–91. Bonnell's argument, however, that in the depiction of the female-headed serpent iconography was influenced by the mystery plays (the latter adopting the tradition for practical convenience) is not supported by the relative chronology of art and drama; cf. Réau, *Iconographie*, ii, i, 84.

28 Cf. J. B. Trapp, 'The Iconography of the Fall of Man', *Approaches to Paradise Lost*, ed. C. A. Patrides (London, 1968), 241–2.

29 Peter Lombard, *Lib.* ii *Sent.*, xxi, 2, ed. cit., 404; Bonaventura, *Opera omnia*, ii, 495; Thomas Aquinas, *Scriptum super libros sententiarum*, ii, 532.

30 *Speculum humanae salvationis*, ed. J. Lutz and P. Perdrizet (Mulhouse, 1907–9), ii, pl. 2; cf. Trapp, op. cit., pl. 12. The accompanying text says only that the serpent then went upright and had a female head. It is possible that the ambiguity of the Latin term *draco* (used, for instance, by Vincent de Beauvais in the *Speculum naturale* instead of the Vulgate *serpens*) combined with the recollection of the dragon (Vulgate: *draco*) of Revelation xii, led to the serpent acquiring dragonish features. The influence of the classical sirens (half-woman, half-bird) has also been suggested (Réau, op. cit., 84).

31 Cf. J. M. Evans, *Paradise Lost and the Genesis Tradition* (Oxford, 1968), 82–3.

32 The translation is that of Kirkconnell, *The Celestial Cycle*, 368.

33 'Perhaps with persuasive words, which the Bible being silent, leaves to be imagined', P.L. 34, 445. Few medieval writers, however, dared to imagine it: the author of the *Cursor mundi*, for instance, evades the issue entirely; where authors did comment, they suspected feminine guile (an interpretation that Milton later took up with supreme skill): the author of the French text of the *Speculum humanae salvationis*, for instance, says, 'elle le flatoit de doulces parolles', ed. cit., i, 5; cf. Peter Comestor, *Historia scholastica*, P.L. 198, 1072.

34 'Out of a certain friendly good-will'; cf. *Summa theologica*, ii, ii, 163, 4.

35 *The Ancient Cornish Drama*, ed. and trans. Edwin Norris (Oxford, 1859), i, 19.

36 Cf. R. Woolf, 'The Fall of Man in *Genesis B* and the *Mystère d'Adam*', *Studies in Old English Literature in Honor of Arthur G. Brodeur*, ed. S. B. Greenfield (Oregon, 1963), 187–99.

37 'You are delicate and tender and fresher than is the rose; you are whiter than crystal or than snow falling upon an icy valley. The Creator made an ill-matched pair: you are too tender and he too hard. Nevertheless you are the wiser and your mind is filled with abundant wisdom', ed. cit., 12–13.

The devil similarly flatters Eve after failing to tempt Adam in a fifteenth-century play from Bologna, *Laude drammatiche e rappresentazioni sacre*, ed. V. de Bartholomaeis, III (Florence, 1943), 193–8.

38 *Summa theologica*, I, xciv, 4.

39 Ibid., I, xciv, I.

40 For the allegorisation of Adam and Eve as reason and senses see Evans, op. cit., 69–77, and D. W. Robertson, Jun. *A Preface to Chaucer* (Princeton, 1963), 74–5, and as body and soul, Woolf, *Religious Lyric*, 101–2.

41 E.E.T.S. S.S. I, 18. In this play after the allegorical figures of Dolor and Misery have asserted their dominion over man, the Holy Ghost appears to comfort them, promising them the joys of heaven provided they have faith in Christ and put on the whole armour of God, the first condition having a distinctively Protestant ring.

42 *The Caedmon Manuscript* with an introduction by Israel Gollancz (Oxford, 1927), f. 7.

43 Cf. Trapp, op. cit., 259–60.

44 Gregory the Great, *XL Homiliarum in evangelia libri duo*, I, xvi, P.L. 76, 1136; cf. Donald Howard, *The Three Temptations* (Princeton, 1966), 44–56 and, for the relation of this theme to *Paradise Regained*, E. M. Pope, *Paradise Regained: The Tradition and the Poem* (Baltimore, 1947). The Temptation in the Wilderness is associated with the Fall in all the main compendiums of typology in the Middle Ages; cf. Trapp, loc. cit., 246–7.

45 Cf. Thomas Livius, *The Blessed Virgin in the Fathers of the First Six Centuries* (London, 1893), 35–59; L. Cignelli, *Maria nuova Eva nella Patristica greca* (Assisi, 1966), and Anselm Salzer, *Die Sinnbilder und Beiworte Mariens*, 476–87.

46 E. Guldan, *Eva und Maria: eine Antithese als Bildmotiv* (Graz-Cologne, 1966), pls 51–78.

47 For further discussion and bibliographical references see above, pp. 138–9.

48 This list, now chiefly familiar from *Sir Gawain and the Green Knight*, 2414–19, is already found in the eleventh-century *Carmen de contemptu mundi* of Roger of Caen; cf. Robert Bultot, *La Doctrine du mépris du monde. Le XIe siècle* (Louvain-Paris, 1964), 64–5. It was thereafter repeated in Abelard's *planctus* for Samson and in the Correspondence between Heloïse and Abelard; cf. Philippe Delhaye, 'Le dossier antimatrimonial de l'*Adversus Jovinianum* et son influence sur quelques écrits latins du xiie siècle', *Mediaeval Studies*, xiii (1951), 65–86. For further examples cf. I. Siciliano, *François Villon et les thèmes poétiques du moyen âge* (Paris, 1934), 366–70, Owst, op. cit., 385, and Dronke, *Poetic Individuality*, 123–8.

49 *English Lyrics of the Thirteenth Century*, ed. Brown, no. 52.

50 *De carne Christi*, 17, Corpus scriptorum ecclesiasticorum, lxx (1942), 233; cf. Guldan, op. cit., 19.

51 Ibid., pl. 3.

52 *Religious Lyrics of the Fifteenth Century*, ed. Carleton Brown (Oxford, 1939), no. 83.

53 *Piers Plowman*, B Text, v, 612.

54 'But it was necessary that he should fall gradually and by steps'. *Summa theologica*, II, ii, 163, 3.

55 It is only in German plays, in which typological significances are usually made explicit, that the lamb is commonly related to Christ; for references see G. Duriez, *La Théologie dans le drame religieux en Allemagne au moyen âge* (Lille, 1914), 124.

56 Outside English drama, Genesis iv. 10, is occasionally dramatised in a direct allegorical way, the blood itself crying out: in the Cornish *Origo mundi* God's statement that he hears the blood of Abel calling was preceded by some cry, as a stage-direction specifies, 'Vox clamat' (ed. cit., I, 44); in the *Mystère du viel testament* (ed. cit., I, 105) and in the *Passion* from Semur (ed. Roy, 18), an invisible voice, personifying the blood, makes a lyrical plea for vengeance.

57 Ed. cit., 34–6. In the *Mystère de la Passion* of Arnoul Greban (ed. cit., 17) the parallel with Christ is made through Abel's dying prayer which anticipates one of the Words from the Cross:

> Ha! roy du souverain empire,
> a ce grand besoing te reclame:
> ayes huy pitié de mon ame;
> en ta garde la recommande.

58 P.L. 198, 1077; cf. O. F. Emerson, 'Legends of Cain', *P.M.L.A.*, xxi (1906), 849.

59 Cf. P.L. 198, 1070, and for further comment, Evans, op. cit., 169, 262.

60 Ed. cit., I, 113–14 (for the French influence on the Chester plays see above, p. 371, n. 18). There were other ways of getting round this difficulty: in the *Origo mundi* Cain returns alone to Adam who then guesses what has happened (*Cornish Drama*, I, 46–7) and in Greban's *Passion* Adam and Eve go to the fields where they find Abel's dead body (ed. cit., 18–19).

61 Cf. Réau, *Iconographie*, II, i, 98.

62 Ed. cit., 46–9.

63 On the Wakefield Master see A. C. Cawley, *The Wakefield Pageants* (Manchester, 1958).

64 Cain's hatred of Abel's virtue was first stressed by Ambrose in *De Cain et Abel*, 'formam speciemque virtutis expressam ferre non potuit'. This and other interesting points are made by J. E. Bernbrock, 'Notes on the Towneley Cycle *Slaying of Abel*', *J.E.G.Ph.* lxii (1963), 317–22, where, however, the influence of Ambrose is only posited for the Towneley Play.

65 The meaning of Cain's words, 'My farthyng is in the preest hand/Syn last tyme I offyrd', is not plain, though the churlish tone is unmistakable. It is possible that Cain is refusing to make the burnt offering on the grounds that he has already paid his tithes to a grasping priest.

66 Cf. Owst, op. cit., 364–70, 491.

67 There had already been an element of this in the *Mystère d'Adam* where Cain's objection to tithing is: 'De dis ne remaindront que noef./Icist conseil ne valt un oef', ed. cit., 33.

68 Cf. Cawley, op. cit., 93.

69 For a brief account see George Duckworth, *The Nature of Roman Comedy* (Princeton, 1952), 249–53.

70 Ed. Mario Roques (Paris, 1912).

71 'La Scène de l'aveugle et de son valet', *Romania*, xli (1912), 346–72.

72 Cf. Cawley, op. cit., 94.

73 For texts see M. C. Spalding, *The Middle English Charters of Christ* (Bryn Mawr, 1914).

74 'Now that the sun has risen one should instantly have a drink', cf. Paul Lehmann, *Die Parodie in Mittelalter* (Stuttgart, 1963), 127. The first line is that of the hymn 'Jam lucis orto sidere/Deum precemur supplices . . .', which was sung at the office of Prime.

75 These translations are taken from Plautus, *The Pot of Gold and Other Plays*, trans. E. F. Watling (Penguin Classics, 1965), 154.

76 Cf. *Répertoire du théâtre comique en France au moyen âge* (Paris, 1886), 220–1.

77 *Noveau recueil de farces françaises des xve et xvie siècles*, ed. Émile Picot and Christophe Nyrop (Paris, 1880), 182–3.

78 *Ancien théâtre français, ou collection des ouvrages dramatiques les plus remarkables depuis les mystères jusqu'à Corneille*, ed. E. Viollet le Duc, II (1854), 303–25.

79 Ibid., 292–302.

80 The treatment of the comic servant in the York play of Cain and Abel cannot profitably be compared since the text is too fragmentary for any conclusions to be drawn from it. Contrary to earlier assumptions, it has been suggested that the servant was already in a York play known to the Wakefield Master; cf. M. G. Frampton, 'The Brewbarret Interpolation in the York play the Sacrificium Cayne and Abell', *P.M.L.A.*, lii (1937), 895–900. Whilst, however, it is right not to take for granted that the Brewbarret episode is necessarily as late as the sixteenth-century hand in which it is written, the probability remains that the comic servant was invented by the Wakefield Master (who again shows knowledge of farces in the shepherds' plays, see below, pp. 188–9), rather than by any of the poets who worked on the York cycle before the time of the Wakefield Master, since there is nothing in the rest of York to suggest knowledge or interest in French religious or secular drama.

VII Types of the Redemption

1 Ed. cit., I, 203–6. That Genesis vi. 2 referred respectively to the descendants of Seth and Cain was accepted from Augustine onwards; cf. *The City of God*, xv, 23.

2 The 'gossips' of Noah's wife who appear fleetingly in the Chester play are technically an exception; but they are introduced to suggest the worldly pleasure which Noah's wife refuses to forsake rather than the wickedness of the world which led to the Flood.

3 On these allegorical significances see J. Daniélou, *Sacramentum futuri* (Paris, 1950), 69–94, and J. P. Lewis, *A Study of the Interpretation of Noah and the Flood in Jewish and Christian Literature* (Leiden, 1968), 156–80. The allegorisation of Noah's wife is found in the *Bible moralisée conservée à Oxford, Paris et Londres*, ed. A. de Laborde, 1 (Paris, 1911), pl. 9, 'Noe significat Christum, uxor eius beatam Mariam'.

4 It is interesting to note that the play of Noah in the lost London cycle probably belonged to this branch, cf. *Canterbury Tales*, A, 3538–43.

5 Ed. Liebenow, 20–1.

6 E.E.T.S. 57, 108; cf. A. J. Mill, 'Noah's Wife again', *P.M.L.A.*, lvi (1941), 613–26.

7 'Not unto us, O Lord, not unto us, but unto thy Name give the praise' (Coverdale). In the Vulgate this verse begins the second part of Psalm cxiii.

8 P.L. 198, 1079, and P.L. 113, 101–2. The story arose from a rationalisation of Genesis iv. 23–4.

9 The scene is also found in England amongst the carvings in the south porch at Malmesbury and the Norwich roof-bosses.

10 Little is known of how Noah's ark was constructed for the stage: Anna Mill has inferred from the records of the Hull Gild of the Trinity that in Hull the ark was a solidly built and roomy sailing ship; cf. 'The Hull Noah Play', *M.L.R.*, xxxiii (1938), 489–505. Towns that were not ports may not have aimed at such naturalism, and in some instances a façade may have been sufficient. In the *Holkham Bible Picture Book* the ark is made on a wooden frame with wicker-work (for an explanation cf. Hassall, op. cit., 73–4), which would not have been difficult to reproduce upon the stage. It is reasonable to infer from the texts (except the *Ludus Coventriae*) that the ark was assembled from prepared sections rather than brought on to the stage complete.

11 Cf. Lewis, op. cit., 163–5.

12 Hugh of Saint-Victor, *Selected Spiritual Writings* (London, 1962), 64–5.

13 In York Noah says, 'Ful wayke I was and all un-welde,/My werynes is wente away', and in Towneley Noah at the end acknowledges divine help (ll. 283–6).

14 The eastern legends have been interestingly investigated and summarised by Mill, op. cit., to which the following summary is indebted.

15 E.E.T.S. S.S. 1, 19–31.

16 Cf. Craig, *English Religious Drama*, 304.

17 Roy, *Le Mystère de la Passion*, 17.

18 Cf. August Wulff, *Die frauenfeindlichen Dichtungen in den romanischen Literaturen des Mittelalters bis zum Ende des xiii Jahrhunderts* (Romanistische Arbeiten, IV [1914]); F. L. Utley, *The Crooked Rib* (Columbus, 1944). Owst, *Literature and Pulpit*, 376–404.

19 For manuscripts see H. Walther, *Initia carminum ac versuum medii aevi posterioris latinorum* (Göttingen, 1959), no. 18302. Lydgate's translation (inc. 'Glory unto God, laude and benysoun') is in E.E.T.S. 192, 456–60.

20 *The Art of Courtly Love*, trans. J. J. Parry (New York, 1941), 201. This list, as Owst pointed out, derives ultimately from Proverbs vii. 10–12.

21 'For every woman is ready to anger, deceitful, envious and never meek; her husband is turned into a little donkey, enduring all burdens', *The Latin Poems commonly attributed to Walter Mapes*, ed. Thomas Wright (London, 1841), 82.

22 Per Nykrog, *Les Fabliaux* (Copenhagen, 1957), 193–207, relates the characterisation of women in the fabliaux to the list of vices in the *Art of Courtly Love* and under *inobediens* notes a number which illustrate this characteristic.

23 *Epistola*, xv, 2, P.L. 22, 355. 'If anyone is not in the ark, he will perish when the Flood prevails.'

24 Trans. Parry, 205.

25 Owst, op. cit., 390.

26 Ibid., 389–90.

27 A. Långfors, 'Le Dit de Dame Jouenne', *Romania*, xlv (1919), 99–107. For further references to this motif see Hj. Crohns, *Legenden och medeltidens latinska predikan* (Helsingfors, 1915), 155.

28 On this formula see Norman Davis, 'A Note on *Pearl*', *R.E.S.*, n.s., xvii (1966), 403–5.

29 *Recueil général et complet des fabliaux des XIIIe et XIVe siècles*, ed. A. de Montaiglon and G. Raynaud, i (1872), 97–111.

30 The E.E.T.S. edition, which is followed by Sisam, *Fourteenth Century Verse and Prose* (Oxford, 1955), inserts a stage-direction, 'They enter the ark' after the last quarrel of Noah and his wife at l. 414; no explanation, however, is given of what action takes place at l. 371, where Noah's wife says, 'Into ship with a byr therfor will I hy/ffor drede that I drone here'. At this point Cawley inserts the stage-direction, 'Rushes into the ship', and therefore interprets 'from doore to mydyng' to mean 'a single step' and 'will' presumably to imply custom: the sentence thus becomes a general statement of obstinacy without particular reference to what is happening. It is, however, possible to assume that 'doore' refers to the door of the ark (as the earlier editors must have taken it) and 'mydying' (sc. dunghill) to be an abusive reference to the inside of the ark. In that case the action would be as follows: Noah's wife at l. 371 rushes up to the entrance of the ark, perhaps by a ladder as shown in many illustrations, and having thus achieved temporary safety above the supposedly rising waters, hesitates once more, and the last quarrel would take place within a fairly large doorway. Either interpretation of the text is possible: regard to the religious pattern suggests that the latter is the correct one.

31 Kolve, op. cit. 150.

32 The stage-direction, which at this point is much more typologically explicit than that of the *Mystère du viel testament* (i, 332), reads, '. . . Abraham, offerens Calicem cum vino et panem super patinam'; Lot offers only 'Cuppam cum vino et panc'.

33 'Whether God the Father delivered up Christ to the Passion'; 'God did not spare His own Son but for all of us delivered Him up'; III, xlvii, 3. For more detailed comment on the typological significance of Abraham, and also of Isaac, see 'The Effect of Typology on the English Mediaeval Plays of Abraham and Isaac', *Speculum*, xxxii (1957), 805–25.

34 'In short I will in no way remit the death of my Son Jesus: at this hour by irrevocable judgment I condemn Him.' Ed. cit., II, 15.

35 'My will shall be shown forth and prefigured in Abraham, who himself without hesitation will smite his only son of true lineage.' Ibid., 16.

36 Op. cit., 257–9.

37 'Whether Christ died out of obedience'; 'He became obedient to the Father unto death'; 'For as by one man's disobedience many were made sinners, so by the obedience of one shall many be made righteous.' (A.V.); *Summa theologica*, III, xlvii, 2.

38 'This I shall do, and furthermore I shall expressly make a prefiguration of the obedience of Jesus Christ in Isaac, who, utterly innocent, when his father wishes to put him to death, will accept this willingly without rebellion or anguish'; ed. cit., II, 16.

39 *Heidelberger Passionsspiel*, ed. Milchsack, 221–32.

40 Cf. Carleton Brown, 'The Prioress's Tale', *Sources and Analogues of Chaucer's Canterbury's Tales*, ed. W. F. Bryan and G. Dempster (London, 1958), 465–6.

41 *Inferno*, XXXIII, 61–3.

42 *Gesta Romanorum*, ed. Hermann Oesterley (Berlin, 1872), 414–15; cf. E.E.T.S. E.S. 33, 12–13.

43 For the last three references see Owst, *Literature and Pulpit*, 34.

44 Hardin Craig, *English Religious Drama*, states that the Brome play is a skilful reworking of Chester (p. 309), and Chester in turn based upon the *Mystère du viel testament* (II, 17–79). The arrangement of episodes in Chester, which includes Melchisedek and Lot, is undoubtedly influenced by the French but, despite the incident (which they have in common) of Isaac asking for his eyes to be bandaged that he may not see the blow, the scene of the sacrifice in general does not derive from the French. The view that the Chester play derived from Brome is argued by J. B. Severs ('The Relationship between the Brome and Chester *Abraham and Isaac*'), *M.P.*, xlii (1945), 137–51.

45 On this subject see M. E. Wells, 'The Age of Isaac at the Time of the Sacrifice', *M.L.N.* lxiv (1939), 579–82.

46 On poems that have these words as a refrain see Woolf, *English Religious Lyric*, 333–6; for the attribution of them to Christ see *The Early English Carols*, ed. R. L. Greene (Oxford, 1935), nos 370–2.

47 'My soul is exceeding sorrowful, even unto death' (A.V.), Matthew xxvi. 38; cf. the exposition of this text in the *Vita Jesu Christi* of Ludolf the Carthusian, IV, 13–14, and the *Summa theologica*, III, xlvii, 2. For Christ's fear of death during the Agony in the Garden see above, pp. 235–6.

48 Cf. R. Brotanek, 'Abraham und Isaak: ein mittelenglisches Misterium aus einer Dubliner Handschrift', *Anglia*, xxi (1898), 21-55, and *The Non-Cycle Mystery Plays*, ed. O. Waterhouse, E.E.T.S. E.S., 104, l-liii.

49 The contents of the Brome Manuscript are printed in *A Commonplace Book of the Fifteenth Century*, ed. L. Toulmin Smith (London, 1886), and the poetical contents of the Northampton manuscript are published in *Mittelenglische Dichtungen aus der Handschrift 432 des Trinity College in Dublin*, ed. Rudolf Brotanek (Halle, 1940). The most recent discussion is that of Norman Davis, op. cit., xlvii-liii and lviii-lxiii.

50 It is worth noting that a play or plays on the subject of Abraham's Sacrifice was acted at various places in France from 1505 onwards (cf. Petit de Julleville, II, 86, 91-2, 110); the date of 1505 of course provides only a *terminus a quo*.

51 The religious pieces in the Dublin manuscript include versified exempla, a miracle of the Virgin, and a complaint of the Virgin against swearers; those in the Brome manuscript include a version of the Fifteen Signs of the Last Judgment, a Life of St Margaret and a carol of the Annunciation.

52 The example of Abraham is cited by Jerome in one of his consolatory epistles, that to Paula on the death of her daughter, 'Abraham unicum filium laetus interficit, et tu unam de pluribus quereris coronatam?' (*Ep.* xxxix, P.L. 22, 472). That *The Pearl* is a *consolatio* has been argued by V. E. Watts, '*Pearl* as a *Consolatio*', *Medium Aevum*, xxxii (1963), 34-6, and by Ian Bishop, *Pearl in its Setting* (Oxford, 1968), 13-26. Neither author, however, fully infers from this the probable conclusion that a major theme of *The Pearl* is the progress from rebelliousness in the face of loss to religious resignation.

53 Ed. Lutz and Perdrizet, ch. xxxi, pl. 61; cf. *Vita Jesu Christi*, IV, 170.

54 Ed. cit., III, 283-4. Aaron is also present in the Cornish cycle, trans. Norris, I, 113-17. Two lost cycles, Newcastle and Norwich appear to have had plays of the Exodus (Chambers, II, 424-5), but the naming of Aaron in the Norwich description of the play ('Moises and Aaron with the Children of Israel and Pharo with his Knyghts'), suggests that it was differently designed from York. It is worth noting that the York play does not conform to the description in Burton's list, 'Moyses exaltans serpentem in deserto, Pharao Rex, viii Judei admirantes et expectantes' (ed. cit., xx): in this earlier play the stress will have been upon the brazen serpent as a type of the Crucifixion.

55 Cf. E. J. Dobson, 'The Etymology and Meaning of *Boy*', *Medium Aevum*, ix (1940), 121-54.

56 Ed. cit., III, 407-22.

57 Cf. Young, II, 150 (Laon), 159 (Rouen), 175 (Benediktbeuern).

58 Ed. K. Brunner, E.E.T.S., 191, 27-32.

59 Whilst there were minor variations in prophets and prophecies the known lists are fairly consistent (cf. Anderson, *Drama and Imagery*, 40, É. Mâle, *L'art religieux de la fin du moyen âge* [Paris, 1949], 246-65, and M. Meiss,

French Painting in the Time of Jean de Berry [London, 1967], 135–40 and notes
p. 385). Only two of the six prophets and prophecies in Chester correspond
with these lists, Isaiah vii. 14 for the Nativity and Joel ii. 28 for Pentecost.
An oddity of the Chester episode is that whilst the expositor expounds six
prophecies ending with Joel, the series actually ends with a seventh, Micah,
who does not fit the pattern since he prophesies the Incarnation (in the
Creed list Micah follows Joel, but with a prophecy of the Church). The
number seven and the unusualness of the list makes one wonder whether
one of the author's sources was a set of seven prophets corresponding to the
Seven Gifts of the Holy Ghost as well as to the articles of the Creed: Professor Wind has shown that this is the typological arrangement of the
ceiling of the Sistine Chapel (E. Wind, 'Michelangelo's Prophets and
Sibyls', *Proceedings of the British Academy*, li [1965], 47–84); it may be noted
that five of Michelangelo's seven prophets correspond to those of Chester,
Isaiah, Ezekiel, Jeremiah, Jonah and Joel.

60 Cf. J. K. Bonnell, 'The Source in Art of the so-called Prophets' Play of the
Hegge Collection', *P.M.L.A.*, xxix (1914), 327–40. Anderson, *Drama and
Imagery*, 37, points out that the list of kings and prophets (save for the last
two) corresponds to those of the Jesse window now in St Mary's Church,
Shrewsbury (cf. H. T. Kirby, 'The Jesse Tree Motif in Stained Glass', *Journal
of the British Society of Master Glass-painters*, xiii [1960], 318–19). On the
iconography in general see Arthur Watson, *The Early Iconography of the
Tree of Jesse* (Oxford, 1934).

61 There is no evidence that York ever had a prophets' play: Burton's list of
1415 does not record one. The Doctor's prologue was apparently rewritten
in the sixteenth century, as a marginal note records; cf. ed. cit., 93.

62 The lyrical quality of David's prophecy has been praised in an illuminating
article: E. C. Dunn, 'Lyrical Form and the Prophetic Principle in the
Towneley Plays', *Mediaeval Studies*, xxiii (1961), 80–90.

63 This common interpretation of the prophecy was based on the association
of the star prophesied by Balaam with the star which guided the three kings:
it is thus that the Chester expositor expounds the prophecy (ll. 445–8).
It may, however, just be worth noting that if the *Stella* was understood as the
Virgin herself, as it often was (cf. Salzer, *Die Sinnbilder und Beiworte Mariens*,
410–11, and *Speculum humanae salvationis*, ch. iii, ed. Lutz and Perdrizet, I,
9), then it would lead more suitably into the Annunciation.

64 I do not assess here the alternative Chester version with the series of prophecies, since it ends with an inferior and irrelevant dramatisation of the whore-
dom of the Israelites (related in Numbers xxv), which is shown to be
brought about by the guileful advice of Balaam. This is clearly a late and
bad extension of the play (it may be noted that Numbers xxv is not dramatised in the *Mystère du viel testament*).

VIII Nativity Plays, I

1 *The Golden Legend or Lives of the Saints as Englished by William Caxton*, ed. F. S. Ellis (London, 1900), I, 27; *Speculum humanae salvationis*, I, ch. viii, ed. cit., II, pl. 16; cf. Mâle, *L'art religieux de la fin du moyen âge*, 255. The Tiburtine sibyl, who prophesies the birth of Christ, is distinct from the Erythraean sibyl who in the twelfth-century prophets' plays foretells the Last Judgment.

2 P.L. 198, 1539.

3 A suggestion for this occurs in the Chester author's main source, *The Stanzaic Life of Christ* (E.E.T.S. 166), where it is said that the emperor was wise 'And thoʒt wel that he was dedly': this detail does not occur in either of the works on which the *Stanzaic Life* is chiefly based, Higden's *Polychronicon* and the *Legenda aurea* (for comment see *Speculum humanae salvationis*, I, 193).

4 The character of the emperor is by tradition sympathetic and he receives the prophecy with delight and devotion. There is, however, a parallel to the Towneley Augustus in the *Nativité* from the Bibliothèque Ste Geneviève (*La Nativité et le geu des trois roys*, ed. Ruth Whittredge [Bryn Mawr, 1944], 118–19).

5 This view was at odds with the more learned understanding of the Islamic religion in the fifteenth century, but had been preserved in romances. For a historical account of the subject, see R. W. Southern, *Western Views of Islam in the Middle Ages* (Cambridge, Mass., 1962).

6 All three are printed successively by C. Tischendorf, *Evangelia apocrypha* (Leipzig, 1876), 1–121; for a translation of the *Protevangelium* see M. R. James, *The Apocryphal New Testament* (Oxford, 1953), 38–49. A helpful account of the legends is given by Yrjö Hirn, *The Sacred Shrine* (London, 1958), 157–94.

7 *Speculum historiale* (*Speculum maius*, III), VI, lxiv–lxvi, lxxii–lxxiii (Venice, 1591), 66–7.

8 *The Golden Legend*, V, 96–111.

9 E.E.T.S. 174; the editor argues that one of these, that in the Minnesota MS, was the sole source of the plays in the *Ludus Coventriae*. This theory rests upon a misunderstanding of what the distinctive characteristics of the dramatic cycle are. That the author of the *Ludus Coventriae* drew upon this poem as one of his sources is a reasonable hypothesis: the verbal correspondences adduced by the editor are, however, too slight to prove it.

10 Ed. J. A. Lauritis, R. A. Klinefelter and V. F. Gallagher (Pittsburgh, 1961). The editors do not discuss the possibility of the *Ludus Coventriae* being influenced by this work though it is likely. In particular it would have provided a model for the slightly illogical placing of the debate between the Four Daughters of God immediately before the Annunciation and therefore

after the Betrothal. In the *Meditationes vitae Christi* the account of the Virgin's devout life in the Temple comes after the debate, and this order is observed also in the French plays which combine these themes.

11 Cf. E. W. Tristram and M. R. James, 'Wall-Paintings in Croughton Church, Northamptonshire', *Archaeologia*, lxxvi (1926–7), 179–204; M. R. James, *The Sculptures in the Lady Chapel at Ely* (London, 1895); Rushforth, *Medieval Christian Imagery*, 270–5.

12 E.E.T.S. 59, 582–621.

13 Cf. Petit de Julleville, II, 427–30.

14 This example is quoted by Anna in her prayer for fruitfulness in the *Protevangelium* (James, op. cit., 39), and a longer list of miracles of this type occurs in the angel's address to Joachim in the *De nativitate Mariae* (Tischendorf, op. cit., 115).

15 E.E.T.S. E.S. 81, 342–4.

16 Cf. The *Gospel of Pseudo-Matthew*, Tischendorf, op. cit., 61.

17 Cf. Hans Giese, *La Passion de Jésus-Christ jouée à Valenciennes l'an 1547*, 10–12.

18 For other examples see Woolf, *English Religious Lyric*, 291–3.

19 This discrepancy has been taken as evidence that the play of the Betrothal belongs to an earlier stage of the cycle and is by a different hand (E.E.T.S. E.S. 120, xxi–xxii). There was an iconographic tradition that Mary was brought up in her parents' home and there taught to read by St Anne (Réau, op. cit., II, ii, 168–9): the author of the Betrothal could therefore have been following this late variation in the story. It should, however, be noted that in the Croughton frescoes, dated 1280–1300, a scene of Mary being led from her parents' home intervenes between representations of the Presentation in the Temple and the Betrothal (*Archaeologia*, lxxvi, 198–9). The explanation probably lies in the statement in the *Evangelium de nativitate* that the maidens brought up in the Temple were sent home at the age of fourteen to prepare for their marriage (Tischendorf, op. cit., 117). It would be reasonable to infer from this that Mary also returned home after the revelation to the high priest, though this is not explicitly stated.

20 Cf. E.E.T.S. E.S., 120, xxi–xxii.

21 That Contemplacio signifies contemplation of the scriptures has been plausibly suggested by Sister M. P. Forrest, 'The Role of the Expositor Contemplacio in the St. Anne's Day Plays of the Hegge Cycle', *Medieval Studies*, xxviii (1966), 60–76. The use of this figure may have been suggested by Nicholas Love's translation of the *Meditationes vitae Christi*, in which the injunctions to meditation in the Nativity sequence are accompanied by the marginal notate, *Contemplacio*.

22 This scene is discussed by Duriez, *La Théologie dans le drame religieux*, 187–91.

23 Giese, op. cit., 12–13. Hope Traver, *The Four Daughters of God* (Philadelphia, 1907), 102, n. 10, observes that in the Netherlandish play, *Die eerste Blijshap van Maria*, two allegorical figures appear in this scene, *Bitter Ellende* (Bitter suffering) who moves the pity of *Innig Gebet* (Inner prayer), who in turn

makes her way to heaven (cf. *Vijf geestlijke Toneelspelen der Middeleeuwen*, ed. H. J. E. Endepols [Amsterdam, 1940]), 93-6.

24 'O saviour of the world, promised of the prophets, when will you come to visit your poor friends, who so much desire your coming.' Ed. cit., 25.

25 'Come then O sovereign dew, come gentle and delightful flower, to repair the loss by which we are damned and which, without you, cannot be redeemed.' Ed. cit., 28.

26 'Come and deliver us, Lord God of Hosts'; ed. cit., 3; cf. *Sarum Breviary* I, xl.

27 Cf. Sicard of Cremona, *Mitrale*, P.L. 213, 215 and Durandus, *Rationale*, 411-12.

28 'Come and save mankind'; 'Come and lead the captive from the house of imprisonment.'

29 Cf. *Vita Jesu Christi*, IV, 177, and *Wisdom*, 996 ff. (E.E.T.S. 262, 146, and note on p. 215).

30 Trans. Ragusa and Green, 5-6.

31 '. . . having recognised his infirmity, he might cry out to the physician and seek the help of grace'; *Summa theologica*, III, i, 5.

32 Though the Four Daughters are portrayed once at an early date in a Tree of Jesse in the Lambeth Palace Bible, they only appear more commonly from the fifteenth century onwards, when they become part of illustrations of the Annunciation in French *horae*; cf. S. Chew, *The Virtues Reconciled* (Toronto, 1947), 60-8.

33 In the iconography of the scene the Trinity is signified either by an aged man, a younger man and the dove between (a symbolism impossible to the plays since the Holy Ghost speaks) or by three identical figures; for an example readily transferable to the stage see Mâle, *L'art religieux de la fin du moyen âge*, 44.

34 St Thomas in answer to the question, 'Utrum efficere conceptionem Christi debeat attribui Spiritui Sancto', replies that the whole Trinity effected the conception of Christ's body, but nevertheless it is attributed to the Holy Ghost for three reasons, of which one is that 'Spiritus enim Sanctus est amor Patris et Filii'; *Summa theologica*, III, xxxii, I.

35 'The angel awaits your answer: for it is time for him to return to God who sent him. And we also, O Queen, wretches oppressed by the sentence of damnation, await your word of compassion. And behold the price of our salvation is offered to you; if you agree to it we shall be immediately set free. We have all been created by the eternal Word of God, but see we die: our restoration to life hangs on your short answer . . . O merciful Virgin, this supplication is made of you by the wretched Adam, exiled from paradise with his poor descendants: it is the plea of Abraham and of David, and of all the other patriarchs, your very ancestors, who also live in the land of the shadow of death. This is the answer which the whole world awaits, kneeling before you. For upon your innocent lips depends comfort for the wretched, redemption of the captive, release of the

condemned, in sum the salvation of all the sons of Adam, of all your race. O Virgin, hasten to give your answer. O Queen, speak the word for which earth, hell and heaven are waiting.' P.L. 183, 83.

36 'Ave Maria,/gratia plena,/dominus tecum,/Virgo serena', *Lateinische Hymnen des Mittelalters*, ed. F. J. Mone, II (Freiburg-im-Breisgau, 1854), 112–13.

37 Joseph's doubts are described in Matthew i. 19–24 and the Visit to Elizabeth in Luke i. 39–56: therefore no chronological order is given in the Bible.

38 This interpretation occurs, for instance, in St Bernard's second homily on the *Missus est* (P.L. 183, 69–70), and in the *Speculum humanae salvationis*; the *Glossa ordinaria* on Matthew i. 19 (P.L. 114, 70–1), however, had simply said, 'Sciebat [Joseph] illam esse inculpabilem, sed unde vel quid esset ignorabat'. The mystery play treatment of St Joseph is of course not compatible with the cult of St Joseph which developed in the course of the fifteenth century: his feast was introduced into the Roman Calendar in 1479.

39 Cf. A. S. Cook, 'A Remote Analogue to the Miracle Play', *J.E.G.Ph.* iv (1902), 421–51.

40 G. La Piana, *Le Rappresentazioni sacre nella Letturatura Bizantina dalle Origini al Secolo IX, con Rapporti al Teatro Sacro d'Occidente* (Grottaferrata, 1912), 160–5.

41 'It could be that someone disguised himself as an angel of the Lord and deceived her'.

42 *Decameron*, Day IV, Novella, 2.

43 *The Early English Carols*, ed. R. L. Greene (Oxford, 1935), nos 465–6; cf. John Stevens, *Music and Poetry in the Early Tudor Court* (London, 1961), 249–50, 400–1.

44 Cf. Salzer, *Die Sinnbilder und Beiworte Mariens*, 476–87, and Hirn, op. cit., 372–3.

45 The translation is that of Cook, *J.E.G.Ph.* iv, 444; cf. P.G. 98, 335. In this dialogue, as in others, the parallelism with Eve had already been made explicit in the scene between Gabriel and Mary at the Annunciation: Mary had rebuked Gabriel, 'I surmise that thou art come to lead me astray like the former Eve, but I am not such as she', and Gabriel had reassured the Virgin, 'I am not he who beguiled Eve'.

46 *J.E.G.Ph.* iv, 438.

47 Pseudo-Chrysostom, *Homily on the Annunciation*, quoted and translated by Cook in *J.E.G.Ph.*, iv, 429; cf. P.G. 60, 755.

48 This subject seems particularly to have interested Lydgate: he makes the Trial one of the Virgin's fifteen sorrows and her triumphal emergence from it one of her fifteen joys; E.E.T.S. 107, 271 and 275.

49 E.g. the magic horn from which a cuckolded husband cannot drink without spilling the wine in *Le Lai du cor* (ed. H. Dörner, Strasbourg, 1907), and the mantle that will shrink when worn by an unchaste woman in the *Le Conte du mantel* (ed. F. A. Wulff, *Romania*, xiv [1885], 343–80); for further references see *Arthurian Literature in the Middle Ages*, ed. R. S. Loomis (Oxford, 1959), 114–15, and Joseph Bédier, *Les Fabliaux* (6th ed., Paris, 1964), 465.

50 J. A. Bryant, Jun. 'The Function of *Ludus Coventriae* 14', *J.E.G.Ph.*, lii (1953), 340–5, comparing ll. 117–28 of this play with *Mankind*, ll. 452–8, argues that at this point a collection of money from the audience was made. The Summoner's speech, however, is explicable in purely literary terms, and since there is no other evidence that the audience of the mystery plays contributed money, it is too large a hypothesis.

51 The second *detractor* is called *bakbytere*. The word was no longer used exclusively of one who defamed another person behind his back but had been extended to cover any slanderer. In the Parson's Tale five kinds of backbiting are distinguished, of which one is: '. . . if a man be good, and dooth or seith a thing to good entente, the bakbitere wol turne al thilke goodnesse up-so-doun to his shrewed entente' (*Works*, ed. Robinson, 289); cf. *M.E.D.* s.v. *bak-biten* and *bak-biter*, and Owst, op. cit., 450–8.

52 For the Latin poems see Raby, *Secular Latin Poetry*, I, 295–7 and II, 34; and for the fabliau Montaiglon and Raynaud, op. cit., I, 162–7; cf. Bédier, *Les Fabliaux*, 460–1.

53 For the archery image see above, p. 384, n. 43.

54 *English and Scottish Popular Ballads*, ed. F. J. Child (London, 1904), 98–100.

55 Tischendorf, op. cit., 87–88; cf. *Cursor mundi*, E.E.T.S. 59, 669–70 and the *Holkham Bible Picture Book*, f. 15.

56 E.g. 'Go forth, O Mary, return to thy home; seek out the thief of thy maidenhood, and be taxed along with him', translated and quoted by Cook from a pseudo-Athanasian dialogue, *J.E.G.Ph.*, iv, 427.

57 For the possibility that these were later insertions see above, pp. 309–10.

58 Cf. P. J. Nordhagen, 'The Origin of the Washing of the Child in the Nativity Scene', *Byzantinische Zeitschrift*, liv (1961), 333–7.

59 *Revelationes sanctae Brigittae*, olim a Card. Turrecremata recognitae nunc a Consalvo Duranto notis illustratae, VII, xxi (Antwerp, 1611), 560.

60 'Vile to relate, viler to hear, vilest of all to see', *De miseria humanae conditionis*, ed. Michele Maccarrone (Lugano, 1955), 14.

61 For the relation of the *Stanzaic Life* to its sources, cf. E.E.T.S. 166, xx–xxviii, and for passages from the *Stanzaic Life* and the Chester Nativity set out in parallel columns to indicate the verbal correspondences, ibid., xxxi–xxxiv.

62 The presence of the ox and the ass is first mentioned by the Pseudo-Matthew who relates it to Isaiah i. 3. The text from Habbakuk appears in the Pseudo-Augustinian sermon (Young, II, 127–8) and thereafter in all prophets' plays that include Habbakuk; cf. also the response 'O magnum mysterium' and versicle 'Domine audivi' for the nocturns of Christmas Day (*Sarum Breviary*, I, clxxx).

63 *Revelationes*, ed. cit., 560; for the influence of this description on iconography see H. Cornell, *The Iconography of the Nativity of Christ*, Uppsala Universitets Årsskrift, 1924.

64 The treatment that comes closest to the York play is that in the first part of the Chantilly *Jeu de la Nativité* (*Nativités et moralités liégeoises du moyen-âge*, ed. Gustave Cohen [Brussels, 1953], 169–71).

65 The Nativity sequence of Jean Michel's *Passion* is a good example of this type of construction.

66 E.E.T.S. E.S. 87, 6–11.

67 The York Nativity is evidently a revision as the description of it in Burton's 1415 list includes an *obstetrix*. It is possible therefore that it was influenced by some of the Nativity lyrics that appear from the end of the fourteenth century onwards. The earliest to have a similar tone is recorded c. 1375 (cf. Woolf, *English Religious Lyric*, 152).

IX Nativity Plays, II

1 These traditions are, for instance, followed by Ludolf the Carthusian, who gives as the first two reasons for the angelic appearance to the shepherds rather than anyone else: 'Primo, quia pauperes, propter quos Christus veniebat, secundum illud Psalmistae: *Propter miseriam inopum, et gemitum pauperum*, etc. Secundo, quia simplices, juxta illud Proverbiorum: *Et cum simplicibus sermocinatio ejus.*' (*Vita Jesu Christi*, I, 72).

2 The collection of glosses in the *Catena aurea* (II, 31–2) on Luke ii. 3, illuminates this point: 'Sed hi erant sinceri, antiquam conversationem Patriarcharum, et Moysis colentes' (Chrysostom); 'Illi prae ceteris videre sublimia merentur qui fidelibus gregibus praeesse sollicite sciunt' (Gregory); 'Significant enim mystice pastores isti gregum, doctores quosque ac rectores fidelium animarum. Nox cuius vigilias custodiebant super gregem suum, pericula tentationum indicat, a quibus se suosque subiectos custodire non disistunt.' (Bede); cf. also the passage from Bruno of Asti quoted by D. W. Robertson and B. F. Huppé, *Piers Plowman and the Scriptural Tradition* (Princeton, 1951), 152.

3 For medieval knowledge of the eclogues see *The English Library before 1700*, ed. Wormald and Wright, 97.

4 *Analecta hymnica*, ed. G. M. Dreves and C. Blume (Leipzig, 1886–1922), xxxi, 207; cf. Woolf, *English Religious Lyric*, 282.

5 I have not mentioned ll. 76–89 (a brief comic dispute about the angel's song) since it is self-evidently an interpolation: indeed it is difficult to see how the play could be convincingly acted with such a disordered interruption of narrative continuity. There seems no particular reason to connect this interpolation specifically with Chester, as Block does (ed. cit., 148): the joke was widespread in England and occurs already in the *Holkham Bible Picture Book* (f. 13r and notes pp. 89–90), and therefore probably in the London cycle.

6 It has been suggested that in some instances at least the simple gifts, like the offerings of the Three Kings, had allegorical significances: E. B. Cantelupe and R. Griffith, 'The Gifts of the Shepherds in the Wakefield *Secunda pastorum*: An Iconographical Interpretation', *Mediaeval Studies*, xxviii (1966), 328–35.

7 The quotation is taken from the translation of Nicholas Love (which here follows the original closely), *The Mirrour of the Blessed Lyf of Jesu Christ* (Roxburghe Club, 1908), 48.

8 In the comments that follow upon the establishment of the shepherds within a contemporary setting I am very indebted to Miss Barbara Harvey, who gave me much helpful information.

9 *The Play called Corpus Christi*, 151-5.

10 *Il Bucolicum Carmen*, ed. Antonio Avena (Padua, 1906), 119-31.

11 M. Wilmotte, *Le Wallon. Histoire et littérature des origines à la fin du XVIIIe siècle* (Brussels, 1893), 95.

12 Ibid. Cf. W. M. Manly, 'Religious Unity in the Towneley "Secunda Pastorum"', *P.M.L.A.*, lxxviii (1963), 154.

13 Op. cit., 159-66.

14 The theme may be introduced in a variety of ways: as an actual meal as in the English plays and the *Passion de Semur* (ed. Roy, 52-3), though in the latter there is no comic list; as a list for which the pretext is the shepherds' discussion of a present for the Christ-Child (Wilmotte, op. cit., 95); or as a list in the form of a prayer as in the *Erlauer Passionsspiel* (cf. Duriez, op. cit., 247). Professor Cawley has pointed out the comic contrast between aristocratic and plebeian delicacies in the list of the *Prima pastorum* ('The "Grotesque" Feast in the *Prima Pastorum*', *Speculum*, xxx [1955], 213-15).

15 For glosses on John xxi, 16, see the *Catena aurea*, II, 590, where Augustine, for instance, is quoted: 'Pascere autem oves est credentes in Christo, ne a fide deficiant, confortare.'

16 Traditions about the Land of Cokayne are discussed by Elfriede Ackermann, *Das Schlaraffenland* (1944); cf. also V. Väänänen, 'Le "Fabliau" de Cocagne', *Neuphilologische Mitteilungen*, xlviii (1947), 3-36. For the Middle English poem on this subject see *Early Middle English Verse and Prose*, ed. J. A. W. Bennett and G. V. Smithers (Oxford, 1968), 138-44.

17 In none of these three plays are the shepherds keeping watch when the angels appear, a variation from the gospel text the more remarkable for the fact that their watchfulness was so allegorically significant. Ludolf the Carthusian, for instance, gives as a third reason for the revelation to the shepherds, 'Tertio, quia vigiles, secundum illud Proverbiorum: *Qui mane vigilant ad me, invenient me*', and adds later 'et custodiunt vigilias noctis super gregem suum, ne infernalium luporum morsibus pereant', *Vita*, I, 72-3. For further comments upon the allegorical significance of keeping watch see above, p. 353, n. 21 on the treatment of the parable of the Wise and Foolish Virgins in the *Sponsus*.

18 Op. cit., 156-8.

19 *A Hundred Merry Tales*, ed. P. M. Zall (Lincoln, Nebraska, 1963), no. 24, pp. 87-8; *The Mad-Men of Gotham* in *Shakespeare Jest-Books*, ed. W. C. Hazlitt, III (London, 1864), 4-5. For the identification of these analogues see H. A. Eaton, 'A source for the Towneley *Prima Pastorum*', *M.L.N.*, xiv (1899), 265-8.

20 Cf. L. Petit de Julleville, *Répertoire du théatre comique en France au moyen âge* (Paris, 1886), 311–12.

21 Gil Vicente, *Obras completas*, I (Lisbon, 1942), 127–63; cf. Shergold, *History of the Spanish Stage*, 41.

22 *Sir Walter Scott's Minstrelsy of the Scottish Border*, ed. T. F. Henderson, IV (Edinburgh, 1902), 389–94; cf. the appendix by Kölbing in E.E.T.S. E.S. 71, xxxi–xxxiv.

23 A. Banzer, 'Die Farce Patelin und ihre Nachahmungen', *Zeitschrift für neufranzösische Sprachen und Literatur*, x (1888), 93–112, included the Mak episode in his survey of imitations of *Pathelin*: this extreme view was shown to be false by L. Wann, 'The Influence of French farce on the Towneley Cycle of Mystery Plays', *Transactions of the Wisconsin Academy of Sciences, Arts and Letters*, xix (1918), 356–68. There is, however, undoubtedly a family resemblance between the sheep-stealing episode and *Pathelin* and other French farces which turn upon fraudulent tricks of similar style.

24 The story of Moll, for instance, is common in collections of exempla (cf. G. H. Gerould, 'Moll of the Prima pastorum', *M.L.N.*, xix [1904], 225–30); whilst an analogue to the Mak story is found in a late fifteenth-century collection of Italian *novellae* (cf. A. C. Baugh, 'The Mak Story', *M.P.*, xv [1918], 729–34).

25 See above, pp. 128, 130.

26 It has been ingeniously suggested by A. C. Cawley, 'Iak Garcio of the *Prima pastorum*', *M.L.N.*, lxviii (1953), 169–72, that Iak Garcio and the third shepherd are identical. This theory, which if true would require substantial emendment of the text, rests largely upon literary judgment: Cawley speaks of 'the absence of any good reason for bringing him [Garcio] into the play at all', whereas on our interpretation his presence is part of a carefully conceived design. There is also the question of whether the fact that the third shepherd pours his meal on to the ground instead of over a bridge absolves him from a charge of folly; the absence of the bridge is anyway dictated by the limitations of the stage; it is also not clear that meal (though it is coarser than flour) would be readily and satisfactorily recoverable from the ground, nor that ll. 174–5 are an order to the shepherds to recover the meal rather than their wits (the second shepherd certainly understands these lines in the latter sense).

27 Some illuminating articles have been written on this subject: see, for instance, M. M. Morgan, ' "High Fraud": Paradox and Double-Plot in the English Shepherds' Plays', *Speculum*, xxxix (1964), 676–89; F. J. Thompson, 'Unity in *The Second Shepherds' Tale*', *M.L.N.*, lxiv (1949), 302–6.

28 Cf. T. M. Parrott, 'Mak and Archie Armstrang', *M.L.N.*, lix (1944), 297–304, who rightly points out that in all versions of the trick oath, the deception is successful. If the trickster is to be punished, as in *Pathelin*, this is brought about by some further twist in the plot.

29 Cf. H. A. Watt, 'The Dramatic Unity of the *Secunda pastorum*', *Essays and Studies in Honor of Carleton Brown* (New York, 1940), 158–66.

30 The modern custom of referring to the two plays as the *Prima* and *Secunda pastorum* is misleading in its implication that both were performed, which is a very unlikely hypothesis. The manuscript incipits refer to the *Prima* as *Pagina pastorum* and the *Secunda* as *Alia eorundem*, which bears out the more probable hypothesis that the *Secunda* was provided as an alternative.

31 *Mystère de l'Incarnation et Nativité de nostre Sauveur et Rédempteur Jésus-Christ, représenté à Rouen en 1474*, ed. P. Le Verdier, ii (Rouen, 1885), 101–34, 147–58, 192–201, etc. Some account of shepherds' scenes in French drama is given by Millicent Carey, *The Wakefield Group in the Towneley Cycle* (Göttingen and Baltimore, 1930), 132–42, but this topic merits a more ample investigation.

32 It is interesting to note that if the dramatists had conceived the *pastores* as genuine shepherds, the practical description of the good shepherd in treatises on estate management would have fitted well with religious idealisation: 'It profiteth the lord to have discreet shepherds, watchful and kindly, so that the sheep be not tormented by their wrath but crop their pasture in peace and joyfulness; for it is a token of the shepherd's kindness if the sheep be not scattered abroad but browse around him in company. Let him provide himself with a good barkable dog and lie nightly with his sheep' (quoted by Eileen Power, *The Wool Trade* [Oxford, 1941], 27).

33 It has been suggested by Frances Foster that the Chester dramatist's debt to the *Stanzaic Life* extends to the Old Testament play of Balaam and the Melchisedek episode (E.E.T.S. 166, xlii); whilst there are no parallels in style and structure, it seems possible that the *Stanzaic Life* suggested the dramatisation of these subjects to the author, though the Melchisedek could be coincidence.

34 *The Golden Legend*, i, 45; cf. the *Speculum humanae salvationis*, ii, pl. 16, and for comment, i, 195.

35 For a discussion of the originally eastern motif of the *Sternengel*, see H. Kehrer, *Die heiligen drei Könige in Literatur und Kunst* (Leipzig, 1908–9), 75–9.

36 Though the attribution to St Bernard is a common one, it seems to rest upon a mistaken reference to his *Sermo I, In Epiphania Domini*, P.L. 183, 142–7.

37 The Chester author, however, says that myrrh signifies 'death that man hath bodylie' (l. 103), instead of 'overcomyng of our fleschlie wille' (*Stanzaic Life*, 2090).

38 The number of the Three Kings, which became fixed by tradition (it is not given by Matthew and early traditions had varied), reflected the Trinity, (cf. Kehrer, op. cit., 22–5). The more devotional amplification here found is made for instance, by Ludolf, 'tum scilicet Trinitatis fidem et mysterium revelantes, et in Christo Trinitatem adorantes' (*Vita*, i, 93).

39 See above, pp. 11, 12.

40 This harmonisation appears invariable in medieval art and narrative: for a typical statement with the emphasis upon exact chronological order see Higden's *Polychronicon*, iv, i (ed. cit., 266–9).

41 This combination has appeared odd. Though the order of events depends on Luke and both Chester and Coventry have large inclusive plays, it still seems strange to combine unrelated events with a lapse of many years between them in one play: as we have said before, the passage of the wagons effectively indicated the passage of time. The explanation here is probably the purely practical one that both episodes took place in the same *locus*, namely the Temple, and could therefore very conveniently be acted upon the same wagon.

42 On the reasons for the Purification see Ludolf, *Vita*, I, 99.

43 In the *Ludus Coventriae* this is rendered as 'ffyff pens' (l. 178).

44 For this prayer see *The Sarum Missal*, 249; in the *Meditationes* this is one of the chants sung by the procession as it circles the altar (trans. Ragusa and Green, 58–9).

45 Réau, op. cit., II, ii, 264, notes that the procession with candles is already found in the twelfth-century glass at Chartres; the *Meditationes* describes the procession but without candles. In the Digby episode (ed. cit., 19–20) there is a full procession with candles, including the virgins (one is given a speaking part) who also often appear in art.

46 This prayer derives from the *Meditationes* (trans. cit., 60) but does not there have a similar colouring of pathos and irony.

47 *English Lyrics of the Thirteenth Century*, ed. Carleton Brown, no. 51; for some discussion of lyrics of this type see Woolf, *English Religious Lyric*, 103–6.

48 For an illuminating discussion of this point see Dunn, *Mediaeval Studies*, xxiii, 87–8.

49 Cf. the *Nativité* from the Bibliothèque Ste Geneviève, ed. Whittredge, 34.

50 Cf. E.E.T.S., 166, xxvii–xxviii.

51 Cf. *Speculum humanae salvationis*, ch. x, ed. cit., I, 23: 'Maria enim candelam Domino in sua purificatione offerebat,/Quando Simeon lumen ad revelationem gentium concinebat.'

52 Cf. *Stanzaic Life*, ll. 2877–84; the further allegorisation of ll. 2957–72 is followed (though not necessarily from this source) in Digby, ll. 489–92.

53 'Senex puerum portabat, puer autem senem regebat'; *Sarum Breviary*, iii, 144. This responsory is quoted and expounded by Ludolf, *Vita*, I, 102.

54 It has been sensitively praised by Kolve, op. cit., 249–53.

55 These miracles, first found in the *Protevangelium* and the *Gospel of Pseudo-Matthew*, were sometimes dramatised on the Continent. The inclusion of some in the *Holkham Bible Picture Book* (ff. 14r–15r) raises the possibility that the London cycle included them.

56 This miracle, often illustrated in art, was given authority by its inclusion in the *Historia scholastica* (P.L. 198, 1543).

57 Cf. Duriez, op. cit., 263.

58 Cf. ll. 132–4, 'And sertis I drede me sore/To make my smale trippe,/Or tyme þat I com þare'. The editor's summary, 'I dread the trip' cannot be correct, since whatever the *trip* is, it will have happened before the arrival

in Egypt; the *N.E.D.* also does not record the sense of 'journey' for trip before 1699 (except for this reference). It may be conjectured that 'trip' here has the sense of 'stumbling', and that 'To make my smale trippe' is a euphemistic phrase for 'die'. 'Trip' or 'trippet' (noun) and 'trip' (verb) are often used in a causative sense with reference to death, cf. *Ludus Coventriae*, p. 174, l. 188, and *Castle of Perseverance*, l. 3425.

59 Cf. York, p. 43, ll. 93-4, *Ludus Coventriae*, p. 164, ll. 57-8.

60 'Their suffering consisted of this: it was a distant land and unknown to them, and they had to travel by hard ways, for which they were unfitted, our Lady on account of her youth, Joseph on account of his old age, and even the Child himself, whom they had to carry, for He was still very young.' Ludolf, *Vita Christi*, I, 116.

61 The raging would probably consist of furious shouting and violent gestures. An allusion in the *Paston Letters*, ed. Norman Davis (London, 1963), 243, also shows that Herod's violence had continued to be a commonplace in the fifteenth century.

62 For references see Duriez, op. cit., 76-7.

63 It has been ingeniously suggested by Stephen Hussey, 'How many Herods in the Middle English Drama?', *Neophilologus*, xlviii (1964), 252-9, that Herod's claim to godlike powers in the plays was influenced by the description of another Herod in Acts xii, 22-3, who was acclaimed as a god and died eaten of worms. There is an obvious similarity between the two deaths, but the conflation or confusion had taken place much earlier. The resemblance in the two Herods' willingness or determination to be accepted as a god may be coincidental, since this dramatic treatment of Herod arises from the modelling of him upon the pattern of the devil (see below, pp. 391-2, n. 64); at most Acts xii might have suggested to the dramatists that such a treatment was historically realistic as well as doctrinally and aesthetically satisfactory. As Mr Hussey points out, it is unlikely that the dramatists were actually confused about the Herods. Indeed they were probably far clearer about them than we are today, as every commentary, recognising a possible source of confusion, distinguished between them with absolute clarity.

64 See above, p. 109. Herod's resemblance to the devil is stressed by commentaries; the *Catena aurea*, for instance, quotes from a sermon of Leo, 'Herodes etiam diaboli personam gerit', and the sixteenth-century commentator Cornelius a Lapide says precisely, 'Tropologice Herodes est diabolus' (cf. Duriez, op. cit., 76). It has been plausibly inferred from the reference to 'black Herod' in the Beverley records (A. F. Leach, 'Some English Plays and Players, 1220-1548', *An English Miscellany Presented to Dr Furnivall* [Oxford, 1901], 213) that at Beverley and conceivably elsewhere Herod's face was painted black or that he wore a black mask to indicate his devilish affiliations, though a figurative usage of *black* cannot be entirely ruled out. If the Beverley Herod's face was painted black, it would make the passage quoted above ostentatiously ironic (additionally

so, if the God the Father had worn a gilded mask). The resemblance between Herod's praise of his own beauty and Lucifer's speech in Towneley i, 77–93, has already been noticed by W. E. Tomlinson, *Der Herodes-charakter im englischen Drama (Palaestra*, 195 [1934], 43), but Tomlinson through making the improbable assumption that Herod is the 'father' of all the wicked characters in the plays, is led to supposing that Lucifer was modelled on him rather than vice versa.

65 *Page, gedling, congeown* and *ribald* are all terms of abuse with roughly identical meaning, i.e. low-born fellow or scoundrel; *marmoset,* here probably means not a monkey, but a grotesque figure, in which sense it is applied in a derogatory way to heathen idols.

66 Elsewhere, as in Towneley xvi, 226–34, Herod abuses the councillors who repeat the prophecies, but not the prophets themselves.

67 Cf. *Biblia Pauperum*, ed. J. Ph. Berjeau (London, 1859), VII, and 2 Kings xi. 1.

68 *Literature and Pulpit*, 494–5, 331–4.

69 Watkin has attracted much critical attention and has been variously compared to Unferþ, Sir Kay, the Miles Gloriosus, and Ralph Roister Doister; cf. Daniel C. Boughner, *The Braggart in Renaissance Comedy* (Minneapolis, 1954), 126–7, and Tomlinson in *Palaestra*, 195, 45.

70 For further discussion of the game metaphor see below, pp. 254, 255.

71 The association of the Innocents with Christ is not made in patristic commentaries, but is found, for instance, in the *Revelations* of St Bridget, where Christ says, 'Quod vero infantes occisi sunt, signum passionis meae futurae erat', ed. cit., 392–3. Commentaries, however, consistently saw in the Innocents the first martyrs for Christ (and in a general sense all martyrs are reflections of Christ), and sometimes following the liturgy they identified them with the 144,000 who follow the lamb and were the 'primitiae Deo et Agno' (Revelation xiv, 1–5), an association made by the liturgy. Amongst the plays only Towneley (xvi, 487–8) alludes to it.

72 Cf. Young, II, 110–14.

73 Cf. Anderson, *Drama and Imagery*, 136–7. Wooden dolls, which were used elsewhere (cf. Hildburgh in *Archaeologia*, xciii, 61), would obviously not serve in this scene.

74 Young, II, 110–13.

75 *Wille of wane:* completely lost.

76 *Merchant's Tale*, E, 2364–6. For the colloquial exclamations cf. Chester, x, 'Out! out! and well away' (l. 325) and 'Out! out! and woe is me!' (l. 345), and Towneley, xvi, 'Out!, alas! and waloway!' (l. 362).

77 Passages of French are found in many of the court scenes in the cycles to indicate the grand manners of the characters and their pretentiousness; it is, however, used sparingly in this play (see Cawley, ed. cit., note to l. 171), and at this point probably refers to Herod's French form of farewell, *adew*, in the preceding line.

78 Cf. Hussey, *Neophilologus*, xlviii, 257; the play is peppered with allusive hints lying beneath the surface meaning: some have been noted by Charles

Elliott, 'Language and Theme in the Towneley Magnus Herodes', *Mediaeval Studies*, xxx (1968), 351-3.

79 Cf. Réau, op. cit., ii, ii, 276.

80 E.g. Herod ordered the slaying of all male children under two just as Pharaoh had ordered midwives to kill all new-born male babies (Exodus i. 16-22); for a full series of parallels see Ludolf, *Vita Christi*, i, 120-1, and the *Speculum humanae salvationis*, ch. xi, ed. cit. i, 25.

81 'Nam febris non mediocris erat, prurigo intolerabilis in omni corporis superficie, assiduis vexebatur colli tormentis, pedes intercutaneo vitio tumuerant, putredo testiculorum vermes generabat, creber anhelitus et interrupta suspiria, quae ad vindictam Dei ab omnibus referebantur'; P.L. 198, 1546.

82 Cf. *The Golden Legend*, ii, 182.

83 Cf. *Piers Plowman*, B Text, vi, 88-9, and for general comment, E. C. Perrow, *The Last Will and Testament as a Form of Literature* (Transactions of the Wisconsin Academy of Sciences, Arts, and Letters, xvii, i [1913], 689-90); both the Chester and Digby authors were probably in the first instance influenced by the statement in Peter Comestor, 'Tunc inscripsit testamentum Herodes'; P.L. 198, 1545.

84 The stage-direction says simply, 'Mors interficiat herodem et duos milites', but to do so he must have carried a weapon, in all probability a spear (cf. for instance, the *Pardoner's Tale*, C, 671-7). The alternative, a dart (cf. The Raising of Lazarus, l. 63, 'When deth on me hath shet his dart') seems less practicable on the stage. Death probably wore a skeleton mask, but ll. 272-3 suggest that his costume had worms (outsize as on many tombs) painted on it.

85 Cf. Tomlinson, *Palaestra*, 195, 49.

86 The figure of death appears, for instance, in the Valencia play of Adam and Eve (cf. Shergold, op. cit., 67), and in the *Alsfelder Passionsspiel* at the death of Lazarus (Froning, op. cit., 644-5).

87 The following themes stand out: the omnipotence of death (ll. 181-4), the suddenness of his coming upon those who think that they will live for ever (ll. 195, 248-55), the poverty of the grave (279-80), and the devouring worms (ll. 281-4); for lyrics spoken by a personification of death see Woolf, *English Religious Lyric*, 336-40.

X The Life of Christ

1 E.g. the *Heidelberger Passionsspiel* and the *Alsfelder Passionsspiel*, except that the latter has a preliminary scene with devils.

2 That the Christ-Child was represented by a doll and not a living baby is a proposition proved by common-sense; on the evidence for this from alabasters see Hildburgh, *Archaeologia*, xciii, 62. There is, however, one instance of the Christ-Child speaking in the Adoration of the Magi: it occurs in two

manuscripts of the Chester cycle (ed. cit., 183) and is probably a later addition. If the play was ever acted with this insertion, a much older child must have impersonated the baby.

3 Cf. Carleton Brown, 'The Towneley *Play of the Doctors* and the *Speculum Christiani*', *M.L.N.*, xxxi (1916), 223–6.

4 See above, p. 155.

5 Chester, xi, 242 and Towneley, xviii, 64. York, xx, 90, which has *we* for *he*, presents an inferior reading.

6 On this topos see Peter Dronke, *Medieval Latin and the Rise of European Love-Lyric*, i (Oxford, 1968), 181–92: the normal context would be in the literature of love whether human or religious.

7 'All wisdom comes from the Lord God'; Ecclesiasticus i. 1.

8 *Summa theologica*, iii, iii, 8.

9 See above, pp. 220–1.

10 Cf. R. Woolf, 'The Theme of Christ the Lover-Knight in Medieval English Literature', *R.E.S.*, n.s., xiii (1962), 1–16.

11 Cf., for instance, Lydgate's poem on the fifteen joys and sorrows, E.E.T.S. E.S. 107, 276.

12 *Passion*, ll. 9449–508.

13 *Sarum Breviary*, i, cccxxxvi–cccxxxvii.

14 Cf. Didron, *Christian Iconography*, i, 318–26.

15 Cf. *Vita*, i, 183, and also the antiphons for the octave of the Epiphany, 'Babtizat miles regem; servus dominum suum' (*Sarum Breviary*, i, cccli) and 'Baptista contremuit et non audet tangere sanctum Dei verticem sed clamat cum tremore, Sanctifica me Salvator' (ibid., ccclvii–ccclviii); the latter antiphon is sung by the choir in the *Alsfelder Passionsspiel*, ed. Froning, 584.

16 On the relation of this tradition to *Paradise Regained* see E. M. Pope, *Paradise Regained, The Tradition and the Poem* (Baltimore, 1947).

17 *Libri IV Sententiarum*, iii, xx, 1–4, ed. cit., 640–2.

18 Cf. Timothy Fry, 'The Unity of the *Ludus Coventriae*', *Studies in Philology*, xlviii (1951), 527–70.

19 *Passion*, 138–40.

20 *Vita*, i, 199–200; in the *Holkham Bible Picture Book* (f. 19v) Christ is shown with His feet resting upon a narrow parapet whilst with His arms He holds on to a finial. In the York cycle, presumably for convenience of staging, Christ remains upon the pinnacle for the third temptation and seems to remain there until the end of the play.

21 Ed. cit., 177–9.

22 i.e. befuddled-beard.

23 See above, p. 111.

24 Satan's appearance is not specified in stage-directions to this play in any of the cycles though the Chester banns describe how Christ was tempted by 'the devill in his fethers, all ragger and rente'. It may be assumed that the devil appeared in his fallen shape, and did not adopt human disguise as one tradition (familiar from *Paradise Regained*) affirmed.

25 Eger on the second day proceeds almost immediately to the Raising of Lazarus.

26 'Then come two Jews with the woman taken in adultery in order to tempt Christ.'

27 The Chester banns do not mention the Woman taken in Adultery as part of the play of the Temptation in the Wilderness, just as they do not include the Purification with the Doctors in the Temple, but their silence has little significance.

28 A gathering has been lost from the manuscript and there is a corresponding lacuna in the Raising of Lazarus.

29 'O wicked broodmare and filthy hag'.

30 In Burton's list the subjects form separate plays; cf. ed. cit., xxii.

31 *Stotte, scowte* and *bych clowte* are terms of abuse applied only to women, *bysmare* (wretch) and *brothel* (lecher or harlot) are applied to either sex. The idiom 'to keep one's cut' (cf. *N.E.D.* s.v. *cut*) is slightly obscure; it appears in respectable contexts meaning something like to keep one's distance though the context here arouses the suspicion that there may be some obscenity lurking in the phrase.

32 Cf. Woolf, *English Religious Lyric*, 214–18.

33 Peter Meredith, ' "Nolo Mortem" and the *Ludus Coventriae* Play of the *Woman Taken in Adultery*', *Medium Aevum*, xxxviii (1969), 38–54; the author has pointed out that the play begins with these words and has illuminatingly stressed the relationship between story and antiphon (the two had already been brought together in the *Vita*, ii, 284).

34 Ed. C. Blume (Leipzig, 1930), 7; cf. E.E.T.S. 158, 6–7.

35 See above, p. 151.

36 *Yorkshire Writers*, ed. C. Horstman (London, 1896), ii, 449–53.

37 A rubric in Towneley, however, specifies, 'Et lacrimatus est ihesus', but when rubrics consist of quotations from the Bible it is difficult to tell how literally they were taken as stage-directions.

38 P.L., 39, 1929 and P.L., 198, 1597.

39 For a full discussion of the *Visio Lazari* see Max Voigt, 'Beiträge zur Geschichte der Visionenliteratur im Mittelalter', i, *Palaestra*, cxlvi (1924), 1–42. An English translation of it (made from the French) may be read in the sixteenth-century *Kalender of Shepherdes*, ed. H. O. Sommer (London, 1892), iii, 67–73.

40 Cf. Roy, *Mystère de la Passion*, 57*–9*.

41 Ed. cit., 205. 'O my sister Martha, it is a place void of happiness; were all the tongues in the world to describe them without ceasing, they could not recount all the torments, bitter, appalling and vile, with which this unhappy place is filled. It is an abyss of wretchedness, a hideous gulf of misery where all unhappiness abounds.'

42 *The Pricke of Conscience*, ed. Richard Morris (Berlin, 1863), 176.

43 *Mystères provençaux du XVe siècle*, ed. A. Jeanroy and Teulié (Toulouse, 1893), 86–8.

44 Although Christ in this play, as in those in the other cycles, gives his biblically based order that Lazarus should be released from his grave-clothes, it seems likely that this was not carried out; one should therefore imagine Lazarus, as he is, for instance, depicted in fourteenth-century frescoes at Pomposa, standing with stillness in his grave-clothes, arms wrapped across his body, and facing, not Christ, but the beholder.

45 *A shete . . . nowche:* The winding sheet shall be your fine robes, toads your jewellery; *lyre:* complexion; *byke:* nest of bees; *paddokys:* toads; *ffor you then sorows . . . goode:* For he who now has inherited the most of your possessions is the one who grieves for you least.

46 The three Synoptic gospels relate the healing by Christ of two poor men who were blind on His way to Jerusalem but before His entry on the ass; both cycles have therefore placed the incident at a later point in time, and York has made it more representative of Christ's earlier miracles by making one of the poor men lame.

47 See above, pp. 186, 188. For some account of the occurrence of the theme of the Good Shepherd in medieval art and thought see Anton Legner, *Der gute Hirte* (Düsseldorf, 1959), 24-32.

48 That the ass was an animal reserved for the use of poor men is stated by the *Meditationes* (trans. cit., 306). This interpretation is followed by the author of the *Ludus Coventriae* (ed. cit., 237-8), where the *burgensis* at first refuses the the ass to the disciples, since, 'but only foor pore men to releve/this Asse is ordayned as I ȝow say'. The same idea seems to lie behind the description of the animals in York as *comen,* that is public property shared by the members of the community.

49 'He garte corne growe with-outen plogh,/Wher are was none', ll. 137-8; for an account of this miracle see the *Holkham Bible Picture Book,* notes to f. 14v.

50 See, for example, the allegorical exposition of the healing of the man born blind in the *Vita Jesu Christi,* II, 297-8.

51 Cf. *The Sarum Missal,* 96.

52 The identification of the woman who was a sinner in Luke vii, 37-8 with the woman in Matthew xxvi. 6-7 was well established, as was also the identification of the latter with Mary the sister of Martha (cf. John xii. 1-3). The discrepancy between Matthew which places the episode in the house of Simon the Leper and John which has it in the house of Martha and Mary, is reconciled by the Chester dramatist (as often elsewhere) by having Simon, Martha, Mary and Lazarus all present at the supper.

53 For an interesting interpretation of the role of Mary Magdalene here see E. Prosser, *Drama and Religion in the English Mystery Plays* (Stanford, 1961), 110-46. Her suggestion, however, that Mary Magdalene was present throughout the Last Supper and the Agony in the Garden is too large a supposition to be safely inferred from negative evidence.

54 Towneley, as far as I know, is unique amongst western European drama in not including the institution of the eucharist. Occasionally a Continental

cycle excluded the Last Supper altogether, as does Kunzelsau, where no doubt the fictional representation of the consecration of the sacrament would have seemed jarring, when the consecrated Host was itself being borne in procession and had been honoured at the beginning of the play.

55 A harmonisation of Matthew and Mark on the one hand with Luke on the other had led to the common view that Christ twice predicted Judas's betrayal, once before the institution of the eucharist and once afterwards. Amongst the extant English cycles, however, the author of the *Ludus Coventriae* alone follows this tradition. Whilst many Continental dramatists depict the double prediction (cf. Duriez, op. cit., 326), the effect in their work is largely of repetitiveness.

56 For a survey of the patristic traditions see Franz Nikolasch, *Das Lamm als Christussymbol in den Schriften der Väter* (Vienna, 1963). Amongst medieval works, the allegorisation of the eating of the lamb of the Passover is found, for instance, in the *Vita*, III, 350. It is probable that the paschal lamb lay upon the table as a stage property: some late York accounts refer to the mending of the *lam*, see A. J. Mill, 'The York Bakers' Play of the Last Supper', *M.L.R.*, xxx (1935), 152.

57 This iconographic type did not become common in the west until the seventeenth century when it served the end of religious polemic. In the Middle Ages the moment in the Last Supper normally depicted in art is, as Mâle pointed out, Judas's betrayal. If it is a eucharistic one, then it is the actual moment of the consecration (as for instance in the painting of Dirk Bouts, cited by Mâle, *L'Art religieux de la fin du moyen âge*, 58–60 and fig. 31). Mâle suggests that here iconography was influenced by the drama, a possibility since the French cycles normally specify the use of eucharistic vessels; they do not, however, lay stress upon the act of communion as does the *Ludus Coventriae*.

58 The dramatist draws upon the exegetic tradition which associated the lamb of Abraham's sacrifice (cf. Isaiah liii, 7) and the Lamb of the Apocalypse. It may be noted that there is a similar association between the Lamb of the Apocalypse and the eucharistic lamb in *The Pearl*, 861–2.

59 Cf. *Meditationes*, trans. Ragusa and Green, 317 ff. and the *Vita*, IV, 1 ff.

60 For this devotion see Woolf, *English Religious Lyric*, 222–7.

61 Though the speaker is described as *Trinitas*, it was probably the figure of God the Father, since He addresses Christ as 'son', though it is of course possible that the dove of the Holy Ghost was also represented. In the *Holkham Bible Picture Book*, f. 28v, it is God the Father who appears to Christ during the Agony in the Garden.

62 For the iconography of the scene see Réau, op. cit., II, ii, 427–31, and for a more detailed account Marie Bartmuss, *Die Entwicklung der Gethsemane-Darstellung bis um 1400* (Halle, 1935).

XI The Passion

1 *Meditationes*, 318–19.
2 *Digby Plays*, 53–90.
3 'For in hell is no redemption', *Sarum Breviary*, II, 278; York xxxvii, 285–8; cf. note to *The Castle of Perseverance*, 3096–7, E.E.T.S. 262, 200.
4 The stage-direction in *Wisdom* reads: 'And aftyr þe songe entreth Lucyfer in a dewyllys aray wythowt and wythin as a prowde galonte', E.E.T.S. 262, 125 and note to l. 324.
5 Cf. B. Spivack, *Shakespeare and the Allegory of Evil* (London, 1958), 151–61.
6 The porter (*janitor*) first appears in the Middle English poem on the Harrowing of Hell, E.E.T.S. E.S. 100, 13; in the York and Towneley Harrowing of Hell the devil named Rybald has in part the duties of the porter and a devil in the Towneley Last Judgment refers to 'Oure porter at hell yate'. The idea of the porter of hell gate, however, seems to have been commoner than these meagre references would suggest, since it is referred to incidentally in Heywood's *The Four PP* (ll. 823–48) and in *Nice Wanton* (l. 224). For a connection with the porter in Macbeth see J. B. Harcourt, 'I Pray You, Remember the Porter', *Shakespeare Quarterly*, xii (1961), 393–402, and Glynne Wickham, 'Hell-Castle and its Door-Keeper', *Shakespeare Survey*, xix (1966), 68–74.
7 *Onhanged harlott*: this is a better editorial presentation of the text than 'Say on, hanged harlott' as in L. T. Smith; cf. York, xxxii, 186, 'Þou onhanged harlott . . .'. The meaning is clearly 'a scoundrel worthy to be hanged', though neither the *N.E.D.* nor the *M.E.D.* record this abusive use of the past participle of either *anhang*, *anhangen* or *hang*, *hongen*; for the use of the verb in imprecations or expressions of anger see *M.E.D.* s.v. *hongen*, 2a (d) and 2b (c). *Uncomely to kys* was probably also a traditionally insulting alliterative phrase; cf. 'þou3 art unsemly for to se,/Uncomli for to cussen suwete', 'Þe desputisoun bitwen þe bodi and þe soule', ed. W. Linow, *Erlanger Beiträge zur englischen Philologie*, i (1889), 41.
8 In astrological treatises Judas was sometimes classified as a child of Saturn, his avarice and suicide being characteristic of the melancholy temperament (cf. R. Klibansky, F. Saxl, E. Panofsky, *Saturn and Melancholy* [London, 1964], 121, 286). The violence inherent in robbery and suicide, however, also made him appropriately a child of Mars; 'The pykepurs' and 'The sleere of hymself' are, for instance, depicted upon the walls of the Temple of Mars in *The Knight's Tale* (ll. 1998, 2005).
9 A play described as *Suspencio Jude* is included in the second of Burton's lists (Davies, op. cit., 235, and York, p. xxiv, n. 1).
10 According to the editor the play is written in a later hand than the rest of the manuscript. It nevertheless seems probable that the play itself is of an earlier date and related to the lost York play.

11 For an account of the apocryphal legend of Judas see P. F. Baum, 'The medieval legend of Judas Iscariot', *P.M.L.A.*, xxxi (1916), 481-632, and E. K. Rand, 'Medieval Lives of Judas Iscariot', *Anniversary Papers by Colleagues and Pupils of G. L. Kittredge* (Boston, 1913), 305-16.

12 Greban, *Passion*, 285-8.

13 Greban, *Passion*, 144-5; *Didot Passion*, 22-8; *Semur*, 124-5, where the story is related by Judas's wife (mother). It seems to be only in the late *Freiburger Passionsspiel* that Judas summarises his history (briefly) at the time of his suicide ('Freiburger Passionsspiele des xvi. Jahrhunderts', ed. Ernst Martin, *Zeitschrift der Gesellschaft zur Beförderung der Geschichts-, Altherthums- und Volkskunde von Freiburg, dem Breisgau und den angrenzenden Landschaften*, iii [1873-4], 69-70).

14 Ed. Evelyn Underhill (London, 1950), 171 ('And feel sin a lump'), and 179 ('thou shalt always feel sin, a foul stinking lump thou wottest never what, betwixt thee and thy God: the which lump is none other thing than thyself').

15 Though passages of dumb show occur in the moralities (cf. Dieter Mehl, *The Elizabethan Dumb Show* [London, 1965], 15-16), they do not occur in any mystery cycle save the *Ludus Coventriae*, where in the Passion sequence they are fairly frequent.

16 Folio 30 and notes p. 129. One may compare the stage-direction specifying a brief dumb show after Judas's despairing monologue in the *Frankfurter Passionsspiel*: 'Judas recedit suspendens eius ymaginem. dyabulus ex ventre eius capit animam' (Froning, op. cit., 472).

17 This dream is mentioned briefly in Matthew xxvii. 19, and a little more amply in the *Gesta Pilati* (James, op. cit., 98), where the Jews interpret it as a piece of sorcery worked by Christ. Peter Comestor in the *Historia scholastica* attributed the dream to the activity of the devil: 'Iam Dei nutu poterat cognoscere diabolus mysterium crucis, et ideo laborabat, ne Christus moreretur. Forte jam gaudebant sancti in inferno, unde hoc notavit', P.L. 198, 1628. This explanation thereafter became the accepted one in narrative and drama.

18 Greban, *Passion*, 304-7. For similar motivation cf. Frankfurt, 3125-32 (Froning, 487). The source was probably Peter Comestor (see previous note) or others who had followed him, such as Nicholas of Lyra who suggested that the devil recognised Christ 'forte per sanctorum patrum in lymbo existentium exultationem' (quoted by Roy, op. cit., 229).

19 The York dramatist passes over the devil's recognition that Christ will redeem man so speedily (xxx, 163-5) that the issue of the reason for this does not arise. In view of Craigie's demonstration that the dramatist was influenced by the Middle English *Gospel of Nicodemus* (see below, p. 400, n. 24), it is worthwhile noting that he did not adopt the quite convincing reason for the devil's attempt to undo the Crucifixion, found in this poem (E.E.T.S. E.S. 100, 34), where it is the apocryphal miracle of the soldiers' standards which bow to Christ against the will of their bearers that gives the

devil his sudden insight. In York the miracle of the standard-bearers occurs considerably later than Procula's dream, an arrangement that departs from the *Gesta Pilati* and is therefore unlike that of the two Continental plays which include the two episodes (Mercadé, *Passion* and Alsfeld), as these follow the order of the *Gesta*.

20 P.L. 114, 173.

21 An illuminating account of the realistic style is given by J. W. Robinson, 'The Art of the York Realist', *M.P.*, lx (1963), 241-51; but the scenes between Judas and the porter and Pilate and his wife should not, as here, be explained solely in terms of realism.

22 For the two traditions of Pilate see Arnold Williams, *The Characterization of Pilate in the Towneley Plays* (Michigan, 1950).

23 The source of this incident is unknown: the passage in the *Northern Passion* cited as the 'germ' of the episode is insufficient (cf. E.E.T.S. 147, 83).

24 As Craigie has shown ('The *Gospel of Nicodemus* and the *York Mystery Plays*', *An English Miscellany presented to Dr. Furnivall* [Oxford, 1901], 56-7) the dramatist was indebted to the Middle English *Gospel of Nicodemus* for this incident: the chief resemblance consists of the fact that in both Pilate threatens the new standard-bearers with death if they cannot hold the standards straight, rather than the former standard-bearers (as in the *Gesta*) who would be proved liars if the miracle did not repeat itself; there are also unmistakable verbal echoes. It may be noted, however, that the York treatment of this point occurs also in Alsfeld (Froning, op. cit., 711-12, and cf. Duriez, *Les Apocryphes dans le drame religieux en Allemagne au moyen âge* [Lille, 1914], 19-22), and in the *Passion* of Mercadé (ed. cit., 157-8) though in these Pilate threatens the first group of standard-bearers, Annas threatens the second.

25 Cf. Enid Welsford, *The Fool, His Social and Literary History* (London, 1935), 119-24.

26 Whilst the style is the dramatist's own, the accusation at this point that Christ was born of fornication goes back to the *Gospel of Nicodemus* (James, op. cit., 98).

27 *Corpus juris canonici*, ed. Friedberg, II, 1066.

28 Craigie in *An English Miscellany*, 54, notes the resemblance between these lines (xxxvii, 229-33) and the Middle English *Gospel of Nicodemus*, ll. 25-7; he did not, however, observe the resemblance between xxxvii, 229-33 and xxix, 51-4.

29 In German drama distinguishing titles are used: in Frankfurt they are *Iudei* and *milites*, and in Alsfeld *Iudei* and *flagellatores*. In French drama, however, these characters are not referred to as members of a generic group, but are given proper names.

30 Even if the weapons used in the Buffeting were cloth or leather bags filled with wool, as Hildburgh suggests (*Archaeologia*, xciii, 78), the blows cannot have been struck with realistic violence.

31 Cf. Owst, *Literature and Pulpit*, 510–11, and Kolve, *The Play Called Corpus Christi*, 185–8 *et passim*.

32 This motif has been noted by H. P. Goodman, *Original Elements in French and German Passion Plays* (Bryn Mawr, 1951), 67–8. Her most striking example is from the *Tyrol Passion*, ll. 2128–31.

33 *Memorials of St Edmund's Abbey*, ed. T. Arnold, I (Rolls Series, 1890), 15.

34 'He is so defaced by spitting from head to foot that I feel very sad to look at him.' *Passion*, 273.

35 For a different view see Kolve, op. cit., 180–90.

36 *Meditationes*, 326 and 329.

37 *Cornish Drama*, I, 323–97.

38 E.g. Eger, 172–93.

39 *Meditationes*, 333–4; *Vita Jesu Christi*, IV, 96–7; *Dialogus Beatae Mariae et Anselmi de Passione*, P.L. 159, 282–3.

40 Cf. for instance, the stage-direction from Alsfeld, 'Et sic Judei corizando per crucem cantant' (Froning, op. cit., 775).

41 For the image see W. Gaffney, 'The Allegory of the Christ-Knight in *Piers Plowman*', *P.M.L.A.*, xlvi (1931), 155–68, and R. Woolf, 'The Theme of Christ the Lover-Knight in Medieval English Literature', *R.E.S.*, n.s., xiii (1962), 1–16, and for the use of the image in Towneley, Sister Jean Marie, 'The Cross in the Towneley Plays', *Traditio*, v (1947), 331–4.

42 'Master, God save you! By the garland on your head you resemble a young gallant; and by your arms thus outspread it seems that you want to dance, shame on you, Jesus, shame on you I say.' Ed. Roy, 150.

43 Cf. Woolf, op. cit., 41.

44 'Jesus, quickly build a new temple: for in place of a hammer you have the three nails with thick points thrust through your hands and feet; and in place of wood to work with you can use the cross which so pulls your nerves and veins apart.' *Passion*, 329.

45 Cf. *R.E.S.*, n.s., xiii, 11–14.

46 *Religious Lyrics of the XIVth Century*, ed. Carleton Brown, revised G. V. Smithers (Oxford, 1957), 67.

47 See A. Wilmart, 'Le grand poème bonaventurien sur les sept paroles du Christ en croix', *Revue Bénédictine*, xlvii (1935), 235–78, and for English poems on the subject, Woolf, op. cit., 220–2.

48 'O vos omnes' is sung twice in the liturgy of Holy Week, on Good Friday and Holy Saturday (*Sarum Breviary*, I, dccci); 'Popule meus' and 'Quid est quod debui ultra facere' are part of the *Improperia*, sung on Good Friday (*Sarum Missal*, 112–13); 'Vulpes foveas habent' is in the office of nocturns for Passion Sunday (*Sarum Breviary*, I, dccxvii).

49 It is possible that there is an early example of the influence of the lyric tradition on narrative treatments of the Crucifixion in the *Northern Passion*, 1757–64 (E.E.T.S. 145, 204–6). The first four lines of this brief complaint appear as an independent lyric in MS. Harley 7322 (E.E.T.S. 15, 232). Whilst this record is considerably later than the earliest texts of the

Northern Passion, the manuscript is no indication of date and the verse could have been composed a century earlier. It is in general more probable that the author incorporated and expanded a lyric than that he was influenced by the Latin works cited by Frances Foster (E.E.T.S. 147, 66-7). It is interesting to note that the *Cursor Mundi* also includes a long complaint (E.E.T.S. 62, 978-82), undoubtedly influenced by the vernacular lyric, though it is not in its historical place.

50 Mercadé, *Passion*, 15806-56. A crucifixion complaint is copied at the end of the *Passion de Biard* (ed. Grace Frank, S.A.T.F. 1934, 145-7), but there seems no reason to suppose that this ever formed part of the play: the rubric specifies that it is spoken by Christ on the Cross, whilst the conclusion of the play proper is the Appearance to Mary Magdalene and Christ's didactic farewell to the audience. The fact that, according to Grace Frank, this is a version of the play designed for reading would make this kind of accretion very simple. For a discussion of the complaint see note to ll. 2057 ff. (ed. cit., 165-7), and for occurrences of other versions of the poem, Jean Sonet, *Répertoire d'Incipit de prières en ancien français* (Geneva, 1956), no. 2107.

51 For the references see Duriez, op. cit., 414-15.

52 Ed. Froning, 791-2.

53 Towneley xxiii, 233-94, contains the following themes: 'O vos omnes' and 'Quid ultra debui facere' (both used in complaint lyrics from the thirteenth century onwards); 'Vulpes foveas habent' (not a typical lyric theme); a reproach based upon man's ingratitude in the face of God's inestimable gift of creating him in His likeness (a topic of the later lyric, cf. for instance, *Religious Lyrics of the XVth Century*, ed. Carleton Brown [Oxford, 1939], 160); and a contrast between Christ's sinlessness and sufferings and man's guilt (a commonplace of the lyrics). It is only the paraphrase of 'Vulpes foveas habent', that is characteristic of complaints in the drama as opposed to the lyrics: it occurs also in York, xxxvi, 192-5, and as we saw above, in the Alsfeld complaint. There was, however, in all probability a meditative source for this dramatic use, as this antiphon does not occur in the *York Breviary*. A verbal resemblance between Towneley at this point and the *Northern Passion*, ll. 1638-9, has been noted (F. H. Miller, 'The *Northern Passion* and the Mysteries', *M.L.N.*, xxxiv [1919], 91), but the *Northern Passion* does not provide a sufficient model, as the quotation from Luke is only partial and it does not form part of a complaint.

54 The *Meditationes* had provided alternative meditative forms for the nailing to the Cross: according to the first (trans. cit., 333-4), Christ ascended the Cross by a ladder and extended his arms upon it; at this moment He made his speech of self-offering to the Father; in the second, the executioners 'furiously cast Him on to the Cross on the ground, taking His arms, violently extending them, and most cruelly fixing them to the Cross' (trans. cit., 334). This second meditative form became the accepted version in later Latin meditations, vernacular literature and art.

55 *Meditationes*, 308-9; Greban, *Passion*, 231. This episode was also common in German drama; cf. Duriez, op. cit., 353-8, and Theo Meier, *Die Gestalt Marias im geistlichen Schauspiel des deutschen Mittelalters* (Berlin, 1959), 199-205.

56 Much more commonly, in the tradition of the *Meditationes* (trans. cit., 326), it is St John who brings the news of Christ's arrest to the Virgin.

57 *English Lyrics of the Thirteenth Century*, ed. Brown, 88.

58 Whilst the description of the weeping women who followed Christ on his way to Calvary (Luke xxiii, 28) perhaps initially suggested the encounter between Christ and the Virgin with her companions (*Meditationes*, 331-2), in meditations and iconography they were not identified; nor were they normally identified in Continental drama. In Greban, for instance, there are four daughters of Jerusalem (each given a proper name) as well as the Virgin and the three other Marys (*Passion*, 314-27). It seems likely that this identification was made out of practical necessity: the exigencies of a small stage and the need to reduce the number of characters for a play which, by English standards at least, already required a large cast.

59 Christ's rebuke was a key text both for Lollards (it is used in the Lollard sermon referred to above, pp. 85, 86) and later Protestants, who denied the value of a compassion for Christ in his sufferings. Some commentators, such as Ludolf (*Vita*, IV, 88-9), explain at length that it should not be interpreted in this way, and soften the harshness of the biblical tone. Mercadé is exceptional amongst dramatists in embodying exegetic comment in the speech so that its effect is less alien (*Passion d'Arras*, 186-7).

60 For the legend see P. Perdrizet, 'De la Véronique et de sainte Véronique', Seminarium Kondakovianum, Prague (1932), 1-15. The incident is included in the three great French *Passions* and Mâle argues that these dramatic representations account for the sudden appearance of St Veronica in late medieval iconographic representations of the road to Calvary (*L'Art religieux de la fin du moyen âge*, 64). The handkerchief bearing the face of Christ appeared amongst the instruments of the Passion; cf. E.E.T.S. 46, 170-3.

61 For the relation of the Latin *planctus* to twelfth-century Latin drama see Young, I, 496-539. For English lyrics see Woolf, op. cit., 249-52.

62 For parallels in the vernacular lyrics, see Brown, *Fifteenth Century Religious Lyrics*, nos 6, 7.

63 The meaning of *Processus talentorum* is the play about the coins or money; since, however, the soldiers do not dice for money, this is an inappropriate description. The probability that for *talentorum* one should read *talorum* (dice) is very strong.

64 Williams, op. cit., 8-9.

65 Ed. Hartl, 227.

66 Cf. *York Plays*, ed. L. T. Smith, xxv.

67 M. G. Frampton, 'The Processus Talentorum (Towneley xxiv)', *P.M.L.A.* lix (1944), 646-54, argued that the Towneley Talents was the lost York play, twice revised at Wakefield, the second revision being partly by the

Wakefield Master. This theory has been denied by Martin Stevens, 'The Composition of the Towneley *Talents* Play: a Linguistic Examination', *J.E.G.Ph.*, lviii (1959), 423–33, who argues on linguistic evidence that the Talents did not originally belong to York. Whilst, even without the linguistic argument, one would not readily accept that Towneley xxiv was substantially the lost York play, it is nevertheless certain that Towneley was influenced by York, for coincidence here would be beyond the bounds of probability.

68 Owst, *Literature and Pulpit* (for page references see Index s.v. *dice-playing*).

69 Mercadé, *Passion*, 191; Greban, *Passion*, 335–6. Duriez points out that the detailed descriptions of the game of dice in many German plays were influenced by the homiletic background (op. cit., 423–4).

70 'et quod beata Virgo propriis suis manibus eam [tunicam] fecerit; et quod cum Jesu crescente paulatim etiam creverit'. *Vita*, IV, 104.

71 Cf. *R.E.S.*, n.s., xiii, 11–12. An *aketoun* was a padded or quilted tunic worn by knights beneath their armour.

72 Cf. *Vita*, IV, 105.

73 Cf. Woolf, op. cit., 395–400.

XII Triumphal and Eschatological Plays

1 For evidence that Chester, Newcastle and Beverley had a play of the Assumption and for the probability that Towneley also included one, see below, p. 409, n. 55, p. 410, n. 57, n. 59.

2 For the *Gospel of Nicodemus* see M. R. James, *The Apocryphal New Testament*, 117–44. There are various translations of it, some verse, some prose, in English, French, German, etc.

3 A number of scriptural texts (all traditionally taken to apply to the Harrowing of Hell) contributed to its iconography: the doors are primarily from Psalm xxiii. 7–10, but the heavy iron locks are from Psalm cvi. 16; both the jaws of leviathan and the cauldron derive from Job xli. In earlier art these features are not realistically related. In the *St Albans Psalter* (ed. cit., pl. 30b), for instance, the broken gates lie before the mouth of hell, but there is no architectural structure into which they once fitted. The artist of the *Holkham Bible Picture Book* has ingeniously ordered these divergent features into a consistent whole that could well have a correspondence upon the stage. For discussions of the iconography of hell see D. C. Stuart, 'The Stage Setting of Hell and the Iconography of the Middle Ages', *Romanic Review*, iv (1913), 330–42, and L. Maeterlinck, 'L'Art et les mystères en Flandres', *Revue de l'art.* xix (1906), 308–18.

4 The emphasis in York, however, upon Christ's bringing of light, 'A light I woll þei have', suggests that perhaps some stage property was used. In art the light was sometimes indicated by the representation of the sun (see for instance the Harrowing of Hell in *St Swithin's Psalter* (E. G. Millar,

English Illuminated Manuscripts from the Xth to the XIIIth Century [Paris and Brussels, 1926], pl. 44), and it would have been easy to hang a painted sun upon the stage at the appropriate moment.

5 *Piers Plowman*, B text, xviii, 304-5.

6 For the theological distinction see the *Summa theologica*, III, lii, 2; cf. Eger, ll. 7592-663 and Alsfeld, ll. 7248-98.

7 This supposition depends upon the view that the present play is not that described in Burton's list of 1415. The latter says, 'Jesus spolians infernum, xii spiritus, [vi] boni et vi mali'. Eleanor Clark has argued ('The York Plays and the *Gospel of Nichodemus*', *P.M.L.A.*, xliii [1928], 156-7) that the inaccuracy of the numbers, if this is the same play (there are seven patriarchs and five devils), is too slight a difference to be significant; moreover ll. 385-400, which require the presence of St Michael, who is not mentioned by Burton, could be a small, late addition (this passage is not in Towneley). But there is something radically odd about Burton's list of *personae*, for it would be strange to use the term *spiritus* generically to refer to two distinct orders of beings, the souls of the patriarchs and the devils: one may compare the description of the Last Judgment where there are 'iv spiritus boni et iv spiritus maligni, et vi diaboli'. It is possible therefore that there was some error in Burton's list, which has been compounded by modern editorial correction (i.e. the insertion of 'vi' before *boni*). The cast of an earlier play could conceivably have included 'xii spiritus boni et vi diaboli'. It may also be remembered that the present York Harrowing is related in literary intention to the play of Pharaoh, which is later than Burton's list (see above, pp. 154, 379, n. 54).

8 For Klosterneuburg see Young, I, 423-5; Duriez (*Théologie*, 512-13) notes only three German plays, the Frankfurt Scenario, Augsburg and Kunzelsau, which place the Harrowing before the Resurrection. Amongst the many German plays to reverse the order are Eger, ll. 7412-697, and Alsfeld, ll. 7028-298.

9 Cf. J. G. Wright, *A Study of the Themes of the Resurrection in the Mediaeval French Drama* (Bryn Mawr, 1935), 84-5; Semur and the late *Passions* place the Harrowing before the Resurrection.

10 The most acceptable theory is that of Duriez (*Théologie*, 512) who assumes it to have sprung from the exigencies of dramatic representation. A commonly stated explanation, however, is that there had been a theological dispute as to whether Christ harrowed hell as a spirit before the Resurrection or in His body after the Resurrection, and that dramatists therefore had the licence to choose. This explanation is given by Wright, op. cit., 84, Young, op. cit., I, 152, n. 1, and by Young's source, W. Meyer, 'Fragmenta Burana', *Festschrift zur Feier des Hundertfünfzigjährigen Bestehens der Königlichen Gesellschaft der Wissenschaften zu Göttingen*: Abhandlungen der philologisch-historischen Klasse, 1901, 62, 99-100. There seems, however, to be no evidence for the existence of such a theological dispute. For an account of patristic and scholastic views on

the Person and the time of the Harrowing see *Dictionnaire de théologie catholique*, s.v. *Descente de Jésus aux enfers*, 585–96. Réau, op. cit., II, ii, 532, also cites the theory of the theological dispute in connection with iconography, but without giving any dates for the latter. The Harrowing of Hell is rare in art until the twelfth century; in the New Testament pictorial sequences of the patristic period it does not occur (one notices its absence, for instance, in the sixth-century mosaics in S. Apollinare Nuovo in Ravenna). In the psalters of the twelfth and thirteenth centuries the position of the Harrowing of Hell is variable. English psalters, such as that of St Albans, place it before the Resurrection, but on the Continent it often appears after the Resurrection or the visit of the three Marys to the tomb, e.g. the *Ingeborg Psalter*, a psalter from Amiens (B.N. MS. lat, 765), and MS. Bibliothèque de l'Arsenal 1186. All of these manuscripts are late enough for the influence of drama to be postulated.

11 *La Passion du Palatinus*, ed. G. Frank, ll. 1235–553 (ed. cit., 48–60). A similar arrangement is found in the fourteenth-century *Salisbury Psalter*, where the order of the miniatures is Crucifixion, Harrowing of Hell, Descent from the Cross, Burial, Resurrection (cf. Leroquais, op. cit., II, 46).

12 Cf. Young, I, 423, 435 and 441.

13 *Passion du Palatinus*, l. 1716; Alsfeld, l. 7036.

14 *Passion*, 381. 'Here the soldiers fall asleep, and then the angels remove the stone from the entrance to the sepulchre; then Christ rises carrying a red cross, and the angels remain seated on the stone from the above-mentioned monument.'

15 The singing of the antiphon 'Christus resurgens' is prescribed by a late marginal note: this note is clearly a good correction and not an innovation, for the soldiers later refer to the *melodie*, and the Towneley version has the stage-direction, 'Tunc cantabunt angeli "Christus resurgens" . . .'. Furthermore, as W. W. Greg noted, the form of the York stage-direction shows that it was accompanied by something, but he wrongly inferred that it was a complaint of the kind found in Towneley and Chester (W. W. Greg, 'Bibliographical and Textual Problems of the English Miracle Cycles', *The Library*, 3rd series, v [1914], 285, n. 1).

16 On the iconography of the Resurrection see H. Schrade, *Ikonographie der christlichen Kunst, Die Auferstehung Christi* (Berlin, 1932), and in particular pls 17, 22, 23, etc. For an English example see *The Luttrell Psalter*, ed. E. G. Millar (London, 1932), pl. 32b. This iconographic form co-existed with more realistic types, in which Christ is in the process of movement or reacts to his surroundings. In the *Holkham Bible Picture Book*, for instance, Christ is gazing to his right at two startled soldiers, whilst in the alabaster tables discussed by Hildburgh (*Archaeologia*, xciii, 90–93 and pl. XXI), Christ as he steps upon the back of a crouching soldier, is obviously caught in a moment of active movement.

17 *The Harrowing of Hell*, ll. 27–30, E.E.T.S. E.S. 100, 4; 'Harde gates I have go', Advocates MS. 18.7.21, f. 119r.

18 *Religious Lyrics of the XVth Century*, ed. Brown, no. 102; cf. Woolf, op. cit., 202-5, for a discussion of the poem and further comment on iconographic parallels.

19 The change of metre in the Chester complaint suggested to Greg that it had been an independent poem (*The Library*, 3rd series, v, 284-5). Only the first stanza, however, is likely to have formed part of an independent lyric; the remainder with its didactic emphasis upon the eucharist is different in content and tone from complaints of the lover-knight or complaints of Christ in general, but resembles the second stanza of the complaint in the *Ludus Coventriae* which is probably an addition of the dramatist. The content is appropriate to a complaint bringing to a close the Passion sequence which began with the Last Supper.

20 Both drama and art vary in the interpretation that they follow. In York the soldiers are frozen with astonished fear, as is seen from ll. 369-70: the stage-direction in L. T. Smith's edition, 'The soldiers sit down and fall asleep', is unfounded; the guard should rather strike attitudes of terror and dismay, as in the *Holkham Bible Picture Book*. In Chester the soldiers seem to be struck into a trance, cf. l. 247, 'but such a slepe on us he [Christ] sett'. It is only in the *Ludus Coventriae* that the soldiers (as in many of the later French plays, Semur, Greban, etc.), grow sleepy and one by one lie down to rest. It may be noted, however, that there is a discrepancy between this scene and the later account of it given by the second soldier to Pilate (ll. 1536-43).

21 There is an inconsistency in the text, in that, whilst Pilate summons four soldiers by name (as in the Continental drama), only three speak: either number is in accord with tradition. One manuscript omits ll. 78-82.

22 As was first pointed out by E. Falke, *Die Quellen des sogenanten Ludus Coventriae* (Leipzig, 1908), 84-5, this treatment of the soldiers is related to that in a poem on the Resurrection (inc. 'When Jhesu was in grave leyd') published by C. Horstmann, 'Nachträge zu den Legenden', *Archiv*, lxxix (1887), 441-7. Falke assumes the poem to be the source of the play, but, in terms of date, either could be the source of the other, or, more probably, both could be indebted to a common original which might well have been French.

23 Cf. É. Picot, 'Le Monologue dramatique dans l'ancient théâtre français', *Romania*, xvi (1887), 518-26, and L. Petit de Julleville, *Répertoire du théâtre comique en France au moyen âge*, 268-70.

24 Cf. Wright, *Resurrection*, 66-9, and Duriez, *Théologie*, 502-4.

25 Alsfeld, ll. 6929-30.

26 For further discussion of this type of characterisation see below, pp. 316, 318.

27 For Klosterneuburg see Young, I, 426; cf. Duriez, *Théologie*, 508.

28 Cf. John A. Yunck, *The Lineage of Lady Meed* (Notre Dame, Indiana), 268-9.

29 Cf. Gregory I, *Homelia in evangelio*, I, x, P.L. 76, 1111 and Leo I, *Sermo* LVII *de Passione Domini*, vi, P.L. 54, 330. For these references and others see *The Christ of Cynewulf*, ed. A. S. Cook (Boston, 1900), 195-7.

30 *Cornish Drama*, I, 467: the centurion here argues Christ's divinity from the marvels accompanying his death. A more agreeable, but non-dramatic, version of the theme occurs in the *Cursor mundi*, E.E.T.S. 62, 959.

31 *Golden Legend*, I, 93–4; *Stanzaic Life*, E.E.T.S., 166, 257–8. The appearance to the Marys is based upon Matthew xxviii. 9–10; Chester follows the *Stanzaic Life*, which harmonises this appearance with that to Mary Magdalene (not recorded by Matthew), by omitting the latter. The appearance to Peter derives from Luke xxiv. 34 and 1 Corinthians, xv, 5; common tradition placed this appearance on Easter Sunday.

32 For various lists see the *Historia scholastica*, P.L. 198, 1637; *Golden Legend*, I, 93–96; Ludolf, *Vita*, IV, 191–245. There were three apocryphal appearances: to the Virgin, to Joseph of Arimathaea and to St James the Less. For Greban and his sources see Roy, *Passion*, 234.

33 Cf. Wright, *Resurrection*, 135, Duriez, *Théologie*, 521–22, and Theo Meier, *Die Gestalt Marias*, 207–9. On the scene in English poetry and art see Woolf, op. cit., 138–9.

34 Ed. Norris, II, 34–41.

35 For the theme of the armour of Christ see *R.E.S.*, n.s., xiii, and for the image of writing on the heart, Woolf, *Religious Lyric*, 163.

36 Cf. G. Cohen, 'La Scène des pèlerins d'Emmaüs', *Études d'histoire du théâtre en France au moyen-âge et à la renaissance* (Paris, 1956), 107–25.

37 Cf. Duriez, *Théologie*, 516–17.

38 *Biblia pauperum*, ed. Berjeau, xxxiii; *Meditatio in passionem*, P.L. 184, 759.

39 The implication of Genesis xxxii. 24–30, is that Jacob recognised the man whom he wrestled with as God when the mysterious stranger blessed him; so in Luke xxiv. 13–32, the disciples constrained (*coegerunt*) their unidentified travelling companion to remain with them and recognised him when he blessed the bread.

40 For references to Mercadé and Greban see Wright, *Resurrection*, 125–6.

41 The *Legenda aurea*, for instance, gives as the fourth reason why Christ appeared first to Mary Magdalene, 'for because that like as a woman was messenger of death, so a woman should be messenger of life', *Golden Legend*, I, 93.

42 Cf. for example, *Religious Lyrics of the Fourteenth Century*, ed. Carleton Brown, no. 84.

43 The use of music throughout the cycles to symbolise divine order and divine intervention is demonstrated by John Stevens, 'Music in Mediaeval Drama', *Proceedings of the Royal Musical Association*, lxxxiv (1957–8), 81–95; for discussion of the theory of heavenly music and of angel-musicians in art see R. Hammerstein, *Die Musik der Engel* (Bern, 1962), and K. Meyer-Baer, *Music of the Spheres and the Dance of Death* (Princeton, 1970).

44 For the iconography of the Ascension see H. Schrade, *Zur Ikonographie der Himmelfahrt Christi* (Leipzig, 1930); cf. Anderson, *Drama and Imagery*, 151–2.

45 This is the interpretation of the *Glossa ordinaria*, P.L. 113, 1306, and the dialogue is set out elaborately in the sermon on the Ascension in the *Legenda aurea* (*Golden Legend*, I, 113-15); cf. *Stanzaic Life*, E.E.T.S. 166, 305-6. Isaiah lxiii is similarly used in the Cornish plays (ed. Norris, II, 188-95); it occurs also in two Provençal plays at the end of the Harrowing of Hell when Christ leads the patriarchs to heaven, cf. Wright, *Resurrection*, 99-104; the argument (loc. cit., 102) that Chester and the Cornish and Provençal plays had a source in common other than the *Legenda aurea* is based on the misleading statement that the Chester Ascension, like the other plays, ends with the welcome of God the Father (a detail not found in the *Legenda aurea*).

46 For the iconography of Pentecost see Stephan Seeliger, *Pfingsten, Die Ausgiessung des Heiligen Geistes am fünfzigsten Tage nach Ostern* (Dusseldorf, 1958); in English iconography the dove may be seen, for instance, in the representation of Pentecost in the *St Albans Psalter*, pl. 33 and *Queen Mary's Psalter*, f. 291.

47 'And I will pray the Father, and he shall give you another Comforter' (*A.V.*); cf. *Sarum Missal*, 160, and *Sarum Breviary*, I, dccccxciv.

48 *Meditationes*, 384.

49 Mercadé, *Passion*, 279; Greban, *Passion*, 435-6.

50 *Golden Legend*, I, 122.

51 Cf. Seeliger, op. cit., 27-9 and pl. 26. The illuminated S is the first letter of the Pentecost versicle, 'Spiritus domini replevit orbem terrarum', cf. *Sarum Missal*, 161.

52 Though the *Legenda aurea* makes the relevant theological point, it seems likely that this is one of the New Testament scenes in which the dramatist drew upon a French source.

53 Both metre and sense indicate that there are two lines missing from Christ's six-line speech. The stage-direction which follows l. 158 is also out of place, since it should clearly come after l. 152, before the beginning of the scene in the heavens.

54 It is possible to re-apportion the monologue so as to eliminate the inconsistency in speaker, the Son beginning to speak from ll. 191ff. It is just possible, however, that the Father's reply originally ended at l. 174, and that the further sixty-four lines, which, apart from their confusion and tediousness, also rather randomly demand the presence of a company of patriarchs and prophets, is a later and inept addition.

55 The lost Beverley and Newcastle cycles also included the Assumption, for records show that the former had a Coronation and the latter a Burial of Our Lady (cf. Chambers, II, 341, 424); neither subject would be performed without the Assumption.

56 In enumerations of the five joys of the Virgin the fourth was her happiness as she beheld the Ascension, and if the list of joys was extended to seven or fifteen, her happiness when she was with the apostles at the descent of the Holy Spirit was included. Medieval iconography almost invariably

recorded her presence on both occasions, though works such as the *Meditationes* describe her presence only at the Ascension (pp. 376–7). For references see Woolf, op. cit., 140.

57 Twelve leaves are missing which would have contained about 1,200 lines. With the ending to the Ascension and the opening of the Last Judgment lost, this would allow for two more plays, most probably those of Pentecost and the Assumption. It has been suggested, on account of the omission of the latter, that these leaves were torn out after the Reformation; cf. Martin Stevens, 'The Missing Parts of the Towneley Cycle', *Speculum*, xlv (1970), 254–65.

58 See further, p. 310 above.

59 A play of the Assumption is included in the banns copied in MS. Harley 2150 and in a list of plays in MS. Harley 2104; cf. W. W. Greg, 'The Lists and Banns of the Plays', *The Trial and Flagellation with other Studies in the Chester Cycle* (The Malone Society Studies, 1935), 137, 171. A curiosity of these texts is that the performance of the plays is attributed to the *wyffys* (or *wyfus*) of Chester instead of one of the gilds. This is difficult to believe. Though women's parts might be occasionally acted by women, the supposition that they acted the parts of the apostles, angels and of Christ is surely impossible. Since the documents giving this information are all sixteenth-century copies of earlier texts, it seems likely that the 'wives' are the 'weavers', the gild which in York acted the Assumption. Admittedly the Chester lists attribute the Last Judgment to the weavers; but in York there were two gilds of weavers (wool and linen) with separate plays, and this could have been so in Chester as well, or it is possible that a careful re-examination of the Chester documents would suggest some other possible source of confusion.

60 *Golden Legend*, IV, 234–41; for a translation of the Latin text attributed to Melito see James, *Apocryphal New Testament*, 209–16.

61 It is certain that the play of the Assumption had an origin distinct from that of the rest of the cycle, since it is written on different paper and in a different hand, cf. *The Assumption of the Virgin. A Miracle Play from the N-Town Cycle*, ed. W. W. Greg (Oxford, 1915), 5. It should also be noted that the Proclamation does not mention the Assumption, though it includes all the plays on the conception and early life of the Virgin.

62 D'Ancona, *Origini*, I, 282.

63 Salter, *Mediaeval Drama*, 50; Anna J. Mill, 'The York Plays of the Dying, Assumption and Coronation of Our Lady', *P.M.L.A.*, lxv (1950), 870–1.

64 Comparison may be made between the Assumption of the *Ludus Coventriae* and that of the York cycle written for performance on a wagon. Whereas in the opening of the former an angel descends from the heavens to the temple where Mary is at prayer, in the latter the angel is already present with Mary when the play begins. Again in the *Ludus Coventriae*, at the death of Mary, Christ *cum omni celesti curia* descends and re-ascends (though the latter is not specified); in York it is not entirely clear what

happens (there could be no movement at all), but at most Christ alone descends and re-ascends.

65 Cf. Shergold, *Spanish Stage*, 66–7 and 78–80; for an account of a modern but traditional performance of the Assumption from Elche, see F. Pedrell, *La Festa d'Elche* (Documents pour servir à l'histoire des origines du théâtre musical, Paris, 1906).

66 Cf. Shull, *P.M.L.A.*, lii, 957–65; the earliest reference to the play in the expense accounts is 1458–9 but the play could be earlier.

67 The two stage-directions read, 'hic cantabunt organa' and 'et hic assendent in celum cantantibus organis'. The meaning of *organa* is uncertain as it can refer either to the organ or to a consort of musical instruments. If the play was performed in church, then the organ could have been meant.

68 Cf. Yvonne Rokseth in *Ars Nova and the Renaissance 1300–1540*, ed. Dom Anselm Hughes and Gerald Abraham (Oxford, 1960), 412–14.

69 Both the question (from Canticles viii. 5) and the answer are part of the liturgy for the feast of the Assumption, cf. *Sarum Breviary*, ii, 688–9.

70 *Laude drammatiche, e rappresentazioni sacre*, ed. V. de Bartholomaeis (Florence, 1943), I, 381–97.

71 For references to this play see A. J. Mill in *P.M.L.A.*, lxv (1950), 866–76.

72 A helpful account of the antecedents to this play is given by Carolyn Wall, 'The Apocryphal and Historical Backgrounds of "The Appearance of Our Lady to Thomas" (Play XLVI of the York Cycle)', *Mediaeval Studies*, xxxii (1970), 172–92.

73 It may be noted that in the play of the Assumption and Coronation no apostles guard the tomb of the Virgin, though their presence is described in the *Transitus Mariae*, and normally in all subsequent works, whether pictorial, narrative or dramatic. Since their presence would have led to a glaring discrepancy between the two plays if acted successively, the omission of them seems too fortunate to be a matter of chance.

74 For English examples see E. G. Millar, *English Illuminated Manuscripts of the XIVth and XVth Centuries* (Paris and Brussels, 1928), pls 1, 13, 23, 29, 35 and 38.

75 The concluding lines of the play (ll. 111–60) should all be assigned to Christ, though the manuscript assigns them to six angels. L. T. Smith observes that the five joys should be narrated by Christ, but she emends the text minimally and her footnote is confusing.

76 A useful survey of plays about the Antichrist is provided by E. Roy, *Le Jour du jugement* (Paris, 1902), 175–203.

77 Mätzner, *Altenglische Sprachproben*, II, 232.

78 *Golden Legend*, I, 12–17; W. Heist, *The Fifteen Signs before Doomsday* (East Lansing, 1952), 168–9, gives the *Legenda aurea* as the source of the Chester Fifteen Signs.

79 Ezekiel xxxvii, 1–14, provides the chief Old Testament prophecy of the general Resurrection: in the type of concordance where an item of the creed was assigned to an apostle and accompanied by a prophecy, part of

Ezekiel xxxvii. 12 corresponded to the Resurrection of the dead (for references see p. 358, n. 24 above). This passage from Ezekiel also provided the *lectiones* in the York Breviary for the last Sunday before Advent (Advent was associated with the Last Judgment). Ezekiel had also provided the source for what in Chester and in the *Legenda aurea* is the Eleventh Sign, i.e. the opening of the sepulchres.

80 For an account of the Antichrist legend see W. Bousset, *The Antichrist Legend*, trans. A. H. Keane (London, 1896); Roy, *Le Jour du jugement*, 7–48; Urban Lucken, *Antichrist and the Prophets of Antichrist in the Chester Cycle* (Washington, 1940).

81 For the Lucerne play see K. Reuschel, *Die deutschen Weltgerichtsspiele des Mittelalters und der Reformationszeit* (Leipzig, 1906), 209–320; a helpful analysis is given by Duriez, *Théologie*, 594–610.

82 Rudolf Klee, *Das mittelhochdeutsche Spiel vom jüngsten Tage* (Marburg, 1906), 69–81.

83 For a discussion of the Signs and of the works enumerating them see Heist, *The Fifteen Signs*, and *Les quinze Signes du jugement dernier*, ed. Erik von Kraemer (Commentationes humanarum litterarum, Societas Scientiarum Fennica, 1966).

84 Cf. F. Harrison, *The Painted Glass of York* (London, 1927), 177–9 and pl. facing p. 178.

85 Cf. E.E.T.S. E.S. 87 (1957), 99.

86 Petit de Julleville, *Les Mystères*, ii, 460–1. This play remains unprinted.

87 *Die Kildare-Gedichte*, ed. W. Heuser (Bonn, 1904), 100–5; *The Minor Poems of John Lydgate*, ed. H. N. MacCracken (E.E.T.S. E.S. 107, 117–20).

88 *Sarum Missal*, 342.

89 The legend of the Antichrist lent itself to topical application, often of a chiliastic kind, and thus used was a favourite theme of the Middle Ages. The Tegernsee *Antichrist* is usually assumed to have some political content (cf. Young, ii, 390–3); a later German play, *Des Entkrist Vasnacht* (*Fastnachtspiele*, ed. A. von Keller, ii [Stuttgart, 1853], 593–608) is a satire on greed and avarice in various walks of society. Sixteenth-century plays of the Antichrist are part of the religious polemic of the period, and matter of this kind seems to have been added to the Chester expositor's speeches (cf. stanza 30 of the banns).

90 *Le Jour du jugement*, for instance, begins with a council of devils, during which Angingnars takes upon himself the enterprise of begetting the Antichrist, and there follows a scene between Angingnars and the mother of Antichrist (ed. Roy, 218–22).

91 *The Apocalypse of St John the Divine from a manuscript* [*Auct. D. iv. 17*] *in the Bodleian Library* (Roxburghe Club, 1876), ff. 8v–9v. For illustrations of the Antichrist in illuminated manuscripts of the Apocalypse see M. R. James, *The Trinity College Apocalypse* (Roxburghe Club, 1909), 9. The Bodleian manuscript presents an interesting parallel to Chester in its illustration of the Antichrist's miracle against nature of making trees

grow upside down with flower-bearing roots: though Heist, op. cit., 93–4, has been shown by Kraemer (*Les quinze Signes du jugement dernier*, 23–4) to be wrong in associating this miracle exclusively with an Irish tradition, this pictorial emphasis upon it has not been noticed.

92 The only other instance of this that Lucken was able to find (op. cit., 55) is in *The Pricke of Conscience*, v, 4290–5: even this, however is not an exact parallel, since Chester xxiii, 193–6 (with the following stage-direction and Latin words, which are an adaptation of Ezekiel xviii. 31), is a blasphemous travesty of Chester xx, 65–9, which dramatises the first occasion on which Christ bestows the holy spirit upon the apostles (cf. John xx. 22), not of Pentecost.

93 Chief amongst the biblical authorities for the trumpets of the Last Judgment are Zephaniah i. 16 (part of the passage on which the *Dies irae* is based) and 1 Corinthians xv. 52.

94 Cf. p. 410, n. 57, above.

95 Cf., for instance, *Le Jour du jugement*, where the damned consist of bishop, abbess, king, bailiff, provost, lawyer, queen, usurer, and the usurer's wife, servant and child: almost identical characters are found in the Dance of Death, cf. *La Danse macabré*, ed. E. F. Chaney (Manchester, 1945), and E.E.T.S. 181.

96 Amongst almost innumerable examples are the twelfth-century tympanum at Autun, a twelfth-century English psalter (MS. B.N. lat. 10433) and the Last Judgments of Roger van der Weyden and Memling. An unsatisfactory compromise sometimes found between the theologically appropriate nudity and a desire to indicate social position, was to give to the dead their appropriate headdress, papal or royal crowns, mitres, etc. An example is the Last Judgment of the *Holkham Bible Picture Book*, f. 42r.

97 Cf. *Summa theologica, Supplementum*, lxxxviii, 4.

98 For accounts of the iconography of the Last Judgment see, amongst many, the following works: Mâle, *L'Art religieux du xiie siècle*, 406–19, Réau, op. cit., II, ii, 731–57; Jean Fournée, *Le Jugement dernier* (Paris, 1964).

99 Cf. *Jour du jugement*, ll. 830–7; Kunzelsau, ed. cit., 213, etc.

100 This theme was condemned in the sixteenth century, but it is interesting to note that, according to Caiger-Smith, the figure of the Virgin was obliterated from a wall-painting of the Last Judgment at Penn, Buckinghamshire, in about 1460 (*English Mediaeval Mural Paintings*, 35).

101 Cf. ll. 185–216.

102 The supposition that the angels were present is supported by the angelic singing prescribed by the final stage-direction.

103 The Chester stage-direction (p. 440) reads: 'Stabunt Angeli cum Cruce, Corona, Spinea, lancea, aliisque Instrumentis, omnia demonstrantes'. It is clear from the silence of the stage-directions that angels with the instruments of the Passion are not included in the *Ludus Coventriae*: neither are the apostles, except for St Peter, who keeps the gates of heaven. This role for St Peter is rare in the iconography of the twelfth and thirteenth centuries,

NOTES TO PAGES 297–303

but became fairly common by the fourteenth, cf. Millard Meiss, *French Painting in the Time of Jean de Berry* (London, 1967), I, 68 and n. 8, p. 377; amongst the Last Judgments to include it is that in *Queen Mary's Psalter*.

104 The seven works of mercy are the six enumerated in Matthew xxv. 35–6, to which was added in the Middle Ages the burial of the dead from Tobit i. 21. In the York play the visiting of those in prison has become obscured through a textual error, which I have corrected on the basis of Towneley, emending *presse* to *prison*. It will also be noted that York does not include the seventh and additional work: this could be on account of fidelity to Matthew, but perhaps also because the burial of the dead is awkward in the first-person structure. Chester abandons the list after the first three, and the *Ludus Coventriae* successfully includes it only because the first person form has not been adopted, 'To bery the deed pore man wold ȝe not gon'.

105 In Continental drama the theme of the seven deadly sins is introduced in a variety of ways: in the Middle High German play of the Last Judgment, Christ in his address to the saved first praises them for not having committed the seven deadly sins (ed. Klee, 89–90); in the *Dì del Giudizio* of Feo Belcari, the rejection of the damned is followed by pairs of speeches between wicked souls, each guilty of one of the seven deadly sins, and good souls, each saved through one of the opposing virtues (*Rappresentazioni Sacre*, ed. A. D'Ancona, III [Florence, 1872], 511–17); in a late Provençal Last Judgment personifications of the seven deadly sins are taken off to hell (*Mystères provençaux du XVe siècle*, ed. Jeanroy and Teulié, 255–83). Clifford Davidson, 'An Interpretation of the *Wakefield Judicium*', *Annale Medievale*, x (1969), 117, draws attention to a semi-allegorical Judgment at Trotton, Sussex, in which the good man is surrounded by little scenes of the seven works of mercy and the bad man by scenes of the seven deadly sins; cf. Caiger-Smith, *English Mediaeval Mural Paintings*, 51, 53, and pl. xviii.

106 The stage-direction reads, 'Et sic facit finem cum melodia angelorum transiens a loco ad locum'. Christ evidently returns to the higher stage from which he has descended for the second scene; whilst the stage-direction does not specify that the apostles and the saved mounted with him, the final tableau would be odd if they remained below.

107 Cf. Kunzelsau, 197–202.

108 E.g. the *Tragedia des jüngstens Gerichts* of Hans Sachs (1558) and *Ein gar schöne Christliche und liebliche Comedia von dem letzten Tage des jüngsten Gerichts* of Philip Agricola (1573); cf. Roy, *Jour du jugement*, 190–1.

XIII The Four Cycles

1 For the documents which name Higden as author, see Salter, *Mediaeval Drama in Chester*, 37–8; for the alternative attribution to Henry Francis, see below, p. 415, n. 6.

2 See above, pp. 169, 172 and 195, 196.

3 Burton's list of 1415 is printed in the edition of L. T. Smith, pp. xix–xxvii the second, undated list, is most recently printed by M. G. Frampton, 'The Date of the "Wakefield Master" Bibliographical Evidence', *P.M.L.A.*, liii (1938), 102–3. The descriptions in the second list are usually too brief for changes of substance within the plays to be detected.

4 Whereas in the play there are two servants, the list gives only one, *garcio cum bosco* (ed. cit., xx).

5 Frampton's plausible argument (loc. cit., 93–7) that the Appearance to Mary Magdalene is a later revision rests firstly upon the inaccurate description of the play in Burton's list as 'Jesus, Maria Magdalena cum aromatibus', and secondly upon comparison with Towneley xxvi, where a briefer treatment of the subject concludes this play of the Resurrection. It seems possible that originally the York Resurrection (which is long for an unrevised play) was divided in such a way that the second half included the Visit to the Sepulchre (hence the spices) and the Appearance to Mary Magdalene.

6 This attribution is made in William Newhall's Proclamation of 1532 (Salter, op. cit., 33) and Salter finds it acceptable (ibid., 41–2). Theo Stemmler, 'Zur Datierung der *Chester Plays*', *Germanisch-Romanische Monatsschrift*, xlix (*N.F.*, xviii, 1968), 308–13, also accepts this attribution, but argues that the plays were written during the pontificate of Clement VI (1342–52), this earlier date being more possible than Salter supposed because he had confused two men of the name of Henry Francis, one a Benedictine monk who was senior enough to sign documents between 1377–82, the other a Carmelite who was made papal chaplain in 1389. As Salter reasonably maintained, the attribution to Henry Francis, unlike that to the famous Randolf Higden, will not have been an invention obvious for the sixteenth century, but there is nothing to rule out the possibility that it is a false attribution of earlier origin or, more probably, represents a sixteenth-century embellishment of some earlier reference to Henry Francis. It would indeed be fortunate if a correct attribution had survived over a period of 150 to 200 years.

7 Cf. Baugh, *Schelling Anniversary Studies*, 35–63, and p. 371, n. 18 above. The exact date at which the *Mystère du viel testament* was composed is not known, but no French scholar has disputed the judgment of its editor, James de Rothschild, that it took its present shape in the course of the fifteenth century and should be associated with the *Passions* composed c. 1450; cf. *Le Mystère du viel testament*, i, iv, vii–viii.

8 It should be noted that if Stemmler's conjecture that the Chester plays were written between 1342 and 1352 is correct, then it is likely that the New Testament series was also entirely rewritten, as this date would scarcely be consonant with the influence of the *Stanzaic Life of Christ* (cf. E.E.T.S. 166, xlii–xliii).

9 French influences on post-Old Testament subjects can be chiefly seen in

plays, such as the Harrowing of Hell, Pentecost and the Last Judgment, where the *Stanzaic Life* could not provide a model.

10 *Specimens of the Pre-Shakspearean Drama*, ed. J. M. Manly (Boston, 1897), I, 353–85.

11 For analyses of these discrepancies and resultant theories see E.E.T.S. E.S. 120, xi–xxxv, Esther L. Swenson, *An Enquiry into the Composition and Structure of Ludus Coventriae* (Minneapolis, 1914), and Kenneth Cameron and Stanley J. Kahrl, 'Staging of the N-Town Cycle', *Theatre Notebook*, xxi (1966–7), 122–38, 152–65.

12 *The Digby Mysteries*, 1–24.

13 Cf. Swenson, op. cit., 51. There is an *explicit* and space left blank at this point in the manuscript, and, unlike those of the Passion play, the stage-directions from here on are brief and in Latin (those of the Resurrection sequence are mixed, sometimes English, sometimes Latin).

14 Ibid., 35–6.

15 If the Contemplacio sequence were a self-contained play, it would be without parallel. The *Sündenfall* (see above, p. 354, n. 45), which begins with the Fall of Man, ends at the Presentation in the Temple: otherwise all those beginning with the Conception of the Virgin extend to the Nativity or beyond. The supposition that the Contemplacio group was originally a St Anne's Day play (cf. Craig, *English Religious Drama*, 79–80) is probable in itself, since this feast of 26 July would provide a convenient summer occasion for performing a Nativity play it would not, however, justify the exclusion of the Nativity. In France St Anne's Day was a common alternative to Whitsun for the performance of the *Passions*, and in England the St Anne's Day cycle, of which the Digby Massacre of the Innocents and Purification is the only surviving part, extended at very least to Christ before the Doctors.

16 In the last stanza of the Proclamation (l. 527) the *vexillatores* announce a performance of the play 'In N. town', the N standing for a proper name to be inserted, as appropriate, by the speaker; for similar contemporary usages see *N.E.D.*, s.v. *N*, 2.

17 Norwich was suggested by Chambers (op. cit., II, 421). The dialect, which is that of Norfolk, would support this theory (cf. E. J. Dobson, *Medium Aevum*, IX [1940], 152), as would the fact that the late Norwich plays of the Fall of Man show peculiarities of treatment, which, amongst surviving texts, associate them exclusively with the play of the Fall in the *Ludus Coventriae* (see above, p. 117). As against this, however, there are some major differences between the contents of the *Ludus Coventriae* and that of the Norwich cycle insofar as it can be reconstructed (cf. E.E.T.S. S.S., I xxix–xxx). Furthermore, whilst there is no evidence that the Norwich cycle was ever acted other than by the trade gilds, there is no evidence that the *Ludus Coventriae* ever existed in a version divisible into small acting units. The arguments for supposing the *Ludus Coventriae* to be the lost Lincoln cycle have been set out by Craig (op. cit., 265–80) and reaffirmed with

additional detail by Kenneth Cameron and Stanley J. Kahrl, 'The N-Town Plays at Lincoln', *Theatre Notebook*, xx (1965), 61–9. Differences in dialect are not an obstacle to this theory since the Cotton manuscript is not an official register of plays (see above, p. 309). But so much remains obscure about the method of performing the Lincoln plays and the history of the *Ludus Coventriae* is so conjectural, that this identification, though attractive, remains very uncertain. Since this chapter was written the provenance of the *Ludus Coventriae* has been discussed by Mark Eccles, '*Ludus Coventriae*: Lincoln or Norfolk?', *Medium Aevum*, xl (1971), 135–41.

18 For the evidence that the manuscript of the Towneley plays is a register, see Cawley, *The Wakefield Pageants*, xii–xvii.

19 For the Chester banns see F. M. Salter, 'The Banns of the Chester Plays', *R.E.S.*, xv (1939), 432–57, and xvi (1940), 1–17, 137–48. The Beverley record is quoted by A. F. Leach, 'Some English Plays and Players, 1220–1548', *An English Miscellany presented to Dr Furnivall*, 215.

20 It has been argued by Esther Swenson, op. cit., and Craig, op. cit., 243–9, that the banns describe the cycle at its earliest stage. Their arguments derive from the fact that four subjects are omitted in the banns, namely, the Conception, the Presentation in the Temple, the Purification and Assumption, and two subjects, the Trial of Joseph and Mary and the Nativity, are enumerated in a different metre: all these are therefore said to be later additions. But a cycle, which contained a Betrothal, so large that it was in two parts, but no Nativity or Purification would be so freakish, that it is difficult to believe that it sprang from conscious literary design at any period. More interesting is the problem of the relationship of the banns to the Passion sequence, for it would be helpful to know whether they relate to a different version, divided into acting units, or whether a not very competent versifier has simply done the best he could to divide the action up into individual stanzas of narrative, arbitrarily numbering them as he went along. The difficulty lies in the fact that, on the one hand the banns preserve some of the distinctive features of the existing Passion play, the division of the Harrowing of Hell into two parts and Christ's Appearance to the Virgin, whilst on the other hand they omit obvious features, such as the Trial before Herod (which would readily make a narrative unit), whilst giving a stanza to Judas's suicide, which has only eight lines of text. The problem is irresolvable, but it is worth noting that the banns mention the presence of 'thre þevys' in the first trial before Pilate, whereas in the text they appear in their proper place during the second trial, when the presence of Barabbas will be relevant to the action. The banns at this point cannot relate correctly to any version, and it therefore seems that whoever wrote the banns had only a partial grasp of the material that he was asked to put into verse. It is therefore reasonable to conclude that when the banns relate correctly to the text, this is significant, but when incorrectly, nothing can be inferred from this, since the discrepancy may have resulted from the incompetence of the versifier.

21 Cf. W. W. Greg, *Bibliographical and Textual Problems of the English Miracle Cycles* (London, 1914), 143.

22 The changes in paper, indicated by differences in watermark, are fully set out by the editor (E.E.T.S. E.S., 120, xi–xv). Whilst it is possible to build too elaborate a theory about the antecedent history of the text from this kind of evidence, it is clear that the fact that part I of the Passion play and part II (up to l. 1243) are written respectively on paper of different watermarks from the rest of the cycle, indicates that they were written both at a different time from the cycle and at a different time from each other.

23 This classification is only approximate. Cain and Abel could, for instance, be included among the plays of the Wakefield Master, whilst the list of plays showing major and distinctive revision could be extended.

24 For the history of Wakefield see J. W. Walker, *Wakefield, its History and People* (Wakefield, 1939).

25 Cf. Marie C. Lyle, *The Original Identity of the York and Towneley Cycles* (Minneapolis, 1919).

26 For the evidence that the York Pharaoh, the Doctors, the Harrowing of Hell and the Last Judgment were all revised after 1415, see above, p. 379, n. 54, p. 405, n. 7 and p. 296; for the Resurrection see Frampton, *P.M.L.A.*, liii, 93–7. Frampton also shows that other Towneley plays, such as the Magi, were influenced by York plays revised after 1415, and he plausibly concludes that York exerted its main influence between 1415 and some point in the third decade of the century.

27 Cf. Cawley, *Wakefield Pageants*, xiii.

XIV The Decline of the Plays

1 *The Digby Mystery Plays*, 53–136.

2 Cf. Erich Auerbach, *Literary Language and its Public in Late Latin Antiquity and in the Middle Ages*, trans. R. Manheim (London, 1965), 25–66.

3 Cf. Greg, *Trial and Flagellation*, 159 (referred to by Kolve, op. cit., 31). For the same type of phenomenon in France see Raymond Lebègue, *Le Mystère des Actes des Apôtres* (Paris, 1929), 163–7, and in Germany, Joseph E. Gillett, 'The German Dramatist of the sixteenth century and his Bible', *P.M.L.A.* xxxiv (1919), 486–7, 490–2.

4 A useful account of Luther's views on religious drama is given by Hugo Holstein, *Die Reformation im Spiegelbilde der dramatischen Literatur des sechzehnten Jahrhunderts* (Halle, 1886), 18–25, but with unclear references. All the following references are to the Weimar edition (1883 ff.). Luther's comment upon the suitability of plays about the life of Christ for schoolchildren will be found in his letter to Nikolaus Hausmann (2 April 1530), *Briefwechsel*, v, 271–2, and upon the Passion in *Duo sermones de Passione Christi*, *Werke*, i, 342. Luther was more positive in his approval of plays

based upon the Old Testament, and in the introductions to his translations of the Bible and Apocrypha and in the Table-talk classified the book of Judith as itself a tragedy and that of Tobit as a comedy, cf. *Die deutsche Bibel*, xii, 6, 108, and *Tischreden*, i, 338; iii, 138.

5 *Opera quae supersunt omnia*, ed. G. Baum, E. Cunitz, and E. Reuss, xxviii (*Corpus Reformatorum*, lvi, Brunswick, 1885), 18; for this reference and further comment upon Calvin's attitude to plays see E. K. Chambers, *The Elizabethan Stage* (Oxford, 1923), i, 245–8.

6 Jacques Grévin, *Théâtre complet et poésies choisies*, ed. Lucien Pinvert (Paris, 1922), 51, cited by Petit de Julleville, op. cit., i, 446.

7 For a brief account of these poets and bibliographical references see F. J. E. Raby, *A History of Christian-Latin Poetry, from the beginnings to the Close of the Middle Ages* (2nd ed., Oxford, 1953), 17–18, 77–79, 108–10.

8 E.E.T.S., 57, 8–15.

9 See Barbara Lewalski, *Milton's Brief Epic. The Genre, Meaning, and Art of Paradise Regained* (Providence, Rhode Island and London), 79–80.

10 P.L. 19, 31.

11 Cf. Raymond Lebègue, *La Tragédie religieuse en France. Les Débuts (1514–1573)* (Paris, 1929), 135, and for Aldus Manutius see Lewalski, op. cit., 54, 375, n. 55.

12 *Joseph* (Antwerp, 1536), A 8; cf. Lebègue, op. cit., 477, n. 2. On the play see Charles E. Herford, *Studies in the Literary Relations of England and Germany in the Sixteenth Century* (Cambridge, 1886), 86–7, and Marvin T. Herrick, *Tragicomedy* (repr. Urbana, 1954), 31–3.

13 For a bibliographical list of subsequent editions and references to Hrotsvitha see E. H. Zeydel, 'A Chronological Hrotsvitha Bibliography through 1700 with Annotations', *J.E.G.Ph.*, xlvi (1947), 29–94.

14 Cf. Lebègue, op. cit., 467–8, where he notes that Theodore Beza and Christopher Stymmelius (both authors of a play on the Sacrifice of Isaac) refer to the *Christos paschōn* as an example of Christian drama; so also did Grotius in his preface to *Christus patiens* (Leyden, 1608). It is possible that when Crocus in 1536 named Gregory Nazianzenus in conjunction with Prudentius, etc. (see n. 12 above) he was referring only to the poetry printed by Manutius.

15 The *Jephthae* has been edited and translated by F. H. Fobes (Newark, Del., 1928). For quotations from and comment upon Christopherson's various statements of dramatic theory see Frederick S. Boas, *University Drama in the Tudor Age* (Oxford, 1914), 47–9.

16 L. R. Merrill, *The Life and Poems of Nicholas Grimald* (Yale Studies in English, 69, 1925), 102–5.

17 Cf. Boas, op. cit., 28–9, and for Barptholomaeus, Lebègue, op. cit., 169–89.

18 For medieval influences on Grimald see G. C. Taylor, 'The *Christus Redivivus* of Nicholas Grimald and the Hegge Resurrection Plays', *P.M.L.A.*, xli (1926), 840–59, and Patricia Abel, 'Grimald's *Christus redivivus* and the Digby Resurrection Play', *M.L.N.*, lxx (1955), 328–30.

19 Lebègue, op. cit., 187.

20 Dodsley's *Old English Plays*, revised by W. C. Hazlitt, II (1874), 185-264.

21 *The Stonyhurst Pageants*, ed. Carleton Brown (Göttingen and Baltimore, 1920), 263-302; cf. Hardin Craig, 'Terentius Christianus and the Stonyhurst Pageants', *P.Q.*, ii (1923), 56-62, and *English Religious Drama*, 371-3.

22 The *Theoandrathanatos* was first printed in Milan in 1508; for comment see Lebègue, op. cit., 129-42.

23 On this work see Lebègue, op. cit., 123-8.

24 The *Christus patiens* was first published in Leyden in 1608; an English translation was made by George Sandys and published in 1640.

25 Wild's *Passionsspiel* was published in a collection of his plays, *Schoner Comedien und Tragedien swolff* (Augsburg, 1566); for a more recent edition see *Das Oberammergauer Passionsspiel in seiner ältesten Gestalt*, ed. August Hartmann (Leipzig, 1880), 103-83. For Grimald's influence on Wild see Johannes Bolte, 'Nicholas Grimald und das Oberammergauer Passionsspiel', *Archiv*, cv (1900), 1-9, and Merrill, op. cit., 68-89. Wild's *Passionsspiel* was heavily drawn upon in the text of the Oberammergau Passion play used until 1740.

26 Cf. Lily B. Campbell, *Divine Poetry and Drama in Sixteenth-century England* (Cambridge, 1959), 167-9.

27 Cf. Craig, op. cit., 369. Bale, though a Protestant, was sensitive to some of the moving, dramatic qualities of medieval drama. He has, for instance, been successfully influenced by the medieval portrayal of the patriarchs' urgent longings for the Redemption in his play, *God's Promises*, in which seven typical figures, Adam, Noah, Abraham, Moses, David, Isaiah and John the Baptist, call in turn for mercy and after each plea one of the Advent O's is sung (*The Dramatic Writings*, ed. J. S. Farmer [London, 1907], 85-125).

28 'The Latin Drama of the Renaissance (1340-1640)', *Studies in the Renaissance*, iv (1957), 41. For a more detailed consideration of the story of David and his sons see Inga-Stina Ewbank, 'The House of David', *Renaissance Drama*, viii (1965), 3-40; for Susanna see M. T. Herrick, 'Susanna and the Elders in Sixteenth-century Drama', *Studies in Honor of T. W. Baldwin*, ed. D. C. Allen (Urbana, 1958), 125-35; the same author in *Tragicomedy*, 31-7, gives a brief account of some plays on the subject of Joseph, whilst a full list of both Latin and vernacular plays on the subject of the sacrifice of Isaac is given in the second volume of the *Mystère du viel testament* (S.A.T.F., 1879), xii-xxvi.

29 H. S. Symmes, *Les Débuts de la critique dramatique en Angleterre* (Paris, 1903), 36, notes that Buchanan is mentioned by Ascham, Gosson, Sidney, Webbe, and Wilmot; for some of these references and others see *Elizabethan Critical Essays*, ed. Gregory Smith (Oxford, 1904), I, 24 (Ascham), 68 (Lodge), 194 and 201 (Sidney), II, 322 (Meres). For an account of Buchanan's work see Lebègue, op cit., 195-254.

30 The most recent edition of Beza's play is that of K. Cameron, K. M. Hall

and F. Higman (Geneva, 1967); Golding's translation has been edited by M. W. Wallace (Toronto, 1906).

31 'A Humanist's "trew imitation": Thomas Watson's Absalom', ed. and trans. J. H. Smith (*Illinois Studies in Language and Literature*, 52, 1964). Boas, op. cit., 62–4, 352–65, gives a brief analysis, whilst doubting whether the extant play is Watson's. Smith, however, has shown the manuscript to be in Watson's own writing.

32 Cf. Peter Dronke, *Poetic Individuality in the Middle Ages*, 115. For a useful enumeration and account of works on the subject of Jephtha, medieval, Renaissance and modern, see W. O. Sypherd, *Jephtha and his Daughter. A Study in Comparative Literature* (Newark, Del., 1948).

33 *European Literature and the Latin Middle Ages*, 462.

34 For Grimald's use of the five-act structure in his two plays see T. W. Baldwin, *William Shakespeare's Five-Act Structure* (Urbana, 1947), 350–2.

35 The part assigned to Alecto has its origins ultimately in *Aeneid*, VII, though Grimald borrowed the figure more immediately from the *Christus Xylonicus* of Barptholomaeus in which Alecto (taking the place of *Desesperaunce*) tempts Judas to suicide; cf. Lebègue, op. cit., 180, n. 3, and also Lewalski, op. cit., 56–7 and 65.

36 The keeping of vows was an issue in the religious polemics of the sixteenth century; cf. Lebègue, op. cit., 230–1. Christopherson in his *Jephthae* takes the Roman Catholic view that a vow once made must be kept, in its literary context a simplistic position which weakens the work.

37 Cf. Petit de Julleville, I, 450. For the personifying of the blood of Abel see above, p. 374, n. 56, and the stage-direction in the register from Mons (G. Cohen, *Le Livre de conduite du régisseur pour le Mysterè de la Passion joué à Mons en 1501* [Paris, 1925], 15–16).

38 Lebègue, op. cit., 54.

39 *The Survey of Cornwall*, ed. F. E. Halliday (London, 1953), 145; the story is quoted in Robert Longsworth, *The Cornish Ordinalia* (Cambridge, Mass., 1967), 105.

40 *Chant*, III, 85–6. This much-quoted passage may be found, for instance, in Petit de Julleville, I, 412.

41 On the suppression of the English plays see Gardiner, *Mysteries' End*, 65–93.

42 Since this chapter was written a very useful account of English sixteenth-century biblical drama has been published: Ruth H. Blackburn, *Biblical Drama under the Tudors* (The Hague and Paris, 1971).

Appendix A *The Shrewsbury Fragments and the Plays of the Burial and Resurrection*

1 The most recent edition of these fragmentary plays is in *Non-Cycle Plays and Fragments*, ed. Norman Davis, and it is from this that all quotations are taken. Professor Davis has not sought to reconstruct the original outlines

of the play: his text is therefore complementary to Young's (II, 514–20), which provides a fairly convincing but necessarily conjectural presentation of the Fragments.

2 For the contents of the manuscript see Young, II, 520–1. The opening pages contain some miscellaneous pieces: Psalm cxiii. 6, with an appended alleluia (the whole psalm with an alleluia after each verse was part of the Easter mass, cf. *Sarum Missal*, 137), and some responsories and proses for the office of the Holy Innocents. The only other non-processional piece is the part of the Jews from the Holy Week Passions. For the custom of copying liturgical plays in processionals see p. 21 above.

3 See above, p. 19.

4 Ed. cit., xix–xxii.

5 Cf. Young, I, 382.

6 Ibid., 349.

7 *Vita*, IV, 184.

8 Cf. F. C. Gardiner, *The Pilgrimage of Desire: A Study of Theme and Genre in Medieval Literature* (Leiden, 1971), 89–97.

9 See above, p. 280.

10 See above, p. 281.

11 Cf. Gardiner, op. cit., *passim*.

12 Cf. *Glossa ordinaria*, P.L. 114, 352–3 and *Catena aurea*, II, 314.

13 *Vita*, IV, 210.

14 Réau, op. cit., II, ii, 563, notes that artists often conceived the Supper at Emmaus as *une communion eucharistique*.

15 Ed. cit., 408. Roy, op. cit., 236, cites this as one of the details in the *Passion* influenced by the *Postilla* of Nicholas of Lyra. Cf. *Purity*, ll. 1105–8.

16 The *Gloria* is necessarily included in all the vernacular plays, and the shepherds' journey to Bethlehem remained a possible occasion for liturgical singing; see, for instance, p. 183 above.

17 For fuller discussion see Woolf, *English Religious Lyric*, 263. I there assumed that the Burial had been written as a meditation and that an adaptor had excised the narrative links in order to make it suitable for acting. The possibility, however, remains that the corrector was not adapting but restoring the text to its original form. It may be noted that the Resurrection was either written as a play with a rubric specifying liturgical singing or it has been indetectably adapted for performance. The presence of vernacular rubrics in the Burial and of Latin rubrics in the Resurrection suggests a slightly different textual history, though they are surely two parts of a single work. The more plausible theory now seems to me to be that the works were written for performance in church, but that their meditative character (see below) made them highly suitable for devotional reading and that they were subsequently copied for this purpose.

18 Cf. Young, I, 164–5.

19 Cf. *English Religious Lyric*, 264–5.

20 Cf. Mâle, *L'Art religieux de la fin du moyen âge en France*, 383.

21 'Egressus foras flevit amare, fugiens in caveam, quae modo Gallicantus apellatur', *Historia scholastica*, P.L. 198, 1624 (cf. *The Southern Passion*, ed. Beatrice Daw Brown, E.E.T.S. 169, lxvi). Legends about the tears of St Peter are mentioned by Joseph Szövérffy, 'The Legends of St Peter in Medieval Latin Hymns', *Traditio*, x (1954), 314, 317.

22 *Passion*, 374-5. Cf. Goodman, *Original Elements in French and German Passion Plays*, 10–11.

23 *Opera Origenis Adamantii* (Paris, 1912), III, cxxix–cxxxi. A brief but useful account of the work is given by Victor Saxer, *La Culte de Marie Madeleine en occident* (Paris, 1959), 315, to which should be added the valuable article, recently published, of John P. McCall, 'Chaucer and the Pseudo-Origen *De Maria Magdalena*: A Preliminary Study', *Speculum*, xlvi (1971), 135–41.

24 Cf. Hans Hansel, 'Die Quelle der bayrischen Magdalenenklage', *Zeitschrift für deutsche Philologie*, lxii (1937), 363–88.

25 *The Lamentatyon of Mary Magdaleyne*, ed. Bertha Skeat (Zürich, 1897). I shall be discussing this poem further in a forthcoming essay.

26 'Quare monumentum tunc perseveranter non custodivi . . .' Origen, *Opera*, III, cxxxv; cf, *Lamentatyon*, ll. 26–8 and 281–4, ed. Skeat, 35, 42.

27 Song of Songs vi. 12; Origen, *Opera*, III, cxxxv.

28 For a comparable snatch of love song, used as the burden of a religious carol, see *The Early English Carols*, ed. R. L. Greene (Oxford, 1935), no. 270 (also published in *A Selection of English Carols*, ed. R. L. Greene [Oxford, 1962], no. 58, with fuller notes, p. 225).

29 *Nativités et moralités liégeoises* (Brussels, 1953), 135.

Appendix B   French Influence on the Mystery Plays

1 The separate question of the influence of the *Mystère du viel testament* on the Chester Old Testament sequence has already been discussed by A. C. Baugh (see p. 371, n. 18 above).

2 Cf. Frank, *Medieval French Drama*, 126.

3 Ibid., 146.

4 Ibid. Cf. Petit de Julleville, *Les Mystères*, I, 415–18.

5 Frank, op. cit., 145–6.

6 *Le Mystère de la Passion*, 115.

7 Frank, op. cit., 179.

8 Greban, *La Passion*, ed. Paris and Raynaud, 11.

9 All these records are referred to by Petit de Julleville, op. cit., II, 9–19, 644, save that of Chelles, for which see Gustave Cohen, 'Le Théâtre à Paris à la fin du xive siècle', *Romania*, xxxviii (1909), 587–95, reprinted with some additions in *Études d'histoire du théâtre en France au moyen âge et à la renaissance*, 169–78.

10 See above, p. 407, n. 22.

11 E.E.T.S., 24, 41–57. It is possible that this poem, which begins with a council

of the devils before the Temptation in the Wilderness, was itself influenced by dramatic portrayals of the subject rather than being a primary
influence upon them. It is less likely that it was directly influenced by the
learned tradition of the council in hell; on the latter see Olin H. Moore,
'The Infernal Council', *M.P.*, xvi(1918–19), 169–93, and Mason Hammond,
'*Concilia Deorum* from Homer through Milton', *S.P.*, xxx (1933), 1–16.

Select Bibliography

The aim of the bibliography is to list English plays and plays of other western European countries (which have been referred to for comparison with the English), in the best or most recent editions. Some of the most important secondary sources have been appended to these, chiefly those that provide a conspectus of the subject and further bibliography. The principle of arrangement is according to language; in each section plays come first, then secondary works. The two exceptions to this are that all works relating to Latin liturgical drama are set out consecutively, the distinction between primary and secondary material being here impracticable, and that for Italian and Spanish drama secondary sources only are listed. Other primary sources, literary, theological, iconographic, etc., will be found in the Index, and bibliographical details in the first footnote reference to them.

Latin Liturgical Drama

DE BOOR, HELMUT, *Die Textgeschichte der lateinischen Osterfeiern*, Hermaea: Germanistische Forschungen, N.S. xxii, Tübingen, 1967.

DONOVAN, R. B., *The Liturgical Drama in Medieval Spain*, Toronto, 1958.

HARDISON, O. B., Jr., *Christian Rite and Christian Drama in the Middle Ages*, Baltimore, 1965.

WRIGHT, EDITH A., *The Dissemination of the Liturgical Drama in France*, Bryn Mawr, 1936.

YOUNG, KARL, *The Drama of the Medieval Church*, 2 vols, Oxford, 1933.

Anglo-Norman

Le Jeu d'Adam (*Ordo representacionis Ade*) ed. Willem Noomen, Paris, 1971.

Le Mystère d'Adam, ed. Paul Studer, Manchester, 1918.

La Seinte Resureccion, ed. T. A. Jenkins, J. M. Manly, M. K. Pope and J. G. Wright, Anglo-Norman Text Society, iv, Oxford, 1943.

Cornish

The Ancient Cornish Drama, ed. and trans. Edwin Norris, Oxford, 1859.

The Cornish Ordinalia: A Medieval Dramatic Trilogy, trans. Markham Harris, Washington, D.C., 1969.

English

The Chester Plays, ed. H. Deimling and J. B. Matthews, E.E.T.S. E.S. 62 (1892, repr. 1926, 1959) and 115 (1916, repr. 1935, 1959).

The Digby Plays, ed. F. J. Furnivall, New Shakespeare Society, 1882, repr. E.E.T.S. E.S. 70 (1896, repr. 1930, 1967).

Ludus Coventriae or The Plaie called Corpus Christi, ed. K. S. Block, E.E.T.S. E.S. 120 (1922, repr. 1960).

Non-Cycle Plays and Fragments, ed. Norman Davis, with an appendix on the Shrewsbury Music by F. Ll. Harrison, E.E.T.S. S.S. 1 (1970).

The Towneley Plays, ed. G. England and A. W. Pollard, E.E.T.S. E.S. 71 (1897, repr. 1952).

The Wakefield Pageants in the Towneley Cycle, ed. A. C. Cawley, Manchester, 1958.

The York Plays, ed. Lucy Toulmin Smith, Oxford, 1885 (repr. 1963).

ANDERSON, M. D., *Drama and Imagery in English Medieval Churches*, Cambridge, 1963.

CHAMBERS, E. K., *The Mediaeval Stage*, 2 vols, Oxford, 1903.

CRAIG, H., *English Religious Drama of the Middle Ages*, Oxford, 1955.

GARDINER, HAROLD C., *Mysteries' End*, New Haven, 1946 (repr. 1967).

KOLVE, V. A., *The Play called Corpus Christi*, Stanford, 1966.

PROSSER, ELEANOR, *Drama and Religion in the English Mystery Plays. A Reevaluation*, Stanford, 1961.

SALTER, F. M., *Mediaeval Drama in Chester*, Toronto, 1955.

STEMMLER, THEO, *Liturgische Feiern und geistliche Spiele*, Tübingen, 1970.

WICKHAM, GLYNNE, *Early English Stages*, I, London, 1959.

WILLIAMS, ARNOLD, *The Drama of Medieval England*, East Lansing, Michigan, 1961.

French

GREBAN, ARNOUL, *Le Mystère de la passion*, ed. Gaston Paris and Gaston Raynaud, Paris, 1878 (repr. 1970).

Le Jour du jugement, ed. Emile Roy, Paris, 1902.

[MERCADÉ, EUSTACHE], *Le Mystère de la passion, texte du manuscrit 697 de la Bibliothèque d'Arras*, ed. J.-M. Richard, Arras, 1893.

MICHEL, JEAN, *Mystère de la passion (Angers, 1486)*, ed. Omer Jodogne, Gembloux, Belgium, 1959.

Mystère de l'Incarnation et Nativité de Notre Sauveur et Rédempteur Jésus-Christ representé à Rouen en 1474, ed. P. Le Verdier, Rouen, 1884–6.

Le Mystère du viel testament, ed. James de Rothschild, 6 vols, S.A.T.F., 1878–91.

Mystères et moralités du manuscrit 617 de Chantilly, ed. Gustave Cohen, Paris, 1920; 2nd ed. under the title, *Nativités et moralités liégeoises du moyen âge*, Brussels, 1953.

Mystères inédits du quinzième siècle . . . d'après le MS. unique de la Bibliothèque Ste-Geneviève, ed. Achille Jubinal, Paris, 1837.

La Passion d'Autun, ed. Grace Frank, S.A.T.F., 1934.

La Passion de Semur, ed. Émile Roy in *Le Mystère de la passion en France du XIVe au XVIe siècle*, 2 vols, Paris, 1905.

La Passion du Palatinus, ed. Grace Frank, Paris, 1922.

La Passion provençale du manuscrit Didot, ed. William P. Shepard, S.A.T.F., 1928.

FRANK, GRACE, *The Medieval French Drama*, Oxford, 1954.

PETIT DE JULLEVILLE, L., *Les Mystères*, 2 vols, Paris, 1880.

German

Alsfelder Passionsspiel: Das Drama des Mittelalters: die lateinischen Osterfeiern und ihre Entwickelung in Deutschland. Die Osterspiele. Die Passionsspiele. Weihnachts- und Dreikönigsspiele. Fastnachtspiele, ed. Richard Froning, Stuttgart, 1891–2 (repr. Darmstadt, 1964), 562–859.

Augsburger Passionsspiel: August Hartmann, *Das Oberammergauer Passionsspiel in seiner ältesten Gestalt*, Leipzig, 1880.

Donaueschinger Passionsspiel. Das Drama des Mittelalters: Passionsspiele II, ed. Eduard Hartl, Leipzig, 1942 (repr. Darmstadt, 1966).

Das Egerer Fronleichnamsspiel, ed. Gustav Milchsack (Bibliothek des litterarischen Vereins in Stuttgart, clvi), Tübingen, 1881.

Frankfurter Passionsspiel, ed. Froning, op. cit., 379–532.

Heidelberger Passionsspiel, ed. Gustav Milchsack, Tübingen, 1880.

Innsbrucker Fronleichnamsspiel: Altteutsche Schauspiele, ed. F. J. Mone (Bibliothek der gesammten deutschen National-Literatur, xxi), Quedlinburg, Leipzig, 1841 (pp. 145–64).

Innsbrucker Himmelfahrt Mariä, ed. F. J. Mone, op. cit., 21–106.

Künzelsauer Fronleichnamsspiel, ed. Peter K. Liebenow, Berlin, 1969.

Die Luzerner Passionsspiele, ed. Heinz Wyss (Schriften des schweizerischen Nationalfonds zur Förderung der wissenschaftlichen Forschung, 7), Bern, 1967.

Maastrichter Paachspel, De Middelnederlandsche Dramatische Poezie, ed. H. E. Moltzer (Bibliothek van middelnederlandsche Letterkunde, I, 3), Groningen, 1875 (pp. 496–538).

Das mittelhochdeutsche Spiel vom jüngsten Tage, ed. Rudolf Klee, Marburg, 1906.

Der Sündenfall und Marienklage, ed. Otto Schönemann, Hanover, 1855.

Wiener Passionsspiel, ed. Froning, op. cit., 305–24.

CREIZENACH, WILHELM, *Geschichte des neueren Dramas*, I (Halle, 1911).

MICHAEL, WOLFGANG, F., *Die geistlichen Prozessionsspiele in Deutschland*, Hesperia. Studies in Germanic Philology, 22, Baltimore, Göttingen, 1947.

STEINBACH, ROLF, *Die deutschen Oster- und Passionsspiele des Mittelalters*, Cologne, Vienna, 1970.

Italian and Spanish

D'ANCONA, ALESSANDRO, *Origini del teatro italiano*, 2 vols, Turin, 1891, repr. Rome, 1966.

DE BARTHOLOMAEIS, V., *Origini della poesia drammatica italiana*, 2nd ed., Turin, 1952.

TOSCHI, P., *Le Origini del teatro italiano*, Turin, 1955.

SHERGOLD, N. D., *A History of the Spanish Stage from Medieval Times until the End of the Seventeenth Century*, Oxford, 1967.

Index

Index

The Index is primarily an index of titles and proper names. In addition it includes the names of places connected with liturgical offices and plays (also those where relevant works of art are situated) and the incipits of vernacular lyrics and Latin hymns (but not antiphons, responses, etc.). The English mystery plays are not included, as references to them were too copious, and for the same reason references to the Bible have been omitted.